DISCIPLES *of* ANTIGONISH

MCGILL-QUEEN'S STUDIES IN THE HISTORY OF RELIGION
Volumes in this series have been supported by the Jackman Foundation of Toronto.

SERIES ONE: G.A. RAWLYK, EDITOR

1 Small Differences
Irish Catholics and Irish Protestants, 1815–1922
An International Perspective
Donald Harman Akenson

2 Two Worlds
The Protestant Culture of Nineteenth-Century Ontario
William Westfall

3 An Evangelical Mind
Nathanael Burwash and the Methodist Tradition in Canada, 1839–1918
Marguerite Van Die

4 The Dévotes
Women and Church in Seventeenth-Century France
Elizabeth Rapley

5 The Evangelical Century
College and Creed in English Canada from the Great Revival to the Great Depression
Michael Gauvreau

6 The German Peasants' War and Anabaptist Community of Goods
James M. Stayer

7 A World Mission
Canadian Protestantism and the Quest for a New International Order, 1918–1939
Robert Wright

8 Serving the Present Age
Revivalism, Progressivism, and the Methodist Tradition in Canada
Phyllis D. Airhart

9 A Sensitive Independence
Canadian Methodist Women Missionaries in Canada and the Orient, 1881–1925
Rosemary R. Gagan

10 God's Peoples
Covenant and Land in South Africa, Israel, and Ulster
Donald Harman Akenson

11 Creed and Culture
The Place of English-Speaking Catholics in Canadian Society, 1750–1930
Edited by Terrence Murphy and Gerald Stortz

12 Piety and Nationalism
Lay Voluntary Associations and the Creation of an Irish-Catholic Community in Toronto, 1850–1895
Brian P. Clarke

13 Amazing Grace
Studies in Evangelicalism in Australia, Britain, Canada, and the United States
Edited by George Rawlyk and Mark A. Noll

14 Children of Peace
W. John McIntyre

15 A Solitary Pillar
Montreal's Anglican Church and the Quiet Revolution
Joan Marshall

16 Padres in No Man's Land
Canadian Chaplains and the Great War
Duff Crerar

17 Christian Ethics and Political Economy in North America
A Critical Analysis
P. Travis Kroeker

18 Pilgrims in Lotus Land
Conservative Protestantism in British Columbia, 1917–1981
Robert K. Burkinshaw

19 Through Sunshine and Shadow
The Woman's Christian Temperance Union, Evangelicalism, and Reform in Ontario, 1874–1930
Sharon Cook

20 Church, College, and Clergy
A History of Theological Education at Knox College, Toronto, 1844–1994
Brian J. Fraser

21 The Lord's Dominion
The History of Canadian Methodism
Neil Semple

22 A Full-Orbed Christianity
The Protestant Churches and Social Welfare in Canada, 1900–1940
Nancy Christie and Michael Gauvreau

23 Evangelism and Apostasy
The Evolution and Impact of Evangelicals in Modern Mexico
Kurt Bowen

24 The Chignecto Covenanters
A Regional History of Reformed Presbyterianism in New Brunswick and Nova Scotia, 1827– 1905
Eldon Hay

25 Methodists and Women's Education in Ontario, 1836–1925
Johanne Selles

26 Puritanism and Historical Controversy
William Lamont

SERIES TWO IN MEMORY OF GEORGE RAWLYK
DONALD HARMAN AKENSON, EDITOR

1 Marguerite Bourgeoys and Montreal, 1640–1665
Patricia Simpson

2 Aspects of the Canadian Evangelical Experience
Edited by G.A. Rawlyk

3 Infinity, Faith, and Time
Christian Humanism and Renaissance Literature
John Spencer Hill

4 The Contribution of Presbyterianism to the Maritime Provinces of Canada
Edited by Charles H.H. Scobie and G.A. Rawlyk

5 Labour, Love, and Prayer
Female Piety in Ulster Religious Literature, 1850–1914
Andrea Ebel Brozyna

6 The Waning of the Green
Catholics, the Irish, and Identity in Toronto, 1887–1922
Mark G. McGowan

7 Religion and Nationality in Western Ukraine
The Greek Catholic Church and the Ruthenian National Movement in Galicia, 1867–1900
John-Paul Himka

8 Good Citizens
British Missionaries and Imperial States, 1870–1918
James G. Greenlee and Charles M. Johnston

9 The Theology of the Oral Torah
Revealing the Justice of God
Jacob Neusner

10 Gentle Eminence
A Life of Cardinal Flahiff
P. Wallace Platt

11 Culture, Religion, and Demographic Behaviour
Catholics and Lutherans in Alsace, 1750–1870
Kevin McQuillan

12 Between Damnation and Starvation
Priests and Merchants in Newfoundland Politics, 1745–1855
John P. Greene

13 Martin Luther, German Saviour
German Evangelical Theological Factions and the Interpretation of Luther, 1917–1933
James M. Stayer

14 Modernity and the Dilemma of North American Anglican Identities, 1880–1950
William H. Katerberg

15 The Methodist Church on the Prairies, 1896–1914
George Emery

16 Christian Attitudes towards the State of Israel
Paul Charles Merkley

17 A Social History of the Cloister
Daily Life in the Teaching Monasteries of the Old Regime
Elizabeth Rapley

18 Households of Faith
Family, Gender, and Community in Canada, 1760–1969
Edited by Nancy Christie

19 Blood Ground
Colonialism, Missions, and the Contest for Christianity in the Cape Colony and Britain, 1799–1853
Elizabeth Elbourne

20 A History of Canadian Catholics
Gallicanism, Romanism, and Canadianism
Terence J. Fay

21 The View from Rome
Archbishop Stagni's 1915 Reports on the Ontario Bilingual Schools Question
Edited and translated by John Zucchi

22 The Founding Moment
Church, Society, and the Construction of Trinity College
William Westfall

23 The Holocaust, Israel, and Canadian Protestant Churches
Haim Genizi

24 Governing Charities
Church and State in Toronto's Catholic Archdiocese, 1850–1950
Paula Maurutto

25 Anglicans and the Atlantic World
High Churchmen, Evangelicals, and the Quebec Connection
Richard W. Vaudry

26 Evangelicals and the Continental Divide
The Conservative Protestant Subculture in Canada and the United States
Sam Reimer

27 Christians in a Secular World
The Canadian Experience
Kurt Bowen

28 Anatomy of a Seance
A History of Spirit Communication in Central Canada
Stan McMullin

29 With Skilful Hand
The Story of King David
David T. Barnard

30 Faithful Intellect
Samuel S. Nelles and Victoria University
Neil Semple

31 W. Stanford Reid
An Evangelical Calvinist in the Academy
A. Donald MacLeod

32 A Long Eclipse
The Liberal Protestant Establishment and the Canadian University, 1920–1970
Catherine Gidney

33 Forkhill Protestants and Forkhill Catholics, 1787–1858
Kyla Madden

34 For Canada's Sake
Public Religion, Centennial Celebrations, and the Re-making of Canada in the 1960s
Gary R. Miedema

35 Revival in the City
The Impact of American Evangelists in Canada, 1884–1914
Eric R. Crouse

36 The Lord for the Body
Religion, Medicine, and Protestant Faith Healing in Canada, 1880–1930
James Opp

37 Six Hundred Years of Reform
Bishops and the French Church, 1190–1789
J. Michael Hayden and Malcolm R. Greenshields

38 The Missionary Oblate Sisters
Vision and Mission
Rosa Bruno-Jofré

39 Religion, Family, and Community in Victorian Canada
The Colbys of Carrollcroft
Marguerite Van Die

40 Michael Power
The Struggle to Build the Catholic Church on the Canadian Frontier
Mark G. McGowan

41 The Catholic Origins of Quebec's Quiet Revolution, 1931–1970
Michael Gauvreau

42 Marguerite Bourgeoys and the Congregation of Notre Dame, 1665–1700
Patricia Simpson

43 To Heal a Fractured World
The Ethics of Responsibility
Jonathan Sacks

44 Revivalists
Marketing the Gospel in English Canada, 1884–1957
Kevin Kee

45 The Churches and Social Order in Nineteenth- and Twentieth-Century Canada
Edited by Michael Gauvreau and Ollivier Hubert

46 Political Ecumenism
Catholics, Jews, and Protestants in De Gaulle's Free France, 1940–1945
Geoffrey Adams

47 From Quaker to Upper Canadian
Faith and Community among Yonge Street Friends, 1801–1850
Robynne Rogers Healey

48 The Congrégation de Notre-Dame, Superiors, and the Paradox of Power, 1693–1796
Colleen Gray

49 Canadian Pentecostalism
Transition and Transformation
Edited by Michael Wilkinson

50 A War with a Silver Lining
Canadian Protestant Churches and the South African War, 1899–1902
Gordon L. Heath

51 In the Aftermath of Catastrophe
Founding Judaism, 70 to 640
Jacob Neusner

52 Imagining Holiness
Classic Hasidic Tales in Modern Times
Justin Jaron Lewis

53 Shouting, Embracing, and Dancing with Ecstasy
The Growth of Methodism in Newfoundland, 1774–1874
Calvin Hollett

54 Into Deep Waters
Evangelical Spirituality and Maritime Calvinist Baptist Ministers, 1790–1855
Daniel C. Goodwin

55 Vanguard of the New Age
The Toronto Theosophical Society, 1891–1945
Gillian McCann

56 A Commerce of Taste
Church Architecture in Canada, 1867–1914
Barry Magrill

57 The Big Picture
The Antigonish Movement of Eastern Nova Scotia
Santo Dodaro and Leonard Pluta

58 My Heart's Best Wishes for You
A Biography of Archbishop John Walsh
John P. Comiskey

59 The Covenanters in Canada
Reformed Presbyterianism from 1820 to 2012
Eldon Hay

60 The Guardianship of Best Interests
Institutional Care for the Children of the Poor in Halifax, 1850–1960
Renée N. Lafferty

61 In Defence of the Faith
Joaquim Marques de Araújo, a Comissário in the Age of Inquisitional Decline
James E. Wadsworth

62 Contesting the Moral High Ground
Popular Moralists in Mid-Twentieth-Century Britain
Paul T. Phillips

63 The Catholicisms of Coutances
Varieties of Religion in Early Modern France, 1350–1789
J. Michael Hayden

64 After Evangelicalism
The Sixties and the United Church of Canada
Kevin N. Flatt

65 The Return of Ancestral Gods
Modern Ukrainian Paganism as an Alternative Vision for a Nation
Mariya Lesiv

66 Transatlantic Methodists
British Wesleyanism and the Formation of an Evangelical Culture in Nineteenth-Century Ontario and Quebec
Todd Webb

67 A Church with the Soul of a Nation
Making and Remaking the United Church of Canada
Phyllis D. Airhart

68 Fighting over God
A Legal and Political History of Religious Freedom in Canada
Janet Epp Buckingham

69 From India to Israel
Identity, Immigration, and the Struggle for Religious Equality
Joseph Hodes

70 Becoming Holy in Early Canada
Timothy Pearson

71 The Cistercian Arts
From the 12th to the 21st Century
Edited by Terryl N. Kinder and Roberto Cassanelli

72 The Canny Scot
Archbishop James Morrison of Antigonish
Peter Ludlow

73 Religion and Greater Ireland
Christianity and Irish Global Networks, 1750–1950
Edited by Colin Barr and Hilary M. Carey

74 The Invisible Irish
Finding Protestants in the Nineteenth-Century Migrations to America
Rankin Sherling

75 Beating against the Wind
Popular Opposition to Bishop Feild and Tractarianism in Newfoundland and Labrador, 1844–1876
Calvin Hollett

76 The Body or the Soul?
Religion and Culture in a Quebec Parish, 1736–1901
Frank A. Abbott

77 Saving Germany
North American Protestants and Christian Mission to West Germany, 1945–1974
James C. Enns

78 The Imperial Irish
Canada's Irish Catholics Fight the Great War, 1914–1918
Mark G. McGowan

79 Into Silence and Servitude
How American Girls Became Nuns, 1945–1965
Brian Titley

80 Boundless Dominion
Providence, Politics, and the Early Canadian Presbyterian Worldview
Denis McKim

81 Faithful Encounters
Authorities and American Missionaries in the Ottoman Empire
Emrah Şahin

82 Beyond the Noise of Solemn Assemblies
The Protestant Ethic and the Quest for Social Justice in Canada
Richard Allen

83 Not Quite Us
Anti-Catholic Thought in English Canada since 1900
Kevin P. Anderson

84 Scandal in the Parish
Priests and Parishioners Behaving Badly in Eighteenth-Century France
Karen E. Carter

85 Ordinary Saints
Women, Work, and Faith in Newfoundland
Bonnie Morgan

86 Patriot and Priest
Jean-Baptiste Volfius and the Constitutional Church in the Côte-d'Or
Annette Chapman-Adisho

87 A.B. Simpson and the Making of Modern Evangelicalism
Daryn Henry

88 The Uncomfortable Pew
Christianity and the New Left in Toronto
Bruce Douville

89 Berruyer's Bible
Public Opinion and the Politics of Enlightenment Catholicism in France
Daniel J. Watkins

90 Communities of the Soul
A Short History of Religion in Puerto Rico
José E. Igartua

91 Callings and Consequences
The Making of Catholic Vocational Culture in Early Modern France
Christopher J. Lane

92 Religion, Ethnonationalism, and Antisemitism in the Era of the Two World Wars
Edited by Kevin P. Spicer and Rebecca Carter-Chand

93 Water from Dragon's Well
The History of a Korean-Canadian Church Relationship
David Kim-Cragg

94 Protestant Liberty
Religion and the Making of Canadian Liberalism, 1828–1878
James M. Forbes

95 To Make a Village Soviet
Jehovah's Witnesses and the Transformation of a Postwar Ukrainian Borderland
Emily B. Baran

96 Disciples of Antigonish
Catholics in Nova Scotia, 1880–1960
Peter Ludlow

DISCIPLES *of* ANTIGONISH

Catholics in Nova Scotia 1880–1960

PETER LUDLOW

McGill-Queen's University Press
Montreal & Kingston • London • Chicago

ISBN 978-0-2280-1087-6 (cloth)
ISBN 978-0-2280-1088-3 (paper)
ISBN 978-0-2280-1311-2 (ePDF)
ISBN 978-0-2280-1312-9 (ePUB)

Legal deposit third quarter 2022
Bibliothèque nationale du Québec

This book has been published with the help of a grant from the Federation for the Humanities and Social Sciences, through the Awards to Scholarly Publications Program, using funds provided by the Social Sciences and Humanities Research Council of Canada.

Funded by the Government of Canada | Financé par le gouvernement du Canada | Canada

Canada Council for the Arts | Conseil des arts du Canada

We acknowledge the support of the Canada Council for the Arts.
Nous remercions le Conseil des arts du Canada de son soutien.

Library and Archives Canada Cataloguing in Publication

Title: Disciples of Antigonish : Catholics in Nova Scotia 1880–1960 / Peter Ludlow.
Names: Ludlow, Peter, 1977– author.
Series: McGill-Queen's studies in the history of religion. Series two ; 96.
Description: Series statement: McGill-Queen's studies in the history of religion. Series two ; 96 | Includes bibliographical references and index.
Identifiers: Canadiana (print) 20220233233 | Canadiana (ebook) 20220233314 | ISBN 9780228010883 (softcover) | ISBN 9780228010876 (hardcover) | ISBN 9780228013112 (PDF) | ISBN 9780228013129 (ePUB)
Subjects: LCSH: Catholic Church. Diocese of Antigonish (N.S.)—History. | LCSH: Catholics—Nova Scotia—History. | LCSH: Catholic Church—Nova Scotia—History.
Classification: LCC BX1423.A7 L83 2022 | DDC 282/.716—dc23

This book was typeset in 10.5/13 Sabon.

For

Fr Father John Joseph "J.J." MacDonald (1928–2019)

Fr Edward J.R. "Ed" Jackman, OP (1940–2021)

Contents

Tables and Figures

TABLES

FIGURES

Acknowledgments

This book – an exploration of events that have long been discussed and debated by generations of Catholics in eastern Nova Scotia – has been many years in the making. In both rural St Andrews, Antigonish County, where I was raised, and in my father's native parish of New Aberdeen, a famously militant section of the Glace Bay mining community, the symbiotic relationship between Church and community was evident. It was often a "mix of facts and myth, criticism and romance," as the late Fr Ed MacIsaac once told me, but Catholics in the region were always aware of the activities of the Church outside of the sanctuary.

I owe a great debt to a historian whom I have never met. Fr Angus Anthony ("A.A.") Johnston died on 18 September 1977 at St Martha's Hospital in Antigonish town. Two weeks later, I was born under that same roof and so we missed each other by a mere fortnight. Quiet, cerebral, and courteous, Johnston was a legendary figure, tramping through the tall summer grass in search of weathered gravestones, studiously researching in the Vatican archive, and spryly climbing the many stairs to his office in the Angus L. Macdonald Library on the campus of St Francis Xavier University. He not only wrote several parish histories and two superb volumes on the history of Catholicism in eastern Nova Scotia but also left an exhaustive archive from which I have benefited.

My friend Fr Edward J.R. Jackman, OP, who died in June 2021, funded the research for this book. Besides his commitment to the Canadian Catholic Historical Association, Fr Jackman and his dedicated associate, Valerie Burke, have helped many historians pursue the history of religion in Canada. I count myself as one of the "wise men" who sought Fr Ed's support and I regret that he did not live to see "the job done." Another important figure who did not live to see the book in print was Fr John Joseph ("J.J.") MacDonald. Although we never met in person, we carried on a robust correspondence over the final years of his life, and I found myself watching the post for his insightful letters on the history of the region and his personal recollections.

It is difficult to write about the Catholic Church without access to institutional records. I am indebted to Archbishop Brian Dunn (now of Halifax) for supporting this project and for literally providing a key to the Antigonish diocesan archive. I enjoyed our many conversations and was aware that while I was immersed in the church construction, subsidiarity and diocesan growth of the nineteenth and twentieth centuries, he was at work in the twentieth-first century dealing with church closures and decline in attendance. Despite the contrast in eras, however, it was always evident that the basic pastoral work has remained unchanged.

There were many priests within the Diocese of Antigonish who provided assistance, let me borrow books from their libraries, or provided answers to various queries. From the Tracadie glebe house, Fr John Barry read the manuscript, provided materials from his own archival collection, and sent many encouraging messages. Fr Paul Murphy at Whitney Pier also commented on the manuscript and offered his hospitality while I was researching in Sydney. I am also very grateful to Fr Anthony O'Connor, Fr Patrick O'Neill, Fr Charlie Cameron, Fr Duaine Devereaux, and Fr Bill Burke.

While writing a biography of Archbishop James Morrison some years ago, I was privileged to spend several evenings talking history with the former president of St Francis Xavier University, the late Fr Malcolm MacDonell. This time around, I was fortunate to spend similar time with his sister, the Gaelic scholar and historian Sister Margaret MacDonell, CND. Not only did Sister MacDonell read the manuscript and sit for two long interviews at her home in Sydney, but over the phone or over lunch she passed along recollections of the diocese, stories about the "big personalities" like Sister St Veronica, CND, and her experience as a woman serving the Church.

The largest collections of materials related to Catholicism in eastern Nova Scotia are housed in Antigonish and Sydney. The Antigonish Diocesan Archive, which was once stored at the

St Francis Xavier University Library, was transferred back to the Chancery Office in the 1990s and catalogued by the late (and very formidable) Sister Mary Roderick MacMullin, CSM. Due to the aforementioned symbiotic relationship between Church and community, these archives are a rich resource for historians interested in various aspects of society. During my time in the "vault," I was kindly aided by Cathy Walsh and Jennifer Wadden, and helped further by Cathy Farrow at the Pastoral Centre in Sydney and a summer student, Kenzie MacNeil.

Across Antigonish town at St Francis Xavier University, the archive, located in the basement of the Angus L. Macdonald Library, is a rich hybrid of institutional and Church records. As college faculty and administrators were also priests and women religious, the range of topics discussed in a collection of presidential papers might, for example, range from the college convocation to the plight of fishermen on Isle Madame. Over the years, the archive's long-time gatekeeper Kathleen MacKenzie, with the aid of Jennifer Clifton and others, has committed considerable time and resources in helping me comb through the vast collection, and I am grateful.

In Sydney, the Beaton Institute, which is located on the campus of Cape Breton University, is another rich and diverse repository of records. The foundation of this important collection was built by the late Sister Margaret Beaton, CND, who recognized the need to preserve the history of Cape Breton Island. It also houses the papers of important priests like Fr James J. Tompkins. I am grateful to Sister Beaton's successor, Catherine Arsenault, and to Anne Marie MacNeil, who made arrangements for me to examine large volumes of material in a short time frame.

Other archivists who have aided the research are Mary Flynn (Congregation of the Sisters of Charity), Marie-Claude Fortier (Congregation of Notre Dame), Sister Florence Kennedy and Melanie Secco (Congregation of the Sisters of St Martha), Father Art O'Shea (Diocese of Charlottetown), Jocelyn Gillis (Antigonish Heritage Museum), Sharon Riel (Archdiocese of Halifax), and Michelle Gait (University of Aberdeen).

One of the joys of historical research is the relationships one makes with other scholars. Dan MacInnes read chapters and shared his vast knowledge of the Antigonish Movement and Gaelic culture. Colin Barr secured for me a visiting fellowship at the Rice Library at the University of Aberdeen so that I could examine the early

Scottish Catholic Records. Terry Murphy lent his encouragement and impressive knowledge of Maritime Catholicism, while Edward G. MacDonald, who has probably read more of my work than anyone else, provided many helpful criticisms.

I am blessed with a wonderful network of colleagues and friends who have aided and contributed to the project in various ways. My thanks to Paul Armstrong, Joe Ballard, Peter Baltutis, James Cameron, Ron Chisholm, Gord Cunningham, Robert Dennis, John Gabriel, John Gillis, Jackie Gresko, M.C. Havey, Fr Seamus Hogan, Bill Landry, Paul Laverdure, Brian Lazzuri, Basil and Dorothy Ludlow, Heidi MacDonald, Pauline MacIntosh, Barry MacKenzie, Lewis MacKinnon, Patrick Mannion, Fred McEvoy, Mark G. McGowan, Peter Meehan, Tom Roach, Paula Romanow, Bart Sears, Rankin Sherling, Laura Smith, Veronica Steinburg, and William Sweet.

There are so many people who helped me in many significant ways; opening churches so I could have a look around or offering bits of ephemera. Representative of these kind individuals are Gary Cusack, who generously provided funding for digital recording equipment, Charles "Bunker" Bowman, who led me through the complicated backroads of Afton to locate the childhood home of Bishop James Boyle, and John Prosper and Robert Pictou, who gave me a tour of St Anne's in Paqenkek as the community was busy preparing for the Feast of St Anne.

Recognizing the historic relationship between the Catholic Church in eastern Nova Scotia and its former college, subventions in support of publication were provided by both the Diocese of Antigonish and St Francis Xavier University. I am very grateful to Bishop Wayne Kirkpatrick of Antigonish and to Murry Kyte and Wendy Langley of the St Francis Xavier University Advancement Department for securing this generous financial support.

Working with McGill-Queen's University Press is always a pleasure, and I am thankful to Kyla Madden and Kathleen Fraser for all their assistance and advice. I am also grateful to Donald H. Akenson for his work as editor of MQUP's Studies in the History of Religion Series. Through his partnership with the late Fr Jackman, the series has provided many scholars, like myself, an opportunity to get their work into print. Finally, I would like to thank copy editor Jane McWhinney, whose skillful edits helped transform the manuscript into a much more pleasing read.

When writing a biography of Antigonish bishop John R. MacDonald in the 1970s, Fr Peter Nearing habitually apologized for the length of time it took to complete the manuscript. "I don't know how it could have been otherwise," he explained to Msgr William Gallivan, "unless, like Fr Johnston, I had locked myself in a room, coming out only for meals and sleep." While I was slightly more accessible, I am grateful to my wife, Kerry, daughter, Payson, and son, Rory – born in the first months of research – for their unwavering support and patience. Sometime after my first book was published, Payson was asked in her nursery school what her father did for a living. She answered, "My dad is a publisher, and he works for Bishop Morrison." Historical projects can have that kind of effect on family.

DISCIPLES

of

ANTIGONISH

Introduction

The first question that any prospective reader might ask is: why write a history of Roman Catholicism that focuses intensively on a portion of a small province within a politically and economically marginalized region of Canada? How can an exploration of eastern Nova Scotia between 1880 and 1960 add to our understanding of Catholicism in North America? My answer is that the ecclesiastical territory that eventually became known as the Diocese of Antigonish had – and still has – an ethnic composition and lived experience that is unique within the Canadian Church. The mainland Nova Scotia counties of Pictou, Antigonish, and Guysborough, as well as Cape Breton Island, may have lacked the demographics, finances, and political clout of larger Catholic centres like Toronto, Montreal, and Saint John but, thanks to the "adult education for action" of the famous "Antigonish Movement," they were by the 1950s as celebrated as any Catholic constituency in the country. In fact, young men sent to Toronto's St Augustine's Seminary after the Second World War recalled the spiritual director, Monsignor (Msgr) John Corrigan, praising them as natives of the "mighty big and strong Antigonish."[1] It was also well known that Archbishop Giovanni Panico, the apostolic delegate in Ottawa from 1953 to 1959, considered Antigonish "the best diocese in Canada."[2]

While these sentiments may be considered mere opinions, they offer a witness to a region that is certainly worthy of scholarly attention. Although the Canadian Catholic narrative has been dominated by the experiences of the anglophone Irish and the francophone Québécois, eastern Nova Scotia was never controlled by either ethnic group. After Jesuit missionaries were welcomed into Mi'kma'ki in the seventeenth century, the faith was cultivated and protected by the Indigenous Mi'kmaq, further buttressed by French-speaking Acadians in the eighteenth century, strengthened by Gaelic-speaking Catholic migrants from Ireland and the Highlands of Scotland in the early nineteenth century, and then topped up by Newfoundlanders, Italians, and eastern Europeans in the early twentieth century. As a result, the Catholic population of eastern Nova Scotia was an amalgam of ethnic groups with challenges and attitudes that reflected the richness and diversity of the Canadian Catholic experience. While many tend to think of dense North American cities like Boston and Toronto as centres of Catholic multiculturalism, by the time of the Great War the languages spoken at the dinner tables of Catholic households in eastern Nova Scotia ranged from Mi'kmaw, French, and Gaelic to Polish and Italian. In all these homes the Church was both an instrument for spiritual sustenance and salvation, and a tool to help safeguard and promote language and culture.

The unique demographics and rich cultural diversity of the Catholics of eastern Nova Scotia were evident as early as the 1840s. As the great ultramontane movement of devotionalism and uniformity took hold of the global Church in that period, Irish prelates ministering in British North America, like the gentrified William Walsh of Halifax, grumbled to Roman bureaucrats that things were not quite right in the eastern corner of the colony. To the Dublin-born Walsh, the old customs of the Mi'kmaq, Acadian, and Highland Scottish faithful were outdated and anathema to the new impulse toward standardization of the modern ultramontane program. The priests of eastern Nova Scotia such as the Rome-educated bishop Colin Francis MacKinnon managed to keep ecclesiastical control of the fledgling diocese (Walsh had wanted the mainland counties for Halifax), but between 1850 and 1880 the region was thoroughly Romanized. Where itinerant pastors like Fr William Chisholm (1779–1818) and Fr James Duffy (1798–1860) had once offered the sacraments within the crude barns of scattered settlements, graduates of Rome's celebrated Urban College such as Fr Daniel MacIntosh MacGregor and Fr (later bishop) John Cameron soon dominated the important ecclesiastical offices in the shade of a large stone Romanesque cathedral – completed in 1874 – which was adorned with Italian artwork.

In a recent book, Luca Codignola has demonstrated that the Romanization of the North American seminarians sent to Italy for training was designed for them to learn to "regard the ways of the

Holy See as an ideal to be followed and reproduced as much as possible in one's new surroundings."[3] Ultramontanists like Cameron, who in 1877 succeeded Mackinnon as archbishop, affirmed papal authority among the farmers and fishermen of the region and encouraged piety and devotionalism within a strong Catholic subculture that integrated almost seamlessly with the state. Faithful and "submissive to the teachings of the Church," dedicated to building churches, schools, and hospitals, and willing to be guided by the clergy even against their partisan political instincts, Roman Catholics in eastern Nova Scotia made great gains throughout the nineteenth century. It is not a coincidence that the first Catholic prime minister of Canada, Sir John S.D. Thompson, was the representative for Antigonish county.

As the hand-picked political candidate of Bishop Cameron, Thompson, a convert to Catholicism, brought the Catholics of eastern Nova Scotia to national attention. By the last decade of the century, however, a new generation was beginning to push back against the quasi-monarchical and authoritarian ultramontane system. Between 1896 and 1910, nationwide political disputes such as the Manitoba Schools Question, as well as the more parochial issues of parish boundaries and church construction, generated so much acrimony between Bishop Cameron and his flock that the apostolic delegate was repeatedly obliged to intercede. Far from being the "best diocese in Canada," Antigonish in the early twentieth century may well have been the most troubled.

Making matters worse, by 1900 the agricultural and coastal districts of the Maritime provinces (then the economic backbone of the diocese) were locked in a generational struggle for survival, and their geographic proximity to the "Boston States" enticed thousands of young people to outmigrate. At the same time, the burgeoning coal mines and fledgling steel mills of Cape Breton Island were attracting thousands of Catholic immigrants from the countryside of eastern Nova Scotia and further afield – Newfoundland, Italy, and eastern Europe. While the injection of Catholic labour into the region steadied Church coffers and supported great physical expansion in the industrial centres of Pictou County and Cape Breton, the social and economic realities of a twentieth-century industrial community presented Catholics with a host of new problems.

Facing these new economic and social challenges, the Church in eastern Nova Scotia did something remarkable. It used its strong subculture, which had been carefully nurtured by the ultramontanists decades earlier, as the foundation for a new program of social Catholicism that would make the region famous. By the time the Great War broke out, leaders such as Fr James J. Tompkins, Fr "Little Doc" Hugh MacPherson, and Mother M. Faustina, CSM, envisioned a role for the Church that went well beyond Sunday Mass. It was a daring pivot away from ultramontanism toward subsidiarity, toward valorizing on the basis of local rather than central authority. Diocesan organizations such as the Congregation of the Sisters of St Martha (CSM), initially formed to prepare the meals and clean the rooms of undergraduates at the diocesan college, were soon ministering to the faithful through hospitals, schools, and orphanages, while farmers in rural parishes like Christmas Island, St Andrews, and Iona were as likely to get clerical instruction on crop rotation as on Church doctrine.

While visionaries like Fr Tompkins deserve credit for this turn toward subsidiarity, Catholics in eastern Nova Scotia had little choice but to press forward with a program of economic and social action. By the 1920s a further downturn in the Maritime economy forced another generation of young people to leave for New England or western Canada, and a series of devastating coal strikes in the colliery towns of Cape Breton produced a level of human suffering that could not be ignored. In 1928, after a few years of social conferences and local agitation, the diocese used its college, St Francis Xavier University (St F.X.), to create an extension department to educate the laity on economic issues, facilitate group action at the parish level, and help people become "masters of their own destiny."[4] Through study clubs, credit unions, and cooperatives, the Antigonish Movement – as the program became known – captured the attention of journalists and educators around the world. There were failures and setbacks, of course, but by the 1930s the St F.X. Extension Department had changed the circumstances of thousands of people. By the 1940s the Vatican had issued special commendations, and stories of clerical leaders like Msgr Moses Michael Coady filled the pages of newspapers, books, and magazines.

Catholics across Canada were enthralled by the successes of "the giants of Antigonish" and, as the region had exported so many of its previous generations, the diocese had many followers. Eastern Nova Scotia had also supplied the rest of Canada with bishops, priests, and nuns. Before clergymen like Archbishop Neil McNeil of Toronto and Archbishop John Hugh MacDonald of Edmonton assumed the nation's highest episcopal offices, they had learned how to baptize and to give sermons in parishes like West Arichat and New Waterford. There were eastern Nova Scotian priests ministering on the prairies, women religious teaching in Alberta's Crow's Nest Pass, and enough former residents scattered throughout the country to keep even the most homesick Catholic in good spirits. As Mark McGowan has noted, the region had been instrumental in constructing a great "pan-Canadian" Catholic network.[5]

Heartened by the tremendous success of the Antigonish Movement and guided by the "Mystical Body" in action, the Church – now spoken of as laity, priests, and women religious – had by the 1950s broadened its frame of reference and was influencing policy on a range of issues related to mental health, prison reform, and even substance abuse. Not only did the rank and file continue to follow the liturgical schedule and build schools, hospitals, and orphanages (one Richmond County pastor exclaimed after a fundraising drive, even "the poor came across to a man") but they also supported new initiatives like the Mabou Family Life Institute and various local Family Welfare Councils.[6] As a result, when the first national Catholic Social Conference (English section) was held in 1953 to discuss the parish as the "basic cell of social life" in Canada, it was no surprise that five hundred delegates travelled from across Canada to eastern Nova Scotia for a gathering on the St F.X. campus.

Despite such achievements, like any institution governed by human beings, the Church in eastern Nova Scotia was not without its flaws. In some cases, priests were severe; in other cases, Catholics struggled to find God's love amid the rules and regulations. While eastern Nova Scotia was multicultural, some ethnic communities had to fight harder than others for a voice within the diocese. Recently, the painful legacy of the residential schools has come to greater attention in Canada. While not under the control of the Antigonish hierarchy, as we shall read, young Indigenous Catholics from the region were sent to the Shubenacadie Indian Residential School, and their experiences are as much a part of the region's Catholic history as the Antigonish Movement. The failures are as significant as the accomplishments.

This book covers a broad time span (some eighty years) in order to track the monumental changes that occurred within the Canadian Church in this region. From ultramontanism, which concentrated power in hands of bishops, to the lay apostolate, which encouraged participation by the laity in the Church, change was slow but steady. When this book begins, most Catholics were aware of their place *within* the Church, but by its end their grandchildren were being told that they *were* the Church.

I have ended with the events of 1959–60 for three reasons. First, by the 1960s many of the prominent personalities who had influenced the Church in eastern Nova Scotia through the early twentieth century had died. Second, the changes in personnel and leadership (which included having a Montreal native as bishop), as well as the changes brought upon the Church after Vatican II (1962–65), require an in-depth study of their own. Finally, and perhaps most important, by the 1960s it was evident that the Church's role as the purveyor of social programming was under siege in the face of secularism, state intervention, and technology. The subsidiarity that made "mighty big and strong Antigonish" so remarkable was on the wane, supplanted by the influence of government bureaucrats with seemingly unlimited financial resources.

I am not, of course, the first historian to engage with the region's Catholic history. The tattered pages of the one-time diocesan newspaper, *The Casket*, carefully preserved in the St F.X. University archive, are full of notations from generations of historians who have mined its columns. Through the short publications of intellectuals like Fr (later bishop) Ronald MacDonald, the genealogical musings of Fr Duncan Joseph "D.J." Rankin, the numerous parish and community histories, the work of Fr Anselme Chiasson, the "greatest fisherman of oral and written traditions of Cheticamp," and later clerical biographies by such writers as George Boyle and Fr Peter Nearing, the story of the diocese has mostly been told in increments.[7]

By far the most famous Catholic historian of the region was Fr Angus Anthony ("A.A.") Johnston. Appointed as diocesan historian in 1953, Johnston began his painstaking research into two volumes of history covering 1611 to 1879. An expert in liturgical music, Johnston proved a keen student of the past and spent decades diligently combing archives, glebe attics, and graveyards in search of its stories. He published in newspapers and scholarly journals, and wrote several parish histories and biographical sketches. The first volume of *A History of the Catholic Church in Eastern Nova Scotia* was published to great acclaim in 1960, as was the volume that followed in 1971.

If Johnston had a flaw, however, it was his reluctance to either criticize or analyze. As a cleric-historian, he was in a difficult position and left uncomfortable analysis to "some future historian."[8] In fairness, his colleagues would have accepted nothing less. One former Antigonish priest, for instance, when asked to comment on the priests who opposed Bishop Morrison during the infamous university merger dispute of the 1920s, pointed out in 1967 that "people are not edified by stories (even reliable ones) about the doings of the clergy when they gang up on their bishop."[9] Another cautioned his interviewer "not to revive the dissensions of yesteryear."[10] Fr Michael Gillis (nicknamed "the old cooperator" for his work on rural cooperatives), seemed to excuse the lack of hard analysis in Fr Peter Nearing's 1975 biography of Bishop John R. MacDonald with his comment that Nearing "couldn't well go into detail."[11]

This attitude began to be challenged in the late 1960s when a young Raymond A. MacLean was hired by the St F.X. History Department to focus on Canadian history.[12] While MacLean waited a few years before plunging into the regional Catholic narrative, throughout the 1970s and 1980s he aided the research of other influential historians who recognized the importance of the Catholic story in eastern Nova Scotia. *The Man from Halifax: Sir John Thompson, Prime Minister*, published in 1985 by the eminent Dalhousie University professor P.B. (Peter Busby) Waite, described in great detail the experience of the first Roman Catholic prime minister of Canada.[13] This scholarly study, which highlighted the relationship between Thompson and Bishop John Cameron, prepared the way for MacLean to write *Bishop John Cameron: Piety & Politics* in 1991. Examining that complex and controversial figure some twenty years after Fr Johnston's second volume, the thoughtful MacLean had more freedom to be critical of Bishop Cameron's ultramontane authority. His literary predecessor, he wrote understatedly, had been "quite sympathetic."[14]

As MacLean was challenging local Catholic historiography, historians of religion in Canada were redirecting their focus away from bishops and priests toward the homes and workplaces of parishioners. Naturally, the grassroots Antigonish Movement provided much material. Former fieldworkers of the Extension Department published memoirs, and sociologists and historians began to highlight the importance of the role of the laity (and especially women) within cooperatives and credit unions. Scholarship on the Catholic social action of eastern Nova Scotia was so pervasive within Canadian Catholic historiography that one prominent historian noted in the mid-1990s that "the only Catholic activity outside of Quebec seemingly worthy of mention [was] the Antigonish Movement."[15]

By the late 1970s a new generation of social and labour historians was also pursuing new lines of inquiry in regional scholarly journals like *Acadiensis* (scholarship on which this book relies heavily). While this body of work had positive things to say about the Antigonish Movement, it mostly criticized or ignored other activities of the Church in the nineteenth and twentieth centuries. Some historians were critical for ideological reasons – always writing of Catholic positions as "ambiguous" or even "reactionary" – but most struggled in vain for access to the materials housed in diocesan archives, which were too often closed to researchers. Of course, in some cases critical scrutiny of the Church in Atlantic Canada offered a fair analysis of an institution that was all too human; however, a lack of deep engagement with the archives meant that the actions and motives of the priests and women religious were regularly misrepresented by myth and confusion. This was especially true within the often-hagiographic accounts of the region's labour leaders.

Such misconceptions were no more evident than in the historiography of the Cape Breton labour movement. Without a solid scholarly analysis of Church activities in the colliery towns, writers like John Mellor, who in 1983 published *The Company Store: J.B. McLachlan and the Cape Breton Coal Miners 1900-1925*, were dependent on largely unreliable oral history. The belief, for example, that the diocese opposed the working-class movement in Cape Breton became so entrenched in the region's historiography that popular writers and activists would suggest that in communities like Whitney Pier the Catholic Church used its power "to keep the workers from taking political stands or action, preaching the virtues of accepting hardship in this life for a reward in the next."[16] It did not seem to matter that Whitney Pier was the parish of cooperators like Fr (later bishop) James Boyle and labour activists like Fr Michael "Micky" MacDonald; nor that Whitney Pier was the home turf of one of the Church's most outspoken advocates for the rights of labour, Fr Thomas O'Reilly Boyle.

The historical perspective began to change in 1996 when St F.X. historian James Cameron published *For the People: A History of St Francis Xavier University*. Thanks to the symbiotic relationship between the diocese and its college, the St F.X. story was the most comprehensive history of Catholicism in the region since Fr Johnston's groundbreaking volumes. Most important, it was the first publication to offer more objective analyses of the careers of famous priests like Fr James Tompkins, the prickly university merger question of the 1920s, and the creation of the St F.X. Extension Department.

By the early 2000s, interest in the Catholic Church in eastern Nova Scotia still focused mainly on the Antigonish Movement, but the analyses were more robust. Recent years have seen the publication of a history of the congregation of the Sisters of St Martha, biographies of Fr Tompkins and Msgr Moses Coady, and a large-scale study of the St F.X. Extension Department that critically analyzed the vision and institutional framework of that fabled program. My previous book, *The Canny Scot: Archbishop James Morrison of Antigonish*, which appeared in 2015, re-examined what we knew (or thought we knew) about the Catholic leadership in the region through a study of an important bishop who had been relegated to the rank of one of the great "sinners" of the period.

Yet, while the careers of bishops and priests such as Archbishop Morrison and Msgr Coady are tremendously important, the need for a broader social history of Catholicism in the region became clear. It was a challenge to write. The Church is hierarchical, and the archives embody this reality. Historians who go to archives looking for the voices of local people mostly find accounts of parish life that were penned by the local pastor, despatched to the local bishop, and then finally reorganized for distribution to bureaucrats in Rome. There is much of value in this episcopal correspondence, but one must be wary. Church relationships were often based on power, and subordinates hesitated to write candidly. Yet all historians are at the mercy of archives and, while I wanted to tell the story of Catholicism from the farmhouse, company home, and fisherman's cottage, I have been obliged to rely significantly on material generated in the vestry, glebe, and bishop's residence.

Although this book was written over three years, it leans heavily on almost two decades of research. In a region like eastern Nova Scotia, it takes time to unravel the complex web of relationships and networks. Knowing that Mother Faustina (Mary MacArthur), the long-time superior of the Congregation of the Sisters of St Martha, was the sister of St F.X. governor and influential Glace Bay lawyer Neil MacArthur changes the way one reads their correspondence.

Small details and minutiae can also trip up even an experienced chronicler. The second Roman Catholic premier of Nova Scotia, Angus Lewis Macdonald ("Angus L."), for instance, spelled his surname name with a lowercase "d," whereas his brother, Fr Stanley MacDonald, and his sister, Sister St Veronica, CND, spelled their surname with an uppercase "D." A trivial detail perhaps, but not to readers in Inverness County.

Finally, this study recognizes that in the nearly five decades since the publication of Fr Johnston's second volume, historians have begun to ask many new questions to supplement their traditional topics of inquiry. Scholars of religion now are also interested in the contribution of women, questions about labour and language, and the narrative of Indigenous communities. I have attempted to weave these accounts together while demonstrating the great importance of faith to generations of Catholics in eastern Nova Scotia.

1

Building a Catholic State
1880–1889

In the late winter of 1883, a brief obituary in a local newspaper reported the death of Patrick Flynn, the 109-year-old native of Salmon River Lake, Guysborough County. Besides a few fragments about his life (he was born in Waterford, Ireland), the announcement noted his dedication to the small mission of Guysborough Parish – the shamrock-festooned St Thomas Church. Incredibly, until his final years, the centenarian walked the three long miles to mass each Sunday.[1] The retired carpenter had witnessed the maturation of the Diocese of Arichat (soon to be renamed Antigonish) and warmly evoked the visits of the rugged Scottish Highlander Bishop William Fraser, who regularly traversed the dense forests and freshly cleared fields of eastern Nova Scotia on horseback. Until his last breath, Flynn, like most of his generation, remained deeply devoted to the Roman Catholic faith.

By 1883 the Diocese of Arichat, which comprised the Nova Scotia mainland counties of Pictou, Antigonish, Guysborough, and the entire island of Cape Breton, had been in existence for only thirty-nine years (considerably fewer than Mr Flynn), but it had progressed steadily since it was founded by Rome's Sacred Congregation for the Propagation of the Faith in the tense ecclesiastical months of 1844.[2] At that time, ethnic bickering and disputes over authority between the Highland Scottish settlers of the eastern counties and the Irish in the capital at Halifax obliged Rome to partition the Diocese of Nova Scotia into the Archdiocese of Halifax and the Diocese of Arichat. The institutions of the Archdiocese of Halifax – which became the Metropolitan in 1852 – were housed in a wealthy and politically relevant port city, whereas Arichat's

75,000 Catholics and its humble institutions were mostly spread among small rural and coastal villages.[3] Despite its French name and the position of its cathedral on the Acadian-dominated Isle Madame in Richmond County, the diocese was considered a Scottish enclave in a regional sea of Irish ecclesiastics. When the bishop of Arichat appealed to Rome, as he frequently did, it was always on behalf of the "poor Highlanders."

Emigration from the highlands and scattered rainswept Hebridean islands of Scotland, which had begun in the 1770s, had transported thousands of indigent families to the poetically described "gloomy forest[s]" of North America and transformed the demographics of eastern Nova Scotia.[4] By the 1870s Archbishop Colin Francis MacKinnon, the son of two émigrés from the small Isle of Eigg, claimed that he had more Catholic Scots among his flock than existed in Scotland itself.[5] A few years later, MacKinnon's successor, Bishop John Cameron, whose family hailed from Fort William in Inverness-shire, made a similar claim, boasting that he had "more Catholic Highlanders than any four dioceses in Scotland put together."[6]

Yet, despite this large Scottish population, in contrast to the many Catholic communities in North America that were ethnically homogenous, Arichat was always multicultural. Long before wooden ships such as the *Nora*, *Aurora*, and *Dove* had conveyed sea-weary Scottish émigrés into the region, the Indigenous Mi'kmaq had welcomed and forged relationships with the French missionaries who arrived in Mi'kma'ki and were responsible for preserving the faith through some difficult (and often violent) periods. More than two hundred years after their initial contact with missionary priests such as Fr Antoine Gaulin from Ile d'Orléans, Mi'kmaq from communities such as Malagawatch and Wagamatcook still made annual summer pilgrimages to Cape Breton's historic Chapel Island to celebrate their singular bond with the Church and to blend Catholic rites with their ancient spiritual customs.[7]

And in rural francophone communities – D'Escousse and Pomquet, for instance – Acadians maintained "the sweet language of their Gallic ancestors" that had been spoken in Nova Scotia since the seventeenth century.[8] These redoubtable Catholics had endured the *Grand Dérangement* of the 1750s and gradually renewed their culture in coastal communities like Cheticamp and West Arichat. Meanwhile, in Sydney, St Peter's, and Guysborough, and at the foot of the stately hills of the Margaree Valley, the descendants of pre-famine Irish émigrés, most of whom had arrived via the fertile fishing grounds of Newfoundland, ensured that St Patrick's Day was a prominent date in the ecclesiastical calendar.

It was this diverse assemblage of Catholics who built the infrastructure of Arichat in the nineteenth century, attended Mass, constructed primitive wooden sanctuaries, steered their children into religious life, and offered their meagre resources for the priest's upkeep. As we begin this book, however, most of this pioneer generation, including Archbishop MacKinnon, have passed on to the next life. Mi'kmaq elders such as John Lulan of Boat Harbour (Pictou Landing), who had watched the steady stream of Scottish immigrants push eastward from Pictou, and early settlers such as Jessie Campbell of Black River, Inverness County, who had been born at sea on a rickety emigrant vessel, now lay in the small overgrown graveyards that dotted the picturesque countryside.[9]

ARICHAT TO ANTIGONISH TOWN

As the Church in eastern Nova Scotia gradually matured, so too did its institutional ambitions. One growing desire was to transfer the diocesan Seat from the coastal Cape Breton cathedral parish of Arichat to the mainland town of Antigonish.[10] The imposing unofficial Romanesque stone "cathedral," which had been built in Antigonish town between 1867 and 1874, was the most obvious sign of this imminent shift. There had, however, been intimations, as Archbishop MacKinnon had been candid about his preference for the mainland and even petitioned Rome for permission to live in the inland parish of St Andrews.

Archbishop MacKinnon had also worried that the Archdiocese of Halifax would annex the mainland counties and leave him on the island of Cape Breton (Archbishop William Walsh of Halifax, who had battled MacKinnon's predecessor, had indeed raised the issue with Rome on numerous occasions).[11] MacKinnon had therefore moved the budding seminary, St Francis Xavier College (St F.X.), from Arichat to Antigonish town in 1855, and would have transferred his cathedral Seat had Walsh not blocked him in Rome.[12] Behind closed curtains, it was well known that St Ninian's Cathedral had been built in Antigonish as the future Seat of the diocese and that it was only bureaucratic hurdles that kept the imposing *Tigh Dhe* (Gaelic for "House of God") from assuming that function.[13]

Figure 1.1 | Our Lady of Assumption, Arichat, c. 1900

Over the years, it has been insinuated that ethnicity which, as we will read, was a major problem within the Canadian Church, played a factor in the transfer of St F.X. to the mainland. Although period correspondence notes only complaints about the weather of Arichat and the cost of rent, the belief that Bishop MacKinnon did not want to educate his mostly Scottish seminarians in an Acadian village would never really wane. "When the college was taken from Arichat years ago," Fr Leo Keats wrote eighty-two years later, "a narrow prejudiced pocket of north-east wind carried it in a south westerly direction to Antigonish."[14]

Bishop John Cameron, who succeeded MacKinnon as bishop in 1877, had no fear of a pending Halifax takeover, spoke fluent French, and enjoyed living in Arichat, "the mistress of the seas"; but he was also keen to finalize the relocation of diocesan infrastructure to Antigonish town. While the 1860s had been "golden days" for the Isle Madame community, the opening of St Peter's Canal in 1869 diverted much of the maritime business to Sydney and the city lost its prominence as a port. It was, of course, not inconsequential that Cameron was also a native of Antigonish county; however, the decision to relocate to the mainland in the autumn of 1880 was mostly pragmatic.[15]

Figure 1.2 | St Ninian's Cathedral

Once described by Thomas Chandler Haliburton, the famous author of *The Clockmaker*, as "one of the prettiest" in eastern Nova Scotia, the town of Antigonish was ready to become the centre of Catholic episcopal authority. While it lacked the splendour of larger cathedral towns like Halifax or Charlottetown, it was home to a college and the diocesan newspaper, *The Casket*, and had made steady improvements to its infrastructure. By 1883 an impressive two-storey bishop's residence, of which the locals were rather proud, was erected on a hill behind St Ninian's Cathedral. "From its windows," noted one travel writer, "the view is beautiful."[16]

Despite Bishop Cameron's relocation to the mainland, Arichat's historic Our Lady of Assumption Cathedral remained the Seat of the diocese until August 1886, when a Pontifical decree changed both the name and the Seat to Antigonish.[17] In the meantime, Fr James Michael Quinan (one of three brother priests) remained on Isle Madame as the rector of Our Lady of Assumption.[18] An erudite native of Halifax, and a capable and distinguished pastor who occasionally wrote for the local newspapers, Quinan was an asset to the parish; nevertheless, the loss of the Seat and the bishop was a bitter blow to Arichat's fortunes. When the American author and artist S.G.W. Benjamin visited the coastal community in 1883, he could already sense this transformation as the gravestones in the cemetery seemed "to read the sad story of a society once happy and prosperous, but now gone to decay."[19]

While Bishop Cameron's transfer to Antigonish town was popular in some quarters, for countless Cape Breton and Acadian Catholics it was a disappointment.[20] Resentment intensified with the news that the construction of St Ninian's Cathedral had saddled the diocese with an enormous debt of forty thousand dollars.[21] The imposing Romanesque *Tigh Dhe*, while aesthetically pleasing, was terribly expensive. As Archbishop MacKinnon had always intended the stone edifice to serve as the diocesan cathedral, most of the construction debt was borne by the diocese and not by St Ninian's parish. Antigonish town got the church but Catholics in the whole diocese bore the responsibility for the payments.

Although Bishop Cameron had once complained to Rome of the cathedral's enormous cost – and it was one reason for securing Archbishop MacKinnon's resignation in 1877 – he stubbornly defended the decision to decentralize the financing of the *Tigh Dhe*. "It was sheer folly," he grumbled in an 1879 circular, "to hold the parish of St. Ninian's answerable for the cost of the church."[22] Born in the rural parish of St Andrews, Cameron appreciated penury but, desperate to avoid defaulting on diocesan loans, he taxed the parishes eighty cents per household. Even when priests ministering to penniless coastal parishes begged him to "leave a part of the debt for another generation," he insisted on payment.[23] Although cash-strapped Catholics across the diocese were prudent, they complained continually about financing infrastructure in Antigonish town.

BISHOP CAMERON'S ULTAMONTANISM

While debt was a serious issue under any circumstances, Bishop Cameron had important reasons for quickly paying off the cathedral liabilities. The dark evergreen forests and freshly cleared fields of eastern Nova Scotia might have been a long way from the paved piazzas of Italy, but the prelate could feel the pedantic Roman bureaucrats breathing down his neck. Within the ancient corridors of the governing Curia, cavalier spending and indebtedness, whether in Paris, Dublin, or Port Hawkesbury, garnered a black stain of incompetence. Cameron may have been native to a small rural parish along the meandering South River, but by the time he graduated from Rome's Urban College of the Congregation de Propaganda Fide he was a thoroughly Roman convert to the philosophy of "ultramontanism" (beyond the mountains) that dominated the Church in the second half of the nineteenth century.

"It is difficult," notes Jeffrey von Arx, SJ, for people "to understand the depth of commitment to the ultramontane cause of so many Catholics in the century and a half before Vatican II."[24] Demanding obedience to the papacy and strict uniformity in practice and dogma, ultramontanism was a monarchical system that filtered power downward from the pope to his bishops and priests.[25] Through this submission to the authority of Rome and the exercise of piety through devotionalism, ultramontanists worked to create a robust Catholic subculture that would keep the Church free from domination by the modern secular state.[26] By tightening bureaucratic and operational procedures around the globe, the Catholic Church moulded itself into "a state within a state."[27]

While the farmers of eastern Nova Scotia barely stirred when the first Vatican Council of 1869–70 voted to endorse the infallibility of the pope when speaking *ex cathedra*, Bishop Cameron was ecstatic. In the 1850s, as local Catholics attended parishes staffed by graduates of the old Quebec seminary, Cameron sat in the "benches" at the Urban College at the feet of some of the Church's most influential intellectuals and cultivated the personal networks useful for promotion. His evident intelligence and strong character earned the young priest powerful friends. Like his ultramontane colleagues throughout the Catholic world, Cameron had lofty ambitions, and presiding over a diocese plagued with debt was not part of his plan.

Bishop Cameron personified the maturation of Catholicism in eastern Nova Scotia. Although young and inexperienced when he was sent to the Eternal City in the late 1840s, he returned with poise and ambition. When he took ecclesiastical control of Antigonish, the region was immediately thrust into the national and global Catholic conversation. Of course, Cameron's predecessors had their own Roman networks, but his contacts were more influential. Bureaucrats such as the Irishman Bishop George Conroy, the first apostolic delegate to Canada, had befriended Cameron at the Urban College and had aided him loyally. It was Conroy who essentially ousted Archbishop MacKinnon from his position (and residence) as bishop of Arichat in 1877, and it was Conroy who got the "poor old man" his ceremonial appointment as titular archbishop of Amida.[28]

Yet Bishop Cameron and Bishop Conroy – who died unexpectedly on a visit to Newfoundland in 1878 – were more than just friends and alumni of the celebrated Urban College; they were also both mentored by the powerful Paul Cardinal Cullen, rector of the Pontifical Irish College in Rome and later archbishop of Dublin. Through this friendship, Cameron was part of a global ultramontane network committed to developing a devotional brand of Catholicism. Historian Colin Barr has demonstrated that from 1832 Cullen "set out with great success to mould the Roman Catholic Church in the English-speaking world to his vision."[29] Through a vast network of Irish clergy ministering in Europe, Australia, and the North American colonies (Archbishop Walsh of Halifax was one of his early appointments), Cullen produced a "Hibernio-Roman" empire among Anglo-Catholics in the new world.[30]

As Barr has noted, Cardinal Cullen preferred his global network of prelates "to be both Irish *and* Roman," but in Cameron's case it was enough to be both *Scottish* and Roman.[31] Cameron was devoted to Cullen (he once asked his father to send money from St Andrews to Rome to buy his mentor a set of leather-bound books) and later stated that he owed more to the Dublin prelate "than to any other man living or dead."[32] In May 1870, while in the Holy City, Cameron was consecrated as coadjutor bishop for Arichat at the hands of the cardinal, and promptly given a seat at the Vatican Council, where he "stoutly supported the majority judgement on the question of papal infallibility."[33]

Cameron returned to the Maritime provinces as a confident and aggressive ultramontanist, sporadically attacking his regional colleagues, especially those who did not support Cullen's agenda, as being infatuated with a vanity "into which the Gallican bishops had decoyed them."[34] No other Canadian bishop "enjoyed more fully the confidence of the Holy See," and even Cameron boasted that he was "favorably known at the Vatican."[35] On one trip to Rome, a number of American prelates condescending observed "the rustic from backwoods Nova Scotia," only to be shocked by the warm welcome he received from Curia officials.[36]

Cameron's ultramontanism had important consequences for eastern Nova Scotia. First, it propelled the local Church into the regional and national spotlight. Rome was eager to hear from the Nova Scotian prelate, and the personal sentiments of local clergy on both regional and national issues were parcelled into annual reports sent back to Italy. Cameron also supplied Rome with information on his episcopal colleagues, and the Curia regularly asked him to intervene in the affairs of regional bishops. His colleagues were of course often asked to do the same; but Cameron's pen wielded greater authority. In 1871 he settled a quarrel in Newfoundland, and when a dispute erupted between Archbishop Michael Hannan of Halifax and the Congregation of the Sisters of Charity in 1880, he was sent to conciliate. His investigation, which favoured the Charities, was instrumental in having Hannan, technically his superior, "admonished" by the Sacred Congregation.[37]

Like any good ultramontanist, Cameron judiciously controlled local institutions, eyed expansion, and demanded submission from the flock. Although Archbishop MacKinnon had taken great pains, under pressure from Halifax and the Curia, to Romanize the diocese in the 1850s, Cameron adopted a system of formality, ecclesiastical discipline, and devotionalism that was unparalleled. "You stood as much chance of changing the Gulf Stream," recalled one contemporary, "as his Lordship's mind once he declared it officially."[38] Significantly, the methods of the old Scottish and Quebec-born priests who had ministered in the pioneer days, and any sign of initiative on the part of the laity – even the use of the fiddle in the sanctuary – were discarded.[39] "A choir of singers and an organ" is needed at Arisaig, noted Fr Ronald MacGillivray. "The old fiddle doing duty" must be "banished from the holy place for ever."[40]

Notwithstanding Cameron's concerns about debt, it is astonishing how quickly he was able to foster a unified and standardized Catholic culture within the region. Everything from the artwork to the liturgy was Romanized and the people happily went along. There is nowhere, he noted proudly, "a diocese in which the faithful are more submissive to the teachings of the church, more respectful of the clergy, or less affected by the paganizing influences of the nineteenth century."[41] Now was the time for expansion.

RAILROADS AND COAL

During this decade, in parallel with this transformation of the Church toward ultramontanism, the Province of Nova Scotia was trying its best to revamp and modernize its economy. Although the Maritime region of Canada had the greatest rate of industrial expansion in the country, it still suffered the highest rate of outmigration.[42] While explanations for the exodus vary, historian Julian Gwyn describes Nova Scotia in this period as "a noted exporter of human beings."[43] As one Cape Breton newspaper commented in the rainy spring of 1883, going west was "the order of the day."[44]

Despite the resulting reduction in manpower for cultivating the soil and the need to seek foreign markets (often with high tariffs) for cattle, fish, and produce, Nova Scotia workers maintained their dignity.[45] "Although our Catholics are poor," one priest boasted, "paupers are comparatively few."[46] When subscriptions and other financial offerings were sent to Rome, the purse was not always bursting – but never from a lack of enthusiasm. "When we take into consideration the failure of our fisheries and the backwardness of the coal traffic," Bishop Cameron explained after sending a particularly light purse to the Propagation of the Faith in 1884, "the wonder is that they have done so well."[47]

Another major problem was the lack of transportation infrastructure. Parishioners habitually complained of the "horrid roads" in their parishes, and getting from Pictou to Cape Breton or Canso was gruelling.[48] "Most roads were rough and dusty in the summer," notes one historian, "impassable with deep snow in the winter, and deep in mud in the spring."[49] Although the provincial government had ambitious plans for the railroads that would eventually connect Yarmouth with Sydney, progress was slow.

While the eastern extension of the Intercolonial Railway ultimately connected Pictou County with the Strait of Canso, travellers from the mainland to Sydney still had to ferry across the strait and then ride in cramped coaches to West Bay, Inverness County. From there the steamer *Neptune* took them across the Bras d'Or Lake.[50] To save Bishop Cameron this arduous journey on his confirmation tours, wealthy Catholics would often place a steamer at his disposal, but trips to parishes like Ingonish and Bay St Lawrence were long and taxing.[51]

It is not surprising, therefore, that Ottawa's decision to build a railway through Cape Breton as part of a nationwide infrastructure investment in 1886 was met with excitement.[52] Local priests aided survey teams and even became embroiled in heated debates over the route that trains should take across the island. As the central route would cross the Barra Strait at Grand Narrows, and the southern route would travel through St Peters, the economic stakes for residents were high and recriminations rampant (the central route was the winner). When Fr Martin MacPherson, the pastor at Little Bras d'Or, aggressively supported the route that would bring the train closest to his native community of Big Pond, opponents objected that his real goal was to get his brother elected to parliament.[53] From East Bay, Fr Neil MacLeod benignly mused that the people "were going mad about the railway," but priests with connections actively lobbied for employment opportunities.[54] "Mr. John MacIntosh, (Father Daniel Joseph MacIntosh's brother) made application for the position of Baggage Master at North Sydney Station," Cameron enquired of a local politician, "and he is now very anxious to learn whether his application will be entertained."[55]

Besides providing more comfortable transportation, the railway was critical for the industrial development of the Sydney area. Sir John A. MacDonald's 1876 "National Policy," which introduced high tariffs on imported manufactured items, created pockets of industrial growth throughout the Maritime provinces, raising optimism that the region would become the industrial centre of Canada.[56] Sydney's plentiful coalfields stretched for thirty miles along the northeastern shore of Cape Breton and, although bituminous coal had been extracted in the mines since the late eighteenth century, operations had recently intensified to supply eager central-Canadian markets.[57] Catholics from the countryside, mostly low-skilled labourers, were increasingly joined by imported workers from Britain and Newfoundland in the damp collieries of the crown monopoly, the General Mining Association.[58]

By Canadian standards, Sydney's industrial expansion was remarkable. Coastal communities like Glace Bay, which had been a "bleak collection of four collieries at the far end of the island," were soon teaming with miners.[59] Yet this expansion came at a social cost. Obliged to live in hastily fabricated company houses and purchase supplies in company stores, workers were vulnerable to having their credit cut off, "leaving families with no provisions."[60] Although the coalfields were decades away from the famous labour-capital tumult of the twentieth century, work stoppages were already common.

When strikes closed the pits, foreign replacement workers were hurriedly recruited, soldiers sent from Halifax, and picketers often forced to emigrate.[61] For many Catholics, work conditions and threats of violence had physical, emotional, and spiritual consequences.

Ministering among the miners, priests such as Fr Alexander Chisholm of Glace Bay, who hailed from the rural mainland parish of St Andrews, were aware of grievances but had scant experience with industry and little guidance from Rome. There is no record of the clergy's opinion on the Provincial Workmen's Association, which was formed at Springhill, Cumberland County, in 1879, and no formal comment can be found on the struggle for legislative recognition that the union waged throughout the latter decades of the nineteenth century.

While the Church had some minor spats with the General Mining Association, the relationship was in general cordial, and the clergy for the most part cooperated with the company responsible for the newfound industrialization. This collaboration was evident in 1883, when the diocese agreed to exempt miners from attending mass on saints' days "in return for the collection of church dues at the pay office."[62] The ability to gather dues directly from the miners' pay envelopes ensured a steady stream of revenue to support the expansion of Catholic infrastructure. After this agreement on the "check-off," new parishes opened at Sydney Mines (1884), Bridgeport (1885), and Victoria Mines (1887). At North Sydney, home to 1,200 Catholics, Fr Daniel Joseph MacIntosh built the impressive St Joseph's Church in the "most conspicuous location of the town."[63]

DEVOTIONALISM IN THE 1880S

While all this new construction was financed mainly by the combustible sedimentary rock taken from the coal mines – even in the heavily Presbyterian County of Pictou, new Catholic parishes were opened at Thorburn (1884) and New Glasgow (1885) – Catholics sponsored these churches in myriad other ways as well.[64] Parish picnics among the miners of Stellarton and the farmers of Christmas Island attracted enthusiastic crowds and yielded excellent profits, while few Catholics in Antigonish town missed the springtime excursion to St Ninian's Cathedral with "horses and carts to level and beautify the grounds."[65]

Aside from its daily labour, life in parishes like West Arichat "revolved around the Church," and in an ultramontane setting Catholics were keen to demonstrate their devotionalism. Priests introduced their flocks to the mystical riches of the Middle Ages, and worship that might have seemed "superstitious or magical" to earlier generations was vigorously promoted.[66] Community newspapers published the regulations for the Lenten season in late winter, autumn winds brought October devotions, and December flurries signaled the beginning of Advent.[67] Not to mention the Holy Days to observe, the catechism to study, and the societies to patronize. In all cases, the "grandeur" and "truth" of the faith was celebrated.[68]

Pushing back against old customs of venerating local saints or indulging in regional or ethnic traditions, ultramontanists promoted devotions that would appeal to all Catholics. The "heart and soul" of this movement was the Feast of Corpus Christi (first celebrated in 1264). Popular in parishes around the globe, the Eucharistic procession allowed church-goers to symbolically follow their Redeemer through the streets and publicly demonstrate their loyalty and faith. One of the more memorable local processions was held in the sweltering June heat of 1884, when the people of Frenchvale, Cape Breton, "spared neither pains nor trouble" preparing for their parade.[69] Before hundreds of spectators, many of whom had poured in from surrounding parishes, the Blessed Sacrament was reverently carried under a beautiful canopy through "magnificent arches" in a pageant led by the North Sydney Catholic band.

Daily life, of course, was never quite as virtuous or as solemn as these displays of piety would suggest. While one historian of Cape Breton claimed that "there were almost no mixed marriages, either from a religious or ethnic point of view," the archives tell a different story.[70] When a young Arichat woman married a Protestant without the blessing of Fr Quinan, the priest laid down the doctrine of the Church "as [he] had never had occasion to do before."[71] From Glace Bay, Fr Alexander Chisholm, an Urban College graduate, confessed that although his flock was "full of faith," mixed marriages were a persistent annoyance. In fact, he often baptised two- or three-year-old children of Catholic mothers who had not attended Mass since their marriage to a Protestant.[72] Priests may have "presided over a people to whom loyalty was a virtue and submission a yoke to be borne," as one historian has put it, but the rate of mixed marriages and church absenteeism in the parishes at the time nonetheless evinced a level of non-compliance.[73]

Obtaining the obedience of Catholic elites could also be difficult. One interesting example is that of the prominent politician Senator William Miller. Born in Antigonish town in 1835, Miller practised law in Arichat, represented Richmond County in the Nova Scotia Legislature, and in 1867, at the age of thirty-two, was appointed to the Canadian Senate. While respected in the political world, he regularly ran afoul of his parish priest in Our Lady of Assumption Parish. In fact, Fr Quinan complained that the senator "functionally lived as a Protestant." He often attended the Protestant Meeting House and even purchased a plot in the Protestant burial ground.[74] A political friend of Bishop Cameron, Miller had served the diocese loyally, but he made the clergy uneasy; it was difficult to obtain the submission of the flock while appearing to have one rule for the poor and one for the rich.

Notwithstanding Fr Quinan's complaint against Senator Miller, relationships between Catholics and their Protestant neighbours were generally peaceful. When the mission church at Thorburn was ransacked and the communion chalice thrown into the stove, it was seen as an isolated incident.[75] Sectarian battles were more often waged in ink or from the podium. When the *Eastern Chronicle*, a Presbyterian newspaper printed in New Glasgow, published some cynical attacks on a popular Catholic author and created a local "anti-Jesuit tempest in a teapot," the "controversialist, lecturer, and journalist" Fr Daniel M. MacGregor gave a fiery lecture in that heavily Protestant town to publicly counter the rhetoric.[76]

A much greater threat to the Catholic community than mixed marriages or sectarianism was drunkenness. As many families were painfully aware, alcoholism spared neither ethnicity nor creed, and "the drink" plagued most communities. Although taught that "no drunkard [would] inherit the Kingdom of God," overzealous parish picnic-goers had a field day with homebrew and rum when they decided to partake in a wee *dileag*.[77] Throughout the diocese, temperance societies such as Fr Theobald Mathew's "Crusade," which had begun in the misty southwest of Ireland in 1838, were kept extremely busy. The "single most extraordinary social movement that occurred in pre-famine Ireland," Father Mathew's Crusade was introduced into eastern Nova Scotia by the County Leitrim native Fr James Drummond, who had made Nova Scotia his new home.[78] Pastor at Main-à-Dieu-Louisbourg, and later Sacred Heart in Sydney, Drummond famously administered the pledge to Bishop William Fraser in 1841 in the presence of a crowd of witnesses in Antigonish town.[79]

Although many "Father Mathew Medals of Sobriety" had been pinned on the chests of teetotalers across the region, by 1885 the crusade had been supplanted by the Catholic Total Abstinence Society, known as the League of the Cross. The league, which had been organized in England by Cardinal Henry Edward Manning, archbishop of Westminster, was introduced to the diocese by Fr John Shaw, pastor in Glace Bay, after he had audience with the cardinal in 1881.[80] In the ultramontane environment, the connection of Father Mathew's crusade with Ireland was problematic, and priests like Shaw ensured that the old Father Mathew Society properties were sold (when Shaw became priest at Arisaig, the society's property at Malignant Cove was immediately listed for sale).[81] By the end of the decade, the League of the Cross was established in Antigonish town and in Presbyterian-dominated New Glasgow; over the next fifty years, it would become the diocese's most influential Catholic society.[82]

THE CONGREGATION OF NOTRE DAME AND THE SISTERS OF CHARITY

While devotionalism, fundraising picnics, processions, and temperance were critical to the development of the ultramontane subculture, Rome knew that only Catholic education could safeguard the Church's long-term survival. Although Nova Scotia Catholics had failed to organize a separate system of denominational education, the convent schools of the Montreal-based Congregation of Notre Dame – whose members had once taught at Fortress Louisbourg – offered young girls in communities like Arichat (1856) and West Arichat (1863) access to a high-quality curriculum in a strict Catholic environment.[83] Since the early days of Archbishop MacKinnon's administration, the congregation had brought the diocese stability and prestige, and the expansion of its influence and visibility was central to Bishop Cameron's agenda.

So, when plans for a new public grammar school were unveiled in the heavily Presbyterian town of Pictou, the priest at Stella Maris parish hurriedly petitioned the Congregation of Notre Dame to build a convent school close by. The resulting brick convent and Young Ladies Academy opened in 1880 under the supervision of Sister St Maurice (Frances Liberia Collins), the daughter of the pioneering Toronto Catholic journalist Francis Collins.[84] When construction began on yet another convent school next to St Ninian's Cathedral in Antigonish town, Bishop Cameron was so excited that he personally donated a crucifix, some ornate chairs, and even a wood stove. Saint Bernard's Convent, "one of the most beautiful houses among the many missions of the Sisters," was opened in the autumn of 1883 before a capacity audience.[85] "I hope [the] Antigonish convent is doing well," wrote one priest. "God knows it was needed."[86]

The rapidity of the Congregation of Notre Dame's expansion throughout eastern Nova Scotia was noteworthy. Convent schools were opened at coastal Port Hood (1884), an expanding Sydney (1885), heavily Protestant New Glasgow (1887), and in rural Mabou (1887). By agreeing to teach the young girls of the community, the sisters were taking a great burden off the priests. According to the archives of Sydney's Holy Angels Convent, when Fr Quinan greeted the first cadre of teaching sisters at the train station, he received them as if they were "angels descended from Heaven."[87] In all cases, the laity generously supported the women with money, furniture, and even feather pillows.[88]

Having the Catholic children of villages like Port Hood educated by members of an esteemed Montreal congregation reinforced the subculture and demonstrated the capacity of the Catholic state. These convent schools, noted one Pictou historian, were symbols "of magnificent religious, civic and material accomplishment."[89] The influx of members of the Montreal congregation also injected a vibrancy – even an exoticism – into the region, as the teachers, often multilingual, came from many different parts of Canada. The sisters also trained girls to teach in the public-school system, and prepared them to raise "respectable" families.[90] Writing from Pictou in the autumn of 1887, Sister St Lucilla noted that she "didn't think there [could be] any Catholic girls going to the public schools," as the mission had such a "good effect."[91]

As Catholic parents petitioned for more convent schools, Bishop Cameron sought out another women's order to meet the demand. From 1879 to 1881, he had defended the Halifax-based Sisters of Charity against their archbishop in a quarrel over jurisdiction and, ironically, their desire to open a teaching academy.[92] Granted apostolic jurisdiction over the sisters in 1880, Cameron appointed Fr William B. MacDonald, pastor at Stellarton, as superior-general, and within three years the "Charities" had laid the cornerstone for a convent in his parish.[93] It was not long before Fr Daniel J. MacIntosh persuaded them to open a publicly funded young ladies' academy in North Sydney.[94] Like the other convent schools, Mount St Joseph offered its patrons a "solid and refined education."

With so many students in these schools, the Congregation of Notre Dame and the Sisters of Charity had a ready supply of new recruits.[95] Like young men who were inspired to enter the seminary by the example of their parish priest, young women who entered convents "were led to the path by somebody who was already a member of a religious congregation."[96] The first to leave for the Congregation of Notre Dame motherhouse in Montreal was Ellen Chisholm of Antigonish town, who became a "brave solitary postulant" in 1876 (she professed her vows in November 1878 but died shortly afterward).[97] In 1882 Isabel Gillis of South West Margaree took the "Brown Habit" as a Charity novice at Mount St Vincent in Halifax before beginning her short career as a teacher in Yarmouth County (she died in 1885 at the age of twenty-six). "What better way to build ties with a geographic area," notes historian Doreen Vautour, "than to attract the daughters of local families to the congregation?"[98] Eventually even Bishop Cameron boasted five nieces in the Congregation of Notre Dame.

PROVINCIAL PUSH-BACK

In Halifax the bureaucrats of the provincial government, mostly Protestant, watched the expansion of the convent schools with some dismay. The complex Education Acts of the 1860s had created in Nova Scotia a system of state-sponsored "free schools" that were administered under the vigilant eye of a provincial education superintendent. Schools were controlled by a committee of local trustees and were subject to compulsory provincial assessment. So, while there was no formal system of denominational education, local trustees had authority to hire Catholic teachers and approve religious instruction in their own buildings.[99] As a result, while Saint Bernard's Convent School in Antigonish town received funds from the trustees, Stella Maris Convent School in Pictou, a heavily Protestant town, did not.

While the Congregation of Notre Dame accepted the trustee arrangement – they financed Stella Maris themselves – the women refused to sit the Nova Scotia teaching accreditation examination. While the exam ensured that the province's teachers had an educational baseline, the sisters of the Congregation were already assessed by a rigorous panel of examiners appointed by the archbishop of Montreal.[100] As more teaching sisters entered Nova Scotia classrooms (and became visible in mixed communities), however, Halifax was under considerable pressure to standardize qualifications.[101]

This question of teaching accreditation demonstrates the periodic tension between the Catholic subculture and the secular state. While government intentions were honourable (although some detected sectarian undertones), bureaucrats did not understand the nuances of religious life. The Montreal-based Congregation staffed convent schools throughout Canada, and their teachers might even be relocated on short notice. Not only was travelling to Nova Scotia for an accreditation exam an inconvenience, but if a sister were to teach in a number of provinces during the term, she would have to sit several accreditation exams.[102]

While the Catholic press acknowledged the benefits of standardizing teaching qualifications, they understood the importance of the Congregation of Notre Dame to the Catholic sub-state and proclaimed the exceptionality of the women religious instructors. Unlike those who used teaching as "a steppingstone to marriage" (only to abandon the profession after tying the knot), teaching sisters devoted their lives to the classroom and staffed some of the nation's finest academic institutions. If the province forced these women to sit the exam, there was a real possibility that the Congregation would leave the region. This Bishop Cameron would not allow. "As I grow older, and draw nearer to death and judgement," he confessed, "my disapproval and dread of Godless education becomes more and more intense."[103]

Fortunately, the accreditation issue was resolved – if only temporarily – by the new provincial superintendent, Dr David Allison, former president of Mount Allison University, who "resisted the desire to make public education an instrument of progressivist reform." Described by Cameron as a "fair-minded friend," Allison agreed to review the credentials of the teaching-sisters on an individual basis. By 1886 Saint Bernard's Convent in Antigonish town had qualified for government support as an "academy," was renamed Saint Bernard's

Young Ladies Academy, and added grades nine to twelve.[104] "Polished education, and gentle manners," noted the inspector of schools for Antigonish County, "distinguished [its] graduates."[105]

THE DIOCESAN COLLEGE

Directly across from Saint Bernard's Young Ladies Academy (separated only by St Ninian's Cathedral) stood the small diocesan college, St Francis Xavier University. In his history of St F.X., James Cameron titled the second part "The Bishop and his College," rightly acknowledging the importance of the institution to Cameron's ultramontane agenda. From its founding in 1853, the school had three important goals: to enhance the reputation of the diocese, provide a steady flow of young men into the seminary, and create a lay Catholic elite that the community could be proud of.[106]

St F.X. had never been an easy project; it was always a challenge to support a small Catholic college without the aid of teaching orders like the Jesuits or the Irish Christian Brothers. In the 1840s there was province-wide talk of one "colonial seminary," and by the 1880s Archbishop Hannan of Halifax had even proposed a merger of the small Catholic colleges into a central institution at Pictou.[107] Nevertheless, most Catholics considered St F.X. the benchmark for the general health of the diocese, and the progress of the college was proudly noted in the diocesan press and cited in reports to Rome. When a three-storey brick wing was attached to the original seminary building in the summer of 1880, the campus looked more stately and the future promising.

St F.X. was funded primarily through parish collections and a substantial annual grant from the province. When the various Christian denominations in Nova Scotia rejected an 1881 proposal to support a non-sectarian University of Halifax, however, the legislature retaliated by withdrawing the annual funding for denominational colleges. Although the loss of this subsidy was a serious blow, Cameron demanded money from the parishes, as he had done with the cathedral debt, and quickly raised some $20,000.[108] The "excessive boldness" of this drive, he proudly reported, "startled the Protestants who were watching for the welcome moment when the [Catholic] seminary would have to indefinitely close."[109]

Determined to create an endowment fund, the bishop decided to incorporate a board of governors and place more "responsibility on their shoulders."[110] While the new board was full of clergy, it was under the aegis of the provincial government and, importantly, offered considerable financial and administrative powers to some prominent laymen. Cameron maintained personal and cultural power over the institution, of course, but St F.X. "ceased legally to be a bishop's college."[111] It meant little in the short term, but would have consequences in years to come.

A CATHOLIC PREMIER FROM ANTIGONISH

The struggle over teaching accreditation and college grants demonstrated the value of political influence in Halifax. The ultramontane movement needed a political star in the legislature and, since 1877, Bishop Cameron had been grooming his own bright light. In books and scholarly journals, generations of historians have described the extraordinary political partnership between the bishop and Sir John S.D. Thompson.[112] The two had been introduced at the Halifax residence of Archbishop Thomas Louis Connolly, and by the early 1870s Cameron had become a mentor to the aspiring Conservative politician.[113] While the men had compatible personal characteristics, their bond was solidified by Thompson's conversion to Catholicism.[114] The bishop's own father had converted to Rome from Presbyterianism, and his paternal uncle, Rev. Ewan Cameron, was an outspoken minister of the Kirk in Port Stanley, Ontario.[115]

While John Thompson pined for a seat in the provincial legislature, there was no opening in the electoral district of Halifax County. Recognizing a golden opportunity, Cameron and the quasi-Catholic senator William Miller invited him to run for the Conservatives in the 1877 Antigonish County provincial by-election.[116] Some immediately recognized the dangers of a bishop parachuting in a candidate from another district, and clergy such as Fr Ronald MacDonald in Pictou were concerned about optics.[117] "A county, which at this moment feels itself for the first time emancipated from the political oligarchy of a quarter of century," he opined, "must be handled delicately."[118]

The heavily Catholic Antigonish County had only become a provincial riding in 1867 and, although Fr MacDonald supported Cameron's agenda, he also knew that voters enjoyed freely electing their own local representatives. Even the rector of St Ninian's Cathedral, the popular Fr Hugh Gillis, felt Thompson had little

Figure 1.3 | Bishop John Cameron

chance of victory. In fact, it was not until Bishop Cameron persuaded Angus MacGillivray, the most popular potential Liberal candidate, to drop out of the contest that Thompson's fortunes changed.[119]

Antigonish County sent two members to the provincial legislature, and so it was easier to convince the heavily Liberal constituency to vote for a candidate supported by the episcopacy (even one from the opposite party). In the ultramontane environment, priests easily made the election about the bishop's episcopal authority. Fr Ronald MacGillivray, later known as *Sagart Arasaig* for his historical and genealogical musings in the local press, wrote that, although cautious not to employ his sacred influence at the St Joseph's polling station, he was clear that "it would be a sorry day for the people if they were to abandon their natural leaders."[120] Others, including St F.X. professor Fr Daniel MacGregor, bluntly told Thompson's opponents that "he was going to do all he could against them in the election."[121]

With this outspoken clerical support, a Liberal already holding the other Antigonish seat, and a popular Liberal candidate on the sidelines, the Conservative Thompson was elected by 517 votes.[122] One brave disenchanted Grit mused that "it would be just as well for the bishop to elect his man off-hand himself, as the late election was only a farce." But Bishop Cameron was elated.[123] When, after the 1878 provincial election (Thompson was returned alongside the popular Angus MacGillivray, who had stepped aside in 1877), his candidate was offered the position of attorney general in the Simon Holmes government, the prelate felt vindicated and empowered.

As patron of Nova Scotia's attorney general, Bishop Cameron enjoyed many benefits. From college grants to the incorporation of St F.X., the recently converted Thompson liberally employed his office on behalf of his surrogate diocese. "As I understand that Dominick Farrell, Esq., is soon to vacate his position as Commissioner of the Provincial Board of Charity," Cameron wrote to Thompson in 1881, "you would greatly oblige by giving the place to Dr. Duncan Fraser."[124] The attorney general also served as a purveyor of news and gossip, not only within the inner circles of the government but also within the echelons of the archdiocese of Halifax.

With his political star in cabinet, Cameron soon became an unabashed political broker who reigned as sovereign of two worlds. "Former residents of his diocese," mused one historian "wrote to ask for his [Cameron's] intercession, not with God, but with the Hon. John Thompson."[125] Cameron sincerely believed that his partnership with Thompson was promoting "God's glory" and he even took to calling local Liberal critics – many of them upstanding Catholics – "chickens."[126] He also believed that Thompson's career was guided by a divine hand. When Premier Holmes unexpectedly resigned to accept a lucrative bureaucratic post, the attorney general was called upon to form a government. By the end of May 1882, Cameron's candidate had been sworn in as the first Roman Catholic premier of Nova Scotia.

Thompson's elevation to the premier's office was a historic moment for Nova Scotian Catholicism. It was also short-lived. When the fledgling government went to the people a few months later they fared poorly. Although Thompson won his Antigonish County seat, his government faced a minority situation in the legislature. For a short time, he was able to cobble together a feeble coalition, but his poor showing and desire to be rid of the "rum and whisky – cards and fiddles" of Antigonish made it more fitting for him to accept a position on the Nova Scotia Supreme Court.[127] Cameron's protégé had been premier of Nova Scotia for a mere fifty-four days.[128]

DIOCESAN CLERGY

The elections of John Thompson demonstrated the loyalty and submission of the diocesan clergy; if some were uneasy with their superior's politicking, they kept quiet. Bishop Cameron counted on these men to be the backbone of the Catholic state and it was a demanding vocation. Priests not only had to maintain their church, administer the sacraments, and keep their parishes debt-free, but they also had secular responsibilities. Second only to physicians (if there was one in the parish) in level of education and often possessing a considerable library, they might also hold several administrative roles.

In period correspondence with their superiors, most clergymen began their missals with apologies for tardiness. The usual reason was the abundance of mentally taxing confessions. One priest endured a week that saw him confessing at a rate of 150 parishioners a day. In the confessional box all Saturday afternoon, Fr Quinan of Arichat returned to find the bishop's letter on his desk, but "it was then near dark and [he] had besides to go immediately to the head of the harbour on a sick call." Sunday was even busier, and only after vespers "could [he] get a spare half an hour."[129] Even Bishop Cameron maintained a strict schedule to cope with his daily commitments. "If a royal prince was spending the evening with him," recalled barrister and historian John L. MacDougall, "just when the minute hand of the clock pointed to half-past nine," the bishop would announce that "it was bedtime."[130]

Priests also noted the strain of ministering amid domestic worries, disease, and death. Life in nineteenth-century Nova Scotia was arduous. Parents struggled to feed and clothe their children and had to face illness and terrifying rates of infant mortality. In 1881 diphtheria devastated the village of Arichat, and two years later, as the *North Sydney Herald* lamented, infections had carried off "many little ones" at Broad Cove and North East Margaree.[131]

The success of any clerical assignment depended greatly on a match between the temperament of the priest and the spirit of the congregation. In some situations, priests unable to build a harmonious rapport with their parishioners had to be quickly transferred, whereas others, like Fr John MacDougall, pastor of Red Islands/Johnstown, ministered in their parishes for decades. When the new pastor of Port Hawkesbury, Fr Ronald MacDonald, visited a section of his flock reported to be uncooperative, he was struck instead by their great generosity. "So, after all," he wrote his bishop, "these people are not the 'stubborn' set they were represented to be."[132]

On rare occasions disputes became messy. At Mabou, the indefatigable Fr Kenneth MacDonald, known for his "very strenuous exertions in the cause of temperance," regularly condemned various sins among his flock and even tried banning the fiddle (he clearly failed).[133] "The ex-M.P. of Inverness [Samuel McDonnell] and Fr Kenneth ... are at war again," warned one anxious priest in the spring of 1883. "This time it is a lawsuit in which the former claims $10,000 damages."[134] Although some defended Fr Kenneth, even his apologists acknowledged that he could not distinguish between the sin and the sinner.[135] When one brave parishioner was asked if he was afraid of anything, he replied, "*Tha, tha an t-eagal orm ro' dà rud: Maighstir Coinneach agus an tàirneanach*!" [Yes, I'm afraid of two things: Fr Kenneth and thunder!][136]

In most cases, however, devotion to the local pastor was unwavering. When East Bay's Fr Neil MacLeod celebrated fifty years in the priesthood in 1887, for instance, his appointment as a domestic prelate, the diocese's first *monsignor*, was announced to thunderous applause.[137] After Fr William Chisholm died at Pomquet in 1884, crowds of parishioners braved the cold to attend his funeral at Heatherton; on one of the bleakest days in memory, a hundred carriages followed his casket and mourners led a procession "well nigh a mile long."[138]

Parochial appointments were complicated. Some parishes were wealthier, located in more attractive settings, or easier to administer. When one clergyman found himself appointed to a "rougher" rural Cape Breton parish, he had his doctor write a medical opinion avowing that the assignment, due to its physical demands, would be a "death warrant."[139] Personality clashes could also make assignments awkward. When Fr Hugh Gillis, the long-time rector of St Ninian's Cathedral, was hesitant to share the new episcopal residence with Bishop Cameron, the prelate was personally offended (Gillis finally moved in at Christmas 1883).[140]

As with parishioners, alcohol abuse could be a nagging problem among the clergy. If a priest succumbed to the drink, a strict administrative process was initiated. At first, a colleague would attempt an intervention; oaths were administered and reliable parishioners given charge of the sacramental wine stores. In extreme cases, clergy would have their faculties removed, be compelled to enter a retreat at a monastery, or be withdrawn from their parishes altogether. Sadly, more than one man received a letter from his bishop that began with the lines "with a heavy heart and with deep sorrow…"[141] In some unfortunate cases alcoholism destroyed careers; but there were also stories of redemption.

If a young man discerned a call to the priesthood, he was most often sent to the Grand Seminary of Quebec. Almost half – thirty-nine – of the clergy serving in Antigonish during this period were ordained in Quebec City, while ten had studied at the Grand Seminary in Montreal, nine at the Urban College in Rome, and four at Nicolet, Quebec. This education was expensive, and Bishop Cameron confessed that the amount of monies "already owe[d] to the seminary at Quebec [was] enough to frighten [him]."[142]

All aspiring seminarians had to fill out a questionnaire with two sorts of queries: spiritual (did the candidate understand the responsibilities of the apostolic ministry?) and physical (had the candidate ever contracted smallpox or been inoculated?).[143] In *A Bit of Autobiography*, Bishop Alexander "Sandy" MacDonald left an account of his vocation discernment. MacDonald, one of the brightest students at St F.X., and Angus J. Chisholm of Heatherton parish, the "luminary in mathematics," were recruited to the college's faculty in 1878. "Neither of [them]," recalled Bishop Sandy, had yet "felt the call to study for the priesthood." Yet, while working in the library, he found a small book of meditations by Saint Alphonsus Liguori titled *Preparation for Death*, which began with the words, "Consider that thou are dust, and unto dust thou must return."[144] These vivid words made a powerful impression on him.[145] While the professors assumed that the brilliant Chisholm would get the scholarship for Rome, Bishop Cameron wanted to send a Cape Bretoner to Italy. So it was the young MacDonald who soon found himself in the benches at the Urban College.[146] Chisholm was sent to Quebec.

As Sandy MacDonald soon learned, the Urban College was no place for the academically challenged or the distracted, and not every student made it to ordination. The men were expected to perform, and their grades and conduct were reported to their bishop. Catholics took a keen interest in the progression of "[their] boys." When the newly ordained Fr Sandy returned from Rome in the summer of 1884, a local newspaper noted his impressive accomplishment, as the "degree of D.D. [had] recently been made much more difficult."[147] Other reports noted that Lauchlin "Lachy" MacPherson of Cloverville, Antigonish County, had "distinguished himself as a successful student" in Quebec, that Angus Chisholm "took a leading part in theological discussions" at that same seminary, and that Amable Monbourquette of Lower L'Ardoise had won several prizes at St Joseph's College, Memramcook.[148]

These young curates who returned to the diocese after 1880 were spoiled for mentors. One was the "impressive" Fr Ronald MacDonald of Pictou. Fr MacDonald had been an early graduate of the St F.X. seminary, and the first local priest from the college sent to shepherd another diocese; in a heavily Protestant county he had guided his besieged flock for nineteen years. In mid-summer 1881, virtually hand-selected by Bishop Cameron, he was appointed bishop of Harbour Grace, Newfoundland. Was it perhaps to needle those very Highland Scottish Presbyterians that his consecration ceremony was held in Pictou town "in all its impressive solemnity" in front of five regional prelates and nearly a thousand onlookers?[149]

As a new bishop, MacDonald succeeded the unpopular Italian bishop Enrico Carfagnini, who had clashed with the powerful Benevolent Irish Society in Harbour Grace. MacDonald offered his new diocese diplomacy and conciliation. His experiences in Protestant Pictou were useful in his new surroundings, although nothing prepared him for the sectarianism of Newfoundland. During the violent "Harbour Grace Affray," a sectarian clash in 1883 between local Irish Catholics and members of the Loyal Orange Order – five killed and seventeen injured – MacDonald was "insulted and harassed" while trying to reach a critically injured parishioner.[150] He described all these events in long missals to Antigonish priests, and, as a regional ally of Bishop Cameron, he remained "interested in the affairs and the people of [his] former diocese."[151] Significantly for young Antigonish seminarians, MacDonald demonstrated that a career in the Church was ripe with possibility beyond the local altar.

JOHN THOMPSON GOES TO OTTAWA

Had the provincial election campaign of 1882 been John Thompson's last, whatever hostility existed between Bishop Cameron and local Liberals would have been lost to history. Less than two years after Thompson's resignation as premier of Nova Scotia, however, Sir Charles Tupper, the Nova Scotia representative in the federal Conservative cabinet of Sir John A. MacDonald, resigned his parliamentary seat to accept a position as Canadian high commissioner in London. While there was no shortage of possible replacements from the province (including the errant senator Miller), Bishop Cameron sensed an opportunity to regain political power.

Getting Thompson to Ottawa took considerable manipulation. First, to open a parliamentary seat in Antigonish County, the Liberal incumbent, Angus MacIsaac, in Ottawa since 1873, was enticed to abandon politics and support Thompson in exchange for a county judgeship. Although patronage was then a tolerated component of the political system, it came as a great surprise to local Liberals that their MP had accepted a judgeship from a Conservative administration. While the appointment could be defended on its merits – the previous Liberal government had failed to appoint a single Roman Catholic to any of Nova Scotia's seven vacant county court judgeships – Liberals were annoyed.[152]

To motivate local voters, Bishop Cameron ordered Thompson not to "accept any other position – even temporarily – than that of Minister of Justice."[153] Satisfied that prominent Antigonish County Liberals would not oppose a Catholic cabinet minister, he instructed the prime minister to make the appointment.[154] On 24 September

1885, Angus MacIsaac was installed as a county court judge, and two days later Thompson was sworn in as Canada's minister of justice. A by-election for Antigonish County was called for 16 October.

The federal by-election of 1885 was a turning point for Bishop Cameron's ultramontane movement. While voters respected their bishop's religious authority and John Thompson's political talents, sending the justice to Ottawa had been, in the opinion of the *Yarmouth Herald*, a "disgusting shuffling of judgeships."[155] More crucially, having made assurances to the prime minister that Thompson would "not have much, if any, trouble in Antigonish," Cameron had to deliver.[156] Unlike the provincial campaigns, in which Antigonish County elected two representatives, the federal seat allowed only for a single victor. Nothing was left to chance; when Thompson's train arrived at the Antigonish town station, the bishop's carriage was waiting.

Although Bishop Cameron had the guarantee of Judge MacIsaac and other prominent Liberals not to oppose Thompson, these men had few political friends left. Some local Conservatives were also troubled that the plum patronage position of county judge had gone to a long-time rival. Even the Conservative MP for Inverness County, Hugh Cameron, distanced himself from the arrangement and aggressively denied charges that he had brokered the deal.[157] In the workplace, the shops, and the churchyard, Catholics spoke of themselves, often passionately, as victims of both John Thompson's ambition and Angus MacIsaac's selfishness.

As a movement to mount an independent campaign intensified, a popular candidate came forward.[158] Dr Alexander MacIntosh, a respected physician from Lower South River, was an early graduate of St F.X. to earn a medical degree and was revered locally for having once risked his life to treat smallpox in the village of Pomquet. Although MacIntosh was initially "satisfied with the arrangement," and confessed to having his "share of fun" teasing and generally irritating his Liberal friends, by the end of September he had an abrupt change of heart. The doctor now felt that "the people had a better right to select their candidate than the govt."[159]

The news that Dr MacIntosh had become a candidate for the Antigonish parliamentary seat enraged Bishop Cameron. Not only had the physician given his word that he would not oppose Thompson, but contesting the seat as an independent was a crafty method of upholding the commitment not to back a Liberal while rounding up support "whip and spur" from local Grits.[160] One can only speculate on Dr MacIntosh's motives, but his decision to enter the 1885 campaign forced Cameron to shift from firm supporter to rank partisan.

The bishop had great political power and deep connections. Wallace Graham (later knighted), an Antigonish town native and emerging Halifax attorney, was recruited as Thompson's campaign manager.[161] To attract the Acadian vote, Senator Pascal Poirier and MP Pierre-Armand Landry, both from New Brunswick, gave speeches to francophone audiences, while Charles Hibbert Tupper helped rally the small but important Protestant vote. Local priests also exploited the bigoted sentiments of the *Toronto Globe*, which decried Thompson as a "wicked papist."[162]

Yet, as Thompson's biographer, P.B. Waite, uncovered, "not all the clergy were enthusiasts for Thompson."[163] As with the provincial campaigns, some priests wanted nothing to do with politics, and some, like the rector at St Ninian's Cathedral, were rumoured to be secretly campaigning for Dr MacIntosh. In the main, however, men like Fr Ronald MacGillivray in Arisaig, Fr James Fraser in Georgeville, and Fr James Quinan in Arichat, stoutly supported Thompson on the principle of clerical obedience. In early October, Fr MacGillivray wrote that the "the gulf is going to do well for Thompson," while Fr John Shaw was sanguine about a large majority at Arisaig.[164] One Halifax reporter later noted that the candidate was "surrounded by priests on the platform."[165]

As an 1874 federal law declared that an election result could be nullified "upon proof of 'undue influence,'" Thompson's clerical supporters had to be cautious.[166] On 4 October, Cameron sent a letter as a "devoted friend and father" to the parishes to be read from the pulpit. It was, he asserted, a privilege to have a "fervent convert to the Catholic Church" as Canada's attorney general and it would be a public disgrace not to elect him as their member of parliament.[167] Others used the pulpit to compare the Liberal attacks on Thompson to "what the atheists of France [were] doing and [had] been doing for some years."[168] If Thompson were defeated, Fr MacGillivray harangued his St Joseph's parishioners, it would mean "disgrace to the Catholics of Antigonish."[169]

On 11 October, Bishop Cameron pushed harder, issuing a circular that attacked MacIntosh directly.[170] In the quiet leafy village of Heatherton, some eighteen kilometres from Antigonish town, the forty-five-year-old Fr John Joseph Chisholm surveyed the situation with unease. A Heatherton native, Chisholm knew that the Scottish and Acadian farmers in his parish were indignant at Cameron's personal attacks on Dr MacIntosh and he was concerned that the bishop had gone too far.[171] With some consternation, the erudite graduate of the Grand Seminary of Montreal had read the circular of 4 October, highlighting Thompson's qualities as a worthy statesman, but the 11 October circular was a different matter. He simply could not disparage a respected Catholic physician. As he walked into Immaculate Conception church, Chisholm put the note back in his pocket. The following morning, he confessed to his superior that he would obey any command "in consistency with truth and justice" but, knowing that Dr MacIntosh denied "one, at least, of the principal statements" made in the circular, he could not read the letter from the pulpit.[172]

Fortunately for Cameron, when the polls closed on 16 October 1885, Thompson had won his parliamentary seat by 228 votes. Although Dr MacIntosh had taken the poll in St Andrews, Heatherton, and Antigonish town (by two votes), he was soundly beaten elsewhere. A relieved Cameron congratulated his flock for saving themselves from "a lasting disgrace." But the accusations and resentment from the election simmered. In November, he defended himself in the provincial press and even made his pre-election correspondence with Dr MacIntosh public. Cameron's agenda had been upheld – but at a cost. Cracks had appeared in the ultramontane state.

2

Piety and Politics 1890–1899

In the spring of 1890, some 73,000 Catholics worshipped in 58 parishes and 38 mission churches scattered throughout eastern Nova Scotia. While the construction of new parishes was underwritten mainly by the expansion of mining in both Cape Breton and Pictou County, much of the area was still engaged in farming or fishing. In coastal parishes, next to the sacraments, the rhythms of the fishery were the primary focus of the Church. There was, as the twentieth-century writer George Boyle noted, a "fellowship of the spirit" through a shared economic struggle.[1] Newspapers reported on the "quality of herring" and the "plentiful codfish," but also described the gloomy periods of poor fishing. When news of bountiful hauls was reported from Cape North, the diocesan newspaper expressed hope that "the anxious fishermen [would] soon be satisfied."[2]

Nova Scotians were always at the mercy of nature. When freezing temperatures hampered the ability of the D'Escousse fishermen to get their catch to Halifax, Fr Angus Chisholm asked his colleagues to pray for better weather, as the frigid cold "will go hard with [the] poor people."[3] Tempestuous storms frequently pulverized equipment and, after a ferocious gale "wrought sad havoc" on the lobstermen along St George's Bay, one journalist noted the "great loss to the poor people."[4] Given the paucity of resources or social programs, poor fishing seasons taxed families and emptied parish coffers. "Hard indeed is the lot of the fisherfolk," noted Fr Chisholm. "God in his kindness has given them light hearts; no class of people need them more."[5]

Of course, when the nets were empty or when the crops failed, priests still had to meet expenses. Writing in his diary at Christmas

1890, Fr Chisholm confessed his aversion to collecting the annual church dues at D'Escousse as "it was hard for some of the poor people to meet their bills." He "hat[ed] to receive money" from hard-working Catholics who needed that cash for their own families.[6] At Little Bras d'Or, the burly Fr Martin MacPherson also admitted the difficulty of collecting monies from farmers during poor growing seasons. "They are trying to meet bills," he wrote sympathetically in the winter of 1896, but had large debts "incurred in buying hay for the last few years."[7]

FURTHER INDUSTRIAL EXPANSION

While rural communities pursued their perennial struggle for survival, the colliery towns of Cape Breton continued to expand. Although there were periods of "dullness," the coal mines were generally "taxed to their utmost capacity."[8] In 1893 Boston financier Henry M. Whitney created a partnership to invest in the Sydney coalfields, "revive the lost coal trade to New England," and restore Nova Scotia's dwindling provincial revenues.[9] He formed the Dominion Coal Company (DOMCO), consolidated most of the fledgling Cape Breton operations under an umbrella corporation, and negotiated a ninety-nine-year lease with the province.[10] A mammoth new shaft was built near Glace Bay, and more towns and villages developed as the company established an extensive network of railways, shipping piers, coalyards, and company houses.[11] By 1898 DOMCO was producing 1.5 million tons of coal a year.[12]

While DOMCO attracted regional workers who might otherwise have outmigrated, the company still faced periodic labour shortages.[13] Newfoundlanders who traditionally fished the north Atlantic or hunted seals on the floes off Labrador were attracted to Cape Breton by advertisements in the *Evening Telegram* and the *Twillingate Sun* that promised transport and work for all men who left for Glace Bay.[14] Newfoundlanders were soon a recognizable group in the local churches, and the ferry SS *Bruce*, which linked Cape Breton with Newfoundland, kept the two islands in close contact.[15]

Most Newfoundlanders who disembarked from the ferry at North Sydney had few resources other than their labour. One customs clerk noted the futility of searching the baggage of passengers, for most "had nothing down there to bring up."[16] In some cases, migrants had family connections who aided the transition into Cape Breton,

Figure 2.1 | St Anne's Church, Glace Bay

but those without networks found themselves in boarding houses or DOMCO's makeshift "shacks."[17] These shacks, furnished with a basic metal bunk, stove, and table, would soon gain notoriety.[18]

Although most Catholic migrants into the colliery towns were single males, some were accompanied by their wives and families. Many of these were young mothers who came from large families and understood the economic realities of mining. In fact, one prominent historian called them "the greatest financier[s] in the world."[19] The single females who entered the paid labour force were generally limited to employment as domestic servants in boarding houses or hotels.[20] Like their male counterparts, they were enticed by prospects of good wages. "Girls for Cape Breton, Nova Scotia and New Brunswick," read one advertisement in the *Evening Telegram*, "first-class families, passage money advanced."[21]

One of the best places to seek employment, housing, and even companionship was the local parish. More than a space for spiritual worship, churches like Sydney's Sacred Heart were literal sanctuaries from the grim realities of industrial life. They offered a permanency in an otherwise transitional and unfamiliar environment and, as Catholics poured into the colliery towns, new edifices were hastily constructed to cope with the large Sunday crowds. In 1893 the spacious St Anne's Church was opened at Glace Bay, in 1895 the new parish of St Joseph's swung open its doors in Reserve Mines, and in 1899 Immaculate Conception at Bridgeport, funded by miners who donated hard-earned wages, was finally dedicated.[22]

After Mass in parishes like St Anne's, miners would linger around the churchyard discussing family, finances, and work. Although men flocked to the collieries for wages, they toiled under harsh and terrifying conditions. "Ten months arduous and continuous labour down in the bowels of the earth," proclaimed one miner, was "about as much as the human system [could] bear."[23] Viral infections such as "slow fever" and typhoid ravaged new migrants, and accidents were common.[24] In June 1899, eleven miners lost their lives at the Caledonia Mine in Glace Bay and, months later, two men from St Anne's parish were killed at the international pier near Sydney. When a lump of coal crashed down upon Alexander Beaton of Sydney Mines, he lived only long enough for a priest to perform the last rites.[25]

In 1891, amid the Sydney coal boom, Pope Leo XIII released the encyclical *Rerum Novarum* ("Of New Things"), his celebrated dictum on the condition of the working classes. It was, as Lawrence Elliott writes, "a dramatic call for the righting of old wrongs, and new regard for those who toiled with their hands for a livelihood."[26] Principally composed for a European audience, whose "passion for revolutionary change" seemed perpetually aroused, the document initially had a smaller a following in North America.[27] Although excerpts were printed in the diocesan press and there were occasional references to labour from the pulpit – in December 1897, for instance, Fr Daniel MacGregor, the former pastor at Bridgeport, gave a lecture at Victoria Mines entitled "Capital, Labour and the State" – there was little intellectual engagement with an encyclical that dealt with issues of subsidiarity, solidarity, and private property.

Had more Catholics studied *Rerum Novarum*, however, they would have discovered that the document addressed many of the issues already plaguing the colliery parishes. When the Gowrie mine at Port Morien was closed in November 1897, the diocesan press commented that the miners had legitimate complaints against their employer, but added nothing about the encyclical's demand that the state safeguard the interests of the worker.[28] The following year, there were reports of a "strong sentiment among the miners against [those company] stores" that exploited hungry mouths.[29] Yet there was no comment in the press on the encyclical's call for "natural justice," or its condemnation of the compulsion of workers to accept conditions against their will. When the mine near New Victoria closed in 1898, reports noted that "no account [was] taken of the misery into which poor, honest miners and their families [were] plunged."[30] Yet, once again, there was no comment on *Rerum Novarum*'s demand that "special consideration be given to the weak and the poor."[31]

The lack of engagement with *Rerum Novarum* can be attributed to two factors. First, as there was no aggressive labour movement in the region, the clergy were not yet forced by radicals seeking the downfall of capitalism to confront the social and economic realities of the coalfields. Although the Provincial Workmen's Association (PWA) was active in protesting company stores and advocating for better working conditions, it was mostly a Protestant organization. While the Catholic press gave the association fair-minded coverage, it could not advocate for an organization dominated by freemasons and Orangemen.[32]

The second factor was the need to cooperate with DOMCO. Unlike the agricultural districts, where the farmer mostly relied on good weather and his own hard work, industrial workers depended on the fortunes of a large corporation to earn their livelihoods.[33] Even civil society was reliant on the goodwill of the company – in Sydney Mines, the local Catholic fraternal society could not have constructed a hall without the company placing the "dock and railway at [their] disposal" – and so, as had been the case with the General Mining Association, a stable relationship with DOMCO was critical.[34]

To investigate the increasingly important coal industry, the diocesan newspaper hired a "Bridgeport correspondent" – the future deputy minister of marine and fisheries, Alexander Johnston – who even ventured a mile down the Reserve Mines shaft to report on conditions.[35] The relocation of the diocesan Seat from Arichat to Antigonish town had put important episcopal institutions on the mainland, but coal made Cape Breton the centre of Catholic life once again. When the new church was dedicated at Bridgeport, locals bragged that the building had a seating capacity "equal to that of the diocesan cathedral."[36]

DEVOTIONS AND SOCIETIES

As today's reader has read about (and lived through) decades of church closures, it is difficult to appreciate the excitement and controversy that could be generated by church construction in this period. While a church had stood at West Lake Ainslie, Inverness County, since the 1870s, in 1893 the area was designated a parish to alleviate the demographic pressure on the church in neighbouring Mabou.[37] A few years later, Fr Alexander Chisholm, who had recently been transferred into the parish from Glace Bay, complained that the people at West Lake lacked the resources to sustain a resident priest, and relocated his home to neighbouring Brook Village.[38] When he announced plans to build a church in the new location, there was considerable outrage.

Of course, annoyed Catholics could grumble about these decisions but in a strict ultramontane environment they were "utterly ineffectual."[39] Although one historian speculated that "fear, and not love," often underlay the compliant attitude toward the clergy, the reality is that most people were fiercely committed to their parishes.[40] In 1891 the priest at Heatherton said three masses on Christmas day and his parishioners "devoutly attend[ed] the services throughout."[41] "We are all church goers here," one miner proudly remarked from Glace Bay.[42]

One popular period expression of love and fidelity was devotion to the Sacred Heart of Jesus. Traced to the mystical revelations of a seventeenth-century French nun, devotion to the Sacred Heart was symbolic of the "burning love of Christ" and of loyalty to the diocese.[43] According to historian John McGreevy, the image of the Sacred Heart had a "fleshy, realistic character," which fostered both obligation and empathy.[44] With cool breezes from the Northumberland Strait offering reprieve from the midsummer heat of 1890, the church at Georgeville was "crammed to the door" as 150 youth were consecrated to the Sacred Heart. The following morning, another large group – with statues and prayer cards – was consecrated down the road in Maryvale.[45]

Devotion to the Virgin Mary by praying the Rosary was also encouraged in the month of October, as the encyclical *Octobri Mense* of 22 September 1891 instructed. "How grateful and magnificent a spectacle," the document urged, "to see in the cities, and towns ...

many hundreds of thousands of pious people uniting their praises and prayers ... saluting Mary, invoking Mary, hoping everything through Mary." Soon afterward, the rector of St F.X. told an overflowing crowd at St Ninian's Cathedral that the rosary was not only a "garland of prayer and praise ... in loving homage to their heavenly queen," but it was also "a powerful weapon."[46] Soon, rosary prayers were ubiquitous in churches, and rosary beads as common in Catholic homes as the kerosene lamp.

Along with devotionalism, inter-diocesan fellowship became widespread. With improvements in rail transport, Catholics travelled longer distances to attend social events and in 1896 the Intercolonial Railway even issued complimentary tickets to convey revellers to the great bazaar at St Ninian's Cathedral.[47] In the colliery towns, the popular band from Bridgeport's Immaculate Conception parish regularly led merrymakers in their own rendition of the popular Irish tune "The Bells of Shandon."[48] Deriding the excessive alcohol consumption, more than one priest wanted "to see church picnics abolished," but they were much too popular to strike from the social calendar.[49]

The attitude toward entertainment in this decade was always cautious, to the extent that, when a billiards hall opened in Antigonish town, the local priest quickly curtailed its business.[50] While some attacks were a self-righteous assault on pleasure, many legitimately worried that the youth were not properly prepared for modern Canadian society. Complaining that only a handful of young Catholic professionals worked in Nova Scotia banks, one correspondent to *The Casket* cited the Young Men's Christian Association of America (YMCA) as an examplar of Protestant determination. "What can be said of the banking institutions can be said of all mercantile business," he observed. "Our Catholic young men are sadly left in the background."

One way of organizing the laity was through Catholic societies. The League of the Cross, which continued its fight against the demon rum, remained tremendously influential.[51] New halls, often capable "of holding five to six hundred," went up throughout the region. "Before the inauguration of the League, people of [our] town had an evil reputation as a dram-drinking populace," noted one member of the 225-strong North Sydney league, but now "the Catholics [were] a sober class."[52] When Thomas McDonald was killed tragically by lightning near the Sterling colliery in Glace Bay, *The Casket* noted that he had been a member of the society since the age of eleven. To retain the loyalty of the youth, branches had libraries carefully stocked with the latest magazines.[53]

While total abstinence appealed to priests like Fr John Francis MacMaster in Mabou, who spent considerable energy trying to stamp out the illicit "black pots" in his Celtic parish, few had issue with a wee glass.[54] When a priest on Isle Madame asked his congregation to swear off the rum, "the men did not seem anxious to come forward."[55] By early December, when fierce snow storms forced the same priest to "put off the pledge" for some weeks, he joked that his flock were overjoyed that "X-mas will have come and gone before they [were] obliged to pledge themselves to total abstinence."

Despite its good intentions, the League of the Cross demanded sacrifice and a good deal of self-control. The Catholic Mutual Benefit Association, on the other hand, required much less discipline and may have provided more benefit. Organized in the State of New York in 1876, the association was a fraternal society that focused on life and health insurance (it satisfied a great need among the Catholic working classes).[56] Following new Nova Scotia divisions at Halifax and Amherst, in the spring of 1890 North Sydney welcomed the association into eastern Nova Scotia. Selling policies as far afield as Cape Breton was a noteworthy achievement for the association, and the names of the North Sydney officers were published in Ontario's *London Record*.[57] The local spiritual director, Fr Daniel Joseph MacIntosh, spoke of the virtues of cheap life insurance and ensured that most parish libraries stocked the association's monthly newsletter, *The Canadian*. While historians have demonstrated that the Catholic Mutual Benefit Association upheld "Irish Catholic identities" in cities like Buffalo, in eastern Nova Scotia its members embraced Canadian values and regional collaboration as "excursions" to functions in Charlottetown, Halifax, and Springhill became commonplace. [58]

SIR JOHN THOMPSON BECOMES PRIME MINISTER

All this activity in the parishes was reported in the Antigonish County newspaper, *The Casket*. Although Catholic and published in the cathedral town since 1852, *The Casket* respected "the other man's point of view."[59] It was not officially the diocesan newspaper,

Figure 2.2 | Fr Neil McNeil

but its editors were guided by the bishop and followed the party line closely. When the paper was purchased by the Saint John native Michael Francis Donovan in 1889, *The Casket* had a circulation of some 1,600, which was not nearly enough to defend the Catholic subculture or to make a respectable profit. Although Bishop Cameron would have liked the paper to be both Catholic and sympathetic to the Conservative Party, Donovan knew that political partisanship would hurt sales.

Although respectful to Bishop Cameron, believing in Pope Leo XIII's famous dictum that Catholic newspapers had "a perpetual mission," Donovan asked the thirty-nine-year-old rector of St F.X., Fr Neil McNeil, to strengthen the paper as editor.[60] The Hillsborough, Inverness County, native, and former editor of the defunct newspaper *The Aurora* was experienced, respected, and objective; but more important, he was a known Liberal sympathizer.[61]

While the news of McNeil's hire made for good optics, behind closed curtains some worried that *The Casket* could not maintain its impartiality if Bishop Cameron fervently continued to support Canada's attorney general John Thompson. Despite Donovan's ethics, the "temptation [for *The Casket*] will be too strong," warned one correspondent, and it will "sooner or later drift away from its moorings."[62] With the federal election of March 1891 looming, national Liberal newspapers began revisiting Cameron's participation in past contests. Besides reopening old wounds, the articles hinted that local Catholics were busy preparing formal complaints to Rome.[63] Characteristically, Cameron penned a measured response for publication in *The Casket*; to the bishop's astonishment, however, due to its prejudice against a Liberal candidate, editor McNeil refused to publish it. "Dr McNeil is such a dyed-in-the-wool Grit," Cameron shot back, "as to blind him to the fact that he is a Grit first and Catholic afterwards only!"[64]

In the following weeks, Bishop Cameron hinted that an "Antigonish clique" had taken up arms against him. James Cameron, in his history of St F.X., notes that the bishop's reaction to the editorial policy "revealed the power of his political loyalties," which had "seduced him into abandoning reason for prejudice."[65] Yet the bishop did not consider his support of Thompson to be strictly partisan; rather, loyalty to the attorney general represented an extension of his episcopal office. His fears of an atheistic Liberal conspiracy might have been an attempt "to cloak a political salvo in sacred garb," as one historian has aptly argued; but he sincerely believed that the attorney general was indispensable to his ultramontane agenda. "As to gratitude, I am his debtor, not he mine," he said of Thompson, "for he has done incomparably more for the welfare of this diocese since he was sent to the Commons than I could have reasonably expected."

The 1891 election in Antigonish County was rancorous, but Thompson was re-elected by a substantial majority.[66] Invigorated, Bishop Cameron asked his priests to sign a memorandum declaring him innocent of partisanship.[67] One priest who refused to sign was Fr Neil McNeil. While he recognized that he had become *persona non grata*, he was nonetheless staggered by his September transfer to the Acadian parish of West Arichat (he would not be the last St F.X. administrator to be abruptly transferred to a rural parish). Yet McNeil, like Cameron a graduate of the Urban College, had powerful contacts within the Roman Curia, and was not on Isle Madame long before sending a formal protest to the Vatican. In a scathing letter, he noted that "clergy should not get mixed up in these political affairs when the defense of the church or moral principles do not require it."[68] Catholic newspapers like *The Casket*, he asserted, served a higher purpose than mere partisanship.[69]

The transfer of Fr McNeil to rural Cape Breton did some damage to *The Casket's* reputation and hurt clerical morale.[70] When, the pastor of D'Escousse, Fr Angus Chisholm – who believed that politics was "too a dirty a business" for the Church – was offered the position of editor (he had filled in for six months), he turned it down. He felt it would be a burden "of great annoyance and distraction" and would hurt his standing among the people. While he wanted *The Casket* to prosper, he could not, he said, work for a newspaper that pursued a policy "calculated to foster unhappy dissensions among Catholics and to compromise the clergy."[71] His sympathies were with Thompson, but *The Casket* was too important to squander on politics.

Just when it seemed that some Catholics were poised to challenge the authority of their bishop, circumstances intervened once again. In November 1892, the ailing prime minister, Sir John Abbott, resigned his post and the Antigonish member of parliament, who "[held] the keys to the future" was on his way to meet the governor general.[72] Leaving Rideau Hall, Thompson, now the new prime minister of Canada, wrote to Bishop Cameron to acknowledge the propitious moment for the Canadian Church. "Whatever may be done," Thompson confessed, "I can say with a clear conscience that I am not seeking the place or seeking my own welfare solely."[73] Cameron was jubilant. He had made history.

While the elevation of Thompson to the prime ministership vindicated Bishop Cameron, it also increased his paranoia. By the spring of 1893, he saw any political opposition as rebellion and considered membership in the Liberal Party to be a "moral malady." The prelate even compared local Grits to the violent Italian revolutionaries who had so disturbed Rome in the 1850s.[74] "No *Casket* last night," wrote Fr James Quinan to the rector of St F.X. from Arichat. "I hope Mr. [Michael] Donovan has not been put *hors de combat* by the Liberals!"[75]

LANGUAGE AND CULTURAL SURVIVAL

The rancorous election campaigns of Sir John Thompson demonstrated that Catholics in eastern Nova Scotia struggled to manage the competing loyalties of faith, ethnicity, and politics. Within ultramontanism, cultural distinctiveness was downplayed, and the Church had a complex relationship with such issues as ethnicity and language. While Scottish Gaelic catechisms, for example, still offered "as much of the Catholic doctrine [as] the young people [could] master," the use of Gaelic in churches had long been discouraged.[76] In fact, as was the case in countries like Ireland at the time, many in Nova Scotia felt that the decline of the language was inevitable.[77] "Without meaning any disparagement to my mother tongue or to those who speak it," Bishop Cameron confessed, "I must remark that Gaelic is fast dying out, and giving way to the English, and that, even were not this the case, its importance is nowise to be compared to that of the French."[78]

At the same time, despite the primacy of Rome and the uniformity of worship, Catholics were proud of their respective cultures, and if negative assessments of the Scottish community persisted in the late nineteenth century, as one historian has claimed, it was not apparent in the local press.[79] The link between the rainswept Scottish Highlands and eastern Nova Scotia was continually validated by *The Casket* and by the clergy. "I hope I shall have the time and means to see at last 'auld Scotia,'" wrote the Roman seminarian D.C. Gillis before taking a trip to the United Kingdom. "I retain a wanton attachment to old Scotland so much so that the strongest patriotism that I possess is in consequence of 'The filial band that knits me to the rugged land.'"[80] In letters, homilies, and after-dinner speeches, Scottish Catholics evoked the "peculiarly bitter" fruits of the Scottish reformation, or illustrated the kinship connections between the late Bishop Fraser and the Highland aristocrat Lord Lovat.[81]

Gaelic speakers were sticklers for elocution. When Bishop Ronald MacDonald of Harbour Grace made his first sojourn to Rome in 1885, he visited the Scots College to meet some of the Highland students.[82] To his astonishment, the "Scottish" scholars had surnames like Meehan, Murphy, and Doherty. When the college's rector, Fr James Campbell, called upon a young seminarian by the surname of MacKenzie to converse with MacDonald in Gaelic, the student committed, to the bishop's "utter disgust," countless mistakes "against the grammar of the dear old language of [his] mother."[83]

This kind of incident became part of the oral culture and inspired students like East Bay's Donald MacAdam to promote Gaelic as part of a St F.X. education.[84] While some complained that his tongue lacked "the right 'Blas,'" and others criticized his vocabulary, MacAdam brought awareness to the precarious state of the language.[85] Having enrolled at Harvard University's summer school before entering the Grand Seminary of Montreal, when the newly ordained MacAdam joined the St F.X. faculty in 1893, he offered a gold medal to the top Gaelic student, planned a weekly *ceilidh*, and started the Gaelic society *Comunn an Fhraoich*.[86] "The more loyal sons of the heather are just now jubilant," quipped *The Casket*, "over the fact that they have succeeded, despite the strong classical atmosphere of St. F.X., in getting a class in their own beloved Gaelic started ... they are able to inhale pure Celtic air three times a week."[87]

Language preservation was also critical in the French-speaking parishes, where Acadians were gradually experiencing their own cultural awakening. Although English predominated in Nova Scotia schools, the indefatigable Fr Pierre Fiset had experimented with bilingual readers in Cheticamp's elementary classrooms, and more French-speaking teachers – including the future bishop of Chatham, New Brunswick – were hired.[88] "We feel the absolute necessity of knowing English, wrote one Acadian correspondent in *The Casket*, "but we wish to retain our own language."[89]

Yet Acadian students faced a dilemma. Learning in their native tongue was vital but without adequate immersion in English, young people were left with only a "mechanical" understanding of the dominant language. Lacking the language skills to matriculate in English universities, Acadians feared that a child of their culture would be "ever looked upon as a dunce ... or a mere hewer of wood and drawer of water."[90] When two students left D'Escousse for St F.X. in

1890, Fr Angus Chisholm prayed for their success, as "the Acadians [did] not make that showing in the diocese to which their number would entitle them."[91]

Dan MacInnes has noted that the "ministration by Irish/Scots priests" in Acadian parishes also hurt the development of the French language.[92] By 1890 *The Casket* noted that the Acadian parishes were "nearly all in the charge of Scotch and Irish pastors."[93] The lack of French-speaking priests was so acute that seminarians sent to Quebec and Montreal were expected to become bilingual.[94] Yet for many English speakers, the French language proved tremendously difficult to master. "I am wholly incapable of taking charge of a French parish," confessed the Mabou native Donald J. Cameron from the Grand Seminary of Montreal in 1891. "This is not a mere opinion ... It is the judgement of my superiors. 'You are perfectly unable to perform the ministry in French,' are Fr [Charles] LeCog's words to me this morning."[95]

Without native-born priests, Acadians were often served by clergy on temporary loan from Quebec. In the summer of 1892, for instance, a priest from Rimouski spent three weeks assisting Fr Guillaume LeBlanc at Friar's Head (St Joseph du Moine), meeting with Acadian cultural societies and presenting lectures.[96] Others, like Fr Louis Chatillon, wandered between New Brunswick and Nova Scotia pastoring Acadian parishes for brief periods, while Fr Joseph Lafond, a native of Drummondville, spent almost two years as a curate at Arichat.

While some Quebec-born priests were "disinterested" in Acadian culture, others, like Fr Pierre Fiset, saved parishes from anglicization.[97] Born in L'Ancienne-Lorette, near Quebec City, Fiset had been recruited by Archbishop MacKinnon directly from the seminary and ordained in Antigonish town in 1864. "Faithful to the culture of his race," he served first as a professor at St F.X, and then ministered among the DeCostes and Fougères of Havre Boucher. Transferred to northern Inverness County in 1875, he "served – and ruled – in Cheticamp for 34 years."[98]

While there is ongoing debate over Fiset's legacy, Dan MacInnes notes that "the stamp of his powerful presence was everywhere."[99] An early cooperator, he opened a general store to provide his parishioners with an alternative to the company stores of the fish merchants, bought a lobster cannery on Cheticamp island, was active in agriculture (he worked the fields himself), and recruited his brother Napoléon as the community's first resident physician.[100]

While not an ideal solution to the Acadian clergy shortage, the religious pipeline between Antigonish and *la belle province* had aesthetic repercussions.[101] Fr Fiset brought with him a passion for Quebec culture, and when the people of Cheticamp began to build a new sanctuary, the blueprints included a "silver-coated spire" more likely to be found along the mighty St Lawrence River then in Cape Breton.[102] Built primarily of stone, the Church of Saint-Pierre was designed in the French-Canadian neo-classical style by Quebec architect David Ouellet.[103] With the harbour before it and the majestic mountains of the Cape Breton highlands as a backdrop, the new church celebrated its first Mass in December 1893.[104]

Scottish and Acadian Catholics understood that cultural preservation often depended on the activities of clergy like Fr MacAdam and Fr Fiset, as they had the education and the authority to effect real change. In the Indigenous community, however, where there were no native clergy, language retention was even more difficult. Although it was responsible for maintaining a Catholic foothold in Nova Scotia during the tumultuous eighteenth century, migration from Scotland and Ireland had changed the region's demographics and weakened the influence of the Mi'kmaq within the Church. In lieu of priests, by the 1850s the community were granted special indulgences by Pope Pius IX stating that, in the absence of a clergyman on Sundays and Holy Days, those who recited public prayers either in a church "or in their wigwams" received an indulgence of three years.[105] The community could also delay their Easter Duties until the annual summertime Feast of St Anne. While convenient and demonstrative of the unique relationship between the Mi'kmaq and Rome, these indulgences also isolated the Mi'kmaq during a period of great transformation and growth of the Catholic sub-state.

When particular attention was given to Indigenous Catholics, it was always during the Feast of St Anne. Every July 26, celebrations were held throughout the diocese, but the most famed was at historic Chapel Island on the beautiful Bras d'Or lake. The former headquarters of the celebrated eighteenth-century missionary Fr Pierre Maillard, who first put the hieroglyphic symbols of the Mi'kmaw language into print, the island on the salt water lake was also an ancient burial ground.[106] During the celebration honouring the grandmother of Jesus and the patron saint of the community, Chapel

Island's spiritual significance was magnified.[107] With participants hailing from as far afield as Newfoundland, the Feast of St Anne was a time for faith, family, duty, governance – and fundraising.

The accounts of attendees to the feast noted the encampments around the church, the impressive attire, and the general sense of antiquity. The latest chapel, constructed in 1884 and finished in 1891, contained an eighteenth-century altar that had been used at the mission of the Recollect Fathers at St Peter's and was saved from destruction after the fall of Louisbourg.[108] The well-attended Mass was performed by the Scottish-born Fr John MacDougall of Red Islands, who had ministered at the gathering since 1868.[109]

Although this was a sacred Mi'kmaq celebration, white Catholics also attended the feast, ferried to Chapel Island from St Peter's, Baddeck, and Grand Narrows. One visitor remembered the "endless varieties of dresses ... incessant crackling of guns ... and the sweet strain of voices as [Catholics] chanted their hymns of praise in honour of their patron."[110] At Summerside, Antigonish County (Paqtnkek), Bishop Cameron confirmed forty candidates during the 1892 festival and watched the new chief be elected to a "deafening fusillade."[111] In July 1897 a picnic, and a well-attended tug-of-war match between Mi'kmaw and local Scots was held on Indian Island, Pictou County (Pictou Landing). As with the regular practice for parish picnics and bazaars, the Intercolonial Railway offered travel discounts to all revellers.[112]

While large numbers of white Catholics attended the Feast of St Anne and were conscious of the "time honoured" traditions of the Mi'kmaq, the diocesan newspaper occasionally exhibited period attitudes toward the "poor Indians," which created racial divisions in a Church that was theoretically universal.[113] Also worrisome was that by the 1890s the diocese was gradually ceding to Ottawa its material responsibility for the Indigenous faithful. For many generations, priests had acted as a liaison between the government and the Mi'kmaq, conducting population counts and conveying messages during religious festivities.[114] Bishop William Fraser had been appointed as the regional commissioner for Indian affairs in 1844, and thirty years later, when Ottawa divided the administration of the Mi'kmaq people into districts, the responsibility for two of the four districts in eastern Nova Scotia went to Catholic clergymen (in 1878, that number rose to six). The clerical-Indian agent was selected solely on the basis of geography; if ministering at Pictou, for example, the priest also acted as the agent for the community of Pictou Landing.

While agents did valuable administrative work and were vocal about freeholders trespassing on Mi'kmaw property, having priests accountable to both their bishop and federal bureaucrats had serious consequences. In November 1891 Fr Michael MacKenzie, who had served the Salmon River, Richmond County (Potlotek) Mi'kmaq from his parish at River Bourgeois, was transferred to East Bay. The previous month, he had been relieved of his spiritual responsibility for Potlotek by the thirty-seven-year-old Fr John C. Chisholm, pastor of the newly built and geographically closer parish of St Peter's. During that month of October, however, there was confusion about jurisdiction over Potlotek, and both priests appointed their own teacher to the local day school.

Although Fr Chisholm did not have a formal appointment as an Indian agent when he made his hire, he and Bishop Cameron maintained that his federal authority over Potlotek began with his appointment to the parish of St Peter's. Confused, locals sought clarification from John Denny, grand chief of the Mi'kmaq on Cape Breton. Denny was not only highly respected but had a hereditary claim to his office, which, according to one bureaucrat, carried "great weight" in the community.[115] While sympathetic to all parties, the chief demanded that federal guidelines be respected. As the official agent in the month of October, Fr MacKenzie was the only person with hiring authority.[116]

With Chief Denny and Bishop Cameron in disagreement, the Catholics of Potlotek were in an awkward predicament. Understandably keen to foster harmony between Ottawa, Fr Chisholm, and their grand chief, they closed the school to both teachers. Chief Denny was outraged. The school was closed, he objected, on the instruction of their priest, "whose advice they were bound to take."[117] When Ottawa eventually ruled that Fr MacKenzie's teacher was the lawful hire, it was now Fr Chisholm and Bishop Cameron who were angry.

Although a tempest in a teapot, the decision to uphold federal guidelines against the wishes of the diocese had significant consequences. Catholic clergymen were in good standing among the Mi'kmaq, but their temporal authority was fragile. While the "cruel wrong" done to Fr Chisholm was soon forgotten, incidents of this kind pushed the Indigenous flock further outside the Catholic subculture. Since they already lacked a native parish or priest, the perception that Ottawa was responsible for the needs of the people only furthered a growing alienation from Church leadership.

MOUNT SAINT BERNARD AFFILIATES WITH ST FRANCIS XAVIER

Back on the mainland, the Rome-educated intellectual Fr Daniel A. Chisholm, who had replaced the exiled Fr Neil McNeil as rector at St F.X., was dealing with his own controversies.[118] Physically delicate, Chisholm had a sharp intellect, an ability to adapt, and big plans for St F.X.[119] With a reputation as a disciplinarian, "Dr. Dan" was in fairness more of a headmaster than a college president. When parents sent their children to St F.X. (136 were enrolled for the college courses in 1892), they expected him to keep a stern eye on the freshmen and extend them a guiding hand. Many parents assumed their sons would go on to the seminary and, when a vocation did not materialize, their frustration was intense. "Had I known when I sent him to your college that he had no desire of studying for the priesthood," wrote one exasperated father, "I should never have sent him there."[120] Mostly, however, Catholics recognized St F.X's importance. It had some prominent graduates and, by 1894 a new alumni association was actively raising monies for infrastructure.[121]

At the adjacent Saint Bernard's Ladies Academy, the students shared access to St F.X.'s facilities and faculty, but males and females remained segregated. George B. Oland, future owner of New Brunswick's Moosehead brewery, remembered taking piano lessons in the convent. The piano was in a room off the auditorium and when he finished his lesson, he was forced to walk back through the auditorium that by then was filled with girls. "'Running the gauntlet' was nothing," he later recalled, "compared to my trip through the hall and I practically ran all the way."[122]

Yet by 1894, scholars at "the Mount," who were mostly being trained for provincial teaching licenses, began to challenge this educational segregation. While senior level women students had access to the lectures of St F.X. professors, they were eager to trade their teaching diplomas for Bachelor of Arts degrees. When a young woman from a prominent local Protestant family applied for admission to St F.X., she was told to go to Dalhousie. Of course, the sisters could not counsel a Catholic girl to do the same. Sensing an opportunity, Sister St Maurice, CND, and Sister St Margaret of the Cross (Jane Thompson), CND, persuaded Rector Chisholm that post-secondary education for women was a looming reality. These clever and resolute women impressed upon him the undesirability of

Catholic students training at Protestant institutions, and soon "the convent girls [were] allowed to take the same course as the young men."[123] Affiliation was an important moment and, according to James Cameron, was "a noteworthy expansion of higher educational opportunities for the region's Catholic women."[124] While St F.X. lagged behind Protestant institutions like Mount Allison University, which first admitted female students in 1862, St F.X in 1897 became the first Canadian Catholic college to confer the degree of Bachelor of Arts on a class of female scholars.[125]

THE CONGREGATION OF THE SISTERS OF ST MARTHA

Rector Daniel Chisholm's desire to grow and transform St F.X. had created several logistical problems. Higher enrollment demanded more domestic staff to prepare meals and clean rooms, and Chisholm asked Bishop Cameron to recruit an order of women religious for an on-campus housekeeping mission. When the initial plan to enlist a congregation serving at St Hyacinthe College in Quebec fell through, the bishop asked the Halifax Sisters of Charity to train a special auxiliary.[126] With convents throughout the diocese, and still indebted to Bishop Cameron for his spirited defence of their congregation in the 1870s, the Charities were happy to oblige. "After much casting about," Cameron excitedly informed the parishes, "we have at length, through the large-hearted and broad-minded kindness of the Reverend Mother M. Bonaventure ... settled upon a plan that, with God's blessing, will answer our purpose most satisfactory."[127] In the autumn of 1894, Bonaventure, a close friend of Sir John Thompson, who had served at Stellarton from 1882 to 1886, opened the Charity novitiate at Mount St Vincent to new recruits for the Sisters of St Martha.

The news of the new auxiliary generated both excitement and anxiety. Priests were told to search their parishes for women who were "fit to join the new order," and they felt under pressure to find candidates quickly. It required two years of intense training in Halifax before the recruits could begin their work, and there was little time to waste. In the meantime, Rector Chisholm had to allay the fears of the Congregation of Notre Dame then staffing seven teaching convents in the region, that the Charities would "take up all the work" and deliver a "death blow" to their missions.[128]

Figure 2.3 | Fr Michael and Elizabeth MacAdam (Sister Mary Francis, CSM)

The initial response was encouraging; letters of recommendation for girls with a "fondness for prayer" poured in from the parishes.[129] Fr Alexander L. MacDonald, pastor of Port Hawkesbury, wrote that he knew a "strong and apparently a fit subject" (Caroline McNamara) who would make a strong candidate.[130] Allan MacAdam, the father of Elizabeth "Betsy" MacAdam of Eskasoni, wrote that his daughter had been "speaking of religion" for a decade, and this was a perfect opportunity for her to enter religious life (her brother Michael entered the seminary shortly afterward).[131]

The first recruits to leave for Halifax had to overcome some obstacles. Most of the girls had never spent a day away from the hearth and relocating to Halifax was frightening. "I never was away from home much, and don't know what travelling is," confessed an anxious Elizabeth MacAdam.[132] As the recruits had to "supply themselves with wearing apparel and bedding," it meant that they required financial means.[133] In a forthright letter to the college, Fr Lachy MacPherson, pastor of L'Ardoise, was concerned about the onerous financial conditions. "Parents, at least in places like this," he complained, "imagine that the mere giving of a daughter, without further responsibility, should be sufficient."[134] In coastal parishes like L'Ardoise, the financial drawback had the effect that many qualified women were prohibited from a vocation.

Once at the Mount St Vincent motherhouse, the postulants' schedules were strictly controlled. Roused from sleep in the wee dark hours, the women spent the day in meditation, at Mass, and undergoing domestic training. They also participated in retreats, spiritual conferences, and even observed long periods of silence.

All of this would have been endured with dignity but for the mean-spirited remarks that were directed at the "uneducated young ladies from eastern Nova Scotia."[135] Sadly, some Charities, training to be teachers, belittled the Marthas' domestic ministry. The Charities were prominent in Halifax, and were teaching as far afield as Roxbury, Massachusetts; they clearly felt superior. "I fear dear father," Mother Mary Fidelis Eustace confessed to Rector Chisholm, that "while the ignorant regard work as a degradation ... we will have the same prejudices to combat." More plainly, the Marthas were "doing the house work" while the other sisters were in the classroom.[136]

Meanwhile, despite the initial interest in the Marthas, by 1895 enthusiasm in the parishes had waned and the number of recruits dwindled. Many of the letters that crossed Rector Chisholm's desk still opened with, "I have a Martha for you," but few girls wanted a religious career in domestic service. Moreover, as Fr Neil MacDonald in Johnstown acknowledged, there was the constant danger of a young girl "getting a *fellow*," and so the window to recruit local girls was brief.[137]

In the warm summer of 1897, the first brave cadre of Marthas, under the supervision of three senior Charities, returned to Antigonish and moved into the new three-storey brick residence on the St F.X. campus[138] The "handsome structure" on St Ninian Street was attached to a new modern kitchen facility that had been prepared for their arrival. Working under strict regulations (they were to be respectful of priests and cautious of male employees) the women were kept busy with huge piles of laundry, and cooking meals for college functions that created "near panic in the kitchen." In the evenings, they depended on kerosene lamps and had to haul heavy buckets of coal up from the basement. The sisters fed the students, mended their clothes, nursed them when sick, and cleaned their rooms.[139] As one Martha later recalled, "prayer time [came] as a blessed relief."[140]

As surrogate mothers to homesick – and sick – students, the Marthas left a lasting impression of their piety on the undergraduates.[141] In March 1899, the twenty-four-year-old Sister Lucy Maillet, a native of Weymouth, Digby County, died of tuberculosis.[142] Her death lingered in the memory of alumni who recalled the Marthas "standing by her side and gazing intently at the pale image of death." During her requiem Mass, the sisters held lighted candles and then slowly followed the remains to the cemetery. "It seemed," noted one onlooker, "that they kept their sorrow from the view of the public."[143]

DEATH OF PRIME MINISTER THOMPSON

News of the Marthas' early days had regularly been passed along in the letters between Bishop Cameron and Prime Minister Thompson. This was good news in correspondence dominated by one of the great storms in Canadian political history.[144] When Manitoba entered Confederation in 1870, the francophone Catholic majority and anglophone Protestant minority were guaranteed equal rights for bilingual and denominational education. By 1890, however, English-speaking migration from Ontario had flipped the demographics and the Liberal government, supported by the now Protestant majority, prohibited the use of French in civil service and ended denominational education.[145]

By 1894 the "Manitoba Schools Question" had assumed sectarian overtones that impeded any negotiated settlement. According to P.B. Waite, Manitoba Protestants were an "ungenerous majority," while some Catholics like Archbishop Alexandre-Antonin Taché, the missionary bishop of Saint Boniface, were inflexible.[146] As a Roman Catholic, Prime Minister Thompson faced tremendous pressure to defend his coreligionists in Manitoba, but he was terrified of upsetting Protestant Ontario. "Because of his Catholicism," argued J. Murray Beck, "Thompson may have been a little too ready to appease the Ultra-Protestant wing."[147]

Bishop Cameron aggressively defended his friend's reputation against Catholic critics who pressured the Conservatives for remediation, especially in Quebec. In the spring of 1894, Fr Albert Lacombe, the Quebec-born missionary to the Canadian West, and Paul LaRocque, the bishop of Sherbrooke, Quebec, came to eastern Nova Scotia to seek the prelate's signature on a petition. The document was already signed by Cardinal Elzéar-Alexandre Taschereau, and demanded remedial legislation from the Thompson government.[148] In a fascinating account, Cameron described how he gave both men a "piece of [his] mind" and rejected those Catholics who questioned the prime minister's commitment to denominational education.[149]

Although the bishop earnestly defended Thompson's integrity, he still signed Fr Lacombe's petition. "The petition is not at all to my liking," he confessed to the prime minister, "but were it less so, I would have signed it under the circumstances."[150] He wagered that his autograph would ensure a "friendly attitude" toward the Conservatives from the Quebec hierarchy. Grateful, the prime minister thanked his friend for admonishing Fr Lacombe, who "had been going from place to place speaking most unjustly of the gov't out of his zeal to get the petition signed."[151]

As the Manitoba controversy intensified, doctors grew concerned about the prime minister's health. Lack of exercise, a poor diet, and work-related stress had made his friends very "uneasy." On 12 December 1894, a telegram at the bishop's residence conveyed the "very very sad news" that Thompson had died while visiting England's Windsor Castle.[152] He had crossed the Atlantic to be sworn in as a member of Her Majesty's Privy Council by Queen Victoria. Although the ceremony lasted only twenty minutes, onlookers noticed that the prime minister was ill at ease. When the guests sat down for lunch, he fainted. He was revived by a glass of brandy but, upon returning to the feast, he complained of a pain in his chest and a few moments later his heart stopped.[153]

For the next week, the telegraph office in Antigonish town was awash in condolences from across North America. One of the warmest messages came from Lady Aberdeen, the wife of the governor general, who suggested that Cameron spend some time at government house so that they could grieve together. "The mutual condolence of such friends is something to be dearly prized," Cameron replied. "It is like the lingering halo of light that has gone out, but it still serves to brighten in some degree the darkness of our own grief."[154]

THE "HEATHERTON STAMPEDE"

While Catholics throughout eastern Nova Scotia were saddened by the death of the prime minister, many hoped that Bishop Cameron's political aspirations had died with him. The prelate supported the Tory candidate in the ensuing by-election, but this time he only "hinted" that the flock follow his example.[155] Many did so, of course, but the majority voted for the Liberal C.F. MacIsaac, the brother of Angus, who had accepted the judgeship that had first opened the parliamentary seat for Thompson. There was some politicking on the part of the clergy (Fr John Anthony Fraser of St Joseph's defended his neutrality in the pages of *The Casket*) but nothing on the scale of previous contests.[156]

Shortly after the voters of Antigonish County had filled Thompson's parliamentary seat with a Liberal – a blow to Thompson's legacy – Fr Neil McNeil, who had defied Cameron when editor of *The Casket*, was plucked from Isle Madame and appointed vicar apostolic of the West Coast of Newfoundland.[157] He was consecrated in St Ninian's Cathedral (a first for that building) on 20 October 1895 and soon sailed for Newfoundland.[158] The elevation of McNeil, an "assiduous scientist and successful educator," like that of Bishop Ronald MacDonald, should have further signalled the growing reputation of the Antigonish clergy.[159] Yet Cameron, still mourning his dead friend, took McNeil's appointment as a personal rebuke. Although he received several telegrams congratulating him on the "outgrowth from [his] diocese," there was little celebration. His complaints to the Curia about McNeil had fallen on deaf ears. Was his authority in the Holy City waning?

Yet no sooner had Bishop McNeil departed for windswept St George's than the veteran Nova Scotia Conservative politician Sir Charles Tupper, returned to Canada as "Prime Minister in waiting."

Although personally opposed to denominational education, Tupper had once brokered a compromise in Nova Scotia and believed that the Manitoba Act of 1870 had made promises to the Catholics of that province that must be honoured. When he decided to contest the parliamentary seat for Cape Breton in a February 1896 by-election, the Manitoba Schools Question was once again thrust upon the voters of eastern Nova Scotia. Annoyed that Tupper was facing criticism in the Liberal press, Archbishop O'Brien of Halifax begged Bishop Cameron to "offset the balance."[160] In response, Cameron penned a letter to be read in the churches of Cape Breton County, stressing the importance of remedial legislation for Manitoba.

With Catholic rights at stake, *The Casket* called for unity against the "stark mad" accusations of broadsheets like the *Halifax Chronicle*.[161] "We are still utterly unable to understand," fumed one editorial, "how any Catholic with the least particle of loyalty to his principles ... could endorse the condemnation of his representatives for voting to do those co-religionists that justice to which the Queen's Privy Council declared they were entitled."[162] Columns that once advocated for Sir John Thompson were now busy defending the faith.

In the lead-up to the June 1896 federal election, Tupper and the Conservative Party formally promised to restore the Catholic school board in Manitoba. When Wilfrid Laurier announced that a Liberal government would not do likewise, the Canadian episcopate formally backed the Tories. A joint letter, signed by several prominent bishops, asked Catholics to vote for Conservative candidates but, according to Terrence Fay, Bishop Cameron demanded that the draft be made "more forceful."[163] In Quebec, the joint letter was read on 17 May, and in eastern Nova Scotia, Cameron's version was published in *The Casket* on 10 June. "To vote for a Liberal in this crisis," the letter warned, "is practically to vote against justice for the Manitoba minority."[164] Not even the most hardline prelates in Quebec "[were] so blunt in [their] approach."[165]

Historians Paul Crunican and Roberto Perin have contended that the Canadian Catholic hierarchy's support for the Conservatives in 1896 was "neither misguided nor partisan," but after years of episcopal meddling in their elections the people of eastern Nova Scotia could see it no other way.[166] On Sunday 21 June, two days before the election, Fr Sandy MacDonald, the erudite professor of Latin, English, and philosophy at St F.X. who had been so affected by the meditations of St Alphonsus Liguori as a student, stood at the pulpit of Immaculate Conception Parish in rural Heatherton and read another address from the bishop. It was the duty, so the letter stated, of every conscientious Catholic to vote for Tory candidates. No Catholic – priest or layman – had the right to dispute this edict.[167] Before MacDonald finished his missal, the sound of three loud stomps on the wooden floor echoed throughout the sanctuary. At that moment, some forty to fifty men, principal members of the Heatherton community, walked out of the building in silent protest. A smaller but similar scene occurred at Mabou, when two members of the congregation left the church in defiance.[168]

Two days later, Wilfrid Laurier's Liberals defeated Charles Tupper's Conservatives. In Quebec, where episcopal support for Conservative candidates was strongest, the Liberals took 49 of the 65 seats. Even in Antigonish County, directly under the vigilant eye of Bishop Cameron, the Liberal incumbent was re-elected with a 110-vote majority. "The party that went to the country on the issue of maintaining the Constitution, in the interest, as it happens, of an oppressed Catholic minority in Manitoba," *The Casket* groaned, "has been driven from office for its pains."[169]

In the following weeks, Cameron and his Quebec colleagues remained stunned by the election results. *The Casket* rummaged for excuses; at one point arguing that Quebec Catholics preferred a prime minister of their own ethnicity, rather than one who would defend their faith. The paper also chastised the "wilful partisan blindness" of Catholics in eastern Nova Scotia as "simply and absolutely sinful."[170] No matter that voting had generally gone along traditional party lines (Tories were elected in Cape Breton, Victoria, Richmond, and Pictou counties), Cameron was exasperated by his flock.

Deeply humiliated, the bishop was determined to punish the rebels at Heatherton and Mabou. While the Mabou walk-out consisted of two daring parishioners, the Heatherton "stampede" was large and coordinated. The spokesperson for the Heatherton rebels, the barrister and future leader of the Nova Scotia Liberal Party, William Chisholm, sent a carefully crafted explanation to Bishop Cameron that only worsened the prelate's mood. When the "stampeders" arrived for Mass the following Sunday, they were told that they could neither enter the confessional nor receive communion without a public apology.

As the Easter season of 1897 approached, the farmers of Heatherton and Mabou faced a difficult choice: if they wanted to fulfill their Easter Duties, they had to bend the knee.[171] In desperation, one of the Mabou rebels pleaded that he only exited the church once Fr John Francis MacMaster had begun to comment on the circular, claiming that he had spurned his pastor's sentiments and not his bishop's letter. Denied entry to the Mabou confessional, he received the sacrament of reconciliation from Fr Alexander Chisholm down the road in Brook Village under the condition that he immediately "settle" the issue.[172]

The incident also engulfed Heatherton's pastor, Fr Roderick Grant, who was blamed for failing to bring his parishioners to heel. Emotions heightened when Cameron learned that the priest's brother had participated in the stampede. Alarmed, Grant foolishly assured his superior that his brother was away that fateful morning. When the bishop learned that John Grant was not only a stampeder but also one of the ringleaders, he seethed with anger.[173]

Fr Grant was physically large, had a "massive frame," and was capable of great feats of strength, but by the spring of 1897 he was browbeaten and exhausted. In correspondence with Cameron, he reiterated that he not only opposed the stampeders but had "condemned their actions as shameful." He had also pressed his parishioners to sign a letter of apology, but the stubborn men of Heatherton refused.[174] When the inevitable letter of transfer to Ingonish arrived in the summer of 1898, Grant opted to retire.

Excluded from the sacraments through 1898, most of the Heatherton stampeders stubbornly refused to confess to sins that their "consciences did not accuse them." One petition, signed by forty-six farmers from Heatherton, Afton, Black Avon, Fraser's Grant, and New France, begged that they be allowed to fulfill their Easter Duties without affixing their names to a letter of apology.[175] "In that circular letter as we understood it, we were asked to support a political party," they maintained, "a party that we believed to be corrupt, the policy of which was ruinous to the best interests of our common country."

The Heatherton farmers' challenge to Cameron's ultramontane agenda came as Rome sought a new spirit of conciliation in Canada. In the spring of 1897, Msgr Raphaël Merry del Val, the London-born son of a Spanish diplomat, was dispatched to Ottawa with instructions to investigate the Church's role in the Manitoba schools controversy. While the future cardinal supported the Manitoba minority, he found that the aggressive clerical support for the Conservatives had damaged the reputation of Catholicism.[176] In response, Pope Leo XIII issued an encyclical, *Affari Vos*, which called for "moderation, gentleness, and brotherly love" among Canadian Catholics. Although he declared the recent Ottawa-Winnipeg settlement in Manitoba to be "a harmful law" (bilingual instruction could be given in French-dominated schools only), he also expected his bishops to seek conciliation.[177]

Weeks after the release of *Affari Vos*, Cardinal Mieczysław Halka Ledóchowski, prefect of the Sacred Congregation of the Propaganda, told Bishop Cameron to stop meddling in politics. "The more priests are detached from the ephemeral cares of this world," the Polish bishop advised, "the better they will fulfill their sacred ministry."[178] Soon afterward, Rome established a permanent apostolic delegation in Ottawa, providing Catholics like the farmers of Heatherton and Mabou a mechanism for submitting their grievances directly to the pope's representative.

When Archbishop Diomede Falconio arrived in Canada, Cameron tried to disperse "the clouds of misrepresentations and half-truths" and, in a classic Roman power play, noted that all the local graduates of the Urban College were loyal supporters.[179] He also demonstrated a level of contempt for his flock, arguing that the stampeders of Heatherton were "illiterate and Gaelic-speaking farmers." The tide was slowly turning against the ultramontane prelate. By 1897 there were even rumblings in the Protestant press that the bishop was opposed to the progressive policies of Leo XIII and hostile to "the changed condition of the times."[180]

In the spring of 1900, the Heatherton farmers, deprived of the sacraments for four years, petitioned the apostolic delegate for permission to make their Easter Duties. While refusing to publicly submit to Cameron, they admitted that their 1896 stampede had been "rash and sinful."[181] They also noted that many of the twenty holdouts – the backbone of the dissension, as Fr Donald Chisholm described them – had received the Eucharist while in Newfoundland (transporting cattle from the port of Bayfield to St John's) or when working in New England. Not only had Cameron's bans failed but they claimed the support of many "good priests and good theologians."

When the stampeders learned that Archbishop Falconio would visit Antigonish town during his tour of the Maritime provinces, Fr Chisholm persuaded them to make a "sufficient" verbal apology to him.[182] While Cameron warmly welcomed the future cardinal to St Ninian's Cathedral as a representative of the Holy Father, such snooping "apostolic visitations" were awkward. While no account of the negotiation survives, by the autumn of 1900 the Heatherton stampeders had given "an oral submission to the document of apology" composed by the delegate, and were promptly readmitted to the sacraments. The men returned to their farms, but the ultramontane subculture had been further shaken.[183]

3

Institutional Growth 1900–1909

As a new century dawned, a progressive impulse was infiltrating Canadian society; citizens sensed a need for a more scientific and efficient management of humanity.[1] Although this impulse has been described most prominently in its manifestation through the Protestant "Social Gospel" movement, it also percolated through Catholic parishes (although without the liberal theology).[2] It was an era, writes Ernie Forbes, when industrialization and urbanization generated "a host of social ills" that required an organized response.[3]

In the first decade of 1900 the ongoing emigration of Nova Scotia youth to the United States and Ontario continued to strip the region of its finest minds and most productive workforce. Where marriage announcements had once dominated the pages of local newspapers, departure notices now bade farewell to the young people who went south "to Uncle Sam's territory to seek their fortune."[4] These young migrants toiled in lumber camps, worked as domestic servants, staffed hotels and factories, joined police forces, and became train conductors. One of the more dangerous jobs was that of the electrical lineman; many young men returned from New England in coffins after being electrocuted on the jobsite.[5]

The clergy were wary of the conditions that awaited parishioners who moved to American cities. "There are five or six promising young girls in this parish," wrote Fr Ronald Beaton from Georgeville, "for whom a little assistance just now to acquire an education means another life altogether from the one which must be theirs if they are allowed to grow up and go to Boston."[6] Yet those who returned home for summer visits spoke of gold in the streets and almost always brought one or two friends back with them.

Table 3.1 | Outmigration from Select Rural Parishes

Parish	Families with Absent Child	Sons	Daughters	Boston	Other
Pomquet	28 (17%)	30	13	27 (63%)	8
Ingonish	19 (18%)	15	12	22 (81%)	3
Iona	38 (18%)	10	39	34 (69%)	6
St Peter's	61 (28%)	43	64	52 (49%)	55
Judique	45 (22%)	32	39	36 (51%)	34

(*Source:* Antigonish Diocesan Statistics)

By 1906, 20 per cent of families in rural parishes like Pomquet, Ingonish, Iona, St Peter's, and Judique had at least one child residing outside Nova Scotia. Most of these young people worked in the vicinity of greater Boston. Almost 70 per cent of the outmigrants from the parish of Iona, for example, lived in that New England city. In fact, there were so many Nova Scotians in Boston, that a Civil War monument in the middle of Boston Common, a meeting place for Nova Scotian expatriates, was fondly known as "Nova Scotia Hill."[7] The money that these expats sent back to the region was critical to parish coffers. Whether fundraising for a monument to the late Fr James Fraser at St Andrews, or raffling off a gramophone to raise monies for the church at Baddeck, former residents bought tickets "by the thousands."[8]

COAL IS KING

Those who remained at home on the farm were keen to increase production. Although the province sent experts into the countryside to lecture on cattle raising and soil cultivation, the clergy were gradually taking a greater interest in agricultural issues.[9] Fr Sandy MacDonald, ministering among the Scottish farmers at St Andrews, remarked that agriculture was "older than civilization and [would] remain as long as life endures," but he stressed the need for training.[10] The travelling dairy school that meandered through Cape Breton each summer and the model orchard that was planted in Antigonish town were a good start.[11]

Pointing out that "a neglected farm [was] a poor inheritance," priests like Fr MacDonald expressed confidence that this new focus on rural education would not only help farmers deal with pesky invaders like "knap-weed," which spread quickly and destroyed pasture land, but also demonstrate that the problems of the countryside were manageable.[12] There was a similar awakening within coastal communities, as the region's inshore fishermen began to organize. In 1909 the new Fisherman's Union of Nova Scotia established "stations" throughout the region to push back against "grasping monopolists," and preserve the inshore fishery.[13]

The diocese was also forced to focus more closely on Cape Breton's booming coalfields. The bituminous coal extracted from the island collieries was well suited to the manufacture of good quality metallurgical coke used in making steel. As large deposits of iron ore had become available across the Cabot Strait in Newfoundland, DOMCO had in 1898 purchased the mining rights to Bell Island in Conception Bay. Soon afterward, the Dominion Iron and Steel Company (DISCO) was formed, and construction began on a large modern steel plant in Sydney. The Nova Scotia Iron and Steel Company soon built another plant across the harbour in Sydney Mines.[14] The Sydney steel plant was the most modern integrated operation in the British Empire and, according to the *Glasgow Herald*, it would soon rival Clydebank and Belfast as an industrial centre.[15] By August 1900, local newspapers bragged that seven thousand tons of coal a day were shipped from Whitney Pier.[16]

The heavy migration of Catholics into the Cape Breton colliery towns kept the clergy busy. At Reserve Mines, Fr Roderick MacInnis, only five years removed from the seminary, established a convent and a beautiful modern church but struggled to cope with the workload.[17] In 1900 Fr Ronald MacDonald of Glace Bay was asked by his former St F.X. classmate Fr Joseph Murphy to travel to Holy Cross Parish in Holyrood, Conception Bay, and collect a hundred men to work in the Glace Bay mines.[18] When MacDonald was transferred from Glace Bay to Reserve Mines in 1906, most of the signatures attached to a petition asking the bishop to rescind the transfer were from men with whom he had crossed the Cabot Strait.[19]

Figure 3.1 | Miners at Donkin, c. 1903

Soon "foreigners" were arriving in the colliery towns from much farther away than Newfoundland. In the autumn of 1901, "about 450 workmen came from Boston," noted Fr James W. MacIsaac from Sydney, and "with a few exceptions, they are Catholic and some of them are very practical Catholics at that."[20] Later, *The Casket* noted the influx of "skilled iron workers from Austria," as well as families from Poland, Russia, Hungary, and even parts of Asia.[21]

There were also some three hundred arrivals from Italy.[22] Interestingly, most of those who signed on to work in the mines were from northern Italy, while those destined for the steel mill hailed primarily from the southern region. This division applied also to housing; the northerners resided in Dominion and New Waterford, while the southerners settled primarily in Whitney Pier.[23] Despite this geographic and occupational segregation, when a southern-Italian labourer was "fearfully crushed" at the steel mill in the spring of 1901, his funeral at Sydney drew a large crowd from both groups.

As the priest at Sacred Heart did not speak Italian, Fr Alexander Thompson, fluent in the language since his days at the Urban College, presided over the funeral mass. Following the service, he was asked to write to the dead man's widow back in Italy. In conversation with the men, the priest learned that DISCO had initiated no investigation into the fatality; nor was any compensation awarded to the man's family.[24] In concern, he met with some barristers, who quickly petitioned the Italian Consul in Montreal to establish a vice-consul at Sydney.

While priests and women religious were doing a valiant job of attending to the needs of the Cape Breton immigrant community, their inability to speak the newcomers' languages was problematic. In 1905 a wealthy Hungarian nobleman-cum-clergyman writing a book on expatriates in Canada met with Bishop Cameron en route to interview some of his countrymen employed at Sydney.[25] While he wanted Cameron to aggressively recruit Hungarian and Italian clergy for eastern Nova Scotia, that was much easier said than done.[26]

In 1907 New York City resident (and Prince Edward Island native) Fr Neil MacKinnon, SJ, arrived in Antigonish town to conduct the annual clerical retreat.[27] Since he ministered among Italian immigrants in Manhattan, he was asked to find an Italian priest willing to go north. In the damp spring of 1908, he wrote that a recent arrival, Fr Domencio Viola, a native of the bustling Adriatic port of Bari, was on his way to Glace Bay. With no parish and no stable income, the twenty-eight-year-old had to serve large congregations of Italians scattered around the colliery towns.[28] But he was a tireless organizer, and within months he had formed the Santa Rita Society at Glace Bay and even organized a popular brass band.[29]

While priests "from away" like Fr Viola occasionally battled sterotypes, the presence of foreign Catholics did not elicit the kind of sectarianism that was common in other industrial cities. But in fact, there was a large contingent who had little good to say about newcomers, regardless of their religious affiliation. All foreigners, even Newfoundlanders, faced bouts of discrimination. One railway contractor in Sydney, for example, characterized his Newfoundland employees as "miserable half-starved pirates" and argued that Italians were "princes" compared to those from *Terra Nova*.[30]

Immigrants poured into Sydney so rapidly that the local infrastructure could not keep up. In 1903 the *Sydney Post* reported that the population of Glace Bay was so congested that it was "almost impossible to rent a home of any size or description."[31] Cases were not uncommon of "boarding houses [being] hammered up to shelter fourteen hundred men, two to a bed."[32] Rows of cookie-cutter company houses, often described politely as "miner's cottages,"

Table 3.2 | Catholic Population Increase in Industrial Cape Breton (1897–1906)

Town	Population in 1897	Population in 1906	Increase
Bridgeport	1,421	2,379	67%
Sydney Mines	1,515	2,373	57%
Sydney	1,347	2,622	95%
Glace Bay	1,659	3,294	98%

(*Source:* Antigonish Diocesan Statistics)

made streets virtually indistinguishable from one another.[33] Those without permanent lodgings lived in the makeshift "shacks."[34] While many of the seasonal migrants tolerated the shacks as a temporary inconvenience, typhoid and smallpox were a serious problem, and the sick and injured were "left all day without care."[35]

The Catholics among these migrants filled the parishes, and Sacred Heart in Sydney and St Anne's in Glace Bay both doubled in size. They crammed the pews, crowded the parish picnics, and joined societies in record numbers. The opening ceremonies of the 1901 mission at St Anne's were witnessed by over two thousand people.[36] "I am positive that large numbers of the men do not come to Mass," wrote an anxious curate at Sacred Heart, "simply because they cannot get into the church. God help us if these people come to Easter Duties."[37]

To cope with the population explosion, three new parishes were opened in the colliery towns: St John the Baptist in New Aberdeen (1902), Holy Redeemer in Whitney Pier (1902), and St Anthony's in Dominion No. 4 (1903). The land for churches was usually donated by wealthy patrons but in New Aberdeen miners rented a building from DOMCO until they could purchase property of their own.[38] The Scottish-born Fr John Cameron, responsible for the multi-ethnic parish of St John the Baptist, in 1902 collected New Aberdeen's first subscription, which was generously supported by local colliers (including many Protestants).

The Casket frequently boasted of this Catholic expansion. "As the rising of the morning star," noted one roused correspondent, "so is the aspect of the Church of the Holy Redeemer on the heights of Whitney, yea, over [the] smoke, flames and materialism."[39] Amid the bustle of construction, resolute priests were working "with the spirit of self-sacrifice utterly unknown and unacknowledged by the so called 'Captains of Industry.'"[40] The clergy were full of optimism as large congregations of miners and steelworkers financed new infrastructure. "My father's name was on three lists," recalled one resident, "the company pay-roll, the voter's list, and the list of pew holders in the church."[41]

With so many unmarried young men carrying coin in their pockets, the clergy were kept busy battling anti-social behaviour and crime. One person later recalled that "those who weren't selling liquor in the town [Glace Bay] were drinking it." Notices of brawls and even deaths due to alcohol abuse appeared regularly in the press. One obituary read simply: "William Tobin, Spanish Bay, Newfoundland – Alcoholism."[42] Liquor provided an easy source of income for bootleggers, and the long hard days of mining coal created eager customers. Ships full of Jamaican and Cayman Island rum regularly slipped past Canadian customs, the barrels brought ashore and transported to old mine tunnels where their contents were transferred into bottles.[43] When under chase, rum runners would occasionally throw their cargo overboard. In 1902 several casks were found floating along the shores of Lingan Beach near Dominion. According to the *Sydney Daily Post*, "they were very quickly taken charge of and many in that town were yesterday feasting at the bacchanal table."[44]

As with the Town Council of Sydney Mines, which pledged to wage a "relentless war" on liquor, the League of the Cross continued to fight against the drink.[45] A "Grand Council" was organized in Sydney in 1900, and the league's magazine, *The Total Abstainer*, was in most Catholic homes.[46] Seeking alternatives to the public house, one branch of the league offered members the use of a pool table, a small gymnasium, and a reading room containing the works of Charles Dickens and Walter Scott.[47] In 1904 the League of the Cross at St Anthony's parish in Dominion No. 4 (Glace Bay) opened "the small hall" and, despite its name, which Fr Ronald H. MacDougall declared he detested, it made a large contribution.[48] After the 1903 midnight Mass in Sydney, Fr MacAdam bragged that "the odor of liquor could scarcely be detected among all that crowd."[49]

ST JOSEPH'S HOSPITAL, GLACE BAY

Despite the pledges that were administered throughout the colliery towns, it was difficult to face health and addiction issues without proper access to medical care. As early as 1893, Fr James Quinan in Sydney had proposed a "home for the infirm" and "a bed or two ... for wounded miners," but by 1902, when John Morrison of Arichat had a serious injury while moving ore at the blast furnace, there was still not enough equipment in the company infirmary to save his life.[50] Responding to the acute need for a hospital, Fr Ronald MacDonald of Glace Bay and Fr Charles W. MacDonald of Bridgeport began touring Catholic infirmaries in Massachusetts and Quebec, while soliciting funds through the miners' check-off.[51]

In the summer of 1901, Governor General Lord Minto turned the first sod for St Joseph's Hospital on a property situated on Chapel Hill, midway between Bridgeport and Glace Bay. By the festive Christmas season, project fundraisers were in full swing. Opening a large bazaar at the CMBA Hall in Glace Bay, Mayor D.M. Burchell paid special tribute to Fr MacDonald and prophesied that the hospital "would be a monument to his Christian zeal and indomitable pluck long after he [had] passed this life."[52]

On Dominion Day 1902, Fr MacDonald stood before a crowd of three thousand on the veranda of the new seventy-five-bed hospital (the fifth in the province), and offered its services to "suffering humanity."[53] The first patient, Patrick Royal of Newfoundland, had his mutilated leg amputated by doctors after a load of coal fell upon him at Caledonia Mines.[54] The new hospital was never short of patients. In the heart of the industrial district, mishaps were frequent and injuries severe. "There was probably a larger percentage of 'industrial surgery' here than in any other part of the Maritime provinces," recalled one physician; "the conditions were similar to those that made Leeds [England] such a center of the best surgical work."[55]

THE 1909 COAL MINERS' STRIKE

Despite advances in medical care and infrastructure, the Church could do little to alter the mood of the miners. Extremely "craft conscious," many veteran colliers hated working alongside low-skilled foreigners, claiming that "two pairs of old hands ... could outpace seven pairs of imported novices."[56] The steel company frequently used seasonal labour to suppress wages and in 1903 they reduced the salaries of steelworkers while simultaneously recruiting new workers in Newfoundland.[57] Employees fortunate enough to have regular shifts often struggled to save money. A new DOMCO weighman at Reserve Mines, after waiting a month to receive his wages, found that the "backdraw" regulations held back two weeks' pay until the day he left the company's employ.[58] Lacking cash, families had no choice but to purchase their supplies on credit from the company store. It was not long before the *Sydney Post* exposed the "truck system" of withholding a miner's pay to satisfy a company bill as nothing more than slavery.[59]

Among Nova Scotia farmers and fishermen, long experienced in the nature-dependent processes of their occupations, few were familiar with such terms as "arbitration." With little local expertise available, the diocesan press looked for guidance to intellectuals like Bishop Wilhelm Emmanuel von Ketteler of Mainz, Germany, whose social teachings on labour were published as *The Social Question and Christianity*.[60] At the same time, reports of European socialism were beginning to percolate. There were rumours that socialists were organizing in communities like Sydney Mines, and clergy studying in Europe wrote of increasing radicalism in European cities. "The Marxists are making such a propaganda in Munich," wrote one priest studying in Germany in 1909. "The disease has spread among the people."[61]

While the Church had historically opposed socialism, it did not support the abuses of industrial capitalism. A policy of that nature would have been suicidal. *The Casket*, while not exactly a "fearless advocate" of the rights of labour, like Boston's *Sacred Heart Review*, editorialized that the appetite of the rich to capitalize power and flout restraint would bring ruin.[62] The people were within their rights to support government control over telegraphs, railroads, gas, and water, but the not the suppression of private capital and private enterprise.[63]

As the Nova Scotia economy relied increasingly on industry, politicians feared strike action. "If a nineteenth century strike was a nuisance," notes one prominent labour historian, "a large coal strike in the twentieth century was a calamity."[64] In June 1904, fifteen hundred employees of DISCO, reacting to a wage reduction and long working hours, went on the picket line. In response, the company temporarily closed portions of the steel plant. Amid a prolonged heat wave, old issues of xenophobia and scab labour resurfaced as a group of Hungarians were stoned by an angry crowd of "young strike sympathizers."[65]

Two years later a strike at Westville, Pictou County, put a thousand miners on the picket line, and by 1907 provincial papers were commenting on the mounting discontent.[66] Priests consistently preached conciliation and, for the first time, a few began to reference the encyclical *Rerum Novarum* more regularly.[67] "Capitalists may ignore the maxims of justice now," warned *The Casket* in September 1909, "but the day shall come ... when the people will compel governments to regulate and control the activities of the industrial world by means of legislation."[68]

In 1908, frustrated by the impotence of the Provincial Workmen's Association (PWA), thousands of miners opted to join the United Mine Workers of America (UMW) instead.[69] The largest union in North America, organized in 1890, had been bloodied by major strikes at Pennsylvania, Colorado, and West Virginia, and although it was an American entity, its opening of an Alberta district in 1903 signalled international aspirations. Nova Scotia miners had flirted with the American union for some time – they had appealed for strike support in 1904 – but opting to leave the old provincial union for an American organization was audacious.[70]

By Easter 1909, UMW's District 26 was organized at Sydney and some 2,600 of the 4,500 miners in Cape Breton had quickly signed UMW cards. DOMCO, fearful of the powerful new union, began to harass its supporters, and closed the mine at Dominion No. 6 until such time as "a small number of men rejoined the PWA."[71] As the lodges of the provincial union disintegrated, UMW leaders were blacklisted and its supporters fired. By early July, District 26 had called its first strike.

The 1909 work stoppage, the "first of the great strikes," was effectively a civil war among the miners which divided communities in Sydney, Glace Bay, and Inverness.[72] It pitted UMW supporters against both DOMCO and the PWA. While the PWA claimed that 40 per cent of the men remained on the job, support for the UMW was clear. At Caledonia and Dominion No. 4, 70 out of 900 miners arrived for work on the first day of the strike, and at No. 2 and No. 9 around 100 of 1,600 men continued with their jobs.[73] With rival union members living on the same streets, violence was inevitable. Men on their way to the work at New Aberdeen were "forced to run a gauntlet of shouts and yells, backed up by flying stones and eggs."[74] There were also sensational claims about a bomb in the Bridgeport mine, and in a particularly sad incident, two former friends, now on opposite sides, got into an argument that resulted in murder.[75] Passions were further inflamed when the Royal Canadian Regiment and special police constables were brought in to protect company property.[76]

While the Catholic press treated the "foreign" UMW with some suspicion, Bishop Cameron's expressed views on the new union were "quite limited."[77] In the main, most clergy sided with the majority opinion of their parishioners, while others held views shaped by their personal dealings with DOMCO. At St Anne's in Glace Bay, for instance, Fr Thompson became a critic of the company because he had been regularly forced into arbitration and compelled to sell parish property at low prices. By March 1909, DOMCO complained that Thompson was "personally against [them]" and was using his influence as vicar-general to influence his colleagues. Incredibly, the company wanted the bishop to force Thompson to issue a public statement against UMW, and even asked to have the priest "go away."[78]

At St Anthony's in Glace Bay, Fr Alexander Mackenzie allowed the outspoken UMW supporter Andrew Livingstone, who had been evicted from his company home, to live in the parish's former glebe house as the "caretaker."[79] Livingstone and other strikers were also using the local League of the Cross Hall as a headquarters from which to "assault the company's men going to and from work." Once again, DOMCO officials demanded an investigation, but it led nowhere. Fr William Kiely of North Sydney noted in his report that Livingstone had a clean record and was a good tenant. As to the LOC Hall, it was not owned by the diocese but by the temperance society, whose members were all UMW supporters.[80]

As DOMCO tried to drive out the United Mine Workers, financial and moral pressure on parishes was intense. [81] "Nearly all my parishioners are on strike," wrote one clergyman from Glace Bay, warning that there would soon be insufficient monies to support a priest.[82] At St Anne's, Fr Thompson expressed concern that most of his parishioners had "to face the problem of living without knowing whence they [were] to derive their daily bread, their clothing, their fuel, their homes."[83] While *The Casket* generally supported the PWA, it took pains to appear impartial. It admitted that the old provincial union had lost the confidence of its membership,[84] and when UMW president Thomas Lewis visited Cape Breton, it politely described his Glace Bay speech as "elegant and forceful."[85]

BRIDGEPORT "MACHINE-GUN" INCIDENT

On 30 July 1909, all the hard work cultivating the perception of clerical neutrality was undone. The previous day, the town of Dominion, a PWA stronghold, learned that three thousand UMW supporters planned a march through their community.[86] The town council increased security and hastily passed a resolution denying the right to hold public meetings without a permit.[87] The following morning, ignoring the edict, UMW supporters, carrying banners and waving flags, left Glace Bay for Dominion. When the strikers approached Bridgeport's Immaculate Conception Church, they encountered a terrible sight. Members of the Canadian Militia had mounted their rapid-fire gun on the steps of the sanctuary, and soldiers with fixed bayonets waited on the grounds of the Presbyterian Church a few hundred yards away. Fearing for their safety, the marchers turned and fled back toward Glace Bay. By evening, news of the incident had spread throughout the colliery parishes, and a petition was circulated in New Aberdeen demanding the immediate removal of the Bridgeport pastor, Fr Charles MacDonald. Within hours, an ecclesiastical investigation was launched.

Fr MacDonald had ministered for fourteen years at Bridgeport, where he would remain until his death in 1948. He was best known for his work toward establishing St Joseph's Hospital. Although not an ardent supporter of the PWA, he felt duty-bound to avert the "terrible calamity" of the strike. He had preached on the conditions necessary for a work stoppage to be a success: that the men be united, that they have public opinion on their side, and that they have exhausted all other means of settling their grievances. In his opinion, the UMW had not met those conditions. He also claimed that the manager of the Bridgeport mine, "a good Catholic," had warned that a UMW victory would result in the permanent closure of the colliery.[88]

Faced with enquiries from Bishop Cameron, the beleaguered priest stated that he had always tried to "moderate the passions." On the morning of 30 July, he testified, he had been kept busy with hospital business and returned home to find a Captain Almon waiting in his parlour.[89] In a conversation that lasted "hardly a minute," Almon explained that his job was to maintain the peace, and asked permission to place some soldiers inside the church fence so that they would be off the road. The priest insisted that the young captain did not mention a "rapid-fire gun," only that he wanted to station a few men on parish property.

MacDonald claimed that he had only learned of the incident that evening when he returned home from an afternoon appointment.[90] While there was a hive of angry UMW supporters in his parish, he was confident that, after many years of faithful service, his congregation knew him "better than to think that [he] should wish any of them harm." He assured Cameron that "after the first gust of passion," most of those UMW supporters, many of whom were personal friends, would realize that the incident "might indeed have been a mistake."[91] As evidence, he claimed that the petition calling for his removal, which originated in New Aberdeen, had been ignored by the UMW strikers in his parish. "I have heard many ugly lies about myself," he declared, "but I strive to bear them all with equanimity."[92]

Recent historical publications have employed the incident at Bridgeport as evidence that the Catholic clergy supported DOMCO against the United Mine Workers. To some it was a clear illustration of religious collusion with "state power."[93] Others contended that it demonstrated the Church's willingness to "take notorious sides" with "confidence and impunity."[94] Whatever one thinks of the motives of Fr MacDonald – and there are many varied opinions (some local Catholics never got over the incident) – his action did not represent a formal diocese-wide policy.[95] Although the investigation found that Fr MacDonald had acted *ultra vires* and violated the spirit of ecclesiastical law – he certainly had no business negotiating with the military – his colleagues refused to believe that he would have consented to a rapid-fire gun on the steps of his church.[96]

In a contrasting incident in the UMW stronghold of New Aberdeen, Fr John Anthony Fraser, a native of St Andrews, offered moral and material support to his striking parishioners.[97] As pastor in a gritty, multi-ethnic parish, the Urban College graduate was privy to some of the worst conditions in the colliery towns: "I have known many poor miners here to come to myself after pay showing me their pay sheets, in which there was not a cent coming to them and declaring that they had not a morsel of food left in their houses."[98] Fr Fraser loathed DOMCO. In 1908 the priest had been abruptly informed that the school playground encroached on DOMCO property and the "wee children" would have to vacate the space. Adamant that his predecessor had obtained permission to use the land, he contended that the company would "stop at nothing to outrage the poor people."[99]

Later, during a protracted battle with the company, Fraser wrote to Prime Minister Wilfrid Laurier in the hope that Ottawa would safeguard "the liberties of his people."[100] Now, the priest actively encouraged solidarity among the UMW supporters in his parish. "As the chain is no stronger than its weakest link," he wrote in the *Sydney Daily Post*, "neither is your union stronger than you yourselves make it."[101] During the contentious summer months of 1909, he lodged many evicted miners in the church basement, schoolhouse, and rectory. He was a popular figure in his parish, and certainly within the working-class literature of Cape Breton. Years later, one former miner noted that even though he was illiterate he "knew a great deal about Fr John Fraser."[102]

As with the incident at Bridgeport, accounts of Fr Fraser's actions have been noted in several scholarly publications. But also, like accounts of the Bridgeport episode, it has been misinterpreted; his narrative of support for the UMW and his acts of kindness toward the strikers was used to portray the diocese as anti-labour. Deploying testimony from individuals who were either confused or had a poor memory, John Mellor was responsible for circulating the myth that Fr Fraser was chastised and disciplined for his support of the UMW. In *The Company Store*, for instance, Mellor quoted Pat Nicholson, a reporter for the *Glace Bay Standard*:

> Father Jim Frazer [sic], pastor of St. John's Church in the parish of New Aberdeen, took pity on them [evicted UMW miners] and filled the convent, the Catholic schools, the rectory and most of the church with poor, destitute miners' families. But another priest [name omitted by author] travelled all the way to Antigonish on the Nova Scotia mainland to see Bishop Cameron and tell him that the coal company was not only fighting the U.M.W.A., it was fighting the Catholic Church due to the actions of Fr Frazer [sic]. That same evening, Fr Jim received word from Bishop Cameron that he must leave the New Aberdeen parish at once! He was given a new parish in Antigonish County under the watchful eye of the bishop and far away from the strike scene. The strikers and their families were ordered to leave the church forthwith.[103]

"It was shocking but true," Mellor wrote, never having scrutinized his sources for a quotation that was absurd even for a book that was already full of hyperbole. Yet the myth of Fr Fraser's transfer – it would not be the last such enduring fable in the diocese's history – made for good copy. In Mellor's depiction, a brother priest had doomed Fraser, while another claimed it was the mine manager at New Aberdeen. In all cases, the theme remained the same.[104]

Like Fr MacDonald in Bridgeport, Fr Fraser did not face ecclesiastical discipline for taking sides during the strike and, despite the claims of his transfer to a "rural parish," he remained pastor of St John the Baptist until 1916.[105] Fraser's pro-UMW attitude during the strike was supported by some of his colleagues, while others, like Fr MacAdam in Sydney, wrote to the apostolic delegate to complain of his "fiery sermons."[106] The clergy were as divided as the miners themselves.

PROGRESS AND TENSION AT ST FRANCIS XAVIER

For priests ministering to miners at Glace Bay and Bridgeport, problems at diocesan institutions such as St F.X. seemed a world away. Even though few striking colliers and fishermen had the opportunity to attend university, in Bishop Cameron's subculture the first Sunday in October was known throughout the diocese as "college Sunday" and parishes donated generously. All financial contributions were noted in *The Casket* and when the paper bungled figures or omitted names, priests demanded that their flock receive their due recognition.[107] When some parishioners of St Anne's in Glace Bay were left off the list of contributors in 1905, Fr Ronald MacDonald complained that these mistakes would produce rumours of financial impropriety as "people [were] apt to be suspicious even of a priest's honesty in money matters."[108]

In 1900 St F.X. was in the administrative hands of Fr Alexander Thompson; "Doc Dan" Chisholm, who had given St F.X. "a push towards university status," was transferred to North Sydney in 1898.[109] Described as "a man of conviction," Thompson had recently received an honorary degree from the University of New Brunswick and was committed to curriculum renewal.[110] The Sydney coal boom had had fuelled an interest in engineering and chemistry, and Thompson's new Faculty of Applied Sciences challenged "the monopoly held by the traditional liberal-classical education."[111] The rector had even encouraged the newly ordained Fr "Little Doc" Hugh MacPherson, working on graduate studies in France, to take classes at the Polytechnique as he had a "natural aptitude" for science.[112] As the small colleges of the Maritimes were woefully underfunded, St F.X. applied to the American industrialist Andrew Carnegie for funds to purchase laboratory equipment and unsuccessfully lobbied the provincial government to support a mining and engineering school (the Nova Scotia Technical College would open at Halifax in 1907).[113]

Despite this new scholarly direction, finances were tight, and the student body came mostly "from modest social and economic backgrounds."[114] While the college had prominent alumni in religious life, business, medicine, and the law, some clergy still advised their young parishioners to attend wealthier schools in Montreal or Ottawa. This lack of confidence in St F.X. was the result, Rector Thompson opined, "of [the] long oppression" of Scottish and Irish peoples who "recognize themselves as in some manner inferior to what the dominant nation can produce."[115]

While cultural inferiority might have been a factor, many priests were annoyed by the changes to the curriculum and rumours of lax discipline.[116] One man sensationally claimed that young ladies were seen "lowered from the college windows" – although he quickly denied making the statement.[117] Still, when St F.X. celebrated its fiftieth anniversary in September 1905, educators from across Canada toasted the achievements of the small, but important, Catholic institution. At a reception held under beautiful Chinese lanterns that adorned the grounds of Mount Saint Bernard College, the mood was hopeful and the future bright.[118]

Having given St F.X. a philosophical shake-up, Thompson was transferred to Glace Bay in 1906.[119] Although there were rumours that the priest would one day succeed Bishop Cameron, negative clerical sentiments toward the college necessitated a change. Nonetheless, eyebrows were raised when Bishop Cameron announced that the thirty-nine-year-old pastor at L'Ardoise, Fr Hugh Peter MacPherson, would lead the institution into the future. Although MacPherson would spend thirty years at the helm and become known affectionately as the "Old Rector" (and will hereafter be referred to by that name), he was a strange choice. He had an honorary doctorate from Université Laval, but was not a graduate of a Roman seminary – still extremely important – and he had spent most of his career ministering on coastal Isle Madame.[120]

It came as a great relief, therefore, that the new rector quickly proved clever, capable, and friendly. One student, Patrick Joseph "P.J." Nicholson of North Sydney, who would later become president of the college, recalled that MacPherson was a dashing figure, "the cynosure of every eye in any gathering."[121] More important, he "had the brains to understand your deeper thoughts, and the gentlemanliness to listen to you."[122]

With the dashing MacPherson as rector, Bishop Cameron selected the thirty-seven-year-old Margaree native Fr James J. Tompkins to put some iron in the glove.[123] The frail but entrepreneurial Tompkins, vice-president in charge of fundraising, and later director of studies, would soon become one of Canada's most famous priests. He had studied at the Urban College in Rome – although he did not receive the standard doctoral degrees due to illness – and joined the St F.X. faculty in 1902 as professor of Greek and higher algebra. An administrator *extraordinaire*, he had little patience for the quiet academic life and swiftly began gathering opinions about what a small modern college could do for the region.[124] He was bursting with ideas; convinced that "every man had a sermon to preach."[125]

These two capable managers went to work restructuring the faculty, training staff, raising money, and changing attitudes.[126] Of significance was that they began to send scholars abroad for post-graduate training. In the summer of 1907, Fr Cornelius Joseph Connolly, a native of Stellarton and a stand-out scholar at Pictou Academy, St F.X., and the Grand Seminary of Montreal, left for doctoral studies in biology at the University of Munich. His letters from the city of "education, art and music" offer fascinating insights into Bavarian society and German education. Fr Tompkins was so inspired by the details of his laboratory training, that St F.X. soon considered offering a doctoral degree.[127]

SISTERS OF ST MARTHA BREAK FROM THE CHARITIES

Much of the new energy at St F.X. was due to the presence and efficiency of the Sisters of St Martha. By 1900 the relationship (and arrangement) between the Sisters of Charity and St F.X. had deteriorated. The number of recruits was unsatisfactory and the college was forced to hire extra domestic labour.[128] In Halifax, the Charity superior, Mother Fidelis, had become disenchanted with the partnership, resented the responsibility, and felt no obligation to the Antigonish college.[129] Bishop Cameron, unwilling to part with the hard-working women staffing his college, announced that the "Mar-

Figure 3.2 | Fr Hugh Peter MacPherson, "The Old Rector"

thas" would become a new diocesan congregation. In early July, the sisters staffing the St F.X. mission were called to a retreat at Mount St Vincent. Unexpectedly, the archbishop of Halifax arrived to offer them a choice: either remain with the Charities in Halifax or leave permanently for Antigonish town.[130] According to congregation historians, it took tremendous courage for thirteen young women to stand up and volunteer to return eastward.[131]

When some of the St F.X. volunteers were segregated, placed in various Charity convents and pressured to abandon the college, the tension was palpable.[132] "If anybody connected with your community has had the presumption to tell any of the Sisters that the blessing of God is not likely to rest upon her choice of a religious life, when the archbishop assured her that she was perfectly free to make it," a furious Rector Thompson wrote, "I would remind that person that such language, apart from the impertinence of it, is nothing short of diabolical."[133] From the Charity convent in North Sydney, Sister Mary Regis, a warm friend of Bishop Cameron, desperately tried to keep the Marthas in the Charity community. "Will you not wait a little longer my lord before taking the decisive step," she pleaded, "or if taken will you not countermand it for a time at least?"[134] But Cameron was determined.[135]

On 16 July, the new diocesan Congregation of the Sisters of St Martha appointed Sister Innocentia (Caroline McNamara) of Lower River Inhabitants, Richmond County, as their first mother superior.[136] Soon afterward, the sisters opened a novitiate and during the snowy feast of the Epiphany four postulants took the habit in the chilly motherhouse chapel. By the following summer, the congregation had grown to thirty-four members. The new constitution confirmed the congregation's duties at St F.X., and a clerical governance board determined the eligibility of all new applicants. While the Marthas were happy to be free from the authority of Mount St Vincent, they knew they had traded the maternalism of the Charities for the paternalism of St F.X.[137]

One of the great strengths of the Marthas – and one reason that generations of Catholics revered them – was their willingness to get their hands dirty. Their domestic skills might have gone unappreciated by the Charities, but they quickly created new opportunities. By the summer of 1902, the women had been asked to bring their "efficient household management" to the new St Joseph's Hospital in Glace Bay and, while the infirmary was always conducted in a "efficient manner," as one prominent Sydney physician recalled, it "attained a new growth and efficiency" after the Marthas' arrival.[138]

As the Marthas' mission at St Joseph's Hospital began, Catholics across the diocese were demanding better access to healthcare. In 1905 the citizens of Antigonish town petitioned the congregation to open a "cottage hospital," and the following summer a former residence, "Campbell House," which was located across the street from the motherhouse, opened with six beds.[139] Patients quickly outnumbered beds – it was rumoured that a larger infirmary would be built on the St F.X. campus – and by the autumn of 1907 the women purchased a considerable property overlooking the college town.[140]

Through their work of cleaning wounds and emptying bedpans, the Marthas demonstrated that faith went well beyond the pew and they became the vanguard of the Catholic social action that would later make the diocese famous. In the short term, however, class remained a hurdle. Responding as they did to their experiences among the Charities, the women serving at St Joseph's Hospital often felt they were treated merely as "servants for the nurses" and were regarded as "intruders." Sister Faustina (Mary MacArthur) eventually petitioned St F.X. for permission for them to withdraw from the infirmary. "Perhaps the bishop will not approve of us leaving here," she acknowledged, "but if he only knew what this place means for us, I do not believe his Lordship would force us to remain."[141] With typhoid "raging in the hospital," the women did not pursue their grievances that year, but in 1908 they closed the Glace Bay mission.[142]

THE FILLES DE JÉSUS

As the Marthas sorted the early hiccups of their healthcare ministry, a congregation in France was looking for similar opportunities. The Filles de Jésus, founded in 1834 for the Diocese of Vannes in Brittany, had spent decades as teachers and nurses only to find themselves without a home. The government of Pierre Waldeck-Rousseau had passed the "Associations Bill" in the spring of 1901, with the object of ensuring the supremacy of civil over Church powers. It intentionally targeted Catholic institutions, banned teaching orders from the classroom, and shuttered thousands of Catholic schools.[143] "They [the religious houses] are wiped out," declared the *New York Evening Mail*. "Of course a few of them are still here, but they are hiding like rats in their holes."[144]

Just as the harassed women were seeking sanctuary in Quebec – Trois-Rivières became the order's general headquarters – the Congregation of Notre Dame happened to withdraw from its historic Convent of Our Lady of Assumption in Arichat. Although Arichat had fallen on hard economic times, the decision to close the mission came as a "great surprise." By the end of July, much of the convent's furnishings were transferred to the Congregation convents in Mabou and Pictou, while the rest was sold at auction (Our Lady of Assumption Parish bought the organ for $90). By the end of August, the old building was empty. "How sad it looks and how large!" one sister pined; "we pass through the vast rooms with sad and sorrowful hearts."[145]

Responsible for a large empty convent and unable to envision Arichat without resident teaching sisters, Arichat's pastor, Fr Lubin

Joseph Gallant, was elated to learn that the French-speaking Filles de Jésus were looking for new fields of ministry. A native of Grand Etang, Fr Gallant – who would serve as the congregation's chaplain until his death in 1940 – invited the women to Isle Madame, and by the autumn of 1902 they were caring for four elderly members of the Third Order of La Trappe (a congregation organized by Fr Vincent de Paul at the Trappist monastery at Tracadie).[146] Within a year, they were also ministering in Cheticamp. The Filles de Jésus and their boarding school were critical for French-speaking education in places like Richmond County, and young girls, one of whom was Elizabeth Béranger, a schoolteacher at River Bourgeois, found new opportunities to enter religious life.

PAINTINGS, MISSIONS, AND SHRINES

The expansion of the Sisters of St Martha into healthcare and the establishment of new congregations like the Filles de Jésus bore witness to the resilience of the Catholic subculture.[147] This ultramontane self-confidence was expressed from the pulpit, in print, and in the elaborate artwork – much of it imported from Europe – that decorated the churches. Between 1899 and 1903, the renowned Quebec artist Ozias Leduc transformed St Ninian's Cathedral by painting the stations of the cross and beautiful frescoes on the ceiling.[148] Working on scaffolding high above the altar, he tried "to do everything according to rule, and rational order, so that the equilibrium of the various posts might result in a harmonious symmetry."[149]

Leduc's project occasioned various delays, in particular causing the cancellation of the 1903 Good Friday services.[150] Holy week was always a sacred occasion, as was the springtime "Blessing of the Oils." At Stellarton, the "May Devotions" included an energetic and elegant procession to the parish cemetery.[151] By participating in such devotional events, the faithful obtained indulgences that they hoped would reduce the amount of time they spent in purgatory. During October Devotions, a "Rosary Indulgence" could be obtained by publicly reciting five decades, and during the Benediction of the Blessed Sacrament, which was observed at different times during the calendar year, plenary indulgences were granted to those who spent an hour in silent vigil. [152]

To instruct the faithful and bring "loose and lapse[d] Catholics back into the fold," parish missions, commonly supervised by a visiting clergyman, were held during the summertime.[153] An eight-day mission at Reserve Mines drew over thirteen hundred Catholics to Holy Communion, while a mission at Glace Bay was held over a two-week period to accommodate miners who worked day and night shifts on alternate weeks.[154]

In the late summer of 1907, Fr Donald MacPherson and Fr Sandy MacDonald invited the distinguished Jesuit preacher Fr Archibald Campbell of Glasgow to facilitate several missions among the Gaelic-speaking Scots (they had made contact via the Scottish nationalist and Gaelic writer Ruaraidh Erskine).[155] Beginning his spiritual tour in Pictou County, Campbell trekked onward to Cape Breton, stopping in parishes like Thorburn and Lismore to offer the descendants of Highland emigrants "the sublime truths of their faith in their rich native tongue."[156]

After an especially successful mission at Creignish, Inverness County, twenty-five teams of horse-drawn carriages conveyed the beloved missionary over ten miles to Glendale, where he was joyfully greeted by fifty more teams led by a piper. Later, he was proudly piped from East Bay to Boisdale.[157] "Exiles, and children of exiles," proclaimed *The Casket*, "gathered to give a royal Highland welcome to the priest who spoke their tongue, and who knew the people and their 'place'"[158] At Southwest Margaree, the Gaelic poet and diarist Donald Dougal MacFarlane wrote that Campbell's mission had been a "big success."[159] After his tiring excursion, the Jesuit lectured on the romantic scenery of Scotland to an enthusiastic audience in Antigonish town's Celtic Hall. To *The Casket*'s readership in 1909, he wrote effusively: "Before this reaches you, I shall be in Benbecula, and South Uist, telling them of all I have seen of their flesh and blood in East Bay, Boisdale, Christmas Island, and Iona."[160]

While most people attended missions and ceremonies close to home, wealthier Catholics visited shrines such as Sainte-Anne-de-Beaupré in Quebec. Testimony of healing at the shrine harked back to the early days of New France, and a popular publication, *Miracles of Beaupré*, which exposed the more recent sensations, was in every parish library.[161] Captivated by poignant testimonies – an Ontario nun was famously cured of debilitating knee pain – Fr A.E. Monbourquette of Arichat led a group of pilgrims in the summer of 1909 to Beaupré, where hundreds of "crutches, high-soled shoes, braces, and even a wooden leg" left by the "cured" were stacked against a wall.[162]

All this devotional activity was costly, and fundraising was continuous. Pew rentals remained a lucrative, if controversial, source of income (although in River Bourgeois the people "were not averse to paying after all") and clergy often gave their personal monies to fend off creditors.[163] Although every cent taken from the parish was "a direct loss to themselves," there was even some money left over to send overseas for the abolition of slavery in Africa and the Holy Shrines of Palestine.[164] When the devastating "Messina earthquake" struck the Italian regions of Sicily and Calabria in 1908, killing some eighty thousand people, the $746 contribution from eastern Nova Scotia was noted in *L'Osservatore Romano*.

ACADIANS AGITATE FOR A BISHOP

While ultramontanists like Bishop Cameron worked strenuously to mould the people into one unified Catholic body, in the multicultural Maritimes ethnicity remained an obstacle. The sizeable Acadian community continued to be frustrated by the ecclesiastical dominance of the Irish and Scots. Although Acadians constituted one of the oldest Catholic constituencies, Acadian customs and contributions to the Catholic culture were often downplayed within a church that wanted to integrate the francophone population into the English-speaking mainstream. When, for instance, the *Richmond Record* reported that Arichat's popular Corpus Christi parade was "an old French custom," the diocesan newspaper retorted that the parade was not "French" but "Catholic." At the 1900 Acadian National Convention at Arichat, Fr Amable Monbourquette, a native of L'Ardoise, argued that without a community awakening Acadians and their customs would forever remain in the background.

Instrumental in the education of young Acadian priests such as Fr (later monsignor) Alfred Abraham Boudreau of Port Felix, Fr Monbourquette was determined to prove that French-speakers from out-of-the-way parishes could "compete with the best material from more enlightened localities."[165] For this to occur, however, Acadians needed representation within the Maritime hierarchy. At the 1905 National Convention in Caraquet, New Brunswick, Senator Pascal Poirier, a scholar of Acadian history, appealed for "recognition of the importance of their ethnic group within the Catholic Church."[166]

Two years later, the apostolic delegate asked the Maritime bishops to comment on the feasibility of an Acadian diocese at Moncton (territory would be appropriated from the archdiocese of Halifax, and the dioceses of Saint John and Chatham). The reaction was not positive. Much like their counterparts in Ontario who advocated for Catholic integration into the larger English-speaking society, the bishops felt that French Canadian nationalism, whether in Quebec or among Acadians, was a threat to Catholic interests in North America.[167] Although the bishops accepted that French-speaking Catholics had legitimate grievances, they felt that Acadians had overall been treated justly.[168] "Their local centers have had resident priests to attend to their spiritual wants," they noted, and while the community had suffered for the faith in the past, the Irish and the Scots had also been "driven into exile."[169]

In downplaying the need for an Acadian diocese, the Maritime bishops had some pragmatic reasons (finances), and some poor justifications (a fear of liberal philosophies from Europe infecting their educational institutions). Yet behind closed doors, there was anger that the Société l'Assomption had been organized to unify and assist Acadians throughout the region without ecclesiastical approval. Rumours that Prime Minister Laurier had offered support for an Acadian diocese in exchange for votes in New Brunswick did not help. Ironically, however, given the dominance of the Irish and Scots within the regional church, their primary concern was that Acadian nationalism might erode the very critical Catholic unity.[170]

In 1909 another proposal came forward for an Acadian diocese – the Holy See sought to divide the diocese of Chatham, New Brunswick, and create a francophone diocese at Bathurst – but again, the Maritime prelates demurred.[171] At least they were consistent. The harmony among the twenty thousand Acadians within his diocese, Bishop Cameron pointed out, was proof that "racial bigotry [did] not prevail" in the Maritime provinces.[172] The Acadians would have to wait.

THE BOER WAR

One of the more feeble arguments against the establishment of an Acadian diocese was that it would embolden those Protestants who slandered Catholicism as a "foreign faith." In reality, however, the relationship between Christian denominations in eastern Nova Scotia had been for the most part amicable, and if respective newspapers became too antagonistic, the record was usually set straight. Rev. Albert Edward Andrew, for example, the Church of England pastor in Antigonish town (and future Military Cross recipient), once criticized *The Casket* for its inference that his flock countenanced such virulent anti-Catholic writers as the former priest Charles Chiniquy. "I have found that it is not any part of the philosophy of the C of E people," Andrew wrote, "to exalt themselves by damning all their neighbours."[173]

In other cases, Protestants railed against Halifax's *Presbyterian Witness* for its "persistent war on Catholics," and one Presbyterian clergyman wrote that *The Casket* was regularly read by many of his broad-minded parishioners.[174] After the plan to unify the Methodist, Presbyterian, and Congregational churches was proposed (it would not occur until 1925), *The Casket* editorials were impartial and considerate. When Fr John MacNeil in Thorburn suggested a proselytizing mission among local Presbyterians, colleagues suggested that Catholics would be better off focusing on their own problems. "Look at the low standards of morals of so many of our Catholics, especially in the larger towns of the diocese," Fr Ronald MacDonald exhorted. "I venture to say that we have more drunkards, more hooligans, more thieves, and we certainly have more rum sellers in our camp than Protestants have – in proportion to numbers."[175]

Unlike the situation in the northern counties of Ireland, where Catholics confronted physical threats and expulsion from industrial work sites, and even in Newfoundland, where institutionalized sectarianism was firmly entrenched, the good will between Protestants, especially non-ascending ones (i.e., Church of England), and Catholics in eastern Nova Scotia had been formed through a commonality of purpose in the early nineteenth century.[176] In fact, Protestants' perception that their Catholic neighbours were loyal citizens of the British Empire – as opposed to the "disloyal" Halifax Irish – was cemented during the Crimean War in the 1850s when Joseph Howe used ethnicity to drive a political wedge between Catholic voters.[177]

Yet the Boer War of 1899–1902, between the British Empire and the Transvaal Republic and Orange Free State in South Africa, tested this perception.[178] The Maritime region was abuzz with excitement as the second Canadian contingent sailed for the African continent in 1900 with twelve hundred men. Nova Scotians followed the conflict closely, attended public lectures, and devoured newspaper columns that described the fighting in far-off places like Paardeberg.

Colin Howell has noted that many Nova Scotians thought of the Boer War as a crusade to "ring the death knell of political inequality, of race or creed, or nationality."[179] For some Canadian Catholics, the conflict was also an opportunity to display their loyalty to the British Empire, and men throughout eastern Nova Scotia eagerly joined the second Canadian contingent. One young soldier, Charles MacGillivray of Arisaig, sent *The Casket* detailed accounts of the fighting, and after the battle of Leliefontein, a battle-hardened Baddeck native wrote that "bullets and shells were flying around [him] like hail."[180]

Perhaps the most famous Maritime participant in the Boer War was Margaret MacDonald of Bailey's Brook, Pictou County. A graduate of the New York City Hospital, she had previously nursed American soldiers aboard a military vessel during the Spanish-American conflict. One of a select group of Canadian nurses sent to South Africa – an enlistment that her biographer attributed to her father's political connections – she was known for her "old time Highland pluck," and by the time she was injured by shellfire in November 1900, she was well on her way to celebrity.[181]

Not all Maritime loyalties lay with the British, however. Margaret MacDonald may have been patriotic, but her sister Adele, Sister St Mary of Calvary, CND, held decidedly pro-Boer sympathies, which the nurse attributed to her "religious point of view."[182] The newspaperman Neil MacNeil recalled that his grandfather's sympathies "were all with the Boers," while Antigonish seminarians studying in Europe reported deep anti-British sentiments; "The Parisians," they said, were "delighted over the British reverses."[183]

In Toronto, the *Catholic Register* cautiously supported British policy and expressed praise for the heroism of Irish troops; but it was troubled by the war rhetoric. According to Mark McGowan, the cautiousness of the *Register*'s editorial position put the broadsheet at odds with many of Ontario's more patriotic priests.[184] Correspondingly, back in eastern Nova Scotia, *The Casket*'s "clear, vigorous and graceful" critique of the war angered many of its more pro-British readers.[185]

Fearing that Nova Scotian Catholics might appear disloyal, Fr Sandy MacDonald, fiercely attacked *The Casket*'s editor, Joseph Wall, under the pen name "Sacerdos."[186] After Wall wrote that Britain had "refused one reasonable offer after another" from the Boers, the former professor Fr Daniel MacGregor offered a pro-British lecture at St F.X.[187] One man went to the talk convinced that the pope was anti-English, but was quickly "straightened out."[188]

Facing intense pressure from such influential priests, Wall soon left the editor's chair.

The Boer War exposed the complexities of living as a Catholic within the British Empire. In May 1900 *The Casket* congratulated the formidable Queen Victoria on another birthday but made a point of adding that the Virgin Mother, the "crowned Queen of Heaven," was far "more benign and more powerful."[189] When King Edward VII succeeded his mother on the throne in 1901, Catholics again protested that the coronation oath opposed transubstantiation and denounced Catholicism. The Canadian Church sent a forceful complaint to the British Parliament, through Cardinal Herbert Vaughn, archbishop of Westminster, which branded the oath as a remnant of religious intolerance.[190] Anti-oath petitions were signed at bazaars and picnics throughout eastern Nova Scotia and then forwarded to Ottawa.[191] Soon, even New Glasgow's *Eastern Chronicle* editorialized against an oath from which "millions of [King Edward's] Protestant subjects, would, if offered to them, recoil with horror."[192] By 1910 the controversial oath had been amended so that the monarch would merely have to state that he or she was a "faithful Protestant."[193] It was a small change but demonstrated that Catholicity was slowly overcoming "the old-time bigotry."

CATHOLIC SOCIETIES

Notwithstanding the controversy surrounding the coronation oath, Catholic society meetings toasted the new monarch, and sang hearty renditions of "God Save the King." The Catholic Mutual Benefit Association and the League of the Cross, with its attached ladies' auxillaries (who, The Casket admitted, "shoulder[ed] most of the burden"), sponsored family excursions and scholarly lectures, and practised subsidiarity (the CMBA bought the uniforms for Holy Redeemer's Excelsior baseball team in Whitney Pier). Special trains regularly transported members to celebratory diocesan occasions like the commencement exercises at St F.X., and commemorative events were often planned along the route. Returning from a visit to the St F.X. campus in 1902, for instance, the Glace Bay CMBA stopped at Heatherton to lay a wreath on the grave of their former pastor, Fr Finlay Chisholm, who had died in 1898.[195]

In 1903, through the efforts of the women at Mount Saint Bernard College, the first branch of the Society of St Vincent de

Paul was organized in Antigonish town. Its objective was straightforward: to provide the poor with firewood, kerosene, codfish, butter, and clothes.[196] Two years later, Sydney Catholics organized a council of the Knights of Columbus (KOC).[197] An American fraternal association founded in Connecticut, its first Maritime council was established at Charlottetown in 1903 (Fr James Morrison, a future bishop of Antigonish, was a charter member) and it quickly gained popularity. Dedicated to charity, unity, fraternity, and patriotism, the KOC also had an excellent insurance program that was in good measure responsible for its robust membership.[198] A hierarchical organization – each new member was designated a First Degree and through acts of service could rise to a Fourth Degree – its rituals had masonic overtones that initially made some bishops uncomfortable. When several knights from the St Ninian's Council in Antigonish town received their First and Second Degrees from the state deputy in 1906, the philosopher Fr D.C. Gillis noted that the knights "secured for their members all the advantages that forbidden associations could offer while not only avoiding their evil tendencies but promoting the spiritual good of their members."[199]

THE BAILEY'S BROOK/LISMORE AFFAIR

While these Catholic societies encouraged the laity to become more active in their parishes, they remained firmly under clerical control. The rank and file were for the most part quite content to follow the direction of their priests and bishops but, like the farmers of Heatherton, when the authorities went too far, laypeople were ready to push back. An important example occurred in 1903, in Lismore, Pictou County, when the parishioners decided to replace the old St Mary's church. Built in 1834, the "masterpiece of pioneer architecture" designed in the New England Meeting House tradition was now in disrepair, its vestments tattered and the state of its chalice "almost a sacrilege."[200] Fearing a structural collapse, Fr Andrew MacGillivray had the heavy church bell removed from the tower in 1897 and displayed it outside on a timber stand. Assuming that the new church would be built next to the old structure, parishioners were surprised when a wealthy Catholic merchant offered property at Bailey's Brook some five kilometres away – and more astonished when Bishop Cameron agreed to build there.[201]

Bishop Cameron could not have guessed that his decision to build a church at Bailey's Brook would be the beginning of the end for his ultramontane program. On 13 June 1903, a gathering of the anxious "malcontents" – as the pro-Lismore group became known in period correspondence – with the support of their pastor, Fr Alexander Chisholm (who had been at the centre of the church relocation dispute at Brook Village in 1896), passed a resolution in favour of building a new church on the old site at Lismore.[202] Although reverential, they rejected Bishop Cameron's claims that Bailey's Brook was centrally located, and highlighted the disrespect involved in separating the church from the parish graveyard.[203]

When the bishop rejected this appeal, the Lismore malcontents decided to formally address the apostolic delegate. Expanding on the initial resolution, they carefully crafted a new petition that highlighted some sixteen "facts" and argued that the history of the parish "absolutely condemn[ed] the new site."[204] The original copy was dispatched to Ottawa and facsimiles were printed for local circulation.

In a region like eastern Nova Scotia, where many of the clergy shared kinship with their flock, it did not take long for the native-born priests of Lismore to become entangled in the dispute. The parish's first pastor, sixty-six-year-old Fr Daniel MacGregor, who had retired to his native Big Island in Merigomish, was drawn into the fray when asked to provide geographic and historical material for a parish survey. While the priest had promised his bishop that he would not "take much interest in it," he soon became a vocal opponent of the Bailey's Brook site.[205] Not only would his neighbours be inconvenienced but he was particularly concerned about the fate of the old graveyard where his parents and siblings were interred. The public support of Fr Chisholm and Fr MacGregor, both graduates of the Urban College, infuriated Cameron.

The Lismore petition to the new apostolic delegate, Msgr Donato Sbaretti, a former papal diplomat in Asia and the United States, raised detailed questions about customs, roads, and population density. Describing the proposed Bailey's Brook site as "bleak and exposed," the petition also raised the delicate fact that several of Bishop Cameron's "blood relations" resided in that community. Any hint of impropriety, the petitioners warned, would be passed down to generations yet unborn "with the tenacity of popular tradition which is characteristic of the Celtic race." Confident that the delegate would investigate, the Lismore Catholics promised to convey him from Antigonish town to Pictou County in a carriage hauled by "300 strong and willing Highland Scottish hands."[206]

In the autumn of 1903, as the malcontents anxiously awaited word from Ottawa, their sympathetic pastor, Fr Chisholm, was transferred to St F.X. He was replaced by Fr Dugald Cameron Gillis, a native of Lochaber parish and a recent graduate of the Urban College. Lismore was Gillis's first parish, and the future St F.X. philosophy professor and editor of *The Casket* was keen to impress.[207] Despite his authoritative demeanour and ambition, however, Gillis soon acknowledged the hopelessness of the situation. Even a thousand-dollar gift that had been bequeathed to the parish by the uncle of Fr John J. Chisholm for "a new Lismore church" could not be executed because the term "Lismore" was disputed. Did "Lismore" refer to the parish generally, or was "Lismore" a precise geographic position.[208] Frustrated by the uncertainty, Gillis counselled his ordinary to either yield and return to the old site or "strike a stunning blow at once" and build at Bailey's Brook.

The "Bailey's Brook affair," as the events were later labelled by diocesan historians, was ostensibly about the physical location of a new church. Yet along the shores of the Northumberland Strait, the growing influence of the laity within the old Catholic subculture was being tested. While pioneer churches had been run by a "small but rising Catholic bourgeoisie," ultramontanism had diminished their authority.[209] "The priest, whether a stranger to the parish given him or not," wrote one disaffected man in Richmond County, "appoints wardens to suit himself, builds and rebuilds, buys unnecessary ornaments and articles without the sanction of either the parishioners or the dupes he is pleased to call church wardens."[210]

Like the Heatherton and Mabou "stampedes," the dispute became a referendum on episcopal authority. Detecting a "very strong conspiracy," Bishop Cameron charged Lismore Catholics with disloyalty to the "sacred cause of truth," and was particularly harsh in his descriptions of Fathers Chisholm, MacGregor (*cha b'urrainn dha am botal fhagail* ["he couldn't leave the bottle"]), and John J. Chisholm, all of whom had stymied Cameron or counselled the malcontents to "stand by their colors."[211]

With letters from Lismore piling up on his Ottawa desk, the apostolic delegate began to gather facts. Having no knowledge of Pictou

County, he wrote to Bishop Cameron for a detailed account.[212] In the summer of 1904, he briefly visited the diocese but did not even stop over at Lismore, opting instead for a tour of the parishes of St Andrews and Lochaber. Evidently satisfied by Cameron's "conclusive" response to his query, in the autumn he approved construction at Bailey's Brook on the basis of three factors – taken almost verbatim from Cameron's pen – centrality, proximity to shops and post office, and finances.[213] The shocked malcontents protested that Msgr Sbaretti's justification was "rot."[214]

Stirred by the "spontaneous upheaval of the people," retired Fr MacGregor encouraged the faithful of Lismore to appeal to the Sacred Congregation for the Propagation of the Faith. The letter to Cardinal Rafael Merry Del Val, the papal secretary of state, was chiefly composed by MacGregor with the aid of the Antigonish barrister Christopher P. Chisholm and Fr Alexander Chisholm, who worked on the Latin translations.[215] Although the text mirrored the earlier petitions, it leaned heavily on the supreme authority of the pontiff. "We do no dishonor to the other apostles when we invoke St. Peter," they argued. "We are merely giving expression to our Catholic instincts when we protest against a procedure which we suspect to be uncanonical, and which we know to be injudicious."[216] It was as "'staunch Catholics' that [they were] trying to prevent an undesirable Episcopal decision, which enemies attribute to nepotism, from taking effect."[217]

The news of the appeal to Rome generated intense gossip. In response, Bishop Cameron charged Fr MacGregor with intemperance, vagrancy, and other acts of misconduct (a classic strategy for dealing with insubordinate clergy).[218] In the frigid weeks of January 1905, MacGregor replied with a flurry of letters that scoffed boldly at the delegate's verdict, which would have been "laughed out of [any] court."[219] He also warned that the malcontents would apply for a separate parish and then a mortuary chapel (privately supporting a resident priest). Should both be denied, the people were resolved to move to another parish.[220]

Although confident in their episcopal authority, as local support for a church at Lismore was strong, both Cameron and Sbaretti worried that Rome might "let them build it there."[221] In the spring of 1905, the bishop went to Italy and brought his case to Curia bureaucrats. Although many of his former colleagues and classmates were retired or deceased, Rome, as Cameron bragged, remained His country.[222] While there is no evidence that the Antigonish prelate influenced the Propaganda – although he did have an audience with the pope alongside the Irish political leader John Redmond – by October he sensed that a favourable judgment was imminent.[223] At the end of November, Cardinal Girolamo Maria Gotti, prefect of the Propaganda Fide, ruled that the authority to select the site for any new church rested solely in the hands of the diocesan ordinary. "Roma locuta est," the cardinal decreed; "causa finite est."

Vindicated, Bishop Cameron immediately ordered the construction of Mount St Mary's in Bailey's Brook. While his decision was unpopular with "a majority of [his] best friends," and certainly with the Lismore malcontents, it was his view that a bishop need not be popular. "I never was an admirer of Pontius Pilate," he retorted, "who, while declaring Christ to be innocent, condemned Him to the most ignominious of deaths, owing to the dictation of the *majority*."[224] In July 1907, the new church was blessed during a "well attended" ceremony.[225]

In the meantime, the bishop had some mopping up to do. Fr MacGregor, who refused to concede that he had "lost in Rome," was placed under suspension, and those who refused to attend Mass or offer financial support to Mount St Mary's were denied the sacraments. One of the most prominent malcontents, Hugh MacDonald, physically weak and nearing death, submitted to episcopal authority in front of the parish priest.[226] When his son, Fr Ronald MacDonald, pastor of Reserve Mines, learned of the incident he was outraged. With a shaking hand, he wrote that his father was "forced to bargain for the sacraments," and only agreed to submit "through fear which he would likely condemn in his heart."[227]

In this environment, the Mount St Mary's pastor, Fr James A.M. Gillis, who left Bailey's Brook in December 1907, confessed that his days as curate on the rugged and windswept western coast of Newfoundland (he had gone to work with Bishop McNeil), were a delight compared to his previous assignment at Bailey's Brook. "No one but the eternal judge knows what I suffered for the last two years," he wrote wearily. "Night after night I walked my room, sleep refusing to come to my eyes through the trouble of mind."[228] When the apostolic delegate ordered the discontented holdouts to support Mount St Mary's, Gillis prayed that the "final battle of the Great War [was] over."

Behind closed curtains, Fr Gillis placed the blame for the "eternal ruin" of his old Lismore flock on his brother priests.[229] "If it were left with me and my parishioners, there would never have been a schism," he grumbled, "but my work was undermined by the conduct of some priests [MacGregor, Chisholm, etc.] who must have forgotten their priestly vows of obedience." Sending a message to his clergy, Bishop Cameron composed a denunciation of the malcontents and sent Fr Gillis's replacement, Fr John Anthony Fraser, to get it signed by every clergyman who had connections with Lismore or whose names had been drawn into the dispute.

The archbishop of Halifax, Edward Joseph McCarthy, happily affixed his signature to the document, but Fr Fraser had mixed results elsewhere. When he tried to obtain the signature of Archbishop Ronald MacDonald, who had retired to Pictou in the spring of 1907, the prelate became annoyed and "positively refused to lend his signature." Fr Roderick MacDonald of Westville signed only after much hesitation, while Fr William B. MacDonald, pastor of Lourdes in Stellarton, and Fr John Duncan MacLeod, pastor of New Glasgow, signed without protest. In Sydney, Fr M.A. MacAdam and Fr John J. MacKinnon "cheerfully signed," but Fr Ronald MacDonald adamantly refused to "subscribe to any document to relieve Bishop Cameron."[230]

In February 1908, Hugh MacDonald, who had recovered long enough from his terminal illness to recant his submission to Bishop Cameron, finally passed away. When Cameron denied him a Christian burial, Fr Ronald demanded that the apostolic delegate intervene in his father's case.[231] When the priest threatened to appeal to the Holy See directly, Cameron begrudgingly consented to a private burial (but there was some question as to whether the plot was consecrated). In the following months, diocesan unity began to unravel. First, there were rumours that Archbishop MacDonald had counselled the late Hugh MacDonald's wife to "go to confession and never mind the order to the contrary."[232] Later, it was revealed that most of the malcontents had received the sacraments from Fr William B. MacDonald in Stellarton. "Fathers Ronald and William are working hard to cover their tracks in smuggling the sacraments to the rebels of Lismore," Fr Fraser wrote angrily, "and setting all ecclesiastical authority at defiance."[233]

Recriminations among the clergy were now rampant. Ecclesiastical investigations were launched and, to "repair the harm," Fr William MacDonald was ordered to sign a letter of apology – in the presence of witnesses – which was circulated throughout the diocese.[234] Yet by constantly attacking his own priests, Bishop Cameron ensured a steady flow of complaints and petitions from Antigonish to Rome.[235] The old Urban College graduate Fr MacGregor, for example, skillfully attacked the prelate on procedural grounds, arguing that he had every right to aid devout Catholics in an appeal to the Holy Father. It was not grounds for suspension, he declared: "the bishop has stabbed me in the back."[236]

The apostolic delegate never wavered on Cameron's authority to build at Bailey's Brook, but when Msgr Sbaretti reviewed Fr MacGregor's complaints, he realized that Cameron had not followed canon law regulations, and anxiously asked whether the suspended priest had first been given a "summary trial." Pope Pius X had begun to codify the unwieldy mass of past legislation in 1904, and Cameron confessed that in his nine and a half years as a student at the Propaganda College, "canon law was never taught."[237] A few years later, a high-ranking Antigonish priest admitted that no one "kn[ew] beans" about canon law.[238]

Recognizing Cameron's procedural blunders, Sbaretti revoked Fr MacGregor's suspension in the summer of 1908.[239] Hopeful that the priest would abandon his crusade, the apostolic delegate had Macgregor sign a letter acknowledging that Cameron had the right to build at Bailey's Brook and that the malcontents were duty-bound to support Mount St Mary's financially.[240] When news of the lifted suspension reached Lismore, a bonfire was lit and there was "great rejoicing."

By Christmas 1909, the malcontents had purchased the old Lismore property from a private owner and asked the delegate for permission to reopen the sanctuary while still voluntarily paying dues at Mount St Mary's. According to Sbaretti, this demonstrated "a very decided change in the[ir] dispositions" and he hoped that Cameron would accept the compromise.[241] Yet the recriminations were too great and the resentment too strong. The issue would not be resolved in Cameron's lifetime.

BISHOP CAMERON'S FINAL YEARS

Despite his authoritarianism, Bishop Cameron was quite progressive on issues such as education and healthcare, and encouraged his priests to plan for the future. In the summer of 1907, the diocese purchased 208 acres of land overlooking Antigonish Harbour as a retirement home for clerics. The spacious farmhouse overlooked orchards and fields that rolled down toward the stunning estuary. The combination of water, mountain, forest, and meadow made Mount Cameron Farm (named after the bishop) one of "the loveliest spots in the Maritime provinces."[242] Yet, while supervised by the Sisters of St Martha, Mount Cameron was always a better farm than a place of retirement. Visitors to the cancer-stricken Fr Angus Cameron, a one-time rector of St F.X. noted that the old man was well "but he [found] Mount Cameron too cold."[243]

Much like the elderly Fr Angus Cameron, by 1908 eighty-one-year-old Bishop Cameron was confronting the realities of old age. As he was by then too ill to participate in the 1908 Holy Week services, the sacred oils required for the celebrations of the sacraments had to be procured from Halifax.[244] As early as 1904, a group of priests, all Urban College graduates, wrote to Rome requesting a coadjutor bishop to ease his workload. At the time, their preferred candidate was Bishop Neil McNeil of St George's, Newfoundland. "Everyone here," confessed Fr John Fraser, "is praying for the return of Bishop McNeil."[245]

The reality was that the endless battles between the bishop and his flock had taken their toll on the diocese's reputation and clerical morale. "My heart bleeds for the sad condition to which we are reduced," a priest grumbled to the archbishop of Halifax in 1908; "the finger of scorn is pointed to us from every side."[246] In Ottawa, the apostolic delegate was cautious not to upset "the dean of the Canadian hierarchy," and the "oldest living Propagandist in the world," but he acknowledged that change was needed.[247]

Recognizing the inevitability of accepting a coadjutor, in October 1908 Cameron formally requested help.[248] Loyally supported by Archbishop Edward McCarthy of Halifax and by Fr Henry O'Leary (a future archbishop of Edmonton), his agent at the Vatican, in January 1909 the Curia consented to his request, with the hope of "lightening the heavy burden of [Cameron's] episcopate."[249] By the end of that month, Cardinal Merry del Val ordered the delegate to draw up the *terna* of names (typically three candidates) for submission to authorities.

One of the obvious candidates to replace Cameron was the intellectual and writer Fr Sandy MacDonald. A professor of Latin, English, and philosophy at St F.X. from 1894 to 1903, in 1900 he was made vicar-general, and from 1903 until 1908 he ministered

Figure 3.3 | Fr Alexander "Sandy" MacDonald, c. 1901

in the rural parish of St Andrews. First from his room at the college, and then from the St Andrews glebe house, a parish described as "the birthplace of priests and learned," he had gained a devoted readership in the pages of *The Casket*, the *Ecclesiastical Review*, and the *Homiletic Monthly*.[250]

A series of articles that Fr MacDonald wrote on the Apostles' Creed for the *Ecclesiastical Review* were so well received that he had them published as *The Symbol of the Apostles: A Vindication of the Apostolic Authorship of the Creed on the Lines of Catholic Tradition* (1903).[251] He followed this book with *The Symbol in*

Sermons: A Series of Twenty-five Short Sermons on the Articles of the Creed (1903), *The Mercies of the Sacred Heart: Twelve Sermons for the First Fridays* (1904), *Questions of the Day: Thoughts on the Biblical Question* (1905), and *The Sacraments: A Course of Seven Sermons* (1906).

Local Catholics were proud of these books and one correspondent to *The Casket* confessed in 1904 "to a feeling of delight and even pride in having amongst our native clergy a man who can produce such a book as *The Symbol*."[252] Surprisingly, however, as Rome began to search for Cameron's coadjutor, Fr MacDonald was consecrated for the Diocese of Victoria, British Columbia. He was despondent about the appointment and, as he boarded the train for the great journey west, had no inkling of the difficulties that would greet him in his new See. Years later, while reading in the St F.X. library, he wrote a few lines at the bottom of the page of *The Casket* that carried notice of his parting: "my funeral procession passed through the streets of Antigonish on the day of my departure, and woe was me that I lived to be part of it."[253]

With "Bishop Sandy" out of the running, on a bitterly cold February afternoon, a meeting was held at the archbishop's residence in Halifax to discuss the matter. With both Bishop Cameron and Fr Hugh MacPherson, the "Old Rector," in attendance, it was difficult for the prelates to speak openly. When Cameron learned that Bishop Neil McNeil was nominated as "*dignissimus*" (the leading candidate), he alleged a "deep laid conspiracy" to impose upon him a disobedient priest as his coadjutor.[254] In the face of this anger, the bishops replaced McNeil's name with that of the Old Rector, and also offered the names of Fr D.M. MacAdam of Sydney and Fr Donald Chisholm of Heatherton.[255] While all but one felt that Fr MacAdam was the best choice "all things considered," Cameron demanded that the Old Rector be the "dignissimus."

Like everything that Bishop Cameron touched in the final years of his episcopate, the search for his coadjutor was contentious. The Old Rector was clearly respected and colleagues joked that when he was appointed "*episcopus*" they would rush to the college for a blessing.[256] Yet he was also seen as "Cameron's man" and influential voices like Bishop Sandy argued that "the not so flourishing state of the diocese of Antigonish" required fresh leadership.[257] Despite his admiration for Bishop Cameron, the new Bishop of Victoria felt that MacPherson "[stood] for a continuation for the present order of things." Many of the clergy who had clashed with Cameron during the turbulent decade agreed, and there was soon a strong lobby against the Old Rector. The debate was so acrimonious that one priest wrote to the archbishop of Halifax malevolently hinting at a "taint of insanity" in the MacPherson family.[258]

As the long summer days gave way to the cool autumn evenings of 1909, there was no news from the Curia. No stranger to the intrigues of Rome, Bishop Cameron knew that something was amiss. The prelate's agent at the Vatican, Fr O'Leary, wrote that he had heard the name of MacPherson mentioned as a candidate but nothing else.[259] Concerned, Cameron hurriedly dispatched a letter to the Cardinal of the Propaganda in support of Fr MacPherson, but the prelate did not have the power of former days.[260] In December, an irritated Cameron scolded the apostolic delegate: "If I am not without a coadjutor, tis not my fault."[261]

In January 1910, Bishop Neil McNeil, ministering on the rocky windswept western coast of Newfoundland, joined Bishop Sandy in Western Canada as archbishop of Vancouver.[262] As telegrams of congratulation poured into eastern Nova Scotia, Bishop Cameron was confident that news of his coadjutor would soon follow.[263] "So we are losing Bp. McNeil!" mused Archbishop Michael Francis Howley from St. John's, "they are giving him like Bp. McDonald, a great bounce, three thousand miles ... they might almost as well have transferred him to Mars."[264] Although Cameron might have preferred the Mars option, British Columbia was far enough away to ensure that McNeil would not be appointed as his coadjutor.[265]

In the end, it would not matter. Having contracted pneumonia, which he assumed was a merely a bad cold, Cameron struggled to maintain his schedule throughout the spring of 1910. On 6 April, he survived a particularly hectic itinerary and retired to his bed earlier than usual. Checking in on him later that evening, his housekeeper, Mrs Mary Johnston, found the prelate near death. Alarmed, she hurried downstairs to notify Fr Michael MacAdam and Fr Michael Gillis, two young curates who were both reading in the parlour. The priests rushed up the stairs to administer the last rites, and shortly afterward, just before the doctor arrived, Cameron died.[266]

Bishop Cameron had charge of Antigonish for thirty-three years and his death was the end of a historic era. He was a commanding figure and many struggled to accept the reality that he was gone. "The news of Bishop Cameron's death was somewhat startling," wrote one priest studying in Germany. "I was under the impression that he was enjoying excellent health."[267] While he had also been a controversial figure, few did more to build up the Church in Canada. Newspapers like the *Halifax Herald* were right to editorialize that the country was "robbed of its ablest and most distinguished prelate," but it could not be disputed that the ultramontane Bishop Cameron had outlived his time.[268]

The funeral was held on 13 April at St Ninian's Cathedral in the presence of political dignitaries, Mi'kmaq leaders, and a considerable number of bishops. Many hundreds could not gain access to the sanctuary but, as "the day was beautifully clear," they remained outside in silent reverence.[269] Mother Ignatius, CSM, estimated that nearly five thousand people arrived in town to attend the ceremony, and the slushy grounds around the cathedral were packed with mourners.[270] Archbishop McCarthy of Halifax sang the pontifical High Mass, and Archbishop Paul Bruchési of Montreal spoke of Cameron's unyielding principles and his national stature. After the three-hour service, a photograph was taken as the horse-drawn funeral cortège left the cathedral for the cemetery. Unlike his predecessors, who were buried under the altar of St Ninian's Cathedral, Cameron was interred in the good earth. His monument was identical to that of Sir John Thompson in Halifax's Holy Cross Cemetery. The men who had done so much to establish the Catholic subculture were connected even in death.

4

Awakening and War
1910–1919

With Bishop Cameron buried in the damp spring ground, the archbishop of Halifax appointed the *dignissimus* of the *terna* for coadjutor, the Old Rector, as administrator of the Antigonish diocese.[1] Fr Hugh MacPherson's colleagues hoped he was not "killing [himself] with the duties and worries" of his new office and were hesitant to bother him unless absolutely necessary.[2] "As our professors in theology told us," Fr Maurice Tompkins wrote timidly from Guysborough, "in all difficulties to ease our conscience on the bishop's, and as you now stand in *loco episcopi*, I beg to submit the following case."[3]

Everyone assumed that the Old Rector would be Antigonish's next bishop. Writing from Newfoundland, the historian Fr P.W. Browne expressed certainty that the priest's newfound responsibilities would "culminate in further honours."[4] Yet the delay in the expected appointment was unsettling. In early May Fr Robert Fraser, the rector of the Scots College Rome, reported that he had little information. "I went to Cardinal [Gaetano] De Lai and to Mgr [Carlo] Perosi of the Consistorial several times: they listened sympathetically but there the matter ended."[5] Powerless, Fraser noted that had "Scotland and Nova Scotia still been under Propaganda [he] might have had some idea," however the consistorial [was] close to impenetrable."[6] As spring yielded to summer, it seemed that the Old Rector's elevation was no longer certain.

As time passed, there was a segment of clergy who suspected (and hoped) that the vicar-general, the former St F.X. rector and outspoken Glace Bay pastor Fr Alexander Thompson, would be named bishop. "I don't see how Rome can pass over either [the Old Rector] or Dr. Thompson," one Cape Breton clergyman opined. "Really I believe that either of [them] will be the new bishop."[7] By the autumn of 1910, however, letters from Rome suggested that the Curia was vetting other candidates. While making his *ad limina* visit to the Vatican, Archbishop Michael Howley of St John's learned that "the V.G [vicar-general] of another Diocese [was] to be named Bishop of Antigonish." The rector of the Scots College Rome could not recall the name of the diocese, but thought "his name began with an M. It was a Scotch name, but more lowland than Highland."[8]

In Sydney, Fr Donald MacAdam, with his own Roman contacts, was certain that the "M" was Fr James Morrison of Charlottetown. In correspondence with the archbishop of Halifax, he acknowledged that Morrison would be a suitable choice despite his feeble knowledge of Gaelic. Although his ignorance of the old language would trouble those "who look[ed] with disdain on a man of Highland Scotch descent who cannot speak Gaelic," he was confident that Morrison would be welcome.[9]

Although the parishes cried out for direction (Port Felix had been without a pastor for almost a year), the Old Rector, now realizing that he would not be bishop, was reluctant to make decisions. When a flurry of angry letters arrived from Glengarry, Cape Breton, demanding an investigation over a parish matter, MacPherson hesitated. "I wonder if there is any hope of our getting a bishop soon," the anxious administrator wrote to a Roman colleague, as the delay is "hurting the diocese."[10] Soon there was even talk that Rome was thinking of "dismembering" Antigonish and giving the mainland counties to Halifax.[11]

BISHOP JAMES MORRISON

The two-year delay in appointing a bishop for Antigonish was due to those seemingly endless controversies related to ethnicity within the Maritime Church. Since the 1908 rejection of an Acadian diocese, francophone Catholics had continued to pressure Rome for inclusion within the regional episcopacy, while the Irish in Prince Edward Island now demanded a Hibernian prelate in Charlottetown. In 1907 the Irish clergy, led by Fr Thomas Curran, the rector of St Dunstan's College, complained to the archbishop of Halifax that the Scots on the island dominated the seminaries, the parishes, and the hierarchy.[12] Making matters worse, the bishop of Charlottetown was bedridden and there was concerned that he would be soon succeeded by Fr Morrison. The Irish pre-emptively refused to accept this appointment.[13]

The preoccupation of the Holy See in this period, as a leading Canadian prelate understood it, was "to prevent divisions in the Church along the lines of national or racial cleavage."[14] In the spring and summer of 1912, Rome made its moves: Morrison was sent to Antigonish; Bishop Neil McNeil, in Vancouver for only fifteen months, was appointed to the vacant archdiocese of Toronto (the most important English-speaking post); Bishop Timothy Casey of Saint John, New Brunswick, was sent to Vancouver; and the Acadian Fr Edouard-Alfred LeBlanc of Weymouth, Nova Scotia, was made the bishop of Saint John.[15] "I am pleased you have a bishop at last," wrote one Scottish priest to the Old Rector. "I am only sorry that Bishop Cameron's choice was not that of the Holy See."[16]

The news of Morrison's appointment as the fourth bishop of Antigonish quickly filtered throughout eastern Nova Scotia. When asked, MacPherson declared that the new man would "fill the bill admirably."[17] In charge of the consecration ceremony, the Old Rector faced a logistical nightmare and there were even brief rumours of a double consecration with Fr Leblanc.[18] Determined to hold the ceremony before the students returned to St F.X. for the fall semester (otherwise there would be no space for the dignitaries), he managed to get consistorial permission to dispense with the papal bulls and expedite the process.[19]

On 4 September 1912, Morrison processed through the large wooden doors of the stone *Tigh Dhe* to begin his consecration ceremony. The church was brightly decorated in the papal colours, and a large contingent of regional media looked on as Archbishop Edward McCarthy of Halifax, the senior assistant bishop, asked the consecrator, Apostolic Delegate Pellegrino Stagni, to promote Fr Morrison "to the burden of the episcopate." When the ceremony ended, the new prelate prostrated himself and the "Litany of Saints" was sung by the choir. Presented with the staff of pastoral office, and having his episcopal ring blessed, the new bishop was mandated to "receive the gospel and go preach to the people."[20]

Bishop Morrison did not remain in Antigonish for long as he was under strict instructions to remain as administrator of Charlottetown until a successor was appointed there.[21] In late September, he returned briefly to officiate at the funeral of Archbishop Ronald MacDonald,

Figure 4.1 | Bishop James Morrison

who had died in Montreal. Rather overweight, MacDonald had been seriously ill for several weeks and had entered the infirmary of the Grey Nuns. A group of local priests (which included the archbishop's brother, Fr Roderick MacDonald) travelled to Montreal and accompanied the body back east for burial in the "cozy little cemetery" at Maryvale.[22]

By mid-October, administration of Charlottetown was placed in the capable hands of Fr James Phelan (Henry J. O'Leary, Bishop Cameron's agent in Rome, would ultimately be appointed bishop of Charlottetown), and Morrison moved permanently to Antigonish town. In time, he selected Fr Daniel Joseph MacIntosh, pastor at Baddeck, as his vicar-general – the office was not intended to be "a very burdensome one" – and appointed six diocesan consultors to assist with parish boundaries and local disputes.[23]

Although some historians have focused on Bishop Morrison's conservativism (he certainly had authoritarian tendencies), he was a much different administrator than Cameron. Whereas Cameron had studied in Rome under Pope Pius IX during a period of tense anti-papal sentiment, Morrison sat in the Propaganda benches in the papacy of the reformer Leo XII, who encouraged understanding between the Church and the modern world. Aware of the acrimony created by his predecessor, Morrison asked the diocesan press to ease the rhetoric on Catholic schools in Ontario and demanded that the clergy avoid public scandal; all communication was to be done in person or by post and never by public telegraph dispatches. Furthermore, while free to hold their own political opinions, priests were not to employ the pulpit to further partisan agendas.[24] "If ever the time comes when the welfare of our religion is at stake and has to be decided at the polls," he wrote to a priest engaging in partisanship, "we clergymen will have far more influence in directing our people than we could hope to have if the people suspected us of being merely partizans."[25]

To celebrate Bishop Cameron's legacy and cultivate diocesan unity, in February 1916 a statue to the late bishop – with a beretta to cover his baldness – was erected in front of Xavier Hall on the St F.X. campus.[26] While pleased with the likeness of Cameron (the inscription was composed by Fr Alexander Thompson), some found the head leaned much too far forward giving the dead prelate a stooped appearance. "The late Bishop Cameron always stood up straight and in the most erect fashion," Morrison complained, but acknowledged that this detail would soon be forgotten. In private, he also hoped that the ill feelings created in the final years of Cameron's episcopate would also fade from memory.

RESOLVING THE LISMORE/BAILEY'S BROOK AFFAIR

Another issue that needed Bishop Morrison's immediate attention was the situation at Lismore/Bailey's Brook. Although a compromise had seemed possible in 1909, Bishop Cameron had not acted, and thirty families in Lismore remained "practically cut off from the Church." As administrator, MacPherson, the Old Rector, had followed Cameron's hard-line policy and forbidden a monthly Mass at Lismore despite attempts by senior priests like Fr Donald MacAdam to broker a settlement.[27] "If the rebels of Lismore win out," MacPherson threatened at the time, "ecclesiastical authority in this diocese will have received a blow from which it will not recover."[28]

As a leading candidate to replace Bishop Cameron, the Old Rector's chances had likely been jeopardized in Rome by his hardline approach to the Lismore malcontents.[29] With Cameron gone, most of the clergy connected with the community had already given the holdouts both communion and confession – Fr Ronald had secured a Christian burial for his father – and a settlement should have been brokered.[30] "Whilst firmness and authority may conquer in the end," the apostolic delegate chastised the Old Rector, "the Church is a good mother who not only welcomes the returning prodigal but goes forth to meet him on the way."[31]

By 1911 the conciliatory efforts of Arisaig's Fr Donald L. MacDonald and Fr MacKinnon at Bailey's Brook were having their effect. One dying man submitted to the diocese in the presence of Fr MacKinnon and was readmitted to the sacraments. Within a year, the "prospects were brightening" and the MacDonald, MacGillivray, and MacKinnon families of Lismore gradually began to support Mount St Mary's.[32] On 7 January 1913, Bishop Morrison called a meeting at Lismore and announced that the old church would reopen for Divine Worship as a mission of Bailey's Brook. Pacified, the holdouts agreed to surrender the deed to the church property in exchange for the use of the sanctuary as a "mortuary chapel" (regular Mass would be said every third Sunday).[33] To seal the deal, all parish internments would be in the old Lismore cemetery.[34] Within weeks, parish picnics were held on the old Lismore property, and by 1915 *The Casket* referred to the parish as "Bailey's Brook and Lismore."[35]

Notwithstanding all this reconciliation, the "Bailey's Brook affair" was permanently settled only in August 1917, when Mount St Mary's was destroyed by fire. The blaze broke out in the glebe and, with the August heat and gusty winds, soon spread to the church and the adjoining schoolhouse. Most of the artwork and vestments were saved from the sanctuary, although a few parishioners had to be restrained from trying to save more items due to the intense heat.[36] Within days, the old Lismore church was once again in regular use.

FR JAMES J. TOMPKINS AND ST FRANCIS XAVIER

One priest who had managed to stay out of the Bailey's Brook affair was St F.X.'s vice-rector, Fr James J. Tompkins. Absorbed completely with the diocesan college, his focus was directed solely toward Catholic education. While one alumnus recalled that Tompkins could be "quite severe," the priest's correspondence suggests that he was admired by the student body.[37] Like a doting parent, he loaned graduates money and reminisced about their days in his corner-room office on the second floor of Xavier Hall. "Father you are simply a wonder," wrote one alumnus, "and although you are very small in stature you are awfully mighty."[38] His correspondence also reveals a man with a robust sense of humour, once joking about all those younger men who had been made bishops. "Do you know I am beginning to get jealous," he playfully wrote to a friend in Florida. "At my first Mass, my assistant was Dr. Henry O'Leary, and one of the servers, Michael Power. Last summer I travelled on the train with the Rt. Rev. Michael Power, to be present at the consecration of the Rt. Rev. Henry O'Leary."[39]

In the summer of 1912, Fr Tompkins represented St F.X. at the Congress of the Universities of the Empire, which was held at the University of London. In the company of two former St F.X. students, the priest "[did] Oxford up and down" and met with some of the world's most respected educators. During one memorable session, John A.R. Marriott of Worcester College, Oxford, told the assembled that "universities need to train and to influence not the tens of thousands who even now become their matriculated students, but the millions who can never secure that privilege."[40] This rhetoric had a profound effect on Tompkins, who returned to Canada with thoughts of reform.

Most Catholics recognized that St F.X. was central to the well-being of the regional Church.[41] "It seems to me that the most important office in our diocese – more important than that of bishop – is that of Rector of St. F.X.," wrote one alumnus; "the good effects are more far reaching."[42] On Bishop Morrison's first formal visit to the college, Tompkins read an address of welcome and greeted the new chancellor as a "friend, counsellor, and guide." In response, Morrison flattered the staff by acknowledging the great achievements of the small institution and promised to regard the college as the "apple of [his] eye."[43]

Since the early 1900s, the St F.X. faculty had been vocal about the lack of modern laboratory equipment and those alumni sent by the new administration to study in European institutions recognized how pitiful their scientific preparation was. "It is a lamentable fact," Fr James Boyle wrote from Belgium, that the North American Catholic students were "terribly backwards in science."[44] So when the university decided to build a new science hall "quite up to date in every particular," optimism abounded.[45] "I have had a gang of fellows digging, cutting, piping," Tompkins comically wrote to a friend in 1912, "and incidentally swearing, for the past few days."[46]

The campus construction also excited the alumni. I believe there are great days to come for St F.X.," mused Fr C.J. Connolly, while studying for a doctorate in Munich. "It means a struggle but vastly greater fruits."[47] Besides Fr Connolly and Fr Boyle, St F.X. had priest-graduates at Johns Hopkins University and the Catholic University of America. These young men represented a new generation of scholars and there was great camaraderie among them. When the Old Rector sent Fr Connolly a money order to support his final semester in Munich, the young priest, who had sufficient funds, quickly returned it. The cash, he noted, could be put to better use in someone else's pocket.[48]

Exposed to some of the world's finest academic facilities, the clerical post-graduates pushed the St F.X. administration onward. "If our own men only had the opportunities of the good libraries, which are afforded here, they would shine," wrote one priest from Washington: "Fr Tompkins would get fat if he had the congressional library near him."[49] With funding secured for new scientific and recreational facilities, and with clerical graduate students soon ready to bring their academic training back to the Antigonish campus, the foundation of a great institution had been laid.[50]

While Fr Tompkins could be harsh toward "pinheaded fellows" who stood in his way, he enjoyed efficient episcopal support.[51] When the French professor Fr Arsene Cormier mocked the yearning for graduate studies as a "pretentious farce," he soon found himself ministering in rural Larry's River.[52] Fr Tompkins and Bishop Morrison were not close friends but Tompkins was happy to have "a very sensible, considerate man at the head of affairs."[53] Morrison recognized the value of Tompkins's building projects and efforts at modernization, at the same time expressing the hope that St F.X. would produce graduates that "never [grew] tired in proclaiming their faith."[54]

THE ANTIGONISH FORWARD MOVEMENT

Like all skilled college administrators, Fr James Tompkins and the Old Rector recognized that the prosperity of any institution was tied to the economic fortunes of the geographic region it served, and they worried about the ongoing deterioration of the Maritime provinces. The population decline resulting from generational outmigration from Nova Scotia had led to a reduction of seats in the federal parliament in 1892 and 1905, and further losses were expected in 1914. Disheartened, many believed that "more than a pound of flesh [was] being extracted" from the region.[55] Merchants and politicians publicly appealed to Ottawa to uphold the "spirit of the constitution" but were rebuffed.[56]

In a raging sea of angry merchants, farmers, and lawyers bemoaning the status of Nova Scotia within Confederation and blaming Ottawa for the economic woes of the Maritimes, Tompkins rowed an optimistic oar. The subsidy inequality and the disproportionate geographic expansion of other Canadian provinces placed the Maritime region in a weak position, but the priest felt that the local people were ultimately responsible for their plight. While mending the relationship with Ottawa was important, Maritimers, he said, had "to get the western spirit" and fix their own economic problems.

Acting on a progressive impulse, Tompkins helped organize the "Antigonish Forward Movement." With its objective of boosting civic action, encouraging public dialogue, and revitalizing local business in Antigonish town, it was, argues Dan MacInnes, "the first testing ground for the public socio-economic theorizing of the intellectuals gathered at the college."[57] Sensing that regional economic stagnation was rooted in "commercial pessimism," the Forward Movement hoped to rekindle energy in the rural area through new partnerships and technologies.[58]

In early November 1913, the movement began its work. Representatives sent letters to regional businessmen seeking opinions on how Antigonish County might grapple with its economic problems. The response was extremely positive. "One big broad man can make a town wake up," noted one former native; "two or three can make men hear her 'hum.'"[59] The prevailing opinion was that local leadership had to be upfront about what a Forward Movement could realistically achieve. It was pointless to advocate for a "made in Antigonish" solution if the people continued to send their money to Toronto department stores. Public engagement and the distribution of literature were also essential.

In December *The Casket* reported that the frigid air in Antigonish was "charged with optimism." At the first formal meeting of the Antigonish Board of Trade, local businessmen such as Alexander S. MacMillan (a future premier of Nova Scotia) told St F.X.'s Fr Tompkins that the economy was crippled by poor business practices and a leadership deficiency. Members talked about improving the Antigonish harbour, paving Main Street, and countering the "aggressive" young town of New Glasgow. With ideas of a "market day," and cold-storage facilities to unite the town and county, people were challenged to "fill up the vacant farms."[60]

Fr James Tompkins was the spiritual leader, but the public face of the Forward Movement was the Havre Boucher native Peter J. "P.J." Webb. One of the acute real estate men in British Columbia, he had often noted that "the brains of the West were Nova Scotia's." Financially secure and excited by the challenge of revitalizing his native community, Webb opened a real estate office and immigration bureau in Antigonish town to fill vacant farms with former residents and support immigration from the British Isles and Western Europe.[61]

Although one priest described Webb as an "offhand fellow," he was a magnetic and charismatic orator.[62] Speaking at Havre Boucher in February 1914, he told the crowd that the parish's fertile soil and proximity to the railway presented a terrific opportunity for intensive farming. Taking his "audience by surprise," he argued that if a western Canadian community had the resources of Havre Boucher, they would "have the railway running through it in twelve months."[63] At St Andrews, listeners displayed great enthusiasm and frequently applauded the speaker. At Georgeville the discussion focused on the steamers that had once called at Arisaig, Malignant Cove, Livingston Cove, and Ballantyne's Cove but were no longer operational due to the lack of trade and the "dilapidated condition of the wharves."[64]

In parish after parish, Webb supplied eager audiences with stimulating fodder for dinner-table discussion. Speaking of the "enlightened" economy of Denmark, he questioned how the Danes, with similar demographics and geography, managed to export large quantities of agricultural products? Surely Nova Scotians had "as much brains" as people in northern Europe.[65] At St Joseph's, two hundred people attended Webb's meeting and collected the addresses of parishioners living abroad so that the federal immigration office could entice them to return home.[66] "How is Webb?" the young Fr Moses Michael Coady asked Fr Tompkins from the Catholic University of America. "Are you going to get any more people in Nova Scotia? That is what we want."[67]

Crucial to the momentum of the Forward Movement was the appointment of a provincial agricultural representative for eastern Nova Scotia. In the autumn of 1914, a new agriculture building was opened in Antigonish town and forty-two-year-old Fr "Little Doc" Hugh MacPherson, on the St F.X staff since 1900, was appointed district representative. The priest was passionate about agriculture and not afraid of getting dirty. One young bureaucrat recalled travelling the dusty road to South River, Antigonish County, where he found Fr MacPherson "deep into the county's first silo." Making the priest a fieldworker "ought to be a great encouragement to our young men abroad to return to us," editorialized *The Casket*. "If in the past they were handicapped for the lack of scientific knowledge of farming, they will now find it brought to their doors."[68]

One early achievement of this agricultural activity was the expansion of local creameries. Dairy production had been active on Antigonish County farms for generations but, by the time of the Great War, creameries in rural communities like South River were starting to sell their goods to the miners of Cape Breton (the butter was a favourite of Fr Kiely in North Sydney).[69] Before long, farmers along the Gulf Shore organized the Milburn Cooperative Creamery Company, while those from Antigonish town and Havre Boucher banded together to start the Antigonish Dairy Company.[70]

Fr "Little Doc" MacPherson participated in all this activity with satisfaction. He attended the annual autumn agricultural exhibition in Antigonish town and encouraged farmers to exhibit their foodstuffs and "promote the best interests and the good name of his County."[71] He directed short courses, organized seed fairs and, during "Old Home Week" at Grand Mira, lectured on the preparation of soil for potatoes.[72] In the spring of 1915, he and Fr Miles Tompkins, a diocesan agricultural expert, spoke at Grand Narrows on scientific farming, while Webb lectured on the principles of the Forward Movement.[73] "The bunch went down to the Grand Narrows on Monday, and from what I can learn they raised one h--- of a noise," Fr James Tompkins wrote to a friend. "I believe at Christmas Island there were over two hundred men at the various meetings. The Iona meetings were not so large, but they were well patronized."[74]

One reason for the success of the Forward Movement was that it focused on intergenerational unity. Although some of the older folk might have yearned for the "olden days of 'wooden ships,'" they were praised for embracing a progressive impulse. There was, as Webb exclaimed, work for young and old.[75] Activities were covered by regional journals and newspapers, including the *Maple Leaf*, and the *Maritime Merchant and Commercial Review* of Halifax, which editorialized that the program would lead to excellent results.[76] Fr Tompkins at St F.X. was thrilled. "What do you think of the Forward Movement?" he wrote to a colleague. "Isn't it – well – ripping?"[77]

While James Tompkins had praise for Webb and "Little Doc" MacPherson, he knew their success was propelled by strategic and punchy columns in *The Casket*. He understood the power of the media and was a regular contributor to the paper. In fact, *The Casket's* publisher, Michael Donovan, who once described by Bishop Cameron as "a young gentleman of fine judgement," had relied heavily on the vice-rector to turn out articles.[78] Tompkins took propaganda seriously and demanded that Forward Movement columns be composed by competent pens. He had his vast collection of friends watch the newspaper "to see the capers that phlegmatic Scotchmen with all their wisdom [could] cut."[79]

Tompkins had grandiose plans for the Forward Movement, for his college – there was also a St F.X. Forward Movement – and for the diocese. He believed that beautification of the little college town and new construction on the St F.X. campus would awaken Catholics in other communities as well. In November 1914, Hector F. MacDougall, the former MP for Cape Breton, sought a federal salary for Webb. "There must be a lot of energy and hard work," he explained, "and nothing can be done without it."[80] By the winter, people began to respond. Merchants in Sydney, for example, observed that Ottawa was subsidizing mail steamers to carry immigrants up the St Lawrence River on a route that ran parallel with the Sydney-Montreal railway. Why not divert a small portion of that ocean travel to Sydney and give some of the newcomers the option to settle in Cape Breton?

Unfortunately for the supporters of the Forward Movement, however, the outbreak of the Great War soon curtailed their activities. After the devastating carnage at the first battle of the Somme in July 1916, the people of the region settled in for a long and expensive war. As recruiters and fundraisers demanded men and money, the community's attention shifted away from marketing and cold storage to recruitment and victory bonds. When Webb tried to organize a meeting at Sydney in 1916, the board of trade "voted the matter down for the present."[81] At St F.X., Fr Tompkins was not dismayed. The movement had been a success, the new library was almost complete, a new gymnasium was planned, and a new dormitory, skating rink, and administration building were in the works. "Things are howling and booming around here," he noted happily.[82]

HENRY SOMERVILLE AND "FOR THE PEOPLE"

Although the Forward Movement was decelerated by the Great War, the region's progressive impulses were not dampened. "Everything is bubbling and boiling around this country and I should not be surprised if when the war is over there should come a great transformation in these Maritime Provinces," Fr Tompkins enthused in the spring of 1917. "The slow old ways are gradually getting licked out of the people." Noting that the spirit was manifest at St F.X. "more than anywhere else," by Christmas he had plans for a full-page column in *The Casket* to engage directly with social, economic, and educational issues.[83] It was time for the Catholic substate to work for its people.

While Tompkins relied heavily on *The Casket* to propagate his message, his relationship with the paper's editor, Robert Phalen (not to be confused with his brother Fr David V. Phalen, who had been the editor from 1900 to 1909), had deteriorated.[84] In 1915 Phalen had rejected several of Tompkins's articles only to be forced into printing them by Bishop Morrison, who considered the compositions "well worth publishing."[85] Soon, Phalen was under tremendous pressure to print pieces by "other contributing writers." Not only would the inclusion of intellectuals like Tompkins give the paper "more diversity," Morrison noted, but it would also give others the opportunity to train for newspaper work.[86]

In 1918 Fr Tompkins launched into a new column with characteristic energy. Initially he considered calling it "Progress and the People," but settled on "For the People." The plan was to have St F.X. intellectuals and prominent laymen contribute scholarly pieces on history, economics, and sociology. Writing to P.W. Thibeau, a native of River Bourgeois studying education at the Catholic University of America, he explained his desire to train educated Catholics to "bring their leadership before the people."[87] As he wrote to the archbishop of Toronto, "Father John R. [MacDonald] will do his best, Father Dan J. [MacDonald] wants to take a hand in, and Dr Nicholson, tho' working very hard, will probably render us some assistance."[88] The priest also asked Archbishop McNeil for permission to syndicate articles by Henry Somerville, his new expert on the Catholic social teaching, at the *Catholic Register* (for which he paid the English academic $100 out of pocket).[89]

Described by the editor of the *Catholic Register* as "quite remarkable for a young ex-factory hand," the twenty-eight-year-old Somerville was a fascinating figure.[90] Although not physically impressive, he was blessed with "a fine mind and a priestly soul."[91] Born in Leeds, England, in 1890, he left school at the age of thirteen and went to work in a factory. For eight years he saved and "read almost every Catholic book or pamphlet dealing with social questions that [he] could get [his] hands on." After long days at the workshop, he would stop and debate the street corner socialists, anarchists, and atheists, and by the age of twenty-one was writing for a Catholic newspaper and sub-editing the liberal *Manchester Guardian*. Popular within Catholic circles, he was soon awarded a scholarship to Ruskin College, Oxford. In 1915 Archbishop McNeil convinced him to move to Toronto to edit the *Catholic Register*.[92] Fr Tompkins greatly admired Somerville and considered him the "most keenly alive mind" in the Canadian Church; he was particularly attracted to the academic's views on education and the media. Publishing Somerville's thoughts in local papers, he reckoned, might even convince the owners and directors of *The Casket* to "get busy." The question was, would it wake anybody up?[93]

By early January, Fr Tompkins's editorial pen was hard at work. "We are making our bow on the 24th," he wrote to the Halifax barrister John Walker, adding proudly that Somerville would be with them.[94] Soon afterward, the priest went back to the lawyer for an article of his own. "You are in for it now," he wrote playfully, "so that you will only have to set your teeth and face the music."[95] While he eagerly awaited an article from Somerville, he recruited a piece on historiography from the Cambridge-educated W.H. Bucknell, and also a commentary on American bishop Thomas Shahan's recent sermon on education (which he printed for local distribution). Tompkins was a tenacious editor and refused to serve his audience weak material. "If you will permit me to give you a few pointers," he wrote to a young contributor, "your style needs to be clipped down a bit ... Your sentences are too long, and the style sometimes has the fashion of Macaulay – a very difficult style in the hands of anybody but Macaulay." Any idea a man had clear in his mind, he noted, "ought to be able to put clearly before his readers."[96]

The first column of "For the People" was published in *The Casket* on 24 January 1918. A long editorial from Fr Tompkins urged Nova Scotia Catholics to occupy their rightful place within public affairs "to which [their] numbers, [their] principles, and [their] patriotism undoubtedly entitle [them]." He also encouraged readers to organize social study clubs, strengthen civil society, and focus on health and education.[97] Fittingly, Henry Somerville's long-awaited article dealt with Catholic efficiency and the need for an effective Catholic press. Protestants were not "opponents to be beaten" but "neighbours to be loved ... friends to be helped ... souls to be won."[98]

Throughout 1918 the "Second Page" was widely consumed and Fr Tompkins was "discovering talent at every turn."[99] Somerville, who contributed articles under the heading "Life and Labour," was impressed by the quality of the content and purchased a subscription to *The Casket* so that he could dissect it at his leisure.[100] Other contributors to the columns included A.B. MacDonald (agriculture), Patrick M. Dewan (a future minister of agriculture in Ontario), Donald F. MacDonald (Pictou County geologist), Fr Daniel J. MacDonald (economics), and Fr Leo J. Keats, just to name a few.

Despite the general popularity of the page, there were occasional criticisms. At St Agnes in New Waterford, the thirty-seven-year-old

Fr John Hugh MacDonald, a former vice-rector of St F.X., took exception to Somerville's characterization of Catholics as apathetic. While some of the faithful were indeed indifferent to education, the lack of modern schools did not mean that they opposed progress. In MacDonald's opinion, the state of Catholic education could be blamed on Nova Scotia's history of Protestant oppression and its lack of legislative power. "Our people have been asleep so long, or rather, crushed so long beneath the heavy load of persecution," he argued, "that we cannot expect to awaken them all at once."[101]

Fr Tompkins considered this defence of the status quo to be "dangerous" and wanted Fr MacDonald handled "judiciously, firmly and fully." The former vice-rector of St F.X., he urged, ought to be leading "instead of sitting in blissful apathy."[102] Yet, while pressing the New Waterford pastor to reconsider his comments, Tompkins found that they had a common cause. In March 1918, Fr MacDonald's contribution to "For the People" suggested that the region had too many Catholic colleges. In his mind, a single Catholic college for the Maritimes would represent a "magnificent field for co-operation."[103]

It was at this moment that Fr Tompkins's ideas on educational reform began to coalesce around the restructuring of post-secondary education in Nova Scotia. How could he possibly transform St F.X. into a modern institution, he wondered, with brother priests who lacked the "faintest conception" of graduate research and thought of the college only as an incubator of young men for the seminary?[104] If clever boys in less fortunate circumstances wanted to climb, "well and good," he protested to a friend, "and the Catholic body is willing to help them, <u>provided of course</u> they study for the Church; but that the Catholic body should make sacrifices to educate young men for other walks of life – well the idea!"[105]

In the spring of 1918, Fr Tompkins began asking dangerous questions. St F.X. was a central diocesan institution, but what were these Catholic colleges accomplishing? In a stirring letter to a colleague, he argued that many of the older clergy still believed that men such as Fr Daniel MacGregor and Fr Alexander Chisholm (both had taught at St F.X. in the previous century and were closely involved in the Bailey's Brook affair), who had "an indifferent high school education and a half-baked theological training," were better professors in their fields than men who had "devoted three or four years to post-graduate work."[106]

In early April, with Somerville's help, Fr Tompkins began his assault on the status quo. The "Second Page" contrasted St F.X.'s rather shaky finances with the large endowments that had recently been gifted to McGill and Dalhousie. There were also "lessons from Louvain," which demonstrated the importance of that well-endowed university for the progress of the Church in Belgium. If Catholics were to gain their place in the public life of Canada, wrote Somerville, "they must, like the Catholics of Belgium, avail themselves of higher education to train the men fitted to lead and to rule."[107]

In July Fr Tompkins organized a diocesan educational conference at the college (a second one would be held in 1919 and a third in 1920). *The Casket* gave it extensive coverage and characterized the priest as a "human dynamo." At the opening of the forum, Bishop Morrison spoke of the value of the dialogue and the necessity of supporting new ideas. The prelate also gave a paper, which was characteristically practical, and lectured on the necessity of rural education and adequate teachers' salaries.[108] Yet, while talks devoted to "commercial arithmetic" were important, it was Tompkins's ideas on post-secondary training that dominated the agenda. The thirty-one-year-old physics professor Fr P.J. Nicholson, a graduate of Johns Hopkins University in Baltimore (with a degree he earned before entering the seminary), reiterated the call for better research and graduate studies.[109] Moving forward, St F.X. had to "re-seed the ground" from which it had regularly reaped its crops.[110]

By the autumn term, to the excitement of many, Somerville had formally joined the St F.X. faculty to lecture on topics ranging from "social agencies" to the "problems of crime and delinquency."[111] While he was the school's academic superstar, however, his opinions were not universally approved. When he publicly took issue with some of *The Casket's* editorials, editor Phalen retorted that he had been working as a newspaperman long before Somerville "had attained the dignity of wearing long pants." Somerville might have an Oxford diploma, Phalen argued sarcastically, while he had merely "walked out of [his] old school house one fine fall afternoon and never looked back" (he did have a law degree from Dalhousie), but the Englishman's attacks added little to the prestige of that venerable institution.[112]

For generations, historians have been so absorbed by Fr Tompkins's later quarrel with Bishop Morrison over St F.X.'s future that they have overlooked the events surrounding the loss of Henry Somerville. Tompkins was humiliated by the treatment of the Englishman and could not understand why his colleagues did not appreciate Somerville's brilliance. In December he told the editor of the *New Freeman* in Saint John, New Brunswick, that the diocese was "absolutely dead and good for nothing." Phalen even stated in print that Somerville wrote for the *Montreal Star*, when in fact it was the *Toronto Star*. A minor detail perhaps, but it indicated how little the paper knew or cared about its leading columnist.[113] Adding to the insult, Somerville was barely earning a living through his pen. Every article that *The Casket* published was underwritten by Tompkins, and he could not understand why other newspapers were not doing likewise. "God knows it is time for some of our Catholic people to wake up," he exclaimed.

By that November, divisions over Catholic post-secondary education were incubating. While Bishop Morrison had supported the Antigonish Forward movement and Tompkins's newspaper column, he did not share the priest's critical attitude to Catholic higher education. While Tompkins championed the work of public institutions like the University of Wisconsin at Madison, whose administrators held that the boundaries of the university should be the boundaries of the state, Morrison was primarily concerned with organizing practical religious education in his parishes. While Tompkins warned that most of the priest-professors at St F.X. would not "be able to get a job in a modern university," Morrison sought to ensure that the professors at the college were spreading sound doctrine.[114] These were immutable positions.

Walking the forested grounds of his seminary on the outskirts of Toronto in early January 1919, Archbishop Neil McNeil pondered the educational dispute brewing in his native diocese. A few weeks earlier, Fr Tompkins had asked about pressuring Rome to sponsor a commission on the future of Catholic education in Canada.[115] In a fascinating letter, McNeil cautioned the priest that public discussions on Catholic educational leadership would be unproductive, as the Church was often "a composite product of several minds." The lack of liberal education was due more to defective organization than to defective leadership.[116] There would not be national movement. Tompkins would move things along locally.

THE CASKET TAKEOVER

While Fr Tompkins had his column, the harsh treatment of Henry Somerville had exposed *The Casket*'s deficiencies. Tired of editor Phalen, Tompkins spoke forcefully at the annual shareholders' meeting in February 1919 about the need for clerical control of the broadsheet. "I am glad to know that you are thinking of re-organizing *The Casket*," noted a friend, adding that it "was difficult to see how it [could] again attain to the position of authority ... after the Somerville castigation."[117] What's more, he knew that many of his colleagues, especially the Scottish priests of Cape Breton, were unhappy with the paper's direction.

The publisher and proprietor of *The Casket*, Michael Donovan, had faced various complaints in the course of his career (there had been rumours of a takeover bid as early as 1915).[118] One criticism that stuck, however, was the habitual coverage of the events of Ireland.[119] The fifty-seven-year-old Donovan was born in the Irish community of Saint John, and he naturally paid attention to the domestic events of his ancestral homeland. The paper had held mildly anti-British sentiments during the Boer War, and Scottish clergy regularly complained that *The Casket* published too many articles on the "the history of hatred and Orangeism," which threatened the amicable relations between local Catholics and their Protestant neighbours.[120]

After the "terrible beauty" of the failed 1916 Easter rebellion in Ireland, *The Casket* sympathetically suggested that *Sinn Fein* nationalists merely wanted to further a cause of self-help not unlike any "Nova Scotia first" movement.[121] "Before we throw too many stones at German enslavement of the mind," lectured *The Casket* in the midst of the Great War, "let us look and see how much such enslavement there is in our own imperial house."[122] In March 1917 the paper again editorialized that Ireland was still waiting for "the measure of simple justice" that the people of Nova Scotia had enjoyed for years.[123]

The sympathetic coverage of Ireland annoyed those Scots who felt the paper was not fulfilling its cultural and religious mission. *The Casket*, while "Scottish Catholic," grumbled one reader, was spending too much of its space defending the "cause of Irish Nationalism" and editorializing about Home Rule. As one subscriber wrote, "Scotch men from Cape Breton and Eastern Nova Scotia, whom I meet abroad, appear to look upon *The Casket* as their bible ... I am sorry that *The Casket* is so pro-Irish."[124]

In the summer of 1917, there were calls for a Scottish Catholic paper in Cape Breton. Not only were Scottish Catholics "practically helpless" to defend themselves, supporters noted, but *The Casket* had little influence with Protestant elites in Sydney. If a Catholic paper were published in the colliery towns, they claimed, most Protestants in Glace Bay and New Waterford would likely give it a browse. A Scottish paper could also stem the decline of the old language and attract Presbyterian readers by introducing a Gaelic column.[125] The Scots' "well-earned reputation for loyalty," noted Fr MacAdam, would give the paper "more influence than either an Irish or French paper."[126]

As the debate raged on the future of *The Casket*, Donovan found himself in a perilous situation. He accepted some criticism, but he was a businessman, had a young family, and needed to earn a living (one of his older daughters, Alice, would later join the Congregation of Notre Dame as Sister St Ursuline). *The Casket* might have had a specific cultural mission in the eyes of a few Scottish priests, but he had enough trouble getting people to buy his product at the best of times. "The attitude of Catholics in general towards the Catholic paper, is not easy to understand," his editor noted in 1910. "There is a very pronounced tendency among them to belittle the Catholic paper."[127] While eager to provide space for religious tracts, language pieces, and local obituaries, Donovan had to print material that sold papers. Moreover, how could any serious journalist ignore the news coming out of Ireland? Surely a rebellion in the Catholic corner of the British Empire was worthy of ink?

The Casket administration categorically blamed Fr Tompkins for their troubles and suspected that he was leading the attack. As early as 1915, Donovan had refused to hire a typesetter who was recommended by the vice-rector. For "obvious reasons," Donovan confessed, he did not "want anyone whose ear Fr Tompkins has."[128] Phalen, who loathed Tompkins, was angry that the priest had not offered any candid suggestions for reforming the paper under its current ownership. In February 1919, he asked Tompkins for a "frank open and full statement as to what fault is found with [him]."[129] Phalen supported a reform of the paper (under the current leadership) but he wanted Tompkins to face him like a man. "After years of sharp criticism, strong, sweeping and comprehensive," he wrote, "the time has come surely, to say before my face some of the things you have said forcibly behind my back."[130]

In his biography of Fr Tompkins, George Boyle told the story of what happened next. One evening, while dining at the university, Tompkins learned that Michael Donovan had decided to retire. Twenty years later, the priest recalled, "I excused myself. I put on my hat, and I walked straight to the man [Morrison] in charge."[131] This did not tell the whole story. It is true, as Laurence Shook noted, that the priest "encouraged Bishop Morrison" to buy out the controlling shares, but Donovan did not want to retire.[132] In fact, at the shareholders' meeting in early 1919, Donovan faced a hostile takeover, and the attacks on his business acumen and editorial content stunned the newspaperman. "I am your friend, Mr. Donovan," one conciliatory priest wrote to him a few days later, "but Fr Tompkins says that you will not allow a line about the college in *The Casket*."[133]

The diocese offered a speechless Donovan $18,000 for the entire company (stocks and assets) but he was "not at all anxious to sell at the figure."[134] In early March of that year, Fr Tompkins threatened to start a rival paper and put *The Casket* completely out of business. If Donovan did not accept Morrison's offer, Tompkins warned, he "would lose all and go crazy in the end."[135] Faced with this overpowering harassment, the publisher reluctantly accepted the contract. Later, Bishop Morrison falsely contended that "the late manager left on his own initiative."[136] The diocese set the price of the stock and Donovan was barred from starting a rival paper in the area for fifteen years.

The hostile takeover of *The Casket* demonstrated the mounting importance of the Catholic press. Bishop Morrison wanted the paper to speak for his office, Fr MacAdam to promote Scottish culture, and Fr Tompkins to advance his progressive agenda. While the story indicates a close rapport between the bishop and the vice-rector, it also demonstrates that Fr Tompkins could be as aggressive "as the brigands of Mexico" when he wanted something.[137] Although often portrayed as a victim, Tompkins had real clout, and as a friend of Donovan warned, "he had the power to destroy [him]."[138] *The Casket* provided "the pulpit from which the social doctrine of Father Tompkins and Msgr Coady might find expression," as one historian noted, but Donovan's family never got over his treatment.[139] Many years later, the former publisher still wondered if it was right for "Fr Tompkins to threaten [him], to break promises to [him].[140]

In July 1919 the broadsheet formally announced Donovan's retirement and offered him its "sincere thanks," which surely must have stung in the Donovan household.[141] The shares of *The Casket* were dispersed among the Antigonish clergy, and priests constituted fourteen of the twenty directors. All editorial decisions remained at the discretion of the manager but were subject to the approval of the bishop.[142] Yet, while columns were now more focused on diocesan issues, and there was an effort to grow the local audience, especially in Scottish Cape Breton, Dan MacInnes has demonstrated that the new editorials reflected a "liberal ascendency." Fr Tompkins's column "For the People," for example, was changed to "For Social Betterment" and divided into two sections, agriculture and education.[143]

In the meantime, Somerville decided to return to England.[144] While Tompkins now had free rein within the pages of *The Casket*, Somerville warned him that running a newspaper was not an easy business. He thought Tompkins should control the editorship with a firm hand and advised him to broaden his interests. "I think you overdo the cry about education," he counselled. "I know you will not mind my speaking with frankness."[145] It was not the last time that Tompkins would face such criticism.

THE CARNEGIE CORPORATION AND FRENCH CHAIR

In August 1919 Halifax's Dalhousie University, celebrating its centenary, notified Fr Tompkins that they were awarding him an honorary Doctor of Laws.[146] The priest was humbled and elated to be acknowledged by a Protestant institution. Not only did it show that "times [were] changing, and the old-time narrowness [was] surely passing away," but the number of congratulatory letters from Protestant educators, including Rev. A.D. Morton, a noted Methodist who expressed his amazement that Tompkins had accomplished so much from the seclusion of a country town, bore witness to a newfound spirit of collaboration among Christian denominations.

Within his own church, however, there were still many divisions based mostly on ethnicity. Although Acadian Catholics comprised a quarter of the diocesan population, for example, they made up only 6 per cent of the St F.X. enrolment.[147] In fact, most francophone students opted for post-secondary training in colleges in

New Brunswick and Quebec. Having taught school at Cheticamp before entering the seminary, Tompkins understood the challenges that Acadian students faced. So, when Fr Arsene Cormier, pastor at Margaree, his old challenger on the question of post-graduate education, suggested an endowed academic chair in French, the vice-rector made it an administrative priority.[148]

While there was already some financial muscle behind the proposal – a Halifax businessman had offered funding – Tompkins and Cormier hoped that the Carnegie Corporation, the latest of several philanthropic trusts established by the industrialist Andrew Carnegie, would provide the bulk of the financing. They knew that the corporation had been generous to other Maritime colleges through its "British Dominions and Colonies Fund." In November 1919, Tompkins left for New York with his hat in hand.[149] Already a veteran negotiator, the priest swiftly attained a $50,000 grant, with the proviso that St F.X. match the contribution.

While the news of the grant for a French language chair was met with excitement – Bishop Morrison was elated – there were some financial hurdles to overcome.[150] Although Tompkins hoped that "good sense and a little vision" would help Acadians raise the $50,000 match, opinions among the clergy were mixed.[151] "In all sincerity, I can say that the Acadian people [are] too poor to raise that sum of money," the Quebec-born Fr Joseph d'Auteuil fretted, "and Acadian priests are equally poor."[152] The college was advised to seek out wealthy patrons in the United States as "the voice of Evangeline [was] very attractive in New York." But d'Auteuil had misjudged the resolve of local Acadians.[153] Fundraising committees in parishes like Cheticamp and Friar's Head worked enthusiastically to raise the monies, and eventually Professor René Gautheron, a graduate of the University of Paris, was hired in the chair.

Even with the chair, however, some Acadian pastors still refused to send local scholars to St F.X. The opening of the Collège Sainte-Anne at Church Point, Digby County, in 1891 had been hard won, and priests like Fr Monbourquette did not want "to see ... Acadian students quit [the] French colleges and flock to St. F.X."[154] The youth were better off totally immersed in the French language, he contended, "which in several ways helps to preserve their Catholic faith."[155] While Fr Alfred Boudreau felt that the new chair would "lead to closer sympathies and better understanding" among local Catholics, he insisted that Acadian graduates of St F.X. must return to the community and not merely become assets for anglophone society. "We find little pride in a Frenchman who is not able to speak or write his own language," he noted, "who knows not his literature, his history, who takes no interest in the past and present struggles for existence."[156]

ETHNIC PARISHES IN CAPE BRETON

As it was among Acadians in Cheticamp or Isle Madame, newcomers into Cape Breton colliery towns were keen to maintain their own languages and cultures. Still smarting from the strike of 1909 that pitted supporters of the old Provincial Workmen's Association (PWA) against those of the United Mine Workers of America (UMW), the financial and spiritual wounds among these folks were raw. Parishes that had been at the centre of the strike – the multi-ethnic St John the Baptist in New Aberdeen for one – were facing financial ruin. The situation in that parish was so precarious that Fr John Fraser was obliged to call in several personal loans. "I am really sorry to bother you but I cannot help it," he wrote to one debtor. "During the strike practically nothing could be collected."[157]

As people poured into the colliery towns, several new mines (Nos. 12, 14, 15, and 16) had been opened in the area of New Waterford and work camps were at capacity. To minister to these colliers, church halls were built at No. 12 and No 14 under the supervision of the overworked pastor of Victoria Mines, the fifty-seven-year-old Fr George McAuley. Travelling four and a half miles between masses, "the Sundays alone [were] killing [him]."[158] By October 1912, with the population around the No. 14 mine set to double, Fr J.H. Nicholson took charge of the new Mount Carmel Parish and its attached Congregation of Notre Dame convent school.[159]

In the meantime, Fr McAuley continued to serve the Catholics who worked at Nos. 12 and 16 mines (mostly migrants from Inverness County) while advocating for a second parish in New Waterford. The Sydney Mines native even rented a small miner's cottage at No. 12, so that the men could see their priest living "just as they live."[160] As the "the women of the mines" wanted a convent school "oh so bad," the priest obtained permission to build using monies from the check-off. Although Fr McAuley was relieved when a new parish was designated for No. 12, the construction of St Agnes Church kept him "awake at nights" and "turn[ed] the days into agony."[161]

Creating two new parishes in New Waterford among miners mostly of Nova Scotia extraction was one thing, but the desire among immigrant populations for "ethnic parishes" was something quite different. By 1910 pockets of ethnically diverse Catholic populations were worshipping throughout the colliery towns. In Sydney, in addition to the "well instructed" Syrians of the Maronite rite worshipping in the old St Patrick's Church under Fr Louis Soaib, a member of the Missionary Fathers of Craim (pronounced "crime"), there were also 150 "nominal Catholics" from the French-speaking island of Saint Pierre who had abandoned an unproductive fishery for work in the collieries.[162] At Sydney Mines, Fr Colin F. MacKinnon helped a small group of Lithuanians who attended his Mass to organize a benefit society. He was also aware of a community of Austrians, but, as they were of the Greek rite, they attended Mass infrequently.[163]

In 1911 Fr Domenico Viola, ministering to the six hundred Italians who were scattered throughout the mining districts, organized an Italian parish in Whitney Pier (the church was built mostly by men on their "off-shifts" and opened on Christmas day).[164] Construction began while Antigonish was without a bishop and there was some grumbling that the property site had not been approved by the administrator. Two years later, Bishop Morrison and five former students of the Propaganda College, all Italian speakers, were present for the blessing of St Nicholas Church (named for the Basilica di San Nicola in Fr Viola's hometown of Bari).

While pleased for his Italian friends, Fr Alexander Thompson warned from Glace Bay of the hazards of opening an ethnic parish (St Nicholas) within the geographic confines of another parish (Holy Redeemer).[165] In fact, the pastor of Holy Redeemer, Fr Rory MacInnis, who held "held strong opinions on public matters," had already expressed concern that Fr Viola had recruited some of his Polish parishioners with promises "to teach them in their own language." Two priests could not claim jurisdiction over the same flock.[166]

Although the ultramontane Church had been "held firmly together by the bond of faith," ethnic parishes like St Nicholas challenged this uniformity and set a problematic precedent.[167] While Bishop Morrison supported St Nicholas and periodically helped with confessions, priests in New Waterford were annoyed that Italians living within their parish boundaries were obliged to attend Mass at

Whitney Pier. Moreover, during confirmation tours there was often confusion about whether the Italian children were to be "confirmed in the parishes in which they lived or all in one place."[168]

The other problem with creating an ethnic parish for the Italians was that other immigrant populations soon wanted parishes of their own. "There is also a movement afoot by the Poles," Fr MacInnis warned the Old Rector from Whitney Pier, "to follow the example of the Italians."[169] In December 1912 Fr Antoni Plucinski, the curate at Holy Redeemer, got the Polish people "excited about having a parish of their own." Despite his objections, since the "numerically smaller" Italians had been given a parish, Fr MacInnis felt that it was unfair to deny four hundred Polish Catholics the same opportunity. "Seeing the many privileges enjoyed by the Italians," he noted, the Poles "naturally expect similar treatment."[170]

While separating the Polish flock from Holy Redeemer would have its consequences, denying the request for a Polish church could have serious repercussions. Would the community continue to support Holy Redeemer? Might they form their own independent church? "From what I know of these people, the end of this agitation will be that they will open their own church, if not in the regular way, then in some schismatical manner," Bishop Morrison warned, "and I may add that some expressions in their letter scarcely conceal such a possibility."[171]

In mid-January 1913, a respected merchant, S.R. Gwozd, a native of Galicia (Austrian Empire) and a representative of the Poles in Whitney Pier, assured Bishop Morrison that the community had bought "nearly everything that [a] priest require[ed]" for a parish.[172] They had also raised monies to establish the St Michael's Society and erect a first-class hall.[173] This level of community organization impressed diocesan officials, and by the end of 1913 the construction of the Church of the Nativity of the Blessed Virgin Mary, which would be known as St Mary's Polish Church, went ahead.

Like any fledgling parish, St Mary's faced the usual problems with construction and finances. More particular, however, were the squabbling and old world animosities that threatened parish unity and eventually claimed both Fr Plucinski and his successor, Fr Marianus Godlewski, who returned to Massachusetts in 1916 on account of a lack of resources and "national differences."[174] Fortunately, the diocese was able to recruit Fr Camillus Grzybala, who had experience ministering among Polish and Ukrainian newcomers in western Canada, to come to Whitney Pier and restore peace.

Despite the relative success of the ethnic parishes in Whitney Pier, many questions remained. First, how did someone qualify to belong to an ethnic parish? Second, was it reasonable to force a Polish miner working in Glace Bay, for example, to support the church in Whitney Pier? Third, how could any ethnic parish grow in population without sustained immigration from the old country?[175]

Seventeen kilometres away in New Waterford, Fr John Hugh MacDonald reported that most Italians at St Agnes simply could not make the trek to Whitney Pier on Sundays.[176] As an experiment, those Italians (130 souls) were permitted to worship at St Agnes as a special body but not as regular parishioners. When in 1916, an Italian labourer, quarrelling with Fr Viola, wanted his infant baptised at Holy Redeemer, Fr MacInnis was ordered to perform the sacrament, as it would not do "to let the child's soul be lost through any else's fault."[177] Things came to a head in 1918, when Fr MacInnis threatened to resign over the issue. As Bishop Morrison quipped, "one cannot carry his home town around the world with him."[178]

AMALGAMATED MINE WORKERS

The question of ethnic parishes demonstrated the uniqueness of ministering in the colliery towns. Fr Ronald MacDougall, who would later pass away while visiting miners on Bell Island, Newfoundland, felt that he had done his best work among the families of St Anthony's in Glace Bay. If "there should be any opening among the Cape Breton miners," he wrote to his superior from his Christmas Island parish in 1911, "I should dearly love to go back and work among them."[179] But working with miners had its social and political challenges.

In the summer of 1913, James Hare, a thirty-two-year-old Newfoundlander employed at the Sydney steel mill, walked into the Roman Catholic Cathedral at Harbour Grace, Newfoundland, and fired shots at Bishop John March, who was in the midst of celebrating Mass. While March escaped injury, such a violent attack in a Christian sanctuary was unprecedented, even in Newfoundland's sporadic sectarian atmosphere. Although Hare was found insane, "there [was] wide belief" that he had recently "become inoculated with the poison of anarchy and socialism through his time spent amongst the miners of Cape Breton."[180]

Reports of left-wing militancy among Catholic miners embarrassed pastors in Glace Bay and Sydney, who mostly blamed newcomers from eastern Europe. "The Socialists are doing their best to make the people join their ranks," one visiting Polish priest wrote from Whitney Pier, while complaining that DOMCO was unknowingly "employing socialistic interpreters."[181] Relaying this warning to the company, Bishop Morrison recommended that DOMCO hire interpreters that held "safe and sane" ideas.[182] In the meantime, the deed to St Mary's was placed safely in the hands of the episcopal corporation lest some "socialist or other trouble-making gang" take control of the property.[183]

Although DOMCO was confident that its interpreters were trustworthy – most of the men had been loyal during the strike of 1909 – all new hires were now carefully vetted.[184] Over the next few years, the coal company saw threats everywhere and, according to David Frank, security forces watched the collieries "day and night."[185] Clerical reports noted "that business [was] not satisfactory in the steel works" but there were few solutions.[186] Demonstrating some naïveté, Bishop Morrison suggested that the growing radicalism among Catholics was due to a laxity in Mass attendance and poor catechism.[187] His inability to read the men was a recipe for a disaster, which was only averted by the Great War, when "larger prospective markets" were opened up for Cape Breton coal.[188]

From 1914 to 1916, as miners lined up at recruiting depots for service in France, there was little labour unrest. But in 1917 supporters of the UMW once again took aim at the increasingly feeble PWA. In January 1917, the fledgling United Mine Workers of Nova Scotia surfaced at the coal face, and by the spring negotiations were underway with the PWA to dissolve both unions in favour of the Amalgamated Mine Workers of Nova Scotia (AMW). By September, the AMW was negotiating for the men. According to labour historian Ian McKay, for the militant miners who had advocated for the UMW in 1909, it was a "wonderful reversal of fortunes."[189] Radicals, like the Scottish immigrant James B. McLachlan, who was voted secretary of the new union, could scarcely believe that the old PWA had crumbled without a single day on the picket line.

One of the priorities of the new AMW was workplace safety. In March 1917 folks were reeling from the news that a thirteen-year-old lad had both legs severed when he slipped from the workman's train on his way home from a shift in Sydney Mines.[190] Months

Figure 4.2 | Fr John Hugh MacDonald

later, on 25 July 1917, an early morning blast at the No. 12 colliery in New Waterford took the lives of sixty-five miners.[191] Fr John Hugh MacDonald was saying Mass at St Agnes when he was hurriedly called to provide last rites to the dying. Alongside his frantic parishioners who rushed to the pithead for news, MacDonald entered the mine "where men had died and where death still lurked." Accompanied by a group of miners acting as guides, the priest went about "confessing, anointing, consoling" and was twice rendered unconscious by gas.[192] He demonstrated, noted his colleagues, "what the Catholic priest [was] prepared to do in the hour of trial."[193]

The dead miners of New Waterford were housed in a temporary morgue and everywhere "white-faced and weeping women huddled in forlorn groups."[194] At St Alphonse's Church in Victoria Mines, Fr McAuley buried seven men who had recently arrived from Europe. The sight of a mass grave of miners, killed so far from home, was long imprinted in the minds of onlookers.[195] Within days, the AMW demanded the dismissal of three mining officials (they alleged that gas was allowed to accumulate in the mine) and threatened strategic work stoppages.

The AMW agitation for workplace safety happened to coincide with the violent October Bolshevik coup in Russia.[196] Over the following months, news of Russian revolutionaries and European communism were mixed with reports of AMW demands. In this environment, some Catholic miners were keen to tone down the rhetoric of the new union. When AMW leadership adopted a resolution that the superintendent and mine manager of No. 12 colliery be dismissed for not having prevented the New Waterford explosion, the local chapter of the Ancient Order of Hibernians (AOH) condemned the resolution and argued that it had been forced through "against the wishes of men."[197]

Interestingly, the AMW had a good share of supporters within the diocese. Young priests like Fr Daniel J. MacDonald, the Glassburn native who held a PhD from the Catholic University of America (he took some of the earliest courses in sociology), rejected the notion that the Church was anti-labour and criticized priests in Europe for occasionally marching with the "classes rather than the masses."[198] In the pages of *The Casket*, columnists wrote about preserving the miners for the Church and the Church for the miners by supporting collective bargaining and strike action.[199] Frustratingly for Catholic intellectuals, typical miners knew nothing of "the influence of the church" in improving economic and social conditions. They were ignorant of the work of such high-profile social reformers as Bishop Wilhelm Ketteler of Germany, while filled with false doctrines by those who considered religion an enemy of the people.[200] The only way forward was for educated Catholics to fight "every socialist propagandist."[201]

LIFE IN THE PARISHES

The coalfields of Cape Breton were but one destination for Europeans immigrating to Canada. As the Canadian Church expanded westward – by 1914 some three million newcomers had arrived in the western provinces – the Catholic Church Extension Society (CCES) provided spiritual and material support. Seeking "Catholic solidarity from east to west," the CCES (organized in 1908) purchased Toronto's *Catholic Register* and rebranded it as the *Catholic Register and Canadian Extension*.[202] The society circulated literature, built a missionary college, and funded schools and convents. The young Fr Duncan Joseph ("D.J.") Rankin, an aspiring writer ministering in Grand Mira, often contributed articles to the *Register* on Church history that reached a national audience. Although the CCES initially struggled to meet expectations, it was rescued after Neil McNeil, "succeeding with those things to which he sets his hand," was appointed Archbishop of Toronto in 1912.[203]

McNeil, the former editor of *The Casket*, looked east and in July 1915 recruited another former *Casket* editor, Joseph Wall, to take control of the *Catholic Register*.[204] Although the Antigonish diocese could "hardly afford to lose him," the region had bade "goodbye to a great many men" who were called to serve the Church elsewhere.[205] Not only did Wall quickly transform the *Register* into a respected source of Catholic news but he demonstrated the respect that the rest of the country had for *The Casket*.[206] Wall was doing splendid work, Fr Tompkins bragged, "leavening the whole country" and waking up the people.[207]

Other prominent locals who were serving the Church in other parts of Canada in this pre–First World War decade included the Broad Cove native Fr Ronald Beaton in Calgary and Fr Ronald Rankin, the younger brother of the aforementioned Fr "D.J.," who was ministering to Gaelic-speaking Scots in Saskatchewan.[208] The rank and file were proud of these contributions and, when Bishop Sandy MacDonald of Victoria visited St Andrews, his former parish, in 1910, the farmers declared a holiday.[209] Far off in British Columbia, Bishop Sandy was haunted by the literature and landscape of the Maritimes.[210] At Christmas 1909, lonely and homesick, he walked the shore in Victoria's Beacon Hill Park.[211] The sound of the waves breaking on the rocks, "stirred into recollection the sound of another sea, beyond the great mountains and the plains and the lakes, four thousand miles away."[212]

The Victoria prelate soon had other reasons to yearn for home. In 1912 he purchased an expensive piece of land on which to build a new cathedral in Victoria. The old building was in a prime downtown location and was heavily taxed by the city. "Instead of paying

[God] His dues," he groaned in the *Victoria Times*, "the city levies a tax on him."[213] The declining value of MacDonald's property investments, coupled with the high rates of taxation on his churches (and a small decline in the Catholic population), crippled the diocese's finances. He was angry and outspoken, attacking the "single tax" theories of popular philosophers like Henry George, while demonstrating that property owners sacrificed more than those with monies in the bank.[214]

Back east, anxious Catholics began sending money to Victoria to help the beloved MacDonald manage the mounting debt.[215] When the prelate returned during the long summer months, he gave lectures and passed the hat around for donations (his 1918 talk at St Andrews, "Reminiscences of My Boyhood," was later turned into a small autobiographical publication).[216] He even accepted a short-term teaching position in the State of Washington to raise extra monies, compelling the Antigonish clergy to formally organize a subscription.[217] Although happy to contribute, many were embarrassed for the "begging bishop" and could not understand why the CCES had not done more to help.[218]

Privately, Bishop Morrison was concerned that the simultaneous collection of monies for Victoria and the CCES, which was supposed to be aiding the western dioceses, would damage the society's reputation and "... seriously injure future collections." It would be a wise policy, he noted, for the CCES to give a generous donation to Victoria (even if they had to borrow the money) and have Bishop MacDonald's acknowledgment printed in the *Catholic Register*.[219]

Although British Columbia was a long way away, for the cash-strapped Catholics of eastern Nova Scotia the financial problems of Victoria felt very close to home. Keeping churches in good repair stretched resources and, while insurance covered the loss of buildings to fire, rebuilding was a long and difficult process. In the summer of 1913, the church, convent school, and glebe of Holy Redeemer burned to the ground, shocking the Catholics of Whitney Pier.[220] In February 1916, the fifty-five-year-old St Paul's Church at Havre Boucher was also destroyed. Frantically, the curate managed to remove the Blessed Sacrament but, as there was no local fire service, the people could only "stand and witness the destruction."[221] Similarly, when the church at Victoria Mines burned, the crowd watched the inferno with "keenest regret and helplessness."[222] When St Anne's Church (and adjoining glebe and convent) in Glace Bay burned in December 1917, the fire brigade was present, but as the sanctuary was situated in an elevated part of the town there was not enough water pressure in the hoses to put out the flames.[223] In January 1919 the three-storey St John's Church in New Aberdeen burned, and then the church at Judique in August 1919, which was hit by lightning. Every precaution was taken to guard against fire, but it seemed impossible to avoid the flames.[224]

All reconstruction plans were carefully scrutinized. When sketches of a new church at Westville were complete, some worried that they looked "awfully protestant" and might be taken for "an Anglican church of the better class" (Catholic interpretation of Gothic architecture was averse to having the tower and spire at the end opposite the main entrance).[225] Artwork was also carefully vetted, and popular artists such as Charles MacKenzie of Lyons Brook, Pictou County, worked closely with clergy to decorate the sanctuary walls. After honing his trade in the United States, the sixty-three-year-old MacKenzie had by 1910 returned to decorate the Shrine of Our Lady of Lourdes with exquisite reproductions of Heinrich Hofmann's celebrated painting "Christ and the Doctors," Martin Feuerstein's "Nativity," and Liber's "St. Bernard."[226] One could linger over his paintings, noted the *Pictou Advocate*, "and return ... again and again, seeing something new and inspiring at each visit."[227]

Besides the beautiful decorations, the rich liturgy of the Church was on frequent display. One of the most solemn events was the Forty-Hour Devotions, a heartfelt devotional exercise that included the singing of *Pange Lingua*. In August 1916 eight priests presided over the two-day affair at Judique, while at Port Hood some two thousand attended Holy Communion during three days of ceremonies.[228] In 1910 Rome had declared that children as young as seven could receive Holy Communion provided they understood the difference between common bread and Eucharistic bread.[229] Priests, parents, and school teachers instructed the children on the "mysteries of faith necessary for the means of salvation," and First Communion became a memorable day on the church calendar.[230] In 1911, 114 children, most "barely six years of age," approached the Holy Table at Stella Maris in Inverness for the first time.[231]

Clerical scrutiny of everyday life continued to extend well into the private realm. Permission was needed to operate a business on a Holy Day, and Fr William Kiely at North Sydney had to obtain a dispensation so that his flock could be served coffee and cake during

Figure 4.3 | Mount Saint Bernard College

their St Patrick's Day celebrations. "I am inclined to indulge the Irish a little on St. Patrick's Day," he mused, "which always comes on lent."[232] The new cinematic trend of "moving pictures" was disparaged as morally problematic, and when some of the senior girls at Mount Saint Bernard asked to attend an off-campus dance in 1915, Bishop Morrison worried that they might jeopardize the reputation of convent schools across the diocese. Confident in the girls' good senses, he pronounced, he felt that they would "see the propriety of not attending."[233]

The perception of piety in eastern Nova Scotia was often reinforced by the national and international press, as one story illustrates. In 1910 sixteen-year-old Hattie LeBlanc of West Arichat was employed as a domestic servant for a wealthy family in Waltham, Massachusetts. Clarence Glover and his wife, Lillian (also a native

of Cape Breton), often quarrelled, and one morning Clarence was mortally wounded at his laundry business. Delirious, he mumbled the name of LeBlanc. Three days later, police found the girl hiding under her bed at the stately Glover home.

At the sensational trial, LeBlanc claimed that Glover had attacked her, threatened her, and then committed suicide (she had not witnessed the shooting but heard the shot). While prosecutors had a strong case, many were convinced of LeBlanc's innocence because she came from a race of people who "observe the commandments with religious obedience." The *New York Times* described her as "the little Cape Breton servant girl" while other newspapers noted that there was no need for judges or sheriffs on Isle Madame as the parish priest combined the offices of policeman, postmaster, peacemaker, and pastor. When the jury acquitted LeBlanc of murder, the *Rhode Island Visitor* noted that the verdict "was received with unfeigned joy in the old land of the Acadian farmers."[234]

Of course, those who braved the icy wintertime roads to attend League of the Cross (LOC) meetings in communities like Margaree did not take reports of piety too seriously. Despite their noble intentions, many LOC supporters, proudly wearing a little pin with their emblem (a cross and the letters L.O.C.), recognized the futility of their struggle against alcohol. Although the propaganda assured members that a mere "point to the pin" would cease the urges of their neighbours for a tot of rum, most knew it was a more complicated matter.[235] Even Fr Donald MacAdam, who promoted sobriety in Sydney, knew that many of the "very best men" stayed away from the organization because of its insistence on total abstinence. "A man was found dead yesterday," Fr James Tompkins wrote to a soldier overseas. "It may scare some of the other boozers around Antigonish, but I hardly think it will."[236]

FATHER PACIFIQUE

While Catholic societies like the League of the Cross were critical for solidarity and networking in most parishes, they were not prevalent among the oldest Catholic constituency in the diocese, the Mi'kmaq. Although the Indigenous flock had first cultivated the faith in the region (and defended it), the Catholic press periodically labelled them "untrained sons of the forest," "simple soulful hearts," or simply the "poor Micmacs."[237] Even within this environment, however, the devotion of Indigenous Catholics remained strong. Their leaders – both political and spiritual – gathered together in October 1910 to lay the cornerstone of the new "prayer house" at Eskasoni. As reported by *The Casket*, among them were Grand Chief John Denny Jr; chiefs Matthew Francis (Pictou Landing) and Stephen Christmas (Sydney); and captains Simon Basque (Whycocomagh), Stephen Simon (Wagmatcook), P. Bernard (Eskasoni), Noel Jerome (North Sydney), and the thirty-nine-year-old Thomas Marshall (Chapel Island).[238]

The efforts of the Mi'kmaq leadership on Cape Breton to build a church at Eskasoni inspired a similar project across the Bras d'Or Lakes at Whycocomagh. Interestingly, when a diocese-wide collection was initiated in 1910 for the new church, there was an implicit acknowledgment that the Mi'kmaq had been faithful "under some trying difficulties." In fact, advocates noted, "Whites owe[d] something to the pious Mi'kmaq" and that "the descendants of those who obtained possession of the poor Indian's inheritance" were morally obliged to donate monies to construction.[239]

As Whycocomagh Catholics prepared the grounds, donations came in from across the diocese and from places across North America. In the howling wind and rain of August 1912 the community assembled for the dedication of the sanctuary. It was a solemn and impressive afternoon as the congregation walked into the brightly decorated sanctuary past the two *wikuom* that were assembled on the grounds. A spectacular stained-glass window, depicting St Anne instructing her holy daughter, with the words *Nogamitjen alasotmelseoin Setan* ("Our grandmother St Anne pray for us") touched many hearts.[240]

Hoping to be of some use to "our dear Indian brethren,"[241] the Glendale pastor (with spiritual responsibility for Whycocomagh) Fr Donald MacPherson had spent a month in 1910 completely immersed in the Mi'kmaq language in the company of his friend the Capuchin priest, Joseph Buisson, better known as Fr Pacifique de Valigny.[242] Pastor at Ste Anne de Restigouche, Quebec, Fr Pacifique was a keen ethnographer, historian, and publisher of the *Micmac Messenger* (Fr MacPherson suggested the name), a monthly newspaper published in Mi'kmaw. He had also published a collection of Indigenous prayers and devotions and, by 1909, was conducting summertime missions throughout the Maritime region. Once asked if he minded the long days of hearing confessions at places like Chapel Island – they sometimes stretched well into the evening – he replied: "When a man has not been to confession for 150 years, that is to say without an interpreter, then he has a right to be somewhat lengthy."[243]

At Wagmatcook, Victoria County, in the summer of 1916, Catholics from North Sydney, Whycocomagh, Malagawatch, and Eskasoni gathered to hear fathers Pacifique and MacPherson preach, discuss plans for a new church, and offer confession in their native tongue.[244] There was also a growing consciousness of connecting with Mi'kmaq spirituality, recognizing that the great creator Glooskap was "co-existent with creation." Without a deeper understanding of Indigenous culture, however, the priests noted that it was difficult to accomplish more meaningful pastoral work among the Mi'kmaq.[245]

While Fr Pacifique did what he could spiritually for the Indigenous faithful during the long summers, it was clear that the Mi'kmaq needed "to get a boy of their own to become a priest."[246] It was well and good to ensure that White priests ministered at the Feast of St Anne, but without Indigenous clergymen to minister among their people, advocate for permanent parishes, or represent Indigenous interests within diocesan institutions like St F.X., it was impossible for the community to participate fully in diocesan life. This plea fell on deaf ears and, as we will later read, that inattentiveness would have unhappy repercussions.

THE SCOTTISH CATHOLIC SOCIETY

Scottish Catholics were certainly not without priests but, with the retention of the Gaelic language a constant concern, Gaelic-speaking priests needed to be found. By 1900 over half the diocesan population still spoke the old language and in communities like Princeville, Cape Breton – with sixty Gaelic-speaking families – it was "absolutely necessary" that the priest be able to minister in that tongue.[247] Those who could not, did not fare well. "In the first place I can neither preach nor teach in Gaelic," wrote an anxious Fr J.A.M. Gillis, when transferred to Christmas Island in 1907.[248] Although he did have "some knowledge," he could not "do justice to [him]self or the people in that language." He was soon transferred.[249] Requests for Gaelic-speaking clergy came also from western Canadian prelates like Bishop Olivier-Elzéar Mathieu of Regina; however, Bishop Morrison confessed that the language was "disappearing from ordinary use," and he still struggled to meet the spiritual needs of the older Gaelic-speaking people.[250]

While the 400-page Gaelic prayer-book, *Iul A Chriostaidh*, was reproduced every few years, and there were regular notices in *The Casket* about the fight for the language in Scotland, there was a sense that Catholic Scots were unwilling to "stand up for [their] rights." A movement to teach Gaelic in local schools never materialized and, although St F.X. had once contracted Alexander MacLean Sinclair, the retired Presbyterian minister and grandson of the famous Bard MacLean, to teach a Celtic heritage course, a chair in Gaelic had not materialized.[251]

In January 1911 Fr Moses Michael Coady, a young native of Margaree, celebrated a requiem High Mass for John MacDonald (St Rose) of North Inverness. The deceased was known locally as *Iain ban Muideartach* and, until his death at the age of ninety-five, had been a link with the Gaelic-speaking pioneers.[252] Out of concern that the culture was disappearing, a movement was initiated to collect old tales, songs, emigrant stories, and genealogy.

On Dominion Day 1919, a group of priests and laymen met at Iona, the parish of the passionate Scottish antiquarian Fr Rory MacKenzie, to discuss the dwindling fortunes of the Scottish culture. On that afternoon, they formed the Scottish Catholic Society of Canada with the intent of preserving the Gaelic language, propagating an "accurate knowledge of the history of Scotland," and advancing educationally, morally, and socially all Catholics of the Scottish race. Rejoicing in the motto *Gloir Dhe Agus Math Ar Cinnidh* (The Glory of God and the Good of Our Race), their aim was to preserve and study the Gaelic language, literature, and traditions of the Highlands.[253]

Under the leadership of such outspoken priests as Fr Angus R. MacDonald and Fr Donald MacAdam – he once told a relative who thought they had Hibernian blood, "No Irish, all Scot" – the society soon had a publication entitled *Mosgladh* ("The Awakening"), which identified the problem as "of core importance" to the survival of Scottish traditions.[254] Councils were organized throughout the region, and monies were invested in cultural activities.[255] Far from being "simple folk," these men were often critical of industrial capitalism and considered the solidification of the countryside as "of core importance" to the survival of Scottish traditions. Yet, despite their nostalgia for the past, there was nothing anti-modern in their approach to the future. Years later, Fr Michael Gillis recalled that the Scottish Catholic Society were fond of "keeping up the Gaelic singing, the bagpipe music, and that sort of thing," but were also concerned with "getting boys to college."[256]

INDEPENDENCE FOR THE MARTHAS

According to one historian of the Sisters of St Martha, "a goodly number" of the order's members were raised in Gaelic-speaking homes."[257] By 1912 these women were busy both with their St F.X. ministry and their small Antigonish town hospital, where they treated everything from severe burns to tubercular peritonitis.[258] In the meantime, the congregation had embarked on a school of nursing, opened the "House of Providence," a home for elderly women, and staffed the priest's retirement home at Mount Cameron. "You must be very busy up there indeed," Bishop Morrison wrote to Mother Faustina in May 1913. "I am glad to know you are getting some more postulants ... it will be a source of much consolation to see the community grow."[259]

Recruits to the congregation were steady, and high numbers of recruits meant that congregations could be selective. One former postulant, who wanted to re-enter the congregation after a brief period of reflection, was politely turned away. Having "good judgement" when she abandoned the community, it was clear that she did not have a vocation. "For if God meant you for a religious life, he would have called you earlier, and with no uncertain signs," Bishop Morrison wrote, "so that you would not have hesitated or doubted the call when in the convent." Although the girl would be disappointed, he continued, she could still live a "good life in the world" and serve the Church in other ways.

In 1913 Archbishop Neil McNeil of Toronto had begun construction on St Augustine's Seminary on the beautiful Scarborough Bluffs overlooking Lake Ontario. When he asked the Marthas to take on responsibility for the school's domestic services, the congregation seized the opportunity.[260] But when Sister Faustina arrived in Scarborough, everything was in disarray and she felt very much "in the dark."[261] It was a nerve-racking few months of preparation, but the redoubtable Faustina ensured that "both sides of the line [got] fair treatment."[262] When the full complement of Marthas were finally settled into their new home in the rainy autumn of 1914, Faustina confessed that God had been "more than good to [her] in every way."[263]

As a gesture of gratitude for the Marthas' services, Archbishop MacNeil offered the diocese an annual scholarship to his new seminary (John Angus MacPherson of Antigonish County was the first recipient).[264] St Augustine's was a wonderful environment for study, and seminarians strolled the forests along the Scarborough bluffs, harvested maple sugar, planted vegetable gardens and, as one student recalled, ate meals that were "fit for a king."[265] While the women who provided those delicious meals did not usually interact with the seminarians, they kept a close eye on the transplanted Antigonish boys. "Pat N [P.J. Nicholson] looks better than I have ever seen him look," one sister wrote to the Old Rector in 1914, "and he seems in good spirits too."[266] When the young seminarian John R.

MacDonald, Archbishop MacNeil's nephew, visited Toronto, Sister Faustina gave him a tour of the convent and took him out on the roof for a panoramic view of the distant Toronto skyline.[267]

In the following years, the Marthas received offers to staff other colleges like Saint Mary's in Halifax but declined because of a lack of resources. Yet when Bishop Henry J. O'Leary of Charlottetown made a request for help at St Dunstan's in 1915, the Marthas consented to training an independent order because it was important that island women have an opportunity to enter religious life.[268] Between January and August 1915, the first four women from PEI begin their education at the St F.X. motherhouse. While all expenses were supposed to be borne by the diocese of Charlottetown, Bishop Morrison later grumbled that Antigonish got the "heaviest side of the burden."[269]

In the midst of all these new projects, the sisters were asked to resume their domestic and nursing duties at St Joseph's Hospital in Glace Bay (which they had left in 1908). A new Protestant hospital in Glace Bay had forced St Joseph's to rely more heavily on local Catholic support, and many felt that the presence of the Marthas would encourage the "charity of the people."[270] Then, in the spring of 1917, the Marthas took charge of St Mary's Home in Sydney and broadened their ministry to orphans and unwed mothers. Seeing the need for a diocesan orphanage, they purchased the three-acre "Herbert Moseley property" on Kings Road for $16,000 (the Good Friday collection for 1917 was used as financing).

As the Marthas expanded, St F.X. administrators grew increasingly concerned that the congregation was overextended.[271] As the women were already in "great demand," the Old Rector felt that the administration of orphanages and hospitals pulled the Marthas away from their original mandate.[272] There were also ongoing disputes over staffing, finances, policy, and personalities. By 1916 Mother Faustina, who had led the expansion in Toronto and Glace Bay, had already started to pursue "Home Rule" and by March 1917, Bishop Morrison confided to a colleague that the women would soon be "separate from the college."[273]

The formal independence of the Marthas came about in August 1917, with a covenant that reiterated the Marthas' commitment to domestic services at St F.X. but authorized the congregation to direct "its own organization" (this decision was ratified by the provincial legislature in March 1918 and subject to the bishop of

Antigonish).[274] Although the agreement was "weighted in favor of St. F.X," the arrangement generated momentum, and plans for a new motherhouse were soon unveiled.[275] "Now that they have their destiny in their own hands," the bishop noted, "it may be hoped that more progress will be made."[276] "The congregation was wise to press for independence," observed James Cameron, "and the college was prudent to grant it."[277]

MORALE AMONG THE CLERGY

Those who most often sang the praises of the Marthas were the diocesan clergy. By the time of the Great War, the Vatican was working diligently to create a comprehensive law book to regulate conditions both within the Church and among its priests. Bishop Morrison, while adhering to injunctions that priests reject modernity and ecumenism, wanted his clergy to win the people over with greater affection. When one priest, for instance, demanded that parishioners produce a certificate proving that they had been to regular confession, the prelate scolded that such a measure would "drive some people from the sacraments." After an Isle Madame pastor violently pulled a woman from her pew during a rental dispute, the hot-headed clergyman was forced to publicly read a letter of apology asking the "pardon of the congregation." More serious charges of misconduct were sent on to the Holy Office (Congregation for the Doctrine of the Faith) in Rome. When a visiting curate at North Sydney was charged with "kissing women and young girls," he was forced to leave the diocese. Written testimony from the victims was sent to the bishop, and the prelate "felt obliged" to forward it to Rome.[278]

When Morrison arrived in Nova Scotia in 1912, he had found clerical morale to be quite low. The incidents at Heatherton and Lismore had taken a toll, and memories of the death and burial at sea of Fr Martin MacPherson still ruffled feathers. The burly pastor of Little Bras d'Or had been suspended from his clerical faculties and censured by Bishop Cameron in 1907 for refusing to accept the division of his parish. Although the priest had begun celebrating the Mass in "good conscience" after Cameron's death in 1910, he was reprimanded by the Old Rector. Denied a formal diocesan investigation, MacPherson secretly travelled to Rome in November to protest directly to the Curia (he had gone to the Halifax Exhibition and then vanished). It was all rather sensational, and one priest joked that MacPherson would surely return "with the papal flag sticking out of his coat pocket," or be named bishop.[279]

It is not known how Fr MacPherson fared in the Holy City, as he succumbed to heart trouble and died aboard the SS *Canada* on his return. The captain of the vessel made the regrettable decision to bury the pastor at sea, provoking anger from the people of Little Bras d'Or and condemnation from *The Casket*.[280] Making the matter even more awkward was that neither Fr John MacIsaac in Little Bras d'Or nor Fr Joseph MacDonald in Frenchvale was allowed to offer a "Mass for poor unfortunate Father Martin," despite parishioners' demands. "Rebellion against divinely constituted authority," intoned Fr Michael Laffin from the Tracadie glebe house, "must end badly."[281]

Surrounded by negativity, Bishop Morrison decided to honour some of the senior clergy as a means of raising spirits. In the autumn of 1914 the venerable Fr Hugh Gillis, the former rector of St Ninian's Cathedral and onetime nemesis of Bishop Cameron, was made a domestic prelate and "garbed for the first time in the robes of his new dignity."[282] A few weeks later, Fr Daniel Joseph MacIntosh in Baddeck, vicar-general since 1913, received the same honour. When Fr Colin Chisholm, the "soundly instructed theologian" who had spent most of his fifty years in the priesthood ministering in Port Hood, was made a domestic prelate in July 1917, Bishop Morrison scrambled to get official confirmation and lent Chisholm the habiliments of a prelate so that he would look the part for his Jubilee celebration in front of the largest gathering of clergy ever assembled in the county of Inverness.[283]

THE GREAT WAR, 1914–1918

In the years leading up to the Great War, Nova Scotia Catholics paid little attention to the nationalism and militarism that gripped Europe. There was no mention in *The Casket* of conditions in the Balkans where Austria-Hungary and the great Slavic power, Russia, constantly locked diplomatic horns. The paper was also mute on the growing economic and military power of Germany, and took little notice of the various "defensive treaties" like the *Entente Cordiale*, which was negotiated by Britain and France in 1904. In fact, the only news of the German kaiser to reach the diocese directly came from the pen of Fr C.J. Connolly, who described the "angry looking countenance" of the monarch when he visited Munich.[284]

In the dark wet spring of 1914, Bishop Morrison and Fr Donald MacAdam went to Rome so that the prelate could make his first *ad limina* and the priest could tour the Holy City. Throughout their journey, first on the liner *Canopic* and then on the train, the topic of colonies and armies occasionally arose in general conversation, but no one seriously believed that a European war was imminent. News of continental sabre-rattling did not enter the conversation that Morrison and Bishop Sandy MacDonald, who accompanied the Antigonish prelate on his first visit with the pontiff, had with Pope Pius X; nor was any potential conflict on the lips of those dining in Rome restaurants or enjoying Paris cafés. As Morrison later reflected, there "did not seem to be the slightest suspicion of any trouble of this kind."[285]

At the end of June, as priest and prelate sailed for Canada, a young Serbian nationalist, Gavrilo Princip, fired bullets at point-blank range into the stomachs of Archduke Franz Ferdinand, heir to the Hapsburg throne, and his wife, Sophie, both on a state visit to Austro-Hungary's recently acquired province of Bosnia. Within days, Austro-Hungary, backed by the military might of Germany, issued several humiliating ultimatums to Serbia. In response, the Serbs sought the protection of their old ally Russia, and the weak tsar, Nicholas II, unwisely obliged. On 28 July 1914, Austro-Hungary declared war on Serbia, and the following morning the Russians mobilized their vast, if poorly equipped armies. In response to Germany's ultimatum, all the backroom treaties that had received such limited coverage in *The Casket* sprang into effect. When a British ultimatum demanding that the German Army not cross into neutral Belgium was ignored, the Empire also declared war.[286] "What a terrible war is on now in Europe," Morrison wrote to Fr L.E. Perrin at the Canadian College in Rome. "Is it the great Armageddon, or what is it?"[287]

Considering the unimaginable death, misery, and destruction of the Great War, it is notable that the Nova Scotia press gave such little attention to the outbreak of hostilities. Days after the declaration of war, *The Casket* noted that Kaiser Wilhelm was "mad," but the seriousness of the situation was muted. In fact, the newspaper was concerned mainly with a rise in the cost of living.[288] It was not until German troops occupied neutral Catholic Belgium that Antigonish's

Catholics took serious notice of hostilities. By mid-September Premier George Murray had organized a steamer to bring supplies to the beleaguered nation, and Bishop Morrison issued a circular requesting "whatever assistance [could] be given."[289]

Every parish in the diocese collected food and clothing for "plucky little Belgium."[290] In St Andrews, a woman from Meadow Green quilted a parcel of blankets, while a man from Beauly donated a bushel of potatoes. The parishioners of St Patrick's Church in Lochaber, besides offering cash, provided a "good number of well filled boxes" of supplies. In coastal L'Ardoise, the people shipped "about two car loads of fish, potatoes, clothing, shoes, and blankets" – a particularly generous donation considering that the community's fishermen had recently been devastated by a ferocious gale.[291] Each edition of *The Casket* carried up-to-date donor lists, and the Antigonish Forward Movement briefly considered settling Belgian refugees on vacant farms.

Germany took a pillorying in the diocesan press, and while Canadians made a distinction between the Kaiser's militarism and "and the German people, who were oppressed by their leaders," patriotism and xenophobia were often blurred. By 1915 a crusade in the colliery towns to force DOMCO to terminate every German employee gained momentum among the miners.[292] "Just a few bigots behind it," wrote the pastor at New Waterford, "but they are very active."[293]

In December 1914, Fr Tompkins predicted that it was only a matter of time before Germany "would have to give in."[294] He was wrong. Despite naïve patriotic promises that the soldiers would be "home by Christmas," *The Casket* had wisely editorialized on the reality of a long war.[295] While the Von Schlieffen plan had failed to knock the French out of the conflict, it was clear that Germany was prepared to fight. Moreover, reports from Russia had exaggerated the early victories over the Austro-Hungarians. They were welcome military triumphs but not the devastating blow that braggarts had predicted. "If it's a long way to Tipperary," *The Casket* quipped, it was an even "longer one to Berlin."[296]

FIRST WORLD WAR RECRUITING

There are few better examples of the Catholic subculture working effectively for the state than wartime recruiting. In the summer of 1915, Major-General R.W. Rutherford, head of Maritime Provinces Command, asked Bishop Morrison to help recruit soldiers for the Canadian Expeditionary Force (CEF). Not only did the prelate agree but he also chastised Rutherford for the sports, theatre, and excursions that were carrying on "without any apparent concern for the safety of the country."[297] Demonstrating his canny foresight, he warned that it would be a miserable reflection on the manhood of the Empire if conscription was needed due to a lack of volunteers.

There were many reasons why a young Catholic might enlist in the CEF – the lure of a steady income, patriotism, or even "adventure-lust" – but the support of the local priest was often a determining factor.[298] At St F.X., Fr Tompkins encouraged men to "see something of the world," and respond to the primordial "love of adventure." While the Old Rector assured parents that all student enlistments would be "strictly voluntary," one Ottawa mother was furious with the college for permitting a recruiting office on campus, and vowed that her son, Leonard Moran, would "never go back to St F.X." (he was killed in 1918).[299]

Recruiting specifically for the Acadian Battalion (165th) in the spring of 1916, P.J. Webb, the public face of the Antigonish Forward Movement, spoke passionately to the people of Cheticamp and River Bourgeois, stumped for the "Patriotic Fund" throughout Richmond County, and urged young men to enlist.[300] In a thesis on the diocese and the Great War, Fr Charles Brewer noted that initial recruiting in some Acadian communities was disappointing because of the presence of priests on loan from Quebec who refused to become "involved in the recruiting meetings or in the general war activities."[301] Yet the pastor of Arichat, Fr Amable Mombourquette, had his parishioners listen for "the call of their country," and at L'Ardoise, with the sound of the pounding surf behind him, Fr Alfred Boudreau made a "strong plea" on behalf of the 165th.[302] By February 1916, one recruiting officer in the *Sydney Post* noted that enlistments among the Acadians of Cape Breton "were equal to those among British Canadians."[303]

Besides the Acadian 165th, local men filled the ranks of battalions such as the 25th, 27th, 38th, 40th, and 66th, while Cape Breton raised the 185th, commonly known as the Cape Breton Highlanders. With the motto *Siol Na Fear Fearsil* (Breed of Manly Men), the 185th appealed to men in parishes like Judique and Creignish, as they could fight alongside friends and also wear "highland garb."[304] At a patriotic meeting at the convent school in Inverness, the children cheered the Highland Brigade, which was over 50 per cent Catholic, and became ecstatic when one of the pupils enlisted.[305] In colliery towns, enlistment was brisk, and by the autumn of 1915 some twelve hundred miners were in uniform.[306] So many men signed up "to escape the drudgery of the coal mines" that DOMCO worried that it would not have enough manpower to maintain production.[307]

In the mainland counties, most recruits gravitated toward the 85th Battalion (Nova Scotia Highlanders). One notable speaker at recruiting meetings in Antigonish County was the St F.X. graduate and former editor of *The Xaverian*, Lieutenant Angus Lewis Macdonald. The future premier of Nova Scotia gave the usual pitch about duty, Empire, peace, and freedom, but it was his rapport with priests like Fr Tompkins that gave him prominence and garnered public attention (Macdonald's brother Colin would die at Arras in 1918).[308] With further speeches by Bishop Morrison and full-page recruiting supplements in *The Casket*, by April 1916 the 85th was over strength.

With so many young men serving overseas, Catholics became familiar with the topography of northern France. Yet as Canadian soldiers suffered heavy casualties at the bloody battles of the Somme and at Ypres, the cruel realities of war hit home. Correspondence from soldiers at the front described scenes of unimaginable horror. "To find oneself almost in a trap with machines guns blazing forth their messages of death upon you is bad enough," wrote John Ronald MacLellan, a Belle Cote, Inverness County, native, "but to find oneself alone, on no man's land, with a wounded comrade to attend to, makes it still worse."[309] Another young man wrote home to his parents while standing up to his knees in filthy cold water.[310] In January 1915, Fr Jerome (Michael Merour), a former Trappist at the monastery, fighting with the 116th French Infantry, wrote that his entire company (seventy-three men) were killed outright or fatally wounded by a single shell. Miraculously unscathed, he spent an agonizing hour giving last rites to men who only recently had been laughing and joking.[311]

The clergy were unprepared for this anguish. These were not old men that were dying by the hundreds, but rather young men, many only a few years removed from school. At Westville, Pictou County, Fr James Butts spent considerable time at the side of the Carrigan family, which had six sons on active service (five received wounds). At St Ninian's, Fr Michael MacAdam comforted the parents of Pte Joseph Bernard Gillis, who went missing at Passchendaele, while

Table 4.1 | Roman Catholic Enlistment from Nova Scotia in the First World War (1914–1918) and Casualty Statistics by County

County	Number of Parishes/Missions	Enlisted	Killed	Wounded
Antigonish	12	636	67 (10.5%)	88 (13.8%)
Pictou	5	304	31 (10.2%)	52 (17%)
Guysborough	5	247	33 (13%)	31(12.5%)
Richmond	10	441	41 (9%)	45 (10.2%)
Inverness	11	712	77 (10.8%)	46 (10.2%)
Victoria	5	172	19 (11%)	47 (10.2%)
Cape Breton	23	2,280	290 (12.7%)	48 (10.2%)
Total	71	4,792	559 (11.6%)	697 (14.5%)

(*Source:* Antigonish Diocesan Statistics)

Fr Alfred Boudreau at L'Ardoise consoled the family of the late Lt Walter Martell with the news that he had received the Military Medal for non-commissioned officers. "Mr. [John] O'Brian feels deeply the death of his son Alexander," the Old Rector wrote in the autumn of 1917. "However, he has reason to feel proud of him as he died in a good cause."[312] Nor were the clergy immune from their own personal suffering; Ambrose Boyle, the brother of Fr James Boyle, was killed on the third day of the battle for Vimy Ridge in April 1917.

The casualties of war haunted every parish. Statistics gathered after the armistice show that the only parishes not to suffer a fatality were Lochaber (18 enlisted), St Nicholas Italian Church in Whitney Pier (11 enlisted), and West Arichat (24 enlisted). Some of the casualty rates in the smaller parishes were shocking. In Baddeck, seventeen men joined the colours, and by 1918, six were buried in France and six more were nursing serious wounds. Like Baddeck, Victoria Mines had a casualty rate of over 50 per cent, as did St Francis Harbour, Lakevale, and Northeast Margaree.

ARMY CHAPLAINCY

While Bishop Morrison was a committed recruiter, he would not let his recruits depart for a violent fate on a European battlefield without "making all the spiritual provisions for them."[313] After enlistment, chaplains were "the most poignant visible reminder of the Catholic faith"; without assurances that a priest would accompany the battalions overseas, Catholics would not have enlisted as eagerly.[314]

In September 1914, Ottawa formally requested chaplains from the diocese and Fr Donald MacPherson enlisted in the army. By the following year, four more priests, the agricultural expert Fr Miles Tompkins (Mount Cameron), Fr Ronald C. MacGillivray (Port Hood), Fr Michael Gillis (Georgeville), and Fr Ronald MacDonald (Pictou), who had been so involved in the Bailey's Brook affair, had signed on. "Hard pressed for enough priests at home," Bishop Morrison hurried the ordination of Leo Joseph Keats so that he could return as a curate at Inverness, rushed Daniel Hastings Doyle for Sacred Heart in Sydney, and asked P.J. Nicholson to take a teaching post at St F.X.[315] Within days of his 1916 ordination, Placide Arsène LeBlanc, a native of Friar's Head studying at the Grand Seminary of Quebec, was ordered to return home immediately.[316] "Sacrifices [had] to be made," Morrison insisted, "to provide for the spiritual welfare of [the] poor boys who [were] laying down their lives for the safety of the rest of us."[317]

Ministering to a battalion was a singular experience, but it was not completely unlike regular pastoral duties. When Fr Donald MacPherson, attached to the 25th (Nova Scotia Rifles), sailed for England in the spring of 1915, more than half of his regiment was from Cape Breton and so he led "a few Gaelic songs" aboard ship.[318] MacPherson was extremely popular among his boys and at least one young solider wrote to the *Halifax Chronicle* that he was "a fine type of a man."[319] Yet once in England, shortly before his battalion crossed the fabled English Channel, he was abruptly transferred away from his "first love." Shocked by orders to leave for Salonika, Greece (today's Thessalonika), he was told that no chaplain could serve exclusively with a single battalion.[320]

In the eagerness of war preparations, little consideration was given to the overseas organization of the Canadian Catholic chaplains. Ottawa formally requested priests for local battalions and, under the assumption that the priest would remain with their men, the

Figure 4.4 | Fr Donald MacPherson (far left) in Egypt, c. 1916

bishops obeyed. Yet had anyone inquired, they would have found that British Army regulations stipulated that only three Catholic chaplains could be attached to a single division. So instead of one chaplain per battalion, the rule was one chaplain per brigade comprising four battalions.[321] Instead of ministering to the Nova Scotia lads of the 25th, MacPherson found himself in a far-off posting surrounded by adherents of the Greek Orthodox Church.

While most assumed that Fr MacPherson's transfer was a simple administrative blunder, within weeks complaints that "Anglican padres swarmed at the front while wounded Catholic boys were going without the Sacraments," reached Toronto's *Catholic Register*.[322] The chaplains ministering in the muddy trenches of northern France certainly felt that the Church of England was given preferential treatment. For one thing, noted Fr R.C. MacGillivray, "the difference between [his] duties and those of a Protestant chaplain" was considerable, and even though it was impossible to give every soldier the personal attention accorded to a man at risk of death, he should at least be able to "offer the sacraments with greater regularity."[323] In the more extreme cases, Catholic soldiers took on pastoral duties themselves.

Concerned, Bishop Morrison wrote to Senator James Lougheed, a prominent federal cabinet minister, to complain that the treatment of the chaplains was "becoming a matter of public talk."[324] If the government wanted to avoid a scandal, then it needed to leave the priests with their intended battalions. Moreover, should the rumours that soldiers were going without pastoral care persist, Catholics might stop enlisting altogether. In an apologetic response, Lougheed promised to investigate the complaints. From Glace Bay, Fr John J. MacNeil of St Anthony's praised Morrison for his firm stance and grumbled that the 185th, although heavily Catholic, had few Catholic officers.[325]

In Greece Fr MacPherson was continually amazed at the packages that arrived from home with beads, medals, and prayer books, which he passed on to the men.[326] Another chaplain asked for copies of *The Casket* and the *Catholic Record* so that the boys would have "mental and spiritual pabulum."[327] In the pages of *The Casket*, MacPherson detailed his experiences on the Greek island of Lemnos, where he celebrated three Christmas Masses with the aid of some Australians; although he feared that the throng would be "as few as were at Bethlehem," the marquee was crowded.[328] Later, on the back of a camel, he toured the pyramids and the Valley of the Kings, and on the island of Malta, he said Mass at the Convent of the Blue Sisters, some twelve miles from where Saint Paul was shipwrecked.[329]

Although many of these missals read like travel diaries, chaplains were blunt about conditions. In one letter, Fr MacPherson asked his audience to think of an "old time tucking frolie" in Cape Breton full of banter, humour, and fun lightening the labour of pounding the wet cloth on the table, and then imagine that suddenly a sixty-pound bomb fell on the group. That is what had recently happened in the French village in which he was billeted.[330] Fr Miles Tompkins described a skirmish in which his brigade sustained 50 per cent casualties. Acting as a stretcher bearer and comforting the dying, he believed that "only the mercy of God" kept him from being killed. During the battle of Mount Sorrel in June 1916, many wounded men lay for days among the dead, while others were buried alive by shell fire. He witnessed big strong men "shaking like they had palsy and crying like babies." "I am not a coward," he wrote poignantly "but I am scared at times."[331]

While Fr Tompkins did Herculean work with the 9th Canadian Infantry Brigade, which was made up primarily of battalions from Ontario, he was supposed to have been in trenches with the boys of the 40th Battalion. The news of his February 1916 transfer had infuriated Bishop Morrison, as did the recurring letters from France complaining of bias against Catholics. "Our colonel don't believe in anything, especially the Catholic Church," wrote one man enlisted in the 25th, "so I tell you we ain't getting the best of shows." An agitated Morrison wrote to Prime Minister Borden "on behalf of the Catholic soldiers of eastern Nova Scotia and Cape Breton," citing Lougheed's pledge of action.[332] Insisting that the British military would not "turn a deaf ear to any representation made by Ottawa with regard for the welfare of Canadian soldiers," Morrison demanded redress.[333] Discouraged, he even suggested that Fr Tompkins return to Antigonish, as he would be more useful ministering in a parish than away from his boys.[334]

The Canadian chaplaincy service was beset with problems. Besides the obvious prejudice of British Army regulations and the ineptitude of some Canadian officials, there was also the interference of Fr Alfred E. Burke, an ambitious Catholic priest (who had once crossed swords with Morrison in PEI), in the pay of the government and claiming to be the representative of all Catholic chaplains in the CEF.[335] A "renowned imperialist, Conservative and friend of Prime Minister Borden," Fr Burke insisted that Catholics were treated fairly.[336] Yet, despite his assurances, problems persisted; priests from Cape Breton, for instance, were assigned to French-speaking soldiers from Quebec and vice versa. There is a big difference between a hole in a "wet low-lying place with the shells breaking all about, and a room in the Strand Hotel in London," wrote Fr Tompkins in 1916. "I would like to have Burke for one day at the Front. Why he does not know where it is."[337]

By April 1916, the condition of the Catholic chaplains in the war theatre was chaotic, and the fresh battalions recruited to replace those who were bloodied in France were sailing for Europe without priests. At recruitment meetings, the clergy put on a brave face but privately they were apprehensive. When the Cape Breton Highlanders were preparing to sail in the spring of 1916, Morrison decided he could not send local boys across the tempestuous Atlantic without Fr Michael Gillis by their side, even though he was sure the chaplain would be transferred upon arrival.

By the summer of 1916, Morrison's outspoken defence of the Catholic chaplains had made him a national figure. In a letter to Prime Minister Borden he acknowledged that he was initially concerned merely with the welfare of his diocese, but pointed out that the treatment of all Canadian priests had "opened up the situation to a wider range."[338] Further letters arrived at the residence from Fr Wolston Workman, a Franciscan and captain in the 1st Canadian Brigade, providing the bishop with the necessary documentation to support his discussions with Ottawa bureaucrats.[339]

Matters finally came to a head when the 4th Canadian Division, set to depart for France, had a Presbyterian appointed as senior chaplain (the role was expected to go to a Catholic).[340] In response, Ottawa priest Fr John O'Gorman, with the support of his fellow chaplains, refused to obey any further orders from his Protestant superior, and demanded that Fr Burke choose sides.[341] A petition soon made the rounds in France calling the situation of the Catholic chaplains "simply scandalous."[342] "I wrote Bishop Morrison with the chaplain question," Fr O'Gorman told a friend, and hope that he will "demand of the government that we should not be under a Protestant in England."[343]

By January 1917, Bishop Morrison had suffered the Borden government long enough. The situation of the Catholic chaplains in the CEF was "a crying shame," and he demanded an investigation and the immediate appointment of a Catholic senior chaplain. If this was not fulfilled, then he would bring the matter to the people and recruitment would suffer. In Ottawa, the prime minister took Morrison's warning seriously and in an election year he could ill afford to call the prelate's bluff. With pressure on the government mounting, Fr O'Gorman was invalided back to Ottawa to nurse a wound he received at the Somme. With access to Ottawa parishes, he took every opportunity to speak on the prejudice in France.[344] As Mark McGowan notes, not only did O'Gorman's revelations bring about changes to the chaplaincy service but they "also spelled the end of Burke."[345]

The work of the Antigonish chaplains, most of whom had only recently served rural parishes, was quite extraordinary. They were all, noted one officer, "scholarly priests with a repertoire of languages from Italian to Micmac."[346] Even the Presbyterian minister, C.W. Gordon, who wrote books under the pen name Ralph Connor, noted the moving sight of Catholic soldiers "huddled around their padre in the dawn before battle," waiting to make their confessions.[347] Both

Fr Miles Tompkins and Fr Ronald C. MacGillivray were awarded the Military Cross for bravery, and their execution of priestly duties, usually under duress, was legendary.[348] They offered Holy Communion in the mud, gave the last rites to hundreds of mangled and dying boys, heard confessions (many of them final), and comforted the stressed and the homesick. When one English soldier was brought into the hospital tent "riddled with bullets," Fr Tompkins wrote to his brother James, he and the priest prayed together in both English and Latin. Some nearby Catholics joined in, and after the young man died, the doctor was in awe of the "wonderful peace" that filled the room.[349]

CATHOLIC ARMY HUTS

By the end of the Somme offensive in 1916, the Canadian army had suffered severe casualties, and volunteers were scarce. Much like the Boer War, the conflict was an opportunity for Catholics in eastern Nova Scotia to show their patriotism, and many priests supported conscription on the basis that it would provide the final thrust to end the war. Yet, because it was such a contentious issue in Quebec, the news that the Canadian Parliament had introduced the Military Service Act caught everyone by surprise. "No single issue has done more to muddy the political waters," noted one historian, "or to destroy the unity of the nation."[350]

Throughout the war, there was a lot of pressure on young men to enlist, and most had "no easy task to justify [their] abstention."[351] In early January 1917, the clergy employed the pulpit to support the National Service Registration and men (sixteen years or older) were encouraged to fill out personal information cards and return them to Ottawa.[352] By October 1917, exemption tribunals were hard at work taking testimony from men as to why they could not join the army. Even Archbishop McNeil in Toronto joked that he dared not publish the list of students in his seminary as the "conscriptionists might get after [them]."[353]

Although most Canadians volunteered *en masse*, French-Canadian politicians were more skeptical of Britain's war aims. Bitter opposition to conscription in Quebec – in the spring of 1917 a riot broke out in Montreal – put the English-speaking media on the attack.[354] When a Presbyterian minister in Middle River, Victoria County, preached that Quebec Catholics were disloyal, *The Casket* defended his right to criticize recruitment in Quebec but not to "fasten a charge of disloyalty on Catholics, or to galvanize the dead carcasses of anti-popery bogies."[355] "There is a great deal of confusion here on account of the war and conscription," Fr James Tompkins wrote in exasperation to *The Casket*. "I wish to heavens the war would get over, we never know what is next."[356]

While Archbishop McNeil in Toronto argued that Quebec opposition to conscription was racially and not religiously motivated, *The Casket* calmly mentioned that some English-speaking Canadians also opposed the act.[357] Things became more sectarian in the winter of 1917, when the *Halifax Herald* published articles about the treachery of Catholic clergy in Italy, and reprinted pieces from the *Christian Science Monitor* charging Archbishop Daniel Mannix in Australia with disloyalty. Although the *Herald* cleverly added that "Loyal Catholics of Nova Scotia [had] nothing but contempt for the fire-brand tactics and teachings of disloyal Catholic bishops in other parts of the Empire," it was an obvious insult. In response, *The Casket* attacked the *Monitor* (which, they argued, was "neither Christian nor scientific") and the *Herald* (its owner, William Dennis, was "mentally and morally twisted") for printing such bigoted babble. "The blood of too many Catholics and our allies," it declared, had "reddened the soil of France" to stand for it.[358]

Catholics did whatever they could to counter bigoted claims of disloyalty in the press. In February 1916, fuelled mostly by pride, St F.X. formed a stationary hospital unit for active service overseas. Although the unit was a disappointment – by 1917 its commanding officer was dead, the personnel transferred – it demonstrated the college's commitment to the war effort.[359]

In raising the hospital unit, the Old Rector hoped that the staff might also protect Catholic soldiers from moral and physical danger.[360] The lack of Catholic resources within the military was a problem, and most letters sent home from enlisted men were scribbled on paper carrying the emblem of the Protestant YMCA. In fact, the multipurpose YMCA tent was the only place for Catholic soldiers to obtain writing paper or read a newspaper. In 1917 Fr J.J. O'Gorman, still recovering in Ottawa, called upon the Knights of Columbus to finance army huts to serve the recreational needs of Catholic soldiers and offer a space for saying Mass.[361]

In the spring of 1918, local councils of the Knights of Columbus, which were already supporting patriotic causes, sprang into action and began canvassing for the army huts. The drive was taken so seriously that the funding campaign for the diocesan orphanage was halted in order to direct resources into the crusade.[362] When the first hut was opened at Bramshott, England, soldiers wrote home of the "cigarettes, chocolates and biscuits" on the shelves and the wonderful space for Mass and evening prayers.[363] In the early autumn of 1918, a second campaign to raise $100,000 began in the Maritime provinces and within weeks Antigonish had raised $55,000, which was just short of the $65,000 that was collected in the archdiocese of Halifax.[364] In total, Nova Scotians raised over $125,000 of an incredible $1 million raised nationally.

THE GREAT WAR ENDS

When the United States entered the war in April 1917, Fr James Tompkins predicted that the Germans would "feel the squeeze."[365] "It is about time for some of you fellows to start licking the Germans," he wrote playfully to Fr Michael Gillis. "If you don't get after it soon we are going to organize a battalion here soon to go over and lick you fellows."[366] Ten months later, it was Nova Scotia that was to feel a "squeeze." On the morning of 6 December 1917, the SS *Mont-Blanc*, a French freighter loaded with dynamite and other explosives, collided with the Norwegian ship SS *Imo* in the narrows of Halifax harbour. The resulting explosion destroyed the north end of the city, took the lives of an estimated two thousand people, and injured – many were blinded – more than nine thousand. From more than two hundred kilometres away, Bishop Morrison "felt the entire house shake" while he was at his desk writing a letter. At the college, the students in the new Science Hall were also momentarily disturbed by a "very noticeable rumble and shaking of the building resembling what [they] thought might have resulted from a slight earthquake."[367] Within an hour, the bishop received a cable from Truro informing him of the disaster.[368] When he tried to contact Archbishop McCarthy, he found that all communication to the city was cut off.

In the following days, *The Casket* drew attention to the plight of the north-end Halifax parish of St Joseph's, which was almost completely ruined. The parish priest, who had just finished saying Mass at the time of the explosion, had been pinned beneath the debris of his church but miraculously was rescued with only minor injuries.[369]

St Patrick's Church had survived the blast, but its roof was crumbling and its walls unstable. St Mary's Cathedral, safely on the south side of the city and protected by Citadel Hill, sustained the least damage, but its stained-glass windows were shattered, as were the windows of the archbishop's residence. Some victims were received as far away as St Martha's Hospital in Antigonish town.[370] Catholics across eastern Nova Scotia sent money to the Halifax Relief Fund, as well as food and clothing for the injured. "Our people have done splendidly for Halifax," Fr Tompkins exulted. "It showed [the people] what they can do when they get together."[371]

Near the end of the war, the so-called Spanish influenza, which ravaged Europe and killed nearly twenty million people worldwide, invaded eastern Nova Scotia. Deaths were reported across the diocese, and like a "tornado," thirty-three fatalities were reported in the Margaree area in January 1919.[372] Throughout the colliery towns, "many young mothers were carried away," while even sturdy miners like John Gates of New Aberdeen died after only forty-eight hours of illness.[373] "It is a despotic sort of evil," Fr H.D. Barry noted from Little Bras d'Or.[374] In early November, the parishioners of St Anne's in Glace Bay learned that their curate, thirty-year-old Fr Ronald Angus MacDonald, had also succumbed.[375] "Things are kind of blue around here and we miss Fr Ronald dreadfully," Sister Ignatius wrote from St Joseph's Hospital. "We find it hard to realize that he is gone."[376]

When the armistice was formally signed on 11 November, church bells rang out from Pictou to Bay St Lawrence, and *The Casket* reported "Joy!" throughout the region. Despite the government's desire to hold off celebrations in Sydney because of the flu epidemic, bonfires were lit, whistles blown at the steel works, and schools closed. Spontaneous celebrations sprang up everywhere.[377] Each parish organized a thanksgiving service, and at St Ninian's Cathedral, Bishop Morrison, accompanied by thirty priests and altar boys, told the gathered that the danger had passed and that the people had "crowned themselves with glory." Nevertheless, as sorrow had entered many homes, he said, it was right to be mindful of those boys who had not returned, that "God may grant them eternal rest."[378]

5

On the Rocks
1920–1929

In early 1920 the anguish caused by the Great War lingered heavily over eastern Nova Scotia. Hundreds of families, like those of Pte Neil MacDonald in Port Hood and Pte Robert Burns of Guysborough, faced the long horrible silence knowing that their loved ones would not return from the blood-soaked fields of France. To some, there were consolations. In the colliery district of New Aberdeen, the parents of John "Johnny" Bernard Croak proudly displayed the Victoria Cross that their son had won at Amiens in August 1918. Separated from his platoon, the former student of St John's parish school, had managed to capture a machine-gun emplacement (and was wounded in the arm). Later, he rejoined his squad and led them on a charge that resulted in the capture of three more machine guns. Sadly, his second wound proved fatal and he died later that afternoon. To honour men like VC Croak, Bishop Morrison purchased two field guns that had seen action in France and placed them in front of St F.X.'s Xavier Hall.

Many soldiers who survived the carnage had terrible physical and psychological wounds (by 1921 there were reports of war wounds cured at the shrine of St Anne de Beaupré). In many communities, memorials and cenotaphs were erected to serve as places to grieve and commemorate. New buildings were named after soldiers and battlefields, and priest-veterans of the trenches, like Fr Ronald MacGillivray, presided at memorial services. To counter the "whispering and sometimes outspoken criticism" of the Church by Protestant newspapers, the young Fr John R. MacDonald was asked to collect enlistment and casualty statistics from the parishes. In

1920 *Catholics of the Diocese of Antigonish, Nova Scotia, and the War, 1914-1919 with nominal enlistment rolls by parishes* was published by St F.X. Along with the statistics, there were photographs of the dead, biographies of the diocesan chaplains, and copies of Bishop Morrison's wartime circulars. Although the figures were "by no means complete or perfect" – many soldiers from the mining towns were missed – the book sold well.[1]

While Nova Scotians hoped that the postwar era would be one of optimism and progress, the Maritime economy in particular remained at the mercy of economic forces that were hard to control.[2] As John Reid has demonstrated, wars had always produced brief economic stimulation in Nova Scotia, followed by "painful adjustment" to the old realities of peacetime.[3] Weary veterans who returned to the farms and collieries of the diocese hoped for new era of democracy and economic security, but they got "the old realities of galloping inflation, rural depopulation, and governments unresponsive to farmer and labour demands."[4]

In the short term, these veterans either outmigrated – one priest recalled issuing far more birth certificates for migrants than for newborn babies – or accepted the daily struggle.[5] While miners and steelworkers responded with aggressive trade unionism, the province's farmers joined a national movement to elect politicians sympathetic to agricultural renewal. Disillusioned by both the Liberals and Conservatives, the farmers and the miners of Nova Scotia had by the summer of 1920 organized new political parties and had nominated their own candidates for the provincial legislature.

The United Farmers and the Independent Labour Party were friendly but hardly unified. As Murray Beck notes, the United Farmers were poorly organized and, with no manifesto, they "advocated the programme of the Canadian Council of Agriculture."[6] Independent Labour, on the other hand, promoted more left-wing policies on housing and price controls. Yet, despite these differences and the condemnation of the *Halifax Chronicle*, which warned its readers about the hazards of class resentment, in July 1920 the United Farmers elected seven members to the forty-three-seat legislature, while the Independent Labour Party elected four.[7]

While the Catholic press was hostile to Independent Labour's call for the nationalization of utilities and "natural sources of wealth" – its platform had been lifted from the openly socialist Independent Labour

Party in England – it was not surprising that successful Labour candidates, like Joseph Steele, secretary treasurer of the Trades and Labour Council, were elected in the colliery towns of Cape Breton.[8] Although Steele's pastor at Sacred Heart Parish, Fr Donald MacAdam, had preached against the Labour platform and even "rapped" the eventual winner from his Sydney pulpit, he recognized that Steele represented a sizeable block of Catholic voters and even suggested appointing him to the St F.X. board of governors.[9]

The only county in eastern Nova Scotia to elect a United Farmers candidate was Antigonish (the other representatives came from the counties of Colchester, Cumberland, and Hants). This was also not surprising, as local clergy like Fr "Little Doc" MacPherson, the "father of cooperation," had patronized political meetings where long-time Liberal and Conservative voters were asked to turn their backs on "the Lord's own Chosen people, the lawyers."[10] With complaints of poor crop prices and costly supplies, farmers rallied against "selfish politicians and capitalists," and elected the former town councillor Angus J. MacGillivray to the Legislature (although he voted as a Liberal).

While some were wary of a "jumble of parliamentary groups" clogging the business of the assembly and considered multiple parties to be discordant with the "traditions of British responsible government," many others, like the "energetic" Fr John J. MacKinnon of Lismore, felt that a multi-party government was the best tactic for securing political rights for minorities.[11] He even attacked *The Casket* for abusing the United Farmers, and the ensuing front-page debate was rather heated.[12]

Although short-lived, the success of the Farmer-Labour movement demonstrated that many Nova Scotians wanted change.[13] In December 1921, Bishop Morrison wrote to Prime Minister Mackenzie King to complain about the central railway management's "lack of sympathy" for the Maritimes and their obvious bias toward Ontario and the West.[14] These concerns were articulated as part of a new movement of "Maritime Rights," and although, as Ernie Forbes has demonstrated, each occupational group tended to define this movement "in terms of its own particular interest," there were commonalities.[15] The acknowledgment that local people had to assert control over their personal situations was gaining momentum.

THE CATHOLIC WOMEN'S LEAGUE

One group keen to challenge the postwar status quo was women. Although women had always been influential in the parishes, with the right to vote – granted in Nova Scotia in 1918 – females were an emerging political force. In the summer of 1920, several fledgling women's organizations met in Montreal and formed the Canadian Catholic Women's League (CWL). The mandate of the league was to spread "Catholic Feminism," and the organization – with its monthly magazine *The Canadian League* – was hailed as a "dawn of a new era." Catholic women must come forth "from their seclusion," urged one influential contributor, "and assist in the betterment of [the] poor war-torn world." With prominent members like the Irish nationalist and historian Katherine Hughes, who authored a biography of Archbishop Cornelius O'Brien of Halifax in 1906, the CWL confronted complex social questions and lobbied for stricter divorce laws.[16]

Following the second national CWL convention, held in Toronto in June 1921, its first diocesan council was organized at St Ninian's parish in August. A second council was formed only days later at Sacred Heart in Sydney and then another at Holy Redeemer in Whitney Pier (where a similar organization had existed since 1920).[17] To generate enthusiasm, the national executive sent Loretta Kneil of Edmonton (the sister of Katherine Hughes) to address meetings throughout eastern Nova Scotia. At Immaculata Hall at Mount Saint Bernard College, she encouraged women to embrace the league and get down to practical tasks.[18] According to Terence Fay, while "fulfilling the expectation of Catholic women," the ladies at these meetings also wished to be modern and "involved in contemporary society."[19]

As sub-divisions of the CWL sprang up across the region – a diocesan council was organized in 1922 and by 1924 it had a membership of over nine hundred – there was a clear focus on social and family issues.[20] At coastal Mulgrave, card parties and bake sales helped alleviate local poverty, while children from Sydney's St Mary's Orphanage were treated to theatrical plays at the Strand Theatre.[21] With increasing numbers of young women in the labour force, Sydney members also offered chaperoned accommodation in modern "rest rooms." The CWL sponsored lectures on home economics and hygiene, funded scholarships to Mount Saint Bernard College, and organized Catholic Girl Guide troops.[22]

ASSEMBLIES AND SAINTS

Organizations like the CWL signified a new era within Canadian Catholic society, a time of change that extended from lay participation to church design.[23] Many churches were rejuvenated during the decade of the 1920s. When Judique's new "halidom of Catholic Scots," the attractive St Andrew's Church, was consecrated by Bishop Morrison and Bishop Sandy in the summer of 1927 (the first double consecration in the region's history), onlookers revelled at the unique stone sanctuary.[24] At Boisdale, another beautiful sanctuary, the Church of St Andrew, was designed by the celebrated Pennsylvania architect Edward J. Weber. Fr Michael Gillis had read about Weber's work in the *Ecclesiastical Review* and during a visit to Pittsburgh asked the architect for ideas. Weber responded that, although he "would never see Boisdale," with the right facts and contours he would design something memorable. Many churchgoers, like Senator Donald MacLellan, the former MP for Inverness, assumed that St Andrew's was modelled after the cathedral of Argyle on the island of Iona (and there is a resemblance), but it was designed after a church near Oxford, England.[25]

Worshippers in these sanctuaries were proud of their faith, well catechised, and could defend their theology. Keen to express the faith publicly, International Eucharistic Congresses, bearing witness to the real presence of Jesus in the Eucharist, had been tremendous successes in large cities like London and Montreal.[26] In 1924 the first diocesan Eucharistic Congress in the Maritime provinces was held in "glorious weather" on the grounds of the St F.X. campus (the second was held in 1929 at Sacred Heart in Sydney). In an event publicized as a protest against "the growing materialism of the age," the Eucharist was carried from St Ninian's Cathedral to an altar that had been set up in the doorway of Somers Chapel. More than a thousand spectators (many of them elderly) knelt on the lawn for the service, which was followed by speeches and a stirring twilight Holy Hour.[27]

In 1927 a diocesan centre of devotion to the relics of the saints, the best "east of Quebec," was opened at St Joseph's Parish in Port Hawkesbury. Fr Angus Beaton had asked a former St F.X. classmate, a Jesuit working in Rome, to collect the holy relics and ship them to his parish. The centrepiece of the shrine, a statue of Saint Thérèse of Lisieux, was surrounded by many exotic pieces, including a "bit of the bone" of St Andrew, all of which were authenticated under the seal of the Roman congregation. There were also genuine "secondary relics" of St Francis of Assisi, the crypt of Gethsemane, and a few undocumented pieces.[28]

That the cornerstone of the Port Hawkesbury shrine was Thérèse of Lisieux – "the Little Flower" – is not surprising. The twenty-four-year-old French Carmelite nun died in Normandy of tuberculosis in 1897. While she had lived in relative obscurity, the publication of her personal notebooks, *Story of a Soul*, made her a spiritual sensation. Miracles attributed to her intercession were soon reported as far afield as Peru and Alaska, and by 1909 the veneration of Sister Thérèse was so widespread that Rome faced tremendous pressure to forgo the fifty-year waiting period and move immediately toward solemn beatification. When she was canonized in 1925 by Pope Pius XI, the exterior of St Peter's Basilica was illuminated for the first time in fifty years.[29] Back in eastern Nova Scotia, her life-size statue dominated the foyer of St Martha's hospital, and in 1927 her name was given to the new diocesan orphanage.

While saints were blessed role models who helped intercede for salvation, the supernatural sometimes had a darker side. In January 1922, sensationalism gripped the parish of St Andrews (and Nova Scotia generally), when tales of a poltergeist emanated from the small village of Caledonia Mills. Alexander MacDonald, his wife, and their adopted daughter, Mary Ellen, whose father was killed in the Drummond Mine explosion at Westville, Pictou County, in 1907, lived on a remote farm that was plagued by a series of mysterious fires. When further "spontaneous fires" were reported in their home, a local reporter was despatched to investigate.[30] Stories of "spooks" gripped readers of the *Halifax Herald* and the *Boston Globe*, as detectives and reporters descended on the rural community. The fires were likely the result of a wayward human hand, but folks were mesmerized by the stories of superstition. One author has even suggested that Bishop Morrison destroyed documents relating to the fires (or hid them), although such a reaction hardly befitted his personality.[31]

INDUSTRIAL CAPE BRETON

Few were aware of superstitions and omens more than the Cape Breton coal miners. By 1920, the veterans of the Great War who had traded their army fatigues for an Edison electric mine lamp and a pick and shovel, still had much to fear. Conditions in the mines, once described by a journalist as "the cellar of hell," remained squarely in the public eye, as did the price of coal and rates of production.[32] By March 1920 several companies, including DISCO and DOMCO, had merged to create the British Empire Steel Corporation (BESCO) under the direction of Montreal businessman Roy Mitchell Wolvin. As UMW District 26 served notice to the new company that the miners wanted to revise their contract, more than one priest observed that a lack of leadership rendered Catholic miners susceptible to radical representatives like "[Silby] Barrett and [J.B.] McLaughlin [sic] who persuaded them to act in defiance of the Company."[33]

The following month, union president Barrett was defeated in the District 26 election by Robert Baxter, but J.B. McLachlan was re-elected as secretary-treasurer. From the glebe at St Agnes, Fr John Hugh MacDonald felt that Barrett's ouster was evidence that saner opinions had prevailed. He was certain that the miners would also have ousted McLachlan except that he was "elected by acclamation before the climax was reached." Yet, according to McLachlan's biographer David Frank, MacDonald had the analysis backward. In fact, the radical was elected by acclamation due to his overwhelming popularity. In other words, "no candidate was prepared to challenge him." By the end of 1920, McLachlan was considered "king among the coal miners."[34]

Although the diocese still had no formal position on labour-capital relations, the savagery of the Russian Revolution, and the ensuing chaos, made many Catholics leery of District 26's leftward shift. Significantly, however, while *The Casket* was critical of radicals like McLachlan, as Ernie Forbes has noted, the paper "was equally critical of BESCO."[35] It is also clear that by 1923 many priests, such as the former assistant at Sacred Heart Fr John J. MacKinnon, recognized that any "carping criticism of labour" would do tremendous damage to the Church.[36] It was wrong, as one priest noted, to "assume that the Church's only concern [was] to oppose socialism and 'the Reds.'"[37]

In his *Casket* column, Fr Tompkins began reaching out to labour. His scribblings focused on wages, working hours, and housing, while demanding that capital "obey the laws of decency and good order." Perceptively, he recognized that those miners who demanded regular shifts and decent wages were not necessarily advocating class strife or Marxist atheism. As one reporter noted after a union meeting in the 1920s, "the Highlanders can't stand knocking religion."[38] Any attempt to break organized labour, or refuse to deal with the unions, Tompkins warned, was "to travel over the road that Russia has gone."[39]

While the Church opposed socialism, what precisely was meant by socialism – as opposed to the more clearly defined communism – was not always apparent. Although intellectuals employed the phrases "capitalistic system" and advocated the "taking of industry," this lexicon had different meanings in different circles.[40] Even among the editors of *The Casket* there was some confusion. When it became clear that the UMW was "anxious for a trial of strength," the paper editorialized that Ottawa should take over the coal industry to "put an end to the ceaseless conflict between owners and workmen." Although the editor hoped that this policy would weaken radicals like McLachlan, he did not appreciate that the nationalization of industry was the bedrock of any serious socialist platform.[41]

In the spring of 1920, a "Catholic Workman" writing in the Catholics press – likely Fr John Hugh MacDonald – noted that Catholic miners faced a difficult dilemma. On the one hand, they could not abandon District 26 as it was their only means of advocating for better conditions, while on the other, they were being led astray by the radicals who controlled their union. He also scolded those who rebuked radical ideas without replacing them with practical ones. "Does *The Casket* believe that socialists cannot be reformed," he asked, "that labour leaders are hopelessly unchristian, and that low-brows are past praying for?"[42]

In accordance with the late Pope Pius X's dictum that evil was strengthened by the "apathy of the good," the Cape Breton clergy wanted action. As early as 1919, Fr John Hugh MacDonald, Fr Michael Gillis, and Fr James Michael Kiely established a Tuesday evening economic study club to discuss Hansard, micro-economics, and the need for Catholic action.[43] Then in the autumn of 1920, the Glace Bay Knights of Columbus organized an evening school under the supervision of St Anne's curates Fr Peter MacMullin and Fr Ronald C. MacGillivray. In an effort to train and identify "useful and intelligent leaders," the study sessions on mining techniques and finances were conducted by prominent instructors like the Glace Bay lawyer and St F.X. governor Neil McArthur.

As District 26 negotiated its first contract with BESCO – which was known locally as the "Montreal Agreement" – a new column in *The Casket*, "Labour Notes," editorialized on themes like "The War against the Labour Unions" and published commentary on Fr John Ryan's popular pamphlets such as "Capital and Labour."[44] A priest-intellectual in the archdiocese of St Paul, Minnesota, and a lecturer at the Catholic University of America, Ryan was a controversial figure; however, he intrigued Catholic intellectuals with his radical reading of *Rerum Novarum*.[45]

In the early summer, the diocese announced that Fr Ryan would participate in the fourth annual Education and Social Conference scheduled for August. As the priest's books were not readily accessible in the colliery towns, he was also engaged as a sermonist at Sydney Mines, Glace Bay, and Whitney Pier.[46] In the meantime, the Catholic Truth Society flooded the diocese with Ryan's publications such as *Catholic Doctrine on the Right of Self Government* and *A Catechism on the Social Question*.

Recruiting Fr Ryan to speak at the 1921 conference was a real achievement. The delegates were welcomed at Mount Saint Bernard College by Fr Tompkins, who also moderated Ryan's session. The first speaker to the podium was the veteran Halifax longshoreman John T. Joy, who had once been described by J.B. McLachlan as the "best labor man in the province."[47] A member of the royal commission that had investigated DOMCO in 1917, Joy engrossed his audience with a detailed history of trade unionism in Cape Breton and the violent suppression of guilds like the Knights of Labour. Setting the tone for discussions, he also assured the audience that a fear of Bolshevism, regularly expressed in newspapers like the *Glace Bay Post*, was a red herring.[48]

Throughout the afternoon, with the warm summer rain beating down upon the windowpanes, questions of housing, collective bargaining, social insurance, and labour legislation were hotly debated.[49] The speakers came from the judiciary, clergy, academia, and labour. William P. Delaney, the "diplomatic" vice-president of District 26, argued that mistrust was ubiquitous within industrial relations because "the spirit of Christ [did] not govern the actions of men." He condemned compulsory arbitration as undemocratic (fearing that the "cards were stacked" against the miners), and advocated for a system of compulsory investigation that would delay a strike until a public inquiry was convened.[50] Like Joy, Delaney thought that rumours of a Bolshevik revolution were exaggerated.[51]

According to the *North Sydney Herald*, the educational and social conference demonstrated the new relationship between "education and religion," and the need for cooperation between labour and capital.[52] While there was a conspicuous absence of radical voices – one former vice-president of District 26 demanded that the conference hear from the average miner – the delegates challenged the status quo.[53] Months later, one Cape Breton pastor chastised St F.X. for building a fancy new hockey arena while "hundreds of children [in his parish] must stay home from school for lack of clothing." A visit to the "scores of poverty-stricken homes in Sydney," he exhorted, "would surely modify the ideas some have of what this country can afford."[54]

In the autumn of 1921, the *Maritime Labour Herald*, the "organ of the working people," became the official newspaper of District 26. The editor's pen was held by William Ulrich Cotton, a veteran journalist and former publisher of a socialist newspaper in Quebec. Although the *Herald* was "crammed with local news and letters, resolutions from union locals and reports from conferences," its avowed enemy was BESCO (and often capitalism in general).[55] Most distressing was that, on the heels of the educational and social conference, the paper attacked the clergy, Catholic or otherwise, for misusing their authority in speaking on social and economic questions.

While articles on workplace safety and inadequate housing soon raised the circulation of the *Maritime Labour Herald* to some six thousand, in many Catholic homes, the paper's virulent attacks on the bible and on religion itself made it seem a "medium of false propaganda."[56] Roman Catholics were not the only Christians insulted by some of the *Herald*'s editorials. Rev. D.M. Gillis of St Paul's Presbyterian Church in Sydney maintained that the paper should be "burnt unread," while a local Baptist minister warned that its blunt rhetoric would take Canada into a "machine gun millennium."[57]

In December 1921 the "Montreal Agreement" expired and BESCO immediately initiated a wage cut of some 33 per cent. By Christmas, most families were surviving on one or two shifts per week, and "hardship and foreboding" hung over the miners' homes.[58] On 21 January 1922, a man who was denied credit at the company store in New Aberdeen pushed the clerk aside and helped himself to the inventory. Within moments he was joined by other frustrated miners. That night the "Pluck-Me Store" was attacked by a violent mob, and the following evening, whatever supplies remained were looted.[59] The priest at St John the Baptist, Fr J.A.M.

Gillis, was shaken by the raid, and assured his bishop that none of his parishioners were involved. Of course, Catholics had joined the hungry mob, but Bishop Morrison cleverly congratulated the people of New Aberdeen in any case on "their good sense of religious and moral honesty."[60]

The general response to the pillaging at New Aberdeen was surprisingly supportive of the looters. While some grumbled that there was "too much violent demagoguism in the UMW," *The Casket* opined that the men were trapped between "reckless labour leaders" and a company that "plunder[ed] the people's pockets by inflated prices."[61] One farmer from Fraser's Mills in Antigonish County, while not wanting to see a repeat of the New Aberdeen incident, admitted that "necessity knows no bounds."[62]

With BESCO indifferent to the grievances of their employees, the clergy watched over the mood of their parishioners. In the cold and anxious February of 1922, the "very brilliant and very attractive" Fr Thomas O'Reilly Boyle, a native of Placentia, Newfoundland (but raised in Whitney Pier), was sent by St F.X. to organize a People's School at Glace Bay.[63] He was to reach out to Catholics "unable to avail themselves of the benefits of the present educational activities" with a mandate to start an educational effort along "sane Catholic lines."[64]

The Glace Bay People's School focused on everything from literacy to economics. St F.X. professor Fr D.J. MacDonald and agricultural specialist Fr Miles Tompkins drove to Cape Breton to lend their expertise, while Fr John Hugh MacDonald gave lectures on "The Church and the Social Question."[65] "I have to report progress and every indication of success for our venture," Fr Boyle wrote from Glace Bay a year later. "Nearly 300 enrolled on Monday night. On Tuesday 350 showed up for class." The school was "the talk of the town" and the students were enthusiastic.[66] Writing to a Glace Bay barrister, the Old Rector made it known that the People's School was so important that the college was "disposed to make any reasonable sacrifice to it."[67]

Two principal concerns were raised at the People's School: that the "older and saner" miners were not active within District 26, and that the local media gave disproportionate coverage to radical voices.[68] At the annual clergy retreat in the spring of 1922, the Cape Breton priests urged Bishop Morrison to issue a pastoral letter to counter the rhetoric of the *Maritime Labour Herald*. District 26 was due to elect officers in mid-August and the priests hoped that episcopal push-back would benefit the moderate candidates.

In early August, John Moffatt, the former grand secretary of the Provincial Workers Association, warned that the miners were "in a very ugly mood" and that the province should "be prepared for the worst."[69] Realizing that labour were unlikely to listen to "reason and good sense," Bishop Morrison judged that any pastoral letter from his office would be regarded as "playing into the hands of capitalism."[70] The eventual re-election of the radical "Red" Dan Livingstone as president by over five thousand votes and J.B. McLachlan by over six thousand confirmed Morrison's decision that intervention could not have halted the union's "left turn."[71] And when a strike ensued (armed soldiers were once again despatched to Sydney), the response from local parishes was also subdued. As no ecclesiastical statement could check the "revolutionary tendencies" of "professional agitators," the frustrated clergy could merely stock the Catholic Truth Society racks with pamphlets devoted to Catholic principles on labour.[72] It was hardly bold intervention.

In the midst of strikes, anger, and growing resentment, it was clear that traditional reliance on clerical authority and the "good sense" of Catholics was a futile strategy. At St F.X., Fr Tompkins spent the rainy autumn thinking of ways to harness the energy of District 26 and reach out to the radicals. He and J.B. McLachlan even discussed the possibility of a labour college in a new university of the Maritimes that the priest was promoting. Despite McLachlan's communist sympathies, Tompkins thought he was a "clever fellow."[73]

Given the sense of powerlessness among Cape Breton clergy, it is not surprising that a Catholic union was soon proposed. One of its most ardent advocates, Fr John James MacNeil of St Anthony's Parish in Glace Bay, had once worked in a Newfoundland copper mine and understood the realities of working-class families.[74] Convinced that District 26 was failing his parishioners, he demanded a Canadian and Catholic solution.[75] When his former classmates from the Grand Seminary of Montreal noted that Catholic unions in Quebec, rooted in both social Catholicism and French-Canadian nationalism, had been extremely successful, he was hooked.

In the spring of 1923, Fr MacNeil despatched to his bishop a roster of interested parishioners who were "heartily sick of the continued agitation and exploitation."[76] In the short term, the scheme was kept under wraps as there was some danger to supporters.[77] Bishop

Morrison hoped that other Catholic miners would acknowledge the disasters brought on by the "irreligious and Godless tactics of some of the present labour leaders," and suggested that the men have talks with fellow workmen of the faith.[78] By June 1923, other parishes were covertly taking names of supporters, while priests were "feeling out the situation" in New Waterford and New Aberdeen.[79]

Within weeks, the community of Dominion became the heart of the Catholic union movement. In June the St Anthony's LOC publicly objected to the "offensive material" published in the *Maritime Labour Herald* and branded the paper "moral poison."[80] Bishop Morrison, impressed by the courage of the men of St Anthony's, considered them the vanguard for a new labour movement. Nevertheless, despite this momentum, the proposed Catholic union was quickly and aggressively confronted. The first salvo was fired by the Ottawa bureaucrat Eugene M. Quirk, who argued that, although the Cape Breton miner had to deal with a corporation "lacking the touch of human nature or sentiment," Catholic labour associations had little place outside Quebec.

The main problem was that Quebec unions, rooted in French Canadian nationalism, were supported exclusively by French speakers in communities that were almost wholly Catholic.[81] In other words, they were most effective in areas outside of Montreal where Church and ethnicity were essentially synonymous. Imposing Catholic unions on multi-ethnic communities with large Protestant populations, such as Glace Bay or Whitney Pier, would do more harm than good. Upon reflection, others agreed. "It would not only set Protestant against Catholic," wrote one Sydney priest, "but it would also tend to a division among Catholics themselves."[82]

There was also the question of BESCO's response. If Catholic miners left District 26, would they have the clout to bargain for a decent wage? Would the company take them seriously? Would BESCO negotiate with a Catholic Union in good faith, knowing that its members would not resort to strikes or violence? Could BESCO "do the right thing" without labour having to "follow up a belligerent course of agitation?"[83] These were compelling questions from a Church that had once blamed "foreign agitators" for the problems at the pithead.

In late June 1923, BESCO steelworkers went on strike (District 26 also called a sympathetic work stoppage). Reacting to bouts of violence, BESCO asked civil authorities to summon the military, and

Figure 5.1 | Military Encamped at Sydney Steel Plant

some two hundred troops were despatched to the colliery towns. On 30 June soldiers arriving on an armoured train in Sydney were deployed around the entrances to the steel plant. Weeks later, mounted police, known as Premier "Armstrong's Army," attacked steelworkers holding a meeting in Whitney Pier and assaulted other citizens returning from evening church services.[84] As the local clergy tried to calm angry parishioners, the commanding officer of the Royal Canadian Regiment formally requested a chaplain to minister to Catholic soldiers protecting company property.

The military's request for a chaplain illustrates the precarious position of the Church in the colliery towns. Although responsible for the spiritual welfare of all followers, priests would find it "embarrassing" to be seen consorting with the soldiers protecting BESCO's assets. Ill feelings still lingered from the incident of the "rapid fire" gun on church property at Bridgeport in 1909 and, with the news that the militia had fired their guns over the heads of protestors outside the steel plant gate, priests were not keen to cosy-up to the perpetrators. As there was no way to predict how miners would react to soldiers in the pews, it was better to minister to them in their own quarters.[85]

BESCO's eventual victory over the strikers further demoralized the colliery towns. By Christmas 1923, most of the young people in Whitney Pier could not even afford to get married (let alone raise a family).[86] When the pastor at Sydney Mines wrote his Ordinary to complain that another strike was looming in January 1924, Morrison responded that he could never tell "what was behind some of the plans that were being formulated by industrialists."[87] Demanding fiscal transparency from BESCO, Fr MacKinnon was indignant that a town like Sydney Mines should "be allowed to go to ruin."[88]

In August 1924, the influential Fr Donald MacAdam, pastor at Sydney's Sacred Heart Church since 1900, died unexpectedly.[89] The *Halifax Herald* noted the loss of one of the "the most outstanding figures" in eastern Canada, and the mayor of Sydney, James McConnell, wondered how to replace such an "influential personality."[90] Sacred Heart was an important parish at the best of times, but in the tense summer of 1924 Catholic leadership on George Street was critical. For the first time, Bishop Morrison was forced to think strategically about a clerical appointment. In October Fr John Hugh MacDonald was transferred from New Waterford to Sydney. It was a smart administrative decision as the Urban College graduate understood the complexities of labour and was also active in the study clubs.

As Fr MacDonald settled in at Sacred Heart, BESCO continued to face weak markets that necessitated production cutbacks, and families had to survive on one or two shifts per week. The *Maritime Labour Herald* advocated letting the "Miners Run the Mines." *The Casket*, on the *other* hand, retreated from its previous stance on nationalizing the coalfields and now demanded that the provincial government take a proactive role. The time has arrived, it editorialized, "when the mere word of a corporation ... can no longer be reasonably accepted without proof of what they say."[91]

In November 1924, as cold north-Atlantic winds whipped through New Waterford and Dominion, BESCO proposed a contract with a wage cut of some 20 per cent. Throughout the frigid months of January and February 1925 (the colliery towns were covered by deep snow) the men, unwilling to accept such a drastic cut without regular work, toiled without a contract. Angry miners, mistrustful of the company, complained of kick-backs and bribes to hapless politicians.[92] By March, although things had "brightened up around the steelworks," the miners were once again on the picket line.

The strike of 1925, which began on 6 March, was one of the most notorious work stoppages in Canadian history. Having endured months of irregular employment, the families of New Aberdeen, Caledonia, and Dominion No. 6 were denied credit at their local company store (for some, the only source of food). When the men walked off the job, BESCO's vice-president, J.E. McClurg, the former general manager of Halifax Shipyards, uttered one of the most infamous lines in Nova Scotia's labour history. He told a Canadian Press reporter: "We hold the cards. Things are getting better every day they stay out. Let them stay out two months or six – it matters not, eventually they will come crawling to us – They cannot stand the gaff."[93] It was a comment, *The Casket* fired back, that might have been made by "a general manager of a bootleggers' league rather than by a general manager of the biggest employing corporation in [the] country."[94]

According to historian Robert Morgan, the period from 1923 to 1925 "branded the Cape Breton soul."[95] People never forgot the deaths of the elderly from malnourishment, or the sight of children wearing clothes made from flour bags. When news of a spike in infant mortality reached the capital in early March 1925, action was mobilized. *The Halifax Herald* noted the "absolute deprivation" of the community,[96] and the mayor of Sydney told Prime Minister MacKenzie King that his town's resources were "about exhausted."[97] And on 12 March, Bishop Morrison, who had made special trips to the colliery towns to investigate and to confer with the priests and religious sisters in those districts, issued a circular calling upon Catholics to gather financial aid for the striking miners, and begging the people to "come to the rescue of [the] children."[98] In the meantime, a special collection was taken up in the diocese on Sunday March 22 and was distributed by a committee of clergymen in the affected areas (even the professors at St F.X. "passed the hat").[99]

In late March, Morrison went to Halifax to discuss the strike with representatives of the provincial government. The evening session of the legislature was cancelled so that the members of both the executive and legislative council could attend the meeting. Entering historic Province House, Canada's oldest seat of government, he was escorted up the dimly lit staircase and into the ornate Red Chamber, where he was introduced to the council by Antigonish MLA and one-time Heatherton "stampeder" William Chisholm. Sitting at a large table under an impressive chandelier, the men "thrashed the matter out in almost every angle it could be approached."[100]

Throughout the meeting, which went late into the night, Morrison begged the politicians to force BESCO to open its books. In response, officials confessed that while they were anxious for a solution, they were afraid of pushing too hard lest they drive the company into receivership.[101] On his way out of the building, the minister of mines handed the bishop a copy of an internal government memorandum on coal, which suggested that BESCO was bleeding money. Although Morrison hoped that the memorandum might make it into the hands of the miners, he still wanted BESCO to submit to a thorough investigation and asked the government to pay attention to the problem of "watered stock."[102]

Although the meeting with the provincial government offered hope that "some remedy [would] be forthcoming," it was quickly dashed.[103] Two days later, Premier Ernest Howard Armstrong, a former mayor of Yarmouth, voted down a proposal to send aid to Sydney. In an extraordinary interview with the *Halifax Herald*, he argued that the stories of deprivation emanating from Cape Breton were exaggerated. He charged a Protestant clergyman in Glace Bay with spreading embellished myths of starvation and suggested that Morrison was misled.[104] Angry, the prelate remained mum on his meeting with the government, opting instead to focus on the work of the Sydney Relief Committee.[105]

The relief committee had worked tirelessly. By the end of March, some $8,564 had been collected across the region.[106] While individuals gave out of their own pockets, the parish of Pomquet gave $92.50; Giants Like, Guysborough County, $60.43; and even the poverty-stricken parish of Canso, with many fishermen "just as bad off as the [Cape Breton] miners," sent $136.85.[107] Money also came from other parts of Canada. The Archbishop of Toronto sent $50, while the national treasury of the Catholic Women's League sent $100. In Sydney, Fr MacDonald faced the unenviable task of distributing the monies equitably but noted that the funds were but "a drop," as Glace Bay alone required some $11,000 in aid.[108]

During these desperate months, the financial support for the strikers gave the Church credibility on the picket line. Offering money for milk held power that dwarfed pastoral letters and pamphlets. The relief effort, noted one priest, was a "telling rebuke administered to the Red element" that had contended that the Catholic Church was "indifferent" to the welfare of the working class. Many of those "who have been heretofore very critical in this respect," wrote an excited Fr MacDonald from Sydney, "are now loud in their praises of the prompt action taken … by the Catholics of the diocese."[109] Those praises grew louder in April when the president of BESCO accused the diocese of "taking sides" against the company.[110]

Although the clergy found it lamentable that District 26 still associated with a "Red element," there was confidence that radicalism was waning.[111] While the May Day parade of 1925 brought strikers into the streets with banners that read, "Workers of the World Unite! Down with Capitalism," Fr Michael MacAdam at St Anne's stated that the parade was not large. David Frank's analysis in his biography of J.B. McLachlan seems to support MacAdam's claim, as he noted that "the [communist] party's role in the direction of the strike was extremely limited."[112]

In June, to force BESCO's hand in the great card game of its vice-president, J.E. McClurg, District 26 withdrew the maintenance men from the New Waterford power plant. On the evening of 11 June, several BESCO employees and company police went to Waterford Lake to restart the generators. They were confronted by a throng of strikers, and the largely untrained company police began firing. When the smoke cleared, William Davis, a New Waterford miner, lay dead. Some five thousand people attended his funeral. In the resulting anger, the Sydney Mines company store was looted and "smashed to a pile of kindling," while the wash house at the No. 12. colliery in New Waterford was burned.[113] "The struggle," Morrison foresaw, "will be drawn out till some one side is completely beaten."[114]

On 16 July, a new provincial Conservative government, led by Edgar Nelson Rhodes, was sworn into office. Promising to support "rights for labour," and with the backing of the *Halifax Herald*, the Tories had defeated an incumbent and tone-deaf Liberal government that had held power in Nova Scotia for forty-two years. Premier Rhodes immediately went to Sydney and met with both BESCO and District 26. In August the government proposed a six-month temporary contract with a wage cut of 6 to 8 per cent, pending an inquiry into the coal industry. It also agreed to organize a Royal Commission and to return to BESCO one fifth of the annual coal royalties the company had paid to the province. In return, all striking miners would be reinstated without a blacklist.[115]

While the great strike had ended, its effects on both Church and society were profound. When an official with a Catholic union in Quebec offered to "help destroy the Reds" in Cape Breton, Bishop Morrison rejected his "dangerous" rhetoric. The province was finally investigating coal, he countered, and it was best left to the authorities to make judgments on the merits of District 26.[116]

The provincial inquiry into the Nova Scotia coal industry began in September 1925 under the direction of British civil servant Sir Andrew Rae Duncan. Recognizing the contribution of the diocese during the strike, Premier Rhodes asked the Old Rector to sit on the commission (Hume Cronyn a businessman and former MP was the other member). While the Church was pleased to wield some influence, there was some risk in having the St F.X. president serve as a commissioner. Should the miners find the results unpalatable, for instance, or if MacPherson uttered something offensive, the reputation of the diocesan college could suffer.[117]

With the temporary contract due to expire in February 1926, the Duncan Commission hurriedly launched its investigation into wages, work conditions, and BESCO's "capital structure and financial policies."[118] Hearings began on Remembrance Day at the courthouse in Sydney, and witnesses, including Silby Barrett and Roy Wolvin, gave testimony. While the Old Rector asked few questions, he was instrumental in obtaining the testimony of J.B. McLachlan, who was not originally scheduled to appear.[119]

In the meantime, BESCO continued to close collieries. From Sydney Mines, Fr MacKinnon mused that the company was "taking the very efficient means of making Bolsheviks by the hundreds." Although his parishioners had maintained their dignity, he expected some lawlessness. After all, "what [could] be expected for five long months when people will become crazed with hunger?"[120] Even amid an investigation, BESCO seemed unreasonable. "What on earth can the company have in mind by this step at this time of the year?" Bishop Morrison wondered. "It is impossible to understand them."[121]

In the main, the Duncan Commission Report, released in mid-January 1926, was well received. "The more I study it," asserted one priest, "the more I find to give thought to."[122] One of its recommendations was that company police, company stores, and company housing had to go. While it criticized the factionalism of the United Mine Workers and the aggressive rhetoric of the *Maritime Labour Herald*, the commission also recommended that BESCO acknowledge the legitimacy of District 26.[123]

From the Church's perspective, however, the report had a fatal flaw, and that was the recommendation that the "check-off" be abolished. At the bishop's residence, Morrison's phone rang incessantly with protests. Knowing that churches, schools, and hospitals were dependent on the regular contributions from the miners' pay envelopes, it seemed incredible that the Old Rector let the recommendation stand. "What in the world came over Dr. MacPherson when he did not protect the parishes down here?" asked Fr J.H. Nicholson in New Waterford.[124]

Frantically, Bishop Morrison began to lobby for the status quo. Knowing that McClurg, whom he despised, would be happy to "to let the church 'check-off' go with the rest," he stressed that the diocese had always tried to promote harmony between BESCO and the union, "not unfrequently almost compromising their own status with the people, in their efforts along [those] lines."[125]

The truth, of course, was that the abolition of the check-off would be more disastrous to the Church than any communist pamphlet. As one Glace Bay Catholic wrote: "With the check-off discontinued it is useless to undertake the work of the orphanage as far as the mining districts are concerned, and as for talking St. F. X College, we might as well dismiss it."[126] Fortuitously, District 26 president John W. MacLeod, who ironically "owed his election to the radicals," was sympathetic.[127] Knowing that many wanted to maintain the check-off as a means of collecting union dues, Catholics swamped the UMW with letters and petitions.[128] Ultimately, the miners ratified a new contract with BESCO, and voted to abolish the reviled company stores but to retain the Church check-off.

In 1928, still facing shrinking markets, BESCO collapsed into bankruptcy and its resources were reassembled into the Dominion Steel and Coal Corporation (DOSCO). The *Halifax Herald* welcomed the restructuring and declared that Cape Breton could look with optimism to the future. But, as Ernie Forbes has argued in *The Maritime Rights Movement*, this was merely a public relations ploy.[129] Cynicism and gloom hung over parishes like Reserve and Sydney Mines and, while the fear of radicalism remained, the blame for the perpetual problems of the coal mines had slowly shifted – away from the "foreign agitators" onto the industry itself.

THE PEOPLE'S SCHOOL

As the coal miners of Cape Breton fought for better conditions, Fr James Tompkins felt that the moment had arrived for St F.X. to shed its "worn-out tradition[s]," change its mandate, and take education to the people.[130] He had been energized by his fruitful negotiations with the Carnegie Corporation to fund a French chair and was sure he had found a formula for fundraising success. "Nothing in my experiences comes near to this experience," Tompkins confided to Fr "Little Doc" MacPherson. "I have had dejected periods and I have spent a frightful pile of money, thank God, however, it is my own."[131]

Tompkins's enthusiasm also came from the knowledge that his Carnegie friends were willing to sponsor other projects. "Has your Lordship been thinking about that People's School (Danish Type)?" he asked Morrison. "I am almost certain I could get 50 or 100 thousand for that."[132] Envisioning a program that would focus on farming, home economics, and civic education, Tompkins pleaded with the Old Rector to "keep the People's School business booming."[133] Meanwhile, the priest pored over the words of Limerick's Bishop O'Dwyer on the education problem in Ireland and even published an exposé on the Carnegie Corporation in *The Casket*.[134] In private, he bragged that eastern Nova Scotia was "about fifty years ahead of the rest of America."[135]

Although Morrison respected Tompkins's passion and fundraising acumen, he proceeded cautiously. Having studied the Scandinavian People's Schools, he thought that a similar enterprise in Nova Scotia would require "a sustaining effort for upwards of twenty years." Facing a sluggish economy, and dwindling markets for Cape Breton coal, St F.X. needed a "good strong fund to see the proposition through."[136] While sympathetic, Tompkins stressed that "such schools were coming."[137] Learning that the Carnegie Corporation would fund "1 to 4 months in winter to farmers, fishermen ... and 1 week to 2 months in summer to home making, etc," ready to "fall into any plan," he asked the bishop to talk the thing over with "Dr Hugh [the Old Rector] and the Sisters [of St Martha]."[138]

In the spring of 1920, St F.X. was at a crossroads. Despite its many achievements over the past sixty-five years, there was a growing awareness that the "common people" in the fields, on the seas, and in the mines had more expertise on economic and social matters than the professors teaching in its classrooms.[139] The college's mandate to educate young men for the seminary and foster a Catholic elite was no longer adequate. Between 1914 and 1918, to mobilize the citizenry, the government employed mass education effectively, with Red Cross committees, war-loan bureaus, and so forth, to bring the people together "spiritually, physically, and industrially." Now, in a postwar society, the nation's colleges needed to use the same educational extension tactics to solve problems and create opportunities for those people who once faced life with "dull resignation." While there was some opposition – a few of the college's governors dreaded Tompkins's restlessness – most were supportive. Even Morrison, who demanded "specific ideas" and "definite studies," appreciated Tompkins impulse.[140]

In December 1920 Fr Tompkins wrote a pamphlet entitled *Knowledge for the People*, which George Boyle in his biography of Tompkins described as "the key statement of his life."[141] The priest printed 5,000 copies for free distribution. It was a call to St F.X. to embrace a new spirit of education through extension work. If farmers, fishermen, and miners had no chance of attending St F.X., then the college would go to them. Citing the examples of the Workers' Educational Association in England and the Irish Gaelic League, Tompkins envisioned an extension program similar to that of the University of Wisconsin in Madison that had striven since 1891 to "bring education to "every family in the state".[142] Fighting perceptions that clergy should stick to spiritual matters, he wanted the movement led by Catholic priests. When "undertaken by the representatives of the Church," he pointed out, the material improvement of lives would be raised to the spiritual plane.

Knowledge for the People was read widely as a "much needed renaissance in university aims."[143] From Lismore, Fr John J. MacKinnon, a supporter of the United Farmers and no friend of the status quo, foresaw that the pamphlet would do the diocese "much good."[144] With copies circulating through the region, the St F.X. board of governors had a "stunning sweetening" and could not have been "better disposed" or "more alive" to organizing the school. "It is really astounding," Tompkins confided to the archbishop of Toronto, "to see how things are done here when we consider the great possibilities of this institution."[145] Writing to the editor of *The Casket*, Tompkins declared: "the hour has struck when St F.X. must get into the field."[146]

During the Christmas season of 1920, *The Casket* ran a full-page advertisement for an inaugural People's School to be held from 17 January to 12 March 1921. No admission exam was required except that the students be over the age of seventeen and "desirous of improving their education." Scholars would be accommodated in Antigonish town at reasonable rates, while the school itself was free (the provincial agricultural department provided a generous

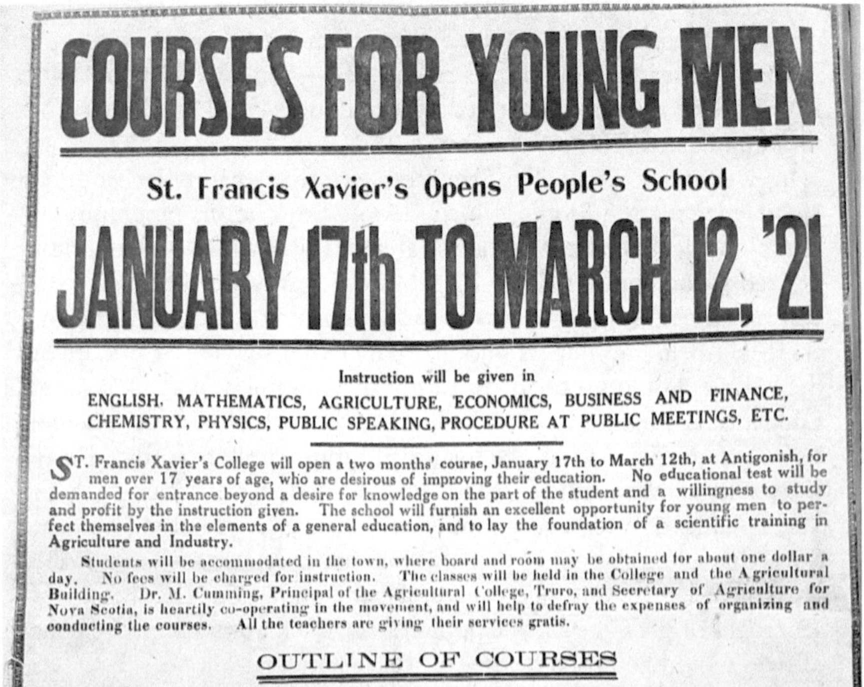

COURSES FOR YOUNG MEN

St. Francis Xavier's Opens People's School

JANUARY 17th TO MARCH 12, '21

Instruction will be given in

ENGLISH, MATHEMATICS, AGRICULTURE, ECONOMICS, BUSINESS AND FINANCE, CHEMISTRY, PHYSICS, PUBLIC SPEAKING, PROCEDURE AT PUBLIC MEETINGS, ETC.

ST. Francis Xavier's College will open a two months' course, January 17th to March 12th, at Antigonish, for men over 17 years of age, who are desirous of improving their education. No educational test will be demanded for entrance beyond a desire for knowledge on the part of the student and a willingness to study and profit by the instruction given. The school will furnish an excellent opportunity for young men to perfect themselves in the elements of a general education, and to lay the foundation of a scientific training in Agriculture and Industry.

Students will be accommodated in the town, where board and room may be obtained for about one dollar a day. No fees will be charged for instruction. The classes will be held in the College and the Agricultural Building. Dr. M. Cumming, Principal of the Agricultural College, Truro, and Secretary of Agriculture for Nova Scotia, is heartily co-operating in the movement, and will help to defray the expenses of organizing and conducting the courses. All the teachers are giving their services gratis.

OUTLINE OF COURSES

ARITHMETIC: (3 hours a week. Rev. Dr. M. M. Coady). Fundamental operations, Fractions, Decimals, Interest, Percentages, Stocks and Shares, Mensuration including plain surfaces and solids, Proportion, etc.

ENGLISH: Language: (3 hours a week. Rev. John R. MacDonald.) Grammar, Composition, Letter-Writing.

Literature: (2 hours a week. Prof W. H. Bucknell, M. A.) Scott: "The Talisman." Shakespeare: "Twelfth Night." Talks on Literature, the object being to develop an appreciation of books and reading.

ECONOMICS: (2 hours a week. Dr. D. J. MacDonald and Mr. F. Coyne.) Early Stages of Industrial Development, Rise of Modern Industry, The Consumption of Wealth, its influence on human welfare, Value and Prices, Forces Fixing Prices, Money and Banking, Production and Labor, Production and Capital, Co-operation, Distribution, Profits, Rent, Wages, Interest, Taxation, The Relation of Government to the Economic Organization.

CHEMISTRY: (3 hours a week. Rev. M. N. Tompkins, B. S. A.) Simple Elements and Chemical Compounds, Detailed Examination of the most Important Elements. Chemistry of Air, Water, Fertilizers, and Foods.

PHYSICS: (2 hours a week. Mr. Fred Ferguson.) Elements of Mechanics, Thermometry and Calorimetry, Optical Instruments; Electricity and Magnetism. The lectures will be directed towards making the student familiar with the application of the Principle of Conservation of Energy. Demonstration will be given of practical devices that illustrate the principle dealt with, such as levers and pulleys, steam and gas engines, the microscope and telescope, the electric generator and motor.

BUSINESS AND FINANCE: (2 hours a week. W. P. Reynolds, Esq., Manager of Canadian Bank of Commerce.) Business and Commerce, Theory of Bookkeeping, Principles of Accounting, Business Correspondence, Investments, Joint Stock and Co-operative Companies, Banking.

PUBLIC SPEAKING: (One session a week. Under the direction of Rev. James Boyle, M. A.) A Debating Club will be organized. Particular attention will be given to the manner of conducting Public Meetings and Debating Clubs.

AGRICULTURE: (1) Stock Breeding: (2 hours a week. Rev. M. N. Tompkins, B. S. A.) Importance of live stock, Types of Farm Animals, the Art of Breeding—Producing Animals of the Required Type,—Cattle, Horses, Sheep, Swine and Poultry. Principal Breeds, and Outstanding Qualities.

(2). Feeding Farm Animals: (3 hours a week. Rev. Dr. Hugh MacPherson). Nutrition, Food Values, Analysis of Farm-Grown Crops and Mill Feeds, Feeding of Young Stock, Feeding for Production, Feeding of Various Classes of Farm Animals will be considered in detail.

(3) Soils and Crops: (3 hours a week. Rev. Dr. Hugh MacPherson). Origin of Soils, Types of Soil, with special reference to soils in Eastern Nova Scotia, Factors and Conditions that constitute the fertility of the soil, Treatment of Soils, Drainage, Cultivation, Rotation, etc., Importance of good seed in crop raising, Seed Selection, Preparation of the ground for the seed, Special Features in Crop Raising such as Spraying, etc.

(4) Veterinary Hygiene: (1 period a week. D. A. MacIsaac, V. S., B. V. Sc.) Sanitary Care of Stock, Ventilation, Water Supply, Milk and Meat Sanitation, First Aid in Sickness, Types, Management and Care of Breeding Animals.

(5) Biology and our Natural Resources: (1 hour a week. Rev. Dr. C. J. Connolly). A Series of Lectures on the Relation of the Science of Biology to the Development and Conservation of our Natural Resources.

Students will register on Monday, January 17th. Classes begin on Tuesday, the 18th.

Applicants will pleas? communicate with

THE SECRETARY, EXTENSION TEACHING,

Box 399 ANTIGONISH, N. S.

Figure 5.2 | People's School Advertisement, December 1920

subsidy). Significantly (and not coincidentally), the courses were mostly taught by St F.X. faculty who had specialized post-graduate training. Fr Moses Coady taught arithmetic, Fr D.J. MacDonald economics, Fr James Boyle public speaking, Fr "Little Doc" MacPherson soils and crops, and Fr C.J. Connolly biology.[147]

Fifty-seven "unusual students," none holding more than an eighth-grade education, were eventually welcomed to the cathedral town.[148] Although Fr Tompkins did not teach a course, he was fond of espousing his favourite formula: "people x resources x education = progress."[149] It is "a perfect joy to see the interest these men take in their work," the priest wrote elatedly to a friend. "Last night about 27 men sat in a classroom discussing country conditions while there was a howling game of hockey going on in the rink and the shouting could be heard. Even a hockey game did not draw them off. We have found the lever that will move the world."[150]

The students were equally pleased with their experience. Richard Boyle of Afton, a brother of Fr James Boyle, wrote that the school was the most progressive step ever taken toward a forward movement in the region.[151] The endeavour was also praised on the floor of the Nova Scotia Legislature, and the *United Farmers Guide* of Western Canada editorialized that its success was so "phenomenal" that there would be no question of its continuation. In Bishop Morrison's mind, it would be a "social crime" against the welfare of the province were such schools "allowed to die in their infancy."[152]

THE UNIVERSITY MERGER QUESTION

While the Old Rector of St F.X., H.P. MacPherson, was the steady hand guiding the diocesan college, after the success of the People's School, everyone knew that Fr Tompkins, the vice-rector, was the "directing genius." Although Tompkins loved his alma mater and had no issue with its clerical mission, he long scoffed at the practice of "know it all" clergy, holding standard philosophy and theology diplomas, teaching complex subjects such as chemistry and physics.[153] It was Fr Tompkins who urged post-graduate specialization and encouraged his gifted senior students to apply for Knights of Columbus scholarships to the Catholic University of America.[154] The roster of those whom Tompkins helped obtain grants is impressive. Students like George Boyle, the future editor of the *Extension Bulletin* and biographer of both Fr Tompkins and Archbishop Neil

McNeil, put the grant to good use (incidentally, in 1926, Peter Nearing of Dominion, the future biographer of Bishop John R. MacDonald, also received a KOC scholarship).[155]

With college administrators like Fr Tompkins regularly applying for funds, in the summer of 1921 the Carnegie Corporation established a commission to investigate post-secondary education in the Maritime region. The commissioners, William S. Learned and K.C.M. Sills (the Halifax-born president of Maine's prestigious Bowdoin College) toured the region's institutions and reported that its schools suffered from chronic underfunding and poor facilities.[156] Like Tompkins, they were also critical of academic standards.[157] The men considered St F.X. a "fairly genuine institution" and praised its fledgling People's School but felt that it, like the other denominational universities, would be better served as a college within a larger Halifax-based university of the Maritimes.[158]

Fr Tompkins, who happened to be in New York when the report was released, became an instant supporter of university merger. James Cameron argues in his history of St F.X. that Tompkins supported the merger because of his high regard for the Carnegie officials, his close rapport with Dalhousie University, and his desire for "higher staff qualifications and specialization."[159] And, according to John Reid, Tompkins also believed that merger would help the region regain its prosperity through "self-help."[160] Yet, for a man so committed to extending the reach of St F.X. into the rural villages of eastern Nova Scotia, a newfound commitment to move the entire enterprise to Halifax came as a surprise to his colleagues.

As Fr Tompkins's educational philosophy evolved, he felt constrained by his office. Put plainly, he wanted to be St F.X.'s president. Years later, friends even cynically suggested that Tompkins might have opposed merger, which seemed anathema to the People's Schools, if he had been made rector of St F.X. in 1920. During the negotiations with the Carnegie Corporation, he had sneeringly referred to the Old Rector as "our leader of higher education."[161] Later, to Fr "Little Doc" MacPherson, he charged that "the college [was] getting sick of H.P. MacPherson," and that it was likely "go to pieces in a few years."[162] Others agreed. Despite its early successes, historian Fr William X. Edwards argued, by 1920 the campus "was in stagnation." Or, as Msgr Hugh Somers put it, the Old Rector had reached a "plateau" and should have been succeeded by his vice-rector.[163]

While studying the particulars of the Carnegie merger report, college administrators like Tompkins had many questions. "There are of course, a vast number of details involved in working out such a scheme as this," Dr Learned explained during a meeting in New York, but it was feasible, especially as "Dalhousie [had] already taken the most generous possible attitude."[164] Confident that the project was doable, the priest wrote to his bishop, unable to contain his enthusiasm: "I shall have some very striking things to say when I get home," as Catholics can look to a new day "if [they] are only alive to our possibilities."[165] On the train back to Nova Scotia, Tompkins's every thought was of merger. He pored over Cardinal John Henry Newman's *The Idea of a University*, and like Newman, he wanted to breathe new spirit into a college that had become complacent. In the following weeks, he talked of merger at every opportunity.

As an answer to Nova Scotia's post-secondary problems, university amalgamation had first been seriously considered in 1874 but was doomed by financial and religious snags (Bishop Cameron thought the scheme "expensive, pretentious and unprofitable"). Yet the federation of ecclesiastical colleges into the University of Toronto, including the Catholic St Michael's College, which entered as a federated member in 1910, demonstrated its feasibility. In fact, Archbishop McNeil, who did not have the resources to support a research university "in the full sense of the term," believed that the University of Toronto was the next best thing.[166] In a letter to his nephew Fr John R. MacDonald, serving as a curate at St Ninian's, he confessed that the Catholics of the Maritime provinces were soon "going to find themselves in a condition of educational inferiority."[167]

Buoyed by the support of prominent Catholics like Archbishop McNeil, Tompkins turned his small corner office into the virtual headquarters of the merger movement in eastern Nova Scotia. According to George Boyle, he kept a small band of "runners" to convey his hastily written correspondence to the train station.[168] In discussions of the proposal with participants of the second People's School held in January 1922, some early followers were Fathers James Boyle, Michael Gillis, C.J. Connolly, Moses M. Coady, John R. MacDonald, "Little Doc" MacPherson, and P. J. Nicholson (although there is evidence that Nicholson played both sides).[169] Other influential priests, including John Hugh MacDonald, Alexander Thompson, James Kiely, Daniel Doyle, Michael MacCormick, and Stanley Macdonald, privately declared their support.[170] It is important to note that most of these priests were still young men in 1922 (seven were in their thirties), and half had completed post-graduate studies abroad. In other words, these "favoured sons of the diocese" had already been exposed to the kind of research-oriented institution for which Tompkins was advocating.[171]

Working on poorly paid contracts, the college's lay faculty quickly passed a resolution in support of merger. A confident Tompkins soon told an audience in Moncton that "the great university is yet to come."[172] He used his column in *The Casket* for propaganda and continued to contrast the feeble endowment of St F.X with those of the wealthier colleges in Maine and Massachusetts. Even one of Nova Scotia's most prominent lay Catholics, Halifax's Nicholas Meagher (Supreme Court justice and author of *Howe and the Catholics*), offered cash for propaganda.[173] "In due time," Tompkins prophesied, Antigonish will be "a center of red-hot enthusiasts for the scheme."[174]

Not far from Fr Tompkins's corner office, Bishop Morrison sat in his own study and carefully mulled over the Carnegie report. He gave merger more thoughtful consideration than historians have presumed, but was never enthusiastic. Nor was the Old Rector, who personally "dread[ed] the scheme."[175] Having attended a meeting between the Carnegie officials and the Maritime college presidents, MacPherson grumbled that the proposal lacked specifics. As an educator, he thanked Dr Learned for helping the people "see the educational situation as it is," but creating a university of the Maritimes seemed both drastic and expensive.[176]

Historians have argued that the bishop and rector were "defending faith and culture" by opposing merger, and there is some truth in that analysis.[177] In fact, some clergy shamelessly fought against merger on the grounds that the rates of venereal diseases were higher among students in secular colleges.[178] In a letter to Archbishop McNeil in May 1922, Fr Tompkins conveyed his frustration at being asked to guarantee that the new university would not teach anything that conflicted with Catholic doctrine.[179] Both Bishop Morrison and the Old Rector had a bias against inter-denominational education, and both feared the loss of "Catholic morals" and the expansion of the "Protestant mentality." Yet this was merely the low-hanging fruit.[180]

The major problem for opponents of merger was that the transfer of resources to Halifax would mean the end of the college in Antigonish town. For generations, St F.X. had provided academic

Figure 5.3 | St Francis Xavier University, c. 1920

prestige, created a class of useful Catholic elites (such as Supreme Court Justice Joseph Chisholm), and supplied vocations to the priesthood. Bishop Morrison, who insisted on strengthening the Latin program so that graduates would not be handicapped in the seminary, truly believed that the college could serve dual roles. A sound Catholic education was useful "not only for those who aspire to become God's holy priests," he declared, "but also for those who are preparing themselves for various spheres of the secular world."[181]

There was also the question of diocesan morale. The archives suggest that merger was unpopular among rank-and-file Catholics and prominent alumni like provincial Liberal cabinet minister William Chisholm. Even one of Fr Tompkins most zealous supporters allowed that Catholics "had contemplated with horror the thought of their university being 'taken away.'"[182] Add the old animosities toward the Halifax-Irish and you had an unsavoury brew of public opinion.

Then there were the financial considerations. St F.X. represented considerable monies for its local economy, and Catholics who had donated their hard-earned finances to the institution were reluctant to have their investment transferred to Halifax.[183] While the Carnegie proposal called for a small junior college (or People's School) to remain in Antigonish town, it would not have been sustainable. It was difficult enough to maintain St F.X. at the best of times – in 1920 the college was "living from hand to mouth" – let alone fund separate campuses two hundred kilometres apart. Moreover, the $500,000 offered by the Carnegie Corporation to build a Halifax campus "would not be enough."[184] Theoretically, money could also come from the other dioceses in the region, but what if they refused financial support?[185] "I make the assertion, and I do not fear the contradiction," wrote one alumnus, "that hundreds of our Cape Breton boys would never have seen the inside of this college, if it had been established in Halifax instead of Antigonish."[186]

St F.X. was not the only college nor was Catholicism the only denomination debating the merger proposition. One representative of Mount Allison University in Sackville, New Brunswick, argued that he would gladly support merger if it would "fling the door open, giving the poor boy or girl the privilege of education," but to his mind the scheme would do the opposite.[187] Echoing these anxieties, Fr Gregory McLellan, rector of St Dunstan's in Charlottetown, ultimately opined that merger would curtail the opportunities of the island's Catholic students. These were powerful opponents.

Hoping to stall Fr Tompkins's momentum, in early July Bishop Morrison took a page out of his predecessor's playbook and reminded readers of *The Casket* that the Maritime bishops were ultimately responsible for the merger question.[188] His problem, however, was that only Antigonish and Charlottetown had stable colleges and so most of his regional colleagues supported the scheme.[189] St Bonaventure's College in St John's could only educate a student to a first-year university level, students at Saint Mary's College in Halifax had nothing "more than good courses in arts," and St Thomas in Fredericton would not receive a university charter until 1934.[190]

The firmest supporter of merger among the episcopacy was Archbishop Roche of St John's, who would be happy, he said, to send his students to any credible school "where the dangers to faith and morals [were] reduced to a minimum."[191] If a Catholic university was not feasible, argued the Irish-educated Roche, merger was the next best thing. After all, "The National University of Ireland was not Catholic in principle."[192] Bishop Morrison now had a serious problem.[193] Making his opinion known to the St F.X. governors and other prominent alumni, he began applying pressure on his clergy. When the priests met for their annual retreat in the summer of 1922, he forbade any discussion of a potential merger. Tompkins, infuriated, described the bishop's actions at the meeting as "autocratic" and "backward."[194]

Although Morrison had invited Tompkins to a meeting of the Maritime prelates earlier that summer, the vice-rector's articles were increasingly denied print by *The Casket*. Frustrated, Tompkins noted that most of the clergy were "disgusted" by the bishop's authoritarianism.[195] Later, he told Carnegie officials that the anti-merger group was an "ignorant spasm of a few backwoods fellows," saving the worst for Morrison, who he believed was imbued with the "St. Dunstan's Spirit" (not meant as a compliment to the island institution!). Of course, not everyone was sympathetic. "When [Tompkins] wanted to put across a point," one priest later recalled, "it was permissible to exaggerate in every possible way."[196]

From St Michael's Palace in Toronto, Archbishop McNeil monitored the situation in his native diocese. He was concerned about the mounting hostility and the fate of his beloved nephew Fr John R. MacDonald. Bright and energetic, Fr MacDonald thought that Tompkins "[was] the man" to reform Catholic education and even made one "embarrassing effort" to sermonize on merger from the pulpit. As a housemate of Bishop Morrison, MacDonald was in a precarious position, and when Archbishop Henry J. O'Leary began recruiting priests for Edmonton, McNeil counselled his nephew to go west (where ironically, he helped organized a Catholic college as part of the University of Alberta).[197]

Throughout the autumn of 1922, Fr Tompkins's initiative faced further setbacks. In early October, another merger supporter, Fr James Boyle, on the college faculty since 1913, was abruptly transferred to the coastal parish of Havre Boucher shortly after returning from graduate studies at Columbia University. As Boyle was representative of the kind of educated Catholic that Tompkins was championing, his transfer was an ominous sign.[198] Then, Bishop John March of Harbour Grace, initially an advocate of merger, visited St F.X. and publicly declared that it was "a fine university"[199]

As Bishop Morrison prepared to board the train for the second summit of the Maritime prelates in mid-October, the Old Rector cautioned him not to "allow a motion of approval to go through," as any hint that the bishops favoured the scheme would "be ruinous."[200] As the prelates were divided, the meeting was tense. Yet, in the sun-lit parlour, Bishop Morrison's canny attributes came shining through. Fighting tenaciously, he quickly recognized that he had allies among the Acadian bishops of New Brunswick, who felt that merger would do little for French-language education.[201]

Against considerable odds, the Antigonish prelate skillfully pushed through a resolution stating that the scheme "appeared" detrimental to Catholicism, while convincing his colleagues to appeal to Rome for final judgment. This was a masterstroke. Returning to Antigonish, Morrison convened a special meeting of the St F.X. board of governors and asked a sub-committee, which had already submitted to his will, to report its findings.[202] With Morrison's personal assurance that the Maritime bishops opposed merger, the governors formally announced that St F.X. would have nothing to do with the scheme.[203] Fr Tompkins was outmaneuvred. On 26 October, *The Casket* declared the matter settled. Without a medium through which to respond, the priest was paralyzed.[204]

Had Fr Tompkins accepted defeat, he might have finished his career at St F.X., but "it was difficult for a man of his commitment and zeal to remain aloof from the fray."[205] The vice-rector had given his life to education and felt that he had a right to "push it for all [he] was worth."[206] Now in open rebellion, he sought a proxy pen. He persuaded St F.X.'s talented alumnus Angus L. Macdonald to take up the torch.[207] An emerging young barrister who was climbing the ranks of the provincial bureaucracy, Angus L. deeply respected the priest – classmates recalled his days in Antigonish town "discussing everything from Aristotle to Fr Jimmy." He agreed to write pro-merger articles for the secular press.[208]

Within weeks, Macdonald's office was bombarded with correspondence (written in pen, pencil, and coloured pencil) from the priest.[209] These "spur-of-the-moment" notes, some of which were scribbled on the back of envelopes and whatever scraps of paper Tompkins had at his disposal, labelled Bishop Morrison and his supporters "Bolsheviks of the worst sort" (which was wonderfully ironic). Tompkins was gambling on Macdonald's powers of persuasion, used so effectively as a military recruiter, to win over the public. "Strong public opinion cannot be ignored," Fr Alexander Thompson once counselled Tompkins, "ergo, stir up public opinion."[210] As Tompkins had told Dr Learned, "[Morrison] never opposes anything the people want."[211]

In late November, Macdonald submitted his pro-merger articles to the secular press, and the major papers in Halifax and Sydney published them. Although he had supporters at *The Casket*, especially the publisher C.J. MacGillivray, however, he had no response from Antigonish town. The importance of *The Casket* on this question cannot be understated. Publishing in the *Halifax Herald* was useful, but making a case to the entire diocesan community was paramount. "Tell me of what value is the verdict of a packed jury," wrote Fr Moses Coady. "You must get it in *The Casket*."[212]

It is ironic that Fr Tompkins, so forceful in wresting control of *The Casket* from Michael Donovan in 1919, was now, when he needed it most, excluded from its pages. Things might have been different if Donovan, with his "sales first" approach, still owned the paper. Now, editor Robert Phalen, who despised the priest, happily obeyed Morrison's command to ignore pro-merger submissions. In a series of demeaning letters, Phalen even demanded that Angus L. expose those priests who supplied him with information and asked sneeringly why "a Catholic layman should have any say in the matter."[213]

Attacking Angus L. Macdonald as a "layman" was particularly rough. In response, the clever young barrister argued that as a Catholic in "good standing," he had every right to intervene on questions of education, and wondered why Phalen, also a layman, was allowed an opinion. Concerned that *The Casket*'s silence had deprived Catholics of the opportunity to examine merger on its merits, he charged the paper with deliberately printing the falsehood that the "clergy [were] behind the bishop." What would it require to get his articles into the paper, he queried. "Possibly my baptismal certificate and a declaration from my parish priest that I attend Mass on Sunday?"[214]

While refusing Macdonald access to print, *The Casket* editorialized aggressively on the pitfalls of merger. The paper made reference to Macdonald's articles in the *Sydney Post* and chastised those "found sneering at those who oppose the scheme," but it interpreted the fight as being about episcopal authority and not education.[215] "The Catholics of this diocese are not going to be stampeded by country election methods into opposition to their bishop," the paper proclaimed. "And they will support him all the more solidly when they see him sniped at by people who do not have the courage to sign their letters with their own name."[216]

In early December, three realities doomed Fr Tompkins. The first was the priest's recent letter to the archbishop of Saint John, leaked back to Antigonish town, in which he argued that Morrison had attempted to "throw dust in the eyes of the people."[217] Second, everyone concerned knew that he was supplying Angus L. Macdonald with fodder for pro-merger articles in the provincial press. Although "the letters in the *Hx. Chronicle* are written by a layman of Halifax," one priest warned, "the ammunition is being supplied from elsewhere."[218] Third, those priests who opposed the vice-rector were growing louder in their demand that he be removed from the college. By early December, Fr Ronald MacDonald wrote to the Old Rector from Judique demanding that the "avowed mergerites" at the college be replaced by loyal assistants or St F.X. "need not expect much sympathy or support."[219]

While the decision to transfer Fr Tompkins from St F.X. was difficult, the Old Rector had convinced Morrison that Tompkins was a shoddy administrator and very much replaceable. He was, according to MacPherson, most effective "where he is not," and his stints as vice-rector, principal of the high school, prefect of studies and registrar had been a failure.[220] On 13 December, Morrison informed Fr Tompkins of his immediate transfer from the college to the isolated windswept coastal parish of Canso, Guysborough County:

> It is of course unnecessary to point out that the first duty of the priesthood of the diocese is the pastoral office, which takes precedence over any other employment of the diocesan clergy, and it is a consolation to know that the priesthood of this diocese fully appreciate this fact and are ever ready to undertake this duty ... and therefore I hereby appoint you to be parish priest of Canso and attached missions.[221]

If Tompkins's removal from St F.X. was foreseeable, his transfer to a poor and remote parish was indisputably retributive.[222]

Fr Tompkins's transfer to Star of the Sea parish sent shockwaves throughout the diocese, and many were "saddened beyond measure."[223] Although Tompkins once mused that the contented man was "the fellow out in a quiet little parish where he [could] let his feet hang," his biographers suggest that he experienced a long period of depression.[224] There were even rumours that he would leave the diocese for the United States to work with Fr Francis Kelley and the Catholic Church Extension Society.[225] "It is far from my wishes to cause any priest to leave the diocese, especially when there is work for him to do here," Bishop Morrison acknowledged, "however, he must leave the college."[226] Writing to Dr Learned in New York, Tompkins bemoaned that he had been "turned out into the wilderness to a place called Canso … a terrible place I understand, where among other things, the sun is not seen for 9 months on account of the fog."[227]

Thirty years after Fr Tompkins's transfer, George Boyle wrote that there was "nothing more intense and tragic than the conflict of honorable men of deep convictions over questions that they hold to be of greatest importance."[228] One friend of Tompkins promised that the priest's "sojourn in the desert" would be brief, "since the pressure of public opinion" would react vigorously to such "ill judgement and arbitrary action."[229] Yet not everyone regretted his transfer. From Bridgeport, Fr Charles MacDonald mockingly wrote:

> It seems that in all the years the fishing industry has been established at Canso no one knew how to cure and look after fish. However, very soon wonderful new methods are to be introduced which will revolutionize that old sleepy town. Then there is too much fog around that coast. As soon as the Carnegie people will have finished their report, that too will be dissipated, for these people will surely give us an infallible remedy.[230]

"I regretted his departure," the Old Rector wrote sardonically a few months later, "but he seems very happy."[231]

The merger debate ended in the spring of 1923 when the Sacred Congregation of Seminaries and Universities officially forbade Catholic participation. By that time, Acadia University had already backed out and Mount Allison was wavering. Only King's College, which had suffered a devastating fire on its Windsor campus, relocated to Halifax. The anti-mergerites were pleased that the Curia's decision was "clear and to the point," leaving no doubt as to the mind of Rome. Nonetheless, while their arguments were "found consonant with the final decision of the Holy See," the battle to save St F.X. came at a great cost.[232]

Might the Canso exile have been avoided? Both Fr Tompkins and Bishop Morrison were outspoken, strong-willed, and shrewd. While Tompkins believed that Morrison and the Old Rector were ruining St F.X., the prelate felt that priest was of a "restless disposition" that was "forever in search of some novel or startling idea [that would] be the final and permanent remedy for some of the world's ills."[233] Among those who lived through the period, some thought that Morrison's "trickery" left the "blackest mark," while others admitted that Tompkins could be "illogical" when dominated by an idea.[234] "He was an extremist," Fr Hugh John MacDonald recalled years later. "You'd have to admit, you know, he was kind of extremist, if you just wanted to be level headed."[235]

The merger controversy left indelible scars, and years later the surviving actors were reluctant to speak about the play.[236] "There was dead silence for years," Fr Michael Gillis noted in 1969. "After Rome gave the decision there was nothing to do but follow it."[237] In retrospect, many of the clergy acknowledged that merger would have been a disaster for the diocese. "I can see that Jimmie was wrong," Fr Lewis MacLellan wrote in 1967. "While the merger might have built a great university at Halifax, the Antigonish diocese would have suffered."[238]

AGRICULTURAL SCHOLARSHIPS

Although a setback, Fr Tompkins's transfer to Canso did not completely dampen the progressive impulses. People's Schools were held at St F.X. in 1923 and 1924, and former supporters of merger, like Fr James Boyle in Havre Boucher, turned to other issues such as the "American exploitation" of the local lobster fishermen.[239] Journalists and historians have declared that Catholic social action in Antigonish was due "almost exclusively to the vision and energy" of Fathers Tompkins and Coady, but there were many contributors.[240]

From the glebe house in Boisdale, Fr Michael Gillis, credited as the "creative mind" behind the social activity of the diocese, demanded a reform of agriculture.[241] Two of his colleagues, the "big, impressive" Fr Angus R. MacDonald at nearby Christmas Island, and the mild-mannered Fr Michael MacCormick at East Bay, shared his concerns. Men like Fr MacDonald, virtually forgotten within the historiography, were vital in the fight for rural rejuvenation.[242]

These men faced considerable pessimism among their priests. Writing to the Old Rector from Judique, one veteran clergyman noted that there were "too many drones among [them] whose only temporal concern [was] their own well-being and comfort." Some priests simply did not care how their parishioners lived, "so long as these [were] able to pay the dues."[243] Others warned that any future rural conferences needed careful organization to avoid the "ramblings" that characterized regular clerical meetings.

In December 1924 the pastor of Christmas Island, Fr Angus MacDonald, gave the opening remarks at the second annual Diocesan Rural Conference. He noted some hopeful signs of progress, such as the "Pomquet Egg Circle" and the cooperative shipping of poultry in Tracadie. But he was troubled by the vacant farms and begged his colleagues to focus on rural resettlement.[244] While the relationship between education and the soil was clear, St F.X did not have the necessary specialists. So, the following year the conference, estimated to include 30 per cent of the clergy, voted to fund twenty-five scholarships to the winter farming course at the provincial Agricultural College in Truro. It was an acknowledgment that Fr Tompkins was right on his call for specialization. However difficult for some to accept, the Church needed help from secular educators to solve the problems of the farm. "There is no more practical way of saluting the flag," wrote Fr Coady, "than to send a boy to Truro."

Not only were the agricultural scholarships something "practical" to bring back to the parishes, but they represented a way forward for those who favoured rural life. "Nothing could be better calculated," argued the *Halifax Herald*, "to arouse ambition and assist in creating a sentiment of pride in the [farming] occupation."[245] As with the People's Schools, the recipients of the scholarships had to be older than seventeen years of age, be of "good moral character," and be in a position to put the newfound knowledge to good use. Candidates were recommended by county committees and then selected by a central clerical commission.[246]

Monies in support of the bursaries poured in from across the diocese. Fr Hugh John MacDonald of Heatherton made a pitch to Catholics in Glace Bay and "they couldn't turn [him] down."[247] Then, at the 1926 conference, the president of the Catholic Women's League announced funding for six young ladies to attend the Agricultural College course on home economics.[248] Cooperation was everywhere. When a Georgeville priest became concerned with the state of agriculture along the Northumberland Strait, he brought some parishioners to meet farmers in Fr Gillis's parish of Boisdale.[249]

ROYAL COMMISSION ON THE FISHERY

While the clergy focused on agriculture, Fr Tompkins found his new parish of Canso to be "on the rocks, literally and otherwise."[250] One woman with six children came to the glebe begging for help as she "had nothing to eat in the house," and prospective grooms had twenty-five-cent pieces fashioned into wedding rings by the local blacksmith.[251] Despite his "exile," Tompkins remained in close contact with his colleagues, many of whom were "back and forth" to visit."[252] According to George Boyle, "even bishops came to see him."[253]

In characteristic fashion, Tompkins educated himself on the problems of a fishery that had lost some six million dollars in value since the Great War.[254] In one particularly stirring story, he slammed the bible closed during a Sunday sermon and informed the people of the small mission community of Dover that there was "sufficient temporal bounty on [those] shores to ensure a full meal on the tables of every home."[255] Yet he shared their frustration over the use of trawler fleets to clear the ocean of fish and flood the market with product. In a letter to his Ordinary, he argued that the Church could "not afford to look on at disease, poverty, hunger and exploitation and take no steps to remedy [those] evils."[256]

In conversation with his parishioners, Tompkins learned that catching the fish was one thing, and getting the product to market was another. Without outside buyers, lobstermen were obliged to sell their catch to local canneries at reduced prices.[257] In 1924 Fr Leo J. Keats at Ingonish wrote despairingly about the poor prices. At one point, prices were so low that many fishers simply released the crustaceans from their traps.[258] "When, for example, here in Antigonish [town] we have to pay around 30¢ for a single mackerel," Bishop Morrison mused after reading a letter from the pastor at coastal Petit de Grat, "it seems to me that it would pay the fishermen to have some kind of distributing agencies in the inland parts of the province."[259]

Perhaps only Fr Tompkins would have had the temerity to ask the Canso Holy Name Society, concerned with stamping out blasphemy, to study the problems of the fishery and cultivate local leadership. By the gusty spring of 1927, the community had already funded three scholarships to the short course at the Fishery School at Halifax and the wharves were full of cultivated outrage. Then on 1 July 1927, as Canada was commemorating the sixtieth anniversary of Confederation, the men of Canso decided to act. It was better to be shot, claimed one indignant participant in a meeting, "than to be starved to death." Within a few days, the *Halifax Chronicle* turned its attention to the beleaguered coastal town.

In the coming weeks, the "shore priests" of the diocese met to discuss the dismal state of the regional fishery. Besides Fr Tompkins, other attendees were Fr Alfred Boudreau of Petit de Grat, later known as "the fisherman's Friend," Fr Placide LeBlanc of Port Felix, and Fr Leo J. Keats. A resolution, eventually signed by forty clergymen, called upon Ottawa to come to the immediate aid of the fishermen and make a thorough investigation of the entire industry. Meanwhile, provincial and federal politicians were "flooded" with telegrams and petitions.[260]

Thanks to this newfound pressure, in October 1927 the MacLean Commission was appointed to investigate the fishery. Fr Boudreau, a descendant of a long line of Acadian fishermen, was anxious that the men and their families be "prepared to meet it." The priest worried that the smaller, but no less important, issues of cost, storage, transportation, and American duties, might be overlooked if not properly presented. He expected his parishioners to prepare their testimony wisely and think carefully about the issues. "Father Boudreau has the right idea," noted *The Casket*. "Let the Fishermen not depend on anybody else ... but let them take jolly good care to see that the commission investigates what they want them to investigate."[261]

Noting that "what was true of agriculture must prove true of the fishers," the diocese announced in the midst of the investigation that it would fund twelve annual scholarships at the Dominion Experimental Station in Halifax. There was finally momentum. St F.X. intellectuals talked of a Fisheries chair at Dalhousie University, and a long line of fishermen waited to give testimony to the Royal Commission. They wanted a separate federal department of fisheries (with a minister from the Maritimes), the appointment of an inspector from the ranks of the local fishermen, a commitment from the Canadian Trade Commission to advertise and expand the foreign market, the abolition of trawlers, insurance for smaller boats and gear, radio broadcasting of weather reports, and better and cheaper transportation.

This was a momentous time and, as Ernie Forbes has noted in *Maritime Rights*, "the hearings themselves were more important, probably, than the commission's recommendations," for they gave the fishers a voice.[262] In Arisaig they spoke of poor transportation facilities, in Malignant Cove they complained of trawlers destroying gear, in Havre Boucher they asked for a bounty on dog fish, and on Isle Madame they demanded affordable insurance for their boats. Not only did clergymen like Fr Boudreau and Fr Tompkins prepare their parishioners to testify, but some even gave evidence.[263] At Tracadie, Fr James McKeough told the commission that his parish once had productive oyster beds but, as the bottom of the beds were raked too clean, there was nothing for the oyster spat to cling to and they were lost.[264]

By early December 1927, Fr Tompkins was working hard with the Fisheries Federation in Canso and there was talk of extending the organization into northern Inverness. Followers acknowledged that Canada was well behind Japan and China in fishing expertise and were sure that education would benefit the coastal communities. A letter that Fr Boudreau had published in the *Halifax Herald* was read to great applause across the region and meetings were full of "optimism and grim determination." A week later, Fr Boudreau attended the Royal Commission hearing in Halifax. Although he was criticized for attending a session outside his district, as two of his parishioners had recently drowned he felt obliged to be present during the testimony.

In May 1928 the Royal Commission conveyed its "grim" findings. The inshore fishermen were at the mercy of forces that could only be countered through careful organization and government intervention. At meeting held at St Peter's, the overflowing crowd of citizens formally approved the report and demanded that the federal government act. In the meantime, *The Casket* continued to call for fishing cooperatives and cold-storage plants so that the fishermen could control their product. It was also imperative that Ottawa appoint a minister of fisheries. In fact, this was so important to Fr Boudreau that he testified to that need before a special standing committee of the House of Commons.

Over the next year, the demands on Ottawa grew louder. Writing to Prime Minister MacKenzie King, Bishop Morrison noted that thousands of fishermen were "pinning their last hope" on the appointment of a minister who was sympathetic to their problems. Having been counselled by Fr Tompkins and Fr Boudreau, he asked MacKenzie King to appoint Cyrus Macmillan, a PEI native and a professor at McGill University, to the post.[265] "I may say that a letter has gone forward to the Prime Minister along the lines you suggest," Morrison wrote to Tompkins in Canso. "I take it that the Fishermen's Unions themselves are taking active measures with the Ottawa authorities in support of the same proposition."[266]

THE ST FRANCIS XAVIER EXTENSION DEPARTMENT

All this agitation energized the rank and file. Since 1926 clergymen like Fr Thomas O'Reilly Boyle, an outspoken advocate for the working class, had regularly attended conferences on home economics and family life.[267] When Fr Michael Gillis returned from a home economics conference at St Paschal, Quebec, he encouraged the Sisters of St Martha to go out to the parishes like Westville to teach the value of "canning, budgeting, and household management."[268] When some warned that a proposal for a central school of Home Economics in Antigonish town would conflict with the Congregation of Notre Dame's new school of Home Economics at Mount Saint Bernard, an exasperated Fr Michael Gillis griped that Mount Saint Bernard "could not train girls for rural life any more than St F.X. could train boys for farm life."[269]

Time and again, it was clear that diocesan institutions moved too slowly. The rural reformers appreciated that St F.X. was the diocese's central educational institution, but they were growing impatient. "We cannot afford to fall down on our plans," one priest noted: "To do so would be to admit, before the public, that we are not united and that we are unable to complete what we set out to do."[270] Bishop Morrison's characteristic caution was also maddening. "[He] rarely gives a definite answer at once," Fr John R. MacDonald wrote to his uncle. "He takes things under 'full consideration.'"[271]

In the glebe house kitchens of Boisdale, Iona, and Christmas Island, advocates of reform decided to jolt the college "into action."[272] When the Mary Stuart Council of the Scottish Catholic Society of Canada (SCS) met at Boisdale in February 1927, besides enjoying the Gaelic stories and songs, they debated the problem of the numerous "maids and bachelors" in the parishes and the impossibility of supporting a family on the farm.[273] At the July 1928 convention, held at Judique, by contrast, SCS delegates like the "pretty aggressive go getter" Fr John Nicholson of New Waterford voted to raise $100,000 (over five years) for an extension program.[274] The SCS had given the university a stiff push.[275]

Although the SCS set "the heather on fire," it is highly unlikely that in the dismal Nova Scotia economy of 1928 they could have raised $100,000 for an extension program. Yet they understood that the very threat of an educational program independent of St F.X. would force Bishop Morrison and the Old Rector to act. The remaining work was to convince the timid that monies could be found. "We have no definite ideas about finance," Glace Bay lawyer, college governor, and extension supporter Neil McArthur told the board of governors, "but I think we can take for granted that if we do something worthwhile for the people, we will easily get remuneration."[276]

In 1928 the college asked a special committee of the St F.X. alumni association, crammed with SCS members, to investigate a program of extension, and in May 1929 they recommended to the board of governors that the school act. As the bishop of the diocese had the final say, this was Morrison's moment. Many prelates in his situation would have demurred, and many others would have opposed for financial reasons or simply out of fear. However, to his enduring credit, he said yes. When the report was delivered, Morrison turned to Fr Coady and asked anxiously "if [he] thought it could be made a go."[277]

The concept of university extension to take education, normally confined to elite campuses, to the people, was first seriously studied in England in the 1870s.[278] In 1892 the University of Chicago opened the first formal extension department in the United States, and in 1912 a similar program began at the University of Alberta. By 1919, nearly a fifth of the University of Wisconsin's operating budget was devoted to extension work in that mid-western state. These examples, along with the knowledge gained through the People's Schools, the work of Fr "Little Doc" MacPherson with local farmers, and more recently the home economics courses of the Sisters of St Martha, offered encouragement.[279]

Yet, unlike those of secular American colleges, the extension program at St F.X. would be modelled on the social teachings of Pope Leo XIII and the thoughts of Frs John Ryan and Charles Plater. No priest would have supported any program that did not follow the Church's tradition of "sane Catholic social action" based on notions of subsidiarity. "The relation between social progress and the spiritual welfare of Catholics," noted the university's alumni association, was "so patent as not to require emphasis."[280]

St F.X. had the perfect person to lead the new program. Intelligent, outspoken, and on friendly terms with local congregations, Fr Moses

Michael Coady was only candidate nominated. Although he was a solid administrator and philosophically compatible, he was initially hesitant to accept a leadership role because of his age (he was forty-eight).[281] But, as Fr Michael Gillis later recalled: "The demand was for Dr Coady. The committee was asked, 'What's your program?' 'We don't know,' was the answer. 'And how are you going to finance it?' 'Well, we don't know that either.' They just asked for Dr Coady to start the ball rolling and to find out, to map out the program."[282] Physically imposing, Coady could be a "ruffian at times," a trait that would serve him well among the rugged farmers, miners, and fishers of eastern Nova Scotia.[283]

As an assistant for Coady, a "little caucus of priests" who met at St Andrews selected Angus Bernard "A.B." MacDonald. A native of Heatherton parish, and brother of Fr D.J. MacDonald, A.B. was one of the most respected laymen in the diocese. Large, handsome, and charismatic, the former inspector of schools for Antigonish and Guysborough Counties commanded attention. "If Mr. MacDonald did not have a single word to say," noted one reporter, "his striking good looks would get him by in any gathering."[284] MacDonald has a celebrated place within the region's historiography, and his willingness to accept the position of Assistant director of the fledgling Extension Department was critical. He already had a steady position with the Department of Education and the new post would come at some financial risk. When the news broke that he had accepted the job, there was considerable excitement.[285] "I think the Extension work is wonderful," the Antigonish native and Acadia University professor D.G. Whidden wrote from Wolfville, and "MacDonald is a good man for the job."[286]

The last great hurdle, and one of A.B. MacDonald's preconditions, was to convince the "hard headed old Scotsmen" of the SCS, all pastors in rural Cape Breton, to surrender their prerogative and support the college's program. This was not an easy task as there was some lingering frustration with St F.X. The person chosen for this unenviable assignment was the agricultural representative for Antigonish-Guysborough, R.J. MacSween. A native of Beaver Cove, Cape Breton, a graduate of the Nova Scotia Agricultural College, and former manager of Mount Cameron farm, he was representative of the kind of educated layperson that the reformers wanted.

MacSween's first stop was Boisdale, where he asked Fr Gillis for help. After lunch and a stroll along the shore, Gillis telephoned his

Figure 5.4 | Angus Bernard ("A.B.") MacDonald, c. 1935

colleagues in the Sydney area and arranged to meet the following morning at the Randolf Hotel. Although the meeting was "a kind of rough session in some parts," the old priests eventually gave their blessing. When his train arrived back at the Antigonish Station, A.B. was there to greet him. "What's the word?" he asked. "They are right behind you," a relieved MacSween replied.[287]

The coming months were devoted to study and organization. Fr Coady investigated extension programs across North America, and A.B. was sent to the University of Toronto to study the history of rural economies in Canada. Later, Coady was selected by the federal government to organize the fishers of the region into a union of United Maritime Fishermen (UMF). Not surprisingly, his first stop in this capacity was to the parish of his double-cousin Fr Tompkins, where he urged the fishermen to put aside their political and sectarian prejudices and band together.[288] Solutions, it seemed, were finally at hand.

THE CULTURAL MOSAIC

The economic awakening in eastern Nova Scotia was precipitated in part by a need for cultural survival. Clergymen like the Eudist priest Msgr Patrice-Alexandre Chiasson, a native of Grand Etang, Inverness County, who was named bishop of Bathurst, New Brunswick, in September 1920, understood the special relationship between the land, faith, and culture. At the Acadian National Convention in 1921, he noted that Acadians had ensured their survival by "grouping themselves around the Church." If the Acadian race did not remain Catholic, he thundered, it should "resign itself to die."[289]

So important was the relationship between land and culture to the Mi'kmaq that they fought constantly for the right, as their needs required, to hunt and fish (or even harvest wood) as stated in the Peace and Friendship Treaty of 1752. According to historian William Wicken, most Nova Scotians recognized these claims, and most newspapers, *The Casket* included, regularly reprinted the treaty as evidence that the Mi'kmaq had general access to local streams and forests.[290] In November 1927, Gabriel Sylliboy, grand chief at Whycocomagh, was arrested on a charge of trapping fox and muskrat for their furs. Even though he invoked the treaty in his defence, he was convicted.[291] Yet his treatment further awakened the community, and by the winter of 1928 they were demanding that their rights and privileges be restored.[292]

These issues were hotly debated at the summertime feast of St Anne, and the "holy land" of Chapel Island, which connected "Cape Breton of to-day and Cape Breton of the past," began to attract more foreign attention.[293] In 1926 the ceremony of "crawling to St Anne" was described in the *Journal of American Folklore* by the anthropologist Elsie Clews Parsons:

> Because of the wet ground, the progressive kneeling ritual began at the church steps, not at some distance from the church. First a prayer was made by the Grand Chief. The men headed the procession of kneelers, who moved forward three or four knee-lengths or strides between prayers, i.e. all moved together and all prayed together, movement and prayer alternating. As persons passed over the door sill, they kissed it. The group moved up the center aisle and then turned to the left to where the images stood, their feet to be kissed and small coins "thrown" to them. It was a devout picture, of a kind rarely seen on this continent.[294]

Such rich cultural practices inspired academics to delve more deeply into the community's history. In 1920 Professor William Francis Ganong of Smith College, Massachusetts, and author of books such as *Historic Sites in New Brunswick*, asked the diocese for help in obtaining a record of all the Mi'kmaw place names in the region (camp sites, fishing places, and so forth), as "even the smallest places, would be worth preserving with care." Priests searched their churches for artifacts, and in 1926 the pastor at Pictou presented the Nova Scotia Archives with a rare copy of a Mi'kmaw "picture book," which had been printed in 1866 and rescued from a period shipwreck.[295]

Throughout this time, clergymen maintained their formal role in Mi'kmaw feasts and governance ceremonies. When the Potlotek native Captain Frances Paul was chosen as the new leader at Paqtnkek (Afton and Summerside) in 1920, he went with Grand Chief Silliboy to Antigonish town to be installed by Bishop Morrison. Having the insignia of his office – a medal (*elegehwi aptung*) – conferred upon him, Chief Paul promised that his community would "always preserve intact the unsullied record of their attachment to the faith."[296]

Yet, in truth, the relationship was also formalized and extremely bureaucratic. If Catholics in Scottish or Acadian parishes wanted to organize a sacred concert, all they needed was the consent of their priest. Catholics at missions like Membertou, however, required the permission of the chief and council as well as the priest (who visited only once a month).[297] Then there were allegations of spiritual neglect. In 1923 Grand Chief Sylliboy made it known that a priest had failed to attend Chapel Island during Pentecost, as was the custom, and expressed regret that they "did not [have] Mass there that Sunday." Apologetic, Bishop Morrison told the pastor at Johnstown that the community had been "so faithful to the Catholic religion" that the diocese needed to be more mindful of these customs.[298]

Retaining culture in communities that had been much reduced by generations of outmigration was difficult. Many Mi'kmaq travelled to Cumberland County in the summertime for agricultural employment. Even the development of the Scottish Catholic Society (SCS) was, as Dan MacInnes has demonstrated, "occasioned by the ravages inflicted upon traditional culture by rapid industrialization."[299] Yet, unlike the Mi'kmaq, the Scots had the demographics and finances to resist cultural decline. By 1922 Gaelic was taught optionally in some rural Cape Breton schools, and the first issue of the bilingual quarterly SCS magazine *Mosgladh* (The Awakening) was available in the parishes. In 1924 James MacNeil, a Sydney steelworker and Gaelic scholar, began publishing the *Scottish Herald* (*Teachdaire Nan Gaidheal*), which by 1926 had a circulation of a thousand.[300] There was also a push for a Gaelic library at St F.X., and missing copies of *Mac-Talla* were collected throughout Canada.

Although Gaelic was still spoken with "remarkable correctness of grammar," by the mid-1920s weekly evening schools sponsored by the SCS opened at the Lyceum Theatre in Sydney and New Waterford to teach the language.[301] Young clergymen like Fr Stanley MacDonald, the brother of Angus L. Macdonald, were regular orators at St Andrew's nights across the region, occasionally speaking at several events on the same evening. Parish dinners on Hallowe'en always had *fuarag* (oatmeal and cream) on the menu, and the *Achadh Nan Gaidheal* column in *The Casket* carried Scottish news from across the region (much of it composed by Professor A.T. MacDonald). It was also not uncommon for priests from the Scots College Rome to ask their Antigonish colleagues to search for Gaelic copies of the Old Testament.[302]

Although many Scottish Catholics belonged to the Self-Determination League for Ireland, a healthy rivalry persisted between Highlanders and Hibernians. Notwithstanding the cultural similarities, the historical narrative of Catholicism in Scotland and

Ireland was very different and those differences sometimes spilled into the pages of *The Casket*. In March 1921, one correspondent, frustrated at the triumphalism of the paper, went on the offensive: "Who abolished the Test Oaths? Uniacke and Doyle and Kavanagh and Kenny, aided by loyalists. Who brought about responsible government? Scotchmen? No! Irishmen and loyalists."[303] While most found these exchanges amusing, one priest resigned his directorship at *The Casket* in protest against the decision to open its columns "to a most dishonest, vulgar and insulting attack on the Scotsmen of Nova Scotia."[304]

In the colliery towns, an active Ancient Order of Hibernians (AOH) continued to organize cultural events and support social causes like the St Mary's Orphanage. The AOH remained very much a Newfoundland society, as it was "Codmen" who continued to trade the "flakes and stages" of the fishery for the mines who sustained the organization.[305] While concerned mainly with fraternity and local parish matters, the AOH in Cape Breton periodically ruminated over the perception of Britain's wrongdoing against Catholic Ireland.[306] In times of political unrest in Ireland, meetings were organized and visiting speakers would preach fierce sermons "favoring Home Rule" or denouncing the unionist activities of "[Edward] Carson the bigot."[307] When Ireland achieved a Free State in 1922, the AOH passed notices of support and attempted to aid the fledgling democracy by promoting Irish migration to Canada.[308] By and large, however, the AOH in Cape Breton was more concerned about events in St John's and Halifax than happenings in Dublin.

WOMEN RELIGIOUS AND SOCIAL SERVICES

Apart from the Mi'kmaq, who would have to wait until the 1950s to get a woman into a local women's congregation, vocations came from female aspirants in all these ethnic communities. Between 1921 and 1930, 163 new candidates entered the Sisters of St Martha alone.[309] Others, like the teacher Ada Attwood of New Waterford, left for the Canadian West to join such congregations as the Ursulines of Jesus, who were teaching and nursing in Edmonton.[310]

The letters from novitiates in Antigonish, Montreal, and Halifax make for fascinating reading. At Christmas 1920, Gertrude MacIsaac (Sister St Helen Marie), the daughter of Antigonish politician Colin

Table 5.1 | Women Religious 1922

Congregation	Sisters	Convents	Schools	Pupils	Hospitals	Patients	Orphanage/ Home
Congregation of Notre Dame	98	9	12	3,505	0	0	0
Congregation of the Sisters of Charity	88	8	8	4,295	2	348	0
Congregation of the Sisters of St Martha	79	2	0	0	3	2,638	1
Filles de Jésus	22	2	2	338	0	0	1

(*Source:* Antigonish Diocesan Statistics)

Francis "C.F." MacIsaac, wrote from the CND motherhouse in Montreal to thank her lonely mother for a recently arrived care package. The novice was nearing the day of her vows and was given permission by the sub-mistress to break her Advent silence. "If you knew how happy I am today, you would not wish me home," she wrote. "Pray that I may make good use of the time from now till Feb 15."[311] As the deadline approached, the girls at Mount Saint Bernard prayed daily for their former classmate.

While there was great pride in sending a daughter into religious life, it was, as the MacIsaac family acknowledged, difficult to bid farewell. When C.F. first took Gertrude to the Montreal motherhouse, he was terribly lonely. Confiding in his friend Senator Lawrence Geoffrey Power of Halifax, he was surprised to learn that similar feelings had once beset the Power family. "Some thirty-five years ago I went to New York with my sister Ella, who was, I think, the flower of the whole Power flock," he confessed, "and it was about as sad a journey as I have ever made."[312]

Figure 5.5 | Bethany Motherhouse, c. 1920s

While nuns are often caricatured by Hollywood as models of sternness (and some were), many were compassionate and vivacious. "I shall never forget the day the father of a dear little boy in my class was killed in the mine while school was in session," one Cape Breton sister recalled. "Our efforts to console the distraught boy reduced us all to tears."[313] These young women were well known in their parishes, and when Mary MacLean of Boisdale, a nineteen-year-old postulant for the Sisters of St Martha, passed away, her funeral drew an overflowing crowd.

In the autumn of 1921, the Sisters of St Martha opened Bethany, their new motherhouse, which was named after the biblical home of St Martha. While not extravagant, it was a commanding building with a beautiful panoramic view of the cathedral town, and plenty of nearby woods and streams for contemplative strolls.[314] It was also an "administrative and hospitality center" that produced everything from church vestments to books.[315]

In addition, Bethany was mission control for the many ventures that the Marthas were supervising. In 1923 they were asked by the "persuasive" Fr Moses Coady to staff a new rural school at Margaree Forks. While this would be a new direction, many of the women had taught in local schools before joining the congregation and were comfortable in the classroom. By 1928 the Marthas were teaching at Bras d'Or, and the school at St Andrew's was considered the most progressive in the region.[316]

The bulk of their work, of course, was in healthcare. In May 1920 the twenty-five-bed Ross Hospital (the name of the institution and its attached nursing school was soon changed to St Rita's) was opened in Sydney.[317] In May 1925 St Mary's Hospital in Inverness opened with fifty beds on the site locally known as "chapel hill" under the supervision of another "brigade" of the Marthas.[318] In the midst of an economic recession, it took considerable effort to maintain St Mary's, as patients often paid their bills in kind, with poultry, dairy, or vegetables. Aid societies were established in Inverness, Broad Cove, Brook Village, Glencoe, and Port Hood to provide bedding and produce and, as Teresa MacIsaac has noted, the sisters even cut up old bedsheets for use as bandages.[319] At Antigonish town in September of that year, the cornerstone for a new modern infirmary was laid. Having literally surrendered their own beds to accommodate patients, the Marthas were proud of the "grand investment" made by Catholics in the mainland counties.[320]

Along with bricks and mortar came a commitment to standardization and scientific training. Nursing sisters travelled to Montreal and Boston to attend courses on dietary preparation and operating-room procedures. At the St Joseph's nursing school graduation in 1924, Fr P.J. Nicholson noted the great strides being made in x-ray techniques and the "isolation of germs." The Glace Bay Hospital soon became the first institution in Cape Breton to administer an insulin treatment for diabetes. When the Maritime Conference of the Catholic Hospital Association was organized in the spring of 1922, Mother M. Ignatius, ministering at St Joseph's, was elected its first president.

One diocesan institution greatly in need of renewal was the orphanage. Each year, hundreds of babies were born to unwed parents, or to families that were, for many reasons, unable to provide for them.[321] Throughout the 1920s, poignant photographs of young children appeared in *The Casket* under the caption, "Who will give me a home?" Advertisements from local children's aid societies sought potential Catholic parents who could provide a reference from their parish priest.[322] This was often a painful process, because, as Fr Peter Nearing noted, "the children of these unmarried mothers bore their parents' stigma. Few wanted to adopt them." Sadly, there was a feeling among the public that aiding unwed mothers and their children was "subsidizing sin and perpetuating promiscuity."[323]

Although Bishop Morrison was occasionally aloof, he was always warm to children and was particularly concerned for the orphans in his flock. He was also sympathetic to the men and women forced to give up their offspring. "There are circumstances," he wrote sensibly, "in which the best parental intentions fail of realization," and therefore it was up to the faithful to care for their children.[324] The prelate had lost his own mother at the age of five (Elizabeth Morrison died during childbirth in 1867) and he keenly understood the children's sense of lonesomeness.[325] Although plans for a diocesan orphanage had been rejected by the provincial government in 1919, by 1925 there was sufficient political sympathy to warrant another attempt.[326]

Working closely with CWL councils in the Sydney area, the Church purchased a twelve-acre property at Bras d'Or, on the banks of the beautiful St Andrew's Channel, and in August 1927 the "Little Flower Institute" (another building named in honour of St Thérèse of Lisieux) was opened as the diocesan orphanage. *The Halifax Herald* noted that the institution, staffed by the Marthas, was of "conspicuous importance."[327] Significantly, the institute represented a movement to "disassociate the children from the stigma of initialized care."[328] The home at Bras d'Or was considered kinder and gentler, full of "spontaneity and laughter," and without the heavy atmosphere of repression that had characterized such institutions in the past.[329] A "Union of St Theresa of the Children of Jesus" was administered by the CWL to raise monies and collect donations. The union had a newspaper, *The Little Flower Messenger*, and membership was open to anyone willing to pay the annual dues of twenty-five cents.

ORGANIZING THE CLERGY

As women religious supervised the diocese's social welfare programs, clergymen worked in a parish environment where discipline was strict and scandals rare. In August 1921 a synod was organized at St Ninian's Cathedral, and copies of the new diocesan regulations, to be strictly observed, were placed in all the churches. A committee of synodal examiners, chaired by the Old Rector, ensured that junior clergy were properly versed and examined in the diocesan constitution and sacred theology.[330] When Fr Angus J. MacIsaac arrived at the glebe in Little Bras d'Or to begin his priestly career, there was a reimbursement cheque from his bishop for seminary charges and a copy of the synodal decrees for him to "study up."[331]

The Priests' Eucharistic League offered the clergy instruction on giving sermons on the Holy Mass and effectively teaching about the Eucharist. Periodically, the men would meet to hear papers and discuss their experiences. One paper, read in 1929 by Fr J.H. Nicholson of New Waterford, focused on the preparation of children for First Communion. Fr James Boyle offered tips on how to teach the catechism.[332]

These efforts toward uniformity did not mean that priests lost their individuality. Some kept chickens and were adapt at making preserves. Fr MacAdam at Sacred Heart, a passionate gardener, repeatedly had to stop parishioners from parking their horses on his little plot of potatoes.[333] The humanity of these priests was remembered well after their deaths. It was no secret, for instance, that Fr John R. MacDonald was afraid of the supernatural and jumpy in the dark. And so, late one evening, in the candlelight of St Ninian's Cathedral, Fr James Tompkins hid behind a pew, waited for the unsuspecting priest to walk past, and jumped out to startle him. Unfortunately for Tompkins, MacDonald was so jittery that he delivered a blow to the prankster's face that almost knocked him out.[334]

The quality of the clergy was such that the Ontario priest Fr John Mary Fraser, "not afraid of attempting big projects," wanted to open a Chinese Seminary in Antigonish town. Although Bishop Morrison thought Toronto "would be more advantageous." However, when the St Francis Xavier China Mission Seminary opened a mere hundred yards away from Toronto's St Augustine's Seminary in the autumn of 1924, the Scarboro Foreign Mission, founded in 1918 to send priests to China, began to comb eastern Nova Scotia for recruits.[335] Pomquet's Arthur Venedam and Glace Bay's James Duncan MacGillivray soon joined Bishop Morrison's half-brother Vincent in the "noble work" among Chinese Catholics.[336] Parishes donated monies to furnish rooms at the seminary and the names of donors were published in the missionary magazine, *China*. "What a wonderful old lad you are," Fr John McRae wrote to Fr Donald MacPherson at Port Hood, "to take the interest you do and the trouble for us."[337]

BISHOP ALEXANDER "SANDY" MACDONALD RETURNS HOME

From Toronto's St Augustine's seminary, Bishop Sandy MacDonald was a regular visitor to the new Scarboro seminary close by. His struggle to have his Church properties exempted from taxation in British Columbia had been successful – in 1921 he won that right at the Privy Council in London – but the Diocese of Victoria remained in financial trouble.[338] More troublesome still was that the "begging bishop" had entered into a protracted and bitter altercation with his Roman superiors on several theological and social questions, including the doctrine of papal authority, which led to his resignation (or removal) while he was visiting Rome in July 1923. "They dealt with your case administratively," one cardinal informed him, although Bishop Sandy felt this was merely "an expression under which injustice may lurk unperceived."[339]

Once MacDonald was appointed titular bishop of Hebron (a defunct see), his episcopal career was effectively over, but he felt he could still contribute academically. He had an appointment as the spiritual director at Archbishop McNeil's seminary, but by 1924 he decided to retire to his native diocese and volunteer to serve as the chaplain for the Sisters of St Martha. Although the "complexity of circumstances" did not permit this request, he was offered rooms in Mockler Hall on the St F.X. campus.[340]

Although Bishop Sandy wished to be "of some service," it was difficult to find him a position.[341] His application for the post of chair of philosophy at the college was denied because placing a faculty member (a bishop) under the authority of the president (a priest) would be "detrimental to the status of the hierarchy." Moreover,

MacDonald's quarrel with Rome had resulted in certain censures, and Bishop Morrison was uncertain whether he would even be permitted to hold a teaching post.

The Antigonish prelate was in a delicate position. Bishop Sandy's many friends and relatives, unaware of the penalties imposed on him by Rome, were extremely "sensitive" to his treatment. If Morrison upheld Rome's punishment (denial of certain faculties, and so forth) it might seem that he was persecuting MacDonald.[342] Concerned that people still considered him an "outsider," the bishop wanted to avoid this scenario at all costs. It was an awkward time for both men – the apostolic delegate sent MacDonald's room and board money directly to Morrison, although the prelate repeatedly asked him not to – and when passing on campus they each addressed the other as "your lordship." In the meantime, Bishop Sandy kept busy giving lectures, and even found time to write another book, *The Apostles' Creed*. Most important, however, was that as a resident on the St F.X. campus he was to have a front-row seat to the application of Catholic action that would soon change the region.

6

A New Movement
1930–1939

By the beginning of the decade of the 1930s, the aspiration for extension work among the 97,887 Catholics of Antigonish had intensified. Facing another gloomy economic forecast, Bishop Morrison noted that federal economists had promised that prosperity was right around the corner; although they did not indicate "how near or how far the corner itself [was]."[1] From Canso, Fr Tompkins wrote that the prospect of a productive fishing season was bleak, while in Petit de Grat, Fr Alfred Boudreau worried that the big companies would "bleed the Fishermen." There was some hope that the new Federal Ministry of Fisheries (for which the Antigonish priests had fought) would improve the "general economic side of the business," but in the meantime, as the fishermen faced inclement weather, Morrison added to the Collects of the Mass (a special opening prayer) *ad postulandam serenitatem* with the hope of calm and bountiful seas.[2] To offset the region's mounting poverty, the prelate sent the Star of the Sea parish a personal cheque for $100.

While acts of charity were certainly welcome, more long-lasting solutions were needed. In the *Sydney Record*, Fr Leo J. Keats, now ministering at coastal St Peters, noted that the work of Fr Coady and the United Maritime Fishermen (UMF) was a "clear call to action" for the twenty thousand men who harvested the waters of the Maritime provinces.[3] The inaugural convention of the UMF was held at Halifax in June 1930, and the *Halifax Chronicle*, now under more sympathetic management, noted that the union was the last chance to save the industry. Things were so bad at North Sydney that most men refused to go out to fish cod as the price was low and the expense of running the motor boats high.[4] Yet, while fishermen could not overcome modern realities like trawlers, or block those greedy vessels from Canadian ports, they could organize at the "easiest phase of the industry" – and that, all agreed, was lobsters.[5]

The focus on lobsters as the departure point for extension work in eastern Nova Scotia was quite logical. Lobsters were abundant and easily stored, and fishermen did not have to compete with the deep-sea trawlers. Moreover, some clergymen in coastal parishes, like Fr Dougald MacEachern of Arisaig, who had studied the fishery while a curate at North Sydney, were already pursuing marketing opportunities. In 1930 MacEachern chartered tank boats to convey live product from St George's Bay to New England's canneries and restaurants.[6]

Fr Coady later claimed that lobstermen were receptive to the message of cooperation because individuals could not obtain results "by going their separate ways."[7] In the summer of 1931, fishermen from Judique and Creignish met with their colleagues across St George's Bay at Havre Boucher to organize a lobster marketing and canning strategy. In a crowded hall full of weathered faces, the outspoken Fr Joseph DeCoste of St Joseph du Moine (and a native of Havre Boucher) spoke of the new cooperative lobster plant in his parish. "Co-operation is applied Christianity," the forty-eight-year-old "advocate of fishermen" told the gathering. The principles of the gospels were about to enter the Nova Scotia fishery.[8]

The remarkable reality is that fishermen and their families were prepared to suffer short-term deprivation as a necessary sacrifice for economic security. Convinced that cooperative canneries were the only means of defeating the fish barons, the people of Dover in 1932 founded their Lobster Cooperative with "more faith than facilities."[9] The results, although heartening, were slow. Shortly after the Havre Boucher cannery opened, the fishermen received 5 cents per pound of product, which was "a little more" than the average factory was paying. Yet, little by little, the price increased, and by 1935 the cannery sold sixty thousand pounds of lobster in the Boston market alone. "A few years ago, we scarcely knew the fishermen existed," noted one writer to *The Casket*. "Today the eyes of all Canada are upon them."[10]

ST FRANCIS XAVIER EXTENSION DEPARTMENT

With the fishermen embracing the message of cooperation, Fr Coady and A.B. MacDonald were anxious to take their extension program to the people. Despite the in-kind contributions of St F.X., they were concerned that the department lacked the finances to function in every parish (the $35,000 grant from the Carnegie Corporation could only be stretched so far). Yet, while some wanted to focus on the most promising parishes, Coady sought diocese-wide implementation. After all, at first glance, Larry's River, Guysborough County, had lacked resources and population, and yet, with the help of Fr Charles Forest, the Acadian parish had already organized a community sawmill.[11]

The "first shot" of the fledgling St F.X. Extension Department was fired at a mass meeting at West Bay Road, Inverness County, on 8 September 1930.[12] From Glendale and the surrounding countryside, people came by the truckload to attend speeches by Extension representatives who hoped to "more or less shock the audience." The message was simple: the local people had to work out their own economic salvation through "group action."[13] Two weeks later, the diarist D.D. MacFarlane noted excitedly that there had been a "meeting on Extension work with the farmers" at the schoolhouse at Southwest Margaree.[14]

After the mass meeting, the next phase of organization was the study club. Critical to the Extension program, these clubs were later described, perhaps hyperbolically, as the lever "to move the world."[15] Although many Catholics, especially those with little formal education, found the name intimidating, Fr Coady wanted to challenge his followers intellectually. To overcome the region's bleak economic realities, people had to face some complex truths. Either they buckled down and embraced education and group action, or they would succumb to further outmigration and decline.

The inaugural study clubs were held in stove-heated kitchens, chilly parish halls, and tiny schoolhouses. Averaging ten to twelve people, members selected their own "enthusiastic" leader to liaise with the Extension office and identify local economic problems. A circulating library provided study materials, and participants were expected to read and discuss the publications. There was no limit on the number of clubs permitted in any given parish, but when five clubs were organized at St Andrews, Fr Coady called a joint meeting to ensure efficiency of study.[16] By 1935 a man from Ingonish boasted that 90 per cent of the people "north of Smokey" were at study.[17]

Through the study clubs, hundreds of Catholics were empowered to examine complex issues of agronomy and finance. The topics were challenging and so Extension stressed precision and clarity.

But above all, members were not to be intimidated. "This should be a very pleasant and informal gathering," Fr Coady emphasized. "A cup of tea – a game of cards – a few songs – a few stories or just a chat will help to break down the reserve of the timid members and prepare all for good discussion and study later on."[18]

In Clydesdale, Antigonish County, members sought scientific strategies for pasture improvement, while junior members organized a "calf club." At MacKinnon's Harbour, Victoria County, merely investigating potato seed varieties increased annual production by 75 per cent. The residents of St Andrews opted to focus on cultural issues and hired a teacher of art and music for the local school. When the study club at Dover tackled literacy, some twenty men fishermen learned to read in a single year.

While the early successes were remarkable – there were 173 active study clubs in 43 parishes by the end of 1931 – as Santo Dodaro and Leonard Pluta remind us, many of these clubs eventually petered out. Participants needed self-discipline and oftentimes a little courage. "They were not only asked to commit to undertaking the difficult task of mutual self-education but were also often subjected to scorn and ridicule by their neighbours, who, at least initially, viewed the whole educational experiment, or program, as naïve, wasteful, and even ridiculous."[19]

Fr Amable Briand wrote a short memoir in the 1970s, describing the obstacles that he had faced as a cooperator in West Arichat. After years of discussing the problems of the pulpwood industry on the island, in 1936 a local cooperative of foresters received the support of the provincial marketing department that inspected and scaled the wood. Within months, the men of Isle Madame were felling local stands of black spruce for the bustling European market.[20] Yet Briand soon discovered that his work was seen as a "threat to existing business" and a "challenge to the old established customs."[21] In fact, certain parties sought to sabotage the foresters by spreading falsehoods about production delays. Worried that the contracted shipments of pulpwood would not be filled, the government twice sent representatives into the evergreen Isle Madame woods to investigate, and on both occasions the inspectors were satisfied that the contract could be met. Indeed, by the end of the year, with the help of Fr George Landry at Louisdale, the first load of pulpwood left for Germany.

Other communities like Inverness County (cranberries) and Port Felix (a general store) overcame the odds in their cooperative endeavours, while Catholics in Sydney established a central marketing organization called the Cape Breton Island Producers Cooperative.[22] By pooling an order of fertilizer totalling some three thousand tons, one Cape Breton cooperative saved $20,000 for local farmers. In the mind of Fr Alfred Boudreau, these cooperative ventures could not eradicate poverty – "the poor ye shall always have among you" – but they could halt the spread of both communism and capitalistic exploitation.[23]

CREDIT UNIONS

With interest in cooperative businesses high, the study clubs soon began to investigate credit unions. Local aspiration for a "people's bank" went back to the Farmer-Labour movement of the 1920s when the party, inspired by "Les Caisses Populaires" of Quebec, made credit unions a feature of its platform. The Quebec movement had been started by the journalist and publisher Alphonse Desjardins, who opened a cooperative savings and loan society at Lévis in 1900 to provide loans to members using the collective savings of the group. Testing the local appetite for such a program, organizers of the 1931 Rural Conference invited Roy Bergengren, a Harvard-educated attorney and crusader for credit unions in the United States, to address the delegates.[24] In a stirring lecture, he invoked those hard-working Americans who had fallen victim to loan sharks because of their inability to secure credit. By the time Bergengren sat down, the delegates were utterly convinced that credit unions were achievable.

After the conference, Fr Coady and A.B. MacDonald took Bergengren on a brief tour of the diocese and asked for a candid assessment of their chances of success.[25] The financial activist was impressed and later claimed that the meeting with the gritty fishermen at Little Dover was "the most interesting credit union meeting" he had ever attended.[26] Extension lobbied the provincial legislature to support a Credit Union Act, and the legislation enacted in the autumn of 1932 brought great excitement.

The signatures on the act were hardly dry when Bergengren returned to help organize. On a "cold, miserable December evening," wearing a heavy fur coat, he joined A.B. MacDonald and Fr Coady on the slippery trek from Sydney to Reserve Mines to address a gathering of miners.[27] The dreary weather foretold an empty hall, but to the organizers' great relief, more than a hundred miners crammed into the hall. After an intense discussion, nineteen families agreed to pool $4.75 of their lifetime savings.[28]

At Broad Cove Chapel, Inverness County, Fr Archie MacLellan, or "Mr Broad Cove" as he was affectionately known, organized a similar gathering in the schoolhouse, and his parishioners voted to establish the Filene Credit Union (named after Bergengren's mentor, Edward Albert Filene). By 1933 St Ninian's Parish had named its credit union after Roy Bergengren himself, while the Catholics of New Aberdeen named theirs in honour of Fr Coady.[29] Extension often loaned the fees for the banking charter, and in the case of New Aberdeen, the money for pass books and deposit slips, but it was all quickly reimbursed.[30]

THE *EXTENSION BULLETIN*

As Extension expanded its remit, it needed to supply educational material to the study clubs, energize the base, and "stimulate study and action." One of the more controversial publications that cooperators were reading was the eight-page *Catholic Worker*, which was published in New York City by the radical journalist and Catholic convert Dorothy Day. Flirting with socialism, Day was printing more than 100,000 copies a month by December 1933.[31] Yet some in Antigonish wondered whether the *Catholic Worker* – not to mention its editor, known as the "Red Convert" – was sufficiently grounded in Catholic teaching. Fr Tompkins thought the paper was somewhat radical, while Bishop Morrison felt Day's writing was "freaky and wild" (although this did not stop Extension from inviting her to speak at the 1938 Rural and Industrial Conference).[32] Extension needed its own broadsheet.

In November 1933 the inaugural issue of the *Extension Bulletin* was available in the parishes. Printed bi-monthly during the school term, the paper included inspirational stories on cooperatives, statistical analysis, and book reviews. "Every time I receive a copy of the 'Extension Bulletin,'" wrote one American cooperator from New York, "I feel as though I were sitting in a theatre witnessing a new play, and at the close of reading the issue want to cry, 'Author, author!'"[33] Priests in Toronto thought the inaugural issue was so good that they asked to reprint a number of columns in the *Catholic Register*.[34]

Most of the articles in the *Bulletin* came from the capable pen of the young St F.X. alumnus George Michael Boyle, a native of Afton,

Antigonish County (as a boy he attended St. Patrick's Church in Merland, a mission of the parish of Tracadie), and a brother of Fr James Boyle and Sister Mary Magdalene of the Sisters of Charity. Boyle had honed his skills as a reporter in Florida and New York City before being thrust into editorial work for Extension; locally he had also published in the *King's County Advertiser* and *The Casket*.[35] Boyle had once been due to join the staff of the *New York Times* but tuberculosis had forced him into a frustratingly long stay in the Kentville sanatorium. Described as a "tall spare handsome man who walked with a slight stoop," he was friendly but quick to "raise Cain about an injustice."[36]

With new canneries, cooperatives, and study clubs active across the region, there was no shortage of potential stories. Boyle later recalled that he received hundreds of letters "bursting with ideas."[37] He spent his weekends at the Havre Boucher glebe house editing his columns with the help of his brother and any priests who dropped in with photos of new factories and wharfs.[38] By 1935 the *Extension Bulletin* had a circulation of some seven thousand.[39]

Although the need to organize women along similar lines as men was acknowledged in the rural conferences, sociologist Rusty Neal has shown that the *Extension Bulletin* often "promoted an idealized female-male dichotomy."[40] The *Bulletin* noted that purchasing, marketing, taxation, credit, and education were "a proper element for the exercise of feminine talents," but gender division was entrenched.[41] Yet, much like the Cape Breton labour leader J.B. McLachlan, who noted in the 1920s that the miner's wife was "the greatest financier in the world," everyone knew that the average Catholic woman was at once a "manager ... a seamstress, a cook, an economist, a plumber ... a nurse ... and a janitor."[42]

Boyle was an astute enough reporter to acknowledge that the *Bulletin* required a female contributor, and he found her in Sister Marie Michael (Mary Sarah MacKinnon) of the Sisters of St Martha.[43] A native of Boisdale and a great friend of Fr Michael Gillis, Sister Marie Michael had entered the Marthas in 1927 and earned degrees from both St F.X. and MacDonald Agricultural College (McGill). When recruited to Extension in 1933, she accepted the task of editing "The Women's Page" in the *Bulletin* and helped organize the department's extensive library, which soon grew to fifteen hundred volumes. MacKinnon was smart and tough and could "hold [her] own in any skirmish."[44]

QUADRAGESIMO ANNO

The staff of the *Extension Bulletin* were keen students of Catholic social teaching and social intervention was sorely needed in the 1930s. The global economic recession had further curtailed the fading fortunes of the coal industry. To "equalize" summer and winter operations, the Dominion Steel and Coal Corporation (DOSCO) closed unprofitable mines, and most parishes faced "what practically amount[ed] to a bread line."[45] Reports to the bishop's office noted that almost every family in Sydney required some form of relief, although most refused charity unless absolutely necessary.[46] Even the executive of UMW District 26 was under fire for failing to represent "anything or anybody."[47] One priest-professor at St F.X. later recalled being "conscious all the time of the recurring crisis in the industrial areas." In fact, many Cape Breton students simply did not return to campus, as their "father hadn't been working."[48]

In May 1931, amid this joblessness and household pressure, Pope Pius XI released *Quadragesimo Anno* to reaffirm and elaborate on the principles outlined in the famous labour encyclical *Rerum Novarum*. As the Great Depression had made life "hard, cruel and relentless," the Church claimed the middle ground between unregulated capitalism and collectivism, and asserted its right to intervene on economic questions.[49]

For the clergy-intellectuals of Antigonish, *Quadragesimo Anno* was a tremendous source of encouragement. George Boyle noted in 1933 that "no actionist could be without the guidance of the *Quadragesimo Anno*," as it put some iron in the proverbial glove.[50] In other words, Catholics could no longer excuse their "indifference to the enforced poverty of [their] fellows with the lazy and selfish reflection that all their troubles [would] be solved beyond the grave."[51] The document received widespread attention within Extension circles, and *The Casket* published the entire text so that local study clubs could engage each sentence.

As with all papal pronouncements, *Quadragesimo Anno* prompted debate. Fr J.H. Nicholson at Mount Carmel in New Waterford, wanting to carefully dissect the encyclical with his parishioners, delivered a series of public lectures to clarify the pope's teaching. Speaking to an audience of struggling miners, he reiterated the need for a "living wage," explained the Church's position on private property, decried the lack of charity, and demanded that the fruits of production be shared among workers. Evoking subsidiarity, he proclaimed it wrong to "permit large corporations to control and perform industrial activities which [could] be carried on well by smaller groups."[52]

Nicholson felt strongly that the diocese could not claim the people's loyalty without embracing "the leadership which belongs to her."[53] If the Church was indifferent to the hardships of those in the pews, then it could not lead in struggling communities like Dominion and New Aberdeen. In his mind, the Church should be the first to "enter the fight" and employ its resources, spiritual or otherwise, to enlighten and aid the people.[54] As Fr Thomas O'Reilly Boyle commented, albeit controversially, "The Church is not pro-Capitalist because it is anti-Communist."[55]

In late September of 1933, Bishop Morrison issued an extraordinary letter directed at the miners of Cape Breton and Pictou County. As priests worked to support their demoralized parishioners – Fr James Kiely of Whitney Pier, for example, wanted to use dispensation fees as a special fund for the distressed – the prelate acknowledged that the Church was now concerned not only with the spiritual welfare of the flock but also with "their social and economic well-being." Blaming "the extremists of both labour and capital," he implored Catholics to study the pope's encyclical. The economic times were difficult but the faithful needed "to keep [their] heads." The "get-rich-quick" schemes of the gamblers on the stock market had taken the savings of the innocent, and those with a "penchant for community strife" had taken advantage of this misery.[56]

The deeper problem, of course, was that the Church had few solutions to the industrial economy. Some young people without work left the region, while others found seasonal employment in other industries. The labour leader George MacEachern, for example, found work among the fishing fleet of Lunenburg, but on his return shortly afterward, he faced "real hunger."[57] Encyclicals were well and good, but men needed jobs. "I have not very good reports," Fr Tompkins wrote to the Extension office from Canso. "They [Catholic miners] look upon you fellows as accomplices in putting things over on them."[58]

One short-term strategy was to have the former Celtic footballer Fergus Byrne, the "Labour Editor" of the *Waterford Times*, print material aimed directly at the Catholic working classes. Fr Stanley Macdonald, assisting Fr Nicholson at Mount Carmel, took clerical responsibility for the column. Although this represented a fledgling attempt at Catholic action, Macdonald was told to avoid anything that might "inflame the people."[59] In the meantime, Fr Thomas O'Reilly Boyle gave a series of lectures on the labour question over CJCB radio. While Fr Boyle was a passionate speaker, his rhetoric sometimes got him into trouble. Writing of the gulag system in Russia, he remarked that "forced labour [with] food was better than forced idleness without food." Many of his colleagues cringed at the reckless and naïve statement.[60]

As temperatures dropped below freezing in January 1932, DOSCO proposed a 12.3 per cent wage cut. Facing political pressure, Premier Harrington, a former mayor of Glace Bay, asked Sir Andrew Rae Duncan to convene another commission into the coal industry. Although Harrington wanted the Old Rector to participate, MacPherson, mindful of the 1925 check-off fiasco, was "disinclined" to take his seat and only consented under relentless pressure from Catholic elites. Other priests understood the labour situation better, but Halifax wanted the Old Rector, and he later noted that Antigonish would have "[lost] ground" if he had not agreed.[61] "You did right in consenting to act on the Royal Commission," Fr John Hugh MacDonald wrote from Sacred Heart, "and our house will be at your disposal during your whole stay here."[62]

Much as in 1925, this Duncan Commission held hearings and took the testimony of some eighty-five witnesses. It recommended an "independent umpire" to settle future disputes, called for a 10 per cent wage reduction and several strategic mine closures.[63] This was not news that unemployed miners wanted to hear. Nevertheless, by May, weary and facing a looming strike, they capitulated.[64] In preparing for mine closures, Fr Miles Tompkins at St Agnes in New Waterford was told to clear all debt as the parish was likely to shut down. Similar instructions were given to Great War veteran Fr Alexander J. MacIsaac in Thorburn.[65] "It was a rather unpleasant thing for me to concur in the reallocation scheme of DOSCO," the Old Rector admitted to a colleague in Glace Bay. But, he asked, was it "better for 2,000 people to be thrown out of employment or for 12,000?"[66]

To deal with the glut of unemployed miners, the provincial government tabled legislation to relocate some families onto abandoned farms. While some balked at the policy, Bishop Morrison and the Extension office felt it "an important step in the right direction."[67] By November 1932, as the Glace Bay Board of Trade fought tenaciously to save the coal industry, over 100 miners had been resettled on farms in the vicinity of Margaree, Boularderie, and Louisbourg. Another 130 waited for placement, while bureaucrats processed 700 new applications. It was a frustratingly slow process as interviews were conducted, suitable farms identified, prices agreed, and grants secured.[68] There were, of course, some successes, but as one official later testified, many of the vacant properties "were not paying farms" and most had not been worked in years.[69]

While Cape Breton priests gradually began to seek practical answers to the problems of industry, the apostolic delegate in Ottawa remained fixated on the threat of communism. Before Joseph Stalin's bloody purges and show trials, some Cape Breton miners looked to the Soviet Union as a workers' paradise.[70] When J.B. McLachlan returned from a trip to Russia, he proclaimed that the average Soviet labourer was "better paid, better fed, and received better treatment than the average Canadian worker."[71] To counter these "reports of rosy conditions in Russia," one frustrated Glace Bay priest obtained up-to-date copies of the Soviet wage scale and had it printed in local papers.[72]

While the delegate was worried about communist sympathizers in Cape Breton, the priests on the ground knew that communist ideology posed little tangible threat to the diocese. While Catholics continued to pray for the conversion of Russia, and publicly refuted atheistic communists who took "base advantage of the stress of the times," these non-believers were mostly just a nuisance.[73] From Whitney Pier and Glace Bay, reports noted that roughly 300 active communists resided in the colliery districts. Some 100 were Canadian-born (or of British descent), while the other 200 were primarily from Eastern Europe (except for a few Belgians and Italians). The great majority of these Europeans were of the Eastern Rite and therefore not under the diocese's jurisdiction.[74] Of the 300 known communists, the clergy surmised that only 70 were enemies of the Church.

One reason that communism was dissipating among the miners was that the Church was finally countering tropes that it was always on the side of the rich and powerful. As one Sydney clergyman charged, radicals had successfully "insinuated that [the clergy] want nothing but the people's money, that they are living in luxury, and that they are everywhere in cooperation with Capital." It was natural that this type of rhetoric still found an eager audience among those who had "nothing but the dole to save them from starvation," but attitudes were changing.

ALEXANDER MACINTYRE AND THE GLACE BAY FIELD OFFICE

In the spring of 1932, the sixty-nine-year-old Fr Ronald MacDonald of New Aberdeen made it known that he lacked the means to support his struggling parishioners. While he was powerless to alleviate local poverty within the weathered row houses of his district, some of the faithful hinted that he was holding back resources.[75] Aware of similar sentiments throughout the town, the Extension Department opened a field office in Glace Bay in August 1932.[76] A few weeks later, the diocesan clergy gathered at the Lyceum building in Sydney for an economic conference that resolved to aggressively recruit the laity through credit unions and consumer cooperatives.[77] By the end of the year, twenty-four study clubs were meeting regularly throughout the colliery towns.[78]

In the meantime, the field office organized "self-help groups," which encouraged idle miners to farm vacant plots of land. Although well meant, it was not an ideal solution. When Fr Tompkins learned that anthracite coal was selling at high prices, he expressed frustration that the men had little work and no money. Bishop Morrison concurred: "It can scarcely be wondered at that the whole capitalist system is being placed on trial before the public conscience when such exploitation is being practiced." By the end of 1932, even the bishop, described by one priest as a "status quo Churchman," agreed that the economic system needed a "fundamental overhauling."[79]

Among the clergy there was also a recognition that the people needed guidance and education in choosing their priorities. In the spring of 1929, Catholics in Reserve Mines had bought into a racehorse named Lambert Todd. When the first community-owned racehorse arrived in town from Ontario, it set off a day-long celebration. While joking that the people had turned to "horse worship," Fr J.J. MacNeil expressed genuine concern for the well-being of parishioners who complained of unemployment and small pay cheques but thought "nothing of losing two shifts to stage the greatest reception and demonstration ever witnessed [in Reserve]."[80]

The Glace Bay field office offered hope that new ideas were possible and that poverty could be overcome. After one meeting at the Knights of Columbus rooms in Sydney, Fr James Boyle wrote excitedly that four newcomers had volunteered to organize study clubs.[81] There was a growing interest in extension work among labour and an "awareness among more of [the] pastors."[82] Yet not everyone was enthusiastic. Labour leader George MacEachern, for one, felt that many ideas, like relocating to the countryside and planting potatoes on vacant lots, were futile. In fact, he maintained that they only served to take pressure off the government.[83]

In 1933, to counter skeptics like MacEachern, Extension hired Alexander S. MacIntyre as a fieldworker. A former vice-president of District 26, and managing director of the *Maritime Labour Herald*, he had been blacklisted after the 1925 strike and faced bouts of ill-health and unemployment. By chance, the former communist sympathizer had attended a study club meeting at New Aberdeen and had articulated the position of the miners so forcefully that the local curate, Fr Sam Campbell, invited him to a meeting with Bishop Morrison.[84] For the diocese to survive, MacIntyre told the prelate, it needed to disentangle itself from forces that made life intolerable for the worker.[85]

MacIntyre was "endowed with great intelligence," but most important, he was dedicated to the working classes. By employing him as a field secretary, Extension gained immediate credibility at the pithead and did much to "enroll the ranks of the miners."[86] Ironically, this collaboration with a former radical fuelled occasional gossip that Extension leaned toward socialism. In response, the *Bulletin* offered a detailed analysis of the differences between cooperation and communism.[87] When the *Halifax Chronicle* published similar charges, one correspondent to *The Casket* noted that the reporting was "bosh."[88]

FAILED COOPERATIVE MINE IN INVERNESS

The elephant in the room of the Glace Bay field office was that, unlike the agricultural sector, mining engendered insurmountable obstacles. Nothing better illustrates this reality then the Inverness Coal Cooperative Limited. By the late 1920s, despite a generous provincial subsidy, the Inverness colliery was operating at a considerable deficit. In order to save the town's primary industry, the province agreed in the summer of 1932 to hand over the mine to the employees on a cooperative basis. The local pastor, Fr Ronald L. MacDonald, an old cooperator and former president of the Nova Scotia Farmers' Association, was appointed to the colliery management board.

Within this cooperative, each miner was a shareholder in the company (no one being permitted to hold more than one share). All concerned were optimistic that Inverness had found the solution to the problem of unemployment. "If this mine can be worked out successfully by the men themselves," noted the Old Rector encouragingly, "it will serve as a useful lesson for Nova Scotia miners generally."[89] Yet, although shared ownership was a good idea in principle, having the local priest intimately connected with the town's primary employer was questionable. First, the board faced the tough job of bringing efficiency to a mine that was haemorrhaging money. Difficult decisions were made, and employees dismissed from the mine (with good reason or not) were likely to blame the priest. Second, the cooperative saw no need for a miners' union. What would be the point of organizing against themselves? The more militant employees were enraged, and one local member of the UMW objected that Fr MacDonald was forcing his flock to choose between a union and God.[90]

When the men of Inverness assembled to vote on UMW representation in the autumn of 1932, they were surprised to find Fr MacDonald mingling in the hall. Denying charges that he had influenced the vote, the priest argued that, as Inverness town was not wholly Catholic, he did not have the power to fix an election. Yet while the miners had overwhelmingly rejected UMW representation, resentment lingered. The biggest problem for the cooperative, however, was that it was unprofitable. In January 1933, the board recommended a 12.5 per cent wage reduction (the same cut that DOSCO had requested). Fr MacDonald did his best to quell the ensuring outrage, promising his parishioners that he was "in this thing with both feet," but by the summer of 1933 the cooperative had failed.[91]

As Douglas Campbell has noted, Fr MacDonald "was a good, well-meaning priest who had the interest of his people at heart," but his venture into the coal industry was doomed to fail.[92] Writing in the 1970s, Dan MacInnes was unable to find any material related to this incident in the Extension archives as it "was the most painful co-operative experience in eastern Nova Scotia."[93] Things didn't improve for the Inverness mine. By the end of the decade, the Nova Scotia premier complained that the men "just [didn't] care whether they [got] out two tons of coal per man per day, or whether they [got] out one and one-quarter tons, or even less than a ton ... A mine cannot be run on a basis like [that]."[94]

FR JAMES J. TOMPKINS TO RESERVE MINES

One person who followed the Inverness mine cooperative closely was Fr James Tompkins. By the autumn of 1934, he was in his eleventh year at Canso's Star of the Sea parish and he continued to agitate for fishermen who had been "holding the fort and suffering for many long years."[95] Although he admired his parishioners, he never got used to the coastal climate, "which he had always considered troublesome."[96] After Tompkins requested a new assignment, Bishop Morrison appointed him chaplain to the Sisters of St Martha, and replaced him in Canso with Fr John Boyd Kyte, a native of River Tillard, Richmond County, who "under[stood] the fishermen's problems very well."[97] Tompkins had gone to Canso in an uproar, but left without a whimper. "Dr. Tompkins is back at Bethany and thinking as hard as ever," a colleague remarked. "He has an enormous lot of ideas in his head and is at present trying to reduce them to order."[98]

Fr Tompkins had a tremendous influence on the younger clergy, who were both awestruck and intimidated. The newly ordained Fr Daniel Roberts, a native of Lingan and curate at Whitney Pier, for instance, once met Tompkins on the train coming from Halifax. They made small talk for a short time and then Tompkins asked, "What are you doing for the people of Whitney Pier?" Being "quite innocent of what he meant," Roberts blurted out that, as the depression was raging, there was little to be done. "That was the worst answer I could have given him," Roberts recalled, "because he immediately went on to tell me what I should be doing for the people."[99]

Now residing back in Antigonish town, Tompkins was a regular visitor to the Extension office. Yet, as his biographer noted, "only ideas interested him, systems never," and he was content to leave the day-to-day bureaucratic burdens to the staff.[100] Incredibly, after a few restorative months with the Marthas, he was "chafing for action again." When Fr Joseph MacDonald of Reserve Mines died in February 1935, the sixty-four-year-old Tompkins requested that parish. Hearing of the transfer, Sister Denis Marie, CSM (Mary Margaret Mulcahey), working in Canso, mused that they would "probably be hearing great things from the miners in the future."[101]

Indeed, Tompkins wasted little time identifying the economic problems of his sprawling new parish. While few could remember a time when so little money was in circulation, the colliery towns presented an opportunity for bold ideas.[102] Reserve Mines had its share of poverty, but it also had four hundred families, a convent, and a school that was staffed by the Sisters of Charity. Like the fishermen along the rugged Atlantic coastline, the miners of Colliery No. 10 were determined to get down to the "brass tacks of helpful endeavour." Tompkins pushed literature on his parishioners and, when scholars were engaged to lecture at St F.X., he recruited them to Sydney for an encore presentation.[103] In preparation for the visit of the American Catholic sociologist Paul Hanley Furfey to the diocese in the summer of 1937, he had his flock read Furfey's *Fire on the Earth* so that they would be "well prepared to hear him."[104]

The colliery towns presented Fr Tompkins with several challenges. On the personal level, he was particularly afraid of a late-night sick call to the mine, but he was also frustrated by local complaints that the cooperative movement moved too sluggishly. Both Fr Coady and Bishop Morrison were aware of this attitude and feared that the miners were not absorbing the message. "Of the seventy-six Extension students who followed the courses at St. F.X. University during the early winter," Morrison observed in 1937, "there was scarcely a male representative from the mining towns, with the exception of New Waterford."[105]

To engage intellectually with his flock, and aware that folks would "read bad stuff if they don't get good stuff," Tompkins opened the first cooperative library in the diocese in 1935 with the help of his dedicated curate, Fr Allan MacAdam.[106] On the glebe house veranda, the priests set up a bulletin board with clippings and quotations from useful publications, and Tompkins sat on the stoop to make sure people took note. To him, libraries were not merely books on shelves but ideas with "hands and feet."[107]

By 1936 the "People's Library" was flourishing and Tompkins was hooked. "I just have one copy of the book [*Social Reconstruction* by Fr John Ryan]," he wrote to a friend, "and it has been going the rounds among miners."[108] Each time a package of books arrived in the post, he felt "like a kid with a new rattle."[109] Few noticed when he lobbied the Cape Breton County School Trustees for a regional library, but when he printed the pamphlet "Why Not a Cooperative Library?" the Extension office got the message. With the desire for books spreading "like scarlet fever," there was little point in opposition, and by 1937 the rector of St F.X. was "a hundred per cent with [him] in [his] effort."[110] The province soon passed the Regional Libraries Act authorizing municipalities to designate library funding.

TOMPKINSVILLE

Fr Tompkins's other major accomplishment in Reserve Mines was a housing cooperative. He was not at St Joseph's long before he recognized the stupidity of instructing people "in singing and all that when they haven't a decent home." He carefully cultivated a cadre of local leaders who wanted to shed their former company homes for modern, affordable residences.[111] In 1937 one protégé, Joe Laben, the leader of the parish study club, gave a rousing talk on the emerging cooperative housing initiative to the Rural and Industrial Conference. Two American cooperators, Mary Ellicott Arnold and Mable Reed, who had visited Reserve Mines a few days earlier, were impressed by Laben's presentation and offered their support.[112] Within weeks, Arnold, the "reformer, builder, cooperator and manager of apartments," was at Tompkins's side organizing and encouraging his flock (she was officially added to the Extension staff in 1938).[113]

Fr Tompkins was naturally confident.[114] Offering the housing project ten acres of parish property previously designated for cemetery expansion, he quipped that while the land would be "a nice resting place for the dead," better it go to the living.[115] The houses were designed to meet the needs of the average mining family, and Arnold and Reed even lived in a "test house" to determine annual household costs. In the spring of 1938, the Arnold Housing Cooperative officially opened "Tompkinsville," so named in his honour, in the presence of hundreds of onlookers. They were not "just workingmen's houses," noted one provincial inspector, "but houses anyone might care to live in."

A CHIEF JUSTICE AND A PREMIER

This spurt of Catholic social action coincided with the upward mobility of prominent Catholic elites throughout the province. In 1931 Joseph Chisholm was appointed the first Roman Catholic chief justice of the Nova Scotia Supreme Court. The St Andrews native and former editor of *The Casket* was a "gentleman of the Old School," and a successful fundraiser for St F.X. This writer and bibliophile was awarded an honorary degree by the college in 1932 and in 1935 was created a Knight Bachelor by King George V.

Another St F.X. graduate increasingly in the public eye was Angus L. Macdonald. Having taught in the Dalhousie Law School since

1924, in 1930 he was recruited by the federal Liberals to contest the parliamentary seat in his native county of Inverness. Although defeated, he was elected leader of the Liberal Party of Nova Scotia a few months later through a "wave of enthusiasm" that dispatched seasoned politicians like Antigonish-Guysborough MP William Duff. Macdonald not only possessed "marked intellectual gifts," noted the *Chronicle Herald*, but he was also politically "clean."

Angus L. was popular among the Catholic rank and file and certainly among the diocesan clergy. His brother, Fr Stanley, was ministering at Sacred Heart in Sydney, and his sister Mary (Sister St Veronica, CND) was studying history at the Catholic University of America. When a priest informed Premier Gordon Harrington that he was transferring "his whole-hearted support to the new and brilliant leader of the opposition," the Tories realized they would have trouble in eastern Nova Scotia.[116]

In the colourful autumn of 1933, Macdonald's Liberals won a landslide victory in the Nova Scotia provincial election, taking twenty-two of the thirty seats in the historic chamber. While the result "reflected the sins of the Conservatives more than the virtues of the Liberals," Angus L. had proven himself a popular candidate with promises of a "New Deal."[117] Like the appointment of Sir Joseph Chisholm as chief justice, Macdonald's election was a watershed moment for Nova Scotia Catholics. Although Angus L. was not the first Catholic premier of the province (an honour earlier held by Prime Minister Sir John Thompson), he was one of them. Upon hearing that the Highland Scottish Liberal premier had been elected, one Cape Breton priest declared: "That means that many of [my] worldly desires shall be fulfilled."[118]

Spirits were high at the Extension office on election night. The Tories had been supportive, but the new premier was practically family and believed that the government could play a transformative role within the economy.[119] Even the Old Rector, whose assessment was that the Tories had been defeated "on account of the depression," knew that Macdonald was not afraid of action.[120] A few months later, the *Extension Bulletin* proudly editorialized that the premier's New Year's resolution was to apply cooperation to industrial and commercial life.[121]

Although Premier Macdonald was a stalwart Catholic, a fourth-degree Knight of Columbus, and supposedly above "crass politics," like all successful politicians he had a long political memory. He had not forgiven Bishop Morrison for his tactics during the university merger debate nor his transfer of Fr Tompkins to Canso and disliked "the man in Antigonish."[122] On his first official visit to the cathedral town, the new premier snubbed Morrison by skipping the customary call to the bishop's residence. "If I do not answer them when some tu'penny ha'penny cracks the whip," he quipped afterward, "it is because I realize that I am not the Catholic premier but the premier of all people."[123] When he did finally visit the bishop some weeks later, he was forced to wait in the hall for an embarrassingly long period and was treated so coldly that he realized it would be a long time before he called upon him again.[124] Things would soon get worse.

THE MASS WINE CONTROVERSY

While the diocesan clergy always encouraged temperance, outright prohibition was never popular. Altar wine was carefully prepared according to code, and the Church did not want bureaucrats tampering with its structure or supply. The wine used in local churches was imported by T.J. Bonner, an Antigonish town grocer and proprietor of "The Catholic Church Supply House." Shipments required an ecclesiastical certificate of authenticity vouching for the vineyard's reliability and a chemical analysis ensuring it met the requirements of canon law.

When the provincial legislature passed the Liquor Control Act, which created the Nova Scotia Liquor Commission in 1930, bureaucrats monitored alcohol imports closely. The new government liquor stores hung up their shingles, and police eventually confiscated most of the remaining illicit spirits.[125] By the summer of 1931, seizures of rum, like the 3,600 gallons taken by authorities at Low Point near New Waterford, were becoming rare. Thanks to the foresight of Catholic politicians, the Liquor Control Act also guaranteed that altar wine importers such as T.J. Bonner could continue their trade unmolested – that is, until November 1933, when Bonner's license was abruptly revoked.

The evident reason for cancelling the license of the Catholic Church Supply House was partisanship. During the August election campaign, Bonner had been critical of the Liberal incumbent in Antigonish County, and the party's local patronage committee removed his government-issued credentials. Bishop Morrison was horrified that the Liberals had not consulted him before acting in retaliation, and appalled that the Holy Sacrifice was left to the narrow-mindedness of "ward politicians." "Is it to be supposed that the furnishing of Mass Wine is to be placed at the mercy of political racketeers?" he asked the Liquor Commission. "And are we to sit quiet while this is being done?"[126]

Despite his "anxiety of thought," Angus L. knew precisely what he was doing. Besides getting even for Fr Tompkins's treatment in 1922, he was also responding to the recent news that his brother, Fr Stanley, had been relieved of his duties at Mount Carmel parish in New Waterford. Rumours that the fifty-year-old priest was being sent to Victoria Mines as a lowly curate enraged the Macdonald family, and friends were convinced that the premier was reacting to an "injustice."[127]

In early December, an agitated Morrison wrote to the premier demanding that Bonner's license be reinstated. Perhaps, he allowed, if the Catholic Church Supply House merely supplied St Ninian's Parish with Mass wine the decision might be begrudgingly accepted, but as the grocer provided wine for the entire diocese it was another matter altogether. Why should Catholics in Glace Bay or Guysborough be at the mercy of the Liberal patronage committee in the town of Antigonish? If Mass wine was going to be made a "political football," he cautioned, the people would not sit as "idle spectators."[128]

In response, Antigonish County MLA Dr John Laughlin MacIsaac, a medical doctor and member of the legislature since 1925 (his sister was Sister St John of Beverley, CND), staunchly stepped up to take responsibility.[129] In a frank and somewhat impertinent letter to Morrison, MacIsaac refused to apologize and insisted that Bonner was solely responsible for his fate. Moreover, as Bonner's replacement, the Liberals had nominated C.F. McNeil, a good Catholic who would maintain the strict wine standards. "Mr. McNeil needs the profits in the business as much as Bonner, and I and the Liberal Party owe it to him to put the favor in his way, rather than leave it with a traitor like Bonner, who during the election campaign, did everything in his power to belittle and injure me politically."[130]

Morrison was enraged. Unaccustomed to receiving curt letters from Catholic elites, he threatened to publish MacIsaac's letter in *The Casket*. Within days, another letter arrived from MacIsaac, more apologetic but no less firm. The politician, who had been raised on a pioneer farm along the Dunmore Road in the parish of St. Andrews, was willing to support legislation that would remove future Mass wine purveyors from the authority of the NSLC, he said, but he would not reinstate Bonner; nor would he be deterred "by any veiled threats from whatsoever source."[131]

The resolve of the Macdonald government to defy the Diocese of Antigonish was gutsy but, while the Liberals were taking a risk, they were also pragmatic enough to recognize that a protracted fight with Morrison might win them supporters among Pictou Presbyterians or Baptists in the Annapolis Valley. Although priests complained of the "Russian and Mexican [i.e., totalitarian] conditions" imposed by Halifax, Morrison was in a no-win position. He could, of course, take his case to the pages of *The Casket* but he wanted to protect the Church from public humiliation and, despite his personal animosity toward Angus L., he recognized the significance of having a Catholic in the premier's office. In a gesture of compromise, he suggested that the NSLC grant licenses to both Bonner and McNeil. Still the government refused to budge.

By the end of January 1934, the clergy were perilously short on wine supply. While some secretly purchased from the new supplier – known as Angus L.'s "minister of Mass wine" – others, like Fr Alfred Boudreau in Petit de Grat, were forced to borrow from a neighbouring parish.[132] Most of these men liked Angus L. personally but resented having to "wait for a Catholic Premier to put over this piece of work." When Morrison charged the Liberals with "degrad[ing] the Mass," priests and politicians were caught in an awkward position. Even the new provincial Liberal member for Cape Breton East, Lauchlin Daniel (L.D.) Currie, was torn between loyalty to his political boss and his parish priest. When informed that the politician would not intervene, the bishop lamented that there was not "better stuff in [Currie] than that."[133]

Knowing how "stolid and determined Angus L. [could] be," Fr John Hugh MacDonald "gently" wrote to the premier seeking a compromise.[134] The priest cautioned his friend that the diocese would fight against political interference in its affairs and warned that a public battle with Morrison would be embarrassing and "injurious to Liberalism" in eastern Nova Scotia. "Have the courage and loyalty," he counselled the premier, "to settle the matter at once."[135]

By May 1934 the volume of altar wine in the diocese was so low that priests had to get supplies from Montreal and Moncton. These imports were illegal, but the clergy were "willing to take a chance on it."[136] When news of this infraction filtered back to Halifax, Macdonald quickly granted permission for clergy to import wine for sacramental purposes.[137] Even Angus L. did not want the police involved. By June, R.D. MacLean, the brother of Fr George MacLean, who owned the Moncton supply house, had applied for the license to sell altar wine in eastern Nova Scotia.

The bad blood between prelate and premier – which would wane over time but never fully disappear – reached its zenith in the summer of 1934. With the wine controversy still lingering, Fr Stanley lodged a formal complaint with the apostolic delegate over his transfer from New Waterford to Victoria Mines. In support of his brother, Angus L. threatened to intervene with Church authorities "to curb the Bishop of Antigonish." "I do not want to be uncharitable," the premier grumbled to an Ottawa colleague, "but it may be that my encounter with Bishop Morrison on the occasion to which I refer may have something to do with his bitterness towards Rev. Stanley now."[138]

Yet on clerical matters, it was Morrison who held the cards. It was well known that Fr Stanley wrestled with drink, and the priest struggled to wage a defence. When the apostolic delegate denied Fr Stanley's appeal, the priest hired a Roman lawyer and took his case to the Curia. Later, when transferred to Pomquet as an assistant, he noted that it was a "manifest attempt to belittle and humiliate [him] still further" (he would serve as a curate for decades until becoming administrator of Big Pond in 1949).[139] Morrison was not through with the premier either. When, in 1938, prominent alumni such as Sir Joseph Chisholm lobbied the college to grant Macdonald an honorary degree, Morrison threatened to boycott the convocation.[140] "[Morrison] puts the Tory stamp on him and a man of his makeup couldn't be anything else," Fr Stanley wrote disparagingly to his brother. "A St. F.X. LLB is not much of an honour and you might be as pleased without it."[141] The college would not grant another honorary degree for eight years.

AMALGAMATED MINE WORKERS

Although the ongoing feud with Bishop Morrison was bothersome, Premier Macdonald had bigger issues to worry about. In the particularly humid summer of 1932, a group of miners had organized the Amalgamated Mine Workers (AMW) and swiftly challenged the dominance of the UMW in the coalfields. As the fledgling union recruited aggressively, the clergy were worried about escalating divisions. "The miners are having their own troubles not only with the management but also with the disrupting activities among themselves," Bishop Morrison wrote to the pastor of Sydney Mines, and it was "regrettable that they cannot remain united ... and thus negotiate more effectively."[142]

In October 1933, Fr Angus MacIsaac, curate at Sydney's Sacred Heart, told a diocesan conference that there was little solidarity among his parishioners. Months later, the Old Rector complained to his former colleague Sir Andrew Rae Duncan, that the AMW was breaking the cohesion of the miners and "doing a lot of harm." Duncan responded that division among the men was "a very disturbing element," as their bargaining position was already weak.[143] Ironically, despite their earlier battles with District 26, the Church and the union were quite friendly. When, for example, William P. Delaney, the former vice-president of the local UMW, died in the summer of 1932, his obituary noted that he was a member of the Glace Bay KOC, the CMBA, and an associate of New Aberdeen's Ancient Order of Hibernians. The militant who, despite his diplomatic demeanour, had fought so tenaciously for the miners in the difficult years of the 1920s, was given a High Requiem Mass at St Anne's in Glace Bay.[144]

As the AMW fought for company recognition, some were irked by its communist leanings and the rhetoric of its newspaper, the *Nova Scotian Miner*.[145] The Catholic press covered AMW-supported strikes and walkouts, like the one at Dominion's 1-B mine in 1934, but these did not garner the headlines of the past.[146] Everyone noticed, however, when J.B. McLachlan publicly argued during the 1935 federal election campaign that communism was the last hope for Cape Breton's working class. His candidacy alone surprised the political elite, yet he finished in third place with over five thousand votes. It "horrified the local middle class," writes Michael Earle, "and for weeks after the election the *Glace Bay Gazette* published the full texts of anti-communist sermons in the town's churches.[147]

After the election, some embarrassed clergymen lashed out at the rebirth of communist sentiment. At St Anne's, Fr Angus A. Beaton pronounced from the pulpit that some of the flock had supported McLachlan, and devoted a sermon to the attitudes of Karl Marx and Friedrich Engels toward organized religion.[148] "The Catholic worker," he noted, was honour-bound "to fight the monster of communism whose strategy was to 'bore from within' their organizations."[149] Yet, at the annual clerical retreat in 1936, Bishop Morrison, while lamenting the "startling vote," maintained that Extension would overcome any new appeal to radicalism. In fact, the Glace Bay field office reported confidently that 90 per cent of the communist vote was "economic" and not "anti-Christian."[150]

While J.B. McLachlan was an atheist, and one of the "greatest enemies" of the Extension program, Alex MacIntyre felt that he had not made any "real or lasting progress."[151] When a Swiss newspaper, *Rorschacher Zeitung*, reported that most Catholic miners in Glace Bay had voted for communism, Bishop Morrison replied that the allegation was laughable. In an extraordinary letter to the apostolic delegate, the prelate claimed that a mere "handful" cast a ballot for the Scottish radical and even admitted some personal sympathy for them. Catholic supporters of McLachlan were not militant atheists, he noted, but rather were "so often cajoled and deceived by the old parties, both Liberal and Conservative, that in disgust they wanted to show their retaliation against the tactics of these old political parties, who for so many years exploited and deceived the miners."[152] What a difference a few decades had made.

THE CO-OPERATIVE COMMONWEALTH FEDERATION

In the hope that *Quadrageismo Anno* would be the start of a new era of Catholic action, the Catholic League for Social Justice, open to those aged eighteen and over, was organized in the spring of 1933 under the leadership of the young St F.X. bursar Fr Hugh Somers. *The Casket* gave social commentators like Fr James Ryan close coverage, noting that he was a "foremost thinker" and not an ardent radical.[153] According to historian Gerald Fogarty, by the 1930s the North American Church had almost no area of thought which was liberal, "except its attitude toward labor and social questions."[154]

It was in this environment that a start-up political party on the prairies – a coalition of farmers, progressives, socialists, and labour groups – attracted interest in the coalfields of Nova Scotia. The Co-operative Commonwealth Federation (CCF), founded in Calgary in 1932, sought to regulate the Canadian economy, add welfare programs, and nationalize key industries. Despite the few radicals in Glace Bay who condemned the reformist policies of the CCF, members of the UMW hastily formed a CCF club, "motivated by their anxiety to find a moderate political force to counter the Communist Party."[155] By August 1933, St F.X. Extension fieldworkers reported that the party's popularity was growing and its manifesto was "causing considerable discussion" in study clubs.[156]

CCF supporters wasted little time linking their party with the Extension message. Some months before the "Regina Manifesto" was proclaimed on the vast Canadian prairie, Extension was rumoured to be in talks with the CCF leader James Shaver (J.S.) Woodsworth. While this was clearly a "piece of propaganda," many felt that the two organizations had a natural synergy on economic issues.[157] The CCF certainly appealed to Glace Bay Extension fieldworker Alex MacIntyre, who was repeatedly asked to stand for election under the party's banner.

But when Woodsworth claimed in the lead-up to the 1933 provincial election that a priest in Nova Scotia was organizing fishermen and miners into cooperative societies in support of his party, a crisis was precipitated. Morrison was outraged. He demanded the priest's identity and publicly refuted the allegation.[158] "To that statement I desire to give a point-blank denial," he indignantly wrote to party officials. "Any social work and Catholic action undertaken by the Catholic priests in this part of the country is solely on its own merits, and has no association whatever either directly or indirectly with the CCF or any other political party."[159] Shortly afterward, in a letter to Fr Leo Keats, he warned that Woodsworth's "mendacious attempt" to link up Extension with the CCF had to be "resisted and guarded against to the utmost."[160]

The popularity of the CCF in the coalfields presented some embarrassing issues for Extension. One of its worst-kept secrets was that many of the clergy were supporters of the Liberal Party, or at least friends of Angus L. Macdonald. If Extension study clubs in the colliery towns openly advocated for a rival political party, how might the Macdonald Liberals react? On the other hand, if Extension officers came out aggressively against the CCF, they would alienate the miners. When a priest attacked the platform of the party from a Glace Bay pulpit, MacIntyre warned that such rhetoric would "drive the people back to communism."[161]

The CCF arrived in Cape Breton at a time of disunity among labour. Although by 1936 the AMW still had its share of supporters, it was unable to achieve company recognition and its members gradually drifted back to UMW District 26. By May the Old Rector optimistically told his friend Sir Andrew Rae Duncan, who had chaired two eponymous royal commissions, that the UMW and AMW on the "Glace Bay side of the harbour" were going to unite.[162] J.B McLachlan, for one, was so disgusted by the capitulation of the AMW that he resigned from the communist party and went into retirement (he died in November 1937). But the victory of the moderates prompted priests like Fr Tompkins to note that "things look[ed] quite promising around the mines."

In the meantime, miners rallied around the CCF as a unifying force, and in 1938 District 26 voted to affiliate with the party (the first union in Canada to do so). Sporadic clerical attacks on the CCF continued to fuel the rift between St F.X. and the Glace Bay field office, and MacIntyre repeatedly asked the Extension director to rein in clergymen whose sermons were "leaving a very bad impression on the workers." Yet Fr Coady refused. "We discussed this situation with Dr. Boyle this morning," A.B. MacDonald wrote, "and he thinks there is no need to worry over it."[163] By 1939 the miners in New Waterford had elected their first CCF representative (in a by-election) to the provincial house.

ARCHBISHOP JOHN HUGH MACDONALD

As Glace Bay Extension fieldworkers monitored the pulse of the colliery towns, priests who understood the local labour movement, like Fr John Hugh MacDonald of Sacred Heart, took on extreme importance. Paradoxically, because these thoughtful and energetic clergymen were so effective, they were susceptible to becoming bishops in other dioceses.

Just after midnight, on 25 May 1934, with his Cape Breton family at his bedside, Archbishop Neil McNeil, now eighty-three years old, died in Toronto. A large contingent of Antigonish clergy took the train to Ontario to attend the funeral at St Michael's Cathedral and the subsequent burial in a tomb on the leafy grounds of St Augustine's Seminary.

While local Catholics mourned the loss of a respected native son, they also watched for the ensuing shuffle of episcopal appointments in the prelude to replacing him. Given the influence of his late uncle the archbishop, it was rumoured that Fr *John R.* MacDonald would be appointed to the vacant diocese of Victoria, British Columbia.[164] So, when the news arrived in August that Fr *John Hugh* MacDonald was the one heading west, there was confusion in the press over which Fr John MacDonald had been selected. "The papers often make mistakes," Fr John R. joked. "Rome, never!"

Fittingly, a contingent of coal miners braved the pouring rain to attend the consecration of the new bishop in St Ninian's Cathedral (some of the best period photographs of St Ninian's were taken just before the ceremony).[165] Bishop Morrison was unhappy to lose such a capable priest as Fr John Hugh, but was confident that the skills MacDonald had gleaned in New Waterford and Sydney would be useful in British Columbia. "Once the machine is lubricated," the canny prelate advised the departing bishop administratively, "matters will go along apace."[166]

Bishop MacDonald would spend less than two years in Victoria – that diocese had watched a spate of bishops come and go – and there was soon talk that he would be returned "to his native province" to succeed the late Archbishop O'Donnell of Halifax.[167] When he was instead appointed coadjutor archbishop of Edmonton in 1936 (he would succeed Archbishop Henry J. O'Leary in March 1938), one Cape Breton native wrote from Alberta that the prelate was "making quite a hit."[168] MacDonald's quick rise through the ecclesiastical ranks demonstrated that Rome was paying attention to the work of priests in the Cape Breton coalfields. Things were moving slowly, but social action was taking root.

EXTENSION GROWS

By 1935 the progress of the "Antigonish Movement," as it was now being called, made leaders like Fr Coady household names. "Dr. Coady is fast becoming one of the most influential men in Eastern Canada," one priest declared. "Discerning people are beginning to call him one of the great Canadians."[169] When the Nova Scotia Royal Commission on Economic Inquiry – the "Jones Commission" – began its investigation in 1934, it relied heavily on Fr Coady and his fieldworkers. Hearings were held throughout the region by the lead investigator Professor J.H. Jones of the University of Leeds, aided by the Toronto economic historian Harold A. Innis (who would write a history of the cod fishery in 1940) and the former deputy minister of marine and St F.X. alumnus Alexander Johnston.[170]

It was anticipated that the commission would help Halifax manage the economic depression and provide a foundation for fiscal and constitutional negotiations with Ottawa.[171] Yet its queries often seemed redundant. At St Peter's, Fr Leo Keats testified that his parishioners were "embarrassed" that their problems were again under scrutiny by outsiders. Nova Scotia had already had "two Duncan Commissions, and certain Apple growers' and fisheries' Commissions," and he wondered how many of the recommendations made by former commissioners had been implemented.[172] In other words, the endless government inquiries by elite Toronto academics and British bureaucrats were merely a "smokescreen" to cover up endemic political and regional inequities.

While the Extension Department believed that people were responsible for their own economic destiny, it was clear that Confederation was partly to blame for much of the region's economic woes. Some high-profile priests such as Fr. D.J. MacDonald advocated for a regional political party to offset Quebec and Ontario's dominance of the Canadian Parliament.[173] Others, like Fr Keats, went so far as to propose that Great Britain should take over administrative control of Nova Scotia much as it had in Newfoundland in 1934.[174] It was hyperbole, of course, but it bore witness to the deep dissatisfaction that pervaded the countryside. The only thing keeping people in Petit de Grat, Fr Alfred Boudreau testified, was the stringent immigration policy of the United States; otherwise his parish would "lose [its] families by the dozen."[175]

While proposed solutions were often vague, Nova Scotians were at least facing their problems. "More and more I realize how many years the locusts have eaten in Nova Scotian agriculture," Premier Macdonald acknowledged to Fr "Little Doc" MacPherson. "There are hopeful signs on the horizon, however, not the least significant of which is an intellectual and spiritual – in the sense of all the faculties of the spirit (loyalty, pride, patriotism and the like) – awakening throughout the province."[176] Even in failure there was victory; intellectual awakening, Fr James Boyle optimistically suggested, was often as important as economic outcomes.[177]

Other countries soon took note of this spirit, and St F.X. was contacted by groups from as far afield as Turkey and the Philippines.[178] From Montreal, Cardinal Jean-Marie-Rodrigue Villeneuve urged

Canadian Catholics to study the Extension message; Archbishop James Charles McGuigan of Toronto sent three priests to Antigonish town to get "sane economic and social direction"; and the Methodist Rev. Dr W.C. Ross of Mount Allison University confessed that Extension appealed to him "more than anything else that [had] happed in the last 10 years."[179] A contingent of foreigners attended the 1938 Rural and Industrial Conference, and some two hundred American cooperators later toured the diocese.[180] By the end of the decade, Extension was at work in Prince Edward Island and in Newfoundland, where the Commission of Government was organizing cooperatives as one approach to economic regeneration.[181]

Extension had supporters within the regional press to champion its agenda. As mentioned above, the English-born William Dennis, president and editor-in-chief of the *Halifax Herald* until 1920, had been, at least in the opinion of the clergy, anti-Catholic.[182] However his nephew, William Henry Dennis, who took control of the paper in 1921, was a "most sympathetic and alert friend."[183] He reported generously (and fairly) on local cooperative projects, and each Christmas sent a $500 donation to be distributed among the needy. Despite the fact that Angus L. had declared Dennis "Public Enemy Number One" for his uncharitable references to Nova Scotia's woeful infrastructure, the paper always made "beautiful reference" to the Extension program.[184] While Dennis understood the power of propaganda, in his enthusiasm he occasionally overlooked protocol, and his plan to have Extension rehabilitate Terence Bay, a fishing community near Halifax, got the Antigonish priests in hot water with the Archdiocese of Halifax.[185]

Perhaps the most important piece of propaganda related to Extension in this period was Bertram Fowler's 1938 book *The Lord Helps Those ...: How the People of Nova Scotia are Solving Their Problems through Co-operation*. In this hyperbolic and hurriedly written volume, Fowler, a former reporter for the *Christian Science Monitor*, described Fr Tompkins as "John the Baptist," and created the enduring and romantic myth that the priest had been transferred to Canso in 1922 due to his support of struggling miners and fisherfolk.[186] In a particularly silly excerpt, Fowler wrote that Tompkins had lost a "bitter battle with evasion and apathy."[187] Writing to A.B. MacDonald, Fowler admitted to having "a kind of Roman Holiday at the expense of the sitters-on-the-fence," but was careful to write "lots of nice things about you fellows."[188]

Fowler was a popular orator and "a great favorite with country audiences."[189] His book was read widely and, as Rusty Neal, a historian of the period, notes, Extension was soon "flooded with requests for information."[190] From Dublin, Edward Cahill, author of *Freemasonry and the Anti-Christian Movement*, mused after reading Fowler's book that Ireland was confronted with problems "somewhat similar" to those of eastern Nova Scotia.[191] The popularity of the manuscript forced Extension to deal with some of the oversimplifications and hyperbole of the text; it was anything but "a cold and dispassionate appraisal of the theories of a movement."[192] The shortcoming of Fowler's book," remarked the *Extension Bulletin* in October 1938, was that the author "having viewed the Antigonish Movement from the standpoint of an outsider, was unable to maintain the proper perspective."[193] It was a piece of propaganda and even Tompkins was a "little embarrassed at the praise" from a book that was "a bit extravagant in spots."[194]

The problem, of course, was that many journalists "wanted Antigonish to be the Promised Land" and Frs Coady and Tompkins their messiahs.[195] Chroniclers like Fowler could not grasp the "great gulf" that had to be bridged between the "ideas of the propagandists of the movement" on the one hand, and the "hard realities of the administrator on the other."[196] They were also unsure how to weigh the role of actors like Bishop Morrison and the Old Rector who did not fit their romantic notions of episcopal hostility. The following years saw many hagiographic commentaries such as Bonaro Overstreet's *Brave Enough for Life*, in which one could read such hyperbolic lines as: "So this is Father Jimmy Tompkins, whose name is spoken with love and honour wherever adult educators or members of the co-operative movement talk of their job as building democracy from the ground up."[197]

Then there were accounts that promoted the work of Extension against an over-simplified and often negative backdrop of extreme poverty and ignorance among the people. *Nova Scotia: The Land of Cooperation* by Fr Leo Ward of the University of Notre Dame was particularly dismissive. Describing an Iona woman wearing "white shoes with tall heels," Ward expected that she was not an "unrealistic person," but rather wore the footwear because "they are the only presentable shoes she possesses."[198] Later, Fr D.J. Rankin would complain that Ward's description of his parishioners at Iona was distorted and that the book would "do very much harm to the cooperative movement."[199]

In response to this "nonsense," Fr Coady decided to write his own account of the movement, which he composed through 1938 and 1939. Funded and encouraged by the General Education Board of the Rockefeller Foundation, *Masters of Their Own Destiny: The Story of the Antigonish Movement of Adult Education through Economic Cooperation* was a "personal report of the Antigonish program." As Coady fought bouts of heart trouble, colleagues like Zita (O'Hearn) Cameron were a tremendous help both in Antigonish and at the Golden Eagle Tavern in Beaufort, South Carolina, the hotel where he went to convalesce.[200] Years later, Msgr Malcolm MacLellan happily recalled his experience of sitting as a "wet nurse" at Coady's bedside "taking notes while he was giving birth to his ideas."[201]

Once the manuscript was approved by the Rockefeller Foundation, Coady took it to the New York publisher Harper & Brothers and then promptly went into the hospital. "Dr Coady left for New York with the manuscript of his new book on cooperation, Fr D.J. MacDonald excitedly informed a friend, "and all say that the book is a humdinger."[202] When *Masters of Their Own Destiny* was released in the spring of 1939, the *Xaverian Weekly* reported that the students had devoured the text.[203] The clergy liked it too, although Bishop Morrison couldn't help joking that the title was bad theology.[204]

Although Fr Coady got the headlines, in fact many people had contributed to the success of the Extension program. Bishop Morrison, for one, was a keen supporter, sought financing, and became an avid student of the cooperative message. When, for instance, Fr George Landry complained about the economy of Louisdale, the prelate pointed out that it was local opposition that had doomed a pulpwood project. "If the people do not work together and cooperate," he responded to Landry, it was "difficult to expect industry to prosper."[205] While supporting a plan in the parish of St Andrews for community health insurance, Morrison told stakeholders that it was better to have "tried and failed then never to have tried at all."[206]

St F.X. administrators also made countless sacrifices for Extension. Juggling the department's needs with those of the college was a challenge. When one professor wanted to coordinate study sessions among the lobster fishermen, substantial rescheduling was required. "I am well aware that although extension work is important," the scholar confessed, but "classes must be carried on as usual" (a substitute was eventually found).[207] When Fr Coady requested that

Fathers James Boyle and Michael Gillis take on more responsibilities in the field (Boyle would work with the fishermen, Gillis with the farmers), clerical faculty were occasionally needed to serve as their replacements for Sunday Mass. There was also a great financial cost, but the board of governors felt that the program "more than justified" the financial outlay.[208]

All these sacrifices were rewarded in April 1938, when the diocese received a dispatch from Eugenio Cardinal Pacelli, the Vatican secretary of state (and future Pope Pius XII), praising and encouraging the work of the Antigonish Movement. Not only was the program effective, Pacelli wrote, but it encapsulated the teachings of both *Rerum Novarum* and *Quadragesimo Anno*. "With eyes uplifted to heaven," the Holy Father bestowed his Apostolic Benediction on the fieldworkers and those "for whom [they] were so profoundly concerned."[209] Elated, Bishop Morrison sent copies to the parishes and the regional newspapers, eager to demonstrate that Rome was "deeply and sympathetically interested in this particular line of Catholic action."[210]

News of the apostolic benediction spread quickly. "We found the letter … of such interest and significance," wrote the *Glace Bay Gazette*, "that we had our editor feature it in our [latest] issue."[211] Congratulatory telegrams poured in from across Canada, including Charlottetown, where Bishop O'Sullivan imagined that "hearts were stirred at St. Francis Xaviers."[212] While there was tremendous excitement at Extension, in Reserve Mines Fr Tompkins reflected "a little grimly about it." He had spent his vocation bellowing for Catholic social action and now the diocese was receiving the "plaudits of the public and the Vatican."[213] Tompkins knew that "Pius XI praised the Antigonish plan," wrote Leo Ward, "but I never heard him make anything of this fact."[214]

STABLE PARISHES

As the work of Extension had helped many parishes stabilize their economies, more monies had come into the parish coffers for construction projects. New churches were built or dedicated at Boisdale (St Andrew's, 1930), Whitney Pier (Holy Redeemer, 1930), and Florence (St Stephen, 1935), and the new church at St Anne's in Glace Bay was finally completed in 1938 (construction having gone on for a decade). The population of industrial Cape Breton continued to expand, and in October 1934 St Theresa's Parish was created to serve the Ashby district of Sydney. When the church was formally dedicated in May 1935, some five thousand onlookers waited outside, while inside the sanctuary Bishop Morrison announced that Sydney's "baby parish" was one of the "important links in the diocesan chain."[215]

Whenever disaster struck, churches became the focal point of community suffering and consolation.[216] In April 1935 seven miners lost their lives in an explosion that destroyed parts of the gassy Allan Shaft in Stellarton. Three of the deceased were respected members of Lourdes Parish and "all the beauty of the liturgy ... and its solemn rituals comforted the [grieving] families."[217] Three years later, the rope (a heavy steel cable) on the rake that lowered the miners into the Princess Colliery at Sydney Mines broke, killing twenty-one men. One witness to the horror confessed that he had seen sights on the battlefields of France "that would not surpass what [he] viewed in that mine."[218] Six of the deceased were parishioners at Immaculate Conception parish (including a father and son), and six priests participated in the solemn Mass of requiem.[219]

The "sudden snuffing out of the lives" of hardworking miners brought feelings of sorrow to the whole region. While loyal to their respective parishes, Catholics in Eastern Nova Scotia were interconnected through kinship and regularly came together for fellowship. In the autumn of 1933, the third diocesan Eucharistic Congress was held at Lourdes in Stellarton. For a community fond of its annual "May Procession," organizing an open-air congress came naturally, and every detail, including the weaving of a replica altar cloth to match the one used at the recent international congress in Dublin, was carefully arranged. Bishop O'Sullivan of Charlottetown crossed the Northumberland Strait to preach, while Bishop Sandy said a special Mass for the children.[220] In all, over six thousand Catholics from across the Maritimes attended, while others were encouraged to go to confession and take communion in their local parishes.[221] Three years later, another successful congress was held at Cheticamp, and like the people of Stellarton, the Acadian Catholics of northern Cape Breton were lauded for their hospitality.[222]

These events helped maintain a strict social and devotional code, and Catholics took regulations seriously. Sunday was always a day of rest and even telegrams were not put through to their recipients until early Monday. In the middle of a lecture that the promoter of cooperatives Wesley Haddon McEwan was giving at Belle Cote, Inverness County, he was stunned to see that, as soon as the Angelus bell began to toll, the audience "immediately knelt down before their chairs with their beads out."[223]

While devotion to popular saints was encouraged, there was also a lively sense of sanctity as an incarnated presence, with many personal exemplars to follow. Families in Mabou, for example, were familiar with the career of Sister Mary of the Cross (Mary Helen MacKillop), who was proposed for beatification in recognition of her ministry in South Australia. Not only had she done Herculean work with the Sisters of St Joseph but she was also the cousin of Mabou's pastor, Fr John Francis MacMaster.[224] Closer to home was thirty-two-year-old Margaret Fougere of Frankville, Antigonish County. After her death in 1931, *The Casket* committed an entire column to her piety. One of eighteen children – three of her siblings had entered the Sisters of St Martha – she had worked since the age of sixteen as a housekeeper for her uncle, Fr Joseph DeCoste.[225] "Prudent, self-effacing and gentle," proclaimed *The Casket*, "Fougere was skilful in both art and music, and like Saint Therese of Liseux, she showed little fear of death."[226]

THE OLD RECTOR RETIRES

There were worthy examples of piety among the clergy as well. In April 1932, H.P. MacPherson, the Old Rector of St F.X, was elevated to the rank of protonotary apostolic, a member of the highest non-episcopal college of prelates (he was henceforth permitted to wear the red (fuchsia) cassock and complementary sash).[227] One of the first to learn of the appointment was the Roman seminarian John Hugh Gillis, who received an unexpected and indirect congratulation from the rector of the Scots College.[228] Writing from Georgeville, Fr J.W. Chisholm noted proudly that the first three monsignors in Antigonish had been Gillis's kinsmen, while the fourth was "one of [his] old professors."[229]

Serving at the helm of the college and acting as Bishop Morrison's vicar-general took a toll on MacPherson's health. During the St F.X. convocation of 1935, he spoke only briefly on account of hoarseness from a protracted flu. The following June, unable to execute all his duties, he resigned. In view of his long and untiring service, he was given a residence on campus and was designated president-rector emeritus.[230] The Old Rector had become "so much of the college itself," noted one alumnus, "that to think of one without the other requires a new orientation."[231] He "always had time for everyone, beggar or scholar," Msgr Malcolm MacLellan later recalled, "and he excelled at putting them all at their ease."[232]

It was not unexpected that it was St F.X.'s vice-president Fr Daniel J. MacDonald who was selected as MacPherson's replacement. Born in the parish of Heatherton and educated at the Urban College, the handsome priest joined the St F.X. faculty in 1912, having earned a PhD in English at the Catholic University of America. A brother of A.B. MacDonald and a great friend of Fr Coady, he knew the Extension program inside out. He was also a political survivor. The son of a "Heatherton stampeder," he had supported Fr Tompkins's program of adult education and community betterment and was considered one of the most radical members of the college staff. Yet he had also opposed university merger in 1922 and was therefore a "safe" choice. While he quickly began to "dream dreams of expansion and further educational conquests," he kept a close eye on the funds.[233]

REGIONAL HISTORY AND LITERATURE

The decade of the 1930s was fruitful for those with a literary or historical bent. As the new college rector, Fr MacDonald lamented that he was so busy with administration that he had no opportunity to expand upon his PhD dissertation on the poet Shelley. But he also had a great interest in the past and spent many evenings discussing the history of his native parish. From Arisaig, writer and genealogist Fr D.J. Rankin used his spare time "searching up old documents" and writing periodically for the *Catholic Register*. While exploring the abandoned farms along the gulf shore, he became keenly interested in the genealogy of their displaced pioneer families and asked readers of *The Casket* to send him their ancestral information.[234] Inspired by the genealogical work of the "thoughtful" barrister J.L. MacDougall at Inverness and A.J. MacKenzie at Christmas Island, Rankin wanted to "awaken in the younger people an interest in the past."[235] In 1929 he published *A History of the County of Antigonish*, with contributions and materials supplied by priests and local historians like Sir Joseph Chisholm. Although it contained many errors and was by no means complete – at least one person joked that it would take a formula from Einstein to decipher the family trees in places – it was an impressive volume.[236]

Later, while ministering in Iona, Fr Rankin published *Our Ain Folk and Others*, his own portrait of a "true Cape Bretoner."[237] He followed it with a novel, *On This Rock*, which offered a spirited defence of the Catholic citizenry of Canada and encouraged vocations to the priesthood (his character, a young Frank O'Kane, ultimately "answers the call").[238] Although contemporary reviewers liked Rankin's work, more recent readers have not been as sympathetic. Historian Ian McKay has suggested that the "fierce[ly] conservative" clergyman's books were "unusually explicit in drawing out the conservative organic ideology of the folk" and had borrowed from the papal encyclicals to create his own ideal construction of the Cape Breton experience.[239]

Rankin had a specific religious and cultural agenda (he was a priest after all), but many of his impressions of agriculture, rural resettlement, and the fisheries fit squarely with the teachings of the St F.X. Extension Department.[240] A folksy writer perhaps, Rankin had worked to develop education in all his parishes, including Grand Mira, and to bring some infrastructure equilibrium within the diocese.[241] Some of his notions were unquestionably romantic – his belief that people could make a "comfortable living" from agriculture and the fishery in this period is contradicted by his colleagues' Royal Commission testimony – but his underlying mentality was shared by many.[242]

The publications of clergymen like Fr Rankin inspired a new generation of historians and folklorists. *The Casket* soon had a "folklore" column that featured Gaelic stories of fairies, witches, mermaids, and forerunners. In 1931 Sister St Thomas of the Angels, CND (Mary L. Fraser) published *Folklore of Nova Scotia*, which stemmed from her PhD research at Fordham University in New York. A native of Antigonish County, she interviewed local Scottish cultural enthusiasts like Bishop Sandy and older residents in the Acadian and Mi'kmaq communities for "tales which have grown up on Nova Scotian soil."[243] Later, in 1937, Fr Richard Valentine Bannon, a Harvard-educated professor of English at St F.X., published a collection of poetry entitled *Eastland Echoes*. Many of his poems dealt with the legends of eastern Nova Scotia such as "A Maryvale Myth," and "The Frenchman's Barn," where "little fairies flung the seed while tides were out a-playing."[244]

While many of these legends were grounded in historical as well as mythical events, more serious research into the history of the Church in Canada was underway. In 1933 the Canadian Catholic Historical Association (CCHA) was established in Toronto and a handful of Antigonish priests were active members (Fr Rankin was one of the founders). Fr Hugh Somers had completed his PhD in history at the Catholic University of America in 1931 with an excellent thesis on Bishop Alexander MacDonell, the first bishop of Upper Canada, and by 1933 he had been "appointed to guard the St. F.X. treasury and to introduce students to history."[245] In the meantime, he dabbled through boxes of papers in church basements and glebe attics and was soon off to Halifax to speak to the Nova Scotia Historical Society on the antiquity of St Andrews Parish.[246]

Another budding historian was Sister St Veronica, CND, the sister of Fr Stanley and Angus L. Macdonald. While she was at the CUA in Washington, her professors noticed her scholarly gifts and St F.X. was keen to have her on its faculty. Although St Veronica was interested in Canadian history, the administration wanted her to focus on another field as they already had two Canadianists on staff.[247] Undeterred, the young academic was determined to write her master's thesis on a "British-Canadian or European-Canadian 'problem.'" In 1937, her degree in hand, she was appointed as an associate professor of history, the first female faculty member at St F.X.

For local historians like Fr Anthony A. Johnston, it was also an exciting period. A "keen student of the French missionary efforts in Nova Scotia," Johnston was known for walking through overgrown cemeteries, notepad in hand, searching local glebes for material relating to a diocese's early history. "The searcher for historical truth," he later commented, "will not neglect the tiring task of visiting all the cemeteries in his diocese and copying the inscriptions."[248] He also began to write short histories of local parishes for publication in *The Casket* under headlines such as "Stella Maris Church has Interesting Career." By 1937 local Catholics hoped that Johnston, a stickler for detail, might write a detailed history of the Catholic pioneers of the region.[249]

In 1935 Glace Bay plumber Albert Almon, a bibliophile, art collector, and early amateur historian of Fortress Louisbourg, who had published *Louisbourg: The Dream City of America*, presented the mission church at Lingan with a two-hundred-year-old chalice that had been found near Cadegan Brook in Bridgeport.[250] The artifact, presumed to have been lost by a missionary, was stored in a miniature oak tabernacle taken from the French man-o'-war *Célèbre*, which had sunk in Louisbourg harbour in 1758.[251] A devout Catholic and a great friend of the historians at St F.X., Almon had provided the college with copies of maps and other ephemera from the crumbling and forgotten fortress. He was also active in reclaiming some of the Acadian heritage of the province and outspoken in his demand to have the Louisbourg Cross, which adorned Gore Hall at Harvard University, returned to Nova Scotia (the cross was finally returned in 1995).[252]

Scottish history enthusiasts found a champion in John Lorne Campbell, a historian, folklorist, farmer, and environmentalist who nourished a lifelong fascination with the region. While working on a graduate thesis at St John's College, Oxford, Campbell carried on correspondence with the Old Rector, and in 1932 he toured the region "to discover the lie of the land."[253] Interested in all things Gaelic, Campbell was enthralled with the people, the landscape, and the work of the Scottish Catholic Society and its newspaper, *Mosgladh* (which was generously supported by Senator John MacCormick of Sydney Mines). Later, he asked the clergy to complete a survey on the use of Gaelic in their parishes and had a very "remarkable response."[254]

From the Hebridean island of Barra (he would soon purchase the island of Canna), Campbell maintained a friendly correspondence with Bishop Sandy, sought "Barramen" throughout Cape Breton, and was particularly captivated by the area around Grand Narrows, known locally as *Caolas nam Barrach* (Barramen's Strait). On publishing his first book, *Highland Songs of the Forty-Five*, in 1933, Campbell had several copies sent to St F.X. for sale, although the Old Rector feared that most would be "debarred from the pleasure of having it" because of the Depression. While working to revive Hebridean fishing through the "Sea League," Campbell became a devotee of the Extension program and even contributed a piece to the *Extension Bulletin* in 1934.

The folklorist also became a lifelong correspondent of Fr P.J. Nicholson (whose ancestors hailed from Barra). As well as being a passionate student of physics, Nicholson was an outstanding Gaelic scholar with an interest in translations (Sir Joseph Chisholm had him translate some musings for publication it in a western newspaper).[255] While Campbell wanted to collect traditional Gaelic music using his

Victor recorder, Nicholson cautioned him that there was "practically nothing in circulation by way of old songs." The priest had watched diligently for material over the years but as all the *seanachaidh*s had "passed beyond" little was still extant.[256] Yet Campbell was persistent, and throughout 1937 he carried his recorder to places like Upper South River and Mabou, seeking songs from local bards like Angus "the Ridge" MacDonald. During one six-week stint in the region, he and his wife, Margaret Shaw, recorded ninety-five traditional songs and three originals (an account of their travels was later published in the *Scots Magazine*).[257]

DEFENDING CHAPEL ISLAND

While touring the region, Campbell was also drawn to the Indigenous narrative and was keen to collect songs and stories from the local Mi'kmaq. He interviewed Grand Chief Gabriel Sylliboy, "an intelligent and middle aged man" who, in his native tongue (he also spoke Gaelic), recounted his grandfather's story of sighting the first Scottish settlers while he was spearing eels in Bras d'Or Lake.[258] The chief also described the challenges of cultural retention, and Campbell noted that the community were "remarkably faithful to their language."[259] While the Campbells recorded several traditional "plain-song hymns" that Mi'kmaw worshippers sang during religious services, he had less luck gathering secular songs.

One of Campbell's great regrets was that he had to return to Scotland before the annual Feast of St Anne. It was still a popular religious event, and priests from across the Maritimes arrived to assist in various communities. Because of the economic depression that engulfed eastern Nova Scotia, however, fewer people had the means to attend the ceremonies. The Mi'kmaq were able to carry out their spiritual and governance responsibilities, but fundraising for infrastructure was severely curtailed. As one anxious Mi'kmaw co-ordinator noted, the Depression had "hit the White people so hard they [had] no money to come by steamer or car to our mission."[260] The loss of the income usually generated by White visitors was a serious impediment to preserving hallowed Indigenous properties. Yet the poor economy was not the only reason Whites stayed away from the feast.

While diocesan officials recognized the spiritual and financial importance of the Feast of St Anne, a paternalistic fear that the moral drawbacks of "'white' civilization" would harm the "splendid

Figure 6.1 | Feast of St Anne, Chapel Island, c. 1930s

fidelity" of Indigenous Catholics was widespread among Catholic elites.[261] At Summerside (Paqtnkek), Fr Hugh John MacDonald asked the visitors to July feast take part in the events "not in a spirit if curiosity and dissipation but in a spirit if reverence and devotion."[262] In 1931 Fr Leo Keats, the pastor at St Peter's on Chapel Island, was angered by the general "lack of morals" of visitors. Citing their drunkenness, he barred Whites, calling them "intruders."[263] Chief Benjamin Christmas of Membertou attributed the "quite disappointing" financial collection for 1931 to their absence. Speaking on behalf of Grand Chief Sylliboy the following spring, he requested that Whites be again welcomed to the feast to pray to St Anne at the shrine and experience the sacred atmosphere.[264] In the meantime, anyone under the influence of alcohol would be escorted off the island.

Although confident that Fr Keats would accept the wishes of the Mi'kmaw leadership by "granting the White visitors another chance to attend," Chief Christmas was concerned.[265] He knew that a segment of clergy would prefer that the annual Chapel Island mission be held every other year, and was also aware of complaints that the feast had become more of a picnic than a religious mission. So he was not entirely shocked when Keats, who argued that visitors attended the mission as a "carnival of sin rather than an exhibition of sanctity," again banned Whites from Chapel Island in 1932.[266]

As complaints poured in, Bishop Morrison mulled over the problem with disquiet. While he felt that unruly visitors to the feast should be "sternly and effectively dealt with," as the Mi'kmaq had assembled on the sacred island for generations, and "as they have a strong self-consciousness in that regard," it was a mistake to tamper with the proceedings. "It can at least be said for them," he noted, "that they have been loyal Catholics, and it would be well to give all possible consideration to their tribal traditions." Chapel Island, he allowed, meant more to the Mi'kmaq than was "fully appreciated by the rest of the people."[267]

The acknowledgment that Indigenous people of eastern Nova Scotia were some of the most "loyal Catholics" makes their Church's role in disastrous federal schemes like the residential schools all the more confounding. In 1926 the federal Department of Indian Affairs announced plans to build a centralized school in Nova Scotia to provide for the "underprivileged Indian Child of Nova Scotia and other Maritime Provinces," including "orphans, illegitimate and neglected children" as well as those who lived "too distant from Indian or public days schools to attend regularly."[268] By February 1930 the Shubenacadie Indian Residential School had opened at Shubenacadie, Hants County, under the administration of the Sisters of Charity.[269] It was Canada's seventy-eighth federally funded Indian residential school and the only such institution east of Ontario.[270] The first students, children from various Halifax orphanages, arrived in February. Despite promises that they would be "comfortably housed," the youngsters faced poor facilities, leaking roofs, and a meagre diet.[271]

In recognition of the longstanding relationship between the Catholic Church and the Mi'kmaq people, Ottawa sought the cooperation of the metropolitan archbishop of Halifax. He appointed a management committee to oversee the institution. Much like the lending of a hand to military recruiters during the Great War, this kind of cooperation, as historian J.R. Miller has noted, represented "the shared authority of Church and State."[272] Ottawa was unquestionably exploiting the Mi'kmaq "attachment to the[ir] faith," and Church officials, firmly believing they knew what was best for the community, went along. As principal of the Shubenacadie school, the Halifax committee appointed Fr Jeremiah B. Mackay, a St F.X. alumnus and priest of Springhill, Cumberland County, to supervise the school on a shoestring budget.

There is little in the Antigonish diocesan archives to suggest that the clergy initially paid much attention to the Shubenacadie school. It was not until the summer of 1934, when the *Halifax Chronicle* printed a story of physical mistreatment at the institution, that White Catholics took notice. Some money had allegedly been stolen from the school's cash box and nineteen children faced punishment. Although it was established that Fr Mackay had struck the children, an investigation supervised by retired federal judge L.A. Audette exonerated the priest of the worst excesses. In an era when priests were rarely questioned, *The Casket* lent its pages in defence of Mackay for confronting the investigation "with dignity." Noting that the strap was used in most Maritime schools (and had been used on those who later became some of the British Empire's greatest leaders), the paper argued that "a weak punishment to [the] Indian pupils would have had no effect."[273]

Perhaps unwittingly, *The Casket*'s editor got to the heart of the matter by arguing that since the laws of the land had changed the environment of the Indians, "they must be taught to adjust themselves to the new environment."[274] That the Church would act on behalf of the state to coerce the very Mi'kmaw peoples who had protected that Church from the state in the eighteenth century was a terrible irony, and a betrayal of a long alliance that stretched back for generations. The widely held opinion that the Mi'kmaq had to be pulled into mainstream society, a view shared by most Canadians, was undeniably detrimental to Indigenous culture. Yet the fact that such federal policies were implemented by members of their own Church would leave Indigenous Catholics with generational scars.

Although the Antigonish diocese had little formal contact with the Shubenacadie School (and no administrative influence), many children from eastern Nova Scotia were enrolled. The stories are poignant. Small children, five to ten years of age, came from Whycocomagh, Barra Head, Sydney, Pictou Landing, Afton, and Inverness. Some travelled to Hants County with the local Indian agent, while others were taken by their older brothers and sisters. Their applications were often accompanied by a small sad notation: "father living, mother dead."

In some cases children in difficult circumstances were able to avoid the institution – the family of the late Louis Smith, Membertou's most "industrious" resident, for instance, was given a temporary raise in its monthly food allowance so that the children could remain with their mother – but many families were separated.[275] In August 1939, an admissions application was sent to Shubenacadie on behalf of a brother and sister aged nine and ten from Pictou Landing. Their mother had died, and they had been left in the care of their seventeen-year-old sister, who had valiantly tried to keep the family together.[276]

In the 1930s a handful of priests served as Indian agents. Of course, dealing with typical agent portfolios like land disputes and finances was one thing, but helping to decide which small children, from a variety of domestic environments, would be sent to Shubenacadie was something altogether different.[277] While the opinion of such clerical agents was an important factor in deciding on admissions (they helped process the applications), as they were not residents of the communities of Eskasoni, Paqtnkek, or Membertou, they rarely had any personal knowledge of particular families or their circumstances.

Although local clerical agents helped enroll children at Shubenacadie, they had limited further authority over students. Ironically, while it was often a child's home circumstances (state of housing, family finances, and so on) that determined their eligibility for admission – and even their permission to return home for a vacation – it was Ottawa that controlled the means of improving local infrastructure. In 1933 the Pictou pastor Fr A.A. Johnston reported the desperate need for repairs to homes at Pictou Landing. With his pleas for funding continually rebuffed, he was told to keep expenses to a minimum. "I believe that the government should give them extraordinary aid in these extraordinary times," he pleaded to the MP for Pictou, "but what can I do?"[278]

As priests had helped to place children in the Shubenacadie school, parents naturally looked to clergymen like Fr Johnston when they sought their release. Their shock at learning that these clerical agents had little influence over school policy often turned to anger.[279] In June 1936 a young John Henry Sapier was accused of stealing the master key to the residential school. He was sent to St Patrick's Home, a reformatory in Halifax, but soon escaped and returned home to his father, Louis, at Pictou Landing. As John Henry was approaching his sixteenth birthday, Louis asked the clergyman's permission to keep him at home to "learn his trade as an Indian craftsman." However, as regulations demanded that the boy return to St Patrick's Home before formally requesting a release, Fr Johnston could merely promise a letter of recommendation. Outraged at the priest's powerlessness, Louis swore to "get in touch with Bishop Morrison."[280]

Fr Johnston, a studious priest, found this work trying and repeatedly asked his superior to release him from duty. However, Bishop Morrison insisted that he remain: a priest, he wrote, could "do more for the welfare of the Indians in [the] province than can be expected from a layman."[281] At Thorburn, Fr Ernest Chiasson was also uncomfortable with his assignment, although as one writer has noted, he still sent children to the school even over the objections of their parents when he thought it was in their best interests.[282]

One young man who had no intention of staying at the institution was Noel Julian of Paqtnkek. In March 1939 he ran away for the fifth time and "took to the deep woods." While the RCMP searched – they were sure that Julian was heading back to his mother's home in Antigonish County – days later, Julian's brother, Joe, also headed for home.[283] Both boys were eventually caught and Noel's head was shaved as punishment.[284]

In a way reminiscent of the diocese's failure to recruit a Mi'kmaw student for the seminary, the residential school represented the attitude ingrained in Canadian society that Indigenous culture was inferior. In a diocese filled with Highlanders and Hibernians ever mindful of historical transgressions against their communities and desperate to hang on to their language and culture, the efforts to assimilate young Mi'kmaq children was hypocritical. Responding angrily to the insinuation of a Halifax newspaper that Gaelic was no longer practical, one Cape Bretoner retorted that the paper needed "an education in the beauties of the language." It is unfortunate that there was not a more sympathetic response to Membertou's Chief Ben Christmas when he complained to Indian Affairs that a boy recently returned from Shubenacadie had lost "his own graceful tongue."[285]

RETENTION OF ACADIAN CULTURE

This indifference to the Mi'kmaq language was also a remnant of the ultramontane revolution that had downplayed ethnic cultural expression. In Acadian communities, the demeaning of old cultures was directed against the old European tradition of Mi-Carême ("mid-Lent"), which involved going door to door in costume to challenge one's neighbours to guess one's identity. As the Lenten season was a time to prepare for Easter, some clergy found the practice irreverent. The priests on Isle Madame had long been divided between those like the "ultra severe" Quebec-born Fr Henri Chouinard, who totally opposed the custom while pastor at Petit de Grat, and the St. Anne's College graduate Fr Wilfrid Boucher of D'Escousse, who was ambivalent. When serving as a priest at D'Escousse in the 1890s, Archbishop Neil McNeil had compromised by asking the "respectable women of the parish" not to open their door to Mi-Carêmes on Fridays.[286] The people were "tenacious of their old customs."[287]

It was not a surprise that Acadian priests such as Fr Boucher and Fr Amable Briand at West Arichat, who had been educated within Acadian institutions like St. Anne's College, appreciated the cultural importance of the Mi-Carême. With the support of organizations like the Société l'Assomption, they also bore witness to the steadfast devotion to the Virgin Mother. In the cold winter of 1932–33 the society petitioned to have the Doctrine of the Assumption of the Blessed Virgin defined as an Article of Faith. Members eagerly collected signatures throughout the region, and those names were among the 100,000 Canadian signatures on a document sent to Rome (the Dogma of the Assumption was ultimately proclaimed in 1950).[288] Active in this work was the former St F.X. professor Fr Arsene Cormier of Margaree. Already serving as general president and grand chaplain of l'Assomption, in 1933 he was named president of the influential St Anne's College Alumni Association. The following year the French Government awarded the fifty-one-year-old priest a "Distinguished Service" medal for his promotion of French culture and contribution to the "general uplifting" of the Acadian people.[289]

CLERICAL LIFE IN THE COMMUNITIES

Many prominent priests like Fr Cormier still hailed primarily from rural districts – the number with roots in Inverness County was remarkable – but the 1930s saw a noticeable increase in seminarians from the Cape Breton colliery towns. When Fr James Duncan MacGillivray was ordained for the China Mission in the Christmas season of 1931, he became the first parishioner from St Anne's in

Glace Bay to enter the priesthood. On a bright June day in June 1935, Fr Edmund Nash celebrated his first solemn high Mass at Sacred Heart in Sydney; Fr Michael McLaughlin said his at St Theresa's; and Fr William Gallivan did the same at Holy Redeemer in Whitney Pier.[290] Within a few years, clergymen from the colliery parishes who, like Fr Robert Donnelly of New Aberdeen, were not "fed from the silver spoon," would be as synonymous with the priesthood as the lads from Margaree.[291]

Clergymen "fed from the silver spoon," or those who lacked a missionary mentality, did not fare well with Bishop Morrison. The prelate lived in one of the most decrepit episcopal dwellings in the Maritimes, and when a Cape Breton priest decided to renovate his glebe house, the old bishop cautioned him to keep the amenities to a minimum. Not only would indulgent priests face criticism from the flock, he said, but young curates would grow accustomed to comforts and become "unfit to meet the conditions of a small parish."[292]

Bishop Morrison was "not an easy man to convince," and he expected his priests to be prompt, polite, and firm.[293] Although Fr Amable Briand, a native of L'Ardoise, objected to his transfer to West Arichat in 1929, knowing that Morrison was "firm and unyielding," he submitted without question. It was "in obedience to [his] bishop," he noted years later, "that [he] laboured there for fourteen years as a victim of duty."[294] When another priest grumbled that a round of clerical appointments left some of the men "sore," the rector of St F.X. replied that the bishop would not be sympathetic.[295]

While the clergy were visible within the community, they were still expected to keep some distance from their parishioners. By the 1930s, growing numbers of young men were playing ice hockey and teams were travelling longer distances for competition. Games between the of League of the Cross of North Sydney and St John's in New Aberdeen always drew large raucous crowds, and the Cape Breton Senior Hockey League had periods of great popularity. At St Andrews, parishioners remembered Fr John R. MacDonald driving friends to games at St F.X. "He loved a good hockey game," noted a friend, "but it had to be good."[296]

Yet watching hockey and playing the sport were altogether different. When Bishop Morrison learned that Fr Angus Beaton, a young curate at Glace Bay, was periodically playing hockey with friends, he was annoyed. Thirty-three years before the "Flying Fathers" began playing exhibition games for charity, the seventy-year-old prelate put an abrupt end to Fr Beaton's hockey dreams. "Hockey," Morrison informed the senior pastor at St Anne's, was "indecorous," and lowered the dignity and respect due to the priesthood. "If Father Beaton wants to have physical exercise," the prelate exhorted, "he can [have] plenty of it tramping through the parish visiting those who need strengthening in the faith."[297]

In October 1936 the PEI-born Fr William T. Trainor, pastor at Main-à-Dieu, was involved in a car accident that resulted in the death of a young man on the reserve road. Not only had the priest been behind the wheel but "a bunch of girls" had also been in the car (and this was not the first such case). Morrison was furious. When the disgraced fifty-eight-year-old Trainor failed to immediately resign his parish, it was swiftly taken from him. "If you imagine that this is going to 'blow over,'" Morrison fumed, "you are very much mistaken."[298]

While Fr Trainor was sent to Inverness to serve his penance as a curate, in other cases discipline was pointless. The former president of St F.X., Fr Alexander Thompson, having lived in retirement in Louisiana for a decade, applied to the St Joseph's Society for financial support, thereby triggering an inquiry into his living arrangements. When Archbishop John Shaw of New Orleans reported that the sixty-seven-year-old Thompson was battling a drug habit, the sickly priest was ordered home. Thompson arrived at St Martha's Hospital in the summer of 1936 and by early August he had died. It was an unfortunate ending for a brilliant man who had once been shortlisted to become a bishop.

By and large, however, Morrison had a solid group of priests who cared deeply about their parishes' social as well as spiritual welfare. In St Andrews, Fr John R. MacDonald worked to upgrade the road leading to Guysborough County, and in 1932, with the help of Fr Hugh John MacDonald, led a drive to extend electrical power from Antigonish town to St Andrews, Heatherton, and Pomquet (assisted by volunteer linemen who had honed their trade in the United States). With the approval of the fledgling Nova Scotia Power Commission, priests served as foremen and organized work parties. "You will be glad to know that the power is now on," Fr John R. MacDonald wrote to his bishop in December, "and we are all enjoying the luxury of electric light."[299] Later, Justice L.D. Currie credited the priests as the men responsible for putting rural electrification in the public eye (the Nova Scotia government passed the Rural Electrification Act in 1937).[300]

Priests were also instrumental in finding men employment. When Fr Domenico Viola left St Nicholas Parish, the Italians of Whitney Pier requested a Nova Scotia–born priest who would have better luck at procuring work for the community. After thirty parishioners were dismissed from DOSCO in 1938, Fr Ronald MacLean had them quickly reinstated.[301] At Sydney, with the help of the Catholic Charities Association, Fr Ronald C. MacGillivray found employment for more than a hundred men in 1937 alone, while at Louisdale, Fr George Landry convinced DOSCO to place an order for forty cars of pit props in his parish, thus securing local employment for an entire summer.[302]

The competence of native-born clergy was also recognized outside the diocese. After receiving a glowing recommendation from Bishop Morrison, the Eudist Fr Patrick Bray was appointed bishop of Saint John, New Brunswick, in 1935. While ministering for decades at Halifax's Holy Heart Seminary, Bray had regularly returned to his native parish of St Andrews where, *The Casket* reported, his appointment was met with great happiness.[303] Later, Brother Abban Phillip (Peter Gagnon of Arichat) was elected assistant to the superior general of the Brothers of the Christian Schools; and the former diocesan priest, Fr Ronald Beaton, was made a domestic prelate in the diocese of Victoria (his brother Patrick was also serving in the west).

All this activity produced a strong camaraderie among the 125 diocesan priests and natives of the region serving elsewhere. "Do not worry about your parish," the Old Rector consoled the hospitalized pastor of Little Bras d'Or in 1934. "Nothing but an earthquake, or a dislocation of the universe will prevent us from supplying if we are at all fit to go."[304] And when Fr Thomas O'Reilly Boyle faced personal problems that affected his health, his colleague at Whitney Pier, Fr James Kiely, and some friends from the parish, offered to "chip in" to pay his expenses in a retreat house.[305]

CATHOLIC CHARITIES

Personal difficulties faced by priests like Fathers Thompson and O'Reilly Boyle drew attention to complex issues such as addiction, which required expert treatment. To gain such expertise, nurses from diocesan infirmaries were regularly sent to teaching hospitals in New England for clinical training. New hospitals like Sacred Heart, which was opened at Cheticamp in 1938 under the supervision of the Filles de Jésus, not only "brightened the outlook" of the community but also offered an unprecedented quality of care.[306] When one Cape Breton United Church minister entered North Sydney's Hamilton Hospital for a heart condition, he confessed that the nurses were not "just 'Sisters of Charity' – they were also 'Angels of Mercy.'"[307]

The availability of hospital infrastructure was one thing, but financing hospital stays needed creative solutions. In 1936 members of the St Andrews cooperative store paid premiums to St Martha's hospital for five weeks' ward accommodation and free ordinary medicine and laboratory service.[308] A few years later, the people of Johnstown banded with the community of Big Pond to promote a similar scheme. The "Socialized Health Association" charged $5 per annum for an in-home doctor's visit and consultations at the physician's office. Drugs and surgeries were offered at reduced rates.[309]

Of course, in many parishes, even a $5 premium would have been prohibitive. At Canso, the Sisters of St Martha, who purchased two houses from the Western Union Telegraph Company for a convent, established the Canso Welfare Bureau to focus on poverty, literacy, and community development.[310] Seeing the need to "revive traditional home industries," four of the sisters went to Quebec in 1933 for a course on handicrafts.[311] They secured passage on a coal freighter bound for Montreal and persuaded the captain to take them ashore in the pilot's launch near Quebec City. With the wind "play[ing] havoc with [their] white and black," Mother Faustina reported, by the time they made it ashore, the brave women were soaked, nauseated, and exhausted.[312]

By easing the financial pressure on households through home economics, or by simply lending a child a book, the Marthas' Canso ministry led to a deeper "practice of faith and religion."[313] One path toward God, they discovered, was to go into the community and deal with "urgent daily problems." In 1935 Sister Baptisa Marie (Catherine MacDonald), a graduate of the Toronto School of Social Work, helped open the Catholic Charities and Welfare Association at Sacred Heart parish in Sydney.[314] Within a broadly defined program, the Marthas collaborated with other city organizations like the Children's Aid Society and with the police to encourage and support Sydney families.

This organizational diversity made the Marthas very attractive to dioceses in western Canada. When Rome approved a new constitution for the congregation in 1932, the "army of zealous workers" were soon at work teaching at St Basil's School in Lethbridge, Alberta, ministering at the Mount Carmel Convent in Canmore, Alberta, and supporting families in Regina with the Catholic Welfare Society.[315] When they took control of a rest home and sanatorium in Banff, Bishop Morrison predicted that they would be "a valuable religious asset for the Calgary diocese."[316]

Despite these great responsibilities, however, women religious in this decade still laboured within an established patriarchy. The credit for successful projects often went to the clergy, and the sisters, many highly educated and outspoken, were frequently reminded of their vow of obedience. As Sister Anselm (Irene Doyle), a Martha and Extension fieldworker, would later recall with some bitterness, "there was one set of values for the sisters." Despite their heroic ministry, the women often endured lectures on frugality and "were supposed to have only so much."[317] When a cadre of teaching sisters went to staff the school at St Andrews, the local priest complained that the modern lights installed in the classroom by the congregation were too ostentatious.

WAR CLOUDS

Mid-twentieth-century Antigonish may have been a small diocese in an eastern corner of Nova Scotia, but it was not isolated from global events. Priests who had studied in Rome had classmates who occupied powerful offices within the Curia, and Bishop Morrison was in regular contact with his agent at the Scots College Rome.[318] The rise of Benito Mussolini and the ensuing violence of his black-shirted fascist followers were much discussed in glebes and parish halls throughout the region. The Lateran Treaty between Fascist Italy and the Holy See, which was signed in 1929, ended generations of hostility between Church and state, put a stop to the escalating violence against priests, and established Vatican City as an independent state.[319]

Although the Second World War ultimately dealt fascism a fatal blow, in the early 1930s many Catholic intellectuals, like the rector of the Catholic University of Milan, were attracted to its critique of liberal democracy. Closer to home, the Ontario-born Fr Charles Edward Coughlin, a member of the Basilian Fathers and a supporter of President Roosevelt's "New Deal," had one of North

America's most popular Catholic radio programs in Michigan.[320] While his hatred for usury gradually devolved into antisemitism, his early message seemed similar to that of the Extension program. In fact, after listing to an "enlightening" talk by Fr Coady, one Massachusetts woman wrote of the similarity "to what Fr Coughlin [was] struggling for."[321]

There were also those who thought that corporatism might end the perpetual contest between labour and capital that plagued regions like Cape Breton. Even the *Extension Bulletin* investigated fascism as a "way of modifying our organization of industry." Obviously, the *Bulletin* was not advocating for a dictatorship, but its editors did feel that "many lessons" could be learned from Mussolini.[322]

The relationship between Italian fascism and the Vatican had always been tenuous. As early as 1931 the *New York Times* reported that blackshirts had trampled the portrait of the pope.[323] It was not long before Mussolini's heavy-hitters violently disrupted meetings of student Catholic action clubs and discouraged new recruits. In response, Pope Pius XI issued an encyclical, *Non abbiamo bisogno*, defending Catholic action against fascist charges of partisanship. By September *The Casket* reported that the clubs were once again operational but limited to purely religious activities.

The situation across the German Tyrol region was not much different. By the time the Vatican signed a concordat with Adolf Hitler's National Socialist government in 1933, the despotic realities of Nazi Germany were becoming clear. Yet unlike Italy, Germany was not synonymous with Catholicism, and so it was easier to condemn Hitler and his stormtroopers. In October 1934 the *Glace Bay Gazette* declared that Hitler, despite his baptism, was clearly not a Catholic. Nor was he a God. "Can anyone imagine Hitler suffering crucifixion for the sake of the Nazis? We rather think he would from his record crucify all his Nazis for the sake of Hitler."[324]

Yet, the Spanish Civil War, which broke out in the summer of 1936, complicated things, as the enemies of fascism were burning churches and murdering priests.[325] In countries like Ireland, Catholic bishops – including Bishop Morrison's friend Francis Wall – reacted to the massacre of Catholic clergy at the hands of Spanish Republicans by raising money for General Francisco Franco and his nationalists.[326] "The secular press stories [on Spain] are so tainted with Red propaganda," *The Casket* publisher C.J. MacGillivray wrote to Fr Micky

MacDonald after a lecture on the subject, "that I am sure your version of the situation will do good."[327]

Writing from his studies at the University of Toronto, Alexander Laidlaw, a Port Hood native and supporter of the cooperative movement, mentioned that the Canadian communist leader Tim Buck drew "quite a crowd on the campus" due to his anti-fascist attitudes, but complained that pro-Franco articles in Toronto's Catholic press only "aggravate[d] the situation."[328] *The Casket* also opposed the Spanish Republicans, and when the "moving picture" *Blockade* (nominated for two Oscar Awards) was shown in Sydney's Capitol Theatre, the Knights of Columbus called for a boycott; any movie depicting a farmer fighting for the republicans, they argued, was designed to create sentiment in favour of communism, and was "historically false."[329]

While pro-Franco, *The Casket* was unquestionably anti-Hitler (despite his anti-communist leanings). In October 1935 it decried the arrest of the bishop of Munster, Clemens August Graf von Galen; and in 1936 it reported that the leaders of Germany's Catholic Youth Group were detained and charged, rather ironically, with "subversive Communist affiliation." The Vatican's 1937 condemnation of nazism, *Mit brennender Sorge* (With Searing Anxiety), which objected to the suspension of the rule of law and the cult of the "heroic" Hitler, was circulated throughout the Catholic world, and the apostolic delegate asked Bishop Morrison to "enlighten, by all possible means, the faithful of [his] diocese, by exposing the gravity of the situation."[330]

As fascism took root in European capitals, the 1937 Rural and Industrial Conference passed a hard-won resolution opposing "Fascism, National Socialism, Communism, and all other such forms of dictatorship."[331] Not everyone supported it. The conference's first speaker, Fr Alex MacKenzie of Westville, stood and proclaimed Mussolini the "man of the hour." Having recently returned from Rome (he was an Urban College graduate), MacKenzie was "in a position to speak with no little authority" and felt that his positive portrayal of Italy's government would surprise those whose sole source of information came from "a biased and anti-Fascist secular press."[332] According to historian Michael Welton, Fr Coady needed a fair amount of "back room" negotiating to get the anti-fascist resolution through the assembly.[333]

That winter, Fr Gelasius Kraus, the German-born prior of the Augustinian community at New York, toured the grounds of the picturesque Monastery of Petit Clairvaux outside Tracadie. Smitten with the woods, fields, and streams of the property, which had been abandoned in 1919 by its resident Trappist monks, Kraus felt that the monastery would make a good asylum for all German Augustinians fleeing Nazi persecution. After purchasing the property in 1938, six brothers arrived to till the soil, open a chapel for public use, and remind locals how easy it was for a dictatorship to fell a country as cultured as Germany.

In February 1939 the outspoken Pope Pius XI died, and weeks later Cardinal Eugenio Pacelli, well known to the Augustinians as the papal nuncio to Germany from 1917 to 1929, was elected Pope Pius XII. Bishop Morrison spent the evening of 2 March listening to the radio for updates, and the proclamation "Habemus papam" from the balcony overlooking St Peter's Square came over the airwaves "quite clearly." While some historians and journalists have argued that Pacelli was the favourite candidate of the fascists, he was well known for his diplomatic experience.[334] He was also an admirer of the Antigonish Movement, and many in eastern Nova Scotia hoped he would provide a "united front against the national and international disturbers of the peace."[335]

In late August the papal secretary of state, Cardinal Luigi Maglione, delivered a Europe-wide diplomatic cable requesting that politicians "abstain from taking any measure that might aggravate current tensions."[336] Yet even the pope could not halt German and Soviet aggression. On 1 September, advanced units of the German *Wehrmacht* crashed into Poland. On 3 September, both France and Great Britain declared war on Germany; a week later Canada followed suit. "These are sad dark hours," one Vatican bureaucrat noted in his diary. "It seems as if a darkness of spirit has spread across the land, thirsty for blood."[337] Cancelling his *ad limina* to Rome, Bishop Morrison remarked, "the war nightmare is with us again."[338]

7

Battles at Home and Abroad 1940–1949

As of September 1939 Canada was officially at war, but it was not until the spring of 1940 that Canadians acknowledged the seriousness of the European conflict. In the interim, there was, as one historian has described it, "a deceptive air of unreality."[1] Information from England filtered slowly into eastern Nova Scotia, and W.H. Dennis at the *Halifax Herald* sent Bishop Morrison copies of his correspondence with the New Brunswick–born Lord Beaverbrook, Winston Churchill's minister of aircraft production, to keep him up to date.[2] Much of the early chatter was of the damage that German U-boats were inflicting in the cold northern waters off Scapa Flow. "We are further from the source of action and feel more secure in Canada," Fr P.J. Nicholson wrote to a friend in Scotland, "but nevertheless we all feel dreadfully grieved over the unfortunate world situation."[3]

Nazi aggression was felt most keenly among the Polish residents of Whitney Pier. In the pews of St Mary's, the news of the brutal German *Blitzkrieg* that had overrun their former homeland in a single ruthless September month was on everyone's lips. During the assault, the Redemptorist seminarian, Neil Corbett of Havre Boucher, studying languages in Tuchow, was fortunate to find passage to Ireland, but most of his Polish colleagues were later murdered.[4] Shortly after the German invasion, the Soviet Union overran the eastern borders of the prostrated Slavic nation and occupied what remained of Free Poland. Within weeks, stories of Church closures, atrocities against the general population, and the massacre of priests filtered back to Whitney Pier. "This is a Polish community," proclaimed the young Fr Leo O'Connell when collecting for the Polish Red Cross, "and we are more than willing to help poor Poland."[5]

Figure 7.1 | St Mary's Polish Church, c. 1919

Much as in 1914, the Canadian declaration of war against Germany was met with patriotic sentiment, albeit with less enthusiasm. In Catholic circles there was considerable anxiety about whether Fascist Italy would fight alongside Germany. When visiting Vatican City in March 1940, Archbishop John McNally of Halifax maintained that he did not meet a single Italian "who expressed a willingness to fight."[6] By May, however, public sentiment had changed. "We are seeing here in Italy," reported one Curia official, "a campaign that promotes Hitler but forgets all religious and moral principles. It is an extremely hurtful spectacle."[7]

When Italy formally emerged as an ally of Germany in June 1940, priests like Fr Michael MacAdam in Glace Bay used the pulpit to proclaim the neutrality of the Vatican.[8] In the meantime, fear mounted that the Vatican would be struck by allied bombers.[9] The British Royal Air Force had already bombarded the northern Italian cities of Genoa, Turin, and Milan, and the British House of Commons was advocating a direct strike on Rome (although the Canadian press expressed certainty that St Peter's Basilica would be spared).

CAPE BRETON ITALIANS INTERNED

Mussolini's decision to fight the war alongside Hitler also had grave repercussions for the hundreds of Italian Catholics in Whitney Pier, Dominion, and New Waterford. Fearing a "fifth column," Ottawa declared thousands of Italian-born residents to be "enemy aliens," suspended *habeas corpus*, and began registering Italian nationals over the age of eighteen. All "nationalistic" cultural and social clubs were closed, and arrest warrants were issued for suspected fascist sympathisers.[10]

In Sydney and Glace Bay, the Royal Canadian Mounted Police quickly compiled lists of local men who had expressed sympathy for Mussolini. Michael LaPenna, an active member of St Nicholas parish in Whitney Pier, was the first man arrested. Within hours, twenty-one others from across the colliery towns, like Romano Scattolon and Bartolo "Burt" Gatto, were rounded up and transported to Moncton and then eventually to Petawawa, Ontario (most were later transferred to Fredericton). While fearing for their incarcerated fathers, families also faced taunts and violence. As one man recalled: "We were also in constant fear. People were throwing rocks at our house; it was hell!"[11]

At St Nicholas, the Rome-educated Fr Ronald MacLean scrambled for information. The Boisdale native had ministered to the Italian faithful since 1926 and none, in his opinion, were enemies of the state. He also dismissed the ridiculous rumours of secret short-wave radios connecting fascist sympathisers in the town of Dominion with Rome. The rise of Mussolini had certainly created tensions within his parish, but they were due to the incessant meddling of the fascist General Consulate for Italy in Montreal and not to any contingent of local black shirts.

In 1937, seeking more control in Sydney, the Montreal consulate had forced the local consul agent, E.J. Giuliani, to resign.[12] His hand-picked replacement, Camillo Vetere, soon arrived in Sydney from Quebec demanding an Italian-born priest for St Nicholas and stirring up trouble. Besides exploiting some petty rifts among parishioners, one of the agent's associates "absconded with funds" belonging to local societies and "succeeded in running up a number of notes as IOUs for monies loaned to him under a false pretense of patriotic zeal."[13] Later Vetere was replaced by the odious Carlo Rezzaghi, who pressured the community to publicly support Mussolini.

By opposing these fascist agents, Fr MacLean ran afoul of the Montreal consulate and a handful of local supporters. While complaints about the priest poured into the bishop's residence, they were quickly dismissed.[14] In defending himself, MacLean noted that he had learned the Italian language, had patronized causes "near and dear" to the community, and had even attended an event in support of Mussolini's 1935 invasion of Ethiopia. Yet he could not remain silent as Montreal escalated its intimidations, black-listings, and "anti-Canadian practice[s]."[15]

Msgr Ildebrando Antoniutti, the apostolic delegate in Ottawa, felt that the friction between the Montreal consulate and Fr MacLean had played a part in the detention of the twenty-two local men.[16] He offered a financial contribution to the detainees' families but, to his utter astonishment, the money was returned.[17] "The wives want their husbands home," MacLean replied, "and they will not accept less."[18] The delegate retaliated by accusing the priest of neglecting his interned parishioners in exchange for an appointment as a chaplain in the Canadian navy. "Only the prisoners of Cape Breton are still all in the internment camp," the delegate complained to Bishop Morrison in February 1942, "and their pastor (who before being a military chaplain showed a certain interest for them) is saying that because of his present situation he cannot do anything."[19]

Morrison did what he could for the internees. He even wrote to Louis St-Laurent, the minister of justice, pointing out that twenty of the prisoners had children aged three to nine years and without their father's regular income they lacked basic necessities. Whatever pro-Mussolini sentiments the men may have had in the past, he said, their round-up and detention was "altogether too drastic and sweeping."[20] When Felice Martinello complained that he had been interned for over two years without a formal charge or conviction, Morrison could only respond that he had pressed his case with Ottawa.[21]

When Fr MacLean finally entered the navy as a chaplain in the late summer of 1943, Fr Emidio Joseph D'Intino was despatched to Whitney Pier. As the first infant baptised at St Nicholas and the diocese's first native-born Italian priest, the recent graduate of Halifax's Holy Heart Seminary was a calming influence on the parish.[22] His pastoral work was challenging as he ministered to families with fathers detained as enemies of the state and others with sons fighting in Europe with the Canadian Army. It was, as Sam Migliore and Evo DiPierro note, a "paradox unresolved."[23]

SCARBORO MISSIONARY PRIESTS AND THE PACIFIC WAR

In defiance of Hitler's earlier non-aggression pact with Stalin, the German *Wehrmacht* launched Operation Barbarossa and invaded the Soviet Union in June 1941. Taking advantage of criminally unprepared Soviet defences and a demoralized officer corps (Stalin had executed most of his senior officers), Hitler's emboldened panzers smashed through the Red Army on three fronts on their way to Moscow. Back in eastern Nova Scotia, there was a sense that the two dangerous foes of Christianity were finally going to clash. "If the Red Army and the Brown would only act as Kilkenny cats," exclaimed Fr P.J. Nicholson, "what a deliverance it would be!"[24] Although everyone wanted to crush Hitlerism, the focus on the twin evil in Moscow was not abandoned. "Enemies of the Church," noted one priest, "[were] still at work trying to replace [the cross] with the swastika or the sickle."[25]

As battle-weary German soldiers pushed toward the snowy Moscow suburbs, on 7 December 1941, the air force of Imperial

Figure 7.2 | Scarboro Priests in China. Fr Louis Venedam, back row centre. Bishop Morrison's half-brother Vincent, front row, second from left.

Japan – with no formal declaration of war – bombed the United States naval base at Pearl Harbour. Eight hours later, the Japanese Army attacked the British Garrison at Hong Kong. They met stiff resistance, but the city was unprepared for a prolonged siege and surrendered on Christmas Day. Nearly half the Canadian forces had been killed and many of the wounded were bayonetted in their hospital beds. Others, like Judique's Pte Archie Peter Gillis and Cpl John Jamieson MacIsaac, survived the battle but faced four brutal and demeaning years as prisoners of war.

The news of the Japanese victories created great anxiety for the families of priests serving in China with the Scarboro Foreign Mission. By the 1930s Asia had come to represent an exciting new opportunity for Catholic evangelization, and young Scarboro missionaries, like Pomquet's Fr Arthur Venedam, frequently toured the Antigonish region delivering "forceful sermons" while seeking money and recruits.[26] In 1932 the mission of Lishui was upgraded to a "prefecture apostolic," and the Newfoundlander Fr William McGrath became its regional superior. Fr Alex MacIntosh of

St Andrews wrote from China that each day "had its own peculiarities," and excerpts printed in the *Glace Bay Gazette* of the letters of Fr James Duncan MacGillivray, a former St F.X. student council president who went to China in 1932, told of the beauty of Asia, the sight of old Chinese junks next to modern battleships in Shanghai Harbour, and baseball games among the children (by 1934, the author had died of malaria).[27]

The Scarboro priests learned of the Japanese attack on Pearl Harbour over the British Broadcasting Empire Service. Having firsthand knowledge of the brutal conditions in Japanese-occupied Manchuria, they were elated that the United States had entered the war and naïvely expected a speedy "mop-up" of Japanese forces. Yet their excitement quickly turned to despair as Emperor Hirohito's battle-hardened divisions seized control of the Chinese coastline from Shanghai to Hong Kong. In the short term, the missionaries, still located in Free China, were unscathed and unmolested, but a Japanese naval blockade left them desperately short of supplies.

Catholic missionaries in Japanese-controlled territories were not so fortunate. After the surrender of Hong Kong, Fr Charles Murphy of Sydney (briefly a curate at Sydney Mines) was detained along with members of the Maryknoll Society. During the siege, he made an attempt to drive a truck full of grain through enemy lines to reach hungry Chinese refugees. He was marched to a hillside for execution, but was spared at the last moment by the British surrender. Along with Bishop Cuthbert O'Gara, the Ottawa-born Passionist vicar apostolic of Yuanling, Murphy was bound and held in a poorly ventilated single-car garage for days.[28] He spent the next three years as a prisoner of war and, when finally repatriated to Canada, was dubbed "the hero of Hong Kong" by the Canadian press.[29]

One bright morning in May 1942, the priests of Lishui awoke to learn that invading Japanese soldiers were a mere fifteen miles from the mission. The streets were quickly awash with anxious refugees and most of the missionaries, including the Grey Sisters of the Immaculate Conception, either fled inland or took to the hills.[30] Chinese civilians suspected of harbouring or aiding American airmen were brutally tortured and executed. "Like a swarm of locusts," recalled one missionary, the Japanese "left behind nothing but destruction and chaos."[31]

When the imperial soldiers finally withdrew from the region in the late autumn, a few priests scrambled back to the mission.

Fr Venedam, serving alone in his little church at Lungchuan, comforted grieving families, opened a rudimentary medical clinic, and even survived a deadly outbreak of bubonic plague. When Fr Harvey Steele of Dominion returned to his mission in January 1943, he was greeted by "nearly 100 Christian converts ... with broad smiles and firecrackers."[32]

The missionaries who made it back safely to Canada offered first-hand accounts of the horrors. When the fifty-one-year-old Fr Donald V. Chisholm, a Boston-born Maryknoll missionary in Korea, returned to stay with relatives in New Glasgow (he would serve the parish briefly as an assistant), he gave talks recounting his treatment at the hands of his captors. To provide context, Fr John Mao, a Chinese priest studying the cooperative movement at St F.X., spoke on the history and geography of Asia. When the Toronto United Church minister Rev. G.K. King, also a former Japanese prisoner of war, arrived at St F.X. in the summer of 1944, he was shocked to find that a fellow prisoner, Fr Michael MacSween, a native of Ironville, Cape Breton, was recuperating at the glebe house in Boisdale. Over local radio, both men noted the bravery of their Chinese friends who smuggled food into the camp and saved the internees from "slow starvation."[33]

WARTIME LIFE

While Nova Scotians did not directly face the horrors of Europe and Asia, the war had a profound effect their on society. Like Bishop Morrison, who cancelled his *ad limina* to Rome, organizations postponed events, and pilgrimages to St Anne de Beaupré were terminated (the trains had been requisitioned for military use). In the meantime, priests referenced the fallen state of mankind from the pulpit, and parish prayer days – Fridays in New Waterford – appealed for victory in Europe.[34]

While priests and ministers happily shared the military recruiting stage, denominational regulations created a few awkward episodes. One prelate, for example, attended a patriotic event on the understanding that there would be no religious ceremony. Yet when his Protestant colleague asked the crowd to stand for a prayer, the embarrassed bishop had to remain seated with his hat on.[35] For the most part, however, the war brought Christians together.

When the Salvation Army began fundraising in New Waterford, Fr Raymond Campbell of St Agnes praised the "splendid" work of the "soldiers."[36]

Young men from all faiths were sent to defend the Nova Scotia coastline, and gun batteries were placed in strategic locations to protect waterways like Sydney Harbour and the Strait of Canso. A barracks was constructed at Victoria Park in Sydney, and a large military encampment was organized near coastal Mulgrave.[37] Although responsible for the spiritual welfare of the Catholic soldiers assigned to these installations, priests also worked to maintain discipline. When soldiers at a coastal battery at Melford expressed dissatisfaction with their officers, Fr R.C. MacGillivray, the great veteran of the First World War and pastor of Sacred Heart in Sydney, went to "restore order."[38]

Having endured the lean years of the 1930s, many men joined the army to escape the drudgery of poverty, and the "first wave of enlistment brought in the worst victims of the depression."[39] As these soldiers fought their way across Europe, letters home described not only new towns and tactics, but the death and destruction familiar to many. In a letter to Fr Donald MacPherson at Port Hood, Lt/Cpl. A.J. MacIsaac did not describe the fighting in detail, as MacPherson had served in the Great War and would understand "just what [their] situation [was]." MacIsaac focused instead on the more humorous episodes and joked that the celebrated Judique fiddler Dan Rory MacDonald, although not afraid of death, was terrified that "he might get his fingers hurt & couldn't play at the dances when he got back home."[40]

Amid the fighting St. F.X. professor Fr P.J. Nicholson lamented that "thirty of the last few years' students [had] already made the supreme sacrifice, including a nephew of [his] own" (Flying Officer Ronald G. MacLean of North Sydney).[41] In the winter of 1942, an officer brought the terrible news to the Sydney home of St F.X. governor Neil MacArthur that his twenty-seven-year-old son Leo had been shot down over Germany returning from a raid on the city of Essen. For weeks, the family held out hope that he had survived the crash, but by June 1943 they learned that their son's body had been buried in Dusseldorf.[42] The following year, the young Fr Bernard Chisholm, ministering at Iona, lost his brother Alexander, who was serving in the American navy. A second brother, Donald, of the Loyal Edmonton Regiment, later died fighting in Italy.[43]

For a time, death seemed to lurk everywhere. In the evening of 13 October 1942, the SS *Caribou*, the ferry to Port aux Basques, Newfoundland, left the pier at North Sydney with 237 passengers and crew. A German U-boat was prowling in the area (a Sydney to Corner Brook convoy had been attacked the previous day), and a navy minesweeper was assigned to escort the ship. At 3:40 the following morning, mistaking the *Caribou* and the minesweeper as a "two-stack destroyer," U-69 fired a fatal torpedo into the belly of the ferry. The ship sank in less than five minutes, drowning many passengers; others died of exposure in the frigid waters of the Gulf of St Lawrence. One of the 137 fatalities was Hugh Gillis, a St F.X. alumnus and popular member of the Sydney Knights of Columbus who worked as a DOSCO superintendent.[44]

A few months after the *Caribou* sinking, a bomber aircraft crashed near the Sydney airfield killing four crewmen. Three days later a requiem service was held at Sacred Heart; the first afternoon Mass in Canadian history.[45] As in 1914–18, the clergy had the difficult task of comforting grieving families, and for younger priests like the twenty-seven--year-old Fr George Topshee, curate at Pictou, it was a terrible way to gain pastoral experience.

SECOND WORLD WAR ARMY CHAPLAINS

In contrast to chaos that reigned among Catholic chaplains in the Great War, the Canadian Chaplaincy Service, in the hands of the capable administrator Bishop Charles Nelligan of Pembroke, Ontario, was by 1939 well prepared.[46] Within weeks of Canada's declaration of war, Nelligan asked permission to enlist Fr Major Michael Gillis and Fr Major R.C. MacGillivray, both of whom had "proved their worth" serving in the trenches of France. Fr Major Donald MacPherson also wanted to enlist but was denied, as the army retirement age was sixty.[47]

Dusting off his uniform, Fr MacGillivray left Sacred Heart parish and went to Halifax to organize the chaplaincy service in the naval port, while Fr Gillis, "the greatest born psychologist," stayed in Cape Breton to minister to troops stationed around Sydney. (From Reserve Mines, Fr Tompkins attended to the Royal Canadian Airforce servicemen at the Sydney airport).[48] Younger priests like Fr James Fraser MacIsaac, pastor at St Theresa's parish, also wanted to serve.

"He is in line for overseas," noted a supportive Fr Major Gillis, "and is quite game to go."[49]

With so many priests keen to enlist, Bishop Morrison faced the inevitable staffing problems at home. In October 1940, Fr Angus Joseph MacIsaac, pastor at Mulgrave, and chaplain to the soldiers in the batteries around the Strait of Canso, had been ordered overseas. Soon afterward, Fr Major MacGillivray was sent to Europe with the 3rd Canadian Division, and Fr Major Gillis was ordered to replace him in Halifax. Finding substitutes for these men was difficult and Morrison objected that it was "high-handed and irresponsible" of the Chaplaincy Service to transfer these priests on such short notice.

Although Morrison allowed Fr Michael E. McLaughlin ("Fr Spotty") to go overseas and Fr Ronald MacLean to enlist in the navy, by 1943 priests were only allowed to serve part-time and could no longer be whisked away to Halifax or England.[50] These regulations frustrated those "who drew on the legend of their Great War forerunners" and wanted to serve.[51] When the St Joseph's native Fr Daniel R. Chisholm enlisted as a full-time chaplain for soldiers in the New Glasgow area, the bishop sabotaged his appointment. Fr Angus C. MacNeil, who had experience with the St F.X. Hospital Unit in the Great War, was told to stay in Glendale; Fr Angus A. Beaton at Southwest Margaree had his enlistment request denied; and Fr Leo Sears managed to sign-up but a spot on his lung quickly ended his military career.[52]

Bishop Morrison's decision to prohibit priests from enlisting as overseas chaplains after 1943 was not due to a lack of patriotism but to a belief that the Canadian Church expected too much from the Maritime provinces. During the Great War, Maritime dioceses had sent sixteen chaplains to France, while the dioceses of Montreal and Quebec together sent nine. With five chaplains enlisted in 1914–18, Antigonish had sent more padres to the blood-stained fields of Flanders than the Archdiocese of Toronto.[53]

The reluctance of Canadian bishops like Morrison to flood the chaplaincy service with priests put tremendous pressure on Bishop Nelligan. When Fr Major Gillis was discharged on his sixtieth birthday in 1943, Nelligan wrote that the need for chaplains was "so acute, that [they were] almost approaching a state of desperation."[54] In some theatres, Catholic soldiers were going without any spiritual ministration at all. "Really Antigonish Diocese hasn't

Figure 7.3 | Hon. Brigadier General, Fr R.C. MacGillivray

given a sufficient number of chaplains," Nelligan wrote to the Old Rector, "and I wish you would point this out very particularly to the bishop."[55]

Of course, few were willing to confront Morrison directly. Even correspondence from chaplains in Europe was somewhat reserved, as younger men like Fr Captain James MacIsaac found it intimidating to write their superior.[56] In fact, none of their descriptions of Europe's battlefields matched those of Fr Miles Tompkins in the Great War. Only Fr Captain Michael McLaughlin went so far as to write understatedly that in June 1945 the 4th Canadian armoured division had advanced through Belgium "with practically no fighting" until the Leopold Canal, where they met a terrible concentration of German machine guns.[57]

In September 1944 Bishop Nelligan, frustrated, resigned because of ill health. He was replaced by the now Brigadier-General Fr R.C. MacGillivray. Evoking his recommendations in the early months of the Great War, MacGillivray pressured his own bishop to rush the ordinations of Antigonish seminarians so that senior priests could replenish the chaplaincy.[58] While the veteran of the trenches had faced many tough scrapes during his military career, trying to force another chaplain out of a stubborn and elderly Morrison was one of his toughest. The army's refusal to pay for the medical care of Fr Captain MacIsaac, who had been sent home with "agitated depression," deeply angered Morrison, and while his letters reached MacGillivray from Antigonish with "words of regret," no more chaplains were forthcoming.[59]

In October 1944 MacGillivray was made a domestic prelate, and two years later he made George VI's New Year's Honours List as a Commander of the British Empire (and in 1948 a companion of the Order of the British Empire). The decorated chaplain, "a treasure house of amusing anecdotes and delightful stories," eventually returned to Sydney to finish his career as pastor of Sacred Heart.[60] Yet, while MacGillivray was a credit to the diocese, Nelligan nevertheless felt that the Canadian episcopate had failed to meet its wartime responsibilities.[61]

CENTRALIZATION OF THE MI'KMAQ

Some 250 Canadian soldiers fighting in Europe, like the decorated paratrooper Lawrence Paul of Membertou, were Mi'kmaq. Before enlisting, many of these young men had survived the difficult 1930s by working in agriculture and the fishery, some traversing the Maritime region in search of economic opportunity. Theirs was a continual fight for economic and cultural survival, and many children from struggling families continued to be sent to the "Micmac Training School" in Shubenacadie.[62]

Coverage of the residential school in the provincial and Catholic press remained mostly benign. "It would scarcely be possible to find a neater, better kept institution than the one that overlooks the beautiful tawny Shubenacadie River," *The Casket* noted in 1941. "A speck of dust or a book out of place would stand out like the proverbial sore thumb." When describing the economic prospects of its graduates, however, the paper was less sanguine. The reality was that most Mi'kmaw young people would find the "social barriers pretty high," while their chances of business or professional success "were out of the question."[63]

Ironically, while Mi'kmaw Catholics faced prejudice in local parishes – some churches still required them to sit in the back pews – the Indigenous experience was frequently used to propagate a favourable view of the Canadian Church. In January 1943 Pope Pius XII venerated Kateri Tekakwitha (1656–1680), an Algonquin-Mohawk convert from Kahnawake, Quebec, known as "Lily of the Mohawks" (she was canonized by Pope Benedict XVI in 2012). One of the miracles attributed to her intercession allegedly occurred at the Shubenacadie School in 1939 during an outbreak of strep throat. With medical treatment found to be ineffective, the staff had the children ask Tekakwitha to intercede. When all temperatures returned to normal, the school physician sent a statement to Rome as evidence of Tekakwitha's saintliness.[64]

This "miracle" at Shubenacadie reinforced the widely held societal conviction that the residential school was a progressive endeavour. Most people knew "what little attention" had been given over the years to the Indian day schools, and so many applauded the federal initiative. After a visit to Shubenacadie, for example, one priest commented that the students had responded favourably to the "refining influence" of the Sisters of Charity, and predicted that, as long as they did not return to the "ugly conditions" of the reservations, they would be successful.[65] The reality, of course, was much different; at least one former student testified that these visits were staged.[66]

For Indigenous Catholics, these were strange and contradictory times. On one hand, the Church fulfilled its historic responsibilities to the community with great attention. When Chief Matthew Francis, the leader at Pictou Landing for over four decades, died in the summer of 1940, for instance, eight priests attended his impressive funeral. Noting that Francis was a "fine Catholic," Fr A.A. Johnston demonstrated the importance of faith within Mi'kmaw governance by preaching that the chief's power "[came] from God."[67]

On the other hand, the Church did little to challenge Ottawa's Indian policies, allowing itself to become involved in schemes that harmed the flock. In 1941 the Mackenzie King government proposed centralizing all of Nova Scotia's Indigenous peoples into two large reservations – at Shubenacadie, Hants County, and Eskasoni, Cape Breton (Prince Edward Island and New Brunswick had similar centralization schemes). As details emerged, it was learned that some Mi'kmaw leaders, Benjamin Christmas at Membertou for one, were completely opposed to the scheme, while others, like Chief Gabriel Sylliboy of Whycocomagh, who was "totally influenced" by Ottawa, seemed to favour it.[68]

Much as with the residential school scheme, centralization was sold as a strategy to "give the Indians themselves a better break," end their cycle of poverty, and ease the stifling bureaucracy that governed the Indigenous community.[69] Throughout 1941–42, the federal minister of mines, and former superintendent-general of Indian affairs, T.A. Crerar, expressed hope that the Church would lend its support, and formally asked Bishop Morrison and Fr Coady to comment on the geographic and economic particulars of the site at Eskasoni.[70] Although the plan had merit on administrative grounds, Morrison cautioned Ottawa to approach the policy with "care and caution."[71]

Privately, Morrison was "decidedly uneasy"; centralization, he wrote, would be a "source of trouble" that might not dissipate for years – "perhaps for generations."[72] The flaws were obvious; despite bureaucratic promises of new homes with electricity, water, and "nice basements," Eskasoni's economy could not sustain a population influx. Extension fieldworkers also warned that the Mi'kmaq would not "consent to sacrifice their present existing opportunities to pioneer in new surroundings." Certain that the Mi'kmaq would resist centralization, Morrison counselled Ottawa to send representatives into the community to explain "the purposes and details" and gauge the reaction. "At all events," he warned in a letter to Crerar, "nothing drastic should be attempted."[73]

While Bishop Morrison personally opposed centralization, the generational marginalization of Mi'kmaw Catholics within their own Church once again had serious repercussions. In the face of some serious government pressure, the diocese offered no formal challenge to the policy, and at least one clerical agent "kind of forced the Indians to move."[74] In a way reminiscent of the refusal to recruit a Mi'kmaw seminarian, the reluctance to halt to the relocation of hundreds of Catholics into centralized communities was a sad reminder that the Church did not always look out for the best interests of its Indigenous flock. Centralization meant the destruction of some of the oldest Catholic communities in the region and flew in the face of economic facts generated by the diocese's own Extension department. And yet the scheme went ahead. Without the "interest and sympathy" of the Church, Robert Hoey of Indian Affairs later confessed, it would have been "exceedingly difficult, if not impossible, to persuade the Indians to abandon their homes."[75]

While some communities, like Paqtnkek, some twenty kilometres from St Ninian's Cathedral, relocated in great numbers – in August 1943, Chief Joseph Sack requested a poignant final mission there – at Membertou, the now forty-seven-year-old chief Ben Christmas reminded his community that "they had a choice." Interestingly, he found an ally in Fr Leo Keats, the priest who had banned White visitors to Chapel Island in 1931.[76] Christmas worried that centralization would hinder Mi'kmaw autonomy and erode culture, and Keats was concerned by the obvious lack of democracy in the relocation process. At Chapel Island in the summer of 1943, the "straight-from-the-shoulder hitting" clergyman declared that Eskasoni was a "concentration camp." With so many of his Mi'kmaw flock fighting the Nazis, he was appalled that they had to "bear the burden of citizenship" without the privileges afforded to other Canadians. "Stand together," he encouraged them, "and do not destroy your unity."[77]

Historians have noted that the fighting record of young Mi'kmaw men in the Second World War created public awareness of "their peculiar situation" and "raised their own expectations."[78] As *The Casket* editorialized: "The Sillaboys, the Goo Goos, the Juliens, the Pauls, have records from world war no. 1, that should dispel all doubt as to the Micmac's place among the warriors."[79] Yet, despite their being considered worthy to die on the battlefields of Holland and Germany, their economic, social, and religious rights at home were seriously curtailed. "You Indian people are often referred to contemptuously as wards of the government. You have no vote. In time of peace, you can get no work," Keats bellowed in 1945. "Now I see before me the long list of Indians killed or wounded in action. Wards indeed! I shout no!"[80]

Fr Keats knew that his diocese had supported centralization on the basis of promises of a new sanctuary and a four-room day school at Eskasoni. For many, it was the only means of rationalizing the Church's support. So, bureaucratic delays, which left many new residents without adequate shelter, were extremely embarrassing.[81] By the spring of 1944, the clergy could do little more than exercise patience. "As we have to depend on the action taken by the department," Bishop Morrison confessed to a colleague, "my hands are tied until we have some definite information."[82]

Ironically, the flawed policy of centralization was responsible for the first regular Mi'kmaq parish in eastern Nova Scotia. In the autumn of 1945, Fr Alexander A. Ross, a thirty-five--year-old native of southwest Margaree, was appointed parish priest at Eskasoni and principal of the day school.[83] When the parishioners of St Anne's (the name was later changed to Holy Family) made their first contribution to the diocese for religious and charitable purposes in December 1945, the historical significance was clear. Pleased that Eskasoni had taken "its place in the diocese in the matter of contributing to the synodal collections," Bishop Morrison praised the "faithful of the parish on this improved position."[84]

It is regrettable that Mi'kmaw Catholics had to experience centralization in order to take "their respectable place in the work of the Church," because the policy flaws were always evident.[85] As veterans returned from Europe, Chief Christmas, serving as president of the United General Indian Council of Nova Scotia, protested that those of them who refused to settle at Eskasoni or Shubenacadie were being denied access to veterans' land grants. Without grants, former soldiers like Gregory Francis, who served three years with the Canadian artillery, struggled to build new lives in communities like Membertou and Pictou Landing. Those who did settle at Eskasoni complained that they were isolated, forced to live in an "artificial social environment," and deprived of economic opportunity.[86] As Mi'kmaq leaders called for a return to the band system, Fr Keats used the 1947 celebration at Chapel Island to reinforce the age-old notion that "there [was] no place like home."[87]

By 1947 the day school at Eskasoni was finally completed and the Sisters of St Martha had established a teaching mission. Incredibly, federal bureaucrats now felt that the "success of the Indian welfare program" depended on the courses of study provided by the diocesan congregation.[88] The Marthas, "surrounded by several dialects of the Mi'kmaq language," worked hard at Eskasoni, provided domestic service training to augment regular studies, and organized a choir and youth groups.[89] Meanwhile, Ottawa wanted Extension to organize Eskasoni's economy on a cooperative basis and expected "opportunities for co-operative bulk purchasing and the co-operative sale or disposal of farm and handicraft products."[90] Yet that expectation never materialized. "With St. Francis Xavier University being so close," Robert Hoey complained from Ottawa, "we had hoped to have fostered some of its extension activities among the Indians. Such activities have not been carried out."[91] Fr Coady too insisted that cooperative strategies represented "better days," but there was little serious action for another decade.[92]

NEW BISHOPS AND ARCHBISHOPS

One of the reasons that the diocese was slow to engage with Eskasoni was that Bishop Morrison had grown old and cautious. By February 1942, rumours were afoot that Rome had appointed a coadjutor to the now eighty-one-year-old prelate. In the autumn of that year, the archbishop of Halifax asked Morrison to recommend an Antigonish priest worthy of episcopal office. Morrison suggested Fr John R. MacDonald, the rector of his cathedral, but was clear that he did not at all feel the need for a coadjutor. Although Fr John R. would be a suitable successor "when in God's providence, the time [came]," that time, he made it known, had not yet arrived.[93]

In early June 1943, it was announced by radio bulletin that Fr John R. had instead been appointed bishop of Peterborough, Ontario. The selection brought further compliments to the "apostolic" Catholicity of eastern Nova Scotia, and the *Peterborough Examiner* noted that the Maritime provinces had long been sending their best sons to other parts of the country, "equipped with ability and culture."[94] "The consecration takes place a week from tomorrow," Fr D.J. MacDonald wrote to a friend in August, "and we shall be so crowded with Bishops, Monsignori, and priests that the place will look like the Vatican."[95]

No sooner had Bishop John R. departed for the rich pastoral fields of Upper Canada than the Antigonish clergy began to lobby for his return. While Morrison sent the new prelate optimistic letters filled with encouragement and advice (lacking a Roman pontifical containing the rites and ceremonies usually preformed by bishops, Morrison sent him a "service worn copy" from the library of the late Fr Michael Laffin), all other extant local correspondence despatched to Ontario was filled with regrets and complaints.[96] "Surely, [Morrison] will resign," wrote an exasperated Fr Michael Gillis.[97]

The Antigonish clergy were mystified by the decision to send Bishop John R. to Ontario, and his absence became a point of contention for those frustrated with the elderly Morrison. While most admired the prelate personally, he was, they judged, no longer capable of providing effective leadership.[98] Throughout the winter of 1944–45, Fr Coady pleaded with both the apostolic delegate and Toronto's Cardinal McGuigan to appoint a young coadjutor who was sympathetic to Extension.[99] Either appoint a local priest, Coady counselled, or bring Bishop John R. home.

Knowing that Archbishop John Hugh MacDonald in Edmonton was deeply interested in the affairs of his native diocese, in 1944 the delegate asked him for advice on the Antigonish problem. From his partially completed cathedral, MacDonald devised a tidy solution. He suggested that Rome use Antigonish's centenary year to appoint the venerable Morrison as an archbishop *ad personam,* while strongly hinting that he retire.[100]

In March 1944 it was announced that Morrison had, as the archbishop had suggested, been accorded the *ad personam* title – making him an archbishop without the burden of an archdiocese. The news was accompanied by a general ecclesiastical shake-up of the Canadian episcopacy. "The best part of yesterday's announcement," wrote the new archbishop of Kingston, Ontario, J.A. O'Sullivan, "was the naming of dear Bishop Morrison as Archbishop. Since he couldn't be named Cardinal in wartimes, this is the highest honour he could get, and no one deserved it better."[101] For local Catholics, including Patrick O'Neill, secretary of the Glace Bay chapter of the Ancient Order of Hibernians, it was a "singular honour" that reflected well on everyone.[102]

When the excitement abated, Archbishop MacDonald gently counselled Morrison that the time had arrived for a coadjutor and, showing great respect, asked him to submit a roster of candidates.

"I am not sure whether he wrote you before receiving my letter," the Edmonton prelate wrote to Bishop John R. "Mine was written on the 6th and the hope expressed therein that he would soon be rewarded with a Coadjutor may have aroused a bit of suspicion."[103] Everyone feared that Morrison would connect the dots (and he did), but it seemed worth the risk. "Whether these hints will fall on favorable ground remains to be seen," the archbishop confessed. "I hope they will, for the benefit of all concerned."[104]

The episcopal shake-up that made Morrison an archbishop also sent Fr James Boyle to Prince Edward Island as bishop of Charlottetown. Boyle, now forty-eight, had ministered among the steelworkers at Whitney Pier since 1938 and was a leading voice of Catholic social action. "I am delighted," one priest noted, "but [Cape Breton] is going to miss him."[105] Boyle's appointment was another indicator of Extension's success; priests who "promoted the movement vigorously in their own parishes" were now being promoted to the episcopate. With some twenty-five cooperative societies active on Prince Edward Island, noted the *Canadian Register*, one of the pioneers of the Antigonish Movement "had gone to guide its destiny."[106]

PARISHES IN THE 1940S

Although the population in Bishop Boyle's former parish of Whitney Pier remained constant, the ever-changing demographics of the Cape Breton colliery towns continued to necessitate boundary changes. St Michael's parish was opened at River Ryan-Scotchtown in 1941, Holy Rosary at Westmount in 1947, and in 1948 Holy Cross at Caledonia (it had been a mission since 1938); in addition, St Alphonsus in Victoria Mines was again raised to parish status.

Then in 1949, Sydney's Sacred Heart Parish was "dismembered," making way for the creation of three new parishes: St Joseph's, St Anthony Daniel (named for one of the seventeenth-century Canadian martyrs who had spent time at St Ann's, Victoria County), and Our Lady of Fatima in Sydney River. That the Sydney River parish took that name was not at the time surprising, as the story behind it was very much in the news. At the height of the Great War, three peasant children had claimed that the Virgin Mary appeared to them in a field near the rural village of Fatima in Portugal. Drawn by accounts of visions and miracles, people flocked to the site and some even witnessed the "public miracle" of the spinning sun. The incident was further popularized by such books as *Vision of Fatima*, published in 1948 by Fr Thomas McGlynn, OP, also an artist who had sculpted her image under the guidance of the last surviving child witness. By then millions of pilgrims had descended on the Portuguese town – Bishop John R. himself attended a candlelight procession there in 1949.[107] As with St Thérèse of Lisieux, images and statues of Our Lady of Fatima soon proliferated; in the summer of 1946 shrines were dedicated to her at Boisdale and at St Anne's Convent in Glace Bay.[108]

Part of the attraction of Marianism, of course, was that Catholics could combine private devotion with public exhibitions of fidelity. On "Mary's Day," large processions of school children paraded through the streets of mixed communities like New Aberdeen with a statue of Mary adorned with a beautiful crown. As vehicles became more accessible, Catholics travelled greater distances to participate in services and parades. In the autumn of 1948, a large diocesan contingent joined eleven thousand of the faithful under the auspices of the Holy Name Society, in a march through the rain-soaked streets of Saint John.[109] Inspired by this fellowship, the following year, three thousand men from the six parishes of Glace Bay walked in their own "Holy Name Rally," from St Joseph's Hospital to Immaculate Conception Church in Dominion.[110]

Parishes in the colliery towns, which had larger populations, offered facilities and services unheard of in the countryside. Youth in New Waterford were well known for their basketball games at the Strand Gymnasium, while the Catholic Youth Organization clubhouse at Sacred Heart regularly hosted Maritime-wide conventions. Even as priests were lamenting that country parishes were petering out because "no children [were] being raised in so many of the homes," by 1946 the first of the "Baby Boom" generation had entered the world.[111] "We speak about great patriots, statesmen and soldiers," said Fr D.J. Rankin at the funeral of a parishioner who had fourteen children; but, he asked rhetorically, "who is more worthy of the praise of his countrymen than the parent of such a large family?"[112]

All the same, attitudes toward family life were slowly changing. In a biography of the St F.X. English professor Fr Roderick MacSween, Stewart Donovan notes that as a young curate the priest-poet would counsel women – through the medium of the confessional – to practise birth control.[113] Catholic women, along with many others, had entered the workforce during the war, and many opted to remain on the job after 1945 rather than undergo multiple pregnancies. As veterans returned to their former lives, post-traumatic stress (then unspoken) often led to alcohol abuse, marital tensions, and family breakups. Divorce and contraception remained generally taboo, but when the Canadian Legion lobbied the provinces to make divorce more accessible, it was clear that change was in the air.[114]

The stereotype of the strict old priest was also slowly fading. Throughout the 1940s, as priests and ministers relaxed their moral grip on the community, liquor profits poured into provincial coffers at astounding rates.[115] And, in the cultural realm, whereas the Church had been "blamed for the death of the old body-contact Eight-Hand Reel" in the nineteenth century according to the Scottish cultural historian John Gibson, by the 1930s organizations like the Scottish Catholic Society were actively promoting music and dance with the clergy's support.[116] In fact, when Fr John James Bryden, the Boston College alumnus, "versatile Gaelic preacher," and business manager of *Mosglaidth*, went to Mabou as a parish priest in 1937, "the quadrille, or square set, was officially condoned" for the first time.[117] Bryden's love of Gaelic music compelled at least one parishioner to complain that the Mabou dances were held with "boot-leggers at the door." The young people, another man muttered, could get "all the devilment they want in Mabou and Brook Village halls."[118] Considering the upheavals of the 1940s, folks could perhaps be forgiven for seeking diversion in dance and drink.

THE RISE OF THE CO-OPERATIVE COMMONWEALTH FEDERATION

As a consequence of wartime austerity – and against the wishes of many stakeholders – Extension closed its Glace Bay field office in March 1941.[119] "I hope you have recovered from the disappointment," the pastor of North Sydney wrote to Rector MacDonald, "and that you will keep your chin up. 'For there will always be a [Cape Breton]' and that sort of rot."[120] However, diocesan charity and welfare associations in parishes like Bridgeport and Sydney continued to combat poverty and strengthen families. In 1939–40 alone, the Sacred Heart Association, staffed by the Sisters of St Martha, made over 1,800 visits to local homes, filled 324 food orders, provided 240 pairs of shoes, operated an employment bureau and youth clubs, and financed summer camps.[121]

All this application of Catholic action brought the Church closer to the people. Fr Stanley MacDonald, for one, felt that he had the trust of the steelworkers and "[stood] pretty well with the miners."[122] In 1937 he had arranged a meeting between his brother, Premier Angus L. Macdonald, and officials of the budding union federation, the Committee for Industrial Organization (CIO).[123] The following year, he congratulated Glace Bay native Fr Michael "Micky" MacDonald for a speech championing steelworkers' union rights.[124] Then, in the spring of 1940, the steelworkers selected Fr Thomas O'Reilly Boyle, curate at Cheticamp, as their representative on the federal conciliation board that was mandated to investigate wage disputes with DOSCO.[125]

The growing confidence of labour in the diocese was in part due to the fact that many priests and seminarians now hailed from the colliery towns. When Micky MacDonald, who had worked as a coal miner before entering St F.X., was promoted from curate at Whitney Pier to parish priest at Ingonish, the secretary of the Steelworkers Union Local 1064 suspected that he had been transferred at the behest of the steel company. "No one approached me either directly or indirectly with such a proposition," Bishop Morrison replied, "and even if this had been done, it would have no effect one way or the other."[126] Under the letterhead of UMW Local 4560, the Whitney Pier miners themselves also protested the transfer, on the basis that they had spent thirty years battling those who sought to "counteract the benefits which accrue from sane administration of a Labour Union." As forces were at work attacking the Christian ideal of brotherhood by preaching "the abolition of private property," the loss of a sympathetic priest could only aggravate the situation.[127]

As young priests like Micky MacDonald came from the ranks of labour, they were very comfortable with the platform of the Co-operative Commonwealth Federation (CCF). In December 1939 Douglas MacDonald of New Waterford was elected for the CCF in the provincial riding of Cape Breton Centre. Even though this win was aided by division within local Liberal ranks, the CCF was now a political reality. In the run-up to the federal election of March 1940, so many Catholics made inquiries about the party's policies that Bishop Morrison was obliged to issue a formal statement.[128] There was nothing in the party's speeches that was antagonistic to religion, he counselled, except in the matter of divorce, but they were not the only politicians "with loose ideas" on that issue. In fact, he added, it was "debateable whether any of the parties could be considered as a true interpretation of democracy."[129]

Representing the CCF in Cape Breton South during the 1940 federal campaign was Clarence "Clarie" Gillis, a one-time associate of J.B. McLachlan, hardened veteran of the Great War (with the shrapnel to prove it) and influential member of District 26.[130] In a close three-way race against David Hartigan, the incumbent Liberal, and J. Clyde Nunn, the popular Catholic intellectual from Whitney Pier, Gillis won the seat by a close 218 votes. Importantly, as Michael Earle has noted, Gillis ran a campaign with "socialistic and patriotic overtones" but was openly opposed to the "more extreme radicalism of the Communist Party."[131] As his biographer has commented, "Clarie was born and remained a Roman Catholic."[132] When one young priest visited Bishop Morrison shortly after the election, he was asked for an opinion on the results. Unsure how to respond, the Sydney native noted that his family considered Gillis's election to be a proud moment for labour. "That's right," Morrison replied, "a feat for the miners."[133]

As Catholics in the colliery towns were free to support the CCF, Glace Bay became the "Liberals' waterloo."[134] With high-profile Extension personalities like Alexander MacIntyre subtly supporting the fledgling party, the CCF captured the ridings of Cape Breton Centre, East, and South in the 1941 provincial election. One of the defeated Liberal candidates, L.D. Currie (he was soon returned to the legislature for Richmond County), was incensed at MacIntyre for attending the poll at Steele's Hill in Passchendaele. According to Currie's section workers, MacIntyre had been "talking quietly against [him]." In a letter to the Old Rector, Fr H.P. MacPherson, Currie grumbled that Extension fieldworkers had campaigned against him because they felt that "the principles of the St. F.X. Extension Movement and the policies of the CCF party were one and the same."[135]

Although it was awkward for St F.X., the perception that Extension and the CCF were natural allies was pervasive.[136] "The election in Cape Breton got us into a lot of trouble with the politicians," Fr Coady confessed to a friend. "The miners more or less identify our movement with the C.C.F. Currie got licked as you probably know."[137] In Halifax the governing Liberals were concerned. Back in 1938 Premier Macdonald had already asked Fr Coady if Extension was "headed to a socialist state."[138] Again in 1942 Angus L., who had resigned the premiership in 1940 to enter MacKenzie King's war cabinet, complained that although George Boyle was thinking of running for the Liberal Party, most Extension fieldworkers were CCF sympathizers. "Any supporter of the CCF," he told Fr Tompkins, "was no friend of his."[139]

Although Fr Coady defended the neutrality of Extension, he refused to distance his movement from the CCF. For one thing, Extension had never felt completely accepted in the colliery towns. In the rural counties of Richmond, Guysborough, Inverness, and Antigonish, where the Extension message was strong, the Grits did well in the 1941 election, but "no Liberal could have won the Glace Bay seat." The miners had voted for non-traditional parties in the past, Coady noted, and "the present flare-up [was] history repeating itself." As everyone knew, organized labour could "swing in a body" and nothing could stop it.[140]

With questions about how the CCF could reconcile its left-wing policies with aspects of Catholic doctrine such as subsidiarity, the Canadian hierarchy met in plenary session at Quebec in October 1943 and decreed that all Canadian Catholics would be allowed to support the party.[141] Little did the prelates know that by freeing the flock to cast ballots for the CCF they had stifled the communist threat in the Cape Breton coalfields.[142] As a viable alternative to both the traditional parties and the radicals, Clarie Gillis was easily re-elected for Cape Breton South in 1945.[143]

In reality, of course, it didn't matter who represented the colliery towns, as Ottawa had little interest in investing in Cape Breton. In fact, during the war the federal government regularly "withheld funds for the modernization and expansion of Maritime Industries."[144] Although steel towns like Hamilton, Ontario, were prepared for the postwar economy, Sydney was ill equipped to absorb returning veterans. "[As for] the boy who has just come back from overseas after fighting a war – in this House we were saying for five years that nothing would be too good for him," thundered Gillis. "He could have a new world, a new heaven, and a new earth … Well, he is back – and he is back on relief."[145]

As Cape Breton steelworkers faced new bouts of unemployment, the United Steelworkers of America demanded nation-wide wage increases and a forty-hour work week. On 15 July 1946, some fourteen thousand Canadian steelworkers walked off the job. When pickets were set up at the entrance to the Sydney steel plant, the men "received wholehearted support" from passersby.[146]

They also received support from the Catholic priests ministering at the Sydney parishes of Holy Redeemer, St Theresa's, and Sacred Heart, who made a $2,000 donation to the strike fund. "You have undertaken a task, the justice of which demands the co-operation of your fellow citizens," read the accompanying note. "Please accept the enclosed as a token of our sympathy." Tom McLachlan, son of the legendary radical J.B. McLachlan, crowed that the "totally unexpected donation" was the most "heartening sign yet of support for the National Wage Campaign outside the ranks of labor organizations themselves."[147]

In late January 1947 District 26 ordered a brief strike in Nova Scotia's collieries (the first strike since 1925); another was called in February. It was a bad time of year to create coal shortages but no miner could raise a family on so few shifts per week.[148] "The priests in the area are very much upset over the whole problem," Bishop Morrison told a colleague in March, adding that he had "several interviews ... as to what procedures should be followed."[149] On 13 March, the Cape Breton County clergy gathered at the Lyceum Theatre to discuss their response. Ironically, one of the first to speak was the eighty-year-old Fr Charles MacDonald, who had been at the centre of the infamous Bridgeport machine-gun incident of 1909. He begged his younger colleagues to find new tactics. "On the spiritual side of the question [they] should make an appeal to almighty God," he advised. But, "on the material side, what were [they] to do?"

By addressing the younger priests in this way, Fr MacDonald acknowledged that members of the older generation were out of ideas. Many of the veteran priests, like the then seventy-seven-year-old Fr James Tompkins, were fed up with the incessant problems of coal and insisted that they were "flying in the face of almighty God" by neglecting to develop the province's other resources. He then gave his colleagues a three-page Novena of Grace in honour of St Francis Xavier and sat down. Everyone respected Tompkins and certainly believed in the power of prayer, but the younger priests demanded something more. By the end of the meeting, a motion was tabled to formally donate to the Miners' Relief Fund from the parish coffers.

Offering an official donation from the Cape Breton clergy was an audacious act (especially to those who worried that the money might "go to Moscow"). Yet the new generation of priests, like the forty-two-year-old Fr Michael J. MacKinnon, were persuasive. The Sydney Mines native had worked closely with Extension, was president of the St Joseph's Hospital Board, and was adamant that the personal donations made to the steelworkers by the Sydney priests in 1946, and a more recent donation to the miners from the parishioners of Sacred Heart, had raised the status of the diocese, even "on the admission of the Communist Party."

Another emerging voice was that of the pastor of St Agnes in New Waterford, the forty-four-year-old Fr Raymond T. Campbell. A native of Sydney whose mother was from that sturdy Newfoundland stock of migrants who had exchanged the cod fishery for the coal mines in the late nineteenth century, he demanded that the Church support its working flock lest they be seen as "favoring the rich." As the clergy were "well-fed," they could surely afford to divert a little money from the parish coffers into the homes of the strikers. As the tone of the meeting shifted, Frs MacKinnon and Campbell were joined by Fr Paul MacNeil of St Michael's parish, who argued passionately that the clergy should "storm heaven" and "march with the masses." The pastor at Sydney Mines, forty-two-year-old Fr Daniel L. MacIsaac, demanded "a special sacrifice," while the historian Fr A.A. Johnston, then ministering at Mount Carmel in New Waterford, reasoned that the priests should "side with the workers." After all, he challenged, it was "the miners who have built [their] churches and [their] schools."

In a historic vote of eight to three (with one abstention), the motion to donate to the Miners' Relief Fund directly from their parish coffers was passed.[150] When Archbishop Morrison, now eighty-six, expressed concern that the donation would be "misunderstood or perverted," Fr MacKinnon used a column in *The Casket* to push back.[151] By early April, the acting president of District 26, Douglas MacDonald of New Waterford, announced that he had received a financial gift from the local Catholic parishes, including a cheque for $1,000 from the priests themselves. It was something that "the miners [would] always remember."[152]

As the younger priests of the colliery towns grew in confidence, charges of diocesan collusion with the CCF resurfaced. In 1948 *The Casket* defended its impartiality but the emerging tension between some Catholic elites and the increasingly left-leaning clergy was obvious.[153] When *The Casket* suggested that socialists were merely seeking a state operating on the principles of Pope Leo XIII, reaction from some quarters was swift.[154] "By associating [socialism] with the names of the highest prelates in the Church," wrote an angry reader from Manitoba, "we inadvertently tend to strengthen the position of our adversary." In his opinion, within any socialist system "the cooperative movement would become superfluous."[155]

In October 1948, an irritated Premier Macdonald took another jab at the CCF, telling the St F.X. political science club that the party was "dictatorial." While government had a role, where did the "planning stop and dictatorship begin?"[156] Yet, the younger clergy still felt it best to support the wishes of their parishioners. *The Casket* may have editorialized that Catholic social action had defeated radicalism, but it was the rise of the CCF that offered an outlet for protest and insulated the region from communism. By the summer of 1949, the paper reported, there were not enough communists in New Waterford, Glace Bay, and Reserve to even "hold a meeting."[157]

CJFX RADIO STATION

Much as Fr Tompkins had done in the 1920s, the clergy recognized that propaganda was key to any program of Catholic social action. By 1940 radio had become an increasingly important platform and priests like Fr James Boyle and Fr R.C. MacGillivray were well-known voices over the Sydney airwaves speaking "*urbi et orbi.*"[158] In Glace Bay, a weekly Knights of Columbus program broadcast over Voice of the Atlantic Seaboard included music stylings from the St Anne's parish choir and religious instruction from high-ranking officials like L.D. Currie and Neil MacArthur.[159] Yet, as the popularity of radio grew – Fr Coady's lectures were often aired over the Canadian Broadcasting Corporation (CBC) – concern arose about the lack of programs to counter the "pagan philosophy of life."[160]

Whereas Fr Raymond Campbell had urged his colleagues to purchase airtime from CJBC in Sydney, Fr James Boyle went even further. Before his appointment to Charlottetown, he suggested that Extension organize its own diocese-wide radio station. A dedicated radio station, he reasoned, would not only uplift people's thoughts but would also counteract the material on the airwaves that was "inane, if not positively vicious."[161] Radio would also support rural sustainability by providing news and entertainment to the most remote parts of the diocese and easing wintertime isolation in parishes like Bay St Lawrence and Georgeville.[162]

Fr Boyle had a supporter in J. Clyde Nunn, a well-known Whitney Pier personality and experienced broadcaster. Years later, one priest mused that "the outstanding success" of local Catholic radio was due more to Nunn "than to any other person, living or dead." Since his teenage years Nunn had been active in Catholic societies and lectured publicly on topics like "what it means to be a good Catholic."[163] Other keen supporters were St F.X. rector Fr D.J. MacDonald and the elderly Alexander Johnston, St F.X. alumnus and former Ottawa bureaucrat who in 1902 had induced Guglielmo Marconi to establish the first transatlantic wireless station at Glace Bay.[164]

As there were no licenses for religious broadcasters and universities were not eligible to hold commercial licenses, a joint stock company – Atlantic Broadcasters Limited (ABL) – was organized in November 1941. It was supervised by three men: Fr Daniel McCormick, a thirty-four-year-old philosopher and Extension official; Fr Alexander J. MacIsaac, pastor of Inverness; and J. Clyde Nunn, who by 1943 was managing director.[165] Since Ottawa prioritized stations with an educational mandate, the ABL application focused on the lack of educational programming in the region and the weak signal of Sydney's CJBC. As Mark McGowan has noted, this strategy exemplified "the ingenuity of some religious groups in bringing their message to a broad audience in spite of government regulation."[166]

The money generated by the 302 shareholders of the ABL, most of them clergy and women religious, paid for the broadcasting license and a modest studio in Antigonish town. Writing to a friend in the United States, an excited Bishop Morrison joked, "Just wait and hear! Seriously, it is intended for more educational work in this part of the country, but if ever the time comes when we have a coast to coast hook up, we shall let you know."[167]

On 25 March 1943, CJFX, the "University of the Air," began transmitting (580 on the dial).[168] As Fr D.J. MacDonald publicly proclaimed, radio was the "most efficient means of communication, and communication is education."[169] The station was on air for sixteen hours a day, and much of the programming was purchased from the CBC through its affiliation with the Dominion Network. This, according to McGowan, helped CJFX complement its local programming with news and public affairs programming produced through the National Religious Advisory Council in Toronto.[170] By 1946 the station's power output was elevated to 5,000 watts and the coverage area was extended to Newfoundland and parts of the northern United States.

Although Santo Dodaro and Leonard Pluta note that much of the early programming was "not highly focused," CJFX proclaimed the Extension message and served "the people it was established to serve."[171] The Sunday afternoon "Labour School of the Air" program, hosted by economist and Sydney native Fr Joseph A. MacDonald, discussed wages and general working conditions.[172] In other segments, St F.X. professors gave lectures on biology, history, and English, while Zita (O'Hearn) Cameron, Moses Coady's assistant at the Extension Department, hosted a popular home economics program called "Your Next Door Neighbour." By May 1943 Rector MacDonald rejoiced that diocesan reception was "better than expected."[173]

CJFX provided Catholic intellectuals with a medium for promoting issues and ideas, and its programs were occasionally picked up by the CBC for national consumption. In February 1943, a series of talks on economic questions by Fr Daniel McCormick, sponsored by the Radio League of St Michael, was broadcast into the living rooms of the nation. Others, like the Sydney-born Danny Gallivan, used the station to report on sports and recreation. By 1947 the brother of Fr William Gallivan and future broadcaster of the CBC's "Hockey Night in Canada" offered thrilling summaries of local, national, and international sporting events. Local musical groups like the Caledonia Male Quartet of New Glasgow became household names, while St F.X. students could study the science of radio with the physicist Fr Ernest Clarke.

Although some programs were more popular than others, CJFX never lost its focus on the Extension message. In 1948, having returned from post-graduate study at the University of Chicago, the Inverness native Allan J. MacEachen joined Fr "Little Doc" MacPherson on the program "Life in these Maritimes." A few weeks later, the recently hired St F.X. economist and future member of parliament, who would wield tremendous political power over Atlantic Canada, was named the station's "Education Chief." With this quality of staff, listening groups expanded across the region and Catholics made "Monday Night [their] Study Night."[174]

INTEREST IN DIOCESE HISTORY

Radio was critical in reinforcing Catholic cultural and historical awareness. In 1941 Fr Hugh Somers was elected president of the English section of the Canadian Catholic Historical Association

(CCHA), in whose journal several Antigonish clergy had by then already published. When Fr D.J. Rankin was asked by the CCHA for a paper on Laurence Kavanagh, the first Catholic to gain a seat the Nova Scotia legislature, Rankin, "who knew nothing about Kavanagh," turned to Fr Leo Keats at St Peter's for assistance.[175] While reading Kavanagh's account books, which were then donated to the Louisbourg Museum, the researcher unearthed a minor scandal. Bishop William Fraser, a famous advocate of temperance, had once purchased a small quantity of rum from the merchant. Not wanting to "offend the inquisitive public," Keats removed the offensive page.[176]

Fr Rankin's publications on Kavanagh garnered great interest. After composing a short article on the politician's career for the *Sydney Post-Record*, Rankin received so much feedback (even from Kavanagh's grandchildren) that he sent similar articles to other regional papers.[177] Interest in the region's Catholic history also led to an awareness of pioneer architecture and cemeteries (local "cemetery days" were set up to recondition gravestones, for instance), and in 1945 the Congregation of Notre Dame erected a monument to their members who had ministered at Fortress Louisbourg in the eighteenth century. The memorial, in what is now a national historic park, was unveiled by a delegation including the Louisbourg mayor, members of the CND and local historian Albert Almon (who received an honorary degree from St F.X. in 1947).[178]

Pioneer Monks in Nova Scotia, a historical account of the old Trappist monastery at Tracadie, was published in 1948 by Fr Luke Schrepfer, OSA. Father Schrepfer, who had lived at the monastery until his transfer to British Columbia in 1947, spent seven years researching his "standing work of tribute" to the Trappist monks and his fellow Augustinians.[179] Shortly afterward, Neil McNeil, the St F.X. alumnus and assistant managing editor of the *New York Times*, published *The Highland Heart in Nova Scotia*, which described his boyhood in the Cape Breton community of Washabuckt and his experience of walking the nine miles to the church at Iona.[180]

With all this interest in the region's history, the Scottish Catholic Society (SCS) had in 1940 financed the post-graduate training of a young Malcolm MacDonell in the history department at Queen's University. Later, they sponsored his theological training, and then further historical studies at the University of Toronto. In return,

St F.X. hired MacDonell to focus on early Scottish immigration and settlement in Nova Scotia (in 1947 he published a scholarly article on the early history of the diocesan college).[181]

At St F.X., Fr P.J. Nicholson, who taught a Gaelic singing class, edited a Gaelic column in *The Casket*, and owned a large collection of Gaelic books known as "Scotland Yard," also wanted MacDonell to also investigate the language of "Adam and Eve." The struggle for the acceptance of Gaelic was never more obvious than during the war when Ottawa banned its use over the nation's airwaves, telegraph wires, and telephone lines.[182] In response, Scottish-born Rev. A.W.R. MacKenzie, the Presbyterian pastor at Baddeck and president of the Cape Breton Island Gaelic Foundation, along with the city of Sydney and the County of Victoria, protested the treatment of Gaelic as a "foreign language."[183]

At picturesque St Ann's, Victoria County, Rev. MacKenzie's new Gaelic college sought to strengthen the region's cultural identity. When the institution opened in 1939, Premier Macdonald, who would soon be elected Grand Noble Chief of the Highland Scottish Clans of New Scotland, proclaimed that it would "pay a debt to Scotland and to the sons and daughters of that land." Soon the college's open-air concerts expanded into "weeklong 'Gaelic Mods,'" with singing competitions and educational lectures.[184]

While many Scots supported MacKenzie's new college, among Catholics there was some unease about yielding responsibility for Highland culture to a Presbyterian clergyman. In response, Sister St Veronica, CND, founded the Mount Saint Bernard Gaelic Choir in 1946 (she would later receive an honorary degree from St F.X. along with Compton MacKenzie, author of *Whisky Galore!*) and although none of the choir girls were Gaelic speakers they all came from homes "where there were still living links with Gaelic."[185] The choir was broadcast to national and international audiences over CJFX, the CBC, and the BBC.[186] From the rainswept Hebrides, Scottish historian John Lorne Campbell watched these cultural developments with great interest. Next to his beloved island of Canna, no region interested him more than eastern Nova Scotia. He was also drawing closer to Catholicism, and in February 1947 the historian was received into the Catholic faith before the young Fr Bernie Chisholm at Somers Chapel on the St F.X. campus.[187]

EXTENSION AND THE WAR

As Canadian soldiers fought their way into Nazi Germany, Extension patriotically offered its knowledge and networks to Ottawa. As financial resources were gobbled up by the war effort, the diocesan collection for fieldwork was discontinued and Ottawa reduced its annual grant. Despite the generosity of benefactors like William Dennis of the *Halifax Herald*, Extension fieldworkers faced serious financial shortfalls, and the Rural and Industrial Conferences were temporarily suspended. In this vacuum, the department gradually ceded jurisdiction to other cooperative entities, and the *Extension Bulletin*, published by the department since 1933, was replaced by the *Maritime Cooperator*, which was funded primarily by local credit unions and cooperatives.[188] As the link between education and economic action blurred, the "seeds of fragmentation" within the regional cooperative movement began to germinate.[189]

It was difficult to preach education with the nation so focused on the war effort. The miners were working at full employment for the first time since 1918, and with others staffing shipyards, or in uniform, it was difficult "to get very much study across." The "people are so busy," noted Fr Coady, "and so many are away in the army and other things."[190]

Yet the slowdown soon had supporters complaining that Extension had lost momentum. "Our credit union is as flat as a prairie," griped the pastor of Brook Village in 1942. "It has been so since last summer and there isn't a member of the Extension Dept. interested enough to ask why."[191] In the winter of 1944 Fr Michael Gillis bemoaned the "general lack of interest" in Extension's message. Replying from Ontario, Bishop John R. tried to console him. "If they could only come here and find what prestige the movement has given St. F.X and Antigonish, they would all take off their coats [and get to work]."[192]

One person still hard at work was Fr Tompkins. He had spent the war ensuring that his parishioners had books "so that they [could] tell a fool when they see one."[193] While bureaucrats dithered on a regional library strategy, the priest drafted Sister Francis Delores Donnelly, a Newfoundlander and member of the Sisters of Charity, who had just completed a degree in librarianship, to work in his Reserve Mines library. "Much against my will and [to my] total dismay in fact," Donnelly recalled, "I was told I was lent out to a man named Dr. Jimmy Tompkins who lived in Reserve – wherever that was."[194] Yet she was soon engrossed in her work, and the little library for children in the basement of St Joseph's School quickly gained recognition from the Department of Education (likely the only school library in the province with a full-time librarian). "One recovers from the 'shock' of finding a coal miner enjoying Mortimer Adler [a philosopher and Roman Catholic convert]," she recounted, "just in time to answer a rather rare request for the Koran or the Confessions of St. Augustine."[195]

By 1945 Catholics in Reserve Mines had access to over five thousand volumes of various genres (it was not all labour economics) as well as subscriptions to periodicals and even the *New York Times*. "We are on the evening of victory," exclaimed Sister Delores as the war came to an end. "Let us hope that in the new world toward which we are all looking there will be more adequate provision of books and libraries for everyone." By 1948 the library, complete with a painting of Andrew Carnegie, was participating in national "book week" programs, and movie versions of Dickens's *Tale of Two Cities* and Stevenson's *Treasure Island* were screened for the local children.[196]

While Fr Tompkins was known favourably throughout the region – the *Glace Bay Gazette* attributed the success of the Antigonish Movement to his philosophical genius – his real celebrity was cultivated by followers outside the diocese. When awarded an honorary Master's degree from Harvard University in the summer of 1941, he was feted for helping "people to become masters of their own economic destiny."[197] In the spring of 1942, the BBC aired a world-wide exposé on the Antigonish Movement, which furthered his personal fame.[198] Likewise, Fr Coady remained in great demand on the lecture circuit; once holding a Winnipeg audience "spell bound" for fifty minutes.[199] His appointment as a domestic prelate in December 1946 gave the new monsignor even more prestige and, when another papal commendation heralded the work of his movement, Cardinal McGuigan noted that the program benefited not only people in Boisdale and River Bourgeois but the "whole Church of God."[200] Crossing the Atlantic Ocean in 1949, one dumbfounded local priest learned that his travelling companion, the Bishop of San Antonio, Texas, not only knew of Extension but had just sent a student to St F.X. for training.[201]

BISHOP JOHN R. RETURNS AS COADJUTOR

These papal commendations and newspaper tributes were all the more satisfying as many of the priests who had built the global reputation of eastern Nova Scotia were nearing the end of their earthy sojourn. One of them, Bishop Sandy, slipped and broke his hip in February 1941, while celebrating his eighty-third birthday at Mockler Hall. Six days later, he died. The eminent scholar who had "shed lustre on the field of literary accomplishment" was buried in the old St Mary's graveyard at Mabou.[202] Hugh P. MacPherson, the Old Rector, spent his retirement at St F.X. reading the exploits of champion boxers and dispensing advice to friends.[203] "Puffing steadily at his big pipe, he now became the sage incarnate," recalled one priest, "an artist in retirement."[204] The Old Rector died two days after Christmas 1949 at the age of eighty-two, and a distraught Msgr Coady (his best friend) wrote that, as far as the people of eastern Nova Scotia were concerned, MacPherson was one "of THE few men of [the] half century."[205]

As the old clerical guard went into retirement, some worried that the diocese itself had lost momentum. Despite the fact that there was "not a penny in sight," diocesan institutions like St F.X. were desperate for infrastructural renewal. In the spring of 1944, the sixty-three-year-old college rector Fr D.J. MacDonald, battling high blood pressure, recognized that the college's postwar renewal would require the skills of a younger administrator.[206] He was replaced by the "conscience of the college," Fr P.J. Nicholson, who had worked hard to build-up St F.X.'s laboratories and science equipment. A teetotaller and "very correct man," Nicholson had a good sense of humour and enjoyed the students. "If you made a hundred in physics," one colleague recalled, "of course, you were everything."[207]

Nicholson faced several daunting challenges and was aware that St F.X. was not equipped for a postwar enrollment boom.[208] The quality of scientific training needed improvement and, especially among those who still considered the college a minor seminary, there was concern that the arts were falling behind.[209] In 1944 a diocesan campaign, the "last general appeal" of Archbishop Morrison's career, was launched to raise $800,000.[210] While excited organizers predicted a collection of a million dollars from local pockets alone, eastern Nova Scotia was not wealthy and there were mumblings about the mounting cost of post-secondary education.[211] At St Peter's, Fr Keats mused that the college administrators still believed in Santa Claus. "They hang up their stockings every night," he joshed, "and expect all sorts of money."[212]

Yet, with so many veterans returning to Canada in 1945, contributors recognized the need for a new residence (Cameron Hall was opened in 1946) and more classroom space.[213] Moreover, Ottawa had enacted a Veterans' Rehabilitation Training Scheme, which provided monies for former soldiers to enroll in colleges across the country. "A little trickle has already begun," Nicholson mused in January 1945. "After demobilization there will be a little deluge."[214] By 1947 veterans made up a third of the student body (for the first time Cape Breton students were outnumbered by those from other areas).[215]

It was difficult to face these realities with the elderly archbishop Morrison at the helm, and some, like Fr Michael Gillis, felt that Morrison's caution was "a tragic hold up." By the spring of 1945 there was hope that Bishop John R. would be transferred back home. If he ever returns from Ontario, predicted Fr Nicholson, "you'll see things hum."[216] Yet from his aging residence, the old archbishop continued to resist the appointment of a coadjutor. Although in his eighties, he was in reasonably good health and discharged his responsibilities without any "unusual fatigue." While Bishop John R. remained his first choice as coadjutor, he felt that it would be unfair to bring him back to Nova Scotia so soon after his transfer to Ontario. "Personally, I would have liked to have had him," he confessed, "but in all fairness I think his own status as Bishop of Peterborough should not be lost sight of ... my opinion is that he should be left where he is."[217]

The proverbial die, however, had been cast. In mid-April, Bishop John R. was transferred back to Antigonish as coadjutor-bishop with right of succession. The reaction in eastern Nova Scotia was positively joyful. "Magnificent," wired Msgr Coady; "Joy of Occasion Inexpressible," chimed in Fr Nicholson; Fr Tompkins simply noted, "Welcome Home." "We owe a deep debt of gratitude to the apostolic delegate," a relieved Fr Michael Gillis confessed.[218] Contemplating the cycle of life from his Glace Bay office, Fr Michael MacAdam wrote his congratulations to a bishop who had once served as his "punctual and obedient" altar boy. "Some comes, and some goes," MacAdam noted, "some rises, and some drops."[219]

GETTING BACK ON TRACK

Bishop John R. returned to Nova Scotia mere weeks after VE Day in May 1945. Newspapers were still filled with accounts of Germany's formal surrender, the global celebrations, and the VE Day violence in Halifax.[220] While the Halifax riot was attributed to alcohol, poor preparation, and poor discipline on the part of the navy, attacks on Italian businesses in New Waterford were more sinister. When a mob congregated, shouting racial insults in front of Peter Favretto's store on Hankard Street, Fr Raymond Campbell and Fr R.J. MacSween fought to protect the property. The two priests stood their ground and narrowly missed being hit by stones (Favretto, who was badly beaten, later moved to Montreal).[221]

Returning to peacetime, intellectuals pondered both the causes and the lessons of the war. Totalitarianism, some argued, was driven by a lack of citizen participation and an economic and cultural shift away from the countryside. In the foreword to George Boyle's book *Democracy's Second Chance: Land, Work and Cooperation*, A.B. MacDonald noted that the trend into the cities was "irresistible and disturbing."[222] The solution was not to be found in urban production, which had only produced tyrannical "supermen" in Europe, but rather in the program of the Extension Department. In 1946 Pope Pius XII came very close to Boyle's stance when he told the farmers of Italy that the national economy was "organic," and that the famers should lead through organization and cooperatives.[223]

One of the most outspoken advocates of the "back to the land movement" was Bishop John R., who advocated the partition of the larger farms so that more people could benefit.[224] When Angus L. Macdonald swept to victory in the provincial election of October 1945 (he was, according to Dalton Camp, like the pope, "infallible in matters of politics"), there was a sense that Extension would soon be moving forward again.[225] Many expected Bishop John R. to push Morrison aside and take up the reins. But it did not take long "for that honeymoon to be terminated." Although he had the fancy title of titular bishop of Ancusa (Fr John MacPherson in St Andrews wondered when MacDonald was going to take him fishing in Ancusa), he was treated like any other priest.[226]

The reality was that Bishop John R. faced a daunting personal and professional challenge as the coadjutor to someone who opposed his appointment. As Archbishop Neil McNeil had noted some two years earlier, coadjutors were difficult to get appointed and "easy to render powerless when appointed."[227] Yet, while some were sympathetic and felt that Bishop John R. "suffered a great deal," others thought that he was too cautious, a kind of "white-haired boy, sitting on the bishop's doorstep, all the time waiting around for his mitre."[228]

At a time when leadership was greatly needed, Bishop John R.'s powerlessness was maddening. Sensing the disappointment in Fr Daniel Roberts after a speech at West Bay Road, the coadjutor said he didn't want to make any statements that might embarrass or upset the archbishop.[229] As the weeks passed, the coadjutor was noticeably irritated with those who had lobbied to bring him back to the diocese. If they wanted him home so badly, he griped, then the onus was on Extension to persuade Morrison of his usefulness. What was the point of grumbling about his ineffectiveness, when they knew he could neither grant permissions nor make appointments?[230]

With St F.X. actively fundraising, the feud between Archbishop Morrison and Angus L. Macdonald, which was in its second decade, was raising questions among the alumni. When King George VI and Queen Elizabeth visited Halifax as part of their royal tour in 1939, Morrison had not been invited to the welcoming ceremony. When his brother, Fr Stanley MacDonald, inquired about the omission, the premier replied that "since the archbishop of Halifax speaks for all Catholics of Nova Scotia, there was no need to invite Bishop Morrison."[231] While the premier was technically correct, it was a needless slight and certainly bad optics.

In March 1946, the retired bureaucrat and St F.X. booster, Alexander Johnston, one of Premier Macdonald's "most trusted advisors," wrote Fr Michael Gillis to complain that Dalhousie, Bishop's, and Queen's universities had each already given the premier an honorary degree and the lack of recognition from St F.X looked "odd."[232] Johnston was aware of the feud but thought it was time to move on. "I always had the active cooperation of Angus, who sometimes had to get a bit tough," Johnston mused, "and he can be tough on occasions."[233]

As university president, Fr Nicholson had the unenviable task of convincing the aging chancellor to offer the degree. Although Bishop John R. and several prominent alumni were in his corner, the short walk from Xavier Hall to the bishop's residence must have felt like a mile. Employing his Celtic charisma, Nicholson persuaded Morrison

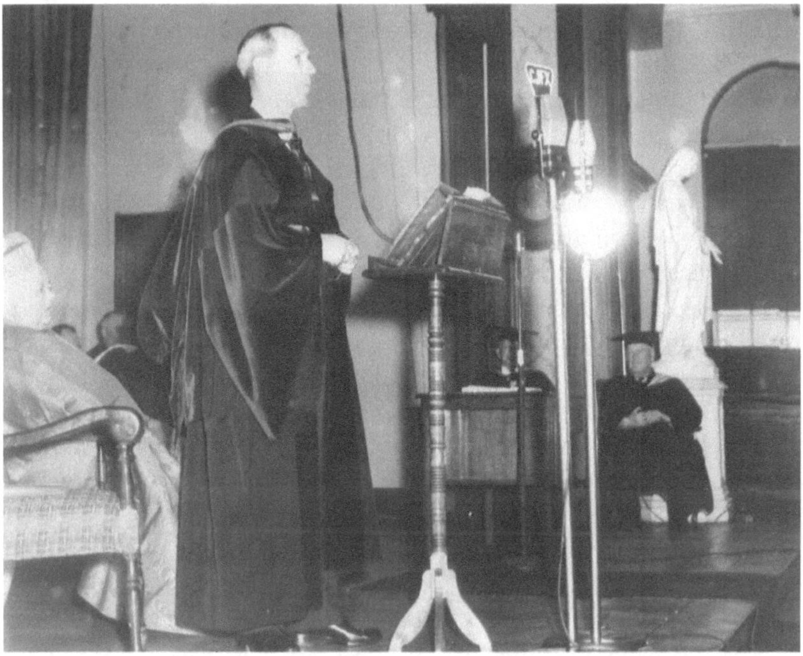

Figure 7.4 | Angus L. Macdonald speaks at 1946 St F.X. Convocation

that the feud with Macdonald was damaging their beloved institution. To soothe hard feelings and to make the convocation less awkward, Nicholson announced that Morrison's old friend, the recently named cardinal, Archbishop James McGuigan of Toronto, would also receive an honorary degree in the spring of 1946.[234]

DEATH OF ARCHBISHOP MORRISON

As it can be with any administrator or politician who remains in office too long, the final years of Archbishop Morrison's extensive and accomplished career taxed the patience of his colleagues. "I am bothering Archbishop Morrison considerably lately," confessed an anxious Fr Michael MacAdam from Sydney, "and there is danger he might get hot under the collar."[235] Another priest observed that Morrison "shuffled about his clerical duties in the same way that he shuffled down the stairway in his carpet slippers when he responded to those who visited his residence."[236] When the frail prelate was admitted to St Martha's Hospital in December 1949, friends recognized that his impressive tenure was over. On 17 January 1950, during a cold snap, Bishop John R. was appointed apostolic administrator.[237] In a letter to the Curia, Msgr Coady expressed a "general feeling of optimism" now that MacDonald was "marshalling the forces."[238]

Amid the springtime snow flurries of 1950, the ailing archbishop grew agitated by the disturbance caused by excavation work for a new wing at St Martha's Hospital. He was transferred up the hill to the Bethany Motherhouse, and the Sisters of Saint Martha ensured that he passed his final days in comfort.[239] In the early afternoon of 13 April, with Fr Nicholson at his bedside, the eighty-nine-year-old prelate, who had administered Antigonish for thirty years, died peacefully. The body of the former Charlottetown priest remained in the parlour at Bethany from Thursday until Sunday, when it was solemnly removed through the slushy streets to St Ninian's Cathedral. As he lay in state, a Knights of Columbus Honour Guard kept a candlelight vigil.[240]

The following morning, Morrison's body was placed in the centre aisle of the *Tigh Dhe*, and for two days long lines of mourners filed past his open casket. The crowds surprised even the most cynical of characters and one onlooker recalled that mothers brought "their babies close so that they could gaze upon his face." For eastern Nova Scotians like Fr Edward Purcell, then serving in the Archdiocese of Edmonton, Morrison's death inspired a moment of personal reflection. From his Alberta parish, Purcell noted that the old bishop had administered Antigonish longer than he had lived.[241] From Ottawa, Toronto, and Halifax, the faithful celebrated the long career of a devoted churchman, while Rome extended to Antigonish "paternal sympathy ... Divine consolation in bereavement."[242]

The funeral, held on 18 April, was covered by several regional news outlets, including CJFX, which broadcast the solemn voice of Fr Cyril Bauer over the airwaves. Loudspeakers were installed outside the cathedral so that the overflow crowd could listen to the Pontifical Mass of Requiem and the sermon of Archbishop John Hugh MacDonald. Speaking to some of Canada's most prominent churchmen, including Cardinal McGuigan, the Edmonton prelate described Morrison as a disciple of the great social encyclicals and an ardent supporter of Extension.

Morrison may not have instigated this Catholic social action but, because all Extension projects required his personal approval, he was "the one mainly responsible for them."[243] In other words, while others played much larger roles, the Antigonish Movement succeeded because Morrison accepted the need for subsidiarity and provided access to the Catholic subculture. As the *Sydney Post-Record* editorialized, the part he played in founding what is known as the Antigonish Movement and bringing it to its position of world-wide renown, was now "a matter of history."[244]

8

New Horizons
1950–1960

On a blustery grey spring morning, Fr Angus J. MacIsaac gazed out of his window at Main-à-Dieu, Cape Breton, across the harbour from the glebe house and out past Scatarie Island Point where his parishioners had set their lobster traps. To the former army chaplain, now in his mid-fifties, the historic parish of Immaculate Conception seemed to be situated between two worlds. Each spring, the priest strolled down to the shore to bless the fleet of local fishermen who plied their trade precisely as their forefathers had done for generations. Yet, while the older men still fished on the deeps, the youth were gradually earning their pay in the modern fish factories down the rugged coastline at Louisbourg. The old weathered boats symbolized the community's traditional way of life, but the small new high school with its auditorium and modern ventilation system represented the new.[1]

The fifty-nine-year-old Bishop John R. MacDonald had been brought back to eastern Nova Scotia from Ontario to face these postwar changes. With a younger man at the helm, there was widespread optimism in the parishes, and the mood at the Extension office was practically jovial as fieldworkers felt the confidence that the prelate would "meet all their wishes."[2] The new boss was a fascinating character. Small in physical stature – his family were known as the "Little Rories" – Bishop John R. was sensitive about his size, was afraid of the supernatural, and occasionally exhibited a ferocious temper.[3] Yet he enjoyed sports (had a strong throwing arm), was an eloquent speaker, had an abiding respect for the priesthood, and above all believed in the great potential of the laity. Unlike his predecessor, who was somewhat aloof and dishevelled, MacDonald was accessible and

Figure 8.1 | Bishop John R. MacDonald

meticulous.[4] Significantly, while Archbishop Morrison had focused solely on eastern Nova Scotia, Bishop John R. had aspirations that went well beyond the Pictou/Colchester County border.[5]

XAVIER JUNIOR COLLEGE

Since Morrison had struggled in his final years to meet the demands of office, Bishop John R. was greeted by "an accumulation of things left undone."[6] One community that felt particularly neglected was Sydney. Since the seat of the diocese was moved from Arichat to Antigonish town in 1886, there had been sporadic grumbling among Cape Bretoners that the "general situation demand[ed] a bishop for Cape Breton."[7] While such discontent was never taken seriously, by the time of Morrison's death enough complaints had been heard to compel the apostolic delegate to seek opinions on "dividing the diocese of Antigonish and erecting another in Cape Breton."[8]

While any consideration of an island diocese was quickly rebuffed – it would kill the Extension program – Bishop John R. was forced to take a hard look at the grievances of Sydney Catholics. By the autumn of 1950, the revamped People's School in Sacred Heart's Lyceum building had an enrollment of seven hundred eager minds, but the younger students had no opportunity for post-secondary education in their city.[9] While many wished to attend St F.X., the Antigonish town campus was some two hundred kilometres away. Just as serious, there were rumours that Halifax's Dalhousie University was going to open a Junior College at Sydney.[10]

As early as 1937 Cape Breton Catholics had spoken of an institution to "teach the first two years of university" and encourage students to attend professional schools on the mainland.[11] At the time, Mount Carmel's Fr Thomas O'Reilly Boyle had investigated the viability of a small college but was warned against it. From St Peter's, Fr Leo Keats cautioned him against his proposal for a Catholic college at Sydney. It would be looked upon, he wrote, "as a slam at authority, a knock at the present college [St F.X.]; it will likely be represented as Protestant in spirit (read the history of university merger), and just when we are on our way with some money spent, anathema and excommunications will float over the heads of the leaders."[12]

By 1950, however, not only was the call for post-secondary education in Sydney growing more forceful but the number of students from the colliery towns enrolling in St F.X. had waned. On a dreary

Figure 8.2 | Xavier Junior College Commencement, c. 1950s. Note St F.X. Extension Office in background.

November evening, Bishop John R. invited St F.X. vice-president Fr H.J. Somers and Fr Malcolm A. MacLellan to his residence to discuss the problem. Despite the obvious financial hurdles, they agreed that the diocesan response to the problems of Cape Breton had often been "too little and too late." On 8 January 1951, the St F.X. governors endorsed a proposal to create Xavier Junior College in Sydney.[13]

Fr MacLellan, the "affable, efficient, serious, and dedicated son of the university," was given the difficult assignment of organizing the new college.[14] Already busy as St F.X.'s dean of students, he was "surprised, even stunned" by the appointment.[15] To provide a campus, Sacred Heart parish donated the Lyceum building, the long-time centre of Catholic cultural life in Sydney (the second choice was the Sydney mansion, Moxham Castle).[16] When the Lyceum was torched by an arsonist during the renovations, Sacred Heart generously contributed its $50,000 insurance payout to complete the facelift.[17]

In its temporary quarters, Xavier Junior College was opened in September 1951 with sixty full-time students and eighty-five part-time scholars (mostly teachers). Months later, on 16 January 1952, the "Lyceum reborn" was formally opened by Bishop John R. in the presence of a crowd "crammed into the top floor auditorium."[18] "We moved into our new building last Thursday and it certainly is a grand place," Fr MacLellan gushed from Sydney. "I believe everything is necessary and not extravagant, but the interior looks beautiful."[19]

Few were more excited about Xavier Junior College than Archbishop John Hugh MacDonald of Edmonton, who felt that "Little X" was "pregnant with promise for the people of Cape Breton County." The former Sacred Heart pastor recognized that the institution would have a profound effect on Cape Breton culture and civil society. Besides its educational programs, the school became a repository of ephemera and archival materials related to the history of the island that otherwise would have been discarded or sent to mainland depositories. Hired as the college librarian in 1955, Sister St Margaret of Scotland, CND (Margaret Beaton), an Edinburgh University–educated bibliophile of Scottish history and literature, gradually built up the exceptional Cape Bretoniana collection. In the words of historian Robert Morgan, "She was a diminutive bundle of energy and charm, who literally browbeat the university, the community, and the staff for books."[20]

SHORTAGE OF ACADIAN PRIESTS

While Xavier Junior College fulfilled an educational need within the colliery towns, Acadians within the region still struggled to access post-secondary schooling. Some had enrolled at St F.X. and others at St Anne's, but the community was still developing "strategies for survival." Acadian children were increasingly taught in francophone schools, but the language and culture remained fragile.[21] One reason for the fragility was that Acadian vocations to the priesthood had drastically dwindled. On the basis of demographics, there should have been some thirty French-speaking clergymen at work in the parishes in 1953, but there were only twelve.[22]

Recruiting seminarians, regardless of ethnicity, was always difficult, as few families could afford to educate their sons for the priesthood.[23] Back in 1942, having come out of the global depression, the Knights of Columbus, through the generosity of members like James MacIntyre, a foreman at the Sydney steel plant, established the Antigonish Diocesan Society to provide interest-free loans to men enrolling in the seminary. With loans secured, those with vocations went to Halifax's Holy Heart Seminary (for the first time in decades, no student was sent to Rome). Holy Heart was the preferred destination, as Antigonish seminarians could build regional bonds with their Halifax counterparts and the "monastic" Eudist Fathers could teach them French.[24] Since so few of these new priests came from Acadian communities, however, any increased fluency in the French language did little for that constituency.

In January 1946, one of the most prominent Acadian clergymen, Fr George Leo Landry, a native of Pomquet and pastor at Louisdale, was appointed bishop of 23,000 Catholics in Hearst, Ontario. An Extension stalwart who had encouraged his parishioners to organize a credit union and a cooperative store, he had worked steadfastly to slay "the dragon of mass-inferiority" among his people.[25] The consecration ceremony, held at Sacred Heart in Sydney, was broadcast over CJFX (Landry's elderly mother was able to listen in from her retirement home) and a few days later, most of Isle Madame gathered at the Church of St Louis in Louisdale to greet the new bishop and attend the first Pontifical High Mass ever celebrated in Richmond County.[26]

Six years later, having tirelessly shepherded his forested and primarily northern francophone diocese, Bishop Landry resigned and took the title of titular bishop of Cnossus. Although he could have retired quietly, at fifty-seven years of age he still had a passion for ministry and volunteered to administer his native parish of Pomquet. He returned home amid the vocation crisis and, although he felt that the diocese was "most sympathetic to the Acadian cause," he found the lack of Acadian seminarians problematic.[27] At Cheticamp, the St Pierre Society, established in 1947 to preserve the parish's language and culture, took action. With their pastor, eighty-five-year-old Fr Patrice LeBlanc, due to retire, in 1953 a delegation met with Bishop John R. to request that the parish be entrusted to the French-speaking Eudists. When Fr Leblanc entered the hospital early that summer, it was the Eudist priest Fr Jules Comeau who took his place. In the view of Cheticamp historian Fr Anselme Chiasson, this was "one of the most important events, if not the most important," in the parish's history.[28]

While grateful for the Eudist contribution at Cheticamp, Bishop John R. did not want to entrust all his Acadian parishes to strangers. In the autumn of 1954, when Fr Amable Briand retired from St Joseph du Moine, he was replaced temporarily by the veteran Scarboro priest Fr Arthur Venedam. On Venedam's return to the Chinese

Mission in British Columbia, the Eudists offered to administer the Church of St Joseph permanently, but Bishop John R. decided to "keep such a good Acadian parish available for diocesan priests."[29]

While vocations may have been in short supply, historical memory was long. In 1955 an overflowing crowd gathered at Arichat in to mark the bicentennial of the *Grand Dérangement*. After the Pontifical High Mass, during which Bishop John R. praised Acadians for their contribution to the "building of the house and family of God," Archbishop Norbert Robichaud of Moncton rode with local clergy in a parade viewed by some five thousand spectators. (At Grand-Pré in King's County, some ten thousand Acadians attended the festivities along with Cardinal Paul-Emile Léger).[30]

Behind the scenes, however, francophone leaders, like the cooperator Dr Remi J. Chiasson (later associate director of Extension), remained vigilant. Bishop John R.'s words were appreciated but Chiasson wanted assurances that the diocese would safeguard Acadian representation in liturgical functions and on the St F.X. board of governors. Others, like the Capuchin priest and historian Fr Anselme Chiasson, worked to capture the diocese's francophone past and strengthen Acadian identity. As Fr Chiasson would later argue, Church, language, and place were intricately connected.

DUTCH IMMIGRATION

While the old Acadian constituency continued its struggle for cultural survival, Catholics continued to arrive in the region from other directions. At the end of the Second World War, European immigration seemed to offer a solution to the problem of the diocese's "empty and deserted" farms.[31] After the liberation of the Netherlands by Canadian soldiers in 1945, nearly two thousand Dutch war brides came to Canada and, following the adoption of the 1947 "Netherlands-Canada Settlement Scheme," Ottawa began prioritizing the entry of Dutch farmers.[32] "From being a country which had never generated a great deal of interest and enthusiasm among prospective Dutch immigrants," commented the historian G.H. Gerrits, "Canada had become, in a few short years, the country of choice for a large percentage of them."[33]

Preparing for this influx, in 1950 a Diocesan Land Settlement Program was organized under the supervision of the thirty-three-year-old

Sydney native Fr Francis "Frank" N. MacIsaac, to settle families on abandoned properties and "set the pace for the natives of [the] diocese."[34] Priests were ordered to identify vacant farms with agricultural potential, lend the newcomers moral support, and help identify financing opportunities. By 1955 half of the 110 Dutch families who migrated into eastern Nova Scotia were at work tilling the soil.[35]

Dutch farmers were a welcome sight in the countryside, but their presence came with administrative challenges.[36] First, there was serious disagreement between Fr MacIsaac, who was instructed to settle families on older abandoned farms, and priests like Fr Daniel Roberts, pastor at southwest Margaree, who wanted new farms cleared in communities like West Bay Road and Brook Village.[37] Second, the Dutch government, needing to focus on reconstruction after years of German occupation, limited the amount of currency that emigrants could take out of the country. This meant that Dutch newcomers were short on capital to make a down payment on a farm so that they could apply for approval and a loan from the Nova Scotia Land Settlement Board. Many families had to cobble together the down payment through diocesan grants and financing from local credit unions. And then, since their early profits went to loan repayment, some families even had to borrow monies from their local priests to buy food.

Like the Newfoundlanders and Italians who had flocked to the colliery towns of Cape Breton at the turn of the twentieth century, Dutch immigrants relied heavily on the local parish for networking, spiritual sustenance, and encouragement. As many lived on isolated rural plots, Sunday was a time to socialize in their native tongue. "I could barely contain myself during the Mass," recalled one woman, "knowing that here I had someone I could talk to who could understand any language."[38]

The Dutch influence also extended into Antigonish town's Mount Cameron farm. Between 1952 and 1956, Fr Peter Renders and a team of Dutch Sacred Heart Fathers worked the property and even wrote an agricultural curriculum for a local school. Although an ambitious plan to have rural students study agriculture at Mount Cameron did not materialize, the presence of the brothers further demonstrated the contribution of the Netherlands to Antigonish's postwar strategy. To quote G.H. Gerrits once again, the Dutch put agriculture in eastern Nova Scotia "back on the map."[39]

A MICRO-MANAGING BISHOP

By creating Xavier Junior College, recruiting the Eudist Fathers, and settling Dutch farmers on abandoned farms, Bishop John R. demonstrated that he was a problem solver. Yet his clergy also found the new prelate to be a cautious micro-manager. You could write a biography of Archbishop Morrison, one priest noted, and then at the bottom of the last page write, "The same thing could apply to Bishop John R."[40] In fact, MacDonald was more obstinate on protocol than his predecessor. Fr John McLaughlin, pastor at Lochaber from 1939 to 1948, recalled going to Morrison for permission to let a Protestant girl stand as a bridesmaid in her sister's wedding (the bride had converted to Catholicism). Waiting for the appointment, Bishop John R. told McLaughlin he was sure the old archbishop would never grant the request and added that he himself wouldn't give it. Yet, as it was a small wedding with little likelihood of a public spectacle, Morrison consented. "When I came downstairs and told Bishop John R. I got permission," McLaughlin later recalled, "he shook his head. He just couldn't understand such permission being given."[41]

Bishop John R. also tightened administrative procedures, stopped publicizing the transfer of curates, and introduced new policies on just about everything.[42] The marriage process was a good example. While Morrison merely wanted to know how long the couple had courted and when the banns would be published, and sought assurance that the lovers were not related, MacDonald introduced a mandatory marriage preparation course, with forms that were to be completed by the couple and then examined and filed. Fiscal rules were tightened, and all parish mortgages had to be transacted through the Chancery Office. Clergy were not permitted more than $500 of credit, and construction projects were delayed until half of the required funds were safely in the bank.[43] These rules caused some bother, as they were "all so new to the priests ... especially the older priests."[44]

Yet, being "a priest first of all and above other things," Bishop John R. implemented a base salary for his clergy, considered building a clerical retirement home (which never materialized), appointed nine new deans to provide senior leadership and, unlike Morrison, who rarely appealed to Rome for clerical honours, pursued the domestic prelacy for his priests at a staggering rate.[45] In 1950, prior to the papal blessing at the Glace Bay Eucharistic Congress, the bishop announced that Frs "Little Doc" MacPherson, James Kiely, and Alfred Abram Boudreau had been appointed monsignors. Five years later, Fr P.J. Nicholson was made a protonotary apostolic, while Frs Hugh Somers, William Gallivan, and Alfred Boudreau were made domestic prelates. In 1957 Frs Malcolm MacLellan, Donald MacPherson, Michael J. MacKinnon, and Alexander S. MacKenzie were also recognized. By 1959 Fr Ronald MacLean, the Roman Catholic chaplain general of the Canadian armed forces (he had previously been chaplain of the naval fleet) was invested as a domestic prelate before a large crowd at St Nicholas Church in Whitney Pier.[46] Shortly after that, Msgr Francis Smyth, working with the Canadian Catholic Conference as director of the Social Action Department, was raised to the rank of papal chamberlain.[47] It was a surprising deluge of awards, but one young priest felt that Bishop John R. had "scored a Roman bull's eye" with all the honours.[48]

THE MARTHAS TO BOSTON

Had the bishop been able to invest the women religious into the domestic prelacy, the list would have been extensive. In 1950 the influential Archbishop Richard James Cushing of Boston, a supporter of Catholic action, was awarded an honorary degree from St F.X. He had been keen to visit eastern Nova Scotia as many of his prominent Boston parishioners, the wealthy businessman Malcolm MacNeil for one, hailed from communities like Grand Narrows, Cape Breton.

While touring the diocese with Msgr Coady, Cushing "discovered the Marthas" and asked if the congregation could expand their social ministry into Massachusetts. Anxious to make an impression on the powerful future cardinal, Bishop John R, who had the ambition of Cushing but not "his bank account," immediately consented.[49] In May 1952, three sisters moved into a stately old brick residence on Boston's Commonwealth Avenue. The St Martha's Catholic Centre, much like their ministries in Bridgeport and in Canso, offered Boston's families counselling and home visitations. Humble and hard-working, the women were popular among the former Maritimers who called Massachusetts home, and a Guild of St Martha was organized with some five hundred members.[50] Surrounded by the Irish pubs of Roxbury, Sister Anselm (Irene Doyle) joked that the women were going to organize either credit unions or "co-op beer parlours."[51]

Although pleased to have a formal connection with the Archdiocese of Boston, Bishop John R. was never entirely comfortable with the Massachusetts ministry. Although the Bethany Motherhouse annals note that the prelate was "insistent that the offer be accepted," the Marthas were aware of his reservations. While there were senseless fears that the congregation would be "Americanized," the reality was that the "sisters were invited to go for their own good and not to meet some urgent and neglected need within the Church."[52] In other words, the Boston ministry was about the Marthas and not the Diocese of Antigonish. Sometimes "[Bishop John R.] would growl and growl about us being up there in Boston," Sister Anselm recalled. "The Diocese of Antigonish needed social workers, why were we there when we were needed at home?"[53] It was a paradox not easily solved.

BISHOP JOHN R. AND THE ARCHDIOCESE OF HALIFAX

With all the activity within the Antigonish diocese, outsiders could be forgiven for not knowing that the Archdiocese of Halifax was the metropolitan of the ecclesiastical province (which also included Charlottetown). When the Halifax archbishop John T. McNally died in November 1952, he left the metropolitan mired in debt. While building a new Saint Mary's University (SMU) campus in the city's leafy south end, McNally flouted canonical procedures and borrowed millions of dollars against diocesan property.[54] An irate apostolic delegate had McNally censured in Rome – a difficult task, considering that McNally was a classmate of Pope Pius XII – and the two churchmen entered into a nasty feud. More ominous, when the parishes were ordered to repay the debt, old ethnic resentments resurfaced. Along the French Shore, Acadians in communities like Clare, already supporting the underfunded francophone Collège Sainte Anne, absolutely refused to finance the anglophone SMU.

In 1951 the Acadian clergy had asked Rome to consider a francophone diocese in western Nova Scotia and, with Halifax facing bankruptcy, their prospects had improved. Although Halifax had an auxiliary bishop, with the archdiocese in turmoil, on the advice of Archbishop John Hugh MacDonald of Edmonton, the delegate announced in June 1953 that Bishop John R. would temporarily administer Halifax while the Curia searched for McNally's successor.

Giving an outsider – especially a Scot from eastern Nova Scotia – authority over Auxiliary Bishop Alfred B. Leverman "created an awkward situation."[55]

Shortly afterward, on 6 July 1953, Rome announced the partition of the Archdiocese of Halifax and the establishment of the Diocese of Yarmouth. The new see included the primarily French-speaking Acadian districts of Digby and Yarmouth counties, as well as the counties of Shelburne, Annapolis, and Kings (the New Brunswick native Albert Leménager was consecrated as bishop). Three weeks later, Bishop Leverman was sent to Saint John to replace the late Bishop Patrick Bray.[56]

With Halifax broken and disillusioned, Bishop John R. faced a mammoth task. Intuitively, he reached out to Harold Connolly, the provincial minister of public health, for advice. Although a native of Sydney, Connolly had spent his career as a reporter and editor for a number of Halifax newspapers, represented the provincial riding of Halifax North, and was friendly with the city's priests. The self-described "legitimate heir" to Angus L. Macdonald, who would become Nova Scotia's third Roman Catholic premier during a brief term in 1954 (he was defeated as Liberal leader by the "brainy and unhandsome" Henry Hicks thanks in large part to the "protestant vote"), Connolly counselled the prelate to go immediately to Halifax and gather the clergy.[57] He also advised MacDonald to wear his "simple and humble" black clericals to create a more friendly atmosphere.

Because of the historical animus between the metropolitan and its suffragan (*The Casket* was absolutely silent on Halifax's financial woes), Bishop John R. went to Halifax "with a strike against him."[58] As the archdiocese began raising monies to repay the crippling debt, there was talk that it would have to sell SMU to Ottawa as there was not "a sufficient Catholic population in Nova Scotia to support two universities."[59] Some wanted St F.X. to purchase the school to broaden the influence of Extension through a Halifax campus. Archbishop MacDonald of Edmonton, in particular, hoped that Saint Mary's might become a Xavier Junior College, which was "devoutly wished, though not spoken *Coram Populo*."[60] Had this happened, the animosity between the Halifax-Irish and the Catholics in the eastern counties or the province that dominated the 1840s would surely have resurfaced. Bishop John R. – he received an honorary degree from SMU in 1952 – wisely refused to sell.

Satisfied to leave the day-to-day responsibilities of Halifax in the hands of its senior clergy, Bishop John R. kept a watchful eye from Antigonish until the installation of the former bishop of Peterborough (MacDonald's successor in that diocese), Bishop Joseph Gerald Berry, as archbishop in February 1954. Addressing his flock, Berry publicly thanked the Antigonish prelate for fulfilling an unpleasant mission with his "well known ability" and leaving the archdiocese in a manner that "promises well for the future."[61] Privately, Halifax's vicar-general, Msgr William J. Burns, bluntly confessed that "Bishop MacDonald saved the Church in Halifax."[62]

EXPULSION OF THE SCARBORO FOREIGN MISSION FROM CHINA

Although local postwar problems such as Halifax's debt required serious consideration, postwar geopolitics forced Canadian religious leaders to turn their attention overseas. While no nation had spilled more blood fighting Nazi Germany than the Soviet Union, the Red Army had merely replaced one totalitarian system with another. As the dreaded NKVD imprisoned and murdered Catholic priests in occupied Yugoslavia and Poland, *The Casket* increasingly covered Soviet crimes and demanded that Canada resettle Europeans fleeing communism.[63]

As Pope Pius XII called upon the Church to "face squarely and fearlessly" the dangers of communism, radical sympathies alienated Catholic audiences. Labour unions were forced "to repudiate the more radical implications of their own history" and even the researcher C.B. Wade, so feared by the clergy for his communistic leanings, found himself ostracized within District 26 and soon out of a job.[64] When the Albanian Workers' Party proclaimed that Stalin was their saviour, *The Casket* noted that the whole idea of deifying a murderer was "so ridiculous that the tendency [was] to laugh."[65] In the parishes, a special "Stalin Novena" encouraged Catholics to pray for prisoners who languished in Soviet jails and, on May Day, sodalities entreated the Holy Spirit to convert the Soviet Union.[66] From the supplications of the packed crowds at the diocesan eucharistic congresses at Tracadie (1947) and Glace Bay (1950) to exhibits on the Immaculate Heart of Mary, Catholics fixated on changing the hearts of communists.[67]

Thanks to the popularity of the Scarboro Foreign Mission, Catholics throughout eastern Nova Scotia paid close attention to the rise of communism in China. After the defeat of Imperial Japan in 1945, China entered into a brutal struggle between Mao Tse-Tung's communists and General Chiang Kai-shek's nationalists. Both sides committed atrocities against citizens and one missionary recalled watching helplessly as three hundred Lishui Catholics were machine-gunned by the Reds.[68] By October 1949, Mao's "People's Republic" had emerged victorious, and Chiang evacuated his government to Taiwan.[69]

While communist propaganda promised freedom of religion, within eight months of declaring the People's Republic Mao "lowered the bamboo curtain."[70] Thousands of Chinese Catholics were arrested (many were executed), while Western missionaries were roughly rounded up and deported. In the spring of 1951, the Canadian Missionary Sisters of the Immaculate Conception, who worked closely with the Scarboro missionaries, were charged with murdering some two thousand orphans in their mission at Canton. Although Canadian prime minister Lester Pearson angrily noted that the indictment was "grotesque and unfounded," the sisters were expelled.[71]

That summer the "long strangulation" of the Scarboro mission at Lishui began with the arrest of Bishop Kenneth Turner.[72] He was imprisoned along with Fr Arthur Venedam of Pomquet, his vicar-general, Fr Paul Kam, a former St F.X. student, and Fr Alex MacIntosh, who hailed from St Andrews.[73] For the native Chinese priests, the sentences were swift and brutal. The imprisonment and deaths of clergymen like the thirty-one-year-old Fr Aloysius Liang (a victim of the "People's" Court) shocked Canadians. Fr Paul Kam, the first seminarian at the China Mission Seminary and former resident of Antigonish town (he was good friends with the Old Rector), languished for six gruelling years in a disease-ridden labour camp. When released, he was physically broken and returned to the former mission headquarters, where he lived in seclusion until his death a few months later. It was a horrifying end for a priest who had been full of energy and optimism while touring eastern Nova Scotia in 1917–18.

Fr Alex MacIntosh was forcibly led out of China with his long list of "crimes" announced in each village through which he passed (mostly that he was a "foreign imperialist"). Recuperating at his parents' farmstead in St Andrews, he warned that the Chinese communists had "even greater disregard for the value of human life" than the Soviets.[74]

He also expressed concern that Catholics were losing their zeal. "If we were as energetic in spreading Christianity as they are in spreading communist ideology," he told a gathering of the Catholic Women's League, "the Red menace would soon disappear."[75]

Fr Arthur Venedam, suffering from malnourishment and failing eyesight, was also expelled from China in May 1954. He spent his first six months of captivity in solitary confinement, and was interrogated every evening by communist officials. While he denied that he was a spy and an officer in Chiang Kai-shek's army, he made no secret of his anti-communist sentiments. He was later transferred to the Hangchow provincial jail, where the interrogations continued. When finally expelled to Hong Kong, he told the international media that he was able to celebrate Mass only once during his confinement. Mysteriously, one frigid morning while sitting on his bunk, a bit of bread and a small perfume bottle of wine were dropped into his cell by a former seminarian serving as a prison guard. Fearing a trap, he waited three days before offering the Sacrifice of the Mass (he pretended he was eating his breakfast). It was, Venedam confessed, "the happiest time" of his captivity.[76]

Exiled Scarboro priests who took temporary positions within the diocese became visible reminders of the lost Asian mission. The St F.X. alumnus Fr Peter Jen-Chung, for example, lived at St Mary's Hospital in Inverness from 1953 to 1955, and later served at New Victoria, Florence, and Dominion.[77] Although described as "living martyr[s]," missionaries like Fr Venedam were disheartened by Mao's destruction of their life's work. "You cannot believe communist promises," he pronounced to a local audience, "for the communist is nothing but a liar, a fraud, and a thief."[78] When a member of the Canadian Senate later stood in Parliament and advocated recognizing Red China, the Glace Bay Knights of Columbus issued a sharply worded attack against recognizing "international banditry."[79]

ANTIGONISH IN LATIN AMERICA

While bitterness against communism remained strong, many of the former Scarboro missionaries who witnessed the program of the Antigonish Movement for the first time gradually recognized the uselessness of offering their Chinese flock spiritual sustenance without material assistance. In retrospect, they realized they had been aloof and not "incarnated in the daily life of the people."

Or, as Archbishop Morrison's brother Vincent noted, the mistake was believing that "our way [was] best."[80] As the Scarboro priests shifted focus to Latin America, the mistakes of the Chinese mission would not be repeated. While still seeking converts and working toward saving souls, young priests like Fr Harvey Steele also brought plans for cooperatives and credit unions. "Foreign missionaries will have to know their Rochdale principles along with their bible," noted one priest, "and their St. F.X. techniques along with their liturgy."[81] By 1950 the feisty Fr Steele had organized fifteen cooperatives in Santo Domingo, Dominican Republic, which were effective in combatting poverty.[82]

Communism, of course, remained a threat – Msgr Coady certainly feared that "South America [would] go communist" – but the voices of men like Fr Henri Langlais, a member of the Missionary Oblates ministering in Haiti, who warned a St F.X. audience in 1950 that poverty was the true menace, were becoming more insistent.[83] In Puerto Rico Fr Steele's cousin, Fr Joseph MacDonald, offered students at the national university classes on the tactics of the Antigonish Movement.[84] He was impressed by the resilience of the local people, and they were fascinated by his ideas (eventually a public park was named in his honour in the city of Río Piedras). Fr Steele also brought scholars from Puerto Rico and Costa Rica back to St F.X. to study Extension concepts. Students like Fr Humberto Munoz of Los Andes, Chile, learned about study club techniques and credit union organization, and explored methods of transferring that knowledge to their own communities.[85]

With so many Latin American students visiting the St F.X. campus, the economic and social problems of countries like the Dominican Republic, Cuba, and Venezuela were soon debated with as much passion as those of Canso, Christmas Island, and Whitney Pier had been decades earlier. As Cardinal Cushing later noted, "it would be hard to find a country in any part of the world that has not had a student [at St F.X.] at one time or another."[86]

POSTWAR CHANGES AT EXTENSION

The export of the Antigonish Movement to Latin America was another feather in Msgr Coady's fabled cap. By the 1950s the apostolic delegate was encouraging seminarians across the county to study the "down to earth" activities of Extension, and all young men in Antigonish destined to be priests were required to attend summer classes on the program's history and philosophy.[87] "If they [are] not interested in the Antigonish Movement, or [feel] that they could not become interested," Bishop John R. decreed, "then I would suggest that they look for another diocese."[88]

Despite his stalwart support of Extension, however, MacDonald the theologian was significantly different from the more philosophical Coady. When the bishop did not want priests to release statements that were not carefully grounded in papal encyclicals (thereby giving the Vatican credit), an irritated Coady responded that "a thing isn't right because the pope said it, the pope said it because it is right."[89] "Coady was thinking in terms of a general public," noted a colleague. "John R. was thinking more in terms of the Church itself."[90] Both men were highly regarded within the regional community and while Extension fieldworkers were frustrated by the prelate's micromanaging, others were sympathetic to his great responsibilities. "It was much easier for [Coady]," Sister Anselm, CSM, later mused, "and he was getting a good name for it. He wasn't losing anything by it, just to be realistic."[91]

By the winter of 1952, the now seventy-year-old Extension director was battling high blood pressure and his legendary energy was waning. Although Coady had spent much of 1951 travelling and lecturing as far afield as Europe, in that frigid January he suffered a severe heart attack and was forced to resign his directorship (effective March 1). "If Dr. Coady is enjoying a well-earned rest," *The Casket* noted encouragingly, "his ideas are not resting. They live on … to challenge ignorance, greed, poverty, and indifference."[92]

Like any organization that loses a commanding and dynamic leader, Extension faced a period of adjustment. While no one could replace the legendary Coady, the forty-six-year-old Sydney Mines native Fr Michael Joseph MacKinnon was the diocese's best option. Not only was the "quiet and shy son of a coal miner" a disciple of Coady but he was also an experienced community organizer, first as the pastor of St Anthony's in Glace Bay and then as head of Extension's Sydney office.[93]

Unfortunately, while MacKinnon had a sharp intellect, it was quickly apparent that he could not match his predecessor's dynamism. They "shared a common mission," noted Joseph Hernon, but "he and Coady were as unlike as two people could be."[94] While Coady commanded the pulpit, MacKinnon preferred to work behind

Figure 8.3 | Msgr Coady, Fr Charles Forest, and Msgr M.J. MacKinnon at Larry's River, Guysborough County

the scenes. "He was no talker," Fr Michael Gillis later recalled. "I knew Mike very well. Two occasions, in all my experiences with him, when he talked."[95]

While Coady had always been most at home among farmers and fishermen, MacKinnon came out of the colliery towns and was keen to take Extension in new directions. In his first year as director, he visited India and Pakistan as part of a United Nations delegation touring housing projects, and inspected the fisheries of Ceylon (Sri Lanka). In 1953 he and Fr George Topshee, the new director of the Extension office in Sydney, spent a month in the Dominican Republic meeting with Scarboro missionaries and speaking at credit union meetings. During discussions with the Italian-born Archbishop Ricardo Pittini Piussi of Santo Domingo, the priests were encouraged by the elderly prelate's knowledge of eastern Nova Scotia. When the nearly blind Piussi expressed a desire for an Extension program in the Dominican, Spanish language classes were organized in Antigonish town and Sydney to prepare priests for service.

These Canadian Catholic inroads into Latin America were supported by both Rome and the United Nations. As early as 1949, Extension's assistant director, Alexander Laidlaw (A.B. MacDonald had moved to Ottawa in 1945 to become the national organizer for the Cooperative Union of Canada), had addressed the delegates to the UN Food and Agriculture Organization (FAO) conference in Costa Rica, while Fr Harvey Steele spoke the following year in Columbia. In 1955 Msgr Luigi Ligutti, Rome's representative at the FAO, asked Fr Steele to organize a three-day program on adult education and cooperatives for the third International Catholic Rural Life Conference to be held in Panama. Steele wasted little time inviting prominent speakers: Bishop John R., Msgr MacKinnon, and Fr Topshee, as well as other noted cooperators like Jerry Voorhis, a former California congressman who had recently been defeated by Richard Nixon.[96]

Scheduled to deliver a keynote address on the Antigonish Movement, an anxious Bishop John R. spent the long ocean voyage to Panama in preparation.[97] "In their stateroom, and even on the deck," Fr Topshee recalled, he "would want to discuss his paper." Not only was this an unprecedented opportunity for a bishop from a small Nova Scotia diocese to speak to a global audience but it was also a chance to offer locally grown solutions to the worldwide problems of poverty and despair.

Back at home, the newspapers reported that Bishop John R. had sung the Solemn Pontifical Mass at the conference, and that his remarks on the Mystical Body and cooperation, conveyed through a translator, had been a tremendous success.[98] Yet this newfound focus on Latin America concerned Extension local fieldworkers. Fighting the same economic battles year after year took a toll on morale, and department reports demonstrated a "surprising sense of complacency."[99] It was well and good to focus on the problems of the Dominican Republic, but Nova Scotia's postwar economy presented complex finance and marketing problems that were not easily remedied. More worrisome was that Extension no longer had all the answers. Before the war it was easier to run labour schools, Msgr Hugh Somers lamented, but in a modern economy, "as soon as you brought these labour leaders along, they started asking questions that Extension couldn't answer."[100]

The older generation's glorification of country living was increasingly seen as mere fantasy. In 1953 Laidlaw gave a speech in England attacking the notion that the rural life was a good life.[101] While advocates of rural living like Fr "Little Doc" MacPherson, George Boyle, and Fr Michael Gillis were disturbed, others were in agreement. "I don't think [Bishop John R.] wanted to hear anything about the, you know, the hard aspect [of rural life] – the less than pleasing aspect," noted sister Marie Michael, CSM.[102] Even the diocesan director of land settlement felt that the bishop was "maddeningly impractical about the consequences of what it meant to live on a farm."[103]

In the meantime, Extension also faced the reality that many of the cooperative organizations that it had "birthed" were now independent. Fieldworkers "shared the field of economic development" with organizations like the Nova Scotia Credit Union League and the Adult Education Division of the provincial Department of Education.[104] While Extension still influenced local consumer cooperatives, most could not get "enough of the consumers to make a good profitable business."[105] In fact, by the autumn of 1956, the two important regional wholesalers, Eastern Coop Services of Antigonish and Cape Breton Co-operative Services, were failing because of shortages of capital, competition from grocery chains, and a failure to market local produce.[106]

In response, the two wholesalers were merged into Eastern Co-op Services. Nothing was spared; the new Sydney-based organization boasted modern cold-storage facilities, a poultry-processing plant, and packaging facilities. Hoping that Eastern Co-op Services would be competitive, the retired Msgr Coady boasted that it was the "synthesis of all our education and all our activity for the whole twenty-nine years of our existence." He was fully convinced that the project would prosper. "The only thing I am interested in is Eastern," Coady wrote movingly in the last years of his life. "The future of the world is hooked up with this pilot plant."[107]

The reality, however, was that the Eastern Co-op Services was "the last stand for [Coady's] Big Picture."[108] As the cooperative model was challenged, Extension was under tremendous pressure to reproduce the energy and results of the past.[109] In the meantime, there had also been administrative stumbles. The expenses for the fisheries grant had not been reported for two years and a growing rift with the provincial department of agriculture jeopardized funding.[110] "There will always be some question as to whether [MacKinnon] was happy in the work he undertook," confided a friend. "There are those who feel that he left his heart in the parishes."[111] In 1958 an exhausted MacKinnon was made executive vice-president of St F.X. (a new position), and forty-seven-year-old Fr John Allan Gillis, the manager of Mount Cameron farm, was appointed director. Extension was faltering.

DEATH OF FR JAMES J. TOMPKINS

Amid the uncertainty within the Extension Department, the life of the man who had done so much to encourage Catholic social action was winding down. Fr James Tompkins had literally "burnt himself out through years of labour in the People's Movement."[112] He battled dementia, his voice gradually became muted, and his reputation, especially among the youth, was diminished. When Fr Francis Marrocco from Ontario arrived on the St F.X. campus in 1945 to study cooperatives, he was flabbergasted that the renowned reformer was so poorly regarded. "I couldn't understand how a man who had really been the creative mind behind so much of what happened in the Antigonish diocese ... could now, when I was on that campus, be talked about as though he was a nut." His questions about the old priest received evasive answers or were ignored, and could only speculate that Tompkins's celebrity had been "swallowed up by the fact that he had been a heretic in this [education] field."[113] It is a part of the Antigonish Movement story not often told.

The sad fact is that the last years of Tompkins's life were rather grim. "In conversation," wrote his biographer, George Boyle, "he was increasingly unable to keep to one subject and forgot what had been said a moment before." Fr Leo Ward described him as "a bit fragile like a shell."[114] As his bright light dimmed, the Reserve Mines library became his refuge from an increasingly frustrating

Figure 8.4 | Fr James Tompkins at Reserve Mines Library

existence.[115] By December 1948, he had retired from pastoral ministry with little fanfare.[116]

As Tompkins began to require constant attention, his cousin Dr M.G. Tompkins of Dominion arranged care for him at the Saint-Jean-de-Dieu psychiatric hospital in Montreal in the spring of 1949. Confused and separated from friends and colleagues, however, he became "lonely and very much distressed." For most of the time he was either locked in his room or tied to his bed, and was frequently bruised or swollen. "It seems rather odd to read articles in *The Casket* and *The Xaverian* and even in *Time Magazine* giving glowing accounts … of Fr Jimmy's services to the world and to Nova Scotia in particular and all the while to know the background," McGill medical professor Dr W.J. McNally wrote to Bishop John R, adding, "I think Cardinal McGuigan was a little surprised to hear that Fr Jimmy was in Montreal." McNally offered to escort the priest home, noting that if Tompkins was left in Montreal, they would all "have failed [their] best friend and certainly … failed one of the best friends of Nova Scotia and of the common people."[117]

In time, the Sisters of St Martha agreed to care for Fr Tompkins at their convent at Margaree Forks. Although the fabled clergyman was unable to participate in the opening of the Tompkins Memorial Library at Reserve Mines in November 1951 (part of the Cape Breton Regional Library system), his friends were relieved to have him home. When Boyle visited the priest to inform him that his biography was almost complete, Tompkins became lucid and said, "there is nothing about me worth writing ... too many duffers writing things nowadays."[118] In 1952 Tompkins was moved to St Martha's Hospital in Antigonish town, where the "deserving apostle of social movement" (as Pope Pius XII called him) celebrated the fiftieth anniversary of his ordination.[119] The following year, on 5 May 1953, the "human dynamo" died at the age of eighty-two.

A great throng of mourners attended the funeral at St Joseph's Church in Reserve Mines and listened intently as Fr Malcolm MacLellan eulogized Tompkins as a soul with a towering instinct for justice and freedom.[120] Msgr Coady noted that his double-cousin's brilliance stemmed from a belief that "donning a religious garb" did not alone qualify a priest to act as an expert in social and economic fields.[121] He was a proud priest, but in Canso he was also a soaking wet fisherman and in Reserve Mines a tired and dust-covered miner. After the funeral, the United Steelworkers of America made a $200 donation to Extension, which was immediately sent to the fishing village of Little Dover.

NEW ECONOMIC OPPORTUNITIES

A year after Fr Tompkins's death, the priest's star pupil and old friend, Angus L. Macdonald, still reigning over Nova Scotia's politics, died of heart failure at his home on Halifax's northwest arm. The funeral service for the "Christian gentleman, patriot, and scholar" was held at the historic St Mary's Basilica, and a hundred thousand citizens quietly gathered along the funeral route to pay their respects.[122] Fittingly, the drapes that had adorned the basilica for the funeral of the province's first Roman Catholic premier were also used at the funeral of the second. "Not since the passing of Sir John Thompson," noted Archbishop Gerald Berry, "has this old church been the scene of the funeral of one of her sons deceased while in the office of a Chief Minister of the State."[123]

Angus L. had a complex relationship with the Diocese of Antigonish. He spoke the language of the Gaels, practised the faith – was a fourth-degree Knight of Columbus – attended diocesan events, and for the most part supported Extension. He was not, however, always on good terms with diocesan leadership, never represented a riding in eastern Nova Scotia, and resented the label of "Catholic politician." His great love within the diocese was St F.X. – he had recently chaired its centenary committee – and the New York newspaper editor Neil McNeil recalled that Angus L. was happiest when visiting the campus. "It will be lonely to come home again, to cross the marshes of Fundy," wrote Fr Malcolm MacDonell to a grieving Sister St Veronica, "to hear his Piper greeting us, to drive along his highways ... and yet to know, to try to realize, that he is no longer with us."[124]

Friends of the late premier also regretted that he did not live to see a causeway linking his beloved Cape Breton Island to the Nova Scotian mainland. Although the "highway ferry" had been adequate for commuters, for decades the bottleneck at the Strait of Canso created delays for freight trains of up to seven hours (those large trains, many carrying coal, were broken up, and individual box cars were slowly ferried across the water). Stakeholders demanded a link.

Although Angus L. rightfully gets credit for pressuring Ottawa to build the causeway as part of a postwar infrastructure scheme – in 1934 the project was rumoured to be closely linked with the designation of the Cape Breton Highlands as a national park – some of its most vociferous advocates came from the Extension study clubs.[125] Priests like Fr Joseph MacDonald (who would soon leave for the Dominican Republic) encouraged the Sydney and Glace Bay clubs to explore bridge and tunnel possibilities and to pester their political representatives for action.[126]

In 1948 a cadre of Sydney businessmen formed the Canso Crossing Association to generate awareness and circulate propaganda.[127] It was an uphill battle, as federal ministers like C.D. Howe, deeply prejudiced against the Maritime provinces, argued against a bridge on account of a general steel shortage. Historians have noted that Howe's obstructionist attitude was typical of Ottawa politicians in this period and, as Ernie Forbes has demonstrated, during the war, "Howe and his controllers went so far as to withhold government funds for the modernization and expansion of Maritime industries" (inexplicably St F.X. gave him an honorary degree in 1954 anyway).[128]

While Cape Breton Catholic organizations demanded a causeway to support industry and tourism, the greatest source of momentum for the project was Newfoundland's decision to join the Canadian Confederation in 1949. The Strait of Canso was no longer just a physical inconvenience for the people of eastern Nova Scotia but an obstacle for interprovincial trade and transportation. By June 1952, bulldozers were at work clearing the ground between Aulds Cove and Mulgrave, and the rocky Cape Porcupine, which loomed over the site, was soon cleared of its trees. In the following months, the mountain was dynamited, and ten million tons of rock were dumped into the strait to gradually close the watery gap with Balache Point, Cape Breton.[129]

In mid-August 1955, during a stifling heat wave, the Canso Causeway was officially opened in front of some forty thousand onlookers (it had been open to vehicles since May). Opinions were divided on the link's significance. On one hand, the causeway opened "pristine" Cape Breton to tourists, while on the other, it offered an opportunity to "revive the faltering coal and steel industries."[130] Residents were proud of the link, and one assistant to the bishop recalled the drives from Sydney to Antigonish town when, "very often, late at night, [the prelate] used to express without fail admiration of the Canso causeway ... with its bright lights, and as the accomplishment it was."[131]

Yet all the "flattery and ceremony" overlooked some grim economic realities. Observing all the cars present at the causeway opening, George Boyle wondered why none were manufactured in Nova Scotia. Perceptive minds knew it would take more than a link across a kilometre of water to restore the economic health of Cape Breton.[132] In fact, as the Presbyterian minister Clarence Nicholson warned, the causeway might become an exit.[133]

Then there were the job losses. Although the new causeway was convenient for tourists and commuters, hundreds of people who had worked on the railroad and ferries, on both sides of the Strait of Canso, were thrown out of work. At Mulgrave, Fr Alexander MacDonald noted anxiously that more than two hundred jobs had vanished.[134] Some of these men found work on the Newfoundland ferry at North Sydney, others in Yarmouth, but many families were forced to outmigrate.[135]

Yet it was not all gloom and doom. The causeway created a year-round, ice-free, deep-water port which many hoped would attract new industry. Seeking to capitalize on the exceptional harbour and the abundant supply of pulpwood, the Four Counties Development Association began courting pulp and paper companies.[136] In 1955 a diocesan delegation of the CWL, led by Margaret Spray, president of the Mulgrave Council, went to Halifax and met with Premier Henry Hicks to discuss prospects for a mill in that coastal community. "If instead of forest resources this were oil or gold or uranium," one Extension official chimed in, "we would be excited, and our leaders would be definitely planning to use the latest methods of utilization and conservation."[137]

In the spring of 1956 Bishop John R. optimistically noted that the "prospect of the new pulp mill at Mulgrave [was] bright."[138] When an agreement with the Scott Paper Company fell through, there was some disappointment, but during the 1958 speech from the throne, the lieutenant governor of Nova Scotia announced that the new premier, Robert Stanfield, had finalized an arrangement with Nova Scotia Pulp Limited (a subsidiary of the Swedish company Stora Kopparbergs) to build a mill at Port Hawkesbury. The province offered the company a fifty-year lease on all the crown land holdings in the region and promised to supply an adequate source of water. When it was announced that the mill would require a quarter million cords of wood annually, Extension began organizing woodlot owners to maximize their economic potential.[139]

To train young people for these new opportunities, Bishop John R. invited another Dutch religious order, the Brothers of Our Lady of Seven Sorrows, to open a vocational school in New Glasgow.[140] While this demonstrated a big commitment – and many grumbled about the cost – few had the resolve to disappoint the bishop or ardent Extension veterans like Fr Michael Gillis.[141] Through the financial generosity of the five Pictou County parishes, in the colourful autumn of 1957, the school opened in the former Aberdeen Hospital with courses in carpentry, electrical engineering, and mechanics.

In an era when state intervention was growing ever more pervasive, Bishop John R. was proud of the Church's action through the vocational school and was "visibly moved" when twenty-one students received their certificates in 1959.[142] Nevertheless, although the Dutch Brothers received further funding from the Department of Indian Affairs to train young Mi'kmaw men, the concern about inadequate finances proved accurate. Not only did the institute place a heavy financial burden on the Catholics of Pictou County, who were still financing their own parochial schools in a time of mounting unemployment, but there was not enough collaboration with Protestants. The Church wanted to foster a new generation of blue-collar disciples but the costs of improving the material life of the flock were soaring.[143]

INDUSTRIAL CAPE BRETON

The vocational school at New Glasgow offered another example of the diocese's evolving relationship with labour. Employees in Catholic hospitals were encouraged to unionize, and Bishop John R. even went underground at the Caledonia Colliery in Glace Bay as a gesture of solidarity with the miners. While previous generations may have treated labour unions with suspicion, priests in Sydney now realized that the youth were "largely ignorant as to why they should be good trade unionists."[144] The bishop went out of his way to stress his sympathy with labour: "I myself come from ordinary working people," John R. wrote to the president of the Nova Scotia Federation of Labour, "and most of my priests come from the homes of industrial workers, farmers and fishermen."[145] At schools like the Catholic University of America, young clerical scholars studied the provincial labour movement, and Fr Philip Mifflen's Master's thesis, which argued that the "dual unionism" of 1898–1900 and 1909–1917 had been "harmful to the miners' best interests," caused great debate.[146]

Most of the younger clergy ministering in eastern Nova Scotia in the decade of the 1950s were, like Fr Mifflen, either natives of industrial Cape Breton or had gained experience as curates in one of the many new churches in the colliery towns.[147] In 1951, after a painstaking diocesan census, parish boundaries were completely redrawn. The following years saw many new parishes: a mission church was constructed at MacKay's Corner (Holy Family Parish would be erected in 1959), St Eugene's Parish was established at Dominion in 1952, the parish of St Pius X was built in Sydney Mines in 1954, St Leo's in Glace Bay was opened in 1957, and in 1959 St. Augustine's parish was established in Sydney. "The young fellows that started the new parishes made a great show," Msgr Coady wrote to a colleague in Alberta. "Father George MacLean has a new Church at Gardiner and started a new one at Dominion. He is just bouncing around with almost uncontrollable energy."[148]

Yet all this optimistic church construction concealed the reality that Cape Breton's industries were in trouble once again. In Inverness, the closure of the mine, the loss of business, and the sale of company homes dramatically altered the town's fortunes.[149] Other fuel sources such as crude oil and hydro-electric power were increasing their share of the national energy market, and Canada regularly imported cheap coal from the United States. Cape Breton miners lacked steady employment, and the American-controlled Dominion Steel and Coal Corporation (DOSCO) was bleeding money. In January 1953, the miners' contract ended and, facing uncertainly, the union agreed to continue working while a conciliation board investigated the industry.

Under the chairmanship of Dr Clarence Nicholson of Pine Hill Presbyterian Seminary in Halifax, the conciliation board ultimately rejected the demands of the colliers but begged labour and capital to cooperate.[150] Despite these pleas, citing absenteeism and low production, DOSCO soon closed the large No. 1-B Coal Mine at Dominion, throwing twelve hundred men out of work (coal-digging machinery was installed in their stead). An angry Fr Walter Roberts of St Eugene's parish immediately sent a telegram of protest to Halifax, demanding that the government reverse the "precipitate action" of DOSCO to avoid social and economic upheaval. Not only did the closure mean economic uncertainty, he wrote, but it also indicated that DOSCO would not be cooperative.[151]

At the annual assembly of the Cape Breton North and Victoria Deanery in 1953, Stephen Dolhanty, the vice-president of District 26, and brother of Fr Francis Dolhanty (curate at New Waterford), begged the priests to pressure the provincial government for solutions to the foundering coal industry.[152] By Christmas over a hundred Glace Bay families were without income and the financial loss to diocesan institutions like St Joseph's Hospital was enormous. Merchants placed "cash only" signs in their store windows, and light and water bills went unpaid.[153] "The Cape Breton miners are not on strike," commented *The Casket*; they are "victims of forces utterly beyond their control."[154]

Throughout the winter, the parish welfare bureaus at Dominion and Bridgeport were swamped by demand. In Sydney, where most miners would take assistance only as a last resort, Catholic charities at St Theresa's Parish had never been busier.[155] At St Eugene's, half of Fr Roberts's parishioners were without work and, with debt on the new church mounting, the parish could ill afford the loss of the Sunday collections. In the spring of 1954, with parishioners already burdened by tremendous household pressure, another disaster struck; the church was burnt to the ground, leaving four hundred families with no school or sanctuary. A dark cloud lingered over the colliery towns.

The 1954 Rural and Industrial Conference was devoted almost solely to the problem of coal. Seeking a high-level discussion, Extension invited top stakeholders to discuss issues of energy development and the use of diesel on the railways. Among them were: the stocky Freeman Jenkins, president of District 26 (who would soon be defeated by Tom McLachlan); H.M.C. Gordon, chief of DOSCO coal operations; Mayor Owen Hartigan of Sydney Mines; and James Morrison, the Acadia alumnus and UMW research director.

Despite the often-passionate debate, the conference delegates had few answers. They could neither control freight rates, move the Sydney Steel mill closer to central Canadian markets, nor find buyers for Cape Breton products. A year later, when still more miners were thrown out of work because of "excessive water" in the No. 25 colliery in Gardiner Mines, many families left for Ontario. Ironically, while Nova Scotia politicians from all parties decried the destruction of industry in the Maritime provinces from the floor of the House of Commons, the miners of Dominion's 1-B were offered courses on urban farming. The Bridgeport Cooperative Small Fruits Association with a cold-storage and processing plant opened in 1957, but without steady orders for Sydney steel it was a hollow victory.[156]

In May 1956 the Trades and Labour Congress of Canada merged with the Canadian Congress of Labour to create the Canadian Labour Congress (CLC). In Toronto, Bishop Francis Marrocco, the former director of the Sydney People's School and subsequent auxiliary bishop in that city, publicly celebrated the union as a "united effort."[157] He also had praise for Donald MacDonald, the CLC's new secretary treasurer and former CCF MLA for Cape Breton South, who, he said, had come up "the hard way." Men like MacDonald, a former coal heaver and Extension study club member, raised hope among the Catholic elite that he would be able to move labour forward.[158]

In the opinion of the Cape Breton clergy, Catholics like Donald MacDonald at the CLC, Ed Corbett among the steelworkers, and Rod MacMullin working with mechanics were "doing heroic things." Not only did they openly oppose the more radical elements, but they had also rallied "a faithful group with them on a common Christian front."[159] The affection for these men revealed the inroads that Extension had made at the coalface. Even skeptics like George MacEachern, who believed the Church still spent too much energy "looking for Reds," were invited to St F.X. to speak. Although MacEachern felt that it was unusual "that they'd allow the left-wing to be represented," parameters were no longer as stark.[160] By 1955 Extension fieldworkers openly boasted that the "prestige of the Movement [was] very high" among labour.[161]

While the arrival of the CCF in Cape Breton had initially worried the Church due to its leftist agenda, by the mid-1950s younger priests like the thirty-three-year-old Glace Bay native Fr Andrew "Andy" Hogan, who brought a left-wing mentality to Extension meetings, were now concerned by the waning fortunes of the party (Hogan would later represent Cape Breton–East Richmond as a member of the New Democratic Party from 1974 to 1980). As the traditional parties reconciled with former supporters, the CCF had become "dangerously inactive" and party membership declined. In the 1956 provincial election, only one CCF politician retained a seat and, soon afterward, the provincial party's newspaper, *Maritime Commonwealth*, moved to Ontario.[162] Yet few could have predicted the defeat of the stalwart CCF MP Clarie Gillis in June 1957 by over a thousand votes (he would lose by a greater margin in March 1958 and had died by 1960). Shortly after Gillis's defeat, DOSCO was purchased by the British corporation Hawker-Siddeley. Although the new management promised "a better, sounder company," the end of the steel mill was drawing nearer.[163]

THE GRAIL MOVEMENT

As industrial Cape Breton entered its "death agony," the Church looked once again to the countryside for stability.[164] When the Congregation of Notre Dame unveiled plans for a new convent in Mabou in 1950, its old building was quickly transformed into a training school designed to instill a "rural mentality" among young women. In preparation for this new ministry, a cadre of sisters visited the

Family Life Institute at St Pascal, Quebec, and then developed a curriculum on home economics. A two-week institute was offered in 1954 (with an emphasis on cooperatives) and, the following year, faculty from Mount Saint Bernard College contributed their expertise to the popular "Mabou Experiment." By 1957 the province had given permission to introduce the program into the local high school on a trial basis. "If I had a million dollars," Bishop John R. mused, "I'd give half of it to Mabou."[165]

While Mabou's Family Life Institute emphasized traditional themes, young women were beginning to ask new questions. One emerging female voice was the Baltimore native and St F.X. professor Dr Doris Boyle, who had come to eastern Nova Scotia through her marriage to George Boyle. Her columns in *The Casket* offered fresh perspectives on an array of societal issues. "While a woman's place was still in the home," she would write strategically, "the home embraces the community, the province, the country, and the world."[166] Smart, witty, and pugnacious, Boyle encouraged women to confront the problems in their own backyards. She even pressured both the churches and the provincial government to treat patients in local mental institutions with more compassion.[167] "With great interest I always read the column of Dr. Doris Boyle," wrote one woman from Sydney. "The May 29th edition of 'Woman's Mission in the World' stirred me very much."[168]

While women had always held sway in parish life, even Catholic intellectuals like Dr Boyle, with large public followings, were expected to maintain traditional gender roles. Recognizing this generational paradox, the Mount Saint Bernard faculty began to educate their students on topics like "women in the parish" and "women in the age of technology." Knowing that females were keen to take active part in and ownership of the liturgy, the faculty were also increasingly gathering information on the emerging American Grail Movement.

The Grail Movement was founded in Holland in the 1920s and by the 1930s its members had taken jobs in factories to preach Catholicism to overworked and exploited employees. By 1940 the movement had been exported to the United States, where followers opened libraries and soup kitchens, taught art and hygiene, and lived communally.[169]

With so many women involved in the work of the Antigonish Movement, it is not surprising that the Grail Movement appealed to local Catholics. By 1952 the Catholic Women's League had

Figure 8.5 | Family Life Program, Mabou, 1957

already sent a diocesan representative to the Grailville School in Loveland, Ohio, while two members of the Congregation of Notre Dame attended "Grail Week" in Philadelphia. There they found an enthusiastic group of women who wanted to expand their role "in theology, catechetics, the arts, international relations, community development."[170] Like the Catholic Women's League, Grail members believed that women exerted a "powerful influence" on the lives of their communities."[171]

For a time, it looked as if the Grail Movement would take hold in the diocese. Plans were prepared to transform the former family farm of Edmonton archbishop John Hugh MacDonald into a Grail training centre in Antigonish County. New York native Evelyn Pugh, invited into the region to lecture, lived in the diocese for six years, working with Extension and sharing her passion for women's ministry.[172] Later, the Grail founder in America, Dr Lydwine Kersbergen, a former associate of radical Catholic activist Dorothy Day, was also invited to lecture and, in 1959 another American Grail member was enrolled at St F.X. [173]

While Pugh was impressed with the Antigonish Movement – she mailed Extension literature back to Michigan for use in the Grail's "Gateway" cooperative program – the possibility of a formal diocesan Grail program was ultimately scuttled by the fear that the Grail would challenge the supremacy of Extension.[174] Msgr Coady "had the greatest admiration for people like Tat Sears, Zita (O'Hearn) Cameron, Kay Tompkins and others, native girls of the Diocese who turned out to be tremendous Extension workers," Fr Topshee recalled. But the attitude was, "Why do we need the Grail if we have these people?"[175]

THE MYSTICAL BODY MOVEMENT

The desire of Catholic women to "live the liturgy" and participate fully within the Church was one example of the "Mystical Body" in action. Back in 1943, Pius XII issued the encyclical *Mystici Corporis Christi* (On the Mystical Body of Christ), which recognized what priests like Fr Tompkins had always believed: that the Church existed for the glory of God but also for the good of the faithful.[176] In response, the faithful would proclaim Christ in their lives, on the street, at dances and sporting events and so on. The idea that all members of the Church were called to help the bishops and priests do God's work in the parishes was so engrossing that two St F.X. professors, Fr John Hugh Gillis and Fr James McMahon, wrote *Our Union in and with Christ* to satisfy the demand for information.[177]

While charity had always been the hallmark of parishes, by the early 1950s the relationship between the responsibilities of the individual within the Church and the responsibility of the Church to the individual was being radically redefined. Bishop John R. was particularly drawn to the encyclical on the Mystical Body and was excited to host the first National Catholic Social Conference (English section) in the late summer of 1953. The theme of the gathering was "The Parish: Basic Cell of Social Life," and some five hundred clergy, women religious, and laity from across Canada came together at St F.X. to discuss the challenges facing Catholic families. Cardinal McGuigan, on the St F.X. campus for the first time since receiving his honorary degree in 1947, represented the Vatican. Speakers debated everything from the responsibilities of the laity to the role of priests in social action. Doris Boyle gave a stirring address on social consciousness of the parish extending to the entire church.

Thanks to the fame of the Antigonish diocese and his own interest in Catholic social action, Bishop John R. was a rising star within the Canadian Church. He was serious about creating a communion of believers and wanted eastern Nova Scotia to become a leading social laboratory. He even asked Bishop Marrocco, by then director of the Social Action Department of the Canadian Catholic Conference (later named the Canadian Conference of Catholic Bishops or the CCCB), to investigate the challenges of family life among the Cape Breton coal miners. Marrocco's blunt report revealed that households were beset by inadequate housing, lack of nutritional awareness, alcohol abuse, and underemployment. In response, MacDonald declared 1953 the "Year of Family Welfare" (a "Family Life Crusade" would follow in 1957), and family welfare councils were organized in parishes like New Waterford's Mount Carmel, where the Family Centre boasted a modern kitchen, meeting rooms, and a library.

CONVENTS, HOSPITALS, AND ORPHANS

Few were better equipped to focus on "family life" in the 1950s than the women religious who were a crucial part of the "Mystical Body" movement. Congregations had faced vocation shortages during the war, but a postwar surge in church attendance had brought many fresh recruits to support new ministries. With an influx of members, the Filles de Jésus acquired the old Notre Dame de L'Acadie convent in D'Escousse, opened a new convent at West Arichat (1953), and began teaching at River Bourgeois (1954). The Congregation of Notre Dame, with 119 active members within the diocese, opened convents and schools at Larry's River (1955) and Port Felix (1956), while the 279-member Sisters of St Martha opened convents or schools at Heatherton (1951), Little Dover (1951), Dominion (1951), East Bay (1953), Trenton (1954), Dingwall (1955), Antigonish town (1956), Guysborough (1958), and St Margaret's Village (1959). "The demands of our own diocese have multiplied so rapidly," Mother Ignatius, CSM, exclaimed to a colleague," that it is almost impossible to keep up with them."[178]

Within the postwar Church, religious sisters also began to look beyond their traditional roles. While most Catholics were used to interacting with the women religious in schools or hospitals, it was now common to see them driving over the dusty and potholed roads of the region. In 1941 Sister Aneas Joseph MacDonald

Figure 8.6 | Mother Ignatius, CSM (Mary Catherine Floyd), c. 1930s

became the first Martha to obtain a provincial driver's license and was soon chauffeuring her colleagues around in a nine-seater bus. "We presume there will be some consternation in our small town," recorded the Bethany annalist, "to see a Sister at the wheel for the first time."[179] When the CND opened their mission at Larry's River in 1955, Bishop MacDonald provided not only an old Volkswagen but driving lessons as well.[180]

Table 8.1 | Catholic Hospitals 1951–1952

Catholic Hospitals 1951–1952	Number of Sisters	Nursing Sisters	Lay Nurses	Patients
St Mary's Hospital, Inverness	8	3	24	952
Saint Martha's Hospital, Antigonish	32	10	109	3,915
St Joseph's Hospital, Glace Bay	22	6	82	3,634
Our Lady of Lourdes Sanatorium, Stellarton	13	1	0	4
Sacred Heart Hospital, Cheticamp	9	6	5	1,029
St Rita's Hospital, Sydney	21	5	35	2,954
Total	129	39	295	14,677

(*Source:* Antigonish Diocesan Statistics)

Women's congregations remained intensively involved in health-care, and continued to acquire new facilities. In the spring of 1954, the Sisters of Charity (with 119 members), long devoted to the people of North Sydney, replaced the old Hamilton Memorial Infirmary with the modern 150-bed St Elizabeth Hospital. Looming over the entrance to Sydney Harbour, the building had "the most delightful views of any hospital in the country." Three years later, the Filles de Jésus acquired the eighteen-bed Isle Madame Red Cross Outpost Hospital at Arichat, changed its name to St Ann's Hospital, and offered both nursing and maternity beds.

Consequently, as provincial bureaucrats took a greater interest in healthcare, they looked to the women's congregations for guidance. They also paid homage to the foundational contribution of nursing sisters like Mother Ignatius, CSM (Mary Catherine Floyd) to the health and well-being of Nova Scotians. When Mother Ignatius professed her vows in 1912, she could not have dreamed that she would one day be granted accolades from the Canadian Hospital Association, an honorary degree from St F.X., and a private audience with Pope Pius XII.

Yet the canny nursing sister, who had been raised on the dusty backroads of Springfield, Antigonish County, could foresee the coming changes to the delivery of healthcare. She understood that, while hospitals like St Martha's maintained a Catholic ethos through sodalities and religious retreats for the nurses, the province was steadily taking administrative control. The Catholic Hospital Council of Canada welcomed all new government subsidies for patient care but questioned its ability to maintain Catholic medical and moral codes within a secular bureaucracy.[181]

The federal Hospital Insurance and Diagnostic Services Act of 1957 forced the province to take stricter administrative control over its infirmaries through a federal-provincial cost-sharing program. The intent of the legislation was to lessen the financial burden of the patient, relieve the hospitals of ceaseless fundraising campaigns, and improve the general quality of care. While the legislation extended care, placed "all hospitals on a firmer financial basis," and took financial strain off the congregations – nurses began receiving better wages – there was a price to be paid.[182] Administrators wanted to maintain the Catholic environment but financial realities had to be faced along with increased patient demand.

Hospitals were not the only institutions into which governments were extending their influence. Whereas priests had once learned "on the job," new leaders like the thirty-two-year-old Fr John Gerald Webb, who supervised the Antigonish Diocesan Charities (ADC), had been trained at institutes like the fledgling Maritime School of

Social Work in Halifax and were influenced by professional "best practices." A degree in theology was no longer sufficient to qualify priests to act as experts on social issues; they now required specialized skills in addition.

By 1952 the diocesan orphanage at Little Bras d'Or was congested, and best practice suggested that the children were too far from the doctors, dentists, and schools of Sydney. During the Institute's Silver Jubilee, the diocese, in collaboration with the CWL, launched a penny-a-meal campaign to replace the overcrowded building. Through penny boxes and bags, which were placed in local schools and restaurants, some two million pennies were donated in the first month alone. On Monday morning of each week, "all these pennies ... were brought to Bethany," one Martha recalled, "and it was the novices' job to count them and roll them and get them ready for the bank."[183]

In the spring of 1953, amid this fundraising, a fire damaged the institute and the Marthas were forced to temporarily place the children in local homes.[184] As plans for a new orphanage on the site of Sydney's old St Rita Hospital (which had burned in 1951) were prepared, new ideas challenged the traditional orphanage model. Experts now believed that the placement of infants in the care of local families was much better for their psychological development. As all the displaced children from the Little Flower Institute were already sheltered within the community, caretakers like Sister Mary Matthew, CSM, were keen to keep it that way.

In June 1956 a much smaller orphanage was opened on Alexandra Street in Sydney, and while the children "seemed happy," the older ones expressed "strong desires for a home and family."[185] By 1958 the Nova Scotia Assistance Act, and later the Mothers' Allowances Act, helped keep more families intact. Best practice now suggested that children were better off remaining in the home, even under difficult circumstances, and infants were admitted to the institute "in cases of emergency only" (mostly for protection purposes).

The province's senior citizens were also a subject of concern. Old age pensions offered some financial relief, but many still lived in poverty.[186] One man writing from Glace Bay noticed the many seniors falling asleep in Mass and begged the diocese for a seniors' home, as "there are a lot of old people trying to live on 40 dollars a month."[187] The young Fr Webb, who had written his graduate thesis at the Maritime School of Social Work on the challenges facing the region's elderly, acknowledged the contribution of the Stella Maris Residence in North Sydney (Sisters of Charity), and St Anthony's Home in Sydney (Filles de Jésus), but the diocese still could not fill the need.

Even alcoholism, which had plagued the parishes for generations, came under increased scrutiny. In 1957 alone, Nova Scotians drank some twenty-nine million dollars' worth of beer, wine, and spirits (not to mention the great quantities of home brew that were available in most rural communities). Although the American organization Alcoholics Anonymous provided some support for addicts, there was a need to shelter and treat those who lives had been destroyed by alcohol. In October 1959, Talbot House, named after a famous recovered alcoholic from Ireland, was opened in the former glebe at Frenchvale, Cape Breton, as a diocesan rehabilitation centre. It was, as one priest noted, "an effort to put some purpose and order back into the lives of these human beings."[188]

THE HOUR OF THE LAITY

All this activity on the social front was supported by a Catholic laity that was gaining in confidence. While historians often suggest that fear of damnation is what motivates folks in the pews, by the 1950s the Church was focusing on motivation through lay formation.[189] In fact, when Fr Gelasius Kraus, the eighty-one-year-old prior of St Augustine's Monastery, entered St Martha's Hospital in December 1952, he left behind a cadre of friars who were as intent on delivering retreats and spiritual formation as they had once been on tending their dairy and crops.[190]

The Augustinians may have been a monastic order, but they had always been forward- and outward-looking. Not only did they have their own preparatory seminary – the Good Counsel Academy – which allowed young men like Andrew Reid of Sydney to take vows or enlist as lay brothers, but they were keen to offer the monastery grounds "with the rich brown soil scented with the odors of growth and summer" for reflection, prayer, or simply a meditative stroll through the woods. Once the Shrine of Our Lady of Grace was completed in 1952, visitors arrived in greater numbers, and the friars were available to pray over the sick or bless the travellers who made the quick detour off the trans-Canada highway on their way to Sydney or Halifax. By 1955 busloads of pilgrims regularly toured the pastoral grounds and made their way along the Stations of the Cross.[191]

This group of Augustinians wanted to accommodate people looking for a "strategic withdrawal" from society or wishing to take a "spiritual inventory" of their life.[192] Their lay retreats, offered since the late 1940s, proved so popular that by 1953 the diocese had opened a retreat centre for the men of Cape Breton County next to St James Church at Gardiner Mines. A year later, the diocese opened Our Lady of Fatima Retreat House at coastal Seabright in Antigonish County, and the Villa Madonna Retreat House at Bras d'Or, both exclusively for women.

To oversee the busy centre at Gardiner Mines, Bishop John R. recruited the Franciscan Friars of the Atonement of Greymor and gave them administrative control of St James Parish. The friars and Fr Theophane Murphy, a "brilliant" native of Newton, Massachusetts, were well known for their weekly radio program, "The Ava Maria Hour," which aired over CJFX.[193] Like the Augustinians, the Greymor Friars also offered vocation opportunities, and by 1956 several Cape Breton men had entered the order's novitiate overlooking the Hudson River in Garrison, New York.[194] "The retreat movement," noted Fr Murphy, "has grown into one of the vitalizing influences of the Church in this area."[195]

Although there was never unanimous official support for the retreat houses – some priests voiced financial concerns, while others thought recruitment by the Atonement fathers was too impulsive – thousands of Catholics used the facilities. In 1954 alone, nearly six hundred Cape Breton women spent time at Villa Madonna.[196] "The two C.B. retreat houses are filled every weekend," noted one clergyman. "The Atonement house recently completed its first year of operation – over 1400 men, many of them coal miners and steelworkers, made a closed retreat."[197]

This was a promising time for the laity, in their role as members of the Mystical Body acting in society. "Bishops and priests cannot save the world," diocesan officials proclaimed. "The whole power of the Church must be brought into action."[198] Soon, the burgeoning Lay Apostolate Movement, which had received serious attention at prominent American Catholic institutions like the University of Notre Dame, dominated the pages of *The Casket*.[199] In an address to the Sydney Knights of Columbus, Bishop John R. compared the Lay Apostolate to a complex military manoeuvre in which the laity fought on the right flank of the clergy. The demands of modern society were too complex to be handled exclusively by priests and nuns, he said. There were many spheres that the Church could not penetrate; at the job site, the hockey rink, and the theatre, laypeople had to shoulder more of the burden.[200]

In recognition of these efforts, prestigious papal honours, once reserved for the clergy (a few medals were awarded for financial contributions in the 1850s), were given to prominent members of the laity. When seventy-nine-year-old John MacDonald of Antigonish town, president of the Antigonish Diocesan Society, was decorated in 1957 with the Papal Cross *Pro Ecclesia et Pontifice*, the highest honour next to a knighthood, the rank and file took note.[201] The following year, Joseph Pickup of Mount Carmel in New Waterford, a retired mine official, was awarded the medal for his forty-seven years of serving the local choir. It was, one reporter commented, "the hour of the laity."[202]

THE SLOW EROSION OF THE CATHOLIC SUBCULTURE

With a properly formed and active laity, and the lively application of Catholic action, the Catholic subculture appeared strong and influential. In the autumn of 1951, the twenty-eight-year-old Fr Terence Lynch, who had studied at St Michael's Choir School in Toronto and later the Pontifical Institute of Sacred Music in Rome, organized the Marion Boys' Choir at St Ninian's parish. Within two years, his choir had matured into an institute to develop musical education and foster a devotion to sacred compositions among the youth. Popular throughout the diocese, the boys were soon touring regionally. One of their first major performances was in January 1954 at the consecration of Bishop Malcolm MacEachern for Charlottetown.

While recruiting new priests had been a challenge in the 1940s, by the mid-1950s the diocese easily met its quota. Fr George Kane, the director of religious education, who held degrees from St F.X., Harvard, and the Catholic University of America, and who had previously worked as an English professor while producing *The Radio League* on CJFX, wrote a popular vocation column in *The Casket* entitled "What Must I Do?" The column was picked up by the *Western Catholic* of Edmonton and the *New Freeman* of Saint John.[203]

Kane had been inspired as a youth by foreign mission magazines, and had a keen interest in the discernment process. From his colleagues he collected several interesting testimonies that were worthy of publication. Hoping to interest a famous collaborator to attract publishers, he wrote to Bishop Fulton J. Sheen, the auxiliary bishop of New York, who had a popular television show called *Life is Worth Living*. Much to Kane's surprise, Sheen replied with a long testimonial to include in the manuscript.

Why I Became a Priest, a "book with a mission," with an introduction by James Cardinal McGuigan, was published in 1952 by the Newman Press.[204] Other contributors were Fr Patrick Peyton of the rosary crusade, the University of Notre Dame's Fr John A. O'Brien, and the intellectual Trappist Monk Thomas Merton. It was an instant success. A contract was quickly signed for publication in the British Commonwealth by Browne and Nolan Limited of Dublin, while the *Catholic Digest* agreed to condense passages for publication (it was eventually translated into German and Italian). By the autumn of 1954 the book had sold an incredible 20,000 copies.

A veritable book factory, Kane published seven more books over the next few years and used the profits to promote vocations (in 1954 he presented $2,238.32 to the chancery office).[205] Before long, his volumes were so popular that he no longer solicited testimonies, but actually had to turn many interesting witnesses away. When he put out the call for testimonies for *Why I Became a Brother*, he received 122 contributions from members of twenty-six different religious communities. In 1957 *A Seal upon My Heart: Autobiographies of Twenty Sisters* sold 18,000 copies in a single month.

Catholics were not only reading books like Kane's *Twice Called: The Autobiographies of Seventeen Convent Sisters* but were also tuning into radio. Some two thousand of the faithful still subscribed to the weekly pre-broadcast bulletins of CJFX's "People's School," which were mailed out in advance of Fr Dan MacCormack's regular program (the show was supported by provincial trade organizations and the Nova Scotia Department of Agriculture and Marketing).[206] In larger parishes like Sydney Mines and Glace Bay, discussion groups continued to complement these radio broadcasts, and feedback was relayed back to the station.

At the same time, another type of literature was having its impact, demonstrating that the Catholic subculture, so carefully nurtured by generations of the faithful, was gradually eroding.[207] In 1953

Liberal Senator J.J. Hayes Doone of New Brunswick asked St F.X. and Xavier College professors to investigate the impact of American magazines on Catholic college students and to use local court records to demonstrate a potential link between obscene literature and youth delinquency. With the cooperation of the Holy Name Society and the Catholic Youth Organization (CYO), the report was personally delivered to Ottawa by George Boyle, who gave a masterful presentation to the Canadian senate.[208]

During the study, researchers became aware of a growing debate over what constituted "obscenity."[209] While the Catholic press praised the colliery town of Dominion for passing an ordinance against "crime comics," others felt that the policy was too aggressive. When CYO members covered over a movie poster in Antigonish town, the St F.X. English professor Fr R.J. MacSween chastised the boys for vandalizing private property.[210] Later, when George Boyle complained of indecent literature to Dr Frank Stiling of the University of Western Ontario, president of the Canadian Authors Association, he replied, "Is there any indecent literature?"[211]

It was increasingly difficult to shelter the faithful from such points of view. The very radio airwaves that carried the news of cooperatives, credit unions, and rosary hours were also challenging Church doctrine. Catholics regularly expressed frustration with the taxpayer-funded CBC for airing segments by intellectuals like Bertrand Russell, who maligned the Catholic teaching. "What we do demand," *The Casket* exhorted, "is that our servants do not seek to run our homes – that the CBC clean up or shut up."[212] Although the national broadcaster offered some obvious benefits, its record, opined the paper, was spoiled by "catering to a small cult of irreligion." [213]

A similar dilemma was presented by television. Not only was the new programming stealing young people away from study clubs, but it was impossible to control the message.[214] In 1952 CBC television executives created an uproar when they decided that Bishop Sheen's popular weekly program *Life is Worth Living* was too controversial, too American, and too Catholic for their airwaves.[215] With Extension seeking a presence within the medium, Fr Andy Hogan in 1957 presided over the production of "The People's School of the Air" on Sydney's CJCB television station (the only station in eastern Nova Scotia). Although there was a desire to move the program onto the screens of the region, "a degree of skill, training, and experience" was required that the diocese did not possess.[216]

As visual media became more accessible, Hollywood productions such as *Going My Way*, and the *Bells of St. Mary's*, starring the likes of Bing Crosby playing progressive clergy who clashed with more conservative colleagues, challenged the traditional caricature of the austere and aloof priest. During the Jubilee of Msgr Donald MacPherson in Port Hood, a special affair was organized for the children. When MacPherson rose to speak, everyone in the hall prepared for a formal lecture on faith and morals, but the old priest surprised them with a performance of "Billy Magee Magaw."

There were three crows sat on a tree,
Oh, Billy Magee Magaw.
There were three crows sat on a tree,
Oh, Billy Magee Magaw.
There were three crows sat on a tree,
And they were black as crows could be.
And they all flapped their wings and cried:
"Caw, caw, caw! Billy Magee Magaw!"

With the children in hysterics, MacPherson finished the song "calling like a crow." "Well, you know," recalled Bishop Marroco, "for a priest to stand up in front of all these children, on his Jubilee, and not to have an apostolic message of some kind but to sing two verses of Billie MacGee MacGaw (sic), seemed the improper thing to Bishop MacDonald. And there was a very pained look on his face ... The children loved it!"[217]

From his residence in Antigonish town, Bishop John R. surveyed these changes with disquiet. He recognized that customs were beginning to wane but struggled to find the appropriate response. Education was a case in point. In 1954 the "Pottier Report" on the state of education in Nova Scotia recommended an educational finance cost-sharing program between the province and the municipalities.[218] Keen to discard the numerous old district schoolhouses that were ruled by local wardens, planners touted school consolidation as an "educational panacea."[219] Some Catholic parents were tempted by the promise of modern classrooms and gymnasiums, but among the clergy there was deep anxiety about surrendering administrative and moral authority to the state.[220] "Our ownership of schools is necessary in most places," warned Bishop John R., "because of the uncertainty of what School Boards might eventually do if they owned all the schools."[221]

In heavily Catholic municipalities like Antigonish County, consolidation went ahead under the direction of priests like Fr Edmund Nash in Tracadie, where eight one-room schoolhouses were consolidated into a modern facility on parish property.[222] Down the road at Havre Boucher, children who had previously studied in four separate buildings were now taught under one roof, while 220 students at the newly consolidated school at Ingonish, Victoria County, were gathered together under the tutelage of the Sisters of St Martha.[223]

Although the monies for these new facilities were borrowed from the Department of Education, the involvement of priests like Fr Nash abated the fears of local ratepayers. The question of district rural high schools, however, was a different matter. For generations, Nova Scotia students had faced a disparity between those who studied under "well-educated urban high-school teachers" and those "studying secondary subjects in the rural common schools, taught by teachers with, *at best*, second class elementary certificates."[224] When Halifax started building modernized non-denominational centralized rural high schools in each county (Riverview Rural High School was built near Sydney in 1950) the Catholic-dominated counties of Antigonish, Richmond, and Inverness were reluctant to accept funding.

Within the parishes, there were logistical concerns over busing teenagers longer distances and fears that the rural students who attended the centralized high school would ultimately abandon the countryside for professional opportunities in the towns and cities (and to some extent this was true). Yet the real concerns were about faith and curriculum. Would, for example, the plan to send Antigonish county students to Mount Cameron farm to study agriculture under the Dutch Sacred Heart Brothers be acceptable to provincial bureaucrats?[225] There was little doubt, noted one educator, that Bishop John R. "was very much afraid that the Church's position might be weakened."[226]

In 1956, after contentious debate, St Andrew, the rural high school for Antigonish County, was opened a short distance from the St F.X. campus.[227] To appease the Church, the school was named after Bishop Colin F. MacKinnon's early grammar school in the parish of St Andrews, three members of the Sisters of St Martha were appointed to the faculty, and the curriculum focused on crops, rural crafts, gardens, and homemaking. "Here at last," wrote the historian and school inspector H.M. MacDonald, "youthful citizens of Arisaig for the first time mingled with those of Havre Boucher and those of Lochaber."[228] Yet, as the province became "dotted with large consolidated regional high schools, junior highs and elementary schools," many Catholics grumbled that they had surrendered their prerogative. Or as one historian put it, these schools were often built over the "protests of parents and local communities."[229]

In the mixed urban communities of the province, higher provincial subsidies for schools created still other problems. As the diocese had built and maintained its own parochial schools (and continued renting them to the province), there was some question as to how the Pottier recommendations would affect this arrangement. Would towns with large Protestant populations permit provincial monies to go toward parochial schools? Could a parish like Mount Carmel in New Waterford sell its school building to the town but maintain the Catholic environment? These were difficult questions and many were unsure whether provincial subsidies were worth the hassle.

As they did on most issues, Catholics found themselves divided. When the City of Sydney took the school-funding question to the people through a plebiscite, Bishop John R., unsure about accepting government monies and worried about sectarianism, forbade his clergy to campaign. At Whitney Pier, Fr Leo Sears felt that the fight to build Catholic schools with tax dollars was "a plain case of justice or injustice" and that his parishioners had "every right to have the City build these schools."[230] Defying their bishop, Fr Sears and a number of colleagues spoke out from the pulpit. They had an effect; the people of Sydney ultimately voted to allow public funding for all schools. Hours after the vote, the bishop "blew in" to the colliery towns and accused the priests of treachery.[231]

There were similar complexities at St F.X. Higher enrollment demanded more faculty and, lacking sufficient priest-professors, the college increasingly relied on lay scholars. Unlike the clergy-intellectuals, who had access to other financial resources, however, these young lay scholars, some of whom had dependants, could not live on poorly paid contracts and needed "something approaching a living wage." Even Fr Nicholson, the college president, confessed that the college's "scale of salaries [was] scandalous."[232] "Dr. Somers is visiting the large Canadian cities in the hope of interesting some of the big corporations in supporting us," Nicholson wrote in 1954. "No doubt you know the cost of educating is soaring."[233]

Table 8.2 | Population of the Diocese of Antigonish in 1960

County	Number of Parishes/Missions	Families	Population
Antigonish	13	2,149	11,651
Guysborough	14	1,056	4,725
Pictou	9	2,159	9,507
Richmond	12	2,208	9,926
Inverness	18	2,535	12,620
Victoria	11	658	3,161
Cape Breton	46	14,597	70,170
Total	123	25,362	121,760

(*Source:* Diocese of Antigonish Yearbook, 1960)

In 1954, as the St F.X. board of governors mulled over further campus expansion plans, the sixty-seven-year-old president, who had been on the college faculty since 1916, was transferred to St Joseph's parish in Sydney and replaced by the historian and financial wizard Fr Hugh Somers.[234] Somers was not terribly interested in the post and felt tremendous pressure to preserve the Catholic environment while modernizing the college.[235] Somewhat reserved and conservative, he recognized that Nova Scotia's universities were at a crossroads and needed to adapt to "contemporary change and demands."[236] The problem, of course, was that the motives of government and wealthy donors did not often match those of the Church.[237] Although Nova Scotia universities would not receive annual grants from the provincial government until the 1960s, St F.X. was slowly becoming more public than private.

Some of the old cooperators questioned the value of higher enrollments, new facilities, and modernization; they felt that St F.X. had lost focus. Fr Michael Gillis, now seventy-one, for example, demanded that the institution revisit the writings of Fr Tompkins, and criticized administrators for graduating a professional elite without addressing the realities that kept eastern Nova Scotia in economic servitude. He also worried that Extension was falling behind. "Some thirty years ago St. F.X. branched out in a new program of adult education," he barked. "The story is well known, interesting and encouraging ... but this department is in urgent need of expansion in personnel and financial aid."[238]

Unfortunately for Fr Gillis, the college and the parishes were often "as far apart as the poles."[239] Behind closed curtains, advocates of modernization saw most veterans of the Antigonish Movement as "old mergerites" and kept them outside the school's inner circle.[240] When Gillis demanded that St F.X. revisit Fr Tompkins's ideas, the board of governors listened in "stunned and respectful silence," and then moved forward with plans for campus expansion.[241] Even the chancellor, a merger sympathizer during the tense months of 1922, felt very much an outsider. And the English professor Fr R.J. MacSween mused, "A priest who used to help at the cathedral was always greeted [by the bishop] this way: 'How are all the PhD's today?'"[242]

DEATH OF MSGR COADY

The gradual erosion of the Extension Department and the Catholic subculture on which it was built came as many of those characters who had made the diocese famous were passing on to the next life. Alex MacIntyre, the one-time radical and District 26 labour leader, passed away in June 1952 at St Martha's hospital. The Extension stalwart and former president of the Nova Scotia Credit Union League, who had first descended into the damp coal mines at the age of fourteen, had retired with honours from some of the region's finest universities.[243] Months later, the handsome A.B. MacDonald from Glassburn in the parish of Heatherton, so long at Coady's right hand, died of heart failure in Ottawa at the age of fifty-nine. He was awarded an honorary degree from his alma mater on his deathbed, and his remains were conveyed back to St F.X. for a Requiem Mass and burial in the picturesque graveyard in his birthplace.[244] Then in early June 1954, Bishop James Boyle fell ill while on a trip to Rome, and received heart surgery in London's historic St John and St Elizabeth Hospital. The sixty-eight-year-old Charlottetown prelate was reportedly "over crisis stage," but then suffered an embolism and "went in less than a minute." In eulogizing his brother, George Boyle summed up the lives of all these men with the words, "If you seek [God's] monument, look around you."

These deaths were particularly difficult on Msgr Coady, who was also battling high blood pressure. By the late 1950s, Coady was frequently hospitalized and when he died in the afternoon of 28 July 1959, at the age of seventy-seven, it was not unexpected.[245] Years later, many could still recall where they were when they heard that the monsignor had died. Unbelievably, Msgr Francis Smyth was actually lecturing on *Masters of Their Own Destiny* at Combermere House in Ontario when the phone rang.[246] Alexander Laidlaw, who had worked so closely with Coady, upon learning the news in the middle of a meeting in Saskatoon, "felt that some kind of world had come to an end."[247]

The great proponent of cooperation lay in state at St F.X.'s Morrison Hall until his body was transferred the few yards to the university chapel for the funeral Mass. His casket was carried out of the church by a steelworker, two fishermen, a coal miner, and two farmers. He was remembered as a "teachers' teacher, with the precious gift of being able to arouse and sustain interest in even the most prosaic subject."[248] Tributes were published in the *Montreal Star*, the *New York Herald Tribune* and the *Halifax Chronicle-Herald*, while the *Maritime Cooperator* printed a moving statement from Coady's long-time secretary, Ellen Arsenault.[249] Time and again, people recalled that Coady's faith had transcended traditional priestly roles. "O.K., have your own pious meetings," Fr Allan MacAdam recalled Coady saying. "We'll work at this."[250]

THE COADY INTERNATIONAL INSTITUTE

Although Msgr Coady was best known for his work among the people of eastern Nova Scotia, his name would soon be synonymous with work overseas. In 1957 Scarboro House, a sanctuary for mission members studying at St F.X., was opened next to the bishop's residence in Antigonish town. It was a symbolic gesture. "Right from the very beginning," noted Scarboro superior-general Msgr Thomas McQuaid, "Antigonish has been the great friend of our society."[251] By the late 1950s, everyone in the leafy college town spoke of this missionary work. "Father McIver, from Scarboro House, has just returned from a three-week visit to South America," noted Fr J.A. Gillis. "He has some interesting stories to tell, and some frightening ones too."[252]

During the final years of Bishop John R.'s life he "talked nothing but Latin America."[253] The prelate's plans for outreach in countries like Costa Rica and Chile were invigorated during his 1959 *ad limina*. In a private audience with the bishop, Pope John XXIII, who had appointed the first-ever cardinals for Japan, Mexico, Africa, and the Philippines, encouraged this ministry, and in 1960 he asked the United States and Canada to send as many priests as possible to Latin America. When Fr Joseph MacDonald requested an Antigonish priest to help his ministry in Puerto Rico, Fr Pius Matthew Hawley, a New Waterford native, was quickly dispatched. Soon, Bishop John R even spoke of Latin America as the "Antigonish obligation."

At St F.X. Msgr Hugh Somers actively campaigned for an "International House for Priests" to train clergy and lay students from around the globe. "Perhaps a better term would be International Institute," noted Somers, "or it could be called the Coady Institute." The training of foreign students had taken place through the usual undergraduate courses and fieldwork, but this process was considered unsuitable for those who already possessed degrees. Moreover, the lack of residence space forced foreign students off-campus, where they felt isolated. "In view of the great service that could be rendered to the Church, and the inadequacy of the present program," Somers wrote to MacDonald, "it is my opinion that now is the time to act."[254]

After Msgr Coady's death, the drive to organize the Coady International Institute gained momentum. Bishop John R. travelled to Montreal to meet with Msgr Smyth, then on loan to the Canadian Catholic Conference, and asked him to return to Antigonish as director of the institute with a special responsibility for training missionary priests. It was the bishop's plan, recalled Smyth, "that a spasmodic, relatively unorganized, uniformalised program be pulled together under one roof and with a director to take charge of it."[255] In early December 1959, the St F.X. board of governors voted to establish the Coady International Institute.

By this time, Bishop MacDonald sensed that his sojourn on earth was coming to and end. In August 1959, having already undergone heart surgery, he suffered a seizure after a short dip in the ocean and was hospitalized for five weeks.[256] Four months later, on 17

December 1959, Archbishop Mario-Joseph Lemieux of Ottawa arrived in Antigonish to discuss his new seminary and to request the services of the Sisters of St Martha. MacDonald was in good spirits as he took Lemieux on a tour of St F.X. and the new R.K. MacDonald Guest House in Antigonish town (where MacDonald planned eventually to retire). The following morning, the men celebrated Mass, ate breakfast, and had a lively chat about the prospects of the Coady Institute and the Church in Latin America, after which Lemieux went to his room to prepare for his meeting with the Marthas. When he returned, he found Bishop MacDonald dead on the sofa. "His death must have been swift and untroubled," Lemieux later recalled, "as his appearance was that of a man asleep."[257]

Antigonish had grown accustomed to funeral Masses and welcomed the apostolic delegate, Sebastiano Baggio, to the cathedral town for the services. As with Archbishop Morrison, MacDonald's body was placed in the centre aisle of St Ninian's, and for days mourners passed by the open casket. The Massachusetts businessman, St F.X. booster, and native of Christmas Island, Malcolm MacNeil, finding that planes to Nova Scotia were grounded due to inclement weather, had his son drive him to the funeral from Boston.[258] MacNeil joined mourners at the prelate's burial in St Ninian's cemetery. Instead of being buried next to the large imposing monuments of Archbishop MacKinnon, Bishop Cameron, and Archbishop Morrison, Bishop MacDonald was laid to rest, rather symbolically, across the way under a modest marker beside Msgr Coady.

A few months later, Msgr Smyth, whose "long standing interest and experience in social action issues ... fitted him well for the daunting new assignment," returned to Antigonish town as director of the Coady Institute.[259] In February 1960, Msgrs Smyth and Somers travelled to Boston to seek financing for a new building to house the Coady Institute. The recently named cardinal, Richard Cushing of Boston, having been unable to attend Bishop MacDonald's funeral, astonished the men with an offer of $200,000 to pay for the building in the late prelate's memory.[260] It was the beginning of a new era for the Catholics of eastern Nova Scotia.

Conclusion

In January 1960, "mighty big and strong" Antigonish was in the hands of the thirty-five-year-old administrator Fr Joseph N. MacNeil. The young canon lawyer (and future archbishop of Edmonton) had been sent to the Canadian College in Rome for legal training in 1955 to ease Bishop John R.'s "matrimonial load," and had returned an expert on *sede vacante*.[1] In May 1960, as Pope John XXIII called a Second Vatican Council (1962–65) to "open the windows [of the Church] and let in some fresh air," the Curia selected the Montreal native William Edward Power as Antigonish's sixth bishop. As a former vice-chancellor of the Archdiocese of Montreal, Power had a socially conscious résumé that seemed to fit seamlessly with the St F.X. Extension program. Yet, while he had worked closely with the Young Christian Workers movement and had managed Montreal's Catholic Men's Hostel, after his installation, as Msgr M.A. MacLellan later noted, "things became totally different."[2]

The selection of an urbane Montreal vice-chancellor as bishop of Antigonish demonstrated that the parishes of eastern Nova Scotia still punched far above their weight (to employ a favourite boxing term of the Old Rector). Yet the books, radio programs, magazine articles, and television documentaries that made the subsidiarity of the region famous concealed some difficult economic and demographic realities that never really waned. Even Bishop John R. MacDonald liked to joke about a former resident who retired to his native community of Port Hood. "Why in the world did you come back here?" asked an old friend. After some thought he replied, "I know of no other place where a man can live on nothing."[3]

In the short term, the Church continued to seek solutions to industrial decline and joblessness, and strengthened its ties to labour. Under Bishop Power, the Extension Department hosted trade union summer schools on the St F.X. campus, and the diocese continued to organize Catholic social life conferences. Yet by the mid–1960s, a new generation was in charge of Extension and, as James Cameron pointed out in his history of St F.X., by the end of the decade very few of the staff had personally known the founding fathers of the Antigonish Movement.[4] People still spoke of the "spirit" of the movement (and still do) but struggled to transpose Msgr Coady's "Big Picture" into a rapidly changing Canadian society.

While Extension's committed fieldworkers still did very important work, some wondered if the diocese's program of subsidiarity had run its course. Was there a need for St F.X. to remain so heavily involved in the community with organizations like the Cooperative Union of Nova Scotia actively pursuing social and economic change? Moreover, as Bishop John R. had foretold, large-scale government material intervention soon dwarfed anything that the Church could offer. With the growth of the regional library movement, for example, by 1966 even the Extension library had closed its doors after twenty-four years. "St. F.X. had three libraries across the province," Director Fr George Topshee told a reporter in 1970, "before the government got into the field."[5]

Through the gradual acceptance of government monies for schools, colleges, and hospitals, the Catholic subculture, so carefully built up by the ultramontane Bishop Cameron, preserved and expanded by Archbishop Morrison, and utilized resourcefully by Bishop John R., became weakened. Diocesan institutions like St F.X. remained "Catholic" in ethos but as the government increased its provision of financial resources, the Church could no longer call the tune. As one prominent Catholic predicted in a 1965 interview: "I think, you're going to see [Bishop] John R's idea [vocational training] obtained and reached within the next ten years, but it will not be under the auspices of the Church. It will be by the constituted state authority."[6] Or, as Bishop John R.'s biographer noted, "the government moved in behind him and took over fields he plowed and seeded."[7] There was no secret as to what was happening but the Church could do little to stop it.

Later, as federal taxpayer-funded entities like the Cape Breton Development Corporation (DEVCO) worked to diversify the local economy, the clergymen who had once organized rural and industrial conferences slowly went back into the sanctuary. Federal ministers like Allan J MacEachen, who once proclaimed the message of subsidiarity from the pulpit of CJFX, now doled out taxpayer monies on one scheme after another. By 1967 even CJFX lost had lost its original focus and its first manager, J. Clyde Nunn, "regretted the departure of the University's educational features from the local airwaves."[8] Priests like Fr Andy Hogan and Fr George Topshee would still make names for themselves as leaders in the Cape Breton colliery towns (Hogan was elected to Parliament in 1974), but they were not capable of effecting change in the way that Msgr Coady had in the 1930s.[9] Consequently, the Church had to struggle to remain relevant in social and economic fields. "There are many people in many foreign countries," observed one priest as early as 1963, "who know much more about this program [Antigonish Movement] than some people in Antigonish itself."[10]

The Church was also changing from within. Although at the time of Bishop John R.'s death the diocese already looked much different than it had during the administration of the ultramontane Bishop Cameron, Vatican II brought further reforms to the liturgy, and the centralization that had placed monarchical power in the hands of men like Archbishop Morrison was challenged. Bishops still had the final word but lay voices would now (theoretically, at least) be heard. Warmer relations with non-Catholics were encouraged and the laity began a new role within the sanctuary as lectors and Eucharistic ministers. There is considerable debate as to what clergymen like Msgr Coady would have thought about these changes. The veteran cooperator Fr Michael Gillis felt that his late comrades would have been "pretty much depressed and discouraged by it," while others felt that Bishop John R. would have been "among the top pushers of the 'renewal.'"[11]

While many Catholics welcomed the renewal brought about by the Vatican Council, some older priests worried that the changes had been too sweeping and that the Church had backed away from the old hard truths. "There is no institution today where you could send your graduates for that Catholic mind training," Fr Michael Gillis commented in one of his last interviews. "No matter where you send them. CUA doesn't have it, Notre Dame doesn't have it, certainly Quebec doesn't have it."[12] The erosion of the old Catholic intellectual position came so rapidly that, within a decade of the Council, many shied away from looking or sounding "too Catholic." This had a tremendous effect on the way people viewed the past activities of the Church, and it became commonplace to praise a diocesan program like the Antigonish Movement for its ecumenism rather than for its adherence to Catholic social teaching. Scholars were right to note that Fr Tompkins didn't believe there was Catholic way to catch fish, but they overlooked the fact that those who attended meetings with him might go home with a copy of the Novena of Grace. As one friend of Msgr Coady noted, "he considered so many of these [faith] truths as obvious and didn't need the bolstering of religion."[13]

On the other hand, those desperate for the renewal of the post–Vatican II Church felt the need for the rank and file to better experience God's love. While it is difficult for historians to find documents that speak to the personal experiences of lay Catholics in the nineteenth and early twentieth centuries, generations of followers in eastern Nova Scotia, like Saint Paul, struggled to rise above the law of the Torah. While the Church was always a "great rallying point," strict adherence to the law affected the way generations of Catholics in Nova Scotia had encountered their faith. As with the woman in the 1940s, abandoned by her husband for decades, who sheepishly wrote to Archbishop Morrison for permission to begin dating again, observing the rules had been paramount.

Yet after the Council, many came to appreciate the law as an instrument to make "love possible." Priests like Archbishop Joseph N. MacNeil, for instance, later recalled that he had been taught to observe the law but "never told why there was a law." Shortly before his death in 1962, Fr John Mary Fraser, the great pioneer of missionary work in China, asked a friend if he thought "all those unbaptized millions out there [were] going to hell." "I never thought that way," his friend replied. "I don't think they are, either," Fraser agreed.[14]

The stereotype of the submissive Catholic being governed by strict rules does not hold up to archival scrutiny in eastern Nova Scotia, however. The people had great reverence for those priests who were active and supportive, and the clergy could only bring Catholics to places where they wanted to go.[15] Even at the height of ultramontanism, when the hierarchy was at the apex of its authority, generations of Catholics in rural villages like Heatherton, Mabou, and Lismore were willing to endure suspension from the sacraments to defend their moral or political positions. Acadians in parishes like Cheticamp may have deferred to their religious leaders but they demanded French-speaking pastors and representation on diocesan committees. The Mi'kmaq were often neglected but they refused to allow the diocese to tinker with the Feast of St Anne.

The view that the Catholic Church was dominated by men is also challenged by the archives. The Mass was of course celebrated by male clergy, and the priest was the most visible member of the parish. But women were always visible and active. The most obvious example, of course, is the often-Herculean work of the women religious. But female voices extended well beyond the sisters' congregations. While Catholic women became better organized nationally after the Great War, they had always influenced their communities on a range of issues. It was a long road from the convent schools of the Congregation of Notre Dame to the Grail Movement, but few in the St F.X. Extension Department were surprised that the Antigonish Movement relied as heavily as it did on the contributions of women.

On matters of dogma, all Catholics were guided by Rome, but on social and economic issues a great variety of opinions were expressed. Within eastern Nova Scotia, attitudes on everything from the Boer War to the Cape Breton labour movement were nuanced and, while there was a common desire for hospitals and schools, Catholics were often divided on those subjects as well. The decision not to oppose the centralization of the Mi'kmaq in 1942, for instance, is a good reminder that the Church may have been universal but Catholics were not always equal. The narrative is rich, often challenging, and always interesting.

Finally, the experience of Roman Catholicism in eastern Nova Scotia ultimately demonstrates that faith went well beyond Sunday Mass. The clergy and women religious were never confined to the sanctuary, and their investment in improving the spiritual and material well-being of the flock gave priests like Msgr Coady a popularity that lasts even to this day.[16] The idea that the Church should confine itself to baptisms and funerals would have been roundly rejected by the Catholics of the early twentieth century, and their great devotion to diocesan projects like the Antigonish Movement was ultimately an expression of love for one another. As Fr Tompkins once expressed it, the Church always took its ideas from the people, "synthesized them," and gave them back.[17] None were perfect, but they were a communion of saints.

Notes

INTRODUCTION

1 Fr J.J. MacDonald to Peter Ludlow, 9 June 2017 (author's collection).
2 Peter Nearing to Francis Smyth, 27 May 1970, St Francis Xavier University Archives (hereafter STFXUA), RG 50-1/1/8872.
3 Codignola, *Blurred Nationalities*, 139–40.
4 "Masters of Their Own Destiny" was the title of Msgr Moses Coady's 1939 book on the Antigonish Movement.
5 McGowan, "The Maritimes' Region," 28.
6 Leo Keats to D.J. MacDonald, 4 November 1937, STFXUA, Daniel J. MacDonald Papers (hereafter DJMP) RG 5/10/1924.
7 *The Globe and Mail*, 9 June 2004.
8 Johnston, *A History of the Catholic Church*, II, 552.
9 Lewis MacLellan to Peter Nearing, 10 May 1967, Antigonish Diocesan Archives (hereafter ADA), Peter Nearing Papers (hereafter PNP), folder 34.
10 Lewis MacLellan to Peter Nearing, 10 May 1967, ADA, PNP, folder 34.
11 Michael Gillis interview, no date, ADA, PNP, folder 65.
12 Malcolm MacLellan to A.A. Johnston, 24 May 1965, ADA, Angus Anthony Johnston Papers (hereafter AAJP), series 3, sub-series 2, folder 6.
13 Waite, *The Man from Halifax*.
14 MacLean, *Piety & Politics*, viii.
15 McGowan, "Life Outside the Cloister," 128.
16 Barlow and May, *Frederick Street*, 48.

CHAPTER ONE

1 *The Aurora*, 14 March 1883.

2 On the division of the Diocese of Halifax see Johnston, *A History of the Catholic Church, II*, 205–15; Ludlow "'Disturbed by the Irish Howl,'" 32–55.

3 On Irish Catholicism in Halifax see Murphy, "Transformation and Triumphalism."

4 "The Gloomy Forest" was a poem composed by the Bard MacLean (1787–1848), who wrote of the harshness of pioneer life at Barney's River, Pictou County. On Scottish immigration to Nova Scotia see Campbell and MacLean, *Beyond the Atlantic Roar*, 22.

5 Although Colin F. MacKinnon was not appointed titular archbishop of Amida (or Amyda) until his resignation on 7 September 1877, he will be called "Archbishop" throughout. Colin F. MacKinnon to Cardinal Alessandro Barnabo, 15 December 1873, ADA, Bishop Colin F. MacKinnon Papers (hereafter BCMP), series 1, sub-series 1, folder 37.

6 John Cameron to John Thompson, 14 April 1881, ADA, Bishop John Cameron Papers (hereafter BCP), series 3, sub-series 1, folder 36.

7 On the relationship between the Mi'kmaq and European settlers in the eighteenth and nineteenth centuries see Patterson, "Indian-White Relations," 23–59; Upton, *Micmacs and Colonists*.

8 MacDonald, *Memorable Years*, 73.

9 *The Colonial Patriot*, 30 April 1828. *The Aurora*, 13 April 1882 & 9 January 1884.

10 Although the Town of Antigonish was not incorporated until 1889, "town" will be used throughout.

11 When, in 1879, Archbishop Hannan of Halifax suggested that St F.X. and Saint Mary's College merge into a new institution at Pictou, most of the Antigonish clergy were wary. "As I have no confidence in the Irish," wrote Fr Kenneth MacDonald from Mabou, "I believe His Grace's object is to take the whole college of Antigonish to himself ... his next step will be to annex the counties of Pictou, Antigonish and Guysborough to the Archdiocese." Kenneth MacDonald to John Cameron, 5 March 1879, ADA, BCP, series 1, sub-series 1, folder 1.

12 William Walsh to Paul Cullen, 18 January 1845, Irish College Archives, Cullen Collection, CUL/1010.

13 Bishop Cameron circular, 1879, ADA, BCP, series 10, sub-series, folder 1.

14 Leo Keats to A. Doucet, 29 January 1937, Beaton Institute, MG 13/53/F1.

15 Johnston, *A History of the Catholic Church, II*, 443.

16 *The Casket*, 31 May 1883.
17 In 1886 the name of the corporation was legally changed to The Roman Catholic Episcopal Corporation of Antigonish. The name Antigonish will be used hereafter.
18 Fr James Michael Quinan (1846–1900) was educated at St Mary's College and the Grand Seminary of Quebec. A nephew of Fr James Quinan who served at Sydney, Quinan and his brother Dr Joseph Stanislaus Quinan (1856–1884) served at L'Ardoise, D'Escousse, and Arichat. He died in Montreal and was buried in the private vault of the Grey Nuns. "What a pity some of us were not able to be present at his funeral," Fr H.P. MacPherson lamented at the time of his death. "All are regretting that he was not buried in the diocese."
19 Tennyson, *Impressions of Cape Breton*, 190.
20 Cameron later confessed that he was actually "not at all as comfortable" on the mainland as he was in Arichat. John Cameron to H. Bludgett, 6 December 1880, ADA, BCP, series 3, sub-series 1, folder 53.
21 *The Casket*, 26 November 1896.
22 Bishop Cameron circular, 1879, ADA, BCP, series 10, sub-series, folder 1.
23 *Silver Jubilee of the Consecration of His Lordship Bishop Cameron*, 29.
24 von Arx, *Varieties of Ultramontanism*, 2.
25 Dolan, *In Search of American Catholicism*, 51.
26 Larkin, "Cardinal Paul Cullen," 62.
27 Raedts, "The Church as Nation State, 484–5.
28 "I congratulate you on the recent negotiations with Dr. MacKinnon," wrote Conroy in 1877. "At the same time you cannot rest on your oars until the resignation and change of residence shall have passed from the shadowy reign of promises to the solid world of facts." George Conroy to John Cameron, 4 August 1877, ADA, BCMP, series 1, sub-series 1, folder 10.
29 Barr, "'Imperium in Imperio,'" 650.
30 Barr, "'Imperium in Imperio,'" 645.
31 For an excellent account of Cardinal Cullen's influence on the global English-speaking Catholic community see Barr, *Ireland's Empire*.
32 *Silver Jubilee Booklet of the Consecration of His Lordship Bishop Cameron*, 36.
33 Johnston, *A History of the Catholic Church, II*, 416.
34 John Cameron to Patrick Power, 27 August 1870, ADA, BCP, series 2, sub-series 1, folder 28.
35 John Cameron to John Thompson, 30 August 1890, ADA, BCP, series 3, sub-series 1, folder 36; see also Ignatius, *Most Reverend John Cameron*.
36 MacLean, *Piety & Politics*, 182.

37 John Cameron to Patrick Power, 11 May 1880, ADA, BCP. For a review of the dispute between Archbishop Hannan and the Sisters of Charity see MacLean, *Piety & Politics*, 80–5; Hanington, *Every Popish Person*, 135–49.
38 J.L. MacDougall, "Cameron Remembered," 28 April 1910, ADA, BCP, series 1, sub-series 1.
39 MacInnes, "Highland 'heather' priests," 85–118.
40 Ronald MacGillivray to John Cameron, 8 January 1886, ADA, BCP, series 4, sub-series 1, solder 86.
41 MacLean, *Piety & Politics*, 76.
42 Fingard, "The 1880s: Paradoxes of Progress," 82.
43 Gwyn, *Excessive Expectations*, 233. See also, Brooks, "Outmigration from the Maritime Provinces," 31; Reid, *Six Crucial Decade*, 135; Thornton, "The Problem of Out-Migration." 3–34.
44 *The Aurora*, 25 April 1883.
45 John Cameron to Propagation of the Faith, 1886, ADA, BCP, series 2, sub-series 1, folder 33.
46 John Cameron to Propagation of the Faith, 1886, ADA, BCP, series 2, sub-series 1, folder 33.
47 John Cameron to Propagation of the Faith, November 1884, ADA, BCP, series 2, sub-series 1, folder 33.
48 John Cameron to John Thompson, 23 May 1887, ADA, BCP, series 2, sub-series 1, folder 36.
49 Campbell and Johnston, *Tracks Across the Landscape*, 30.
50 Sweetser, *The Maritime Provinces*, 161.
51 *The Aurora*, 8 August 1883.
52 Morgan, *Rise Again! Book 1*, 156.
53 Campbell, *With our Hearts and Hands*, 72; MacDonald, *Cape Breton Railways*, 56; John Cameron to John Thompson, 15 November 1886, ADA, BCP, series 3, sub-series 1, folder 36.
54 MacLeod, quoted in John Cameron to John Thompson, 11 November 1886, ADA, BCP, series 3, sub-series 1, folder 36.
55 John Cameron to John Thompson, 31 December 1889, ADA, BCP, series 3, sub-series 1, folder 36.
56 Acheson, "The National Policy," 4.
57 Sydney was incorporated as a town in 1886 and as a city in 1904. Brown, *The Coal Fields and Coal Trade*; Gesner, *The Industrial Resources of Nova Scotia*; Martell, "Early Coal Mining in Nova Scotia," 156–72.
58 Muise, "The Making of an Industrial Community," 80.
59 DeMont, *Coal Black Heart*, 101.

60 Hornsby, "Staple Trade, Subsistence Agriculture," 428.
61 *The Aurora*, 28 March 1883; *North Sydney Herald*, 28 March 1883.
62 Hornsby, "Staple Trade, Subsistence Agriculture," 427.
63 *North Sydney Herald*, 6 October 1886.
64 Other churches constructed in this period were Christmas Island (St Barra's 1883); and mission churches at Reserve Mines (1883), Giant's Lake (1887), and Ballantyne's Cove (1889).
65 *North Sydney Herald*, 22 July 1883; *The Aurora*, 22 October 1884.
66 Raedts, "The Church as Nation State," 492.
67 MacLean, *Piety & Politics*, 110.
68 Larkin, "Paul Cardinal Cullen," 82.
69 *The Aurora*, 18 June 1884; *North Sydney Herald*, 18 June 1884.
70 Muise, "The Making of an Industrial Community," 83.
71 James Quinan to John Cameron, 20 November 1883, ADA, BCP, series 2, sub-series 1. In 1874, Archbishop MacKinnon complained "this important point of church discipline has not been observed with all due strictness." See MacKinnon, *Practical Remarks on the Publication of Marriage Bands*.
72 Angus Chisholm to Propaganda Fide, 7 September 1882, Archives of the Congregation of the Propaganda Fide, Scritture riferite nei congressi, Canada, Volume 22.
73 MacLean, *Piety & Politics*, 110.
74 James Quinan to John Cameron, 28 Nov 1890, ADA, BCP, series 2, sub-series 1, folder 43.
75 *The Casket*, 1 September 1881.
76 John Cameron to John Thompson, 1 June 1889, ADA, BCMP, series 2, sub-series 1, folder 36.
77 Bishop Cameron circular, 1877, ADA, AAJP, series 10, sub-series 1, folder 1.
78 Paul A. Townend, *Father Mathew*, 1.
79 Johnston, *A History of the Catholic Church, II*, 115
80 On the LOC see MacDougall, *The Total Abstinence Movement*.
81 Shaw donated the proceeds from the sale to a monument-fund for the late Fr William Bernard. Fr William Bernard MacLeod (1798–1881) was considered the first native priest of the diocese. Monies were raised for a monument over his grave and a stained-glass memorial window in the sanctuary. On the sale of the Fr Mathew Society property at Arisaig see *The Aurora*, 7 May 1884.
82 There were other temperance societies like the Society of St. Joseph at Stellarton. In March 1885, the society enrolled "thirty young lads" who promised to abstain from alcohol and tobacco. See *The Aurora*, 25 March 1885.

83 On the founding of the CND see Simpson, *Marguerite Bourgeoys and the Congregation of Notre-Dame*. On Louisbourg see Johnston, *Religious Life at Louisbourg*.

84 On Francis Collins see Alfred, "Francis Collins," 51–66.

85 Pope, "Antigonish," 44. See also, *Mount Saint Bernard Centennial*.

86 Ronald MacDonald to John Cameron, 21 October 1883, BCP, series 2, sub-series 1.

87 Campbell, *With our Hearts and Hands*, 73.

88 Coleman, "The Religious Roots of Female Education in Sydney," 39.

89 Stella Maris Parish, *Stella Maris Church, Pictou County*, 7.

90 Andrew, "Selling education," 15.

91 Sister St Lucilla to John Cameron, 21 September 1887, BCP, series 2, sub-series 1, folder 49.

92 On this dispute see Hanington, *Every Popish Person*, 135–49; MacLean, *Piety & Politics*, 80–5.

93 *The Aurora*, 30 May 1883.

94 *The Aurora*, 9 January 1884.

95 By the end of the decade some forty-five women from the Maritime provinces had joined the CND. See Vautour, "Maritime Entrants to the Congregation of Notre Dame," 66.

96 MacDonald, "Entering the Convent," 88.

97 Chisholm was followed in 1877 by: Mary Ann MacLeod of Dunvegan, Inverness County: Elizabeth Thompson of Cloverville, Antigonish County; Catherine Jane Chisholm of St Andrews (the sister of Fr Colin Chisholm); and Mary Isabella Cameron of Upper South River, Antigonish County. Isabella Cameron also died at the Montreal motherhouse in 1882, as did her sister Mary J. in 1893. See Ormond, *A Century Ago*, 68–74.

98 Vautour, "Maritime Entrants to the Congregation of Notre Dame," 157.

99 Xavier, "Educational Legislation in Nova Scotia," 72.

100 Cameron to Joseph Reze, 8 November 1871, ADA, BCP, series 2, sub-series 1, folder 28.

101 Perry, *The Grand Regulator*, 131.

102 John Cameron to John Thompson, 17 November 1881, ADA, BCP, series 3, sub-series 1, folder 36.

103 John Cameron to John Thompson, 13 February 1882, ADA, BCP, series 2, sub-series 1, folder 36. In another letter to Thompson, Cameron was reminded that the CND had laboured for two hundred years without "being asked by the State to undergo such examinations." See John Cameron to John Thompson, 13 February 1882, ADA, BCP, series 2, sub-series 1, folder 36.

104 Cameron, *For the People*, 78; Coleman, "The Religious Roots of Female Education in Sydney," 10.
105 Cameron, *For the People*, 78.
106 Cameron, *For the People*, 68.
107 John Cameron to H. Bludgett, 6 December 1880, ADA, BCP, series 3, sub-series 1, folder 53; Cameron, *For the People*, 66–7; Johnston, *A History of the Catholic Church, II*, 504–11.
108 Shook, *Catholic Post-Secondary Education*, 80.
109 John Cameron to the Propagation of the Faith, 13 November 1881, ADA, BCP, series 2, sub-series 1, folder 33.
110 Cameron, *For the People*, 75; *The Aurora*, 13 April 1882.
111 Shook, *Catholic Post-Secondary Education in Canada*, 80.
112 See Waite, "Annie and the Bishop," 605–16; Gillis "Sir John Thompson and Bishop Cameron," 87–97.
113 Their introduction was described by Lady Aberdeen in her diary. See Saywell, *The Canadian Journal of Lady Aberdeen*, 180–3.
114 For information on Sir John S.D. Thompson see Sutherland, "A Fond but Extravagant Farewell"; Waite, "Sir John Sparrow David Thompson; Waite, *The Man from Halifax*.
115 Discussing the Cameron family, Ewan Cameron wrote: "Neither did your father or uncles, except your uncle Ewan, belong to your church until they came to Nova Scotia. Ewan Cameron to John Cameron, 15 June 1877, ADA, fonds 8, series 10, sub-series 1.
116 Gillis "Sir John Thompson and Bishop Cameron," 88.
117 Waite, *The Man from Halifax*, 72.
118 Miller, *Incidents in the Political Career*, 3.
119 John Cameron to Angus MacGillivray, 27 November 1877, ADA, BCP, series 2, sub-series 1, folder 48.
120 Ronald MacGillivray to John Cameron, 11 December 1877, ADA, BCP, series 2, sub-series 1, folder 48. Fr Ronald MacGillivray (1836–1892) was a noted scholar. He died while bathing at Arisaig.
121 Ronald MacGillivray to John Cameron, 21 December 1877, ADA, BCP, series 2, sub-series 1, folder 48.
122 Waite, *The Man from Halifax*, 75
123 *Halifax Morning Chronicle*, 11 December 1877.
124 Cameron to John Thompson, 10 July 1881, ADA, BCP, series 2, sub-series 1, folder 36.
125 MacLean, "Bishop John Cameron – Political Prelate," 93.
126 Cameron to John Thompson, 4 March 1881, ADA, BCP, series 2, sub-series 1, folder 36.

127 Waite, *The Man from Halifax*, 82.
128 Ibid, 112–13.
129 James Quinan to John Cameron, 20 Nov 1883, ADA, BCP, series 2, sub-series 1, folder 43.
130 John L. MacDougall "The Late Bishop Cameron," ADA, BCP, series 2, sub-series 1, folder 30.
131 *North Sydney Herald*, 18 April 1883.
132 Ronald MacDonald to John Cameron, 6 May 1889, BCP, series 2, sub-series 1, folder 28.
133 On MacDonald's attempts to confiscate the fiddles of Mabou see McDavid, "The Fiddle Burning Priest of Mabou," 115–36.
134 Neil McNeil to Angus MacIsaac, 28 April 1883, ADA, AAJP, series 10, sub-series 1, folder 1.
135 Rankin, "Father Kenneth J. MacDonald," 112–13.
136 Nilsen, "The Role of the Priest," 185.
137 Ordained in 1837, Msgr Neil MacLeod (1807-1891) ministered in Arisaig (1837–38) and at East Bay (1838–91). One of the early native priests of the diocese, he was a great promoter of St F.X. See *The Casket*, 19 November 1891.
138 *The Aurora*, 20 February 1884.
139 J.C. Mcfin to John Cameron, 11 August 1890, ADA, BCP, series 3, sub-series 2, series 2.
140 MacLean, *Piety & Politics*, 79.
141 John Cameron to Father Bourgeois, 23 November 1886, ADA, BCP, series 2, sub-series 1, folder 28.
142 John Cameron to John Thompson, 13 April 1881, ADA, BCP, series 3, sub-series 1, folder 36.
143 D.A. Chisholm, "Answers to Bishop Cameron's Queries," ADA, BCP, series 3, sub-series 1, folder 66.
144 Liguori, *Preparation for Death*, 1.
145 MacDonald, *A Bit of Autobiography*, 23
146 MacDonald, *A Bit of Autobiography*, 24.
147 *The Aurora*, 23 July 1884.
148 *The Aurora*, 26 September 1883; 19 November 1884; 2 July 1884.
149 Bishop Cameron, the consecrating prelate, was assisted by Bishop Sweeny of Saint John and Bishop James Rogers of Chatham, while Archbishop Michael Hannan of Halifax presided. See the *Pictou Standard*, 22 August 1881 and *The Casket*, 24 August 1881.
150 Ronald MacDonald to John Cameron, 19 January 1884, BCP, series 2,

sub-series 1. On the Harbour Grace Affair see Collins, *Harbour Grace Affray*; Keough, "Contested Terrains," 29–70.

151 Ronald MacDonald to John Cameron, 27 November 1881, BCP, series 2, sub-series 1.

152 Miller, *Incidents in the Life*, 14.

153 Waite, *The Man from Halifax*, 130.

154 John Cameron to Joseph Chisholm, 12 October 1885, ADA, BCP, series 2, sub-series 1, folder 48.

155 *Yarmouth Herald*, 30 September 1885.

156 Joseph Pope, *Correspondence of Sir John A. MacDonald*, 353.

157 Hugh Cameron to John Cameron, 7 March 1885, ADA, BCP, series 2, sub-series 1, folder 48.

158 Alexander MacIntosh (1831-1907) was a graduate of St F.X and the Pennsylvania Medical School. His brother, Msgr Daniel Joseph MacIntosh, was vicar-general of the diocese form 1913 to 1925. Active within the local community, he helped raise money for a grave marker to Fr Colin Grant (1784–1839) at the Old Burial Ground in Lower South River. See *The Casket*, 1 April 1886.

159 Alexander MacIntosh to John Cameron, 28 September 1885, ADA, BCP, sub-series 1, folder 48. See also MacLean, *Piety & Politics*, 95.

160 Waite, *The Man from Halifax*, 138.

161 MacLean, *Piety & Politics*, 139.

162 *Toronto Globe*, 28 September 1885.

163 Waite, *The Man from Halifax*, 139.

164 Ronald MacGillivray to John Cameron, 9 October 1885, ADA, BCP, series 2, sub-series 1, folder 48.

165 *Halifax Chronicle*, 3 October 1885.

166 Waite, *The Man from Halifax*, 140.

167 Bishop Cameron circular, 30 September 1885, ADA, BCP, series 1, sub-series 1, folder 48.

168 Ronald MacGillivray to Angus MacGillivray, October 1885 (copy), ADA, BCP, series 2, sub-series 1, folder 48.

169 Ronald MacGillivray to Angus MacGillivray, October 1885 (copy), ADA, BCP, series 2, sub-series 1, folder 48.

170 Waite, *The Man from Halifax*, 140.

171 A native of Heatherton parish, Fr John Joseph Chisholm (1840–1909), was ordained by Bishop J.J. Lynch of Toronto, and first served as an assistant at St Patrick's in Montreal before returning home. See *The Casket*, 3 June 1909.

172 John Joseph Chisholm to John Cameron, 12 October 1885, ADA, BCP, series 2, sub-series 1, folder 48.

CHAPTER TWO

1 Boyle, *Democracy's Second Chance*, 137.
2 *The Casket*, 15 May 1890.
3 Diary of Angus J. Chisholm, 3 December 1890, ADA, AAJP, series 5, sub-series1, folder 19.
4 *The Casket*, 12 May 1892.
5 Diary of Angus J. Chisholm, 3 December 1890, ADA, AAJP, series 5, sub-series1, folder 19.
6 Diary of Angus J. Chisholm, 29 December 1890, ADA, AAJP, series 5, sub-series1, folder 19.
7 Fr. M.A. MacPherson to Daniel Chisholm, 3 Dec 1896, STFXUA, (Daniel Chisholm Papers, hereafter DCP), RG 5/7 /590.
8 *The Casket*, 10 September 1891.
9 Frank, "The Cape Breton Coal Industry," 11.
10 For an interesting examination of the Whitney conglomerate and the Government of Nova Scotia see Fergusson, *Hon. W.S. Fielding*, 126–9 and 234–8.
11 Frank, "The Cape Breton Coal Industry," 11.
12 Beck, *Politics of Nova Scotia, Volume Two*, 10-11.
13 *Globe and Mail*, 13 October, 1900; *The Casket*, 31 August 1899.
14 *Evening Telegram*, 13 March 1903.
15 *Trade Review*, 14 November 1903.
16 Ronald Caplan, "With Frank Jackson at 99," 45.
17 Reeves, "Newfoundlanders in the 'Boston States,'" 43.
18 Beaton, "Housing People and Place," 134.
19 Frank, "The Miner's Financier," 137.
20 Parr, "Women Workers," 79–88.
21 *Evening Telegram*, 21 September 1905.
22 *The Casket*, 28 June 1894. See also, Goodwin, *Immaculate Conception Parish*, 20; Johnston, *Saint Anne's Parish Glace Bay*.
23 *The Casket*, 13 March 1890.
24 *The Casket*, 8 January 1890.
25 *The Casket*, 17 August 1899.
26 Elliott, *I will be called John*, 21.
27 Leo XIII, *Encyclical Letter*, 5.
28 *The Casket*, 25 November 1897.

29 *The Casket*, 15 October 1898.
30 *The Casket*, 14 July 1898.
31 Leo XIII, *Encyclical Letter*, 33.
32 *The Casket*, 27 February 1890; see also McKay, "'By Wisdom, Wile or War,'" 13–62.
33 Boyle, *Democracy's Second Chance*, 3–16.
34 *The Casket*, 18 June 1891.
35 *The Casket*, 3 April 1890.
36 Godwin, *Immaculate Conception Parish*, 18–19.
37 St Peter's (St Peter's, 1891); Larry's River, Guysborough County (St Peter's, 1891); the short-lived Pictou County industrial community of Bridgeville-Ferrona (St Margaret's, 1892); West Lake Ainslie (St John the Baptist, 1893); Brook Village (St John the Baptist,1896) and Lochaber (St Patrick's, 1896).
38 When Fr Alexander Chisholm (1843–1911) died, Bishop Alexander "Sandy" MacDonald wrote: "I owed him a great deal. He was in his prime when I came to Antigonish. He taught me, in translating Latin in to English, to take account of idiomatic terms of thought and expression, and to choose my words with care ... Few men in his day knew the niceties of classical Latin as he knew them, and few persons reared in Nova Scotia could write English as he wrote it." See *The Casket*, 31 August 1911.
39 *MacLean, Piety & Politics*, 122.
40 MacLean, *Piety & Politics*, 121.
41 D.J. Rankin, "Rev. Dr. Dan A. Chisholm," unpublished paper, 1947, STFXUA, William X. Edwards papers (hereafter WXEP), MG 45/2/192.
42 *The Casket*, 27 February 1890.
43 McGowan, *The Waning of the Green*, 93.
44 McGreevy, *American Jesuits*, 111–15.
45 *The Casket*, 24 and 31 July 1890.
46 *The Casket*, 8 October 1891.
47 *The Casket*, 24 September 1896.
48 *The Casket*, 10 April 1890.
49 James Quinan to Daniel Chisholm, 12 November 1895, STFXUA, DCP, RG 5/7 /771.
50 *The Casket*, 8 December 1892.
51 Alexander MacDonald to John J. MacNeil, 9 June 1905, BIA, JJMP, MG 13, 48 (F2).
52 *The Casket,* 7 January 1892.
53 *The Casket,* 17 September 1891.
54 Gibson, *Traditional Gaelic Bagpiping*, 244.

55 Diary of Angus J. Chisholm, 8 December 1890, ADA, AAJP, series 5, sub-series 1, folder 19.
56 Comiskey, *My Heart's Best Wishes*, 180.
57 *The Casket*, 19 June 1890.
58 *The Casket*, 23 July 1896.
59 MacLean, *The Casket*, 132. For information on John Boyd (who operated the paper until 1861) see Stanley-Blackwell and MacLean, *Historic Antigonish*, 82; Johnston, *A History of the Catholic Church*, II, 228, 270, 289.
60 *The Casket*, 20 March 1890.
61 *The Casket*, 17 April 1890.
62 *The Casket*, 20 March 1890.
63 MacLean, *Piety & Politics*, 132.
64 MacLean, *Piety & Politics*, 118.
65 Cameron, *For the People*, 85.
66 MacLean, *Piety & Politics*, 133.
67 Angus J. Chisholm diary, August 1891, ADA, AAJP, series 5, sub-series 1, folder 19.
68 MacLean, *The Casket*, 62.
69 Neil McNeil to Joseph Wall, 7 January 1895.
70 Diary of Angus J. Chisholm, 14 November 1890, ADA, AAJP, series 5, sub-series, folder 19.
71 Angus J. Chisholm to John Cameron, 31 March 1890, ADA, BCP, series 1, sub-series 1, folder 14.
72 Waite, *The Man from Halifax*, 347.
73 John Thompson to John Cameron, 23 November 1892, ADA, BCP, series 2, sub-series 1, folder 46.
74 MacLean, *Piety & Politics*, 14. [It would be helpful to give a bit of the backstory of the "revolutionaries who had disturbed Rome in the 1850s" here.]
75 James Quinan to Daniel Chisholm, 20 Dec 1895, STFXUA, DCP, RG 5/7/775.
76 *The Aurora*, 3 September 1884.
77 MacLean, "Hector's Cargo," 125.
78 John Cameron to John Thompson, 3 March 1879, ADA, BCP, series 3, sub-series 1, folder 36.
79 Little, "A Fine, Hardy, Good-Looking Race of People," 22.
80 D.C. Gillis to Daniel Chisholm, 14 December 1896, STFXUA, DCP, RG 5/7/186.
81 *The Casket*, 20 August 1891 & 16 January 1896.

82 For more on this period at the Scots College Rome see McCluskey, *The Scots College Rome*, 88–92.
83 Ronald MacDonald to John Cameron, 12 February 1885, ADA, BCP, series 2, sub-series 1, folder 32.
84 *The Casket*, 25 April 1891.
85 Patrick Nicholson to John Lorne Campbell, 16 January 1950, STFXUA, Patrick J. Nicholson Papers (hereafter PJNP) MG 2-90-1182.
86 *The Casket*, 29 November 1894.
87 *The Casket*, 29 November 1894.
88 *The Aurora*, 20 August 1884.
89 *The Casket*, 4 September 1890.
90 *The Casket*, 4 September 1890.
91 Diary of Angus J. Chisholm, 23 November 1890, ADA, Fonds 8, series 5, sub-series, folder 19.
92 MacInnes, "The Acadian People," 58.
93 *The Casket*, 4 September 1890.
94 *The Casket*, 17 March 1892.
95 Donald J. Cameron to John Cameron, 21 April 1891, ADA, BCP, series 1, sub-series 2, folder 3. Sadly, Cameron had died by the spring of 1893.
96 Fr Guillaume (William) LeBlanc (1836–1907) was a distinguished Acadian genealogist. See *The Casket*, 17 January 1907.
97 MacInnes, "The Acadian People," 58.
98 Lotz and Welton, *Father Jimmy*, 12.
99 MacInnes, "The Acadian People," 60.
100 Chiasson, "Fiset, Pierre," 341–2; Lotz, *The Lichen Factor*, 115.
101 See MacLeod, "Words Apart."
102 Tuck, *Churches of Nova Scotia*, 98.
103 On Ouellet see Morisset, "Ouellet, David."
104 Work on the interior of the church continued until 1893. See Chiasson, "Fiset, Pierre," 342.
105 Pacifique, *Souvenir of the Micmac Tercentenary Celebration*, 82.
106 On Fr Pierre Maillard see Burns, "The Abbé Maillard," 13–22; Johnson, "Maillard, Pierre."
107 Poliandri, *First Nations, Identity, and Reserve Life*, 206–7.
108 In 1960 Fr A.A. Johnston wrote that the altar was of French construction and was likely brought from France to the Récollet mission at St Peter's, that it was hidden in the woods in 1758 (or 1745) when the English captured Louisbourg, and that the Mi'kmaq found it and presented it to Fr MacDougall. As Johnston noted, however, *The Aurora* mentioned that the altar was located in the St Anne's Church in 1884. Sometime later, it

was moved to vestry at the church in Johnstown and it was then, Johnston claimed, that the painting of the dead Christ was affixed to its front. In July 2015, the altar was returned to Chapel Island. See Johnston, *Sacred Heart Parish,* 11.

109 Born in Arisaig, Scotland, Fr John MacDougall (1823–1891) was the fourth native of the diocese to enter the seminary. Ordained in 1860 by Bishop MacKinnon, he spent his entire career at Red Islands. His successor changed the name of the parish to Johnstown in his honour.

110 *The Casket*, 6 August 1891.

111 *The Casket*, 4 August 1892.

112 *The Casket*, 8 July 1897.

113 *The Casket*, 5 August 1897.

114 Parnaby, "The Cultural Economy," 70.

115 Walls, *No Need of a* chief, 57. See also, Wicken, *The Colonization of Mi'kmaw Memory*, 52.

116 John Denny to John Cameron, 30 March 1892, ADA, BCP, series 1, sub-series 1, folder 18.

117 John Denny to John Cameron, 30 March 1892, ADA, BCP, series 1, sub-series 1, folder 18.

118 *The Casket*, 10 September 1891.

119 Cameron, *For the People*, 87.

120 Charles MacKay to Daniel C, 11 March 1895, STFXUA, DCP, RG 5/7/483.

121 *The Casket*, 9 October 1890.

122 George B. Oland to A.A. Johnston, 4 July 1962, ADA, AAJP, series 3, sub-series 2, folder 6.

123 Lilian MacDonald to Daniel Chisholm, 8 July 1896, STFXUA, DCP, RG 5/7 /1214.

124 Cameron, *For the People*, p.96.

125 *The Casket*, 24 June 1897. The first graduates were Florence MacDonald (Bailey's Brook, Pictou County), Mary Bisset (River Bourgeois), Margaret MacDougall (Antigonish), and Lillian MacDonald (Antigonish).

126 Cameron, *"And Martha Served,"* 4.

127 Cameron, *"And Martha Served,"* 5.

128 Sister St Stanislaus to John Cameron, 17 May 1894, ADA, BCP, series 1, sub-series 2, folder 3.

129 Caroline McNamara to Daniel Chisholm, 1 October 1894, STFXUA, DCP, RG 5/7/524.

130 A.L. MacDonald to Daniel Chisholm, 30 Sept 1894, STFXUA, DCP, RG 5/7/341.

131 Allan MacAdam to Daniel Chisholm, 19 September 1894, STFXUA, DCP, RG 5/7/300.
132 Betsy MacAdam to Daniel Chisholm, 26 Sept 1894, STFXUA, DCP, RG 5/7/303.
133 Bishop Cameron circular, 22 May 1894, ADA, BCP, series 6, sub-series 0.
134 Lauchlin MacPherson to Daniel Chisholm, 8 August 1894, STFXUA, DCP, RG 5/7/580.
135 Cameron, *"And Martha Served,"* 7.
136 Mother M. Fidelis to Daniel Chisholm, 3 September 1896, STFXUA, DCP, RG 5/7/1073.
137 Neil MacDonald to Daniel Chisholm, 23 March 1896, STFXUA, DCP, RG 5/7/385.
138 Maura, *The Sisters of Charity*, 35–6. The three senior Charities were Sister Rita Jones, Sister Gregory Lyons, and Sister Agatha Beaton.
139 J.H. Gillis, unpublished paper on the Sisters of St Martha, 1970, 5, ADA, AAJP.
140 Congregation of Sisters of St Martha, *Sisters of St. Martha*, 5.
141 Cameron, *"And Martha Served,"* 11.
142 *The Casket*, 9 March 1899.
143 "Extract from a Diary kept by a St. F.X. Student, Antigonish N.S., during the Scholastic Year 1898-1899," 5 and 6 March 1899, ADA, BCP, series 6, sub-series 0.
144 See Crunican, *Priests and Politicians.*
145 Morton, "Manitoba Schools," 10.
146 Waite, *The Man from Halifax*, 397.
147 Beck, *Pendulum of Power*, 74.
148 Crunican, "Father Lacombe's Strange Mission," 57–71.
149 John Cameron to John Thompson, 30 April 1894, ADA, BCP, fonds 3, series 2, sub-series 1, folder 36.
150 John Cameron to John Thompson, 30 April 1894, ADA, BCP, fonds 3, series 2, sub-series 1, folder 36.
151 MacLean, *Piety & Politics*, 145.
152 John Costigan to John Cameron, 12 December 1894, ADA, BCP, fonds 3, series 2, sub-series 1, folder 46.
153 Waite, *The Man from Halifax*, 424–5.
154 MacLean, *Piety & Politics*, 146.
155 MacLean, *Piety & Politics*, 147.
156 *The Casket*, 25 April 1895.

157 McNeil was not happy about the appointment. "They have simply blundered," he wrote to his sister. See Neil McNeil to Christanna MacDonald, 9 September, 1895, ADA, AAJP, series 10, sub-series 1, folder 19.
158 McNeil was consecrated by Bishop John Cameron, Bishop James Charles MacDonald (Charlottetown), and the Bishop of St John's Newfoundland. The sermon was delivered by Bishop Michael Francis Howley, his predecessor at Harbour Grace.
159 James Rogers to John Cameron, 6 October 1895, ADA, fonds 3, series 2, sub-series 1, folder 10.
160 Cornelius O'Brien to John Cameron, 23 January 1896, ADA, BCP, series 2, sub-series 1, folder 46. Tupper defeated the Liberal (and future premier of Nova Scotia) George Murray by 500 votes.
161 *The Casket*, 13 February 1896.
162 *The Casket*, 9 April 1896.
163 Fay, *Canadian Catholics*, 133.
164 MacLean, *Piety & Politics*, 151.
165 MacLean, *Piety & Politics*, 155.
166 Perin, *Rome in Canada,* 4.
167 MacLean, *Piety & Politics*, 155. See also, Skelton, *Life and* Letters, 484–5.
168 One Mabou parishioner "went out" while the circular was being read, while the other left once it was finished. John Francis MacMaster to John Cameron, 22 February 1897, ADA, BCP, series 3, sub-series 1, folder 76.
169 *The Casket*, 25 June 1896.
170 *The Casket*, 3 July 1896.
171 The men were asked to sign a letter confessing that they "did deliberately turn [their] backs to the altar, and with contemptuous disgrace of the sanctity of the place and the solemnity of the occasion, did walk out of the church, to the grave scandal of all who were present and of all who, though absent, were sure to be informed of our misbehavior."
172 John Francis MacMaster to John Cameron, February 22 1897, ADA, BCP, series 3, sub-series 1, folder 76.
173 John Cameron to Roderick Grant, 2 March 1897, ADA, BCP, series 3, sub-series 1, folder 76.
174 Roderick Grant to John Cameron June 1897, ADA, BCP, series 3, sub-series 1, folder 76.
175 Parishioners of Heatherton to John Cameron, 16 February 1898, ADA, BCP, series 3, sub-series 1, folder 76.
176 Perin, *Rome in Canada*, 64–5.
177 See Rusak, "The Canadian 'Concordat,'" 209–34.

178 MacLean, *Piety & Politics*, 158.
179 John Cameron to Diomede Falconio, 1898, ADA, BCP, series 2, sub-series 1, folder 76.
180 *Eastern Chronicle*, 9 September 1897.
181 Diomede Falconio to John Cameron, 13 May 1900, ADA, BCP, series 1, sub-series 1, folder 3.
182 Donald Chisholm to John Cameron, 7 June 1900, ADA, BCP, series 1, sub-series 1, folder 3.
183 MacLean, *Piety & Politics*, 159.

CHAPTER THREE

1 Howell, "The 1900s," 156–7.
2 On the Social Gospel Movement see Bland, "The Social Gospel." 381–99.
3 See Forbes, "Prohibition," 11–36.
4 *Eastern Chronicle*, 18 January 1894.
5 Archibald Chisholm of Salt Springs, Antigonish County, had 11,000 volts pass through his body while working in New Haven, Connecticut, and managed to hold on to life for nine days before succumbing to severe burns. *The Casket*, 15 July 1909.
6 Ronald Beaton to H.P. MacPherson, 29 August 1910, STFXUA, HPMP, RG 5/9/588.
7 *The Casket*, 17 July 1902.
8 MacLean, "The Early History of St. Michael's Parish," 114.
9 *The Casket*, 27 June 1901.
10 *The Casket*, 8 June 1905.
11 Similar "laboratories" were organized in the Annapolis Valley. By 1911 the Nova Scotia Experimental Fruit Station was opened at Kentville. See Gwyn, *Comfort Me with Apples*.
12 *The Casket*, 27 August 1903.
13 Candow and Corbin, *How Deep is the Ocean?*, 189.
14 MacEwan, *Miners and Steelworkers*, 8; Caplan, "The Steel Boom Comes to Sydney," 35.
15 *The Glasgow Herald*, 9 June 1899.
16 *The Casket*, 2 August 1900.
17 *The Casket*, 4 September 1902. Three "splendid altars" were made to order from a company in Paris and were the most modern in the diocese.
18 Msgr Joseph Murphy (1862–1944) served as pastor of Holy Cross Parish, Conception Bay, from 1900 until 1907. He and Fr Ronald MacDonald

studied together at St F.X. and they remained close friends. See *Evening Herald*, 27 August 1900; Crawley, "Off to Sydney," 44.

19 Petition of the Parish of St Ann's to Bishop Cameron, 19 November 1906, ADA, BCP, series 1, folder 3.

20 J.W. MacIsaac to Alexander Thompson, March 1901, STFXUA, Alexander Thompson Papers (hereafter ATP), RG 5/8/936.

21 *The Casket*, 17 October 1901.

22 *The Casket*, 11 January 1900.

23 Migliore and DiPierro, *Italian Lives*, 17.

24 Alexander Thompson to A.J.G. MacEachern, 31 January 1901, STFXUA, ATP, RG 5/8/796.

25 "I was in the extreme north of Canada, on the shores of the Atlantic; I had just been visiting a colony of Hungarian artisans working in the iron foundries of Sidney [sic] (Nova Scotia). Although it was a long way back to Chicago, I willingly undertook the tedious journey – occupying three days and three nights – in order to comply with the complimentary request." See Luskod, *The Inner* Life, 181–2.

26 MacLean, *Piety & Politics*, 183.

27 Fr Neil MacKinnon (1842–1907). Born in Grand River, he was educated at St Dunstan's College and the Grand Seminary of Montreal. Besides serving the Italian community in Montreal, Fr MacKinnon taught at Fordham University and is buried on its grounds. See Fr Art O'Shea, *Prince Edward Island Priests Away.*

28 A.S. MacKenzie, "Father Viola," unpublished paper, 27 May 1962, ADA, AAJP, series 2, sub-series 1.

29 A.S. MacKenzie, "Father Viola," unpublished paper, 27 May 1962, ADA, AAJP, series 2, sub-series 1.

30 Heron, *Working in* Steel, 77.

31 *Sydney Post*, 9 March 1903.

32 MacDonald, "A Coal Town Fights," 24–5, 58–63.

33 Moses M. Coady, "Coal Mining in Cape Breton," (unpublished paper, 1953), STFXUA, Moses Michael Coady Papers (hereafter MMCP), RG 30–3/18/55, 6.

34 Beaton, "Housing, People and Place," 156. The newspapers associated the "shacks" with skullduggery, and Austrians and Italians were often singled out. *St John Daily Sun*, 11 November 1901.

35 *Sydney Daily Post*, 6 June 1901. See also Heron, *Working in Steel*, 81.

36 *The Casket*, 21 February 1901.

37 J.W. MacIsaac to Alexander Thompson, April 1901, STFXUA, ATP, RG 5/8/937.

38 The land for Holy Redeemer in Whitney Pier, for example, was donated by a Captain Carlin of Sydney. See *The Casket*, 5 July 1900.
39 *The Casket*, 16 October 1902.
40 *The Casket*, 16 October 1902.
41 Boyle, *Justice through Power*, 195.
42 *The Sydney Record*, 7 May 1901.
43 MacDonald, *Historic Glace Bay*, 101.
44 *Sydney Daily Post*, 15 June 1902.
45 *Sydney Post*, 16 February 1907.
46 *The Casket*, 14 July 1904.
47 *The Casket*, 22 December 1904.
48 *The Casket*, 29 December 1904.
49 Donald MacAdam to Alexander Thompson, 28 December 1903, STFXUA, ATP, RG 5/8/4272.
50 James Quinan to John Cameron, 1893, ADA, BCP, series 1, sub-series 1, folder 3; *The Casket*, 6 February 1902.
51 See St Joseph's Hospital, *Golden Gleanings*.
52 *The Casket*, 23 January 1902.
53 *The Casket*, 3 July 1902.
54 *The Casket*, 31 July 1902.
55 St Joseph's Hospital, *Twenty-Fifth Anniversary*, 16–17.
56 MacLeod, "Colliers, Colliery Safety," 247. See also McKay, "Strikes in the Maritimes," 214.
57 *Daily News* (St John's), 2 April 1904.
58 McSween to Alexander Thompson, 27 June 1903, STFXUA, ATP, RG 5/8/2552.
59 *Sydney Post*, 30 January 1907.
60 *The Casket*, 5 May 1904.
61 Cornelius Connolly to H.P. MacPherson, 30 January 1909, STFXUA, HPMP, RG 5/9/2141.
62 *The Casket*, 5 December 1907.
63 *The Casket*, 19 December 1901.
64 McKay, "Strikes in the Maritimes," 243.
65 *The Casket*, 30 June 1904.
66 *Halifax Herald*, 20 February 1907.
67 *The Casket*, 7 October 1909.
68 *The Casket*, 16 September 1909.
69 John Mellor attributes the desire to dump the PWA for the UMW partially to the increase of foreign workers into the colliery towns – workers who were used to more rigorous union representation. There is evidence to

suggest that this was the prevailing opinion at the time. Mellor, *The Company Store*, 24.

70 Frank, *J.B. McLachlan*, 76–7.

71 Frank, *J.B. McLachlan*, 89.

72 MacEwan, *Miners and Steelworkers*, 23.

73 *The Casket*, 8 July 1909.

74 Frank, *J.B. McLachlan*, 99.

75 *Boston Daily Globe*, 7 July 1900; *Sydney Daily Post*, 11 September 1909.

76 *Boston Daily Globe*, 3 July 1909.

77 MacLean, *Piety & Politics*, 126.

78 Alex Dick to John Cameron, 16 March 1909, ADA, BCP, series 3, sub-series 1, folder 77.

79 Vice-President DOMCO to John Cameron, 14 September 1909. ADA, BCP, series 3, sub-series 1, folder 77.

80 William F. Kiely to John Cameron, 8 November 1909, ADA, BCP, series 3, sub-series 1, folder 77.

81 Alex Dick to John Cameron, 16 March 1909, ADA, BCP, series 3, sub-series 1, folder 77.

82 J.A.M. Gillis to Alexander Thompson 21 July 1909 (copy), ADA, BCP, series 3, sub-series 1, folder 65.

83 *The Casket*, 12 August 1909.

84 *The Casket*, 30 June 1909.

85 *The Casket*, 10 June 1909.

86 Mellor, *The Company Store*, 56.

87 Town of Dominion Council Minutes, 30 July 1909, STFXUA, WXEP, MG 45/2/394.

88 Charles W. MacDonald to John Cameron, ADA, BCP, series 3, sub-series 1, folder 77.

89 The "Captain Almon" is likely Lt Colonel William Bruce Almon (1875–1961). A native of Halifax, Almon served with the Royal Canadian Artillery until his retirement in 1940, and was a member of the Canadian Expeditionary Force that was sent to Russia in 1919.

90 John Mellor noted that the priest "had been away at the time" but argued that few "believed his denial." Mellor, *The Company Store*, 58.

91 In December 1912, MacDonald was feted by his parishioners, at which time they presented him with a "purse of gold." See *The Casket*, 19 December 1912.

92 Charles W. MacDonald to John Cameron, ADA, BCP, series 3, sub-series 1, folder 77.

93 Frank, "Tradition and Culture," 208; McKay, "Strikes in the Maritimes," 43.
94 Donovan, *The Forgotten* World, 43.
95 McKay, "Strikes in the Maritimes," 228.
96 D.C. Gillis to John Cameron, 27 August 1909, ADA, BCP, series 3, sub-series 1, folder 77.
97 MacEwan, *Miners and Steelworkers*, 31.
98 Steele, "The Big Strike," 11.
99 John Fraser to H.P. MacPherson, 17 September 1909, ADA, AAJP.
100 John Fraser to H.P. MacPherson, 17 September 1909, ADA, AAJP.
101 *The Sydney Post*, 10 August 1909.
102 This is an undated, unsigned letter sent to P.J. Nicholson after his transfer from St Joseph's Parish, Sydney to St F.X. in March 1961. The writer was from Dorchester Massachusetts. STFXUA, PJNP, MG 2/1/221.
103 Mellor, *The Company Store*, 51–2.
104 Another source for this myth was a 1977 honours thesis at Mount Allison University. The author quoted an oral interview conducted years after the event. The interviewee was clearly mistaken. See Trenholm, "Radical Labour."
105 Fr John Anthony Fraser (1851–1918) was a native of St Andrews who served multiple parishes during his career. Considered one of the most active priests in the diocese, Fraser was described as "gifted with excellent abilities and ... naturally vigorous and full of energy." See *The Casket*, 25 April 1918.
106 MacDonald, "The Succession," 10.
107 A.E. Monbourquette to Alexander Thompson, 5 May 1902, STFXUA, ATP, RG 5/8/1251.
108 Ronald MacDonald to Alexander Thompson, 6 August 1905, STFXUA, ATP, RG 5/8/721-722.
109 D.J. Rankin, "Reverend Dr. Dan J. Chisholm," unpublished paper, 1949, ADA, AAJP, series 4 sub-series 1.
110 Cameron, *For the People*, 111.
111 Cameron, *For the People*, 118–19.
112 Alexander Thompson to John Cameron, 6 April 1899, STFXUA, WXEP, MG 45/2/157.
113 Alexander Thompson to Andrew Carnegie, 18 March 1901, STFXUA, ATP, RG 5/8/130; Alexander Thompson to Neil MacDonald, April 1901, STFXUA, ATP, RG 5/8/4394.
114 Cameron, *For the People*, 136.

115 Alexander Thompson to R.S. Cronage, 30 October 1900, STFXUA, ATP, RG 5/8/3907-3908. See also Cameron, *For the People*, 118.

116 A.J.G. McEachern to Alexander Thompson, 31 July 1905, STFXUA, ATP, RG 5/8/868.

117 William B. MacDonald to Alexander Thompson, 11 October 1901, STFXUA, ATP, RG 5/8/798.

118 MacLean, *Piety & Politics*, 184.

119 One erroneous report noted that he would soon be made Bishop Cameron's coadjutor. *Globe and Mail*, 19 July 1905.

120 The rector of Quebec seminary, Msgr Paquet, considered the Old Rector to be one of his most brilliant students. The Laval degree was conferred after Mass at L'Ardoise in October 1906. See *The Casket*, 4 October 1906.

121 *The Casket*, 5 January 1950.

122 Boyle, *Father Tompkins*, 38.

123 The literature on Fr Tompkins is vast. See Boyle, *Fr Tompkins*; Lotz and Welton, *Father Jimmy*; Welton, "'Knowledge for the People'"; Welton, "'Fraught with wonderful possibilities.'"

124 Boyle, *Fr Tompkins*, 34.

125 Interview with the CND Sisters of Sydney N.S., 22 June 1965, ADA, PNP, folder 61.

126 William X. Edwards, "The MacPherson-Tompkins Era of St. Francis Xavier University," CCHA, *Report*, 20 (1953), 49.

127 C.J. Connolly to H.P. MacPherson, 25 June 1909, STFXUA, HPMP, RG 9/5/2143.

128 Kennedy, "Family and Gaelic Culture," 9.

129 Mother Fidelis to Daniel Chisholm, 15 July 1897, STFXUA, WXEP, MG 45/2/250.

130 Those who decided to remain in Antigonish were Sisters Thecla Chisholm, M. Innocentia MacNamara, M. Dorothy Beaton, M. Theodore Sampson, M. Ninian Beaton, M. Andrew MacDonald, M. Faustina MacArthur, M. Remegius MacArthur, M. Marcella Beaton, M. Anne MacAdam, M. Benjamina Beaton, M. Potens Landry, and Sister Joseph Agnes MacDonald.

131 Cameron, *"And Martha Served,"* 14–15.

132 In her history of the Charities, Sister Maura makes no mention of this tension. Yet, some ill feelings about their treatment at the hands of the Charities were evident during the fiftieth anniversary of the Marthas. In an article in *The Casket*, the congregation noted that although seven sisters arrived in Antigonish in July 1900, "some sisters were delayed in Halifax by the Sisters of Charity until September 11, in order to give them ample

time to consider the feasibility of the Antigonish project. This course naturally impeded the work of our organization in the new foundation." *The Casket*, 29 July 1950.

133 Alexander Thompson to Mother Fidelis, 24 July 1900, STFXUA, ATP, RG 5/8/309.

134 Sister Mary Regis to John Cameron, 6 July 1900, ADA, BCP, series 1, sub-series 1, folder 4.

135 Cameron, *For the People*, 123.

136 J.H. Gillis, unpublished paper on the Sisters of St Martha, 1970, ADA, AAJP. Sister Innocentia was "carried off by heart trouble" in October 1909 at the young age of thirty-nine. See *The Casket* 21 October 1909.

137 Cameron, *"And Martha Served,"* 18.

138 Cameron, *"And Martha Served,"* 32–4; St Joseph's Hospital, *Twenty-Fifth Anniversary*, 28.

139 *The Casket*, 6 April 1905.

140 Cameron, *"And Martha Served,"* 36–7.

141 Sister Faustina to H.P. MacPherson, 18 September 1907, STFXUA, HPMP, RG 5/9/3465.

142 Sister Faustina to H.P. MacPherson, 30 September 1907, STFXUA, HPMP, RG 5/9/3467.

143 Fortescue, *The Third Republic*, 75.

144 *New York Evening Mail*, 28 May 1907.

145 Quote taken from Annals of the Convent of Our Lady of Assumption, which was quoted in "Arichat," ADA, AAJP, sub-series 6, folder 1.

146 Upon their death, the women were buried in a plot near the Church of Our Lady of Assumption in Arichat. The last four members were Sister Claire (MacDonald) who died on 2 April 1904; Sister Marie Victoire (Doiron) who died on 11 February 1905' Sister Flora (MacDonald) who died on 4 August 1907; and Sister Marie (Levandier), who passed away on 31 December 1917. *The Casket*, 7 February 1918. See also Schrepfer, *Pioneer Monks*, 145–8.

147 Churches constructed in this period were Holy Redeemer in Whitney Pier (1902), St Columba in Iona (1902), St Mary's French Road (1902), Louisbourg, Baddeck, and Westville (1903), Inverness, Louisdale, and Lower River Inhabitants (1904), Big Pond (1905), and River Denys' Station, and East Bay (1908).

148 Art historian Tom Roach suggests that the Stations of the Cross might have been painted by Leduc's assistant Raoul Ducharme. See Tom Roach, "The Work of Ozias Leduc in Antigonish," unpublished paper, 1995, STFXUA. On Leduc see Ostiguy, *Ozias Leduc*.

149 *The Casket*, 3 September 1903.
150 *The Casket*, 16 April 1903.
151 Kirincich, Stephen M. *Our Lady of Lourdes*, 40.
152 *The Casket*, 1 October 1903 and 27 December 1900.
153 McGowan, *The Waning of the Green*, 93.
154 *The Casket*, 3 March 1904; *The Casket*, 9 May 1907.
155 Donald MacPherson to A.A. Johnston, 8 March 1956, ADA, AAJP, series 4, sub-series 1. Fr Archibald Campbell, SJ, was born in Lochaber, Scotland. He entered the Society of Jesus in 1871 and ministered for a time in England and Wales before moving to Glasgow. He had a keen interest in the Scots of Nova Scotia. See *The Casket*, 26 May 1921.
156 *Sacred Heart Review*, 31 August 1907.
157 See Gibson, *Old and New World*, 267-77.
158 *The Casket*, 29 August 1907.
159 D.D. MacFarlane diary, 23 September 1907, ADA, AAJP.
160 *The Casket*, 11 February 1909.
161 Redemptorist, *The Miracles of Beaupré*.
162 *The Casket*, 22 December 1910.
163 H.P. MacPherson to Alexander Thompson, 28 May 1899, STFXUA, ATP, RG 5/8/1188; *The Casket*, 15 February 1900 and 10 January 1901.
164 Michael Laffin to Alexander Thompson, 9 December 1901, STFXUA, ATP, RG 5/8/571.
165 *The Casket*, 12 June 1902; 2 August 1900; Amable Briand to H.P. MacPherson, 24 May 1905, STFXUA, HPMP, RG 5/9/943; *The Casket*, 29 June 1905.
166 LeBlanc, "The Vatican and the Roman Catholic Church in Atlantic Canada," 65.
167 For an in-depth examination of this issue in the Windsor, Ontario, border region, see Cecillon, *Prayers, Petitions, and Protests*, 42–77.
168 For information on the politics surrounding the college of St Louis see Andrew, *Development of Elites*.
169 Maritime Bishops to Donato Sbarretti, 17 January 1908, ADA, BCP, series 1, sub-series 1, folder 3.
170 Leblanc, "The Vatican and the Roman Catholic Church in Atlantic Canada," 69.
171 Donato Sbarretti to John Cameron, 20 November 1909, ADA, BCP, series 1, sub-series 1, folder 3.
172 MacLean, *Piety & Politics*, 180-81.
173 *The Casket*, 14 May 1903.
174 *The Casket*, 19 November 1903.

175 Ronald MacDonald to John J. MacNeil, 22 November 1905, BIA, JJMP, MG 13, 48, (F2).
176 For a good account of the history of Protestant-Catholic relations in Northern Ireland see Parkinson, *Belfast's Unholy War*, and Elliot, *The Catholics of Ulster*. On the institutionalized sectarianism of Newfoundland see Noel, *Politics in Newfoundland*.
177 *The Casket*, 13 August 1857. For a full account see Ludlow, "Disturbed by the Irish Howl," 49–55; Beck, *Joseph Howe, Volume II*, 115–37.
178 Morton, *The Kingdom of Canada*, 399.
179 Howell, "The 1900s," 155.
180 *The Casket*, 5 July 1900; Morgan, *Rise Again! Book* 2, 46–7.
181 Mann, *Margaret MacDonald*, 35–7. See also *The Pictou Advocate*, 28 December 1899.
182 Mann, *Margaret MacDonald*, 46; Sister Saint Mary of Calvary died in December 1950 at the CND motherhouse in Montreal. See *The Casket*, 14 December 1950.
183 H.P. MacPherson to Alexander Thompson, 27 January 1900, STFXUA, ATP, RG 5/8/1187. See also Neil MacNeil, *The Highland Heart*, 103.
184 McGowan, *The Waning of the Green*, 206–7.
185 *The Casket*, 26 September 1918.
186 *The Casket*, 11 January 1900.
187 MacLean, *The Casket*, 78–9.
188 Alexander Thompson to L.J. MacPherson, 23 March 1900, STFXUA, ATP, RG 5/8/1195.
189 *The Casket*, 31 May 1900.
190 *The Casket*, 18 April 1901.
191 Cornelius O'Brien to John Cameron, 8 October 1901, ADA, BCP, series 1, sub-series 1, folder 3.
192 *The Eastern Chronicle*, 26 May 1910.
193 See Richardson, "The English Coronation Oath," 129–58.
194 *The Casket*, 21 January 1909.
195 Fr Finlay Chisholm (1848–1898). Born in Glassburn (Heatherton Parish), Chisholm served at Pomquet (1880–84) and St Anne's Glace Bay (1884–98). *The Casket*, 19 June 1902.
196 *The Casket*, 30 January 1908.
197 On the founding of the KOC see Brinkley and Fenster, *Parish Priest*; Kauffman, *Faith and* Fraternalism, 118.
198 Sydney received its charter on 12 November 1905 and Antigonish on 23 March 1906. New Glasgow would follow in 1912. The driving force to get the council started in Antigonish was the lawyer and senator Edward

Lavin Gerrior. William Landry, "A History of the Knight of Columbus," unpublished paper, 2006, 3.

199 *The Casket*, 8 November 1906.

200 D.C. Gillis to John Cameron, 23 October 1903, ADA, BCP, series 1, sub-series 1, folder 15. On St Mary's see Pacey, *More Stately* Mansions, 40–3.

201 The land for the church (three acres) was part of the farm of the late A.D. MacGillivray.

202 John Cameron to Apostolic Delegate, 22 November 1904, ADA, BCP, series 1, sub-series 1, folder 15.

203 John A MacGillivray to John Cameron, 13 June 1903, ADA, BCP, series 1, sub-series 1, folder 15.

204 Letter from the Parishioners to Lismore to Msgr Sbaretti, 16 August 1903, ADA, BCP, series 1, sub-series 1, folder 15.

205 Daniel MacGregor to John Cameron, 17 July 1903, ADA, BCP, series 1, sub-series 1, folder 15.

206 Letter from the Parishioners to Lismore to Msgr Sbaretti (copy), 16 August 1903, ADA, BCP, series 1, sub-series 1, folder 15.

207 D.C. Gillis to John Cameron, 6 October 1903, ADA, BCP, series 1, sub-series 1, folder 15.

208 The executor of Austen Chisholm's estate, his nephew, Fr John J. Chisholm, pastor of Pictou, told Fr Gillis that construction of a church at Bailey's Brook would forfeit the bequest. The priest was under considerable pressure from Bishop Cameron to release the funds for Bailey's Brook and confessed that the prelate had tried to transfer him to Lismore in 1903 with the specific intent of forcing him to employ "[his] uncle's money for that purpose." John J. Chisholm to S. McDonnell (copy), 20 November 1903, ADA, BCP, series 1, sub-series 1, folder 15.

209 Murphy, "Trusteeism in Atlantic Canada," 128.

210 Duncan Cameron to John Cameron, 31 July 1907, ADA, BCP, series 3, sub-series 1, folder 57.

211 Cameron to Apostolic Delegate, 16 May 1904, ADA, BCP, series 1, sub-series 1, folder 15; Cameron to D.D. MacDonald, 25 May 1904, ADA, BCP, series 1, sub-series 1, folder 15. On the rumour of MacGregor's drinking, see Nilsen, "The Role of the Priest," 187.

212 Apostolic Delegate to Bishop Cameron, 1 May 1904, ADA, BCP, series 1, sub-series 1, folder 15.

213 Apostolic Delegate to J.A. MacGillivray (copy), 6 September 1904, ADA, BCP, series 1, sub-series 1, folder 15.

214 Daniel MacGregor to John Cameron, 17 January 1905, ADA, BCP, series 1, sub-series 1, folder 15.
215 Christopher P. Chisholm (1854–1934) was a barrister who represented Antigonish in the Nova Scotia Legislature from 1891 until 1911. He served on the Legislative Council from 21 February until its abolition in in May 1928. For a brief biography see Elliott, *The Legislative Assembly of Nova* Scotia, 34.
216 Petition to Cardinal Merry Del Val (copy), 9 October 1904, ADA, BCP, series 1, sub-series 1, folder 15.
217 Parishioners of Lismore to Cardinal Merry Del Val (copy), 9 October 1904, ADA, BCP, series 1, sub-series 1, folder 15.
218 John Cameron to Apostolic Delegate, 22 November 1904, ADA, BCP, series 1, sub-series 1, folder 15.
219 Daniel MacGregor to John Cameron, 17 January 1905, ADA, BCP, series 1, sub-series 1, folder 15.
220 Daniel MacGregor to John Cameron, 11 February 1905, ADA, BCP, series 1, sub-series 1, folder 15.
221 The apostolic delegate is quoted in John Cameron to D.D. MacDonald, 19 October 1904, ACA, BCP, series 1, sub-series 1, folder 15.
222 John Cameron to D.D. MacDonald, 14 March 1905, ADA, BCP, series 1, sub-series 1, folder 15.
223 "There is assuredly much to sadden and discourage you, did you look at things from a merely human point of view?" wrote Fr MacNeil's colleague at the Grand Seminary of Montreal, "But, dear Father, is it not clear, is it not evident, that you are doing God's holy will, and that consequently your trials are permitted and ordained by God?" J.S. Dorvaux to John J. MacNeil, 10 November 1905, BIA, JJMP, MG 13, 48 (F1).
224 John Cameron to J.A.M. Gillis, 3 April 1906, ADA, BCP, series 1, sub-series 1, folder 15.
225 In 1977 one parishioner of Lismore recalled that a "raiding party" invaded the old church at Lismore and removed the Stations of the Cross, a picture of Our Lady, an assortment of statues, and the church bell, for transfer to Mount St Mary's. Interview with Roderick W. MacPherson, March 1977, ADA, BCP, series 1, sub-series 1, folder 15.
226 J.A.M. Gillis to John Cameron, 30 September 1907, ADA, BCP, series 1, sub-series 1, folder 15.
227 Ronald MacDonald to John Cameron, 18 October 1907, ADA, BCP, series 1, sub-series 1, folder 15.
228 J.A.M. Gillis to John Cameron, 30 October 1907, ADA, BCP, series 1, sub-series 1, folder 15.

229 *The Casket*, 9 January 1908.

230 John Fraser to Bishop Cameron, 31 January 1908, ADA, BCP, series 1, sub-series 1, folder 1.

231 The telegram to the delegate read: "My aged father who received last sacraments three months ago died suddenly yesterday. No time to call priest. Bishop refuses him Christian burial because he was one of the Lismore Malcontents. No excommunication previously inflected or warning of such given. Can you prevent sentence going into effect? Funeral announced for tomorrow morning. Wire at my expense. "Ronald MacDonald to Apostolic Delegate (copy), 14 February 1908, ADA, BCP, series 1, sub-series 1, folder 15.

232 John Fraser to John Cameron, 3 February 1908, ADA, BCP, series 1, sub-series 1, folder 15.

233 John Fraser to John Cameron. 5 July 1908, ADA, BCP, series 1, sub-series 1, folder 15.

234 "Report of Commission Appointed to Investigate Charge of Administering Sacraments to the Malcontents of Lismore," no date, ADA, BCP, series 1, sub-series 1, folder 15.

235 John Cameron to J.A.M. Gillis, 12 November 1908; J.A.M. Gillis to John Cameron, 28 November 1907, ADA, BCP, series 1, sub-series 1, folder 15.

236 Daniel MacGregor to Apostolic Delegate, 23 July 1908, ADA, BCP, series 1, sub-series 1, folder 15.

237 John Cameron to Apostolic Delegate, 29 May 1908, ADA, BCP, series 1, sub-series 1, folder 15.

238 James J. Tompkins to Moses M. Coady, 25 October 1914, BIA, JJTP, MG 10, 2 (1A, F1).

239 Apostolic Delegate to Daniel MacGregor, 3 August 1908, ADA, BCP, series 1, sub-series 1, folder 15.

240 John Cameron to Daniel MacGregor, 25 July 1908, ADA, BCP, series 1, sub-series 1, folder 15.

241 Apostolic Delegate to John Cameron, 11 December 1909, ADA, BCP, series 1, sub-series 1, folder 15.

242 *The Casket*, 15 August 1907.

243 J.A.M. Gillis to John Cameron, 6 December 1907 & 28 November 1907, ADA, BCP, series 1, sub-series 1, folder 15.

244 MacDonald, "The Succession," 2.

245 R.B. MacDonald, "The Succession," unpublished paper, 1991, STFXUA, 1.

246 Donald MacAdam to Edward Joseph McCarthy, 31 July 1908, Archdiocese of Halifax Archives (here after ACHA), Archbishop Edward Joseph McCarthy Papers (hereafter ABEJMP), Volume 3, #253.

247 Apostolic Delegate to John Cameron, 30 December 1905, ADA, BCP series 1, sub-series 1.
248 Alexander Thompson to L.J. MacPherson, 23 March `1909, STFXUA, ATP, RG 5/8/1195.
249 Apostolic Delegate to John Cameron, 26 January 1909, ADA, BCP, series 1, sub-series 1.
250 *The Casket*, 16 October 1913.
251 For a review see *The Casket* 24 September 1903. His other books were published by the Christian Press and the Willow Press.
252 *The Casket*, 28 January 1904.
253 *The Casket*, 13 May 1909. MacDonald made a similar comment in his *A Bit of Autobiography*. In it he writes, "It was death – that is the only word which fitly describes it. My funeral procession passed through the streets of Antigonish on the day of my departure, and woe was me that I live to take part in it."
254 MacDonald, "The Succession," 3.
255 Fr Donald Chisholm (1844–1916) was born at Glassburn and was the elder brother of Msgr Finlay J. Chisholm. "Under an apparently stern demeanour which was rather accentuated by an upright and dignified carriage," eulogized *The Casket*, "he hid a very kind heart and a humble, quiet and charitable disposition." See *The Casket*, 7 September 1916.
256 Donald Beaton to H.P. MacPherson, 29 March 1909, STFXUA, HPMP, RG 9/59/565.
257 MacDonald, "The Succession," 5–6.
258 McCarthy to Merry Del Val, 10 March 1909, ADHA, ABEJMP, Vol. IV, 340. See also R.B. MacDonald "The Succession," 5–8.
259 Henry O'Leary to John Cameron, no date (1909?), ADA, BCP, series 1, sub-series 1.
260 MacDonald, "The Succession," 8.
261 John Cameron to Apostolic Delegate, 13 December 1909, BCP, series 1, sub-series 1.
262 Nearing, *He Loved the Church*, 11.
263 Bishop McNeil was replaced in Newfoundland by Michael Fintan Power (1877–1920), a Newfoundlander and an alumnus of St F.X. See *The Casket*, 3 August 1911.
264 Michael Howley to John Cameron, 24 February 1910, ADA, BCP. In 1888, Howley wrote *The Ecclesiastical History of Newfoundland*. See Crosbie, "Howley, Michael Francis," 514–22.
265 McNeil was not keen on going to British Columbia. See Boyle, *Pioneer in Purple*, 103.

266 MacLean, *Piety & Politics*, 186.

267 C.J. Connolly to H.P. MacPherson, 25 April 1910, STFXUA, HPMP, RG 9/5/2147.

268 *Halifax Herald*, 13 April 1909.

269 MacLean, *Piety & Politics*, 187.

270 Ignatius, *Most Reverend John Cameron*, 75.

CHAPTER FOUR

1 While executing the late prelate's will – the bulk of the estate was left to family and to St F.X – some kind-hearted priests became concerned about the welfare of Cameron's housekeeper, who had served in the bishop's residence for twenty-five years. Although Cameron had not remembered Mrs Johnston in his will (he had apparently intended to do so), Fr John H. Nicholson, a curate in the bishop's residence from 1907–10, insisted that St F.X. bestow some of the legacy on the woman, as she was "old, homeless, her health poor, and absolutely penniless." This act of charity, he promised, would "return to the college a thousand-fold." Little is known about Mary Johnston (1848–?); see MacLean, *Piety & Politics*, 185; J.H. Nicholson to H.P. MacPherson, 10 October 1910, ADA, HPMP, series 1, sub-series 1, folder 6.

2 Charles W. MacDonald to H.P. MacPherson, 19 February 1911, ADA, HPMP, series 1, sub-series 1, folder 4.

3 Maurice F. Tompkins to H.P. MacPherson, 18 January 1911, ADA, HPMP, series 1, sub-series 1, folder 4.

4 P.W. Browne to H.P. MacPherson, 22 May 1910, STJXUA, HPMP, RG 5/9/994. P.W. Browne (1864–1937) was a noted Newfoundland historian. See Browne, *The Story of Labrador*; "Catholic Education in Newfoundland"; "Irish Bishops in Newfoundland."

5 Robert Fraser to H.P. MacPherson, 10 May 1910, ADA, HPMP, series 1, sub-series 1, folder 11.

6 In 1908, the Propaganda Fide, in charge of the mission territories across the globe, no longer had jurisdiction over Canadian dioceses. Robert Fraser to H.P. MacPherson, 15 September 1910, ADA, HPMP, series 1, sub-series 1, folder 11.

7 John Fraser to H.P. MacPherson, 19 November 1910, ADA, HPMP, series 1, sub-series 1, folder 11.

8 Robert Fraser to H.P. MacPherson, 10 June 1910, ADA, HPMP, series 1, sub-series 1, folder 11.

9 Donald MacAdam to Edward McCarthy, 15 April 1910, ADHA, ABEJMP, Volume 3 #253.

10 H.P. MacPherson to Robert Fraser, 16 November 1911, ADA, HPMP, series 1, sub-series 1, folder 11.

11 MacPherson wrote: "Have you any report to the effect that our diocese was going to dismembered? The report is current in Halifax that the counties on the mainland of NS ..." H.P. MacPherson to Robert Fraser, 16 November 1911, ADA, HPMP, series 1, sub-series 1, folder 11.

12 Petition from Irish Priests in PEI [A.E. Burke, Martin Monaghan, J. F. Johnston, Thomas Curran, P.D. McGuigan, J. T. Murphy, Felix L. Connolly, M.J. Smith.] to Edward McCarthy (copy). 1 November 1907, ADA, BCP, series 2, sub-series 1, folder 32.

13 Thomas Curran to Edward McCarty, 8 February 1909, ADHA, ABEJMP, vol. 2 #155. On this affair see Ludlow, "Raising the Cry of Nationality," 2–10.

14 McNeil, *The Pope and the War*, 20.

15 Rumours abounded that Fr MacPherson was going to be consecrated for the diocese of Charlottetown after the death of Bishop MacDonald, but his lack of Irish blood made this an impossibility. Samuel Doyle to James J. Tompkins, 10 December 1912, BIA, JJTP, MG 10, 2 (1A, F1).

16 Robert Fraser to H.P. MacPherson, 12 August 1912, ADA, HPMP, series 1, sub-series 1, folder 11.

17 H.P. MacPherson to D.J. McIntosh, 10 August 1912, ADA, HPMP, series 1, sub-series 2, folder 17.

18 *The Casket*, 29 August 1912. Morrison had hoped for three months to prepare for the consecration, see James Morrison to Edward J. McCarthy, 13 August 1912, ADA, BMP, letter#10.

19 MacDonald, "The Succession," 18; Robert Fraser to H.P. MacPherson, 12 August 1912, ADA, HPMP, series 1, sub-series 1, folder 11.

20 *The Casket*, 5 September 1912.

21 James Morrison to Donald MacPherson, 19 October 1912, ADA, BMP, letter#7.

22 Archbishop McCarthy celebrated the Pontifical High Mass for the Dead. As there was confusion over the date of the funeral, the number of clergy in attendance was disappointing. *The Casket*, 26 September 1912.

23 James Morrison to D.J. MacIntosh, 10 October 1913, ADA, BMP, letter#805.

24 James Morrison to Robert Phelan, 21 January 1914, ADA, BMP, letter#983.

25 James Morrison to R.L. MacDonald, 15 December 1917, ADA, BMP, letter#4768.

26 The artistic commission was handled by Fr E.L. Perrin, the rector of the Scots College Rome, who provided the sculptor, Paolo Bartolini, with photographs of the late bishop. When Bartolini struggled with Cameron's features, he was advised by Ronald Cameron MacGillivray, a native of St Joseph's Parish studying at the Urban College. James Morrison to Colin F. MacKinnon, 25 May 1913, ADA, BMP, letter#526; James Morrison to Ronald MacGillivray, 7 May 1915, ADA, BMP, letter#2110.

27 D.M. MacAdam to H.P. MacPherson, 14 December 1910, ADA, HPMP, series 1, sub-series 1, folder 4.

28 H.P. MacPherson to Apostolic Delegate, 4 July 1910, ADA, HPMP, series 1, sub-series 1, folder 11.

29 Interestingly, the Old Rector also considered resigning over the conflict but was counselled by Fr Alexander Thompson to remain. Alexander Thompson to H.P. MacPherson, June 1911, ADA, HPMP, series 1, sub-series 2, folder 16.

30 J.J. MacKinnon to H.P. MacPherson, 9 November 1910, ADA, HPMP, series 1, sub-series 1, folder 11.

31 H.P. MacPherson to Apostolic Delegate, 30 June 1911, ADA, HPMP, series 1, sub-series 1, folder 11.

32 J.J. MacKinnon to H.P. MacPherson, 24 January 1912, ADA, HPMP, series 1, sub-series 1, folder 11.

33 James Morrison to J.J. MacKinnon, 10 January 1913, ADA, BMP, letter#157.

34 If a family requested interment at the Bailey's Brook graveyard, the pastor was to remind them that Lismore was the regular parish cemetery; however, if they still demanded burial at Bailey's Brook, "then in God's name let it go ahead." James Morrison to J.J. MacKinnon, 4 March 1914, ADA, BMP, letter#1102.

35 *The Casket*, 2 September 1915.

36 *The Casket*, 16 August 1917.

37 MacNeil, *The Rewarding Path*, 63.

38 Frank White to James J. Tompkins, 12 May 1916, BIA, JJTP, MG 10, 2 (1A, F2).

39 James J. Tompkins to Michael J. Curley, 8 April 1914, BIA, JJTP, MG 10, 2 (1A, F1).

40 Sir John Arthur Ransome Marriott (1859–1949) was a British historian, and Conservative Member of Parliament. He wrote over forty books, including *England Since Waterloo*, and *Anglo-Russian Relations*.

41 Edwards, "The MacPherson-Tompkins Era," 58.

42 C.J. Connolly to H.P. MacPherson, 23 March 1911, STFXUA, HPMP, RG 5/9/2153.
43 *The Casket*, 17 October 1912.
44 James Boyle to H.P. MacPherson, 15 October 1910, STFXUA, HPMP, RG 5/9/880.
45 James J. Tompkins to John C. MacNeil, 9 January 1913, BIA, JJTP, MG 10, 2 (1A, F1).
46 James J. Tompkins to A.J.G. MacEchen, 1912, BIA, JJTP, MG 10, 2 (1A, F1).
47 C.J. Connolly to H.P. MacPherson, 25 April 1910, STFXUA, HPMP, RG 9/5/2147.
48 C.J. Connolly to H.P. MacPherson, 25 July 1909, STFXUA, HPMP, RG 9/5/2145.
49 Moses M. Coady to H.P. MacPherson, 23 June 1915, STFXUA, HPMP, RG 5/9/2010.
50 James J. Tompkins to T.A. Lebbetter, 12 March 1915, BIA, JJTP, MG 10, 2 (1A, F2A).
51 Cameron, *For the People*, 151.
52 Cameron, *For the People*, 150.
53 James J. Tompkins to N.A. MacMillian, 1 December 1912, BIA, JJTP, MG 10, 2 (1A, F1).
54 *The Casket*, 4 May 1916.
55 James Morrison to Robert Borden, 12 February 1914, ADA, BMP, letter#1040.
56 Ernest R. Forbes, *Maritime Rights*, 14–15.
57 MacInnes, "Clerics, Fishermen, Farmers and Workers," 157.
58 *The Casket*, 4 December 1913.
59 *The Casket*, 13 November 1913.
60 *The Casket*, 11 December 1913.
61 *The Casket*, 11 June 1914.
62 Hugh John MacDonald to Peter Nearing, 18 May 1965, ADA, PNP, series 2, sub-series 1, folder 20.
63 *The Casket*, 5 February 1914.
64 *The Casket*, 25 June 1914.
65 *The Casket*, 30 July 1914.
66 *The Casket*, 20 August 1914.
67 Moses M. Coady to James J. Tompkins, 25 October 1914, BIA, JJTP, MG 10, 2 (1A, F1).
68 *The Casket*, 8 October 1914.

69 James Kiely to H.P. MacPherson, 16 October 1919, STFXUA, HPMP, RG 5/9/5559.
70 *The Casket*, 25 June 1914.
71 *The Casket*, 6 September 1917.
72 Ostensibly "Old Home Week" was about cajoling people to return to the vacant farms, but it had little success. At Lismore in the summer of 1914, there was a High Mass, Benediction of the Blessed Sacrament, an open-air concert in Gaelic, a public meeting supported by the Antigonish Forward Movement which dealt with the "opportunities for success on the farm," a children's agricultural fair, and a solemn blessing of the Calvary cross in the cemetery. See *The Casket*, 21 May 1914.
73 *The Casket*, 25 March 1915.
74 James J. Tompkins to John McNeil, 26 March 1915, BIA, JJTP, MG 10, 2 (1A, F2A).
75 *The Casket*, 4 February 1915.
76 Quoted in *The Casket*, 19 February 1914.
77 James J. Tompkins to T.F. Horrigan, 13 March 1914, BIA, JJTP, MG 10, 2 (1A, F1).
78 When Fr Michael MacKenzie died in November 1912, Donovan sent Tompkins word "to get something for him," and Tompkins quickly set out collecting facts on the priest's life. Knowing that he died a poor man, Tompkins wanted "something to say about that and expand on it a little." See James J. Tompkins to N.A. MacMillan, 2 December 1912, BIA, JJTP, MG 10, 2 (1A, F1), and *The Casket*, 5 December 1912.
79 James J. Tompkins to Mother St Margaret, 25 February 1914, BIA, JJTP, MG 10, 2 (1A, F1).
80 H.F. MacDougall to H.P. MacPherson, 29 October 1914, STFXUA, HPMP, RG /5/9/732.
81 Stephen MacEachern to James J. Tompkins, 27 July 1916, BIA, JJTP, MG 10, 2 (1A, F2).
82 James J. Tompkins to J.M.P. Coady, 18 October 1916, BIA, JJTP, MG 10, 2 (1A, F2).
83 James J. Tompkins to D. MacGillivray, 3 May 1917, BIA, JJTP, MG 10, 2 (1A, F3).
84 In 1900 Fr David Vincent Phalen (1866–1909) became editor of *The Casket*, having for a long while contributed to the paper under the pen name "David Creedon." In 1901 he became ill with pulmonary tuberculosis and despite various stints at sanatoria in Canada and the United States, he never fully recovered. See *The Casket*, 8 April 1909.
85 James Morrison to Robert Phalen, 15 April 1915, ADA, BMP, letter#2047.

86 James Morrison to Michael Donovan, 22 April 1914, ADA, BMP, letter#1239.

87 James J. Tompkins to P.W. Thibeau, 6 January 1918, BIA, JJTP, MG 10, 2 (1A, F4).

88 James J. Tompkins to Neil McNeil, 26 December 1917, BIA, JJTP, MG 10, 2 (1A, F3).

89 Neil McNeil to James J. Tompkins, 10 June 1917, BIA, JJTP, MG 10, 2 (1A, F4).

90 Joseph Wall to Nicholas Meagher, 28 October 1915, ADA, AAJP, series 4, sub-series 1, folder 1.

91 Neil McNeil to H.P. MacPherson, 20 August 1917, STFXUA, HPMP, RG 5/9/8385.

92 Henry Somerville to James J. Tompkins, 18 January 1918, BIA, JJTP, MG 10, 2 (1A, F4). See also Beck, "Henry Somerville," 91–108; Sinasac, *The Life of Henry Somerville*.

93 James J. Tompkins to Neil McNeil, 16 January 1918, BIA, JJTP, MG 10, 2 (1A, F4).

94 James J. Tompkins to J.A. Walker, 15 January 1918, BIA, JJTP, MG 10, 2 (1A, F3).

95 James J. Tompkins to J.A. Walker, 6 January 1918, BIA, JJTP, MG 10, 2 (1A, F4).

96 James J. Tompkins to P.W. Thibeau, 21 January 1918, BIA, JJTP, MG 10, 2 (1A, F4). This letter is particularly fascinating, as the priest also explains his theory on learning how to write. "You need to take some very good author, say Washington Irving for instance, and read him very slowly and very carefully – a little every day. In writing it is only safe to write on such subjects as a person has a very clear idea of and which he has very fully mastered."

97 *The Casket*, 24 January 1918.

98 *The Casket*, 24 January 1918.

99 James J. Tompkins to Neil McNeil, 15 February 1918, BIA, JJTP, MG 10, 2 (1A, F4).

100 Henry Somerville to James J. Tompkins, 10 February 1918, BIA, JJTP, MG 10, 2 (1A, F4).

101 *The Casket*, 7 March 1918.

102 James J. Tompkins to Neil McNeil, 22 February 1918, BIA, JJTP, MG 10, 2 (1A, F4).

103 *The Casket*, 7 March 1918.

104 James J. Tompkins to Donald F. MacDonald, 9 March 1918, BIA, JJTP, MG 10, 2 (1A, F4).

105 James J. Tompkins to Donald F. MacDonald, 9 March 1918, BIA, JJTP, MG 10, 2 (1A, F4).
106 Fr Alexander Chisholm was educated at the Urban College Rome and taught at St F.X. from 1866–75 and again from 1877–81, 1885–95, and 1904–07. Fr Daniel MacIntosh MacGregor was also educated at the Urban College Rome and taught at St F.X. from 1865–69 and also 1872–81.
107 *The Casket*, 11 April 1918.
108 *The Casket*, 8 August 1918.
109 The links with the Catholic University of America were deeply rooted in this period. The primary funding for scholarships came from the KOC of Canada. It was a means to send young men "of promise," like P.W. Thibeau who entered as a graduate student in 1917, to the United States for post-graduate work. See *The Casket*, 27 September 1917.
110 *The Casket*, 24 October 1918.
111 *The Casket*, 8 August 1918.
112 *The Casket*, 14 November 1918.
113 James J. Tompkins to B.P. McCafferty, 26 December 1918, BIA, JJTP, MG 10, 2 (1A, F4).
114 James J. Tompkins to Neil McNeil, 5 April 1918, BIA, JJTP, MG 10, 2 (1A, F4).
115 James J. Tompkins to B.P. McCafferty, 26 December 1918, BIA, JJTP, MG 10, 2 (1A, F4).
116 Neil McNeil to James J. Tompkins, 9 January 1919, BIA, JJTP, MG 10, 2 (1A, F4).
117 J.D. Keane to James J. Tompkins, 12 February 1919, BIA, JJTP, MG 10, 2 (1A, F4).
118 H.P. MacPherson to J.C. Bourinot, 2 March 1915, STFXUA, HPMP, RG 5/9/811.
119 MacLean, *The Casket*, 136–44.
120 *The Casket*, 24 September 1914.
121 *The Casket*, 11 May 1916.
122 *The Casket*, 27 July 1916.
123 *The Casket*, 29 March 1917.
124 MacLean. *The Casket*, 124.
125 D.M. MacAdam to James Morrison, 25 June 1917, ADA, BMP, letter#4343.
126 D.M. MacAdam to James Morrison, 25 June 1917, ADA, BMP, letter#4343.
127 *The Casket*, 19 May 1910.
128 Michael Donovan to H.P. MacPherson, 9 March 1915, STFXUA, HPMP, RG 5/9/2838.

129 Robert Phalen to James J. Tompkins, 18 February 1919, BIA, JJTP, MG 10, 2 (1A, F4).
130 Robert Phalen to James J. Tompkins, 27 February 1919, BIA, JJTP, MG 10, 2 (1A, F4).
131 Boyle, *Father Tompkins of Nova Scotia*, 62. Tompkins and local barrister James M. Wall approached Morrison with the takeover plan. As the relationship between Morrison and Donovan had broken down, Donovan sold the company to Tompkins and, the next morning, Tompkins sold it to the diocese. James Morrison to P. Di Maria, 7 November 1921, ADA, BMP, letter #8775.
132 Shook, *Catholic Post-Secondary Education*, 84.
133 Michael Donovan to James Morrison, 6 August 1920 (copy), STFXUA, HPMP, RG 5/9/2849.
134 Bishop Morrison circular, 19 March 1919, ADA, BMP, letter#6147.
135 Michael Donovan to James Morrison, 28 June 1922, ADA, BMP, incoming letter# 9241.
136 James Morrison to D.J. MacIntosh, 4 April 1919, ADA, BMP, letter#6207.
137 Michael Donovan to H.P. MacPherson, 10 December 1920, STFXUA, HPMP, RG 5/9/2854.
138 Michael Donovan to James Morrison, 22 August 1919, ADA, BMP, letter#6549. See also Michael Donovan to H.P. MacPherson, 10 December 1920, STFXUA, HPMP, RG 5/9/2854.
139 MacDonald, *The Builders*, 52.
140 Michael Donovan to James Morrison, 18 July 1923, ADA, BMP, fonds 4, series 4, sub-series 1, folder 1.
141 *The Casket*, 17 July 1919.
142 MacLean, *The Casket*, 143.
143 MacInnes, "Clerics, Fishermen, Farmers and Workers," 166.
144 Sinasac, *The Life of Henry Somerville*, 49.
145 Henry Somerville to James J. Tompkins, 25 June 1919, BIA, JJTP, MG 10, 2 (1A, F4).
146 Howard Murray to James J. Tompkins, 25 August 1919, BIA, JJTP, MG 10, 2 (1A, F4). Interestingly, Tompkins did not want to make a long speech as it was an "aversion" of his.
147 Cameron, *For the People*, 164.
148 James Tompkins to Henry S. Pritchett (copy), 3 December 1919, ADA, BMP; document attached to letter#6818.
149 Reid, "Health, Education, Economy," 66.
150 James Morrison to James J. Tompkins, 14 November 1919, ADA, BMP, letter#6865.

151 James Tompkins to H.P. MacPherson, 15 December 1919, STFXUA, James J. Tompkins Papers (hereafter JJTP), RG 6/5/378.

152 Fr Patrice LeBlanc, ministering in Cheticamp, agreed, noting that "the Acadians are so poor that it is hard to know which way to turn to obtain even a portion [of the matching funds]." Patrice LeBlanc to H.P. MacPherson, 27 December 1919, STFXUA, HPMP, RG 5/9/5813.

153 Joseph d'Auteuil to H.P. MacPherson, no date, STFXUA, HPMP, RG 5/9/2530.

154 On Collège Sainte-Anne see LeBlanc and Laliberté, *Sainte-Anne*.

155 A. Monbourquette to H.P. MacPherson, 20 January 1920, STFXUA, HPMP, RG 5/9/8932.

156 Alfred Boudreau to H.P. MacPherson, 21 January 1920, STFXUA, HPMP, RG 5/9/749.

157 John Fraser to J.W. MacDonald, 5 August 1910 (copy), ADA, HPMP, series 1, sub-series 1, folder 11.

158 George McAuley to H.P. MacPherson, 17 May 1912, ADA, HPMP, series 1, sub-series 2, folder 63.

159 H.P. MacPherson to Apostolic Delegate, 12 June 1911, ADA, HPMP, series 1, sub-series 2, folder 49.

160 George McAuley to H.P. MacPherson, 27 May 1912, ADA, HPMP, series 1, sub-series 2, folder 63.

161 George McAuley to H.P. MacPherson, 6 April 1912, ADA, HPMP, series 1, sub-series 2, folder 63; George McAuley to H.P. MacPherson, 8 December 1912, ADA, HPMP, series 1, sub-series 2, folder 63. For more information on both Mount Carmel and St Agnes see Boutilier, *The New Waterford Story*, 26–9.

162 Donald MacAdam to James Morrison, 13 February 1913, ADA, BMP, letter#241.

163 Colin F. MacKinnon to James Morrison, 18 February 1912, ADA, BMP, letter#244.

164 St Nicholas was blessed in May 1913. See *The Casket*, 8 May 1913.

165 Alexander Thompson to H.P. MacPherson, 19 December 1911, ADA, HPMP, series 1, sub-series 1, folder 7.

166 Roderick MacInnis to H.P. MacPherson, 15 January 1912, ADA, HPMP, series 1, sub-series 1, folder 5.

167 *The Casket*, 21 November 1912; J.H. Nicholson to H.P MacPherson, 12 December 1911, ADA, HPMP, series 1, sub-series 1, folder 6.

168 James Morrison to D. Viola, 30 October 1912, ADA, BMP, letter#22.

169 Roderick MacInnis to H.P. MacPherson, 21 December 1911, ADA, HPMP, series 1, sub-series 1, folder 5.

170 R. MacInnis to James Morrison, 21 January 1912, ADA, BMP, incoming letter#161.
171 James Morrison to Roderick MacInnis, 16 January 1913, ADA, BMP, letter#173.
172 S.R. Gwozd to James Morrison, 17 January 1913, ADA, BMP, incomingletter#179.
173 See David Mullan, "A History of St. Mary's Polish Parish Sydney."
174 James Morrison to S.R. Gowzd, 1 September 1915, ADA, BMP, letter#2369.
175 James Morrison to D. Voila, 30 October 1914, ADA, BMP, letter#1586.
176 John Hugh MacDonald to James Morrison, 22 March 1915, ADA, BMP, letter#1962.
177 James Morrison to D. Viola, 26 June 1916, ADA, BMP, letter#3207.
178 James Morrison to D. Viola, 24 May 1918, ADA, BMP, letter#5244.
179 R.H. MacDougall to H.P. MacPherson, 17 July 1911, ADA, HPMP, series 1, sub-series 2, folder 24.
180 Ludlow, "More than Codmen," 93–4.
181 John M. Chmielinski to James Morrison, 6 July 1914, ADA, BMP, incomingletter#1280.
182 James Morrison to D.H. MacDougall, 8 July 1914, ADA, BMP, letter#1255.
183 James Morrison to R. MacInnis, 14 July 1914, ADA, BMP, letter#1268.
184 D.H. MacDougall to James Morrison, 23 November 1914, ADA, BMP, letter#1604.
185 Frank, *J.B. McLachlan*, 133.
186 James Morrison to R. MacInnis, 17 August 1914, ADA, BMP, letter#1356.
187 James Morrison to Moses Coady, 18 December 1916, ADA, BMP, letter#3760.
188 James Morrison to Gregory McLellan, 15 September 1914, ADA, BMP, letter#1461.
189 McKay, "The 1910s," 219.
190 *The Casket*, 15 March 1917.
191 See *Canadian Mining Journal,* 15 August; 1 October; 15 December 1917; Caplan, "Mine Explosion in New Waterford, 1917," 1–11; MacKenzie, *Blast!*, 79–91; J.A. MacLellan, "Archbishop MacDonald Resigns," *The Western Catholic*, 12 August 1961, XLVII, 31, 79–91.
192 *Boston Daily Globe*, 26 July 1917; *Cape Breton Post*, 26 September 1924; MacLellan, "Archbishop MacDonald Resigns," 31.
193 James Morrison to John Hugh MacDonald, 30 July 1917, ADA, BMP, letter#4438.
194 Mellor, *The Company Store*, 94.
195 Lachlan MacKinnon, "Labour Landmarks," 10.

196 *The Casket*, 18 July 1918. See also Mellor, *The Company Store*, 103.
197 *The Casket*, 3 January 1918.
198 *Moncton Transcript*, 22 March 1917.
199 Sinasac, *The Life of Henry Somerville*, 25.
200 Bishop Wilhelm Emmanuel Von Ketteler (1811–1877) was a social reformer who wrote on the labour question and Christianity. See Hogan, *The Development of Bishop Wilhelm Emmanuel Von Ketteler*.
201 *The Casket*, 16 May 1918.
202 McGowan, "'Religious Duties and Patriotic Endeavours,'" 109–10.
203 *The Casket*, 5 August 1915.
204 McNeil was so desperate for Wall's pen that he asked his uncle, Judge Nicholas Meagher, to find a suitable replacement for Wall at his law firm. Neil McNeil to Nicholas Meagher, 30 May 1915, ADA, AAJP, series 4, sub-series 1, folder 1.
205 *The Casket*, 29 July 1915.
206 McGowan, *The Waning of the Green*, 193. Unfortunately, Joseph Wall would only spend three years in Toronto. He died on 18 September 1918. See *The Casket*, 19 September 1918 and 26 September 1918.
207 James J. Tompkins to J.A. Wall, 26 December 1917, BIA, JJTP, MG 10, 2 (1A, F3).
208 James Morrison to Thomas O'Donnell, 24 April 1916, ADA, BMP, letter#3169.
209 *The Casket*, 22 September 1910.
210 MacDonald, "On Getting the Sack," 18.
211 In many letters home, Bishop MacDonald admitted his homesickness. See Alexander MacDonald to Sister St Olga, 23 April 1918, BIA, (Bishop Alexander MacDonald Papers hereafter BAMP), MG 13, 22 (F1).
212 Alexander MacDonald, *The Primacy of Thought in Poetry*, 80.
213 *The Casket*, 9 August 1917.
214 *The Casket*, 26 July 1917.
215 *The Casket*, 12 September 1918.
216 This talk drew so many spectators that it was moved from the parish hall and into the church. *The Casket*, 5 September 1918. See also MacDonald, *A Bit of Autobiography*.
217 MacDonald, "On Getting the Sack," 18.
218 MacDonald also raised $3,000 in the diocese of Hamilton and $11,000 in the diocese of Brooklyn, New York. Throughout his "begging" tours he raised over $30,000 for Victoria. See "The Bishop of Victoria Personal Statement," BIA, BAMP, MG 13, 22 (F1).

219 James Morrison to Thomas O'Donnell, 24 January 1917, ADA, BMP, letter#3842.

220 At first sight, the fire was not considered serious. When the Ward V fire brigade reached the church, they found their ladders too short and the water pressure too weak to reach the roof. "A History of Holy Redeemer Parish 1901-1984: A Canada Community Development Project Federal Government," unpublished paper, 22 June 1984.

221 *The Casket*, 10 February 1916.

222 *The Casket*, 6 January 1916.

223 *The Casket*, 3 January 1918.

224 In September 1919, a mysterious blaze that began in the dormitory destroyed much of the old wing of the St F.X. administration building. Books from the library, many of them quite rare, were tossed out the window to safety. College authorities suspected an arsonist and in early October *The Casket* suggested the fire was "a deliberate plot to destroy the institution." With the aid of a Halifax detective, a St F.X. student from Sydney Mines confessed and was arrested for arson. H.P. MacPherson to John Francis, 10 November 1919, STFXUA, HPMF, RG 5/9/3699. See also Cameron, *For the People*, 176.

225 James Morrison to Alex MacKenzie, 2 April 1919, ADA, BMP, letter#6198.

226 *The Casket*, 26 May 1910.

227 *Pictou Advocate*, 7 May 1910. Some twenty years before decorating the shrine at Stellarton, MacKenzie (1847–1935) had decorated St. Paul's Church in Havre Boucher. He later also worked in Pictou's Stella Maris Church. See *The Casket*, 26 May 1910.

228 *The Casket*, 3 August 1916 and 13 July 1916.

229 For an interesting discussion on this change see McGrail, *First Communion*.

230 *The Casket*, 8 June 1911.

231 *The Casket*, 30 March 1911.

232 William F. Kiely to H.P. MacPherson, 2 March 1911, ADA, HPMP series 1, sub-series 1, folder 11.

233 James Morrison to Sister St Camillus, 12 May 1915, ADA, BMP, letter#2126.

234 Hattie LeBlanc returned to West Arichat, married, and fell into obscurity. *Alexandria Gazette*, 16 December 1910; *The Casket*, 5 January 1911.

235 *The Casket*, 29 December 1904.

236 James Tompkins to Michael Gills, 2 February 1917, BIA, JJTP, MG 10, 2 (1A/F3).

237 *The Casket*, 13 October 1910.
238 *The Casket*, 13 October 1910.
239 *The Casket*, 31 August 1911.
240 Much of the artwork and vestments was donated from other parishes. Fr Donald MacPherson purchased the statue of St Anthony, Fr Berry of Bras d'Or donated the Stations of the Cross, while the Sisters of St Martha provided the altar linens. See *The Casket*, 29 August 1912; 13 August 1914.
241 Donald MacPherson to H.P. MacPherson, 30 May 1910, ADA, HPMP, series 1, sub-series 1, folder 6; Donald MacPherson to John Cameron, 6 April 1910, ADA, HPMP, series 1, sub-series 2, folder 34.
242 Henri-Louis-Joseph Buisson (1863–1943). Born in Valigny, France, he joined the Capuchins at Carcassonne, France, in 1879, taking the name Father Pacifique. He was ordained in Spain in 1886, and taught there and in Ottawa. In 1894 he began his work as missionary to the Mi'kmaq of the eastern provinces from his home parish in Restigouche, Quebec. See Pacifique, *Le Paroissien Micmac*.
243 Pacifique is quoted in a sermon given by Fr MacPherson, 24 June 1919, BIA, Msgr Donald MacPherson Papers (hereafter DMP), MG 13, 58 (F5A).
244 *The Casket*, 3 June 1915.
245 "A sermon given by Fr MacPherson at the third centenary of the first baptism among the Mi'kmaq at Port Royal," 24 June 1919, BIA, DMP, MG 13, 58, (F5A).
246 Donald MacPherson to H.P. MacPherson, 14 December 1911, ADA, HPMP, series 1, sub-series 1, folder 6.
247 Donald MacPherson to H.P. MacPherson, 22 December 1911, ADA, HPMP, series 1, sub-series 1, folder 6.
248 J.A.M. Gillis to Bishop Cameron, 5 December 1907, ADA, BCP, series 1, sub-series 1, folder 1.
249 J.A.M. Gillis to H.P. MacPherson, 11 May 1908, STFXUA, HPMP, RG 5/9/3875.
250 James Morrison to O.E. Mathieu, 21 April 1915, ADA, BMP, letter#2064.
251 Cameron, *For the People*, 142.
252 *The Casket*, 5 January 1911.
253 "The Scottish Catholic Society of Canada," no date, STFXUA, RG 13/SC/F1.
254 MacInnes, "Scottish Catholic Society," 30–1.
255 (1) St Andrew's Council [St Andrews]; (2) St Margaret's [Glace Bay]; (3) St Columba's [Iona]; (4) Kilbar [Christmas Island]; (5) Bishop Fraser [New Waterford]; (6) St Kentigern's [Sydney]; (7) St Peter's [Port Hood]; (8) St Mary's [East Bay]; (9) Mary Stuart's [Boisdale]; (10) Montrose [Glendale];

(11) Stella Maris [Creignish]; (12) St Margaret's [Arisaig]; (13) St Andrew's; (14) St Joseph's [St Joseph's]; (15) Bishop Cameron [New Waterford]; (16) Bishop Morrison [S.W. Margaree].

256 Michael Gillis interview, 3 June 1965, ADA, PNP, fonds 5, folder 12.

257 Kennedy, "Family and Gaelic Culture," 1.

258 *The Casket*, 27 February 1913.

259 James Morrison to Mother Faustina, 20 May 1913, ADA, BMP, letter#521.

260 See Cameron, *"And Martha Served,"* 50–1.

261 S.M. Faustina to H.P. MacPherson, 19 July 1913, STFXUA, HPMF, RG 5/9/3462.

262 S.M. Faustina to H.P. MacPherson, 14 May 1914, STFXUA, HPMF, RG 5/9/3476.

263 S.M. Faustina to H.P. MacPherson, 20 October 1914, STFXUA, HPMF, RG 5/9/3481.

264 James Morrison to Neil McNeil, 19 September 1913, ADA, BMP, letter#754.

265 Nearing, *He Loved the Church*, 12.

266 S.M. Faustina to H.P. MacPherson, 22 October 1914, STFXUA, HPMP, RG 5/9/3482.

267 Fr John R. MacDonald transferred from the Grand Seminary of Quebec to St Augustine's because his uncle, Archbishop McNeil, had helped him gain an O'Keefe scholarship that covered most of the $250 board and tuition. John R. MacDonald to Christianna MacDonald, 24 June 1914, ADA, BJRMP, series 1, sub-series 1, folder 2.

268 MacDonald, "Social Origins and Congregational Identity," 53.

269 James Morrison to H.P MacPherson, 23 October 1915, STFXUA, HPMP, RG /5/9/9011.

270 James Morrison to Alexander Thompson, 30 July 1914, ADA, BMP, letter#1299.

271 Mother Faustina to H.P. MacPherson, 31 May 1914, STFXUA, HPMP, RG 5/9/3479.

272 H.P. MacPherson to James Morrison, 22 January 1917, ADA, BMP, letter#3858.

273 MacPherson, "Religious Women in Nova Scotia" 51 (1984), 98; James Morrison to Pere Dominique, 5 March 1917, ADA, BMP, letter#1283.

274 Archives of the Sisters of St Martha, *Articles of Agreement*, 7 August 1917.

275 Cameron, *"And Martha Served,"* 65.

276 James Morrison to D.M. MacAdam, 12 March 1918, ADA, BMP, letter#5201.

277 Cameron, *"And Martha Served,"* 66.
278 James Morrison to Emile Roy, 8 September 1916, ADA, BMP, letter#3429.
279 J.W. MacIsaac to H.P. MacPherson, 3 June 1910, ADA, HPMP, series 1, sub-series 1, folder 5; J.W. MacIsaac to H.P. MacPherson, 6 October 1910, ADA, HPMP, series 1, sub-series 1, folder 5.
280 *The Casket*, 8 December 1910.
281 Michael Laffin to H.P. MacPherson, 12 December 1910, STFXUA, HPMP, RG 5/9/5701.
282 *The Casket*, 13 June 1907.
283 *The Casket*, 6 September 1917.
284 C.J. Connolly to H.P. MacPherson, 4 October 1909, STFXUA, HPMP, RG 5/9/2146.
285 Morrison to Gregory McLellan, 15 September 1914, ADA, BMP, letter#1461.
286 For a good account see MacMillan, *The War that Ended the* Peace, 574–631.
287 Morrison to L.E. Perrin, 15 August 1914, ADA, BMP, letter#1352.
288 *The Casket*, 6 August 1914.
289 Morrison to E.M. MacDonald, 19 September 1914, ADA, BMP, letter#1475.
290 *The Casket*, 24 September 1914.
291 Brewer, "Antigonish and World War I," 21.
292 McGowan, *The Imperial Irish*, 86.
293 John Hugh MacDonald to James Morrison, 20 August 1915, ADA, BMP, letter#2406.
294 James J. Tompkins to Flora Hunt, 14 December 1914, BIA, JJTP, MG 10, 2 (1A, F1).
295 *The Casket*, 1 October 1914.
296 *The Casket*, 1 October 1914.
297 James Morrison to R.W. Rutherford, 4 August 1915, ADA, BMP, letter#2318.
298 McGowan, *The Imperial Irish*, 115.
299 P.W. Thibeau to James J. Tompkins, 10 July 1916, BIA, JJTP, MG 10, 2 (1A, F2A).
300 *The Casket*, 12 August 1915.
301 Brewer, "Antigonish and World War I," 52.
302 *Sydney Post*, 9 August 1915.
303 *Sydney Post*, 21 February 1916.
304 Hunt, *Nova Scotia's Part in the Great War*, 123.
305 *The Casket*, 2 March 1916.

306 *Sydney Post*, 10 September 1915.
307 Brewer, "Antigonish and World War I," 54.
308 Brewer, "Antigonish and World War I," 48.
309 MacDonald, *Catholics of the Diocese of Antigonish*, 231.
310 *The Casket*, 23 September 1915.
311 *The Casket*, 28 January 1915.
312 H.P. MacPherson to Joseph Hayes, 30 October 1917, STFXUA, RG 5/9/4714. Alexander O'Brien was the son of J.S. and Mary Ellen (MacIntosh) of Antigonish. He is buried in Villers Station Cemetery.
313 Morrison to A.B. MacDonald, 29 September 1915, ADA, BMP, letter#2487.
314 McGowan, "Harvesting the Red Vineyard," 52.
315 Brewer, "Antigonish and World War I," 40.
316 James Morrison to Placide LeBlanc, 26 May 1916, ADA, BMP, letter#3256.
317 James Morrison to R.H. MacDougall, 17 October 1916, ADA, BMP, letter#3562.
318 *The Casket*, 20 May 1915.
319 *Halifax Morning Chronicle*, 15 February 1916.
320 Newfoundland Catholics faced similar difficulties. See O'Brien, "Out of a Clear Sky." 409–10.
321 O'Gorman, "Canadian Catholic Chaplains," 73; McGowan, *The Imperial Irish*, 170.
322 *Catholic Register*, 13 May 1915; Crerar, "Bellicose Priests," 23.
323 R.C. MacGillivray to James Morrison, no date, ADA, BMP, incoming letter#3397A.
324 James Morrison to James Lougheed, 12 August 1915, ADA, BMP, letter#2336.
325 J.J. MacNeil to James Morrison, 29 March 1917, ADA, BMP.
326 James Morrison to Donald MacPherson, 7 September 1915, ADA, BMP, letter#2404.
327 *The Casket*, 12 April 1917.
328 *The Casket*, 2 March 1916.
329 *The Casket*, 6 July 1916.
330 *The Casket*, 28 March 1918.
331 Miles Tompkins to James J. Tompkins, 13 June 1916, BIA, JJTP, MG 10, 2 (1A, F2A).
332 Ludlow, *The Canny Scot*, 81.
333 James Morrison to Robert Borden, 23 March 1916, ADA, BMP, letter#3051.
334 James Morrison to Miles Tompkins, 20 May 1916, ADA, BMP, letter#3255. Tompkins wrote to Fr James Tompkins, "If the Bishop calls me back, I

suppose I shall have to go, but much against my will." See BIA, JJTP, Miles Tompkins to James J. Tompkins, 13 June 1916, MG 10, 2 (F1A).

335 Crerar, *Padres in No Man's* Land, 42.

336 McGowan, *The Waning of the Green*, 254.

337 Miles Tompkins to James Tompkins, 13 June 1916, BIA, JJTP, MG 10, 2 (1A, F2A).

338 James Morrison to Robert Borden, 11 September 1916, ADA, BMP, letter#3437

339 James Morrison to Robert Phalen, 1 May 1916, ADA, BMP, letter#3185; James Morrison to Ronald MacDonald, 23 April 1917, ADA, BMP, letter#4112.

340 Crerar, *Padres in No Man's Land*, 52.

341 Crerar, *Padres in No Man's Land*, 53

342 Crerar, *Padres in No Man's Land*, 54.

343 John O'Goreman to Fr James J. Tompkins, 17 January 1917, BIA, JJTP, MG 10, 2 (1A,F3).

344 Crerar, "Bellicose Priests," 34–5.

345 McGowan, *The Imperial Irish*, 178.

346 MacDonald, *Catholics of the Diocese of Antigonish*, 39.

347 McGowan, *The Imperial Irish*, 186–7.

348 MacGillivray had two brothers also serving overseas, one of whom, J.D. MacGillivray, was awarded the Military Medal for Bravery. See *The Casket*, 31 October 1918.

349 Miles Tompkins to James J. Tompkins, 13 June 1916, BIA, JJTP, MG 10, 2 (1A, F2A).

350 Heath, "The Protestant Denominational Press," 28.

351 James Morrison to Gregory McLellan, 13 March 1916, ADA, BMP, letter#3026.

352 *The Casket*, 4 January 1917.

353 Neil McNeil to James J. Tompkins, 23 October 1917, BIA, JJTP, MG 10, 2 (1A, F3).

354 Morton and Granatstein, *Marching to Armageddon*, 194.

355 *The Casket*, 19 July 1917.

356 James J. Tompkins to John MacNeil, 9 July 1917, BIA, JJTP, MG 10, 2 (1A, F3).

357 McGowan, *The Waning of the Green*, 278. See also, Brewer, "Antigonish and World War I," 24.

358 *The Casket*, 11 April 1918.

359 The unit's commander and Margaree native, Dr Roderick C. MacLeod, died in January 1917 of anthrax poisoning. "Poor Col. McLeod had a

tragic ending," lamented Fr Tompkins. "Is there any truth in the report that it was a bit of German perfidy?" See James J. Tompkins to J.J. Higgins, 23 January 1917, BIA, JJTP, MG 10, 2 (1A, F3). See also C.R. Blackburn, "Diary of No. 9 Stationary Hospital," Unpublished Paper, STFXUA, WXEP, MG 45/2/79.

360 Cameron, *For the People*, 161.

361 *The Casket*, 29 September 1917. For a complete account of the KOC Army Hut campaign, see Daniel and Casey, *Catholic Army Huts*.

362 James Morrison to J.J. MacNeil, 10 May 1918, ADA, BMP, letter#5212.

363 *The Casket*, 1 August 1918.

364 Cape Breton County ($28,566.50), Pictou ($9,300), Antigonish ($6,628.70), Inverness ($4,764.73), Guysborough ($3,250), Richmond ($1,764.50) and Victoria ($1087). See *The Casket*, 5 September 1918 and 12 September 1918,

365 James J. Tompkins to Flora Hunt, 15 February 1917, BIA, JJTP, MG 10, 2 (1A, F3).

366 James J. Tompkins to Michael Gillis, 23 January 1917, BIA, JJTP, MG 10, 2 (1A, F3).

367 McCarthy, *Times of My Life*, 59.

368 James Morrison to John R. MacDonald, 6 December 1917, ADA, BMP, letter#4742.

369 *The Casket*, 10 January 1918.

370 *The Casket*, 13 December 1917.

371 James J. Tompkins to J.A. Wall, 26 December 1917, BIA, JJTP, MG 10, 2 (1A, F3).

372 *The Casket*, 9 January 1919.

373 Sisters of St Martha, *A General View of the Religious Life*, 12.

374 H.D. Barry to H.P. MacPherson, 16 October 1918, STFXUA, HPMP, RG 5/9/431.

375 *The Casket*, 7 November 1918.

376 Sister Ignatius to H.P. MacPherson, 23 November 1918, STFXUA, HPMP, RG 5/9/5090.

377 Morgan, *Rise Again!* Book 2, 54.

378 *Morning Chronicle*, 12 November 1918.

CHAPTER FIVE

1 Nearing, *He Loved the Church*, 17.

2 Frank, "The 1920s," 235.

3 Reid, *Nova Scotia: A Pocket History*, 123.

4 Forbes, *Maritime Rights*, 38.
5 Nearing, *He Loved the Church*, 25.
6 Beck, *Politics of Nova Scotia, II*, 80–1.
7 Forbes, *Maritime Rights*, 47.
8 On the Independent Labour Party in England see Cohen, *The Failure of a Dream.*
9 Donald MacAdam to H.P. MacPherson, 2 August 1920, STFXUA, HPMP, RG 5/9/5946; Donald M. MacAdam to Hugh MacPherson, 21 August 1920, STFXUA, HPMP, RG 5/9/5946.
10 Coady, *Masters of Their Own Destiny*, 6.
11 Beck, *Politics of Nova Scotia, II*, 84.
12 *The Casket*, 28 July 1921.
13 See also Forbes, *Challenging the Regional Stereotype*, 100–13.
14 James Morrison W.L. MacKenzie King, 14 December 1921, ADA, BMP, letter#8885.
15 Forbes, *Maritime Rights*, viii.
16 On Hughes's fascinating and controversial life see Ó Siadhail, *Katherine Hughes.* See also, Shelia Ross, "'For God and Canada,'" 89–108.
17 Campbell, *With our Hearts and Hands*, 115.
18 *The Casket*, 21 August 1912.
19 Fay, *A History of Canadian Catholics*, 262.
20 On the CWL in the Diocese of Antigonish see Ronan, *History of the Catholic Women's League.*
21 *The Casket*, 13 April 1922.
22 James Morrison to Michael Gillis, 7 August 1920, ADA, BMP, letter#7488. See also Campbell, *With our Hearts and Hands*, 191. The first Scout troop was organized at Whitney Pier by Fr Leo O'Connell in 1920 with an enrollment of sixty boys.
23 During the 1920s new sanctuaries were built at New Aberdeen (St John the Baptist, 1928), Glace Bay (St Anthony's, 1921), Glace Bay (St Anne's, 1921), Havre Boucher (St Paul's, 1920), New Victoria (St Joseph's, 1929), Westville (Holy Name, 1921), Westmount (Holy Rosary, 1923), St Joseph's (St Joseph's, 1927), and the little memorial chapel at Mabou (St Mary Magdalen, 1929).
24 *The Casket*, 4 August 1927 and 18 August 1927.
25 Fr Gillis thought the church was in "Alyford" near Oxford. A church, St Peter and St Paul Church, closely resembling St Andrew's is located in Aylesford.
26 On the importance of these congresses see Devlin, "The Eucharistic Procession of 1908," 407–25; Keogh, *Ireland and the Vatican*, 94–100.

27 *The Casket*, 30 October 1924.
28 *The Casket*, 17 November 1927.
29 Görres, *A Study of St Thérèse of Lisieux*, 12. See also Nevin, *God's Gentle Warrior.*
30 *The Casket*, 19 January 1922.
31 Graham, *Fire Spook*, 97, 112. See also MacIntyre, *The Fire-Spook of Caledonia Mills.*
32 Raine, "Toilers under the Sea," 21.
33 John Hugh MacDonald to James Morrison, 10 December 1920, ADA, BMP, unnumbered.
34 Frank, *J.B. McLachlan*, 168–9.
35 Forbes, *Challenging the Regional Stereotype*, 32.
36 J.J. MacKinnon to H.P. MacPherson, 12 March 1923, STFXUA, WXEP, MG 45/2/553.
37 Nearing, *He Loved the Church*, 27.
38 Frank, "Tradition and Culture," 216.
39 *The Casket*, 22 January 1920.
40 *The Casket*, 23 February 1922.
41 *The Casket*, 21 October 1920.
42 *The Casket*, 8 April 1920.
43 The other clergy involved were Fr Stanley Macdonald (Asst Sydney Mines), Fr Alfred Boudreau (Asst North Sydney), Fr Michael MacCormick (East Bay), Fr Martin Wallace (Louisbourg), Fr Ronald C. MacGillivray (Asst St Anne's Glace Bay), Fr Angus Bryden (Asst Sacred Heart Sydney), and Fr Amable Briand (Asst Little Bras d'Or). Some of the early members of the club were Angus A. MacDonald (druggist), Fred MacInnis (employment agent DOMCO), John MacLean (locomotive fireman), Leo Timmons (pipe fitter), Wilfrid Bates (manager Dominion Utilities), and J.A. Gillis (schoolteacher).
44 Some of Ryan's most popular books were *Capital and Labor*, *A Catechism of the Social Question*, and *Catholic Doctrine on the Right of Self Government.*
45 On Father Ryan see Gearty, *Monsignor John A. Ryan*; Hunnicutt, "A Forgotten Vision," 384–402.
46 *The Casket*, 28 July 1921.
47 Frank, *J.B. McLachlan*, 135.
48 *The Casket*, 4 August 1921.
49 *The Casket*, 17 February 1921.
50 *The Casket*, 4 August 1921.
51 *The Casket*, 1 September 1921.

52 Quoted in *The Casket*, 18 August 1921.
53 *The Casket*, 18 August 1921.
54 Donald MacAdam to H.P. MacPherson, 4 November 1921, STFXUA, HPMP, RG 5/9/5949.
55 Frank, *J.B. McLachlan*, 214–15.
56 Frank, *J.B. McLachlan*, 215; James Morrison to J.J. MacNeil, 1 February 1922, ADA, BMP, letter#9066.
57 MacGillivray, "Industrial Unrest in Cape Breton, 1919-1925," 48. See also *Sydney Record*, 3 July 1922.
58 James Morrison to A.L. MacDonald, 22 February 1921, ADA, BMP, letter#8109.
59 Frank, *J.B. McLachlan*, 237–8.
60 James Morrison to J.A.M. Gillis, 27 January 1922, ADA, BMP, letter#9042.
61 *The Casket*, 26 January 1922.
62 *The Casket*, 16 February 1922.
63 R.J. MacSween interview, 20 July 1965, ADA, PNP, Folder 39.
64 James Morrison to Thomas O'Reilly Boyle, 17 February 1922, ADA, BMP, letter#9126.
65 *The Casket*, 8 February 1923.
66 Thomas O'Reilly Boyle to H.P. MacPherson, 1 February 1923, STFXUA, HPMF, RG 5/9/896.
67 H.P. MacPherson to Neil McArthur, 7 January 1924, STFXUA, HPMF, RG 5/9/6024.
68 James Morrison to R.J. MacDonald, 5 July 1922, ADA, BMP, letter#9416.
69 Frank, *J.B. McLachlan*, 262.
70 James Morrison to J.A.M. Gillis, 31 July 1922, ADA, BMP, letter#9463; James Morrison to Colin F. MacKinnon, 4 August 1922, ADA, BMP, letter#9483.
71 Morton and McKay, "Expanding the Circle of Resistance," 70.
72 James Morrison to Colin F. MacKinnon, 4 August 1922, ADA, BMP, letter#9483.
73 Frank, *J.B. McLachlan*, 271.
74 Fr John James MacNeil (1862–1941) was born at Washabuck (Iona Parish) and had parishes across the diocese. An advocate of temperance, he received a vocation late in life, having also worked as a deep-sea fisherman. See *The Casket*, 30 October 1941.
75 James Morrison to J.J. McNeil, 7 October 1922, ADA, BMP, letter # 9685.
76 James Morrison to J.J. MacNeil, 14 March 1923, ADA, BMP, letter#10174.

77 James Morrison to Donald M. MacAdam, 10 April 1923, ADA, BMP, letter#10230.
78 James Morrison to Michael MacNeil, 5 June 1923, ADA, BMP, letter#10377.
79 James Morrison to Donald M. MacAdam, 8 June 1923, ADA, BMP, letter#10395.
80 James Morrison to Michael MacNeil, 5 June 1923, ADA, BMP, letter#10377.
81 Eugene M. Quirk to James Morrison, 9 July 1923, ADA, BMP, incoming letter #10237.
82 Donald M. McAdam to James Morrison, 12 April 1923, ADA, BMP, incoming letter #10231.
83 James Morrison to D.M. MacAdam, 8 June 1923, ADA, BMP, letter#10395.
84 MacGillivray, "Military Aid to the Civil Power," 102–5.
85 James Morrison to D.M. MacAdam, 18 July 1923, ADA, BMP, letter#10462.
86 *The Casket*, 19 July 1923.
87 James Morrison to Colin F. MacKinnon, 17 December 1923, ADA, BMP, letter#10849.
88 *The Casket*, 29 May 1924.
89 Campbell, *With our Hearts and Hands*, 135–6.
90 *The Casket*, 14 August 1924. See also *Cape Breton Post*, 12 August 1924.
91 *The Casket*, 11 September 1924.
92 *The Casket*, 29 January 1925.
93 Mellor, *The Company Store*, 270; *Canadian Press*, 8 March 1925.
94 *The Casket*, 19 March 1925.
95 Morgan, *Rise Again!* Book 2, 62.
96 *Halifax Herald*, 4 March 1925.
97 DeMont, *Coal Black Heart*, 199.
98 James Morrison circular, 12 March 1925. See also *The Casket*, 19 March 1925.
99 In the cathedral town, for example, clothes "carefully wrapped" could be left at the store of D.D. MacDonald. See *The Casket*, 19 March 1925.
100 James Morrison to John Hugh MacDonald, 20 March 1925, ADA, BMP, letter#12075.
101 James Morrison to John Hugh MacDonald, 20 March 1925, ADA, BMP, letter#12075.
102 James Morrison to William Chisholm, 19 March 1925, ADA, BMP, letter#12071.

103 James Morrison to John Hugh MacDonald, 20 March 1925, ADA, BMP, letter#12075.
104 *Halifax Herald*, 20 March 1925.
105 James Morrison to J.A.M. Gillis, 21 March 1925, ADA, BMP, letter#12079.
106 By May the total reached $11,050.68.
107 James Tompkins to James Morrison, 29 March 1925, ADA, BMP, letter#11928.
108 James Morrison to John Hugh MacDonald, 25 March 1925, ADA, BMP, letter#12087.
109 John Hugh MacDonald to James Morrison, 27 March 1925, ADA, BMP, incoming letter#12212.
110 *Sydney Post*, 27 April 1925; MacEwan, *Miners and Steelworkers*, 136.
111 Michael MacAdam to James Morrison, 8 May 1925, ADA, BMP, incoming letter#12120.
112 Frank, *J.B. McLachlan*, 379.
113 MacEwan, *Miners and Steelworkers*, 140–1.
114 James Morrison to J.A.H. Cameron, 19 June 1925, ADA, BMP, letter#1233.
115 *The Casket*, 6 August 1925.
116 James Morrison to Aime Boileau, 19 August 1925, ADA, BMP, letter#12449.
117 James Morrison to G.S. Harrington, 1 October 1925, ADA, BMP, letter#12547.
118 Frank, "The Cape Breton Coal Industry," 126.
119 Frank, *J.B. McLachlan*, 398.
120 Colin F. MacKinnon to James Morrison, 12 January 1926, ADA, BMP, letter#12787.
121 James Morrison to Colin F. MacKinnon, 14 January 1926, ADA, BMP, letter#1926.
122 Jerome Chisholm to H.P. MacPherson, 27 January 1926, STFXUA, HPMF, RG 5/9/1701.
123 Frank, *J.B. McLachlan*, 428.
124 J.H. Nicholson to James Morrison, 5 February 1925, ADA, BMP, letter#12879.
125 James Morrison to J.E. McClurg, 23 January 1926, ADA, BMP, letter#12853.
126 Alexander MacEachern to James Morrison, 8 February 1925, ADA, BMP, letter#12893.
127 Frank, *J.B. McLachlan*, 371.

128 J.H. Nicholson to James Morrison, 5 February 1925, ADA, BMP, letter#12879.
129 Forbes, *The Maritime Rights Movement*, 184.
130 Boyle, *Father Tompkins*, 79.
131 James Tompkins to Hugh MacPherson, 11 December 1919, STFXUA, WXEP, MG 40/2/402.
132 James Tompkins to James Morrison, 11 December 1919, ADA, BMP, incoming letter#6846.
133 James Tompkins to Hugh MacPherson, 11 December 1919, STFXUA, WXEP, MG 45/2/452.
134 On Bishop Edward O'Dwyer see Morrissey, *Bishop Edward Thomas O'Dwyer*.
135 James Tompkins to James Morrison, 11 December 1919, ADA, BMP, letter#6846.
136 James Morrison to James Tompkins, 16 December 1919, ADA, BMP, letter#6960.
137 James Tompkins to James Morrison, 23 December 1919, ADA, BMP, incoming letter#6869.
138 James Tompkins to James Morrison, 13 January 1920, ADA, BMP, incoming letter#7109.
139 James Tompkins to John Ryan, 17 November 1920, BIA, JJTP, MG 10, 2, (1A, F2).
140 James Morrison to James Tompkins, 14 January 1920, ADA, BMP, letter#7061.
141 Boyle, *Fr Tompkins*, 79.
142 Tompkins, *Knowledge for the People*, 26. https://extension.wisc.edu/about-us/history/
143 *The Casket*, 30 December 1920.
144 Boyle, *Father Tompkins*, 88.
145 James J. Tompkins to McNeil, Archives of the Archdiocese of Toronto, Archbishop Neil McNeil Papers, 20 January 1921 (misdated as 1920), MN AP07.31
146 Cameron, *For the People*, 171.
147 *The Casket*, 23 December 1920.
148 Laidlaw, "The Adult Education Program of St. Francis Xavier University," 83–4.
149 Laidlaw, "The Adult Education Program of St. Francis Xavier University," 64.
150 Archives of the Archdiocese of Toronto, Archbishop Neil McNeil Papers, James J. Tompkins to McNeil, 27 January 1921, MN AP07.31.
151 *The Casket*, 21 April 1921.

152 St Francis Xavier University, *The People's School.*
153 James Tompkins to Neil McNeil, 5 April 1918, BIA, JJTP, MG 10, 2 (1A, F4).
154 For an interesting account of one student's time at the CUA see McCarthy, *Times of My Life*, 77–80.
155 *The Casket*, 30 August 1923.
156 Reid, "Beyond the Democratic Intellect," 286.
157 Brison, *Rockefeller, Carnegie, and Canada*, 47.
158 Learned and Sills, *Education in the Maritime Provinces of Canada*, 25.
159 Cameron, *For the People*, 182.
160 John G. Reid, "Beyond the Democratic Intellect," 288–91.
161 James Tompkins to Hugh MacPherson, 25 December 1919, STFXUA, WXEP, MG 45/2/451.
162 James Tompkins to Hugh MacPherson, 10 January 1920, STFXUA, WXEP, MG 45/2/455.
163 Hugh Somers interview, 11 October 1964, ADA, PNP, series 2, sub-series 1, folder 50.
164 W.S. Learned to James J. Tompkins (copy), 1 December 1921, ADA, BMP, document 8745.
165 James J. Tompkins to James Morrison, 11 December 1921, ADA, BMP, incoming letter#8672.
166 Neil McNeil to H.P. MacPherson, 21 January 1922, STFXUA, HPMP, RG 5/9/8401.
167 Neil McNeil to John R. MacDonald, 11 February 1922, ADA, AAJP, Series 4, Sub-Series 1.
168 Boyle, *Father Tompkins of Nova Scotia*, 98-99.
169 James Morrison to J.H. Nicholson, ADA, BMP, 3 June 1923, letter#10376.
170 P.J. Webb to Angus L. Macdonald, 2 January 1922, Nova Scotia Archives and Records Management (hereafter NSARM), Angus L. Macdonald Papers (hereafter ALMP), F1348/66.
171 Ronald MacDonald to H.P. MacPherson, 31 May 1923, STFXUA, HPMP, RG 5/9/6694.
172 *The Casket*, 22 March 1922.
173 Neil McNeil to Nicholas Meagher, 7 April 1922, ADA, AAJP, Series 4, Sub-Series 1.
174 Cameron, *For the People*, 183.
175 H.P. MacPherson to H. Bourque, 30 June 1922, STFXUA, HPMP, RG 5/9/814.
176 H.P. MacPherson to W.S. Learned, 15 March 1922, STFXUA, HPMP, RG 5/9/5794.
177 Welton, *Little Mosie from the Margaree*, 40.

178 James Tompkins to Angus L. Macdonald, 4 March 1923, NSARM, ALMP, F1348A/143.
179 Neil McNeil to James Tompkins (copy), 13 May 1922, ADA, BMP, incoming letter#9125.
180 James Morrison to Gregory McLellan, 3 June 1922, ADA, BMP, letter#9368.
181 *Red and White*, December 1919, 72.
182 Boyle, *Father Tompkins*, 107; Cameron, *For the People*, 179.
183 In 1909, for example, the parish of St Ninian's alone gave $2,000 to the college. See MacLean, *The Casket*, 109.
184 H.P. MacPherson to M.A.B. Smith, 10 February 1922, STFXUA, HPMP, RG 5/9/11147.
185 H.P. MacPherson to Lewis Hunt, 2 March 1923, STFXUA, HPMP, RG 5/9/5074.
186 V. Mullins to Morrison, 14 November 1922, ADA, BMP, incoming letter#9568.
187 *Minutes of a Conference of Representatives of Maritime Provinces Universities and Colleges* (Halifax: privately published, 1922), 54
188 *The Casket*, 6 July 1922.
189 Welton, "'Fraught with Wonderful Possibilities,'" 118.
190 Hanington, *Every Popish Person*, 188; Apostolic Delegate to James Morrison, 18 March 1924, ADA, BMP, letter#10918.
191 MacLeod, *A History of Memorial University* College, 14–15.
192 Edward Roche to Peter Di Maria, 23 February 1923, Archives of the Archdiocese of St John's (hereafter AADSJ), Archbishop Roche Papers (hereafter ABRP), 107/21/1.
193 James Morrison to Gregory J. McLellan, 3 June 1922, ADA, BMP, letter#9368.
194 Cameron, *For the People*, 184.
195 James Tompkins to Learned, 19 July 1922, BIA, JJTP, MG 10, 2 (6b[I]). See also Cameron, *For the People*, 184.
196 Leo Sears interview, 7 July 1965, ADA, PNP, folder 47.
197 Nearing, *He Loved the Church*, 18.
198 After Bishop Boyle's death in 1954, Fr Coady insinuated in an article for *The Casket* that Boyle had been transferred because of his commitment to merger. The transfer "looked at the time like defeat," wrote Coady, "but it turned out to be a stroke of providence." *The Casket*, 10 June 1954.
199 James J. Tompkins to Edward Roche, 24 October 1922, AADSJ, ABRP, 107/21/3.

200 H.P. MacPherson to James Morrison, 7 October 1922, ADA, BMP, incoming letter#9496.
201 Edward LeBlanc to Edward McCarthy, 16 October 1922, ADHA, ABEJMP, Vol. 3, 175.
202 Neil McArthur wrote: "If it is Bishop Morrison's intention, not to enter this scheme under any conditions, our committee should know it, in order that we may guard ourselves at the meeting from making any statements which might later on, be construed by the public, as expressions of opinion, representing the views of St. Francis Xavier College and the Diocese of Antigonish." Neil McArthur to Morrison, 16 October 1922, AD ADA, BMP, incoming letter#9523.
203 *St. Francis Xavier University Board of Governors Minutes*, 20 October 1922, STFXUA, RG /5/9/12362. See also Cameron, *For the People*, 186–8.
204 *The Casket*, 26 October 1922.
205 Boyle, *Father Tompkins*, 107.
206 James Tompkins to Edward Roche, 16 November 1922, AADSJ, ABRP, 107/21/3.
207 Edwards, "The MacPherson-Tompkins Era," 65.
208 The classmate was the *New York Times* editor Neil McNeil. See *The Casket*, 30 December 1954.
209 To Angus L. Macdonald, Tompkins wrote, "They are only high-schools and they think themselves universities." NSARM, ALMP, James Tompkins to Angus L. MacDonald, undated, F1348A/106.
210 Alexander Thompson to James J. Tompkins, 22 October 1920, BIA, JJTP, MG 10, 2 (1A,F4).
211 Welton, "Fraught with Wonderful Possibilities," 128.
212 Moses Coady to Angus L. Macdonald, 1 December 1922, NSARM , ALMP, F1348/24.
213 Robert Phalen to Angus L. Macdonald, 15 December 1922, NSARM , ALMP, F1287/2.
214 Angus L. Macdonald to Robert Phalen, 22 December 1922, NSARM , ALMP, F1287/5.
215 *The Casket*, 14 December 1922.
216 *The Casket*, 7 December 1922.
217 James Tompkins to Edward Roche, 16 November 1922, AADSJ, ABRP, 107-21-3.
218 Quoted in James Morrison to Charles W. MacDonald, 7 December 1922, ADA, BMP, letter#9833.
219 Ronald MacDonald to H.P. MacPherson, STFXUA, HPMP, RG 5/9/1593.

220 H.P. MacPherson to James Morrison, 7 October 1922, ADA, BMP, incoming letter#9496.
221 James Morrison to James J. Tompkins, 13 December 1922, ADA, BMP, letter#9855.
222 The outgoing pastor at Canso had formally resigned his post in the spring of 1919. James Morrison to J.W. MacIsaac, 31 May 1919, ADA, BMP, letter#6369.
223 Lewis MacLellan to Peter Nearing, 10 May 1967, ADA, PNP, folder 34.
224 James J. Tompkins to P.A. LeBlanc, 28 November 1914, BIA, JJTP, MG 10, 2 (1A, F1).
225 Mifflin, "The Antigonish Movement," 11.
226 James Morrison to J.W. MacIsaac, 18 December 1922, ADA, BMP, letter#9885.
227 Welton, "Fraught with Wonderful Possibilities," 131.
228 Boyle, *Father Tompkins*, 77.
229 Welton, "Fraught with Wonderful Possibilities," 131.
230 Charles MacDonald to James Morrison, 28 December 1922, ADA, BMP, incoming letter#9702.
231 H.P. MacPherson to Lewis Hunt, 2 march 1923, STFXUA, HPMP, RG 5/9/5074.
232 James Morrison circular, 25 May 1923, ADA, BMP, letter#10355.
233 James Morrison to Pietro Di Maria, 24 September 1925, ADA, BMP, letter#12529.
234 Cameron, *For the People,* 192–3; See also Laidlaw, *The Campus and the Community*, 147.
235 Hugh John MacDonald to Peter Nearing, 18 May 1965, ADA, PNP, series 2, sub-series 1, folder 20.
236 Michael Gillis interview, 4 January 1968, ADA, PNP, folder 65.
237 Michael Gillis interview, 1969, ADA, PNP, series 2, sub-series 1, folder 65.
238 Lewis MacLellan to Peter Nearing, 10 May 1967, ADA, PNP, folder 34.
239 James Boyle to C.F. MacIsaac, 12 March 1923, STFXUA, Colin F. MacIsaac Papers (hereafter CFMP), MG 80.
240 Donovan, *The Forgotten World*, 44.
241 Moses Coady to R.J. MacSween, 24 March 1953, STFXUA, MMCP, RG 30/3/2964.
242 Fr Angus R. MacDonald (1868–1953) was born at Broad Cove Marsh, Inverness County. He ministered at Christmas Island for forty-one years, and was described as a "gentleman of the old school" who was devoted to cooperatives, agriculture, and experimental farming. See *The Casket*, 21 May 1953.

243 Ronald MacDonald to H.P. MacPherson, 11 June 1924, STFXUA, WXEP, MG 45/2/411.
244 *The Casket*, 18 December 1924.
245 Quoted in *The Casket*, 24 December 1925.
246 *The Casket*, 24 December 1925.
247 Hugh John MacDonald to Peter Nearing, 18 May 1965, ADA, PNP, series 2, sub-series 1, folder 20.
248 *The Casket*, 18 November 1926.
249 Leo Sears interview, 7 July 1965, ADA, PNP, folder 47.
250 James Tompkins to James Morrison, 6 August 1923, ADA, BMP, letter#10302.
251 James Tompkins to H.P. MacPherson, 29 July 1926, STFXUA, JJTP, RG 6/5/311.
252 Hugh Somers interview, 11 October 1964, ADA, PNP, folder 50.
253 Boyle, *Father Tompkins*, 124.
254 Extension Department, *United Maritime Fishermen*, 11.
255 Boyle, *Father Tompkins*, 122.
256 James Tompkins to James Morrison, 15 December 1923, ADA, BMP, incoming letter#10616.
257 Morgan, *Rise Again!* Book 2, 75–6.
258 James Morrison to Leo J. Keats, 7 January 1924, ADA, BMP, letter#10942.
259 James Morrison to Alfred Boudreau, 20 February 1926, ADA, BMP, letter#12949.
260 Coady, *Masters of Their Own Destiny*, 11.
261 *The Casket*, 15 September 1927.
262 Forbes, *Maritime Rights*, 182.
263 Boyle, *Father Tompkins*, 140.
264 *The Casket*, 17 November 1927. Born at Afton in Heatherton Parish, Fr James McKeough (1870–1939) ministered at Pictou (1898), North Sydney (1898–99), Canso (1899–1915) and Tracadie (1915–39). He was found dead in his bed in 1939, and by 1941 the parish of Tracadie had erected a monument in his memory. See *The Casket*, 12 June 1941.
265 James Morrison to MacKenzie King, 8 March 1929, ADA, BMP, letter#15789.
266 James Morrison to James Tompkins, 8 March 1929, ADA, BMP, letter#15790.
267 Sister Catherine Martyr interview, 7 June 1965, ADA, PNP, folder 59.
268 *The Casket*, 11 August 1927.
269 Minutes of the Fifth Annual Rural Conference of the Diocese of Antigonish, September 28 & 29, 1927, ADA, BMP, letter#14427.

270 John R. MacDonald to Michael Gillis, 21 January 1927, STFXUA, WXEP, MG 45/2/404.
271 Nearing, *He Loved the Church*, 32.
272 Moses Coady to R.J. MacSween, 24 March 1953, STFXUA, MMCP, RG 30-2/1/2963.
273 Mary Stuart Council Minutes, 6 February 1927, ADA, AAJP, series 6, sub-series 2.
274 *The Casket*, 26 July 1928.
275 In 1965 Michael Gillis noted that "there was a discussion, a movement on to get something started in the Sydney area; and I think that's what moved them, the fear of that starting there ... And that forced them to meet the burden of taking on a layman and paying him a good salary" (A.B. MacDonald). Michael Gillis interview, 3 June 1965, ADA, PNP, series 2, sub-series 1, folder 12.
276 Interview with Fr Michael Gillis, recorded in 1967, STFXUA.
277 Moses M. Coady to R.J. MacSween, 24 March 1953, STFXUA, MMCP, RG 30/2/1/2963; See also Coady, *My Story*, 13.
278 Laidlaw, *The Campus and the Community*, 45–56. See also Corbett, *Henry Marshall Tory*, 122–8.
279 Cameron, *For the People*, 212.
280 St F.X. Alumni Association Report, 1928, STFXUA, HPMP, RG 5/9/12384.
281 Moses Coady to R.J. MacSween, 24 March 1953, STFXUA, MMCP, RG 30/2/1/2963.
282 Michael Gillis interview, 3 June 1965, ADA, PNP, series 2, sub-series 1, folder 12.
283 Hugh John MacDonald interview, 9 October 1964, ADA, PNP, series 2, sub-series 1, folder 20.
284 *The Casket*, 8 December 1927.
285 R.J. MacSween interview, 20 July 1965, ADA, PNP, Folder 39.
286 D.G. Whidden to Hugh MacPherson, no date, STFXUA, WXEP, MG 45/2/157.
287 R.J. MacSween interview, 20 July 1965, ADA, PNP, folder 39.
288 *The Casket*, 26 September 1929.
289 The Casket, 25 August 1921.
290 Wicken, *The Colonization of Mi'kmaw Memory and History*, 56.
291 For more on the case see Wicken, "'Heard It from Our Grandfathers," 146–61.
292 *The Casket*, 13 December 1928.
293 *The Casket*, 9 August 1923.
294 Parsons, "Micmac Notes," 468.

295 *The Casket*, 2 September 1926.
296 *The Casket*, 11 November 1920.
297 James Morrison to George Landry, 12 April 1930, ADA, BMP, letter#16713.
298 Sylliboy is quoted in James Morrison to L.J. MacDonald, 31 May 1923, ADA, BMP, letter#10367.
299 MacInnes, "Scottish Catholic Society," 26.
300 *The Casket*, 1 April 1926.
301 MacInnes, "Scottish Catholic Society," 32; Campbell, *With our Hearts and Hands*, 121.
302 *The Casket*, 13 July 1922.
303 *The Casket*, 24 March 1921.
304 Donald MacAdam to James Morrison, 29 March 1921, ADA, BMP, incoming letter#8070.
305 See Ludlow, "More than Codmen," 72–174; Campbell, *With our Hearts and Hands*, 124.
306 In the autumn of 1920, a county board convention of the AOH met for an emergency meeting in Glace Bay to draft a resolution of protest to be presented to the provincial, dominion and British governments protesting the military laws as applied to Ireland. *The Casket*, 20 October 1920.
307 MacKenzie, *The Irish in Cape Breton*, 101.
308 *The Casket*, 1 September 1927.
309 Cameron, *"And Martha Served,"* 92.
310 *The Casket*, 14 February 1924.
311 Gertrude MacIsaac to Mary MacIsaac, 8 December 1920, STFXUA, CFMP, 80.
312 L.G. Power to C.F. MacIsaac, 18 August 1920, STFXUA, CFMP, MG 80. Power's daughter, Sister Maura, was an educator and historian of the Sisters of Charity.
313 MacIsaac, *A Better Life*, 158.
314 *The Casket*, 22 September 1921.
315 Cameron, *"And Martha Served,"* 68.
316 Nearing, *He Loved the Church*, 34.
317 Cameron, *"And Martha Served,"* 74.
318 Sister Mary of the Sacred Heart MacKinnon, Sister Bernardine (Viola) Livingstone, Sister M. Chrisostom (Philomena Loretta) Bates, and Sister M. Veronica (Caroline Campbell).
319 *The Casket*, 2 December 1926. In 1927, for example, Glencoe donated $58.85 along with 10 bags of potatoes, 4 bushels of turnips, 4 pecks beets, 1 peck carrots, 3 tubs butter, 3 cheese, 2 lbs tea, 1 blanket, 1 quarter beef, 14 ½ doz. Eggs, 1 sheet, 1 pr pillow cases, 1 box cookies, and numerous articles for the annual sale. MacIsaac, *A Better Life*, 163.

320 James Morrison to William Clapperton, 7 July 1924, ADA, BMP, letter#11418; *The Casket*, 3 September 1925.
321 For more general information on orphanages in Nova Scotia see Chard, "The Halifax Protestant Orphans' Home," 100–14; Lafferty, *The Guardianship of Best Interests*.
322 One poignant advertisement in November 1921 sought a home for two girls aged three years and sixteen months. Both girls had been born to "married" Catholic parents. The Children's Aid Society was hopeful that they could be adopted into the same family or at the very least be adopted into the same district. See *The Casket*, 21 November 1921.
323 Nearing, *He Loved the Church*, 66.
324 *Little Flower Messenger* (1928), foreword.
325 See Ludlow, *The Canny Scot*, 13.
326 Lafferty, "Modernity and the Denominational Imperative," 117.
327 *Halifax Herald*, 30 August 1927.
328 Lafferty, "Modernity and Denominational Imperative," 107.
329 Cameron, *"And Martha Served,"* 72.
330 James Morrison to H.P. MacPherson, 24 April 1922, ADA, BMP, letter#9231.
331 James Morrison to Angus J. MacIsaac, 24 June 1925, ADA, BMP, letter#12568.
332 *The Casket*, 13 June 1929.
333 Campbell, *With our Hearts and Hands*, 206.
334 Fr J.N. MacNeil interview, October 1964, ADA, PNP, folder 36.
335 James Morrison to J.M. Fraser, 18 November 1918, ADA, BMP, letter#5737. See also H.P. MacPherson to J.J. Tompkins, 24 August 1918, STFXUA, JJTP, RG 6/5/368.
336 James Morrison to Vincent Morrison, 14 December 1925, ADA, BMP, letter#12707.
337 John McRae, to Donald MacPherson, 4 March 1930, BIA, DMP, MG 13, 58 (F3).
338 MacDonald, "On Getting the Sack," 18.
339 "The Bishop of Victoria Personal Statement," 15 September 1922, BAMP, BIA, MG 13, 22, (F1).
340 James Morrison to Alexander MacDonald, 13 September 1924, ADA, BMP, letter#11552.
341 Alexander MacDonald to H.P. MacPherson, 22 September 1924, STFXUA, HPMP, RG 5/9/6214.
342 James Morrison to Apostolic Delegate, 1 December 1924, ADA, BMP, letter#11766.

CHAPTER SIX

1 James Morrison to J.J. Purcell, 16 December 1930, ADA, BMP, letter#17266.

2 James Morrison to James J. Tompkins, 9 January 1930, ADA, BMP, letter#16497.

3 *Sydney Record*, 8 January 1930.

4 James Kiely to H.P. MacPherson, 12 December 1932, STFXUA, HPMP, RG 5/9/5567.

5 Coady, *My Story*, 14.

6 *The Casket*, 10 April 1930. For an interesting account of the lobster industry in New England see Woodard, *The Lobster Coast*.

7 Coady, *Masters of Their Own Destiny*, 29.

8 *The Casket*, 30 July 1931.

9 James J. Tompkins to James Morrison, 11 February 1930, ADA, BMP, letter#16507; Boyle, *Father Tompkins*, 163.

10 *The Casket*, 29 May 1930.

11 Michael Gillis interview, 3 June 1965, ADA, PNP, folder 12.

12 Moses Coady to R.J. MacSween, 24 March 1953, STFXUA, MMCP, RG 30/2/1/2963.

13 Cameron, *For the People*, 218.

14 D.D. MacFarlane diary, 24 September 1930, ADA, AAJP.

15 "The Study Club," unpublished paper, STFXUA, RG 30-3/25/912.

16 *The Casket*, 22 January 1931.

17 *The Casket*, 22 August 1935.

18 Moses Coady to Study Club Leaders, 9 October 1930, STFXUA, RG 30-3/25/815.

19 Dodaro and Pluta, *The Big Picture*, 64.

20 For information pulpwood cooperatives, see Sandberg and Clancy, *Against the* Grain, 74.

21 Amable Briand, "Brief Sketch of my Pastorate in West Arichat, 1929 to 1943," ADA, AAJP, 9. Later, Fr Briand claimed to have faced similar opposition when he organized a local cooperative store.

22 *Extension Bulletin*, 7 November 1933.

23 *The Casket*, 1 March 1934.

24 Roy Frederick Bergengren (1879–1955). Born in Gloucester, Massachusetts, Bergengren was educated at Dartmouth College and Harvard University. In 1921 he was hired by the millionaire Edward Albert Filene (Broad Cove's credit union was named in his honour) to promote the credit union movement. In 1934 the Federal Credit Union Act

was passed by Congress, and Bergengren headed the Credit Union National Association. He resigned that post in 1945.

25 Dodaro and Pluta, *The Big Picture*, 115.
26 *The Casket*, 29 October 1931.
27 *The Casket*, 2 June 1949.
28 Mooney, *Co-operatives Today and Tomorrow*, 108–14.
29 On New Aberdeen's Credit Union see Delaney, *25¢ A Week*.
30 Dodaro and Pluta, *The Big Picture*, 90.
31 See Coles, *A Radical Devotion*; William Miller, *Dorothy Day*.
32 James Morrison to James J. Tompkins, 23 October 1933, ADA, BMP, letter#19842.
33 E.R. Bowen to H.P. MacPherson, 27 November 1934, STFXUA, HPMP, RG 5/9/842.
34 Neil McNeil to H.P. MacPherson, 16 November 1933, STFXUA, HPMP, RG 5/9/8418.
35 Mary Johanna Boyle (1894–1963) entered the Sisters of Charity in 1915 and made her first vows in July 1918. She served in Massachusetts, Halifax, Stellarton, New Waterford, North Sydney, and Glace Bay.
36 John J. McLaughlin interview, 11 August 1965, ADA, PNP, folder 41.
37 Boyle, *Father Tompkins*, 158.
38 H.P. MacPherson to H.D. Barry, 14 July 1934, STFXUA, HPMP, RG 5/9/521.
39 Dodaro and Pluta, *The Big Picture*, 98.
40 Neal, *Brotherhood Economics*, 73; *The Casket*, 3 September 1931.
41 *Extension Bulletin*, 7 November 1933.
42 Frank, "The Miner's Financier," 137; *The Casket*, 29 August 1935.
43 Dodaro and Pluta, *The Big Picture*, 94.
44 Cameron, *"And Martha Served,"* 136.
45 DOSCO to James Morrison, 9 June 1931, ADA, BMP, incoming letter#17915.
46 Labour leader George MacEachern suggested that "only paupers" took relief. See Frank and MacGillivray, *George MacEachern*, 37.
47 A.B. MacDonald to James Tompkins, 21 November 1931, STFXUA, MMCP, RG 30/2/2/2358.
48 Leo B. Sears interview, 7 July 1965, ADA, PNP, series 2, sub-series 1, folder 47.
49 Fay, *A History of Canadian Catholics*, 203. *The Casket*, 21 May 1931.
50 *St Francis Xavier University Yearbook, 1933*, 28.
51 Ryan, *Social Doctrine in* Action, 243 & 289.
52 J.H. Nicholson, "Pope Pius XI's encyclical on Labour," unpublished paper, 1 September 1931, STFXUA, RG 30-3/28/48.

53 J.H. Nicholson, "Pope Pius XI's encyclical on Labour," unpublished paper, 1 September 1931, STFXUA, RG 30-3/28/48.
54 J.H. Nicholson, "Pope Pius XI's encyclical on Labour," unpublished paper, 1 September 1931, STFXUA, RG 30-3/28/48.
55 Quoted in *The Casket* from the *Glace Bay Gazette*, 25 June 1931.
56 James Morrison circular letter, 26 September 1931, ADA, BMP, letter#17993.
57 Frank and MacGillivray, *George MacEachern*, 37.
58 James Tompkins to A.B. MacDonald, 1931, STFXUA, RG 30-2/2/2347.
59 James Morrison to J.J. MacNeil, 25 November 1931, ADA, BMP, letter#18126.
60 O'Reilly Boyle made the comments in the New York publication *The Commonwealth*.
61 H.P. MacPherson to H.D. Barry, 22 February 1932, STFXUA, HPMP, RG 5/9/515.
62 John Hugh MacDonald to H.P. MacPherson, 2 January 1932, STFXUA, HPMP, RG 5/9/6547.
63 Beck, *Politics of Nova Scotia, II*, 143. See also, *The Casket*, 25 February 1932.
64 MacEwan, *Miners and Steelworkers*, 164–5.
65 James Morrison to A.J. MacIsaac, 23 February 1932, ADA, BMP, letter#18426.
66 H.P MacPherson to J.J. MacNeil, 10 March 1932, STFXUA, HPMP, RG 5/9/8301.
67 James Morrison to Gordon Harrington, 22 February 1932, ADA, BMP, letter#18425.
68 H.P. MacPherson to Andrew Rae Duncan, 5 November 1932, STFXUA, HPMP, RG 5/9/3022.
69 Testimony on Farm Resettlement, Sydney Hearings, Nova Scotia Royal Commission on Economic Inquiry, September 1934, STFXUA, Alexander Johnston Papers, MG 35.
70 Frank, *J.B. McLachlan*, 458.
71 Mellor, *The Company Store*, 329.
72 *The Casket*, 29 January 1931.
73 John Hugh MacDonald to James Morrison, 27 May 1932, ADA, BMP, incoming letter#18863.
74 In Whitney Pier four hundred Ukrainians worshipped under the ecclesiastical authority of the Greek Orthodox Bishop Basil V. Ladyka of Winnipeg. In 1913 they built Holy Ghost Church. As the community was too small to build a school of their own, 150 children attended the school

of Holy Redeemer parish. On the Ukrainian Church in Canada see Hryniuk, "Pioneer Bishop," 21–41.

75 James Morrison to Andrea Cassulo, 6 June 1932, ADA, BMP, letter#16675.
76 John Hugh MacDonald to James Morrison, 27 May 1932, ADA, BMP, incoming letter#18863.
77 *The Casket*, 15 September 1932.
78 Extension Department, *Mobilizing for Enlightenment*, 5.
79 James Morrison to James J. Tompkins, 4 November 1932, ADA, BMP, letter#18959.
80 J.J. MacNeil to Donald MacPherson, 6 May 1929, BIA, DMP, MG 13, 58.
81 Alexander MacIntyre to A.B. MacDonald, 16 May 1934, STFXUA, RG 30-2/7/79.
82 Nearing, *He Loved the Church*, 46.
83 Frank and MacGillivray, *George* MacEachern, 46–7.
84 Fr. Michael Gillis interview, Coady International Institute, STFXUA (recorded in 1966).
85 Nearing, *He Loved the Church*, 46.
86 Alexander MacIntyre biography, unpublished paper, STFXUA, no date, RG 30-2/7/271.
87 *Extension Bulletin*, 7 November 1933.
88 *The Casket*, 28 December 1933.
89 H.P. MacPherson to Andrew Rae Duncan, 5 November 1932, STFXUA, HPMP, RG 5/9/3032.
90 Joseph R. Chisholm to James Morrison, 14 October 1932, ADA, BMP, incoming letter#18922.
91 Campbell, *Banking on Coal*, 56.
92 Campbell, *Banking on Coal*, 58.
93 MacInnes, "Clerics, Fishermen, Farmers and Workers," 417.
94 Beck, *Politics of Nova Scotia, II*, 180.
95 James Tompkins to A.B. MacDonald, 29 January 1934, STFXUA, RG 30-2/2367.
96 Boyle, *Father Tompkins*, 170.
97 James Morrison to James J. Tompkins, 24 September 1934, ADA, BMP, letter#20610.
98 H.P. MacPherson to C.J. Connolly, 29 November 1934, STFXUA, HPMP, RG 5/9/2215.
99 Daniel Roberts interview, 14 July 1965, ADA, PNP, folder 46.
100 Boyle, *Father Tompkins*, 172.
101 Denis Marie to H.P. MacPherson, 29 April 1935, STFXUA, HPMP, RG 5/9/2551B.

102 H.P. MacPherson to William Clapperton, 30 May 1935, STFXUA, HPMP, RG 5/9/1970.
103 Daniel J. MacDonald to Eileen Burns, 5 December 1938, STFXUA, DJMP, RG 5/10/396.
104 James J. Tompkins to Daniel J. MacDonald, 2 August 1937, STFXUA, DJMP, RG 5/10/4152.
105 James Morrison to James J. Tompkins, 11 January 1937, ADA, BMP, letter#22586.
106 Boyle, *Father Tompkins*, 177.
107 *The Casket*, 3 September 1936.
108 James Tompkins to A.B. MacDonald, 6 March 1936, STFXUA, RG 30-2/2/2345d.
109 James Tompkins to Kay Thompson, 19 March 1936, STFXUA, RG 30-2/2/2367V.
110 Daniel J. MacDonald to James J. Tompkins, 21 September 1937, STFXUA, DJMP, RG 5/10/4153.
111 See Arnold, *The Story of Tompkinsville.*
112 Mary Arnold and Mabel Reed had a lifelong relationship. See Neal, *Brotherhood Economics*, 125–37.
113 MacKinnon, "Tompkinsville, Cape Breton Island," 51.
114 Harris, "Flattered but not Imitated," 108.
115 Boyle, *Father Tompkins*, 196.
116 J.W. Chisholm to Gordon Harrington, 29 November 1930, ADA, BMP, incoming letter#16970.
117 Henderson, *Angus L. Macdonald*, 56.
118 Beck, *The Politics of Nova Scotia*, II, 140.
119 Henderson, *Angus L. Macdonald*, 47.
120 H.P. MacPherson to Andrew Rae Duncan, 6 March 1934, STFXUA, HPMP, RG 5/9/3038.
121 *Extension Bulletin*, 17 January 1934.
122 Angus L. Macdonald to Stanley Macdonald, February 1937, NSARM, ALMP, F422/4.
123 Beck, *The Politics of Nova Scotia*, II, 166; Henderson, *Angus L. Macdonald*, 49.
124 Beck, *The Politics of Nova Scotia,* II, 166.
125 *The Casket*, 21 August 1930.
126 James Morrison to G.W. Ackhurst, 30 November 1933, ADA, BMP, letter#19931.
127 John Hugh MacDonald to James Morrison, 6 March 1934, ADA, BMP, incoming letter#20375.

128 James Morrison to Angus L. Macdonald, 1 December 1933, ADA, BMP, letter#19934.

129 John Laughlin MacIsaac (1870–1941). Born in Dunmore, Antigonish County, he was educated at St F.X. and attended medical school at the University of Maryland. He was elected in 1925 and served until his death. Two of his sisters, Ann (Sister St Charles Spinola) and Mary Jean (Sister St John of Beverley), were members of the CND. See *The Casket*, 27 March 1941.

130 John L. MacIsaac to James Morrison, 6 December 1933, ADA, BMP, letter#20109.

131 John L. MacIsaac to James Morrison, 8 December 1933, ADA, BMP, letter#20202.

132 Leo Keats to T.J. Bonner (copy), 19 February 1934, ADA, BMP, not numbered.

133 James Morrison to M.A. MacAdam, 6 March 1934, ADA, BMP, letter#20222.

134 John Hugh MacDonald to James Morrison, 6 March 1934, ADA, BMP, incoming letter#20375.

135 John Hugh MacDonald to Angus L. Macdonald (copy), 6 March 1934, ADA, BMP, incoming letter#20375.

136 James Morrison to Colin F. MacKinnon, 8 May 1934, ADA, BMP, letter#20343.

137 Angus L. Macdonald to James Morrison, 15 June 1934, ADA, BMP, letter#20605.

138 Angus L. Macdonald to Alex Johnston, February 1934, NSARM, ALMP, F1397/165.

139 Stanley Macdonald to James Morrison, October 1937 (Copy), NSARM, ALMP, F422/6.

140 Joseph Chisholm to Daniel J. MacDonald, 3 April 1938, STFXUA, DJMP, RG 5/10/526.

141 Stanley Macdonald to Angus L. Macdonald, 25 May 1938, NSARM, ALMP, F422/44.

142 James Morrison to Colin F. MacKinnon, 3 May 1933, ADA, BMP, letter#19495.

143 Andrew Rae Duncan to H.P. MacPherson, 27 December 1933, STFXUA, HPMP, RG 5/9/3036.

144 *The Casket*, 11 August 1932.

145 See Earle, "The Amalgamated Mine Workers of Nova Scotia," 99–137.

146 *The Casket*, 24 May 1934.

147 Earle, "The Amalgamated Mine Workers of Nova Scotia," 104.

148 *Sydney Post Record*, 20 October 1935.
149 *The Casket*, 24 October 1935.
150 Alexander S. MacIntyre to D.J. MacDonald, 19 October 1935, STFXUA, RG 30/2/7/266.
151 Alexander MacIntyre to John McPherson, 1 May 1935, STFXUA, RG 30/2/7/109-111.
152 James Morrison to Andrea Cassulo, 27 February 1936, ADA, BMP, letter#21784.
153 *The Casket*, 20 April 1933.
154 Fogarty, *The Vatican and the American Hierarchy*, 237.
155 Earle and Gamberg, "The Coming of the CCF to Cape Breton," 8.
156 Alexander MacIntyre to A.B. MacDonald, 10 August 1933, STFXUA, RG 30/2/7/59.
157 James Morrison to H.P. MacPherson, 28 November 1932, ADA, BMP, letter#19028.
158 James Morrison to H.P. MacPherson, 30 March 1933, ADA, BMP, letter#19418.
159 James Morrison to James McKenzie, 25 September 1933, ADA, BMP, letter#19790.
160 James Morrison to Leo Keats, 25 September 1933, ADA, BMP, letter#19789. Gregory Baum argued that Extension's political neutrality could be partly explained by pressure from funding sources and detractors accusing the Antigonish Movement of being "socialist." See Alexander, *The Antigonish Movement*, 102.
161 Alexander MacIntyre to A.B. MacDonald, 28 October 1938, STFXUA, RG 30/2/7/162.
162 H.P. MacPherson to Andrew Rae Duncan, 12 May 1936, STFXUA, HPMP, RG 5/9/3052.
163 A.B. MacDonald to Alexander MacIntyre, 31 October 1938, STFXUA, RG 30/2/7/164.
164 Nearing, *He Loved the Church*, 50.
165 John H. Gillis to H.P. MacPherson, STFXUA, HPMP, RG 5/9/3938.
166 James Morrison to John Hugh MacDonald, ADA, BMP, letter#20899.
167 Joseph Chisholm to H.P. MacPherson, 8 February 1926, STFXUA, HPMP, RG 5/9/1840.
168 James McLellan to Daniel J. MacDonald, 18 March 1937, STFXUA, DJMP, RG 5/10/2954.
169 Boyle, *Father Tompkins*, 170.
170 Alexander Johnston's personal transcripts of the testimony are held in the St F.X. University Archives.

171 Henderson, *Angus L. Macdonald*, 61.
172 Testimony of Fr Leo Keats, Port Hood Hearings, Nova Scotia Royal Commission on Economic Inquiry, September 1934, STFXUA.
173 *The Casket*, 6 September 1934. On the commission see Forbes and Muise, *The Atlantic Provinces in Confederation*, 298–9.
174 On Newfoundland's Commission of Government see Chadwick, *Newfoundland: Island into Province*; Long, *Suspended State*.
175 Testimony of Fr Alfred Boudreau, Port Hood Hearings, Nova Scotia Royal Commission on Economic Inquiry, September 1934, STFXUA.
176 Angus L. Macdonald to Hugh MacPherson, 21 January 1938, STFXUA, WXEP, MG 45/2/402.
177 Boyle, *A Middle Way*, 8.
178 *The Casket*, 23 December 1937.
179 *The Casket*, 14 June 1934; 29 August 1935.
180 Daniel J. MacDonald to D.F. MacDonald, 19 August 1938, STFXUA, DJMP, RG 5/10/2302.
181 For an account of cooperative work on Prince Edward Island see Croteau, *Cradled in the Wave.*
182 March, *Red Line*, 149.
183 James Morrison to W.H. Dennis, 21 September 1937, ADA, BMP, letter#23085.
184 H.P. MacPherson to W.H. Dennis, 16 May 1931, STFXUA, HPMP, RG 5/9/2563; W.H Dennis to Daniel J. MacDonald, 31 August 1939, STFXUA, DJMP, RG 5/10/1666.
185 March, *Red Line*, 297–8.
186 Tompkins was later called "John the Baptist" by several writers, including Gustav Francis Beck. See Beck, "The Men of Antigonish," 4; Ludlow, "Saints and Sinners," 100.
187 Fowler, *The Lord Helps Those*, 20–1.
188 Bertram B. Fowler to A.B. MacDonald, 23 April 1938, STFXUA, RG 30/2/2/748.
189 Croteau, *Cradled in the Waves*, 100.
190 Neal, *Brotherhood Economics*, 149.
191 Edward Cahill to Daniel J. MacDonald, 24 July 1938, STFXUA, DJMP, RG 5/10/420. See Cahill, *Freemasonry and the Anti-Christian Movement.*
192 Fowler, *The Lord Helps Those*, vii.
193 *Extension Bulletin*, 18 October 1938.
194 Boyle, *Father Tompkins*, 201.
195 Welton, *Little Mosie from the Margaree*, 95.
196 *Extension Bulletin*, 18 October 1938.

197 Quoted in Boyle, *Father Tompkins*, 204.
198 Ward, *Nova Scotia*, 119. Unfortunately, these negative assessments of people in rural Nova Scotia would be a reoccurring theme among those who moved to eastern Nova Scotia to work with the people or at the Coady International Institute. For a particularly patronizing and damning account see Lotz, *Sharing the Dream*, 152–63.
199 D.J. Rankin to D.J. MacDonald, 28 April 1943, STFXUA, DJMP, RG 5/10/373.
200 For another account of the writing process see Lotz, *The Humble Giant*, 86–99.
201 M.A. MacLellan, "Opening Address at the One Hundredth Celebrations of Dr. M.M. Coady, July 24 1982, Coady International Institute," BIA, MCMP, MG 13, 59 (2D.F4).
202 Daniel J. MacDonald to J.A. Floyd, 30 May 1939, STFXUA, DJMP, RG 5/10/1382.
203 *Xaverian Weekly*, November 1939.
204 Daniel J. MacDonald to D.F. MacDonald, 22 November 1939, STFXUA, DJMP, RG 5/10/2308.
205 James Morrison to George Landry, 2 February 1935, ADA, BMP, letter#20948.
206 *The Casket*, 3 January 1935.
207 Arthur Chiasson to H.P. MacPherson, 3 August 1932, STFXUA, HPMP, RG 5/9/1599.
208 James Morrison to Moses Coady, 12 August 1932, ADA, BMP, letter#18768.
209 Eugenio Pacelli to James Morrison, 8 March 1938, ADA, BMP, letter#24015.
210 James Morrison to Umberto Mozzoni, 12 April 1938, ADA, BMP, letter#23626.
211 D. MacNeil to Daniel J. MacDonald, 25 April 1938, STFXUA, DJMP, RG 5/10/1515.
212 J.A. O'Sullivan to Daniel J. MacDonald, 24 April 1938, STFXUA, DJMP, RG 5/10/3632.
213 Boyle, *Father Tompkins*, 190.
214 Ward, *The Land of Cooperation*, 93.
215 *The Casket*, 30 May 1935.
216 See Zech and Gaunt, *Catholic Parishes of the 21st Century*.
217 *The Casket*, 25 April 1935.
218 MacKenzie, *Blast!*, 117.
219 *The Casket*, 15 December 1938.

220 Bishop Morrison was impressed with the event, describing it as "so excellent." James Morrison to J.A. Butts, 13 December 1933, ADA, BMP, letter#19954.
221 *The Casket*, 7 September 1933.
222 *The Casket*, 17 September 1936.
223 McEwen, *Faith, Hope and Cooperation*, 139.
224 On Saint Mary MacKillop (1842–1909), see Paton, *Mary MacKillop*.
225 Fougere's sisters were Sister Mary Concepta, Sister Mary Aloysius, and Sister Jean de la Salle.
226 *The Casket*, 6 August 1931.
227 In 1930 the eight-two-year-old Fr Finley J. Chisholm was made a domestic prelate.
228 John H. Gillis to H.P. MacPherson 21 July 1932, STFXUA, HPMP, RG 5/9/3920.
229 J.W. Chisholm to H.P. MacPherson, 12 May 1932, STFXUA, HPMP, RG 5/9/1685.
230 James Morrison to H.P. MacPherson, 9 June 1936, ADA, BMP, letter#22020.
231 James Kiely to H.P. MacPherson, 20 June 1936, STFXUA, MG 1/1/1539.
232 M.A. MacLellan, "A Character to Remember," unpublished paper, p. 2, BIA, MCMP, MG 13,59 (2D, F3).
233 Cameron, *For the People*, 241.
234 *The Casket*, 24 April 1924.
235 MacDougall, *History of Inverness County*; Archibald MacKenzie, *History of Christmas Island Parish*; Campbell, *Banking on Coal*, 39; Rankin, *A History of the County of Antigonish*, viii.
236 The then publisher of *The Casket*, C.J. MacGillivray, later wrote to A.A. Johnston about Rankin's confused genealogical connections. See C.J. MacGillivray to A.A. Johnston, 10 October 1943, ADA, BMP, series 3, sub-series 2, folder 5.
237 Rankin, *Our Ain Folk and Others*, v.
238 Rankin, *On This Rock*.
239 McKay, *Quest for the* Folk, 238–9.
240 James J. Tompkins to John Ryan, 17 November 1920, BIA, JJTP, M 10, 2 (1A, F2). Some of these themes would be taken up by George Boyle a decade later in *Democracy's Second Chance*.
241 In *On This Rock*, Rankin noted that when a family faced economic distress, the eldest child was frequently called upon as a breadwinner. See Morton, "Women on Their Own," 97.
242 *The Casket*, 11 December 1930; *The Casket*, 15 September 1932.

243 Fraser, *Folklore of Nova Scotia*, XIII.
244 Bannon, *Eastland Echoes*, 3.
245 Somers, *Rt. Rev. Alexander Macdonell*; Cameron, *For the People*, 251.
246 *The Casket*, 10 March 1932.
247 Daniel J. MacDonald to Sister St Veronica, 1 October 1936, STFXUA, DJMP, RG 5/10/4235.
248 See Johnston, "To Search and Investigate," 11–21.
249 *The Casket*, 28 October 1937.
250 Albert Almon (1872–1960). Born at Glace Bay, Almon was a plumber and amateur historian. "To remember the dead," he wrote in *Rochefort Point: A Silent City in Louisbourg*, is "a holy and wholesome thought."
251 *The Casket*, 30 May 1935.
252 Albert Almon to H.P. MacPherson, 17 September 1911, STFXUA, RG 5/9/65.
253 An account of Campbell's travels through eastern Nova Scotia, and the songs he collected, were later published. See Campbell, *Songs Remembered in Exile*, 2.
254 John Lorne Campbell to H.P. MacPherson, 13 August 1933, STFXUA, HPMP, RG 5/9/1184.
255 Joseph Chisholm to H.P. MacPherson, 23 January 1935, STFXUA, HPMP, RG 5/9/1831.
256 Patrick Nicholson to John L. Campbell, 19 March 1937, STFXUA, PJNP, MG 2/90/1182.
257 Perman, *The Man Who Gave Away His Island*, 66.
258 For comments on the early accounts of interaction between the Mi'kmaq and the Scots see Newton, "The Macs meet the 'Micmacs,'" 67–96.
259 Campbell, *Songs Remembered in Exile*, 48.
260 *The Casket*, 4 August 1932.
261 James Morrison to J.D. MacLeod, 17 May 1915, ADA, BMP, letter#2144.
262 *The Casket*, 2 August 1934.
263 In both May 1921 and July 1931, the grand chief anxiously wrote to Bishop Morrison to ensure that a priest was ready for the mission. James Morrison to R.L. MacDonald, 16 May 1921, ADA, BMP, letter#8352; Gabriel Sylliboy to James Morrison, 14 July 1931, ADA, BMP, incoming letter#17820.
264 Benjamin Christmas to Leo Keats (copy), 20 May 1932, ADA, BMP, letter#18705a.
265 B.E. Christmas to Leo Keats, 20 May 1932 (copy), ADA, BMP, letter#18705A.

266 Leo Keats to B.E. Christmas, 28 May 1932 (copy), ADA, BMP, letter#18705B.

267 James Morrison to Leo Keats, 22 July 1932, ADA, BMP, letter#18729.

268 Miller, Shingwauk's Vision, 313–14.

269 J.A. MacLennan to James Morrison, 17 June 1927, ADA, BMP, incoming letter #14125.

270 For a history of residential schools in Canada see Miller, *Shingwauk's Vision*.

271 Chris Benjamin, *Indian School Road*, 34–6.

272 Miller, "Reconciliation with Residential School Survivors," 135.

273 *The Casket*, 27 September 1934. In her memoir, Isabelle Knockwood recalled that during a special council meeting the assignation of Fr MacKay was discussed. See Knockwood, *Out of the Depths*, 152–3.

274 *The Casket*, 27 September 1934.

275 Joseph MacKinnon to Indian Affairs, 8 September 1939, LAC, RG 10, Volume 6053, file 260-10, part 1, 845.

276 Ernest Chiasson to Indian Affairs, 28 August 1939, LAC, RG 10, Volume 6053, file 260-10, part 1.

277 Duncan C. Scott to J.L. Ilsley, 1 March 1929, LAC, School Files Series – 1879-1953 (RG 10), Volume 6054, file 265-1, 2127-2129.

278 A.A. Johnston to Thomas Cantley, 18 July 1933, LAC, School Files Series – 1879-1953 (RG 10), Volume 6054, file 265-1, 2183-2184.

279 Others soon found that students at Shubenacadie were "wards of the principal." See Knockwood, *Out of the Depths*, 113-114.

280 A.A. Johnston to James Morrison, 12 June 1936, ADA, BMP, incoming letter#22032

281 James Morrison to A.A. Johnston, 13 June 1936, ADA, BMP, letter#22032.

282 Benjamin, *Indian School Road*, 101. Ernest Chiasson to Indian Affairs, 7 December 1939, LAC, RG 10, Volume 6053, file 260-10, part 1, p.922.

283 J.P. MacKay to Neil A. MacDougall, 21 March 1939, LAC, RG 10, Volume 6053, file 260-10, part 1, 843–4.

284 Truth and Reconciliation Commission of Canada, *Canada's Residential Schools*, 588.

285 Benjamin, *Indian School Road*, 127.

286 Thomas D. Morrison to H.P. MacPherson, 14 July 1934, STFXUA, RG 5/9/9320.

287 James Morrison to Amable Briand, 16 March 1936, ADA, BMP, letter#21827.

288 *The Casket*, 24 August 1950.

289 On the Comité France-Acadie see Bosher, *The Gaullist Attack on Canada*, 50–2.
290 *The Casket*, 27 June 1935.
291 *The Casket*, 24 December 1931.
292 James Morrison to James J. Tompkins, 25 March 1933, ADA, BMP, letter#21061.
293 Daniel J. MacDonald to J.E. Brown, 4 August 1936, STFXUA, DJMP, RG 5/10/349.
294 Briand, "Brief Sketch of my Pastorate in West Arichat," 8.
295 Daniel J. MacDonald to Angus A. Beaton, 1 December 1938, STFXUA, DJMP, RG 5/10/72.
296 Nearing, *He Loved the Church*, 40.
297 James Morrison to M.A. MacAdam, 15 February 1930, ADA, BMP, letter#16599.
298 James Morrison to W.T. Trainor, 22 October 1936, ADA, BMP, letter#22321.
299 Nearing, *He Loved the Church*, 39.
300 L.D. Currie to Peter Nearing, 16 May 1966, ADA, PNP, series 2 sub-series 1, folder 6.
301 James Morrison to Umberto Mozzoni, 10 June 1938, ADA, BMP, letter#23721.
302 *The Casket*, 11 May 1933.
303 *The Casket*, 16 July 1936.
304 H.P. MacPherson to H.D. Barry, 29 November 1934, STFXUA, HPMP, RG 5/9/527.
305 James Kiely to James Morrison, 17 February 1936, ADA, BMP, letter#22051.
306 In 1930, the St Anthony's Home suffered a devastating fire. The fire broke out in the home's kitchen and proceeded up the dumb-waiter shaft, rapidly engulfing the residents in smoke. While most of the occupants were evacuated, six bed-ridden seniors were trapped in the upper floors, and the sisters (with the help of the local fire brigade) worked frantically to rescue them. The congregation's superior, Sister Mary Anthony, successfully carried the Blessed Sacrament through the flames, but her injuries ultimately lead to her death some weeks later. After twenty-seven years of administering in St Anthony's Home, the sisters were forced to construct a new three-storey facility. See *The Casket*, 1 May 1930.
307 MacDonald, *Memoirs of an Unorthodox Clergyman*, 24.
308 *The Casket*, 2 April 1936.
309 *The Casket*, 16 November 1939.

310 Cameron, *"And Martha Served,"* 137.
311 The sisters were Mother Faustina, Sister Irene Doyle, Sister Joan of Arc, and Sister Monica Doyle.
312 Mother Faustina to James J. Tompkins, 1933 (copy), STFXUA, HPMP, RG 5/9/3485a.
313 *The Casket*, 25 February 1937.
314 Cameron, *"And Martha Served,"* 10–142.
315 P.J. Monahan to James Morrison, 30 November 1935, ADA, BMP, letter#21809.
316 James Morrison to Sister Maris Stella, 13 February 1932, ADA, BMP, letter#18400.
317 Sister Irene Doyle interview, 3 July 1965, ADA, PNP, series 2, sub-series 1, folder 6.
318 William Clapperton to H.P. MacPherson, 22 October 1931, STFXUA, HPMP, RG 5/9/1953.
319 Kertzer, *The Pope and Mussolini*, 112.
320 On Fr Coughlin see Carpenter, *Father Charles E. Coughlin.*
321 *The Casket*, 15 October 1936.
322 *Extension Bulletin*, 17 January 1934.
323 *New York Times*, 28 May 1931.
324 *Glace Bay Gazette*, April 1934.
325 Huber, *Our Bishops Speak*, 219.
326 *Irish Catholic Directory*, 1938 (579); Whyte, *Church and State in Modern Ireland*, 92.
327 C.J. MacGillivray to Michael MacDonald, 9 November 1936, BIA, MAMP, MG 13,12 (F1).
328 Alexander Laidlaw to Daniel J. MacDonald, 29 November 1936, STFXUA, DJMP, RG 5/10/2060.
329 *The Casket*, 15 September 1938.
330 Apostolic Delegate to James Morrison, 28 September 1937, ADA, BMP, incoming letter#23763.
331 Welton, *Little Mosie from the Margaree*, 109.
332 *The Casket*, 26 August 1937.
333 Welton, *Little Mosie from the Margaree*, 108.
334 The first reference to Pope Pius XII and his connections to the fascist States of Europe came from a 1963 play entitled *The Deputy*, by Rolf Hochhuth. Recently this controversial argument has been made in print in Cornwell, *Hitler's Pope,* and Kertzer, *The Pope and Mussolini.* These arguments have been countered by Blet, *Pius XII and the Second World War*, and Godman, *Hitler and the Vatican.*

335 James Morrison to William Clapperton, 8 March 1939, ADA, BMP, letter #24212.
336 Pighin, *The Secrets of a Vatican Cardinal*, 19.
337 Pighin, *The Secrets of a Vatican Cardinal*, 20.
338 James Morrison to John Hugh MacDonald, 13 September 1939, ADA, BMP, letter#24549.

CHAPTER SEVEN

1 Miller, "The 1940s," 306.
2 On Beaverbrook see Taylor, *Beaverbrook: A Biography*.
3 Patrick Nicholson to John Lorne Campbell, 25 September 1939, STFXUA, PNP, John Lorne Campbell Correspondence (hereafter JLCC).
4 Laverdure, *Redemption and Renewal*, 170.
5 Leo O'Connell to D.J. MacDonald, 14 November 1939, STFXUA, DJMP, RG 5/10/3602.
6 *The Casket*, 21 March 1940.
7 Pighin, *The Secrets of a Vatican Cardinal*, 43.
8 *The Casket*, 22 August 1940.
9 In March 1944, allied bombers mistakenly dropped their cargo on Rome. The bombs fell close to Vatican territory and the *Osservatore Romano* called it a "deliberate irreverence."
10 Thirteen men interred were from New Waterford, seven from Sydney, and two from Dominion. All the men except two were married and all but three had children.
11 Migliore and DiPierro, *Italian Lives*, 110.
12 For more on the Italian Consul Office in Montreal see Salvatore, *Fascism and the Italians of Montreal*.
13 Ronald MacLean to Paolo de Simone, 25 April 1939 (copy), ADA, BMP, incoming letter #24962.
14 Ronald MacLean to James Morrison, 15 March 1938, ADA, BMP, letter#24588.
15 Ronald MacLean to James Morrison, 29 Mary 1939, ADA, BMP, incoming letter#24962.
16 For a good summary of Italian internment across Canada see Iacovetta, Perin, and Principe, *Enemies Within*.
17 Pighin, *The Secrets of a Vatican Cardinal*, 152.
18 Ronald MacLean to Apostolic Delegate, 9 February 1942 (copy), ADA, BMP, incoming letter#27312.

19 Apostolic Delegate to James Morrison, 11 February 1942, ADA, BMP, incoming letter#27312

20 James Morrison to Louis St-Laurent, 31 July 1942, ADA, BMP, letter#26701.

21 James Morrison to Felice Martinello, 11 December 1942, ADA, BMP, letter#26985.

22 Migliore and DiPierro, *Italian Lives*, 180; Donovan, *The Forgotten World*, 65.

23 Migliore and DiPierro, *Italian Lives*, 121.

24 P.J. Nicholson to John Lorne Campbell, 23 June 1941, STFXUA, PJNP, JLCC.

25 *The Casket*, 24 July 1941.

26 On Venedam see Landry, *A Man of Faith*; On Steele's career see Steele, *Dear Old Rebel.*

27 *The Casket*, 19 January 1933; Maxwell, *Assignment in Chekiang*, 31, 109; James MacGillivray to Micky MacDonald, 10 March 1933, BIA, MAMP, MG 13, 12 (F1).

28 *The Casket*, 10 June 1943.

29 Caplan, "Fr. Charles Murphy and Hong Kong," 74.

30 *The Casket*, 12 November 1942.

31 See Schoppa, *In a Sea of Bitterness.*

32 Steel, *Dear Old Rebel*, 70. In 1946 Steele was awarded the "Emblem for Meritorious Civilian Service" by the United States Government for his work with American forces in China in 1944 and 1945. Specifically, he acted as a guide and interpreter and helped locate the bodies of pilots who had crashed in the mountain surrounding Chungking.

33 *The Casket*, 31 August 1944.

34 Mount Carmel Parish, *The Parish Year 1941*, 5.

35 Interview with Sister Catherine Martyr, 7 June 1965, ADA, PMP, series 2, sub-series 1, folder 59.

36 Minutes of Meeting of the Priests of Cape Breton and Victoria Counties, 5 March 1940, ADA.

37 Morgan, *Rise Again!*, Book 2, 118.

38 James Morrison to R.C. MacGillivray, 7 December 1939, ADA, BMP, letter#24777.

39 Hayes, Bechthold, and Symes, *Canada and the Second World War*, 36.

40 A.J. MacIsaac to Donald MacPherson, 24 February 1945, BIA, DMP, MG 13, 58. Dan R. MacDonald (1911–1976) survived the war and went on to record a number of LPs.

41 P.J. Nicholson to John Lorne Campbell, 4 October 1943, STFXUA, PNP, JLCC.

42 Neil McArthur to D.J. MacDonald, 22 June 1943, STFXUA, DJMP, RG 5/10/2190. Leo McArthur was later re-buried in the Reichwald Forest War Cemetery, Kleve, Germany. For Judge MacArthur's obituary, see *The Casket*, 20 November 1945.

43 *The Casket*, 13 January 1944.

44 For more on the *Caribou* sinking see How, *Night of the Caribou.*

45 *The Casket*, 25 February 1943.

46 For more see Hamilton, "Padres Under Fire."

47 C.L. Nelligan to James Morrison, 17 October 1939, ADA, BMP, incoming letter#25485.

48 J.C.F. MacDonnell to John R. MacDonald, 24 January 1950, ADA, BJRMP, series 3, sub-series 1, folder 5.

49 Michael Gillis to James Morrison, 14 March 1941, ADA, BMP, incoming letter#26517.

50 James Morrison to W.V. McCarthy, 13 November 1940, ADA, BMP, letter#254855.

51 Crerar, "In the Day of Battle," 70.

52 James Morrison to R.C. MacGillivray, 2 October 1940, ADA, BMP, letter#25375.

53 James Morrison to Michael Gillis, 2 December 1941, ADA, BMP, letter#26155.

54 Pelletier, "Fighting for the Chaplains," 95.

55 C.L. Nelligan to H.P. MacPherson, 6 April 1943 (copy), ADA, BMP, series 3, sub-series 1, folder 2.

56 In 1944. Bishop Morrison claimed to Fr McLaughlin that the chaplains were "absolutely silent." James Morrison to M.E. McLaughlin, 14 November 1944, ADA, BMP, letter#28436.

57 M.E. McLaughlin to James Morrison, 16 June 1945, ADA, BMP, series 3, sub-series 1, folder 3.

58 R.C. MacGillivray to James Morrison, 18 January 1944, ADA, BMP, incoming letter#30019.

59 James Morrison to R.C. MacGillivray, 7 September 1944, ADA, BMP, letter#28301.

60 M.A. MacLellan, "In Memoriam," BIA, MCMP, MG 13, 59 (2D.F4).

61 Pelletier, "Fighting for Chaplains," 118.

62 Anita Maria Tobin, "The Effect of Centralization," 18, 36–7.

63 *The Casket*, 28 August 1941.

64 *The Casket*, 26 March 1942.

65 Moses Coady to E.A. Arsenault, 26 May 1942, STFXUA, MG 20/1/52.

66 Knockwood, *Out of the Depths*, 141–3.

67 *The Casket*, 4 July 1940.
68 Tobin, "The Effect of Centralization," 65, 67; Patterson, "The Nova Scotian Centralization Policy," 101.
69 *The Casket*, 29 January 1942.
70 T.A. Crerar to James Morrison, 24 September 1941, ADA, BMP, incoming letter#28364.
71 James Morrison to A.R. MacDonald, 29 November 1941, ADA, BMP, letter#26144.
72 James Morrison to D.J. Rankin, 10 January 1942, ADA, BMP, letter#26279.
73 James Morrison to T.A. Crerar, 15 December 1941, ADA, BMP, letter#26195. In 1942, Fathers D.J. Rankin, Angus C. MacNeil, and Ernest Chiasson went to Ottawa to seek information and clarification from federal bureaucrats.
74 Patterson, "The Nova Scotia Centralization Policy," 102.
75 R.A. Hoey to James Morrison, 16 October 1942, ADA, BMP, incoming letter#28043.
76 Patterson, "the Nova Scotia Centralization Policy," 100 & 109.; James Morrison to Hugh John MacDonald, 9 August 1943, ADA, BMP, letter#27424,
77 *The Casket*, 16 September 1943.
78 Patterson, "the Nova Scotia Centralization Policy," 136.
79 *The Casket*, 23 September 1943.
80 *The Casket*, 9 August 1945.
81 James Morrison to R.A. Hoey, 10 December 1942, ADA, BMP, letter#26984.
82 James Morrison to M.M. MacDonald, 2 September 1943, ADA, BMP, letter#27486.
83 Fr Ross was appointed parish priest at Eskasoni on 29 October 1944. Interestingly, his mother died in 1910 and the children were sent to live with a foster family in Southwest Margaree. His father, Colin Francis Ross, joined the priesthood and served in the Diocese of Calgary.
84 James Morrison to A.A. Ross, 10 December 1945, ADA, BMP, letter#29103.
85 James Morrison to A.A. Ross, 26 December 1946, ADA, BMP, letter#29701.
86 Miller, "The 1940s," 345.
87 *The Casket*, 31 July 1947.
88 T.A Crerar to James Morrison, 17 May 1943, ADA, BMP, incomingletter#30751.
89 Cameron, *"And Martha Served,"* 173.

90 T.A Crerar to James Morrison, 17 May 1943, ADA, BMP, incomingletter#30751.

91 R.A. Hoey to James Morrison, 22 December 1947, ADA, BMP, series 3, Sub-series 1, folder 6.

92 Moses Coady to E.A. Arsenault, 26 May 1942, STFXUA, MMCP, MG 20/1/52.

93 James Morrison to Ildebrando Antoniutti, 23 November 1942, ADA, BMP, letter#26942.

94 *Peterborough Examiner*, 14 September 1943.

95 D.J. MacDonald to Ed O'Flaherty, 16 August 1943, STFXUA, DJMP, RG 5/10/3618.

96 Born at Lingan, Fr Michael Laffin (1851–1915) had died thirty years earlier after collapsing and striking his head on the concrete steps at the Tracadie church. James Morrison to John R. MacDonald, 16 September 1943, ADA, BMP, letter#27515.

97 Michael Gillis to John R. MacDonald, 18 February 1947, ADA, BJRMP, series 3, sub-series 1, folder 5; Roderick MacSween interview, 24 July 1965, ADA, PNP, folder 40.

98 Nearing, *He Loved the Church*, 56.

99 Nearing, *He Loved the Church*, 59.

100 John Hugh MacDonald to John R. MacDonald, 13 March 1944, Archdiocese of Edmonton Archives, John Hugh MacDonald Papers (JHMP).

101 J.A. O'Sullivan to John R. MacDonald, 5 March 1944, ADA, BJRMP, series 3, sub-series 3, folder 2.

102 *The Casket*, 9 March 1944.

103 John Hugh MacDonald to John R. MacDonald, 15 March 1944, ADA, JHMP; See also Nearing, *He Loved the Church*, 56.

104 John Hugh MacDonald to John R. MacDonald, 10 March 1944, Archdiocese of Edmonton Archives, JHMP.

105 John R. MacDonald to Michael Gillis, 23 March 1944, ADA, BJRMP, series 3, sub-series 1, folder 2.

106 *Canadian Register*, 17 June, 1944. Yet, according to the cooperator J.T. Croteau, Boyle "seemed to withdraw from active participation in the movement after the first few months" and within a few years he was facing criticism that he was not "spearheading a progressive movement." There were limitations to a bishop's office. See Croteau, *Cradled in the Waves*, 141; Moses Coady to Adolphus Gillis, 16 January 1950, STFXUA, MMCP, MG 20/1/917.

107 See McGlynn, *Visions of Fatima*.

108 *The Casket*, 3 June 1948.
109 *The Casket*, 23 September 1948.
110 *The Casket*, 15 September 1949.
111 P.J. Nicholson to John Lorne Campbell, 17 March 1944, STFXUA, PNP, JLCC .
112 *The Casket*, 23 July 1942.
113 Donovan, *The Forgotten World*, 74–5.
114 Miller, "The 1940s," 316.
115 Beck, *Politics of Nova Scotia*, II, 196.
116 Gibson, *Gaelic Cape Breton Step-Dancing*, 80.
117 Gibson, *Traditional Gaelic Bagpiping*, 334.
118 Mabou Parishioner to John R. MacDonald, 19 December 1945, ADA, BJRMP, series 3, sub-series 1, folder 4. On Bryden's contribution to Gaelic culture see MacDonald, *Mabou Pioneers Volume 1*, 52.
119 Cameron, *For the People*, 247.
120 J.A. Butts to D.J. MacDonald, 30 September 1941, STFXUA, DJMP, RG /5/10/412.
121 *Halifax Herald*, 17 April 1940.
122 Stanley MacDonald to Angus L. Macdonald, 12 February 1937, NSARM, ALMP, F422/2.
123 Henderson, *Angus L. Macdonald*, 78.
124 Stanley MacDonald to Micky MacDonald, 23 November 1938, BIA, MAMP, MG 13, 12 (F1).
125 *The Casket*, 28 March 1940.
126 James Morrison to James Nicholson, 4 November 1940, ADA, BMP, letter#25456.
127 UMW Local 4560 to James Morrison, 31 October 1940, BIA, MG 13/120.
128 Minutes of Meeting of the Priests of Cape Breton and Victoria Counties, 6 February 1940, ADA.
129 James Morrison to C.H. Bauer, 9 February 1940, ADA, BMP, letter#24950.
130 On Gillis see, Harrop, *Clarie*.
131 Earle and Gamburg, "The Coming of the CCF to Cape Breton," 21–2.
132 Harrop, *Clarie*, 6.
133 Author interview with Archbishop Joseph Neil MacNeil, 7 November 2016.
134 Beck, *Politics of Nova Scotia*, II, 183.
135 L.D. Currie to H.P. MacPherson, 9 December 1941, STFXUA, HPMP, RG 30-2/7/29.
136 L.D. Currie to H.P. MacPherson, 9 December 1941, STFXUA, HPMP, RG 30-2/7/29.

137 Moses Coady to Mary Arnold, 5 December 1941, STFXUA, MMCP, RG 30/1/39.
138 Angus L. Macdonald to Stanley MacDonald, 17 October 1938, NSARM, ALMP, F422/47.
139 Angus L. Macdonald to James J. Tompkins, 16 June 1942, NSARM, ALMP, Vol. 1518, F762/1.
140 Moses Coady to J.E. Michaud, 12 December 1941, STFXUA, MMCP, RG 30-3/7/31.
141 *The Casket*, 30 December 1943.
142 *Glace Bay Post-Gazette*, 9 November 1943.
143 Earle and Gamburg, "The Coming of the CCF to Cape Breton," 23.
144 Forbes, *Challenging the Regional Stereotype*, 17–34.
145 MacEwan, *Miners and Steelworkers*, 257.
146 MacEwan, *Miners and Steelworkers*, 261.
147 *The Casket*, 1 August 1946. The letter was signed by Fr R.C. MacGillivray (Sacred Heart), Fr Leo Sears (Whitney Pier), Fr A.A. Beaton (St Theresa's), Fr Allen MacDonald and D.A. Doyle (Sacred Heart), Fr Francis MacIsaac (St Theresa's), Fr Richard Laffin (Whitney Pier), Fr F.J. D'Intino (St Nicholas), and Fr Leo O'Connell (St Mary's).
148 *The Casket*, 30 January 1947.
149 James Morrison to Sam Campbell, 16 March 1947, ADA, BMP, letter#29841.
150 "Meeting of the Pastors of Twelve Mining Parishes of Cape Breton County Held in the Lyceum Theatre, Sydney, March 13, 1947," ADA, fonds 5, series 3, sub-series 1, folder 5.
151 *The Casket*, 27 March 1947.
152 *The Casket*, 3 April 1947.
153 *The Casket*, 1 July 1948.
154 *The Casket*, 12 August 1948.
155 *The Casket*, 2 September 1948.
156 *The Casket*, 14 October 1948.
157 *The Casket*, 1 September 1949.
158 D.J. MacDonald to R.C. MacGillivray, 4 May 1938, STFXUA, DJMP, RG 5/10/2525.
159 *The Casket*, 24 March 1932.
160 D.J. MacDonald to Alex Johnston, 25 September 1940, STFXUA, DJMP, RG 5/10/1882.
161 *The Casket*, 19 September 1940.
162 Minutes of Meeting of the Priests of Cape Breton and Victoria Counties, 3 April 1940, ADA.

163 Minutes of Meeting of the Priests of Cape Breton and Victoria Counties, 10 September 1940, ADA. On J. Clyde Nunn, see Nunn, "Life was his Podium."

164 D.J. MacDonald to Alexander Johnston, 25 September 1940, STFXUA, DJMP, RG 5/10/1882.

165 Daniel McCormack circular letter, 12 December 1941, STFXUA, WXEP, MG 45/2/401. See also James Morrison to Msgr. James M. Reardon, 13 April 1942, ADA, BMP, letter#26460. Other members of the Board of Directors were Fr. A.A. Johnston, Fr Moses M. Coady, Mr Alphonse Sears, and Dr J. Seward Brean.

166 McGowan, "University of the Air," 9.

167 James Morrison to James M. Reardon, 13 April 1942, ADA, BMP, letter#26460.

168 The original staff of CJFX were J. Clyde Nunn, Danny Gallivan, D.F. Campbell, E.F. MacDonald, Ralph Ricketts, John Langlois, Zita O'Hearn Cameron, Terry MacLellan, Patricia Lebbetter, Rosaria Nearing, Irene Gatto, and Nora McKenna.

169 Speech given at opening of radio station CJFX, March 1943, by Fr D.J. MacDonald, STFXUA, DJMP, RG 5/10/680.

170 McGowan, "University of the Air," 14.

171 Dodaro and Pluta, *The Big Picture*, 135.

172 On this program see Miriam, "The Historical Background of the People's School," 2–4.

173 D.J. MacDonald to Alexander Johnston, 1 May 1943, STFXUA, DJMP, RG 5/10/1889.

174 *The Casket*, 21 October 1948.

175 The paper was eventually published in 1941. See Rankin, "Laurence Kavanagh," 51–76. In 1945 Rankin published a brief account of the life of Fr Kenneth J. MacDonald. See Rankin, "The Reverend Kenneth J. MacDonald," 109–16.

176 Leo J. Keats to A.A. Johnston, 30 September 1941, ADA, AAJP, series 10, sub-series 1, folder 2.

177 *The Casket*, 13 November 1941.

178 *The Casket*, 23 August 1945.

179 *The Casket*, 15 April 1948.

180 MacNeil, *The Highland Heart*. See also, Caplan, "Neil MacNeil and the Highland Heart," 32–6.

181 Colin MacKenzie to James Morrison, 20 November 1943, ADA, BMP, incoming letter#29851. See MacDonell, "The Early History of St. Francis Xavier University," 81–90.

182 *The Casket*, 26 May 1949.

183 *The Casket*, 19 December 1940.
184 Lamb, *The Celtic Crusader*, 41.
185 Sister St Veronica, "The Mount Saint Bernard Choir," unpublished report, June 1963, BIA, SMP, MG 13, 13 (F1).
186 *The Casket*, 31 January 1946.
187 In his biography of Campbell, Ray Perman writes that Campbell was received into the Catholic Faith in St Ninian's Cathedral but *The Casket* suggests that it was Somers Chapel. See *The Casket*, 13 February 1947.
188 Dodaro and Pluta, *The Big Picture*, 132.
189 Dodaro and Pluta, *The Big Picture*, 134.
190 Moses Coady to Mary Arnold, 5 December 1941, STFXUA, MMCP, MG 20/1/39.
191 Sam Campbell to D.J. MacDonald, 19 May 1942, STFXUA, DJMP, RG 5/10/466.
192 John R. MacDonald to Michael Gillis, 23 March 1944, ADA, BJRMP, series 3, sub-series 1, folder 2.
193 *The Casket*, 17 November 1949.
194 Lotz and Welton, *Father Jimmy*, 128.
195 *The Casket*, 26 July 1945.
196 *The Casket*, 2 December 1948.
197 *The Casket*, 26 June 1941.
198 *The Casket*, 12 March 1942.
199 Alfred Sinnott to James Morrison, 29 November 1945, ADA, BMP, series 3, sub-series 1, folder 4.
200 James McGuigan to James Morrison, 10 June 1947, ADA, BMP, letter#32498.
201 Bishop John R. MacDonald Diary of Trip to Rome, 1949, ADA, BJRMP, series 1, sub-series 1, folder 15.
202 *The Casket*, 27 February 1941.
203 Michael Gillis interview, 3 June 1965, ADA, PNP, series 2, sub-series 1, folder 12. Coady and MacPherson were best friends. In 1956 Coady told a friend that "the old Rector left a void in [his] life that [could] never be filled." Moses Coady to Sister Anselm, 28 May 1957, STFXUA, RG 30-2/1/43.
204 M.A. MacLellan, "A Character to Remember," unpublished paper, BIA, MCMP, MG 13, 59 (2D. F3).
205 There is a poignant story surrounding the Old Rector's death. For various reasons, he was never overly friendly with Bishop John R. Most felt that it was due to some animosities that he had for MacDonald's uncle, Archbishop Neil McNeil. On his deathbed, the Old Rector asked for the bishop, and John R. immediately rushed to his bedside and forgave any

past transgressions (this was written privately and not for public consumption). Hugh John MacDonald to Peter Nearing, 18 May 1965, ADA, PNP, series 2, sub-series 1, folder 20.

206 *The Casket*, 16 September 1948.

207 Michael Gillis interview, 3 June 1965, ADA, PNP, series 2, sub-series 1, folder 12.

208 Hugh Somers interview, 11 October 1964, ADA, PNP, series 2, sub-series 1, folder 50.

209 Cameron, *For the People*, 268.

210 *The Casket*, 6 July 1944.

211 James Morrison to John R. MacDonald, 25 August 1944, ADA, BMP, letter#28266.

212 Leo Keats to Albert Doucet, 29 January 1937, BIA, ADP, MG 13, 53, (F1).

213 On the new building on the St F.X. campus see Roach, *The Jewel of the Campus*.

214 P.J. Nicholson to John Lorne Campbell, 10 January 1945, STFXUA, PNP, JLCC.

215 Cameron, *For the People*, 268; *The Casket*, 24 October 1946.

216 Roderick MacSween interview, 24 July 1965, ADA, PNP, series 2, sub-series 1, folder 40.

217 Nearing, *He Loved the Church*, 60.

218 Michael Gillis to John R. MacDonald, April 1945, ADA, BJRMP, series 3, sub-series 1, folder 7.

219 M.A. MacAdam to John R. MacDonald, 7 December 1945, ADA, BJRMP, series 3, sub-series 1, folder 4.

220 For more on the riot see Kimber, *Sailors, Slackers and Blind Pigs*.

221 Donovan, *The Forgotten World*, 86.

222 Boyle, *Democracy's Second Chance*, 68.

223 *The Casket*, 28 November 1946.

224 Report of Conference on Rural Rehabilitation (copy), 11 and 12 September 1941, ADA, BMP, letter#27381.

225 Henderson, *Angus L. Macdonald*, 156.

226 Interview with Fr George Topshee, no date, ADA, BJRMP, series 1, sub-series 1, folder 15.

227 Neil McNeil to Nicholas Meagher, 22 February 1920, ADA, AAJP, series 4, sub-series 1, folder 1.

228 Sister Irene Doyle interview, 3 July 1965, ADA, PNP, series 2, sub-series 1, folder 6.

229 Daniel Roberts interview, 14 July 1965, ADA, PNP, series 2, sub-series 1, folder 46.

230 Nearing, *He Loved the Church*, 63.
231 Angus L. Macdonald to Stanley MacDonald, 3 July 1939, NSARM, ALMP, F422/57.
232 Henderson, *Angus L. Macdonald*, 62.
233 Alexander Johnston to Michael Gillis (copy), 22 March 1946, ADA, BMP, series 3, sub-series 1, folder 4.
234 Bishop Morrison was friendly with Cardinal McGuigan's father, George. See Ludlow, *The Canny Scot*, 234; Fisher, *James Cardinal McGuigan*.
235 M.A. MacAdam to John R. MacDonald, 7 December 1945, ADA, BJRMP, Series 3, sub-series 1, folder 4.
236 M.A. MacLellan, "Xavier College, 1951-1964," unpublished paper, BI, MG 13/59.
237 Nearing, *He Loved the Church*, 71.
238 Moses Coady to Cardinal Antoniutti, 10 February 1950, STFXUA, MG 20/1/15.
239 John R. MacDonald to Sisters of St. Martha, 22 April 1950, ADA, BMP, series 7, sub-series 1, folder 7.
240 *The Casket*, 20 April 1950.
241 Edward Purcell to John R. MacDonald, 17 April 1950, ADA, BMP, series 7, sub-series 1, folder 7.
242 Vatican to John R. MacDonald, 18 April 1950, ADA, BMP, series 7, sub-series 1, folder 7.
243 *The Casket*, 20 April 1950.
244 *Sydney Post-Record*, 19 April 1950.

CHAPTER EIGHT

1 *The Casket*, 28 May 1953.
2 Nearing, *He Loved the Church*, 72.
3 Bishop John R. was always mindful of physical stature. In 1954 Fr Peter Nearing wanted to start a society for people with chronic illnesses called "The Little Sick Friends of Villa Madonna," but the bishop objected to the name. "I still don't like 'little,' he grumbled. "Most sick people are adults. Normally, they don't like being called 'little.'" John R. MacDonald to Peter Nearing, 29 December 1954, ADA, BJRMP, series 4, sub-series 1, folder 7.
4 Fr R.J. MacSween recalled hearing complaints from parishioners who liked Archbishop Morrison's simplicity in dress. "I remember speaking to a very old man in the parish, who said, 'Bishop Morrison never cared for his appearance. And this man insists on being the center of everything.' He was a very old man and I didn't think I'd hear such criticisms from him.

And yet it came." R.J. MacSween interview, 24 July 1965, ADA, PNP, Series 2, sub-series 1, folder 42.

5 Leo B. Sears interview, 7 July 1965, ADA, PNP, series 2, sub-series 1, folder 47.

6 Nearing, *He Loved the Church*, 71.

7 Stanley MacDonald to Angus L. Macdonald, October 1937, NSARM, ALMP, F422/25.

8 Apostolic Delegate to John R. MacDonald, 2 May 1950, ADA, BJRMP, series 3, sub-series 7, folder 17.

9 Miriam, "The Historical Background of the People's School," 18.

10 Leo B. Sears interview, 7 July 1965, ADA, PNP, series 2, sub-series 1, folder 47. In his history of Dalhousie University, P.B. Waite does not mention a Sydney junior college but period interviews suggest that the school examined a few potential properties. See P.B. Waite, *Lives of Dalhousie University*, Vol. 2.

11 Morgan, *Perseverance*, 15.

12 Leo Keats to Albert Doucet, 29 January 1937, BIA, ADP, MG 13, 53 (F1).

13 Hugh Somers interview, 11 October 1964, ADA, PNP, series 2, sub-series 1, folder 50.

14 Morgan, *Perseverance*, 22.

15 M.A. MacLellan, "Xavier College, 1951-1964," unpublished paper, BI, MG 13/59.

16 M.A. MacLellan, "Xavier College, 1951-1964," unpublished paper, BI, MG 13/59.

17 Msgr MacLellan lodged at Sacred Heart and recalled Msgr R.C. MacGillivary's many acts of kindness. Recognizing the great stress that the priest was under while organizing Xavier College, MacGillivray would come into his room each evening with a tall glass of whisky and order him to drink it. It was the perfect tonic for the restless man to get some sleep. See M.A. MacLellan, "Xavier College, 1951-1964," unpublished paper, BI, MG 13/59.

18 Morgan, *Perseverance*, 28.

19 Fr Malcolm MacLellan to John R. MacDonald, ADA, BJRMP, series 5, sub-series 2, folder 16.

20 Morgan, *Perseverance*, 32.

21 Morgan, *Rise Again!* Book 2, 196.

22 In the meantime, Antigonish did what it could to procure French-speaking clergy. The Cheticamp native Fr Paul Boudreau returned from Saskatchewan in 1950 to minister at L'Ardoise and Port Felix, but he soon returned to the Diocese of Gravelbourg. Fr Sylvere Gallant was on loan

from Charlottetown to serve at Cheticamp from 1950–52, and Fr Joseph Pelletier, on loan from Quebec, administered D'Escousse in 1959.

23 Michael Gillis to John R. MacDonald, no date, ADA, BJRMP, series 3, sub-series 1.

24 In 1987 Bishop Colin Campbell (1931–2012) became the seventh bishop of Antigonish. Born in Antigonish, he spent his early years in Port Hood before moving to Halifax. A graduate of SMU and Holy Heart Seminary, Campbell served in various capacities as priest of the archdiocese. In 2019 Bishop Brian Dunn of Antigonish was appointed coadjutor archbishop of Halifax. See Campbell, *Adventures of a Parish Priest.*

25 *The Casket*, 9 May 1946.

26 *The Casket*, 9 May 1946.

27 George Landry to Peter Nearing, 16 November 1965, ADA, PNP, series 2, sub-series 2, folder 10.

28 Chiasson, *Cheticamp*, 140.

29 Nearing, *He Loved the Church*, 86.

30 Minutes of General Clergy Meeting, 20 June 1955.

31 Campbell, *Songs Remembered in Exile*, 39.

32 Gerrits, *They Farmed Well*, 21.

33 Gerrits, *They Farmed Well*, 11.

34 *Antigonish Diocese Yearbook*, 1955; interview with Fr George Topshee, no date, ADA, BJRMP, series 1, sub-series 1, folder 15.

35 *1955 Yearbook Diocese of Antigonish.*

36 A.B. MacDonald to James Tompkins, 21 November 1931, STFXUA, RG 30-2/2/2358.

37 D.F. Roberts to Peter Nearing, 18 October 1966, ADA, PNP, series 2, sub-series 1, folder 46.

38 van den Heuvel, "The Dutch Immigrants," 77–83.

39 Gerrits, *They Farmed Well*, 175.

40 John J. McLaughlin interview, 11 August 1965, ADA, PNP, series 2, sub-series 1, folder 41.

41 John J. McLaughlin interview, 11 August 1965, ADA, PNP, series 2, sub-series 1, folder 41.

42 Roderick MacSween interview, 24 July 1965, ADA, PNP, series 2, sub-series 1, folder 40.

43 Nearing, *He Loved the Church*, 79.

44 John J. McLaughlin interview, 11 August 1965, ADA, PNP, series 2, sub-series 1, folder 41.

45 Daniel Roberts interview, 14 July 1965, ADA, PNP, series 2, sub-series 1, folder 46.

46 In 1946, Maclean visited Mexico City and was told of the shrine to Our Lady of Guadalupe. In the spring of 1961, MacLean became pastor at Johnstown, Cape Breton, and commissioned a mosaic of Our Lady of Guadalupe. He had the shrine dedicated at Johnstown in 1963.
47 Michael Gillis to M.A. MacLellan, 20 July 1957, BI, MG 13/59/F3.
48 Malcolm MacDonell to M.A. MacLellan, July 1957, BI, MG 13/59/F3.
49 Hugh Somers interview, 11 October 1964, Our Lady of Guadalupe, series 2, sub-series 1, folder 50.
50 Cameron, *"And Martha Served,"* 209–21.
51 Sister Anselm to Moses Coady, 7 June 1952, STFXUA, RG 30-2/1/33.
52 Cameron, *"And Martha Served,"* 212.
53 Sister Irene Doyle interview, 3 July 1965, ADA, PNP, series 2, sub-series 1, folder 6.
54 See McGuigan, *The Intrigues of Archbishop John T. McNally*. For a more scholarly account on McNally see Bérard, "A Cardinal for English Canada," 81–100.
55 Hanington, *Every Popish Person*, 221; Nearing, *He Loved the Church*, 81.
56 On 17 June 1953, Bishop Bray died at the age of sixty-nine. The native of St Andrews returned home at every opportunity and financed vocations throughout the diocese. "He was ill for a long time and suffered much," noted Bishop MacDonald. John R. MacDonald to James C. McGuigan, 19 June 1953, ADA, BJRMP, series 4, sub-series 2, folder 5.
57 On Connolly see Beck, *Politics of Nova Scotia*, Vol. 2 240; Henderson, *Angus L. Macdonald*, 210.
58 Hugh Somers interview, 11 October 1964, ADA, PNP, series 2, sub-series 1, folder 50.
59 Lewis MacLellan to John R. MacDonald, 15 February 1954, ADA, BJRMP, series 3, sub-series 7, folder 18.
60 John Hugh MacDonald to John R. MacDonald, 14 November 1951, ADA, BJRMP, series 3, sub-series 1, folder 12.
61 *The Casket*, 4 February 1954.
62 Nearing, *He Loved the Church*, 81.
63 *The Casket*, 23 December 1948.
64 Frank, "In Search of C.B. Wade," 52.
65 *The Casket*, 2 February 1950.
66 *The Casket*, 24 April 1947.
67 *The Casket*, 21 August 1947.
68 *The Casket*, 9 September 1954.
69 On this period see Dikötter, *The Tragedy of Liberation*.
70 Steele, *Why Kill a Priest?*, 48.

71 *The Casket*, 29 March 1951.
72 Maxwell, *Assignment in Chekiang*, 143–58.
73 For Venedam's account see Landry, *A Man of Faith*, 10–21.
74 *The Casket*, 11 December 1952.
75 *The Casket*, 22 January 1953.
76 *The Casket*, 3 June 1954.
77 The events in China did not dissuade others from missionary work. In 1949 Fr Alex MacIntosh's brother, James, went to minister in Japan. He and sixteen other missionaries were killed in 1956 when their plane went down in the fog-shrouded Aleutian Islands.
78 Fr Venedam died in British Columbia at the age of fifty-seven in 1958 and his body was returned to Pomquet for burial. See Landry, *A Man of Faith*, 23.
79 *The Casket*, 24 February 1955.
80 Maxwell, *Assignment in Chekiang*, 185.
81 Ward, *Nova Scotia*, 95.
82 *The Casket*, 2 November 1950.
83 *The Casket*, 6 July 1950; Cameron, *For the People*, 333.
84 In 1951 St F.X. gave Cardinal Gregory Peter XV Agagianian, patriarch of Cilicia of the Armenians, an honorary degree. The cardinal was a rising star in the church (later considered a candidate for Pope in 1958) and within a few years would be appointed pro-prefect of the Sacred Congregation for the Propagation of the Faith.
85 For an account of Fr Munez's role in the first legal peasants strike in Chile in 1967 see Pérez, "Rural Guerrilla in Chile," 8–9.
86 *The Casket*, 2 April 1959.
87 *The Casket*, 23 March 1950.
88 Interview with Fr George Topshee, no date, ADA, BJRMP, series 1, sub-series 1, folder 15.
89 Sister Irene Doyle interview, 3 July 1965, ADA, PNP, series 2, sub-series 1, folder 6.
90 A.J. MacLeod interview, 25 November 1965, ADA, PNP, series 2, sub-series 1 folder 33.
91 Sister Irene Doyle interview, 3 July 1965, ADA, PNP, series 2, sub-series 1, folder 6.
92 *The Casket*, 28 February 1952.
93 Cameron, *For the People*, 292.
94 First printed in the *Atlantic Advocate* in February 1960, and condensed and reprinted in Laidlaw, *The Campus and the Community*, 158.
95 Michael Gillis interview, 3 June 1965, ADA, PNP, series 2, sub-series 1, folder 12; Laidlaw, *The Campus and the Community*, 157.

96 Steele, *Dear Old Rebel*, 150–1.
97 *The Casket*, 28 April 1955.
98 Interview with Fr George Topshee, no date, ADA, BJRMP, series 1, sub-series 1, folder 15.
99 Dodaro and Pluta, *The Big Picture*, 171.X
100 Hugh Somers interview, 11 October 1964, ADA, PNP, series 2, sub-series 1, folder 50.
101 The glorification of rural life was common in Catholic communities. In Ireland, Éamon de Valera told a crowd in 1943 that the Ireland of his dreams was "a land whose countryside would be bright with cosy homesteads ... the romping of sturdy children ... and the laughter of comely maidens, whose firesides would be the forums for serene old age." See Fleming, *A Man Who Does Not Exist*, 29.
102 Sister Marie Michael interview, 8 June 1965, ADA, PNP, series 2, sub-series 1, folder 54.
103 Nearing, *He Loved the Church*, 74.
104 Cameron, *For the People*, 342.
105 Michael Gillis interview, 3 June 1965, ADA, PNP, series 2, sub-series 1, folder 12.
106 Dodaro and Pluta, *The Big Picture*, 194.
107 Moses Coady to Sister Anselm, 19 February 1959, STFXUA, RG 30-2/1/49.
108 Dodaro and Pluta, *The Big Picture*, 201.
109 Nearing, *He Loved the Church*, 95.
110 Nearing, *He Loved the Church*, 95; interview with Fr George Topshee, no date, ADA, BJRMP, series 1, sub-series 1, folder 15.
111 Laidlaw, *The Campus and the Community*, 158.
112 *The Casket*, 17 November 1949.
113 F.A. Marroco interview, 14 April 1966, ADA, PNP, series 2, sub-series 1, folder 42.
114 Ward, *The Land of Cooperation*, 89.
115 Boyle, *Father Tompkins*, 217.
116 James J. Tompkins to John R. MacDonald, 8 January 1948, ADA, BJRMP, series 3, sub-series 1, folder 5.
117 W.J. McNally to John R. MacDonald, 3 July 1949, ADA, BJRMP, series 3, sub-series 7, folder 17.
118 Boyle, *Fr Tompkins of Nova Scotia*, 223.
119 *The Casket*, 29 May 1952.
120 *The Casket*, 14 May 1953.
121 *The Casket*, 7 May 1953.
122 *The Casket*, 15 April 1954.

123 *The Casket*, 22 April 1954.
124 Malcolm MacDonell to Sister St Veronica, 13 April 1954, BIA, SMP, MG 13, 13 (F1).
125 *The Casket*, 4 October 1934.
126 C.J. MacGillivray to John R. MacDonald, 18 February 1944, ADA, BJRMP, series 3, sub-series 1, folder 2.
127 See, for example, Canso Crossing Association. *A Permanent Crossing over the Strait of Canso.*
128 Forbes, *Challenging the Regional Stereotype*, 173; Forbes, "Consolidating Disparity," 3–27.
129 Morgan, *Rise Again!* Book 2, 128.
130 Beaton and Muise, "The Canso Causeway," 58.
131 A.J. MacLeod interview, 25 November 1965, ADA, PNP, series 2, | sub-series 1, folder 33.
132 *The Casket*, 11 August 1955.
133 *The Casket*, 28 April 1954.
134 Morgan, *Rise Again!* Book 2, 129.
135 Beaton and Muise, *The Canso Causeway*, 60.
136 Foote, *The Case of Port Hawkesbury*, 33.
137 *The Casket*, 14 April 1955.
138 John R. MacDonald to John Hugh MacDonald, 3 February 1956, ADA, BJRMP, series 3, sub-series 1, folder 12.
139 See Walsh, *We Fought for the Little Man*, 142–51.
140 T.L. Sullivan interview, 2 July 1965, ADA, PNP, series 2, sub-series 1, folder 51.
141 Roderick MacSween interview, 24 July 1965, ADA, PNP, series 2 sub-series 1, folder 40.
142 *Diocese of Antigonish Yearbook, 1959*, 84.
143 Interview with Fr Rod MacPherson, 15 July 1965, ADA, PNP, series 2, sub-series 1, folder 38.
144 Interview with Fr George Topshee, no date, ADA, BJRMP, series 1, sub-series 1, folder 15; Francis Smyth. To John R. MacDonald, 18 February 1949, ADA, BJRMP, series 3, sub-series 1, folder 5.
145 John R. MacDonald to Sidney Oram, no date, ADA, BJRMP, series 3, sub-series 7, folder 21.
146 Mifflen, "A History of Trade Unionism," 71.
147 John J. McLaughlin interview, 11 August 1965, ADA, PNP, series 2, sub-series 1, folder 41.
148 Moses Coady to Adolphus Gillis, 16 January 1950, STFXUA, MG 20/1/917.
149 Campbell, *Banking on Coal*, 86.

150 Pope, *Clarence MacKinnon Nicholson*, 55–7.
151 *The Casket*, 4 June 1953.
152 *Diocese of Antigonish Yearbook, 1954*, 9.
153 *Maclean's Magazine*, "A Coal Town Fights for Its Life."
154 *The Casket*, 10 December 1953.
155 *Diocese of Antigonish Yearbook, 1954*, 29.
156 *The Casket*, 29 August 1957.
157 *The Casket*, 10 May 1956.
158 *The Casket*, 10 May 1956.
159 Francis Smyth to John R. MacDonald, 18 February 1949, ADA, BJRMP, series 3, sub-series 1, folder 5.
160 Frank and MacGillivray, *George MacEachern*, 138–9.
161 Meeting of the General Clergy of Antigonish, 20 January 1955.
162 MacEwan, *Miners and Steelworkers*, 301.
163 Fairley Jr, *DOSCO and the Future*, 13.
164 *The Casket*, 5 March 1959.
165 Nearing, *He Loved the Church*, 107.
166 *The Casket*, 8 May 1952.
167 *Antigonish Diocesan Yearbook*, 1959, 31.
168 Helen Ranni to John R. MacDonald, 5 June 1958, ADA, BJRMP, series 3, sub-series 7, folder 22.
169 Harmon, *There Were Also Many Women There*, 226–7.
170 Grail Movement, *The Grail Movement in America*, 4.
171 Patricia DeFerrari, "Collaborating in Christ's Redeeming Work," 112.
172 Carmel Losier interview, 7 June 1965, ADA, PNP, Series 2, sub-series 1, folder 58.
173 On Kersbergen see O'Brien and Miller, "A Woman of Vision," 95–105.
174 DeFerrari, "Collaborating in Christ's Redeeming Work," 124. Pugh died in 1972 of cancer.
175 Interview with Fr George Topshee, no date, ADA, BJRMP, series 1, sub-series 1, folder 15.
176 Freemantle, *The Teachings of the Popes*, 271.
177 Interview with Sisters of Notre Dame Holy Angels Convent, 22 June 1965, ADA, PNP, series 2, sub-series 1, folder 61. Gillis and McMahon, *Our Union in and with Christ.*
178 Cameron, *"And Martha Served,"* 203.
179 Cameron, *"And Martha Served,"* 189. See also Nearing, *He Loved the Church*, 92.
180 CND Sisters, Holy Angels Convent interview, 22 June 1965, ADA, PNP, series 2, sub-series 1, folder 61.

181 MacDonald, "Increased Health and Social Welfare Funding," 154.
182 Cameron, *"And Martha Served,"* 226.
183 Sister Denis Marie interview, 5 July 1965, ADA, PNP, series 2, sub-series 1, folder 53.
184 Sister Mary Matthew, CSM, interview, 23 June 1965, ADA, PNP, series 2, sub-series 1, folder 55.
185 *Diocese of Antigonish Yearbook, 1956*, 31.
186 See Morton, "Old Women and Their Place in Nova Scotia," 21–38.
187 Godfrey Gibson to John R. MacDonald, 9 February 1956, ADA, BJRMP, series 3, sub-series 7, folder 9.
188 *Diocese of Antigonish Yearbook 1959*, 31.
189 On the perception that Catholics obeyed out of fear see MacLean, *Piety & Politics*, 110.
190 McNeil, "Retreat Movement in Nova Scotia," 107–15.
191 *The Casket,* 14 July 1955.
192 *The Casket*, 22 April 1948.
193 *The Casket*, 9 April 1953.
194 The would-be friars were Angus Rogers of Glace Bay, Earl Vassalo of Dominion, and Robert McLean of Reserve Mines. See *The Casket*, 3 February 1955.
195 *Diocese of Antigonish Yearbook 1956*, 47.
196 John J. McLaughlin interview, 11 August 1965, ADA, PNP, series 2, sub-series 1, folder 41.
197 John R. MacDonald to John Hugh MacDonald, 16 November 1954, ADA, BJRMP, series 3, sub-series 1, folder 12.
198 *Diocese of Antigonish Yearbook 1954*, 49.
199 *The Casket*, 21 August 1947.
200 "The Lay Apostolate," an address by Bishop MacDonald to the Sydney Knights of Columbus, 29 April 1951, ADA, BJRMP, series 2, sub-series 3, folder 19.
201 *The Casket*, 21 February 1957.
202 "Rome and the Lay Apostolate," *Ecumenical Review* 10, 3 (1958), 320.
203 *The Casket*, 1 January 1948.
204 Kane, *Why I Became a Priest.*
205 *Why I Became a Nun* (1953); *Why I Became a Brother* (1954); *Meeting the Vocation Crisis* (1956); *Lay Workers for Christ* (1957); *Melody in Your Hearts* (1958); *Why I Became a Missioner*; *Twice Called: The Autobiographies of Seventeen Convent Sisters* (1959); *What You Can Do* (1959).

206 One of the most popular programs was the Radio League. The league's three principal programs were the "Sunday Evening Program," the "Ava Maria Hour," and the "Sacred Heart Program." Most talks broadcast over the Radio League were published and distributed in the parishes, and so Fr George Kane read these lectures carefully before the show went to air (a difficult task, considering he was residing in Glendale, [80 kilometres away).]

207 George Boyle to John R. MacDonald, 6 November 1952, ADA, BJRMP, series 3, sub-series 1, folder 12.

208 *The Casket*, 25 October 1956.

209 Gauvreau, *Catholic Origins of Quebec's Quiet Revolution*, 120–74.

210 Donovan, *The Forgotten World*, 145.

211 George Boyle to John R. MacDonald, 4 July 1954, ADA, BJRMP, series 3, sub-series 1, folder 12.

212 *The Casket*, 11 October 1951.

213 *The Casket*, 26 September 1951,

214 Dodaro and Pluta, *The Big Picture*, 162.

215 McGowan, "The Fulton Sheen Affair," 22.

216 Dodaro and Pluta, *The Big Picture*, 181.

217 F.A. Marroco interview, 14 April 1966, ADA, PNP, series 2, sub-series 1, folder 42. Another priest recalled that Bishop MacDonald enjoyed reading detective stories at bedtime. "And he'd take two or three of these in his pocket and go off," he recalled, "not admitting to the world that he was reading them."

218 MacDonald, *Memorable Years*, 166–7.

219 Bennett, "School Consolidation in Maritime Canada," 32.

220 James Morrison to J.E. LeBlanc, 10 June 1942, ADA, BMP, letter#26635.

221 Nearing, *He Loved the Church*, 112.

222 Bennett, "School Consolidation in Maritime Canada," 36.

223 *The Casket*, 14 October 1954.

224 Gidney and Millar, *How Schools Worked*, 133.

225 Nearing, *He Loved the Church*, 110.

226 T.L. Sullivan interview, 2 July 1965, ADA, PNP, series 2, sub-series 1, folder 51.

227 Other rural high schools in eastern Nova Scotia were Riverview Rural High, Baddeck Rural High, East Pictou Rural High, and St Mary's Rural High (Sherbrooke, Guysborough County). Eventually, the distance from Antigonish town for students from the eastern portion of Antigonish County was deemed too great and Antigonish East Rural High was opened at Tracadie.

228 MacDonald, *Memorable Years*, 170. MacDonald also wrote *Down Memory Lane*, and *The Rector*.
229 Guildford, "Power, politics, and pedagogy," 5.
230 Leo B. Sears interview, 7 July 1965, ADA, PNP, series 2, sub-series 1, folder 47.
231 Hugh John MacDonald to Peter Nearing, 18 May 1965, ADA, PNP, series 2, sub-series 1, folder 20.
232 P.J. Nicholson to Donald MacPherson, 23 June 1952, BIA, DMP, MG 13/58.
233 P.J. Nicholson to Patrick Nicholson, 23 January 1954, STFXUA, PJMP, MG 2/1/224.
234 Whether Nicholson was "pushed out" or had a "hankering to get into the direct work of the ministry, it was a changing of the guard." Cameron, *For the People*, 304; Donovan, *The Forgotten World,* 127; P.J. Nicholson to Margaret MacIsaac, 25 February 1954, STFXUA, PJMP, MG 2/1/44.
235 Hugh Somers interview, 11 October 1964, ADA, PNP, series 2, sub-series 1, folder 50.
236 Cameron, *For the People*, 309.
237 Cameron, *For the People*, 317.
238 Nearing, *He Loved the Church*, 115.
239 Leo Keats to Daniel J. MacDonald, 4 November 1937, STFXUA, DJMP, RG 5/10/1924.
240 F.A. Marroco interview, 14 April 1966, ADA, PNP, series 2, sub-series 1, folder 42.
241 Cameron, *For the People*, 316.
242 R.J. MacSween interview, 24 July 1965, ADA, PNP, series 2, sub-series 1, folder 42.
243 Having employed his skills in both Newfoundland and British Columbia, MacIntyre retired to Antigonish town (his family operated the Cornish Arms Lodge).
244 *The Casket*, 18 September 1952.
245 "The recent death of Mons Coady was not unexpected because of his frequent heart attacks in recent years, and his serious condition for some weeks before," noted Archbishop John Hugh MacDonald from Edmonton. John Hugh MacDonald to John R. MacDonald, 19 October 1959, ADA, BJRMP, series 3, sub-series 1, folder 12.
246 F.J. Smythe interview, 12 October 1964, ADA, PNP, series 2, sub-series 1, folder 49.
247 Laidlaw, *The Man from Margaree*, 18.
248 M.A. MacLellan, "EUGE, SERVE BONE ET FIDELIS," 1959, BIA, MCMP, MG 13, 59 (2D. F4).

249 Welton, *Little Mosie from the Margaree*, 250–1.
250 Nearing, *He Loved the Church*, 88.
251 *The Casket*, 28 March 1957.
252 J.A. Gillis to Bede MacEachern, 10 December 1960, STFXUA, Fr John Allan Gillis Papers, RG 30-2/8/135.
253 Hugh John MacDonald interview, 9 October 1964, ADA, PNP, series 1, sub-series 1, folder 20.
254 Hugh Somers to John R. MacDonald, 29 March 1959, ADA, BJRMP, series 2, sub-series 1.
255 F.J. Smythe interview, 12 October 1964, ADA, PNP, series 2, sub-series 1, folder 49.
256 Fr Gallivan recalled that CJFX would issue regular updates on his health while in hospital. One afternoon he went to visit the ailing prelate and asked how he was feeling. "I'm not too sure," MacDonald responded. "I haven't turned on the radio yet." William Gallivan interview, ADA, PNP, series 2, sub-series 1, folder 10.
257 M.J. Lemieux to A.A. Johnston, 11 January 1960, ADA, PNP, series 9, series 2, sub-series 1.
258 MacNeil, *The Rewarding Path*, 171.
259 Cameron, *For the People*, 336.
260 F.J. Smythe interview, 12 October 1964, ADA, PNP, series 2, sub-series 1, folder 49.

CONCLUSION

1 A.J. MacLeod interview, 25 November 1965 ADA, PNP, series 2, sub-series 1, folder 33. For years, the diocese relied on the canon law scholar and Port Hood native Fr John Francis "Bede" MacEachen for legal advice. A member of the Franciscan Friars of the Atonement, and a graduate of Columbia University, MacEachen was a brilliant student and worked in Rome for nearly two decades.
2 M.A. MacLellan, "Xavier College, 1951-1964," unpublished paper, BI, MG 13/59.
3 John R. MacDonald to John Hugh MacDonald, 16 November 1954, ADA, BJRMP, series 3, sub-series 1, folder 12.
4 Cameron, *For the People*, 348.
5 *Chronicle Herald*, 4 February 1970.
6 T.L. Sullivan interview, 2 July 1965, ADA, PNP, fonds 5, series 2, sub-series 1, folder 51.
7 Peter Nearing to J.C. Chisholm, 16 May 1966, ADA, PNP, folder 63.

8 J. Clyde Nunn to Joseph N. MacNeil, 8 September 1967, STFXUA, RG 30-2/6/716.

9 On Hogan see Cameron, "The Priest Who Went to Parliament."

10 J.N. MacNeil speech, "Holy Name Society Communion Supper," 31 March 1963, Antigonish, STFXUA, RG 30-2/6/572.

11 Sister M. Crescentia interview, 2 April 1965, ADA, PNP, fonds 9, series 2, sub-series 1, folder 57.

12 Michael Gillis interview, 1969, ADA, PNP, fonds 9, series 2, sub-series 1, folder 65.

13 J.N. MacNeil interview, October 1964, ADA, PNP, fonds 9, series 2, sub-series 1, folder 36.

14 Maxwell, *Assignment in Chekiang*, 164.

15 Kennedy, "Sisters of St. Martha," 60; Dolan, *In Search of American Catholicism*, 47–70.

16 MacDonald, *The Mystical Body of Christ*, 4.

17 Boyle, *Democracy's Second Chance*, 143.

Bibliography

PRIMARY MATERIALS

Manuscript Material

Antigonish Diocesan Archives, Antigonish Nova Scotia (ADA)

- Fonds 2 Archbishop Colin F. MacKinnon Papers, 1851–77 (BCMP)
- Fonds 3 Bishop John Cameron Papers, 1877–1910 (BCP)
- Fonds 4 Archbishop James Morrison Papers, 1912–50 (BMP)
- Fonds 5 Bishop John R. MacDonald Papers, 1950–59 (BJRMP)
- Fonds 7 Monsignor Hugh Peter MacPherson Papers, 1907–25 (HPMP)
- Fonds 8 Fr A.A. Johnston Papers (AAJP)
- Fonds 8 Fr Peter Nearing Papers (PNP)

Archdiocese of Edmonton Archives:

- Archbishop John Hugh MacDonald Papers (JHMP)

Archdiocese of Halifax Archives (ADHA)

- Archbishop Edward Joseph McCarthy Papers (ABEJMP)

Archdiocese of St. John's Archives, St. John's Newfoundland (ADSJ)

- Archbishop Edward P. Roche Papers (ABRP)

Beaton Institute, Cape Breton University (BIA):

- MG 10/2 Father James J. Tompkins Papers (JJTP)
- MG 13/22 Bishop Alexander MacDonald Papers (BAMP)
- MG 13/12 Father Michael A. MacDonald Papers (MAMP)
- MG 13/13 Sister Mary MacDonald Papers (SMP)
- MG 13/53 Father Albert A. Doucet Papers (ADP)
- MG 13/59 Msgr Malcolm C. MacLellan Papers (MCMP)
- MG 13/48 Father John J. MacNeil Papers (JJMP)
- MG 13/58 Msgr Donald MacPherson Papers (DMP)

Irish College Rome Archives
 Cardinal Paul Cullen Collection (CUL)
Nova Scotia Records and Archive Management [NSARM], Halifax, Nova Scotia
 MG 2 Angus L. Macdonald Fonds, [189?]–1954 (ALMP)
St Francis Xavier University Archives (STFXUA):
 RG 5/7 Fr Daniel A. Chisholm Papers (DCP)
 RG 5/8 Fr Alexander Thompson Papers (ATP)
 RG 5/9 Monsignor Hugh Peter MacPherson Papers (HPMP)
 RG 5/10 Fr Daniel J. MacDonald Papers (DJMP)
 RG 6/5 Fr James J. Tompkins Papers (JJTP)
 RG 13 Scottish Catholic Society Fonds
 RG 30/2/1 Monsignor Moses Michael Coady Papers (MMCP)
 RG 30/2/6 Archbishop Joseph N. MacNeil Papers
 RG 30/2/8 Fr John Allan Gillis Papers
 RG 30/3 St F.X. Extension Department
 MG 2 Fr Patrick J. Nicholson Papers (PJNP)
 MG 35 Alexander Johnston Papers
 MG 45 Fr William X. Edwards Papers (WXEP)
 MG 79 Angus MacIsaac Papers
 MG 80 Colin F. MacIsaac Papers (CFMP)
University College Reports / Calendars, 1880–1960.
Board of Governors Meeting Minutes
Fr Michael Gillis Interview, Coady International Institute, St F.X. University, 1966.

Printed Material

Contemporary Newspapers and Journals
Alexandria Gazette
The Aurora
The Boston Daily Globe
Canadian Mining Journal
Canadian Press
The Canadian Register
The Casket
Cape Breton Post
The Daily News (St John's)
Extension Bulletin
The Eastern Chronicle

The Evening Telegram
The Evening Herald
Glace Bay Gazette
The Globe
The Halifax Herald
The Halifax Morning Chronicle
Maclean's Magazine
Moncton Transcript
The Morning Chronicle
New York Evening Mail
New York Times
North Sydney Herald
Peterborough Examiner
The Pictou Advocate
Pictou Standard
Sacred Heart Review
The Summerside Journal
St John Daily Sun
Sydney Herald
The Sydney Post
The Sydney Post-Record
The Sydney Record
The Trade Review
Toronto Globe
The Xavierian
The Western Catholic
Yarmouth Herald

BOOKS AND ARTICLES

Acheson, T.W. "The National Policy and the Industrialization of the Maritimes, 1880-1910." *Acadiensis* 1, 2 (spring 1972): 3–28.

Alexander, Anne. *The Antigonish Movement: Moses Coady and Adult Education Today*. Toronto: Thompson Educational Publishing, 1997.

Alfred, Rev. Brother. "Francis Collins, First Catholic Journalist in Upper Canada." CCHA *Report* 6 (1938–39): 51–66.

Andrew, Sheila. *Development of Elites in Acadian New Brunswick, 1861-1881*. Montreal and Kingston: McGill-Queen's University Press, 1996.

– "Selling education: the problems of convent schools in Acadian New Brunswick, 1858–1886." CCHA *Historical Studies* 62 (1996): 15–32.

Arnold, Mary. *The Story of Tompkinsville*. New York: The Co-operative League, 1940.

Bannon, R.V. *Eastland Echoes*. Toronto: Macmillan, 1937.

Barlow, Maude, and Elizabeth May. *Frederick Street: Life and Death on Canada's Love Canal*. Toronto: HarperCollins, 2000.

Barr, Colin. "'Imperium in Imperio': Irish Episcopal Imperialism in the Nineteenth Century." *English Historical Review* 122, 502 (2008): 611–50.

– *Ireland's Empire: The Roman Catholic Church in the English-Speaking World, 1829-1914*. Cambridge, Cambridge University Press, 2020.

Beaton, Elizabeth. "Housing People and Place: A Case Study of Whitney Pier." PhD dissertation, University of Manitoba, 1996.

Beaton, Meaghan, and Del Muise. "The Canso Causeway: Tartan Tourism, Industrial Development and the Promise of Progress for Cape Breton." *Acadiensis* 37, 2 (summer/autumn 2008): 39–69.

Beck, Gustav F. "The Men of Antigonish: A New St. Gallen." *Journal of Adult Education* (April 1935).

Beck, J. Murray. *Joseph Howe, Volume II: The Briton Becomes a Canadian 1848-1873*. Montreal and Kingston: McGill-Queen's University Press, 1983.

– *Pendulum of Power: Canada's Federal Elections*. Scarborough: Prentice-Hall, 1968.

– *The Politics of Nova Scotia, Volume Two 1896-1988*. Tantallon: Four East Publications, 1988.

Beck, Jeanne M. "Henry Somerville and Social Reform: His Contribution to Canadian Catholic Social Thought." CCHA *Study Sessions* 42 (1975): 91–108.

Benjamin, Chris. *Indian School Road: Legacies of the Shubenacadie Residential School*. Halifax: Nimbus, 2014.

Bennett, Paul W. "School Consolidation in Maritime Canada: The Educational Legacy of Edgar L. Morphet and His Disciples." *County School Journal* 5 (2017): 31–47.

Bérard, Robert. "A Cardinal for English Canada: The Intrigues of Bishop John T. McNally, 1930-1937." CCHA, *Historical Studies* 63 (1997): 81–100.

Bland, Salem. "The Social Gospel and the Reform Tradition in Canada, 1890-1928." *Canadian Historical Review* 49 (1968): 381–99.

Blet, Pierre. *Pius XII and the Second World War: According to the Archives of the Vatican*. New Jersey: Paulist Press, 1999.

Bosher, J.F. *The Gaullist Attack on Canada, 1967-1997*. Montreal and Kingston: McGill-Queen's University Press, 2000.

Boutilier, Ted (ed.). *The New Waterford Story 1913-1963: A Souvenir of New Waterford's Golden Jubilee August 4-8, 1963*. New Waterford, 1963.

Boyle, George. *Democracy's Second Chance: Land, Work and Cooperation*. New York: Sheed & Ward, 1941.

– *Father Tompkins of Nova Scotia*. New York: P.J. Kenedy and Sons, 1958.

– *Pioneer in Purple: The Life and Work of Archbishop Neil McNeil*. Montreal: Palm Publishing, 1951.

– *The Poor Man's Prayer*. New York: Harper & Bros., 1951.

Boyle, James. *A Middle Way*. Antigonish: St F.X. Extension Department, 1937.

Boyle, Thomas O'Reilly. *Justice through Power: A Short History of Labour and its Present Situation*. Toronto, 1961.

Brennan, Sarah. "Revisiting the proverbial tin cup, a study of political resistance of the Mi'kmaq of Nova Scotia, 1900-1969." Master's thesis, Saint Mary's University, 2000.

Brewer, Charles G. "The Diocese of Antigonish and World War I." Master's thesis, University of New Brunswick, 1975.

Brinkley, Douglas, and Julie M. Fenster. *Parish Priest: Father Michael McGivney and American Catholicism*. New York: William Morrow, 2006.

Brison, Jeffrey. *Rockefeller, Carnegie, and Canada: American Philanthropy and the Arts and Letters in Canada*. Montreal & Kingston: McGill-Queen's University Press, 2005.

Brooks, Alan. "Outmigration from the Maritime Provinces, 1860-1900: Some Preliminary Considerations." *Acadiensis* 5 (spring 1976): 26–55.

Brown, Richard. *The Coal Fields and Coal Trade of the Island of Cape Breton*. London, 1871.

Browne, P.W. "Catholic Education in Newfoundland." *Studies: An Irish Quarterly Review* 20, 79 (1931): 374–88.

– "Irish Bishops in Newfoundland (1794-1893)." *Studies: An Irish Quarterly Review* 20, 77 (Mar. 1931): 49–66.

– *Where the Fishers Go: The Story of Labrador*. New York: Cochrane Publishing, 1909.

Burns, J.E. "The Abbé Maillard and Halifax." CCHA *Report* (1936–37): 13–22.

Cahill, Edward. *Freemasonry and the Anti-Christian Movement*. Dublin: M.H. Gill, 1930.

Cameron, Donald. "The Priest Who Went to Parliament." *Globe and Mail Weekend Magazine* (March 1975): 10–12.

Cameron, James. *"And Martha Served": History of the Sisters of St. Martha, Antigonish, Nova Scotia*. Halifax: Nimbus, 2000.

– *For the People: A History of St Francis Xavier University*. Montreal and Kingston: McGill-Queen's University Press, 1996.

Campbell, Brian, and Andrew John Bayly Johnston. *Tracks across the Landscape: The S&L Commemorative History*. Sydney: Cape Breton University Press, 1995.

Campbell, Colin. *Adventures of a Parish Priest*. Hantsport: Lancelot Press, 1983.

Campbell Douglas F. and R.A. MacLean. *Banking on Coal: Perspectives on a Cape Breton Community within an International Context*. Sydney: UCCB Press, 1997.

– *Beyond the Atlantic Roar: A Study of the Nova Scotia Scots*. Toronto: McClelland & Stewart, 1974.

Campbell, John. *With our Hearts and Hands: A History of Sacred Heart Parish*. Sydney: Sacred Heart Parish, 2001.

Campbell, John Lorne. *Songs Remembered in Exile*. Aberdeen: Aberdeen University Press, 1990.

Candow, James, and Carol Corbin. *How Deep Is the Ocean?: Historical Essays on Canada's Atlantic Fishery*. Sydney: Cape Breton University Press, 1997.

Canso Crossing Association. *A Permanent Crossing over the Strait of Canso*. Sydney: Canso Crossing Association, 1948.

Caplan, Ronald. "Fr. Charles Murphy and Hong Kong." *Cape Breton's Magazine* 62 (1993).

– "Mine Explosion in New Waterford, 1917," *Cape Breton's Magazine* 21 (1978): 1–11.

– "Neil MacNeil and the Highland Heart." *Cape Breton's Magazine* 58 (1991): 32–6.

– "The Steel Boom Comes to Sydney, 1899." *Cape Breton's Magazine* 39 (1985).

– "With Frank Jackson at 99." *Cape Breton's Magazine* 34 (1983).

Carpenter, Ronald H. *Father Charles E. Coughlin*. Greenwood Publishing Group, 1998.

Cecillon, Jack D. *Prayers, Petitions, and Protests: The Catholic Church and the Ontario Schools Crisis in the Windsor Border Region, 1910-1928*. Montreal & Kingston: McGill-Queen's University Press, 2013.

Chadwick, St John. *Newfoundland: Island into Province*. Cambridge: Cambridge University Press, 1967.

Chard, Donald. "The Halifax Protestant Orphans' Home: Triumphs and Tragedies in the Life of a Victorian Institution, 1857-1970." *Journal of the Royal Nova Scotia Historical Society* 9 (2006): 100–14.

Chiasson, Anselme. *Cheticamp: History and Acadian Traditions.* St John's: Breakwater, 1986.Chiasson, Paulette M. "Fiset, Pierre." *Dictionary of Canadian Biography* 13 (1994): 341–2.

Coady, Moses. *Masters of Their Own Destiny: The Story of the Antigonish Movement of Adult Education through Economic Cooperation.* New York: Harper & Brothers, 1939.

– *My Story.* Antigonish: St F.X. Extension Department, 1957.

Codignola, Luca. *Blurred Nationalities Across the North Atlantic: Traders, Priests and Their Kin Travelling Between North America and the Italian Peninsula, 1763-1846.* Toronto: University of Toronto Press, 2019.

Cohen, Gidon. *The Failure of a Dream: The Independent Labour Party from Disaffiliation to World War II.* London: I.B. Tauris, 2007.

Coleman, Amy. "The Religious Roots of Female Education in Sydney: A History of the Congregation de Notre Dame and Holy Angels Convent School, 1885-1911." Master's thesis, Saint Mary's University, 2003.

Coles, Robert. *Dorothy Day: A Radical Devotion.* Reading: Addison-Wesley, 1987.

Collins, Patrick J. *Harbour Grace Affray, St. Stephens Day, 1883: The Clash of Two Solitudes: A Story of Riot, Religion and Romance.* St John's: DRC Publishing, 2011.

Comiskey, John. *My Heart's Best Wishes for You: A Biography of Archbishop John Walsh.* Montreal and Kingston: McGill-Queen's University Press, 2012.

Congregation of the Sisters of St Martha. *Sisters of St. Martha, Women of Exodus, Women of Hospitality, Women of Undaunted Hope.* Antigonish: Sisters of St Martha, 2000.

Corbett, E.A. *Henry Marshall Tory: Beloved Canadian.* Toronto: Ryerson Press, 1954.

Cornwell, John. *Hitler's Pope: The Secret History of Pius XII.* New York: Viking, 1999.

Crawley, Ron. "Off to Sydney: Newfoundlanders Emigrate to Industrial Cape Breton, 1890-1914." *Acadiensis* 17, 2 (spring 1988): 27–51.

Creighton, Helen, and Calum MacLeod. *Gaelic Songs in Nova Scotia.* Ottawa: National Museum of Canada, 1964.

Crerar, Duff W. "Bellicose Priests: The Wars of the Canadian Catholic Chaplains 1914-1919." CCHA *Historical Studies* 58 (1991): 21–39.

– "In the Day of Battle: Canadian Catholic Chaplains in the Field 1885-1945." CCHA *Historical Studies* 61 (1995): 53–77.

– *Padres in No Man's Land: Canadian Chaplains and the Great War.* Montreal & Kingston: McGill-Queen's University Press, 1995.

Crosbie, Barbara A. "Howley, Michael Francis." *Dictionary of Canadian Biography*, 14 (1998): 514–22.

Croteau, J.T. *Cradled in the Waves: The Story of a People's Co-operative Achievement in Economic Betterment on Prince Edward Island, Canada.* Toronto: Ryerson Press, 1951.

Crunican, Paul. "Father Lacombe's Strange Mission: The Lacombe-Langevin Correspondence on the Manitoba School Question 1895-96." CCHA *Report* 26 (1959): 57–71.

– *Priests and Politicians: Manitoba Schools and the Election of 1896.* Toronto: University of Toronto Press, 1974.

Daniel, I.J.E. and D.A. Casey. *A History of the Canadian Knights of Columbus Catholic Army Huts.* Ottawa, 1922.

Davis, C. Mark. "I'll Drink to That: The Rise and Fall of Prohibition in the Maritime Provinces, 1900-1930." PhD dissertation, McMaster University, 1990.

DeFerrari, Patricia. "Collaborating in Christ's Redeeming Work: The U.S. Grail and Social Reform in the 1950s." *U.S. Catholic Historian* 16, 4 (autumn 1998): 109–26.

Delaney, Ida Gallant. *25¢ A Week: The Coady Credit Union, 1933-1943.* Antigonish: St F.X. Extension Department, n.d.

DeMont, John. *Coal Black Heart: The Story of Coal and the Lives It Ruled.* Toronto: Doubleday, 2009.

Devlin, Carol A. "The Eucharistic Procession of 1908: The Dilemma of the Liberal Government." *Church History* 63, 3 (September 1994): 407–25.

Dikötter, Frank. *The Tragedy of Liberation: A History of the Chinese Revolution 1945-1957.* London: Bloomsbury, 2013.

Dodaro, Santo, and Leonard Pluta. *The Big Picture: The Antigonish Movement of Eastern Nova Scotia.* Montreal and Kingston: McGill-Queen's University Press, 2012.

Dolan, Jay P. *In Search of American Catholicism: A History of Religion and Culture in Tension.* Oxford: Oxford University Press, 2002.

Donovan, Stewart. *The Forgotten World of R.J. MacSween: A Life.* Sydney: Cape Breton University Press, 2007.

Earle, Michael. "The Coal Miners and Their 'Red' Union: The Amalgamated Mine Workers of Nova Scotia, 1932-1936." *Labour/Le Travail* 22 (autumn 1988): 99–137.

– and H. Gamberg, "The United Mine Workers and the Coming of the CCF to Cape Breton." *Acadiensis* 19, 1 (autumn 1989): 3–26.

Edwards, William X. "The MacPherson-Tompkins Era of St. Francis Xavier University." CCHA, *Report* 20 (1953): 49–65.

Elliott, Lawrence. *I Will Be Called John: A Biography of Pope John XXII*. New York: Reader's Digest Press, 1973.

Elliott, Marianne. *The Catholics of Ulster: A History*. London: Allen Lane, 2000.

Elliott, Shirley B. *The Legislative Assembly of Nova Scotia 1758-1983*. Halifax: Province of Nova Scotia, 1984.

Fairley Jr, A.L. *DOSCO and the Future: Address on Steel by Albert L. Fairley, Jr., President, Dominion Steel and Coal Corporation, Limited, delivered before the Sydney Board of Trade, at Sydney, Nova Scotia, February 24th 1959*. Sydney, 1959.

Fay, Terrence J. *A History of Canadian Catholics*. Montreal and Kingston: McGill-Queen's University Press, 2002.

Fergusson, C. Bruce. *Hon. W.S. Fielding, The Mantle of Howe: The Early Life and Career of a Former Premier of Nova Scotia and Finance Minister of Canada*. Windsor: Lancelot Press, 1970.

– "The Inauguration of the Free School System in Nova Scotia." *Public Archives of Nova Scotia Bulletin 21*. Halifax, 1964.

Fingard, Judith. "The 1880s: Paradoxes of Progress." In *The Atlantic Provinces in Confederation*, edited by E.R. Forbes and D.A. Muise, 82–118. Toronto: University of Toronto Press, 1993.

Fisher, Claude L. *James Cardinal McGuigan*. Toronto: McClelland & Stewart, 1948.

Fleming, Deborah. *A Man Who Does Not Exist: The Irish Peasant in the Work of W.B. Yeats and J.M. Synge*. Ann Arbor: University of Michigan Press, 1995.

Fogarty, Gerald P. *The Vatican and the American Hierarchy from 1870 to 1965*. Wilmington: Michael Glazier, 1985.

Forbes, Ernest R. *Aspects of Maritime Regionalism 1867-1927*. Ottawa: Canadian Historical Booklet, 1983. Forbes, E.R. and D.A. Muise (eds.). *The Atlantic Provinces in Confederation*. Toronto: University of Toronto Press, 1993.

– *Challenging the Regional Stereotype: Essays on the 20th Century Maritimes*. Fredericton: Acadiensis Press, 1989.

– "Consolidating Disparity: The Maritimes and the Industrialization of Canada during the Second World War." *Acadiensis* 15, 2 (spring 1986): 3–27.

– *Maritime Rights: The Maritime Rights Movement, 1919-1927. A Study in*

Canadian Regionalism. Montreal and Kingston: McGill-Queen's University Press, 1979.

– "Prohibition and the Social Gospel in Nova Scotia," *Acadiensis* 1, 1 (autumn 1971): 11–36.

Foote, Raymond L. *The Case of Port Hawkesbury: Rapid Industrialization and Social Unrest in a Nova Scotia Community*. Toronto: PMA Books, 1979.

Fortescue, William. *The Third Republic in France 1870-1940: Conflicts and Continuities*. London: Routledge, 2002.

Fowler, Bertram B. *The Lord Helps Those….: How the People of Nova Scotia Are Solving Their Problems Through Co-Operation*. New York: Vanguard Press, 1938.

Frank, David. "The Cape Breton Coal Industry and the Rise and Fall of the British Empire Steel Corporation." *Acadiensis* 7 (autumn 1977): 3–34.

– "In Search of C.B. Wade, Research Director and Labour Historian, 1944-1950." *Labour/Le Travail* 79 (spring 2017): 9–52.

– *J.B. McLachlan: A Biography: The Story of a Legendary Labour Leader and the Cape Breton Coal Miners*. Toronto: Lorimer, 1999.

– "The Miner's Financier: Women in the Cape Breton Coal Towns, 1917." *Atlantis* 8, 2 (1983): 137–43.

– "Tradition and Culture in the Cape Breton Mining Community in the Early Twentieth Century." In *Cape Breton at 200: Historical Essays in Honour of the Island's Bicentennial 1785-1985*, edited by Kenneth Donovan. Sydney: UCCB Press, 1985.

– "The 1920s: Class and Region, Resistance and Accommodation." In *The Atlantic Provinces in Confederation*, edited by E.R. Forbes and D.A. Muise, 233–71. Toronto: University of Toronto Press.

Frank, David, and Donald MacGillivray (eds.). *George MacEachern: An Autobiography: The Story of a Cape Breton Radical*. Sydney: UCCB Press, 1987.

Fraser, Dawn. *Echoes from Labor's War: Industrial Cape Breton 1920s: Narrative Verse by Dawn Fraser*. Toronto: New Hogtown Press, 1976.

Fraser, Mary. *Folklore of Nova Scotia*. Toronto: Catholic Truth Society, 1931.

Freemantle, Anne (ed.), *The Teachings of the Popes: The Papal Encyclicals in their Historical Context*. New York: G.P. Putnam's Sons, 1956.

Furfey, Paul H. *Fire on the Earth*. New York: Macmillan, 1936.

Gagné, Michael. "'Memorial Constructions': Representations of Identity in the Design of the Grand-Pré National Historic Site, 1907-Present." *Acadiensis* 42, 1 (winter/spring 2013): 67–98.

Gauvreau, Michael. *The Catholic Origins of Quebec's Quiet Revolution, 1931-1970*. Montreal & Kingston: McGill-Queen's University Press, 2005.

Gearty, Patrick W. *The Economic Thought of Monsignor John A. Ryan*. Washington: Catholic University of America Press, 1952.

Gerrits, G.H. *They Farmed Well: The Dutch-Canadian Agricultural Community in Nova Scotia, 1945-1995*. Kentville, Vinland Press, 1996.

Gesner, Abraham. *The Industrial Resources of Nova Scotia*. Halifax, 1849.

Gibson, John F. *Gaelic Cape Breton Step-Dancing: An Historical and Ethnographic Perspective*. Montreal and Kingston: McGill-Queen's University Press, 2017.

– *Old and New World Highland Bagpiping*. Montreal and Kingston: McGill-Queen's University Press, 2002.

–*Traditional Gaelic Bagpiping, 1745-1945*. Montreal and Kingston: McGill-Queen's University Press, 2000.

Gidney, R.D., and W.P.J. Miller. *How Schools Worked: Public Education in English Canada, 1900-1940*. Montreal and Kingston: McGill-Queen's University Press, 2012.

Gilley, Sheridan. "The Roman Catholic Church and the Nineteenth-Century Irish Diaspora." *Journal of Ecclesiastical History* 35, 2 (April, 1984), 188–207.

Gillis, D. Hugh. "Sir John Thompson and Bishop Cameron." *Canadian Historical Association Report* (1955): 87–97.

Gillis, John Hugh, and J.A. McMahon. *Our Union in and with Christ: The Encyclical Mystici Corporis Christi Arranged and Simplified*. Antigonish, 1951.

Godman, Peter. *Hitler and the Vatican: Inside the Secret Archives that Reveal the New Story of the Nazis and the Church*. New York: Free Press, 2004.

Godwin, Catherine A. *Immaculate Conception Parish, Bridgeport, Nova Scotia, 1885-1985*. Bridgeport: Immaculate Conception, 1985.

Görres, Ida Friederike. *The Hidden Face: A Study of St. Thérèse of Lisieux*. San Francisco: Ignatius Press, 2003.

Graham, Monica. *Fire Spook: The Mysterious Nova Scotia Haunting*. Halifax: Nimbus, 2013.

Grail Movement. *The Grail Movement in America 1940-1982, Plus Supplement of Grail Activity 1989-90*. Grail Movement, 1989.

Guilday, Peter. "The Sacred Congregation de Propaganda Fide (1622-1922)." *Catholic Historical Review* 6, 4 (January 1921): 478–94.

Guildford, Janet. "Power, Politics, and Pedagogy: Nova Scotia: Education in Crisis." *New Maritimes* 13, 1 (Sept./Oct. 1994): 11–16.

Gundy, H.P. "Francis Collins." *Dictionary of Canadian Biography*, 1987.

Gwyn, Julian. *Comfort Me with Apples: The Nova Scotia Fruit Growers' Association, 1863-2013*. Berwick: Lupin Press, 2014.

– *Excessive Expectations: Maritime Commerce & the Economic Development of Nova Scotia, 1740-1870*. Montreal and Kingston: McGill-Queen's University Press, 1998.

Gwyn, Richard, *Smallwood: The Unlikely Revolutionary*. Toronto: McClelland & Stewart, 1999.

Hamilton, Thomas. "Padres Under Fire: A Study of the Canadian Chaplain Service (Protestant and Roman Catholic) in the Second World War." PhD dissertation, University of Toronto, 2003.

Hanington, J. Brian. *Every Popish Person: The Story of Roman Catholicism in Nova Scotia and the Church of Halifax, 1604-1984*. Halifax: Archdiocese of Halifax, 1984.

Harmon, Katherine E. *There Were Also Many Women There: Lay Women in the Liturgical Movement in the United States, 1926-59*. Collegeville Minnesota: Liturgical Press, 2013.

Harris, Richard. "Flattered but not Imitated: Co-operative Self-Help and the Nova Scotia Housing Commission, 1936-1973." *Acadiensis* 31, 1 (autumn 2001): 103–28.

Harrop, Gerry. *Clarie: Clarence Gillis, M.O. 1940-1957: A Political Memoir from the Coal Mines of Cape Breton to the Floor of the House of Commons*. Hantsport: Lancelot Press, 1987.

Hayes, Geoffrey, Mike Bechthold, and Matt Symes. *Canada and the Second World War: Essays in Honour of Terry Copp*. Waterloo: Wilfrid Laurier University Press, 2013.

Heath, Gordon L. "The Protestant Denominational Press and the Conscription Crisis in Canada, 1917-18." CCHA *Historical Studies* 78 (2012): 27–46.

Henderson, T. Stephen. *Angus L. Macdonald: A Provincial Liberal*. Toronto: University of Toronto Press, 2007.

Heron, Craig. *Working in Steel: The Early Years in Canada, 1883-1935*. Toronto: University of Toronto Press, 1988.

Hornsby, Stephen J. "Staple Trade, Subsistence Agriculture, and Nineteenth-Century Cape Breton Island." *Annals of the Association of American Geographers* 79, 3 (September 1989): 411–34.

How, Douglas. *Night of the Caribou*. Hantsport: Lancelot Press, 1995.

Howell, Colin. "The 1900s: Industry, Urbanization, and Reform." In *The Atlantic Provinces in Confederation*, edited by E.R. Forbes and D.A. Muise, 155–91. Toronto: University of Toronto Press, 1993.

Hryniuk, Stella. "Pioneer Bishop, Pioneer Times: Nykyta Budka in Canada." CCHA *Historical Studies* 55 (1988): 21–41.

Huber, Raphael. *Our Bishops Speak*. Milwaukee: Bruce Publishing Company, 1952.

Hunnicutt, Benjamin K. "Monsignor John A. Ryan and the Shorter Hours of Labor: A Forgotten Vision of 'Genuine' Progress." *Catholic Historical Review* 69 (1983): 384–402.

Hunt, M.S. *Nova Scotia's Part in the Great War*. Halifax, 1920.

Iacovetta, Franca, Roberto Perin, and Angelo Principe (eds.). *Enemies Within: Italian and Other Internees in Canada and Abroad*. Toronto: University of Toronto Press, 2000.

Ignatius, Sister M. *Brief Sketch of Life of The Most Reverend John Cameron, Third Bishop of Antigonish*. Antigonish: Sisters of St Martha, 1951.

Johnson, Micheline D. "Maillard Pierre." *Dictionary of Canadian Biography*, Vol. 3 (1974).

Johnston, A.A. (Kathleen MacKenzie, ed.). *Antigonish Diocese Priests and Bishops 1786-1925*. Antigonish: The Casket, 1994.

Johnston, Angus Anthony. *A History of the Catholic Church in Eastern Nova Scotia*, 2 Vols. Antigonish: St Francis Xavier University Press, 1962, 1971.

– *The Chisholm Catholic Priests*. Pictou, 1935.

– *L'Indienne and Lingan: Text of Address Given by Rev. A.A. Johnston, P.P., Pictou, N.S., at the Presentation of an Ancient Chalice to Lingan Church on Sunday Afternoon, May 26, 1935*. Lingan, 1935.

– *Sacred Heart Parish, Johnstown, Nova Scotia: Centenary Anniversary 1860-1960*. Johnstown, 1960.

– *Saint Anne's Parish, Glace Bay, Nova Scotia 1866-1966: Centennial Celebration*. Glace Bay, 1967.

– "To Search and Investigate. Report of an Amateur Historical Sleuth." CCHA *Report* 30 (1963): 11–21.

Johnston, A.J.B. *Religious Life at Louisbourg 1713-1758*. Montreal and Kingston: McGill-Queen's University Press, 1984.

Kane, George L. (ed.) *Lay Workers for Christ*. Westminster: Newman Press, 1957.

– (ed.) *Meeting the Vocation Crisis*. Westminster: Newman Press, 1956.

– (ed.) *Melody in Your Hearts: A Sequel to Why I Became a Nun*. Westminster: Newman Press, 1958.

– (ed.) *Twice Called: The Autobiographies of Seventeen Convent Sisters*. Westminster: Newman Press, 1959.

– (ed.) *What Can You Do?* Huntington: Our Sunday Visitor Press, 1959.
– (ed.) *Why I Became a Brother*. Westminster: Newman Press, 1954.
– (ed.) *Why I Became a Missioner*. Westminster: Newman Press, 1958.
– (ed.) *Why I Became a Nun*. Westminster: Newman Press, 1953.
– (ed.) *Why I Became a Priest*. Westminster: Newman Press, 1952.

Kauffman, Christopher J. *Faith and Fraternalism: The History of the Knights of Columbus 1882-1982*. New York: Harper & Row, 1982.

Kennedy, Florence. "Sisters of St. Martha: The Influences of Community, Family and Gaelic Culture on Members of the Sisters of St. Martha who entered the Congregation between 1929-1959." Master's thesis, St Francis Xavier University, 2006.

Keogh, Dermot. *Ireland and the Vatican: The Politics and Diplomacy of Church-State Relations, 1922-1960*. Cork: Cork University Press, 1995.

Keough, Willeen G. "Contested Terrains: Ethnic and Gendered Spaces in the Harbour Grace Affray." *Canadian Historical Review* 90, 1 (2009): 29–70.

Kertzer, David. *The Pope and Mussolini: The Secret History of Pius XI and the Rise of Fascism in Europe*. New York: Random House, 2014.

Kimber, Stephen. *Sailors, Slackers, and Blind Pigs: Halifax at War*. Toronto: Doubleday, 2002.

Kissane, Edward. "Review of Pioneer in Purple." *Christus Rex* (October 1952).

Knockwood, Isabelle. *Out of the Depths: The Experience of Mi'kmaw Children at the Indian Residential School at Shubenacadie, Nova Scotia*. Lockeport: Roseway Publishing, 1992.

Lafferty, Renée. *The Guardianship of Best Interests: Institutional Care for the Children of the Poor in Halifax, 1850-1960*. Montreal and Kingston: McGill-Queen's University Press, 2013.

–"Modernity and the Denominational Imperative: The Children's Aid Society of Halifax, 1905–1925." *Journal of the Canadian Historical Association* 13 (2002): 95–118.

Laidlaw, Alexander. *The Campus and the Community: The Global Impact of the Antigonish Movement*. Montreal: Harvest House, 1961.

– "The Campus and the Community: A Study of the Adult Education Program of St. Francis Xavier University, Antigonish Nova Scotia." PhD dissertation, University of Toronto, 1958.

Lamb, James B. *The Celtic Crusader: The Story of A.W.R. MacKenzie and the Gaelic College*. Hantsport: Lancelot Press, 1992.

Landry, Marion. *A Man of Faith: Father Arthur Venedam*, SFM. Privately printed.

Larkin, Emmett. "Cardinal Paul Cullen." In *Varieties of Ultramontanism*, edited by Jeffrey von Arx, SJ, 61–84. Washington: Catholic University of America Press, 1998.

Laverdure, Paul. *Redemption and Renewal: The Redemptorists of English Canada, 1834-1994*. Toronto: Dundurn, 1996.

Learned, W.S. and K.C.M. Sills. *Education in the Maritime Provinces of Canada*. New York: Carnegie Foundation for the Advancement of Teaching, 1922.

LeBlanc, Phyllis E. "The Vatican and the Roman Catholic Church in Atlantic Canada: Policies Regarding Ethnicity and Language, 1878-1922." In Peter C. Kent and John F. Pollard, *Papal Diplomacy in the Modern Age*. Westport Connecticut: Praeger, 1994.

LeBlanc, René and Micheline Laliberté. *Sainte-Anne, collège et université, 1890-1990*. Pointe-de-l'Église, 1990.

Leo XIII. *Rerum Novarum: Encyclical Letter of His Holiness Pope Leo XIII on the Conditions of the Working Classes*. Boston: St Paul Editions, 1942.

Liguori, Alphonsus (edited by Rev. Orby Shipley). *Preparation for Death*. Philadelphia: J.P. Lippincott, 1869.

Little, J.I. "A Fine, Hardy, Good-Looking Race of People": Travel Writers, Tourism Promoters, and the Highland Scots Identity on Cape Breton Island, 1829-1920." *Acadiensis* 44, 1 (winter/spring 2015): 20–35.

Long, Gene. *Suspended State: Newfoundland before Canada*. St John's, 1993.

Lotz, Jim. *The Humble Giant: Moses Coady Rural Revolutionary*. Toronto: Novalis, 2005.

– *The Lichen Factor: The Quest for Community Development in Canada*. Sydney: Cape Breton University Press, 1998.

– Sharing the Journey. Lawrencetown: Pottersfield Press, 2015.

Lotz, Jim, and Michael Welton. *Father Jimmy: Life and Times of Jimmy Tompkins*. Breton Books: Wreck Cove, 1997.

– "'Knowledge for the People': The Origins and Development of the Antigonish Movement." In *Knowledge for the People: The Struggle for Adult Learning in English-Speaking Canada, 1828-1973*, edited by Michael R. Welton, 97–111. Toronto: OISE Press, 1987.

Ludlow, Peter. *The Canny Scot: Archbishop James Morrison of Antigonish*. Montreal and Kingston: McGill-Queen's University Press, 2015.

– "Disturbed by the Irish Howl': Irish and Scottish Roman Catholics in Nova Scotia, 1844-1860." In *Irish Catholic Halifax: From the Napoleonic Wars to the Great War*, edited by Mark G. McGowan and Michael Vance, 32–55. Toronto: *CCHA*, 2015.

– "More than Codmen: The Newfoundland-Irish in Industrial Cape Breton, 1890-1919." PhD dissertation, Queen's University Belfast, 2010.
– "A 'Primitive Germ of Discord' in the North Atlantic World: Newfoundland-Irish Roman Catholics in Scottish Cape Breton." *Journal of Irish and Scottish Studies* 3, 1 (autumn, 2009): 175–92.
– "Raising the Cry of Nationality: The Struggle for an Irish Bishop of Charlottetown." *The Island Magazine* 80 (autumn/winter 2016): 2–10.
– "Saints and Sinners: Popular Myth and the Study of the Personalities of the Antigonish Movement." *Acadiensis* 42, 1 (winter/spring 2013): 99–126.
Luskod, Count Vay de Vaya. *The Inner Life of the United States*. New York: E.P. Dutton, 1908.
– *Empires and Emperors of Russia, China, Korea and Japan*. New York: E.P. Dutton, 1906.
MacDonald, A.D. *Mabou Pioneers Volume 1: A Genealogical Tracing of Some Pioneer Families Who Settled in Mabou and District*. Halifax: Formac, 2014.
MacDonald, Alexander. *The Apostles' creed; a vindication of the apostolic authorship of the creed on the lines of Scripture and tradition, together with some account of its development and critical analysis of its contents*. Kegan Paul, Trench, Trübner & Co., 1920.
– *A Bit of Autobiography*. Vancouver, 1920.
– *The Christian Passover*. Catholic Truth Society, *1932*.
– *The Primacy of Thought in Poetry*. London: Kegan Paul, Trench, Trübner & Co., 1928.
MacDonald, Carole. *Historic Glace Bay*. Halifax: Nimbus, 2009.
MacDonald, Charles. "On Getting the Sack: Bishop Alexander MacDonald's Departure from Victoria," Historical Papers 1994: *Canadian Society of Church History*, 15–23.
MacDonald, David. "A Coal Town Fights for Its Life." *Maclean's Magazine* 67, 6 (15 March 1954), 24–63.
MacDonald, H.M. *The Builders: Biographical Sketches of the Architects of the Diocese of Antigonish*. Antigonish: The Casket, 1968.
– *Down Memory Lane with Gems of Antigonish to Remember*. Antigonish: The Casket, 1972.
– *Memorable Years*. Antigonish: The Casket, 1964.
– *The Rector: A Biography of Reverend John Schulte, D.D., Ph.D. First President of St. Francis Xavier University*. Antigonish: Formac, 1976.
MacDonald, Heidi. "Entering the Convent as Coming of Age in the 1930s," In *Changing Habits*, edited by Elizabeth M. Smyth, 87–102. Ottawa: Novalis, 2007.

– "The Impact of Increased Health and Social Welfare Funding on the Evolution of Two Congregations of Women Religious in Nova Scotia and Prince Edward Island, 1944-1982." In *Delicate Dances: Case Studies on Public Policy and the Non-Profit Sector in Canada*, edited by Kathy Brock, 147–70. Montreal and Kingston: McGill-Queen's University Press, 2003.

– "The Social Origins and Congregational Identity of the Founding Sisters of St. Martha of Charlottetown, PEI, 1915-1925." CCHA *Historical Studies*, 70 (2004): 29–47.

MacDonald, Herb. *Cape Breton Railways: An Illustrated Edition*. Sydney: Cape Breton University Press, 2012.

MacDonald, J.D. Nelson. *Memoirs of an Unorthodox Clergyman*. Truro: Cooperative Resources, 1986.

MacDonald, John R. *Catholics of the Diocese of Antigonish, Nova Scotia, 1919-1919, with Nominal Rolls by Parishes*. Antigonish: St Francis Xavier University Press, 1920.

– *The Mystical Body of Christ and the Cooperative Movement*. Des Moines, National Catholic Rural Life Conference, 1955.

MacDonell, Malcolm. "The Early History of St. Francis Xavier University." CCHA, *Report* 15 (1947–1948): 81–90.

MacDougall, J.A. *The Total Abstinence Movement and the League of the Cross*. Glace Bay, March 1939.

MacDougall, J.L. *History of Inverness County, Nova Scotia*. Truro, 1922.

MacEwan, Paul. *Miners and Steelworkers: Labour in Cape Breton*. Toronto: Samuel Stevens, Hakkert & Company, 1976.

MacGillivray, Donald. "Industrial Unrest in Cape Breton, 1919-1925." Master's thesis, University of New Brunswick, 1971.

– "Military Aid to the Civil Power: The Cape Breton Experience in the 1920s." In *Cape Breton Historical Essays*, edited by Donald MacGillivray and Brian Tennyson, 95–109. Sydney, UCCB Press, 1980.

McGlynn, Thomas. *Visions of Fatima*. Boston: Little Brown, 1948.

MacInnes, Daniel W. "The Acadian People: Race Memories Isolated in Small Spaces." In *Banked Fires: The Ethnics of Nova Scotia*, edited by Douglas F. Campbell, 41–65. Port Credit: Scribblers' Press, 1978.

– "Clerics, Fishermen, Farmers and Workers: The Antigonish Movement and Identity in Eastern Nova Scotia, 1928-1939." PhD dissertation, McMaster University, 1978.

– "The Legacy of Highland 'Heather' Priests in Eastern Canada." In *Keeping the Kirk: Scottish Religion at Home and in the Diaspora*, edited by Daniel MacLeod and Stuart Macdonald, 85–118. Guelph: Guelph Series in Scottish Studies, 2014.

– The Role of the Scottish Catholic Society in the Determination of the Antigonish Movement." *International Review of Scottish Studies* 8 (1978): 25–46.

MacIntyre, Carroll N. *The Fire-Spook of Caledonia Mills*. Antigonish: Sundown Publications, 1985.

MacIsaac, Teresa. *A Better Life: A Portrait of Highland Women in Nova Scotia*. Sydney: Cape Breton University Press, 2006.

MacKenzie, Anthony. *The Irish in Cape Breton*. Antigonish: Formac, 1979.

MacKenzie, Archibald *The MacKenzie's History of Christmas Island Parish*. Christmas Island, 1926.

MacKenzie, Rennie. *Blast!: Cape Breton Coal Mine Disasters*. Wreck Cove: Breton Books, 2007.

MacKinnon, Lachlan. "Labour Landmarks in New Waterford: Collective Memory in a Cape Breton Coal Town." *Acadiensis* 42, 2 (summer/autumn 2013): 3–26.

MacKinnon, Richard. "Tompkinsville, Cape Breton Island: Co-operativism and Vernacular Architecture." *Material History Review* 44 (autumn 1996): 45–63.

MacLean, Alexander D. "The Early History of St. Michael's Parish, Baddeck, Nova Scotia." CCHA, *Report* 11 (1943–44): 109–16.

MacLean, Raymond A. *Bishop John Cameron: Piety & Politics*. Antigonish: The Casket, 1991.

– "Bishop John Cameron: Political Prelate." *Collections of the Royal Nova Scotia Historical Society* 43 (1991): 12–25.

– *The Casket: From Gutenberg to Internet: The Story of a Small-Town Weekly*. Antigonish: The Casket, 1992.

– "The Scots: Hector's Cargo." In *Banked Fires: The Ethnics of Nova Scotia*, edited by Douglas F. Campbell, 106–30. Port Credit: Scribblers' Press, 1978.

MacLellan, J.A. "Archbishop MacDonald Resigns," *The Western Catholic*, XLVII (August 1961).

MacLeod, Donald. "Colliers, Colliery Safety and Workplace Control: The Nova Scotia Experience, 1873-1910." Canadian Historical Association, *Historical Papers* (1983).

MacLeod, Erna. "Words Apart: Performing Linguistic and Cultural Identities in Cheticamp, Nova Scotia." PhD dissertation, University of Massachusetts Amherst, 2008.

MacLeod, Malcolm. *A Bridge Built Halfway: A History of Memorial University College 1925-1950*. Montreal and Kingston: McGill-Queen's University Press, 1990.

MacMillan, Margaret. *The War that Ended Peace: The Road to 1914*. New York: Allen Lane, 2013.
MacNeil, Malcolm. *The Rewarding Path*. Boston: Christopher Publishing, 1961.
MacNeil, Neil. *The Highland Heart in Nova Scotia*. Toronto: S.J. Reginald Saunders & Company, 1948.
MacPherson, Sarah. "Religious Women in Nova Scotia: A Struggle for Autonomy. A Sketch of the Sisters of St. Martha of Antigonish, Nova Scotia, 1900-1960." CCHA *Historical Studies* 51 (1984): 89–106.
Mann, Susan. *Margaret Macdonald: Imperial Daughter*. Montreal and Kingston: McGill-Queen's University Press, 2005.
March, William. *Red Line: The Chronicle-Herald and the Mail-Star 1875-1954*. Halifax: Chebucto Agencies, 1986.
Marriott, John Arthur Ransome. *England Since Waterloo*. London: G.P. Putnam's Sons, 1913.
– *Anglo-Russian Relations, 1689-1943*. London: Methuen & Co, 1944.
Martell, J.S. "Early Coal Mining in Nova Scotia." *Dalhousie Review* 25 (1945–46): 156–72.
Maura, Sister. *The Sisters of Charity Halifax*. Toronto: Ryerson Press, 1956.
Maxwell, Grant. *China: Assignment in Chekiang*. Scarborough: Scarboro Foreign Mission, 1982.
McCarthy, Joseph P. *Times of My Life*. Privately Printed, n.d.
McCluskey, Raymond (ed.). *The Scots College Rome 1600-2000*. Edinburgh: John Donald, 2000.
McDavid, Jodi. "The Fiddle Burning Priest of Mabou." *Ethnologies* 302 (2008): 115–36.
McEwen, W.H. *Faith, Hope and Co-operation: A Maritime Provinces Story*. Moncton: Maritime Cooperative Services, 1969.
McGowan, Mark G. "The Fulton Sheen Affair: Religious Controversy, Nationalism, and Commercialism in the Early Years of Canadian Television, 1952-1958." CCHA *Historical Studies* 75 (2009): 21–38.
– Harvesting the Red Vineyard: Catholic Religious Culture in the Canadian Expeditionary Force, 1914-1919." CCHA *Historical Studies* 64 (1998): 47–70.
– *The Imperial Irish: Canada's Irish Catholics Fight the Great War 1914-1918*. Montreal and Kingston: McGill-Queen's University Press, 2017.
– "Life Outside the Cloister: Some Reflections on the Writing of the History of the Catholic Church in English Canada, 1983–1996." CCHA *Historical Studies* 63 (1997): 123–33.

– "The Maritimes' Region and the Building of a Canadian Church: The Case of the Diocese of Antigonish after Confederation." CCHA *Historical Studies* 70 (2004): 48–70.

– "The People's University of the Air: St. Francis Xavier University Extension, Social Christianity, and the Creation of CJFX." *Acadiensis* 41, 1 (winter/spring 2012): 5–20.

– "'Religious Duties and Patriotic Endeavours': The Catholic Church Extension Society, French Canada and the Prairie West, 1908-1916." CCHA *Historical Studies* 51 (1984): 107–20.

– *The Waning of the Green: Catholics, the Irish, and Identity in Toronto, 1887-1922*. Montreal and Kingston: McGill-Queen's University Press 1999.

McGrail, Peter. *First Communion: Ritual, Church and Popular Religious Identity*. Cambridge: Routledge, 2016.

McGreevy, John T. *American Jesuits and the World: How an Embattled Religious Order Made Modern Catholicism Global*. Princeton: Princeton University Press, 2016.

McGuigan, Peter. *The Intrigues of Archbishop John T. McNally and the Rise of Saint Mary's University*. Halifax: Fernwood Press, 2012.

McKay, Ian. "'By Wisdom, Wile or War': The Provincial Workmen's Association and the Struggle for Working-Class Independence in Nova Scotia, 1879-97." *Labour/Le Travail* 18 (fall 1986): 13–62.

– *Quest for the Folk: Antimodernism and Cultural Selection in Twentieth-Century Nova Scotia*. Montreal and Kingston: McGill-Queen's University Press, 2014.

– "Strikes in the Maritimes." *Acadiensis* 13, 1 (autumn 1983): 3–46.

– "The 1910s: The Stillborn Triumph of Progressive Reform." In *The Atlantic Provinces in Confederation*, edited by E.R. Forbes and D.A. Muise, 192–229. Toronto: University of Toronto Press, 1993.

McNeil, Evangeline. "The Importance of the Retreat Movement in Nova Scotia." CCHA *Report* 10 (1942-1943): 107–15.

McNeil, Neil. *The Pope and the War*. Toronto, February 1918.

Mellor, John. *The Company Store: James Bryson McLachlan and the Cape Breton Coal Miners 1900-1925*. Toronto: Doubleday, 1983.

Mifflen, Philip. "A History of Trade Unionism in the Coal Mines of Nova Scotia." Master's thesis, Catholic University of America, 1951.

Mifflin, Francis J. "The Antigonish Movement: A Revitalization Movement in Eastern Nova Scotia." PhD dissertation, Boston College, 1974.

Migliore, Sam and A. Evo Dipierro. *Italian Lives, Cape Breton Memories*. Sydney: Cape Breton University Press, 1999.

Miller, Carman. "The 1940s: War and Rehabilitation." In *The Atlantic Provinces in Confederation*, edited by E.R. Forbes and D.A. Muise, 306–45. Toronto: University of Toronto Press, 1993.

Miller, J.R. "Reconciliation with Residential School Survivors: A Progress Report," In *Aboriginal Policy Research Volume VII: A History of Treaties and Policies*, edited by Jerry P. White, Erik Anderson, Jean-Pierre Morin, and Dan Beavon. Toronto: Thompson Educational Press, 2010.

– *Shingwauk's Vision: A History of Native Residential Schools*. Toronto: University of Toronto Press, 1996.

Miller, William. *Dorothy Day: A Biography*. New York: Harper and Row, 1982.

– *Incidents in the Political Career of the Late Sir John Thompson not Contained in Mr. J. Castell Hopkins' Book*. Antigonish, 1895.

Miriam, Sister St Francis. "The Historical Background of the People's School." Bachelor's thesis, St Francis Xavier University, 1955.

Mooney, George S. *Co-operatives Today and Tomorrow: A Canadian Survey*. Montreal: The Survey Committee, 1938.

Morgan, Robert J. *Perseverance: The Story of Cape Breton's University College 1952-2002*. Sydney: UCCB Press, 2004.

– *Rise Again!: The Story of Cape Breton Island, Books 1& 2*. Wreck Cove: Breton Books, 2008.

Morisset, Lucie K. "Ouellet, David." *Dictionary of Canadian Biography* 14 (1998).

Morrissey, Thomas J. *Bishop Edward Thomas O'Dwyer of Limerick, 1842–1917*. Dublin: Four Courts Press, 2003.

Morton, Desmond and J.L. Granatstein, *Marching to Armageddon: Canadians and the Great War, 1914-1919*. Lester and Orpen Dennys, 1989.

Morton, Suzanne and Ian McKay. *The Kingdom of Canada: A General History from Earliest Times*. Indianapolis: Bobbs-Merrill, 1963. Mount Carmel Parish. *The Parish Year 1941: Mount Carmel Parish, New Waterford*. New Waterford, 1942.

– "The Maritimes: Expanding the Circle of Resistance." In *The Workers' Revolt in Canada, 1917-1925*, edited by Craig Heron, 43–86. Toronto: University of Toronto Press, 1998.

– "Old Women and Their Place in Nova Scotia, 1881-1931." *Atlantis* 20, 1: 21–38.Morton, W.L. "Manitoba Schools and Canadian Nationality 1890-1923." In *Minorities, Schools, and Politics: Canadian Historical Readings 7*, edited by Craig Brown. Toronto: University of Toronto Press, 1969.

– "Women on Their Own: Single Mothers in Working-Class Halifax in the 1920s." *Acadiensis* 21, 2 (spring 1992): 90–107.

Mount Saint Bernard College, *Mount Saint Bernard Centennial, 1883-1983*. Antigonish: Mount Saint Bernard, 1983.

Muise, D.A. "The Making of An Industrial Community: Cape Breton Coal Towns 1867-1900." In *Cape Breton Historical Essays*, edited by Don MacGillivray and Brian Tennyson, 76–94. Sydney: UCCB Press, 1980.

Mullan, David George. "A History of St. Mary's Polish Parish Sydney, Nova Scotia." Unpublished paper, 2002.

Murphy, Terrence. "Trusteeism in Atlantic Canada: The Struggle for Leadership among the Irish Catholics of Halifax, St. John's, and Saint John, 1780-1850." In *Creed and Culture: The Place of English-Speaking Catholics in Canadian Society, 1750-1930*, edited by Terrence Murphy and Gerald Stortz. Montreal and Kingston: McGill-Queen's University Press, 1993.

– "Transformation and Triumphalism: the Irish Catholics of Halifax, 1839-1858." In "Irish Catholic Halifax: From the Napoleonic Wars to the Great War," edited by Mark G. McGowan and Michael Vance, 56–81. Occasion Paper, CCHA *Historical Studies* 81 (2015).

Neal, Rusty. *Brotherhood Economics: Women and Co-Operatives in Nova Scotia*. Sydney: UCCB Press, 1998.

Nearing, Peter. *He Loved the Church: The Biography of Bishop John R. MacDonald, Fifth Bishop of Antigonish*. Antigonish: The Casket, 1975.

Nevin, Thomas. *Thérèse of Lisieux: God's Gentle Warrior*. Oxford: Oxford University Press, 2006.

Newton, Michael. "The Macs meet the 'Micmacs': Scottish Gaelic First Encounter Narratives from Nova Scotia." *Journal of Irish and Scottish Studies* 5, 1 (autumn 2011): 67–96.

Nilsen, Kenneth. "The Role of the Priest in the Gaelic Folklore of Nova Scotia." *Béaloideas* 64/65 (1996/1997): 171–94.

Noel, S.J.R. *Politics in Newfoundland*. Toronto: University of Toronto Press, 1971.

Nova Scotia Barristers' Society. "Address of Nova Scotia Barristers' Society to Sir Joseph Chisholm, Kt., LL.D., Chief Justice of Nova Scotia And Reply of the Chief Justice." Halifax, 8 January 1935.

Nunn, Bruce. "Life Was His Podium: A Biography of J. Clyde Nunn." BA dissertation, St Francis Xavier University, 1984.

O'Brien, Mary B., and Patricia M. Miller. "A Woman of Vision: An Interview with a Founder of the Grail Movement in the United States." *U.S. Catholic Historian* 15, 4, "Spirituality and Devotionalism" (autumn, 1997): 95–105.

O'Brien, Mike. "Out of a Clear Sky: The Mobilization of the Newfoundland Regiment, 1914-1915." *Newfoundland and Labrador Studies* 22, 2 (2007): 401–27.

O'Gorman, J.R. "Canadian Catholic Chaplains in the Great War, 1914-1918." CCHA *Report*, 7 (1939–1940): 71–2.

Ormond, Douglas Somers (ed.). *A Century Ago at Arichat and Antigonish: Reminiscences of Mary Belle Grant Ormond (1860-1947)*. Hantsport: Lancelot Press, 1985.

O'Shea, Art. *Prince Edward Island Priests Away*. Charlottetown: Art O'Shea, 2001.Ó Siadhail, Pádraig. *Katherine Hughes: A Life and a Journey: From "Canadian Imperialist" to Irish Republican Activist: From Emerald, Prince Edward Island, to Ireland*. Newcastle: Penumbra Press, 2014.

Ostiguy, Jean R. *Ozias Leduc: Peinture Symboliste et Religieuse. Symbolist and Religious Painting*. Ottawa: National Gallery of Canada, 1974.

Pacey, Elizabeth. *More Stately Mansions: Churches of Nova Scotia 1830-1910*. Hantsport: Lancelot Press, 1983.

Pacifique, Père. *Le Paroissien Micmac*. Quebec, 1903.

– *Souvenir of the Micmac Tercentenary Celebration, 1910*. Sainte-Anne-de-Ristigouche [Quebec]: Frères mineurs capucins, 1910.

Parkinson, Alan F. *Belfast's Unholy War*. Dublin: Four Courts, 2004.

Parnaby, Andrew. "The Cultural Economy of Survival: The Mi'kmaq of Cape Breton in the Mid-19th Century." *Labour/Le Travail* 61 (spring 2008): 69–98.

Parr, Joy. "Women Workers in the Twentieth Century." In *Lectures in Canadian Labour and Working-Class History*, edited by W.J.C. Cherwinski and Gregory Kealey, 79–88. St John's: New Hogtown Press, 1985.

Parsons, Elsie Clews. "Micmac Notes. St. Ann's Mission on Chapel Island, Bras d'Or Lakes, Cape Breton Island." *Journal of American Folklore* 39, 154 (Oct.–Dec. 1926).

Paton, Margaret. *Mary MacKillop: The Ground of Her Loving*. London: Darton Longman Todd, 2010.

Patterson, Lisa Lynne. "Indian Affairs and the Nova Scotian Centralization Policy." Master's thesis, Dalhousie University, 1985.

Patterson, Stephen E. "Indian-White Relations in Nova Scotia, 1749-61: A Study in Political Interaction." *Acadiensis* 23, 1 (autumn 1993): 23–59.

Pelletier, Yves Yvon J. "Fighting for the Chaplains: Bishop Charles Leo Nelligan and the Creation of the Canadian Chaplain Service (Roman Catholic), 1939-1945." CCHA *Historical Studies* 72 (2006): 95–123.

Pérez, Cristián, "Rural Guerrilla in Chile: The Battle at the Farm of San Miguel (1968)." *Estudios Públicos* 78 (autumn 2000): 8–9.

Perin, Roberto. *Rome in Canada: The Vatican and Canadian Affairs in the Late Victorian Age*. Toronto: University of Toronto Press, 1990.

Perman, Ray. *The Man Who Gave Away His Island: A Life of John Lorne Campbell of Canna*. Edinburgh: Birlinn Ltd., 2016.

Perry, George D. *The Grand Regulator: The Miseducation of Nova Scotia's Teachers, 1838-1997*. Montreal and Kingston: McGill-Queen's University Press, 2013.

Pighin, Bruno Fabio (ed.). *The Secrets of a Vatican Cardinal: Celso Costantini's Wartime Diaries, 1938-1947*. Montreal and Kingston: McGill-Queen's University Press, 2014.

Poliandri, Simone. *First Nations, Identity, and Reserve Life: The Mi'kmaq of Nova Scotia*. Lincoln: University of Nebraska, 2011.

Pope, Joseph. *Correspondence of Sir John A. MacDonald*. Toronto: Oxford University Press, 1921.

Pope, William (ed.). *Clarence MacKinnon Nicholson: An Intimate Profile of His Achievement, Thought and Spiritual Leadership*. Hantsport: Lancelot Press, 1981.

Raedts, Peter. "The Church as Nation State: A New Look at Ultramontane Catholicism (1850-1900)." *Dutch Review of Church History* 84 (2004): 476–96.

Raine, Norman Reilly. "Toilers under the Sea." *Maclean's Magazine*, 1 January 1925: 21.

Rankin, D.J. "Father Kenneth J. MacDonald." CCHA *Report* 12 (1944–45): 109–16.

– *A History of the County of Antigonish*. Toronto: Macmillan, 1929

– "Laurence Kavanagh." CCHA *Report* 8 (1940–41): 51–76.

– *On This Rock*. Ottawa: Overbrook Press, 1930.

– *Our Ain Folk and Others*. Toronto: Macmillan, 1930.

Redemptorist, A. *The Miracles of Beaupré: A Collection of the Most Remarkable Cures Wrought at the Far-famed Shrine of St. Anne de Beaupré*. St Anne de Beaupré, 1908.

Reeves, W.G. "Newfoundlanders in the 'Boston States': A Study in Early Twentieth-Century Community and Counterpoint." *Newfoundland and Labrador Studies* 6, 1 (1990): 34–55.

Reid, John G. "Beyond the Democratic Intellect: The Scottish Example and University Reform in Canada's Maritime Provinces, 1870-1933." In *Youth, University and Canadian Society: Essays in the Social History of*

Higher Education, edited by Paul Axelrod and John G. Reid. Montreal: McGill-Queen's University Press, 1989.

– "Health, Education, Economy: Philanthropic Foundations in the Atlantic Region in the 1920s and 1930s." *Acadiensis* 14, 1 (autumn 1984): 64–83.

– *Nova Scotia: A Pocket History*. Halifax: Fernwood, 2009.

– *Six Crucial Decades: Times of Change in the History of the Maritimes*. Halifax: Nimbus, 1987.

Richardson, H.G. "The English Coronation Oath." *Transactions of the Royal Historical Society* 23 (January 1941): 129–58.

Roach, Thomas E. *The Jewel of the Campus: A History of the St. Francis Xavier University Chapel*. Antigonish: St Francis Xavier University Press, 2009.

Robert, Dana L. "American Crusade: Catholic Youth in the World Mission Movement from World War I through Vatican II (review)." *American Catholic Studies* 122, 4 (winter 2011): 92–4.

Ronan, Mary. *History of the Catholic Women's League of Canada in the Diocese of Antigonish 1921-1959*. Antigonish, 1960.

Ross, Sheila. "'For God and Canada:' The Early Years of the Catholic Women's League in Alberta." CCHA *Historical Studies* 62 (1996): 89–108.

Rusak, Stephen T. "The Canadian 'Concordat' of 1897." *Catholic Historical Review* 77, 2 (April 1991): 209–34.

Ryan, John. *Capital and Labor*. Washington: National Catholic Welfare Council, 1920.

– *A Catechism of the Social Question*. New York: Paulist Press, 1921.

– *Catholic Doctrine on the Right of Self Government*. New York: Paulist Press, 1919.

– *Distributive Justice: The Right and Wrong of Our Present Distribution of Wealth*. New York: Macmillan, 1922.

– *Social Doctrine in Action: A Personal History*. NewYork: Harper Brothers, 1941.

Salvatore, Filippo. *Fascism and the Italians of Montreal: An Oral History, 1922-1945*. Montreal: Guernica Editions, 1998.

Sandberg, Anders L. and Peter Clancy. *Against the Grain: Foresters and Politics in Nova Scotia*. Vancouver: University of British Columbia Press, 2000.

Saywell, John T. (ed.) *The Canadian Journal of Lady Aberdeen 1893-1898*. Toronto: The Champlain Society, 1960.

Schoppa, R. Keith. *In a Sea of Bitterness: Refugees during the Sino-Japanese War*. Cambridge: Harvard University Press, 2019.

Schrepfer, Luke. *Pioneer Monks in Nova Scotia*. Antigonish, St Augustine's Monastery, 1947.

Shook, Laurence. *Catholic Post-Secondary Education in English-Speaking Canada: A History*. Toronto: University of Toronto Press, 1971.

Simpson, Patricia. *Marguerite Bourgeoys and the Congregation of Notre-Dame, 1665-1700*. Montreal and Kingston: McGill-Queen's University Press, 2005.

Sinasac, Joseph. *Faithful Passages: The Life of Henry Somerville, Catholic Journalist*. Toronto: Novalis, 2003.

Skelton, Oscar D. *Life and Letters of Sir Wilfrid Laurier, Volume One*. Toronto: Oxford University Press, 1921.

Somers, Hugh J. *The Life and Times of the Hon. and Rt. Rev. Alexander Macdonell, D.D., First Bishop of Upper Canada, 1762-1840*. Washington: Catholic University of America, 1931.

Stanley-Blackwell, Laurie C.C. and R.A. MacLean, *Historic Antigonish Town and County*. Halifax: Nimbus, 2004.

Steele, Harvey. *Dear Old Rebel: A Priest's Battle for Social Justice*. Lawrencetown: Pottersfield Press, 1993.

– *Why Kill a Priest!* Burlington: Crown Publications, 1982.

Steele, Joseph. "The Big Strike 1909-1910." Master's thesis, St Francis Xavier University, 1960.

Stella Maris Parish. *Stella Maris Church, Pictou County: Parish Year Book, 1944*. Pictou, 1944.

St Francis Xavier University. *The People's School*. Antigonish, Nova Scotia, January to March 1921.

St Francis Xavier University Extension Department, *Mobilizing for Enlightenment: St. Francis Xavier University Goes to the People*. Antigonish, 1942.

– *Golden Gleanings: Commemorating the Fiftieth Anniversary of St. Joseph's Hospital 1902-1952 and its School of Nursing 1905-1955, Glace Bay, Nova Scotia*. Glace Bay, 1955.

– *United Maritime Fishermen*. Antigonish, 1945.

St Joseph's Hospital. *A General View of the Religious Life*. Antigonish: Sisters of St Martha, n.d.

– *Twenty-Fifth Anniversary of St. Joseph's Hospital, Glace Bay, Nova Scotia*. Glace Bay, 1927.

Sutherland, David. "A Fond but Extravagant Farewell: The Halifax

Funeral of Prime Minister Sir John Thompson, 1895." *Journal of the Royal Nova Scotia Historical Society* 16 (2013).

Sweetser, Moses F. (ed.). *The Maritime Provinces: A Handbook for Travelers. A Guide to the Chief Cities, Coast, and Islands of the Maritime Provinces of Canada ... Also Newfoundland and the Labrador Coast. With Four Maps and Four Plans.* J.R. Osgood, 1875.

Taylor, A.J.P. *Beaverbrook: A Biography*. New York: Simon and Schuster, 1972.

Tennyson, Brian. *Impressions of Cape Breton*. Sydney: Cape Breton University Press 1986.

Thornton, Patricia A. "The Problem of Out-Migration from Atlantic Canada, 1871-1921: A New Look." *Acadiensis* 15 (autumn 1985): 3–34.

Tobin, Anita Maria. "The Effect of Centralization on the Social and Political Systems of the Mainland Nova Scotia Mi'kmaq (Case Studies: Millbrook–1916 & Indian Brook–1941)." Master's thesis, Saint Mary's University, 1999.

Tompkins, James J. *Knowledge for the People: A Call to St. Francis Xavier University*. Antigonish, 1921.

Townend, Paul A. *Father Mathew, Temperance and Irish Identity*. Dublin: Irish Academic Press, 2002.

Trenholm, Hayden. "Radical Labour and the Catholic Church: The Case of Cape Breton." Honours thesis. Mount Allison University, 1977.

Truth and Reconciliation Commission of Canada, *Canada's Residential Schools – The Legacy: The Final Report of the Truth and Reconciliation Commission of Canada, Volume 1*. Montreal and Kingston: McGill-Queen's University Press, 2015.

Tuck, Robert. *Churches of Nova Scotia*. Toronto: Dundurn, 2003.

Upton, L.F.S. *Micmacs and Colonists: Indian-White Relations in the Maritimes, 1713-1867*. Vancouver: University of British Columbia Press, 1979.

Van den Heuvel, Mary. "The Dutch Immigrants." In *St. Andrews Then and Now*, edited by H. Joseph MacDonald, 77–83. Antigonish: The Casket, 2000.

Vautour, Doreen. "Maritime Entrants to the Congregation of Notre Dame: 1880-1920: A Rise in Vocations." Master's thesis, University of New Brunswick, 1995.

Voisine, Nive. "George Conroy." *Dictionary of Canadian Biography* 10, 1972.

von Arx, Jeffery P. (ed.). *Varieties of Ultramontanism*. Washington: Catholic University Press, 1998.

Waite, Peter B. "Annie and the Bishop: John S.D. Thompson Goes to Ottawa, 1885." *Dalhousie Review* 57 (1977): 605–16.

– *Lives of Dalhousie University, Volume 2: 1925-1980: The Old College Transformed*. Montreal and Kingston: McGill-Queen's University Press, 1997.

– *The Man from Halifax: Sir John Thompson, Prime Minister*. Toronto: University of Toronto Press, 1985.

– "Sir John Sparrow David Thompson." *Dictionary of Canadian Biography* 12 (1990).

Walls, Martha E. *No Need of a Chief for This Band: The Maritime Mi'kmaq and Federal Electoral Legislation, 1899-1951*. Vancouver: University of British Columbia Press, 2011.

Ward, Leo. *Nova Scotia: The Land of Cooperation*. New York, 1942.

Welton, Michael R. "'Fraught with Wonderful Possibilities': Father Jimmy Tompkins and the Struggle for a Catholic Progressivism, 1912-1922." *Studies in Continuing Education* 27, 2 (July 2005).

– *Little Mosie from the Margaree: A Biography of Moses Michael Coady*. Toronto: Thompson Education Publishing, 2001.

Whyte, J.H. *Church and State in Modern Ireland, 1923-1979*. London: Gill & Macmillan, 1971.

Wicken, William C. *The Colonization of Mi'kmaw Memory and History, 1794-1928: The King v. Gabriel Sylliboy*. Toronto: University of Toronto Press, 2012.

– "'Heard It from Our Grandfathers': Mi'kmaq Treaty Tradition and the Syliboy Case of 1928." *University of New Brunswick Law Journal* 44 (1995): 146–61.

Woodard, Colin. *The Lobster Coast: Rebels, Rusticators, and the Struggle for a Forgotten Frontier*. New York: Penguin, 2005.

Xavier, Sister Francis. "Educational Legislation in Nova Scotia and the Catholics." CCHA, *Report* 24 (1957): 63–74.

Zech, Charles E., and Thomas P. Gaunt. *Catholic Parishes of the 21st Century: The Challenges of Mobility, Diversity, and Reconfiguration*. Oxford: Oxford University Press, 2017.

Index

www.ingramcontent.com/pod-product-compliance
Lightning Source LLC
LaVergne TN
LVHW100608130826
845408LV00027B/170

* 9 7 8 0 2 2 8 0 1 0 8 8 3 *